Sleeping price codes

LL	over US$200
L	US$151-200
AL	US$101-150
A	US$66-100
B	US$46-65
C	US$31-45
D	US$21-30
E	US$12-20
F	US$7-11
G	under US$7

Price of double room in high season, excluding taxes.

Eating price codes

♥♥♥	over US$12
♥♥	US$6-12
♥	under US$6

Price of a two-course meal for one person, excluding drinks and taxes.

Rajasthan Handbook

Annie Dare & Victoria McCulloch

Rajasthan is a land of unending variety, in parts painfully touristy, in others completely untouched. Its people range from suave, polo-playing Rajputs and their elegant, jewellery-draped wives, to tall, incandescently turbaned camel drivers, a gold hoop in each ear almost bridged by a luxuriant moustache, the hard-working women often hidden behind a swathe of brilliantly bright fabrics, an inverse camouflage against the surrounding sand.

Its history is one of fierce pride, unflinching chivalry and unequivocal independence until the arrival of the British, who granted the maharajas huge wealth but very little power. As a result, the period under their rule was characterized by the most conspicuous, extravagant consumption. This varied past has left behind a veritable feast of unparalleled riches: a collection of forts, palaces, temples and treasures that no other state can begin to equal.

In recent years, however, Rajasthan has been struggling to find a place in increasingly high-tech India. Rooted in its past but with little identity other than as a tourist destination, it is regarded as backward and parochial by a large number of Indians. Many of the major sites have done little to preserve their valuable heritage, controlled as they have been by well-meaning maharajas with little professional experience. A much-needed transition is now underway, however, with Jodhpur's Meherangarh Fort, freshly enhanced with a superb MP3 guided tour, setting an example for the rest to follow. Whereas tourists were perhaps once seen as an entertaining diversion, their role as the mainstay of the local economy is now being taken far more seriously, with the standards of facilities on offer improving dramatically as a result.

This page Traditional dolls made in Rajasthan.
Previous page Annual elephant festival in Jaipur.

Highlights

1 Magnificent and serene, the Taj Mahal is now officially a Wonder of the World. ▶▶ page 109.

2 Ranthambhore National Park, tiger-spotting in stunning surroundings. ▶▶ page 171.

3 Sundowners at Udaipur lake, when the sky turns golden and the fairytale buildings light up. ▶▶ page 192.

4 A glimpse of how life in a royal palace was lived 200 years ago, at Juna Mahal, Dungarpur. ▶▶ page 208.

5 Ranakpur, with its intricate temples and wonderful setting, is remarkably untouristy. ▶▶ page 214.

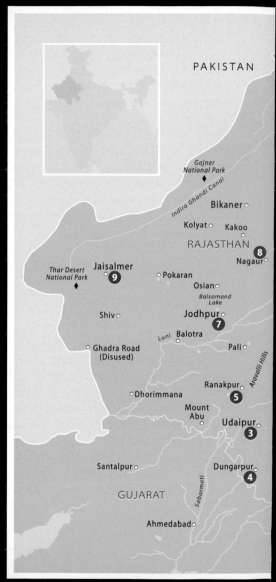

PAKISTAN

Gajner National Park

Indira Ghandi Canal

Bikaner

Kolyat   Kakoo

RAJASTHAN

8
Nagaur

Thar Desert National Park

Jaisalmer
9

Pokaran

Osian

Balsamand Lake

Shiv

Jodhpur
7

Luni   Balotra

Pali

Aravalli Hills

Ghadra Road (Disused)

Ranakpur
5

Dhorimmana

Mount Abu

Udaipur
3

Santalpur

Dungarpur
4

Sabarmati

GUJARAT

Ahmedabad

See colour maps in centre of book

6 The massive fort at Bundi towers over an authentic and hugely atmospheric town. ▶▶ page 230.

7 Meherangarh Fort is Rajasthan's most imperious fort, painstakingly resorted. ▶▶ page 241.

8 Nagaur has an authentic cattle fair and fascinating fort. ▶▶ page 246.

9 Jaisalmer's incredible fort rises so majestically from the flat desert plain that you'll think it's a mirage. ▶▶ page 255.

10 Malji-ka-Kamra, Churu, is one of the best-preserved havelis in Shekhawati, but it's crumbling fast so get there quick. ▶▶ page 283.

Clockwise from top

Jaisalmer.

Nagaur.

Taj Mahal.

Juna Mahal, Dungarpur.

Udaipur lake.

Clockwise from top
Malji-ka-Kamra, Churu.
Bundi.
Ranthambhore National Park.
Ranakpur.

Next page Meherangarh Fort.

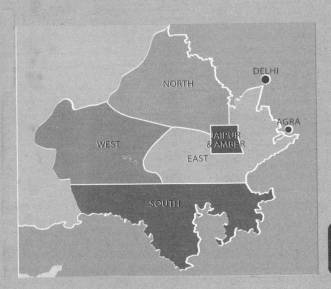

Contents

Footprint features

Essentials

Planning your trip

Where to go

Rajasthan offers an almost daunting range of possibilities for travellers. You could travel for weeks without seeing it all. Here we suggest some possible tours ranging from one-week to one-month trips. Travel networks of road, rail and air are so interconnected that you can combine parts of the routes given below in a range of different ways. Travel agencies, listed through the book, can make the necessary arrangements for a relatively small fee, saving you time and bother, but remember that air and rail tickets can be difficult to get at short notice for some trips, especially during the winter peak season. Allow a little more time if you are planning to travel entirely by road and rail. However, if you use overnight trains for longer journeys you can cover almost as much ground in the same time as you would by flying.

One week

You'll probably need a night or two in Delhi to recover from the flight and adjust to both the time zone and being in India. Most people have the Taj Mahal as a top priority even on a flying visit; if you're keen to see it you could either head to Agra first, or follow these suggestions in reverse and leave it until the end. Wherever you go from Agra it's probably worth stopping off at Fatehpur Sikri for at least a couple of hours on the way. From there you could head to Bharatpur if you fancy some birdspotting in tranquil Keoladeo Ghana National Park or, if tigers are more your thing, make for Ranthambhore, possibly stopping off along the way for a night at the wonderfully wacky Bhanwar Vilas Palace in Karauli. Most tourists head to Jaipur from Agra, or vice versa, on the ever-popular 'Golden Triangle' route. Jaipur is not everyone's cup of tea, however; many feel that the hustle and bustle is not outweighed by the city's attractions. Other options include staying at one of the heritage hotels nearby, at Kanota and Bhandarej, for example, and then heading back towards Delhi on the quieter Alwar road if you're travelling by car, perhaps stopping for the night at Sariska Palace or Kesroli Hill Fort.

If this sounds too relaxed, but you don't fancy spending long in Jaipur, it's possible to get the train to Jaipur and continue on elsewhere from there, to Ajmer/Pushkar, for example. From there you could get as far as Jodhpur or even Udaipur, and then fly back to Delhi.

Two weeks

The extra week could be spent travelling further in one direction; to Bikaner and then Jaisalmer in the west if you felt like taking in some authentic desert scenery and culture; Mount Abu, Ranakpur and Kumbhalgarh to the south if you wanted to see stunning Jain temples, an amazing fort and experience Rajasthan's coolest climate; or Bundi, Kota and Chittaurgarh in the east if you felt like getting off the beaten track and witnessing the Rajasthan of yesteryear.

One month

One month is enough time to complete an entire loop of Rajasthan or, at a more leisurely pace, either an eastern or western loop taking in most of the sights of north and south. This could mean leaving Delhi for Agra, and then on to places such as Bharatpur, Ranthambhore, Bundi, Kota, Chittaurgarh, Dungarpur and then Udaipur. From there you could head back to

Packing for India

You can buy most essentials in larger cities and shops in five-star hotels. Items you might find useful include loose-fitting, light cotton clothes including a sarong (women should dress modestly at all times; brief shorts and tight vest tops are best avoided, though on the beach modest swimwear is fine). It can be cold in the north from December to February, especially in the desert, so warmer clothing is necessary. Comfortable shoes, sandals or trainers are essential. Take high-factor sun screen and a sun hat. Earplugs and an eyemask are also a good idea. Indian pharmacies can be very cheap but aren't always reliable,

so take a supply of medicines from home, including inhalers and anti-malarial drugs (Proguanil is not available). For protection against mosquitoes, take repellent. See also Health, page 44.

Photocopies of documents, passport ID and visa pages, and spare photos are useful when applying for permits, checking into hotels, or in case of loss or theft.

For budget travellers: moquito nets aren't always provided in cheap hotels so take one with you. Take a good padlock to secure your budget room too, though these are cheaply bought in India. A cotton or silk sheet sleeping bag are useful when you can't be sure of clean linen.

Delhi, probably taking in Jodhpur and Jaipur on your way, giving an interesting mix of historical sights, major cities and varied wildlife. Alternatively, you could head through the Shekhawati region from Delhi, perhaps stopping at Neemrana along the way, then continue west to Bikaner, Jaisalmer, Jodhpur, and then on through the Ranakpur/Kumbhalgarh region to Udaipur. A couple of days relaxing by the lake would prepare you for the journey back north, stopping at Ajmer/Pushkar and Jaipur en route. By the end you'd have seen a fascinating blend of desert landscapes and beautiful havelis, religious sites and major cities. Travelling by plane and/or hiring a car with driver will free up more time for sightseeing, making the entire loop possible at a reasonably leisurely pace.

When to go

Late October to early March is the most pleasant period to visit Rajasthan, especially the desert districts of Jaisalmer, Jodhpur and Bikaner, but it's also the busiest time of year, with good accommodation being booked up months in advance. The summer months of April to June get extremely hot while the southwest monsoon (July to September), in addition to being very humid, brings other hazards. European school holidays do create a bustle during August as well, as the light rains take the edge off the heat. Road surfaces are often damaged by heavy rain, most national parks are closed and some remote places become inaccessible. Travelling slightly outside the peak season often means cheaper accommodation and fewer crowds, advantages which can outweigh the less predictable climate.

If you'd like to time your trip to coincide with a festival or two, it's worth noting that while Rajasthan's most famous fair, the Pushkar Camel Fair, takes place in November, January and February see the highest concentration of events. Highlights include the camel fair in Bikaner in January; the boisterous but authentic cattle fair in Nagaur in January/February; the highly regarded Desert Festival in Jaisalmer, also in February; the Jaipur Literary Festival in January; and and the Elephant Festival in Jaipur in March. Remember, however, that prices tend to skyrocket around these events, so try to book well in advance if possible.

Birdwatching

The country's diverse and rich natural habitats harbour over 1200 species of birds of which around 150 are endemic. Visitors can enjoy spotting Oriental species whether it is in towns, in the countryside or more abundantly in the national parks and sanctuaries. On the plains, the cooler months (Nov-Mar) are the most comfortable for a chance to see migratory birds from the hills, but the highlands themselves are ideal in May-Jun and again after the monsoons when visibility improves in Oct-Nov. Bodies of water of all sizes draw visiting water fowl from other continents during the winter.

It is quite easy to get to some parks from the important tourist centres. *A Birdwatcher's Guide to India* by Krys Kazmierczak and Raj Singh (Prion Ltd, Sandy, Bedfordshire, UK, 1998), is well researched and comprehensive with helpful practical information and maps. See also Background, page 335.

Contact www.delhibird.net, www.kolkatabirds.com, www.oriental birdclub.org, www.sacon.org.
Bird Link, biks@giasdl01.vsnl.net.in, is concerned with conservation of birds and their habitat.

Camel safaris

Today's camel safaris try to recreate something of the atmosphere of the early merchant camel trains that travelled through the desert. The Thar Desert, in Rajasthan, with its vast stretches of sand dotted with dunes and its own specially adapted shrubs and wildlife, is ideal territory. The guides are expert navigators and the villages on the way add colour to an unforgettable experience, if you are prepared to sit out the somewhat uncomfortable ride. Jaisalmer has regular camel safaris ranging from short rides on the dunes to long hauls of 6 or 7 days visiting villages, towns, dunes, wildlife areas and scenic places. Facilities vary: simple safaris allow you to spend the night on the dunes, in tents or village huts supplied with bed-rolls, and you get simple Rajasthani food; de luxe ('royal') safaris provide luxury self-contained tents, multi-cuisine meals and camel carts to transport your baggage. Bikaner and Jodhpur have fewer tour operators and hotels offering safaris, at a higher price than Jaisalmer but with less rampant commercialism; if you want to traverse areas where you don't keep bumping into tourists these could be a better options.

Cricket

Cricket has an almost fanatical following across India. Reinforced by satellite TV and radio and a national side that enjoys high world rankings and much outstanding individual talent, cricket has become a national obsession. Stars have cult status, and you can see children trying to model themselves on their game on any and every open space.

Contact India's cricket board (BCCI), www.bcci.cricket.deepthi.com, keeps up to date with all the latest in Indian cricket, and for information and tickets.

Cycling

Cycling offers a peaceful – not to mention healthy – alternative to cars, buses or trains. Touring on locally hired bicycles is ideal if you want to see village life in Rajasthan. As cycles are an important means of transport, it is easy to find repairers for punctures and other problems in towns and cities. These cycles are simple and do not have gears. If you bring mountain bikes and multi-geared cycles for touring with you, be warned that thefts are not uncommon. Delhi-based tour operators arrange de luxe cycle tours of Rajasthan with guide, back-up vehicles and accommodation in good hotels on the way. Mopeds are an alternative to cycling and these can be bought or hired in popular tourist destinations like Jaipur and Udaipur.

Football

Football is played from professional level to kickabout in any open space. The season is Oct-Mar and details of matches are published in the local papers. Top class game tickets are Rs 25, but they are sold for much more on the black market. The crowds generate tremendous fervour for big matches, and standards are improving. African players are now featuring more frequently with Indian teams and monthly salaries have risen to over Rs 40,000 per month, an excellent wage by Indian standards.

Contact www.indianfootball.com, for the latest news.

Horse safaris

These are similar to camel safaris, with grooms (and often the horse owner) accompanying. The best months are Nov to Mar when it is cooler in the day (and often cold at night). The trails chosen usually enable you to visit small villages, old forts and temples, and take you through a variety of terrain and vegetation including scrub- covered arid plains to forested hills. The charges can be a lot higher than for a camel safari but the night stays are often in comfortable palaces, forts or *havelis*. The safaris are only recommended for those who are reasonably adept at horse riding as the trips can be long and tiring, the horses are also quite spirited and require experienced handling. Most routes are planned to include interesting sightseeing destinations within a week or 10-day horse-riding tour.

Jeep safaris

Besides game drives by jeep in sanctuaries and national parks, some hotels and tour operators now arrange jeep safaris, with accommodation in heritage hotels and camps on the way along lesser roads and cross-country trails.

Trekking

The easily accessible parts of the national parks, wildlife sanctuaries and reserved forests provide ample opportunity for walking but if you want to venture deeper you'll need to take a local guide as paths can soon become indistinct and confusing. Some areas require a permit to visit since the authorities wish to keep disturbance to wildlife and tribal communities to a minimum. The government Wildlife and Forestry Departments and private tour operators will be able to set you on the right path but you need to enquire, sometimes as much as a month, in advance.

There are simple lodges and guesthouses in most areas including tribal villages, but more comfortable jungle camps and luxury safari lodges also exist in the national parks, which can be used as a base for day treks.

As the altitudes here are much lower than the Himalaya and the Western Ghats,

First impressions

On arrival at any of India's major cities the first impressions can take you aback. The exciting images of an ancient and richly diverse culture that draw many visitors to India can be overwhelmed by the immediate sensations that first greet you. These can be daunting and make adjustment to India early on in your trip difficult. Even on a short visit give yourself time and space to adjust.
Pollution All cities seriously suffer.
Noise Many find India incredibly noisy, as radios, videos and loudspeakers blare at all times.

Smells India has a baffling mix of smells, from the richly pungent and unpleasant to the delicately subtle.
Pressure On stepping out of your hotel everybody seems to clamour to sell you their services. Taxi and rickshaw drivers are always there when you don't want them. There often seems to be no sense of personal space or privacy. Young women are often stared at, so cover up.
Public hygiene (or lack of it) It is common to see people urinating in public places and defecating in the open countryside.

the focus is on visiting tribal villages and seeing wildlife and birds along the trail, and perhaps a fort or a temple.

Yoga and meditation
There has been a growing Western interest in the ancient life-disciplines in search of physical and spiritual wellbeing, as practised in ancient India. Yoga is supposed to regulate the nervous system and aims to attain union of body, mind and spirit through the practice of *asanas* (body postures), breath control, discipline, cleansing, contemplation and awareness. It seeks to achieve moral purification through abstinence and restraint (dietary and sexual). Meditation, which complements yoga to relieve stress, increase awareness and bring inner peace, prescribes the practice of *dhyana* (purposeful concentration), achieved by withdrawing

oneself from external distractions and focusing one's attention upon consciousness itself. This leads ultimately to *samadhi* (release from worldly bonds).

Hatha Yoga has captured the Western imagination; it promises good health through postural exercises, while the search for inner peace and calm drive others to learn meditation techniques.

Centres across the country offer courses for beginners and practitioners. Some are at special resort hotels that offer all-inclusive packages in idyllic locations, some advocate simple communal living in an ashram while others may require rigorous discipline in austere monastic surroundings. Yoga holidays in Rajasthan can be arranged through **KOKOindia** (www.kokoindia.com) and Yoga on a Shoestring at the lovely Castle Bijapur.

Taking a tour
You may choose an inclusive package holiday or let a specialist operator quote for a tailor-made tour. Out of season these can be worth exploring. The lowest prices quoted from the UK vary from about US$550 for a week (flights, hotel and breakfast) in the low season to over US$3000 for three weeks during the peak season. Most will chalk out individual itineraries and cover the major sights with small groups. For a list of specialist tour operators, who arrange anything from general tours and wildlife safaris to ashram retreats, can see page 51.

Getting there

Air

India is accessible by air from virtually every continent. Most international flights arrive in Delhi or Mumbai and from there you can fly to cities in Rajasthan. Some carriers permit 'open-jaw' travel, arriving in and departing from different cities.

Buying a ticket

Discounts The cheapest fares from Europe tend to be with Central European, Central Asian or Middle Eastern airlines. With these airlines it pays to confirm your return flight as early as possible. You can also get good discounts from Australasia, Southeast Asia and Japan. If you plan to visit two or more South Asian countries within three weeks, you may qualify for a 30% discount on your international tickets. International air tickets can be bought in India though payment must be made in foreign currency.

Stopovers and Round-the-World (RTW) tickets You can arrange several stopovers in India on RTW and long-distance tickets. RTW tickets allow you to fly in to one and out from another international airport. You may be able to arrange some internal flights using international carriers, eg **Air India** sometimes allows stopovers within India for a small extra charge. **Emirates/Sri Lankan** offers some attractive return fares to Australia that allow stops in Dubai, India, Sri Lanka and either Thailand or Singapore. If you plan to visit two or more South Asian countries within three weeks, you may qualify for a 30% discount on your international tickets. Ask your travel agent. International air tickets can be bought in India, often at excellent prices, though payment must be made in foreign currency.

From Europe

The best deals are from the UK (try www.cheapflights.com, which also has lots of useful information). In 2010, a return, off-season flight direct to Delhi from London Heathrow could cost as little as £300, but prices do rise in the high season of Christmas, New Year and Easter. The flight from London to Delhi takes around eight hours. Airlines such as **Jet Airways** offer good deals on internal flights when booked in conjunction with an international leg.

Flight consolidators in the UK offering competitive fares include: **Flight bookers**, T0203-320 3320, www.ebookers.com; and **North South Travel**, T01245-608291, www.northsouthtravel.co.uk (profits to charity). Air India has a companion-free scheme for routes from India to the USA/Canada/UK/Europe and also to other destinations in Asia and the Middle East (valid until 31 December 2010, one-way and return trips).

From Australasia

Flights cost anything from Aus$1500-2500 in the high season, falling to Aus$1000 in the low season. Availability can be particularly low around September and Christmas. The cheapest deals generally involve a change in Southeast Asia.

From North America

Flights cost anything from US$1300/US$1500 in the high season from New York/Los Angeles, falling to US$1000/US$1200 in the low season. Availability can be particularly low around September and Christmas. Several airlines fly direct from New York to Delhi and Mumbai, including **Air India** and **Jet Airways** (15-16 hours). From the west coast, it is best to fly via Hong Kong, Singapore or Thailand using one of those countries' national carrier.

Departure tax

Rs 500 is payable for all international departures other than those to neighbouring SAARC countries, when the tax is Rs 250 (not reciprocated by Sri Lanka). This is normally included in your international ticket; check when buying. (To save time, 'Security Check' your baggage before checking in at departure.)

Ticket agents

Abercrombie & Kent, www.abercrombie kent.com, www.abercrombiekent.com.au.
Adventure Company, T0800-554 7016, www.adventurecompany.co.uk. Quotes competitive fares.
Adventure World, www.adventureworld.com.au.
Ebookers, T0203-320 3320, www.ebookers.com.
Flight Centres, www.flightcentre.com.
North South Travel, T01245-608291, www. northsouthtravel.co.uk. Profits go to charity.
Peregrine, www.peregrine.net.au. Adventure tours for small groups.
STA, London, T0871-230 0040, www.sta travel.co.uk. Over 100 offices worldwide.
Trailfinders, London, T0845-058 5858, www.trailfinders.com. Worldwide agencies.
Travel Corporation of India, www.tcindia.com.
Travel Cuts, www.travelcuts.com. US and Canadian agent.

Websites

www.expedia.co.uk
www.lastminute.com
www.travelocity.com

Airlines

Air India, www.airindia.com
British Airways, www.ba.com
Cathay Pacific, www.cathaypacific.com
Emirates, www.emirates.com
Gulf Air, www.gulfair.com
Jet, www.jetairways.com
Kingfisher, www.flykingfisher.com
KLM, www.klm.com
Kuwait Airways, www.kuwait-airways.com
Lufthansa, www.lufthansa.com
Malaysian Airlines, www.malaysiaairlines.com
Qantas, www.qantas.com.au
Royal Jordanian, www.rj.com
Singapore Airlines, www.singaporeair.com
Thai Airways, www.thaiair.com
Virgin Atlantic, www.virgin-atlantic.com

Road

Crossings between India and its neighbours are affected by the political relations between them. Get your Indian visa in advance, before arriving at the border. Several road border crossings are open periodically, but permission to cross cannot be guaranteed.

Getting around

Air

Deregulation of the airline industry has had a transformative effect on travel within India, with a host of low-budget private carriers offering sometimes unbelievably cheap fares on an ever-expanding network of routes in a bid to woo the train-travelling middle class. Promotional fares as low as Rs 9 are not unknown and, on any given day, booking a week or two in advance, you can hope to fly between Delhi and Mumbai for between Rs 1500 and Rs 3500 one way. Competition from the efficiently run private sector has, in general, improved the quality of services provided by the nationalized airlines. It also seems to herald the end of the two-tier pricing structure, meaning that ticket prices are now usually the same for foreign and Indian travellers. The airport authorities too have made efforts to improve handling on the ground.

The best way to get an idea of the current routes, carriers and fares is to use a third-party booking website such as **www.cheapairticketsindia.com** (toll-free numbers: UK T0800-101 0928, USA T1-888 825 8680), **www.cleartrip.com**, **www.makemytrip.co.in**, or **www.yatra.com**. Tickets booked on these sites are typically issued as an email ticket or an SMS text message – the simplest option if you have an Indian mobile phone, though it must be converted to a paper ticket at the relevant carrier's airport offices before you will be allowed into the terminal.

All the major airlines are connected to the central reservation system and there are local travel agents who will book your tickets for a fee if you don't want to spend precious time searching online or waiting in a queue. Remember that tickets are in great demand in the peak season on some sectors particularly between Rajasthan and Delhi (eg Udaipur–Delhi) so it is essential to get them weeks or months ahead. If you are able to pre-plan your trip, it is even possible to book internal flights at the time you buy your international air ticket. This can be done through an agent or direct with the airline (eg Air India, Jet Airways). Both Jet and Indian offer a variety of flight passes (details available on their respective websites), valid on certain sections of their networks; these can be useful if you plan to travel extensively and quickly in areas beyond the reach of the budget airlines.

National airlines

Air India, www.airindia.com. The nationalized carrier with a wide network of domestic routes.
Indigo, T099-1038 3838, http:book.goIndigo.in. Comparable to SpiceJet.
Jet Airways, T1800-225522, www.jetairway.com. This long-established airline, offers full-service domestic flights.

Jetlite, www.jetlite.com. Comprehensive coverage of the country.
Kingfisher, T0124 284 4700 (T0843 080 1010 in the UK), www.flykingfisher.com. Similar service and prices to Jet.
SpiceJet, T1800-180 3333, www.spicejet.com. No-frills service between major cities.

Rail

Trains can still be the cheapest and most comfortable means of travelling long distances, saving you hotel expenses on overnight journeys. It gives access to booking station Retiring Rooms, which can be useful from time to time (see page 31). Above all, you have an ideal opportunity to meet local travellers and catch a glimpse of life on the ground. Remember the dark glass fitted on air-conditioned coaches does restrict vision.

High-speed trains

There are several air-conditioned 'high-speed' **Shatabdi** (or 'Century') **Express** for day travel, and **Rajdhani Express** ('Capital City') for overnight journeys. These cover large sections of the network but due to high demand you need to book them well in advance (up to 90 days). Meals and drinks are usually included.

Royal trains

You can travel like a maharaja on the *Palace on Wheels*, www.palaceonwheels.com, which gives visitors an opportunity to see some of the 'royal' cities in Rajasthan during the winter months for around US$300-400 per person per day. The diesel-pulled carriages are fitted out with plush fabrics, and include restaurant cars, a library and bar. It departs Delhi every Wednesday from October to April and gets booked up usually six months in advance. The itinerary includes Jaipur and Amber Fort, Chittaurgarh, Udaipur (**Lake Palace Hotel**), Jaisalmer, Jodhpur (**Umaid Bhawan Palace**) and Bharatpur, ending with trips to Fatehpur Sikri and Agra before returning to Delhi. You travel overnight in cabins fitted out with luxurious private baths and personal attendants. It is a well packaged tour, but rather compressed for some of the key sites. Travelling by night means that you don't see much of the countryside. Bookings via **Rajasthan Tourism** ① *Bikaner House, New Delhi, T011-2338 1884, www.rajasthantourism.gov.in.*

There is now also the *Royal Rajasthan on Wheels*, www.royalpalaceonwheels.com, taking in Jaipur, Jaisalmer, Jodhpur, Sawai Madhopur, Udaipur, Bharatpur and Agra. It's stunningly decorated including one carriage that's a spa on wheels.

The world's oldest working steam engine, *Fairy Queen*, built in 1855, runs a weekend tour for 50, twice a month in the winter. It travels from Delhi to Alwar with a transfer by road to the (now tigerless) Sariska Tiger Sanctuary, and accommodation at **Sariska Palace**; US$165 per person twin-share. Bookings via the **International Tourst Office at New Delhi Railway Station** ① *T91-11-234 0515, or email itbnrind@hotmail.com, http://indianrailways.gov.in/tourist/fairy_queen.htm.*

Classes

A/c First Class, available only on main routes, is very comfortable (bedding provided). It will also be possible for tourists to reserve special coaches (some air conditioning) which are normally allocated to senior railway officials only. **A/c Sleeper**, two and three-tier configurations (known as 2AC and 3AC), are clean and comfortable and good value. **A/c Executive Class**, with wide reclining seats, are available on many *Shatabdi* trains at double the price of the ordinary **a/c Chair Car**, which are equally comfortable. **1st Class (non-a/c)** is gradually being phased out (now rather run down but still pleasant if you like open windows). **Sleeper Class** provides basic upholstered seats and is a 'Reserved' class though tickets are sometimes 'subject to available accommodation'. **2nd Class** (non-a/c) two- and three-tier (commonly called Sleeper), provides exceptionally cheap and atmospheric travel but can be crowded and uncomfortable, and toilet facilities can be unpleasant; it is nearly always better to use the Indian-style squat loos rather than the Western-style ones as they are better maintained. At the bottom rung is **Unreserved 2nd Class**, with hard wooden benches. You can travel long distances for a trivial amount of money, but unreserved carriages are often ridiculously crowded, and getting off at your station may involve a battle of will and strength against the hordes trying to shove their way on.

Train touts

Many railway stations – and some bus stations and major tourist sites – are heavily populated with touts. Self-styled 'agents' will board trains before they enter the station and seek out tourists, often picking up their luggage and setting off with words such as "Madam!/Sir! Come with me madam/sir! You need top class hotel ...". They will even select porters to take your luggage without giving you any say. For a first-time visitor such touts can be more than a nuisance. You need to keep calm and firm. Decide in advance where you want to stay. If you need a porter on trains, select one yourself and agree a price before the porter sets off with your baggage. If travelling with a companion, one can stay guarding the luggage while the other gets hold of a taxi and negotiates the price to the hotel. It sounds complicated and sometimes it feels it. The most important thing is to behave as if you know what you are doing!

Indrail passes

These allow travel across the network without having to pay extra reservation fees and sleeper charges but you have to spend a high proportion of your time on the train to make it worthwhile. However, the advantages of pre-arranged reservations and automatic access to 'Tourist Quotas' can tip the balance in favour of the pass for some travellers. Tourists (foreigners and Indians resident abroad) may buy these passes from the tourist sections of principal railway booking offices and pay in foreign currency or by major credit card. Fares range from US$57 to US$1060 for adults or around half that for children. Rail-cum-air tickets are also to be made available. Indrail passes can also conveniently be bought abroad from special agents. For people contemplating a single long journey soon after arriving in India, the half- or one-day Pass with a confirmed reservation is worth the peace of mind; two- or four-day passes are also sold. The UK agent is **SD Enterprises Ltd** ① *103 Wembley Park Drive, Wembley, Middlesex, HA9 8HG, UK, T0208-903 3411, www.indiarail.co.uk*. They make all necessary reservations and offer excellent advice. They can also book Air India and Jet Airways internal flights.

Cost

A/c First Class costs about double the rate for two-tier, and non-a/c Second Class about half. Children (five-12) travel at half the adult fare. The young (12-30 years) and senior citizens (65 years and over) are allowed a 30% discount on journeys over 500 km (just show your passport). Fares for individual journeys are based on distance covered and reflect both the class and the type of train. Higher rates apply on the Mail and Express trains and the air-conditioned *Shatabdi* and *Rajdhani Expresses*.

Rail travel tips

Bedding It can get cold in air-conditioned coaches when travelling at night. Bedding is provide on second class air-conditioned sleepers. On others it can be hired for Rs 30 from the Station Baggage Office for second class.

Berths It is worth asking for upper berths, especially in second class three-tier sleepers, as they can also be used during the day when the lower berths are used as seats. Once the middle berth is lowered for sleeping the lower berth becomes too cramped to sit on.

Credit cards Some main stations now have separate credit card booking queues – even shorter than women's queues!

Delays Always allow plenty of time for booking and for making connections. Delays are common on all types of transport. The special **Shatabdi** and **Rajdhani Express** are generally quite reliable. Ordinary Express and Mail trains have priority over local services and occasionally surprise by being punctual, but generally the longer the journey time, the greater the delay. Delays on the rail network are cumulative, so arrivals and departures from mid-stations are often several hours behind schedule. Allow at least two hours for connections, more if the first part of the journey is long distance.

Food and drink It's best to carry some though tea, bottled water and snacks are sold on the platforms (through the windows). Carry plenty of small notes and coins on long journeys. Rs 50 and Rs 100 notes can be difficult to change when purchasing small food items. On long-distance trains, the restaurant car is often near the upper class carriages.

Getting a seat It's usually impossible to make seat reservations at small 'intermediate' stations as they don't have an allocation. You can sometimes use a porter to get you a seat in a 2nd class carriage. For about Rs 20 he'll take the luggage and get you a seat!

Internet services Much information is now available online via the websites www.railtourismindia.com, www.indianrail.gov.in and www.trainenquiry.com, where you can check timetables (which change frequently), numbers, seat availability and even the running status of your train. Another useful website for checking availability and planning itineraries is www.erail.in. Internet tickets can theoretically be bought on www.irctc.co.in, though a credit card is required; foreign cards are accepted, but persistence is needed with the website when registering. Easier still is using www.makemytrip.co.in, where you can view train info and make bookings. An alternative is to seek out a local agent who can sell e-tickets, which can cost as little as Rs 5-10 (plus Rs 20 reservation fee), and save hours of hassle; simply present the printout to the ticket collector.

Left luggage Bags can be left for up to 30 days in station cloakrooms. These are especially useful when there is time to go sightseeing before an evening train. The bags must be lockable and you are advised not to leave any food in them (rats!).

Ladies' compartments A woman travelling alone, overnight, on an unreserved second class train can ask if there is one of these. Lone female travellers may feel more comfortable in air-conditioned sleeper coaches, which require reservations and are used extensively by Indian families.

Ladies' and seniors' queues Separate (shorter) ticket queues may be available for women and senior citizens. Travellers over 60 can ask for a 30% discount on the price.

Overbooking Passengers with valid tickets but no berth reservations are sometimes permitted to travel overnight, causing great discomfort to travellers occupying lower berths. Wait-listed passengers should confirm the status of their ticket in advance by calling enquiries at the nearest computerised reservation office. Or you can check online and click on PNR status for update. At the station, check the reservation charts (usually on the relevant platform) and contact the Station Manager or Ticket Collector.

Porters These can carry prodigious amounts of luggage. Rates vary from station to station (sometimes listed on a board on the platform) but are usually around Rs 10-25 per item of luggage.

Pre-paid taxis Many main stations have a pre-paid taxi (or auto-rickshaw) service which offers a reliable service at a fair price. Search these out on arrival, they can save you from nasty disagreements.

Quotas A large number of seats are technically reserved as quotas for various groups of travellers (civil servants, military personnel, foreign tourists, etc). Tourist quota is available at main stations. As a tourist you are not obliged to use it, but it can get you on an otherwise 'full' train; you will need your passport, and either pay in US dollars or pounds sterling or in rupees with a currency encashment certificate/ATM receipt. In addition, many stations have their own quota for particular trains so that a train may be 'fully booked' when there are still some tickets available from the special quota of other stations. These are only sold on the day of departure so wait-listed passengers are often able to travel at the last minute. Ask the superintendent on duty to try the 'Special' or 'VIP Quota'. The 'Tatkal' system releases a small percentage of seats at 0800 on the day before a train departs; you pay an extra Rs 75-200 (depending on class and season) to get on an otherwise heavily booked train.

Security Keep valuables close to you, securely locked, and away from windows. For security, carry a good lock and chain to attach your luggage.

Tickets and reservations Unreserved second-class tickets are available at any station by queueing at the window – a skill in itself – and represent the quickest way to get on a train that is about to depart. On most trains (not Rajdhani or Shatabdi Express) you can attempt to upgrade an unreserved ticket by seeking out the Station Manager's office, or the black-suited TTE (Travelling Ticket Examiner, pronounced 'tee-tee') if the train is at the platform, and asking if a seat is available; an upgrade fee is payable. This can save time waiting in the slower line for reservations.

It is possible to reserve tickets for virtually any train on the network from one of the 520 computerized reservation centres across India. It is always best to book as far in advance as possible (usually up to 60 days). To reserve a seat on a particular train, note down the train's name, number and departure time, and fill in a reservation form while you line up at the ticket window; you can use one form for up to four passengers. At busy stations the wait can take an hour or more; you can save a lot of time and effort by asking a travel agent to get yours for a small fee, usually of around Rs 50-100. If the class you want is full, ask at the ticket window if special 'quotas' are available (see above). If not, consider buying a 'wait list' ticket, as seats often become available close to the train's departure time; phone the station on the day of departure to check your ticket's status. If you don't have a reservation for a particular train but carry an Indrail Pass, you may get one by arriving about three hours early. Be wary of touts at the station offering tickets, hotels or money changing.

Timetables Regional timetables are available cheaply from station bookstalls; the monthly 'Indian Bradshaw' is sold in principal stations. The handy 'Trains at a Glance' (Rs 30) lists popular trains likely to be used by most foreign travellers and is available in the UK from SD Enterprises Ltd (see under Indrail passes, page 21).

Road

Road travel is often the only choice for reaching many of the places of outstanding interest in which India is so rich. For the uninitiated, travel by road can also be a worrying experience because of the apparent absence of conventional traffic regulations. Also, in the mountains, especially during the rainy season, landslides are possible. Vehicles drive on the left – in theory. Routes around the major cities are usually crowded with lorry traffic, especially at night, and the main roads are often poor and slow. There are a few motorway-style expressways, but most main roads are single track. Some district roads are quiet, and although they are not fast they can be a good way of seeing the country and village life if you have the time.

Bus

Buses now reach virtually every part of India, offering a cheap, if often uncomfortable, means of visiting places off the rail network. Very few villages are now more than 2-3 km from a bus stop. Services are run by the State Corporation from the State Bus Stand (and private companies which often have offices nearby). The latter allow advance reservation and though tickets prices are a little higher, they have fewer stops and are a bit more comfortable.

Bus categories Though comfortable for sightseeing trips, apart from the very best 'sleeper coaches' even **air-conditioned luxury coaches** can be very uncomfortable for really long journeys. If you're booking a 'sleeper' bus, try and book a berth downstairs near the front, and for solo women travellers book a single berth near the front. Often the air conditioning is very cold so wrap up. Journeys over 10 hours can be extremely tiring so it is better to go by train if there is a choice. **Express buses** run over long distances (frequently overnight), these are often called 'video coaches' and can be an appalling experience unless you appreciate loud film music blasting through the night. Ear plugs and eye masks may ease the pain. They rarely average more than 45 km per hour. **Local buses** are often very crowded, quite bumpy, slow and usually poorly maintained. However, over short distances, they can be a very cheap, friendly and easy way of getting about. Even where signboards are not in English someone will usually give you directions. Many larger towns have **minibus** services which charge a little more than the buses and pick up and drop passengers on request. Again very crowded, and with restricted headroom, they are the fastest way of getting about many of the larger towns.

Bus travel tips Some towns have different bus stations for different destinations. Booking on major long-distance routes is now computerized. Book in advance where possible and avoid the back of the bus where it can be very bumpy. If your destination is only served by a local bus you may do better to take the Express bus and 'persuade' the driver, with a tip in advance, to stop where you want to get off. You will have to pay the full fare to the first stop beyond your destination but you will get there faster and more comfortably. When an unreserved bus pulls into a bus station, there is usually an unholy scramble for seats, whilst those arriving have to struggle to get off! In many areas there is an unwritten 'rule of reservation' using handkerchiefs or bags thrust through the windows to reserve seats. Some visitors may feel a more justified right to a seat having fought their way through the crowd, but it is generally best to do as local people do and be prepared with a handkerchief or 'sarong'. As soon as it touches the seat, it is yours! Leave it on your seat when getting off to use the toilet at bus stations.

Car

A car provides a chance to travel off the beaten track, and gives unrivalled opportunities for seeing something of India's great variety of villages and small towns. Until recently, the most widely used hire car was the Hindustan Ambassador. However, except for the newest model, they are often very unreliable, and although they still have their devotees, many find them uncomfortable for long journeys. For a similar price, Maruti cars and vans (Omni) are much more reliable and are now the preferred choice in many areas. Gypsy 4WDs and Jeeps are also available, especially in the hills, where larger Sumos have made an appearance. Maruti Esteems and Toyota Qualis are comfortable and have optional reliable air conditioning. A specialist operator can be very helpful in arranging itineraries and car hire in advance.

Car hire With a driver, car hire is cheaper than in the West. A car shared by three or four can be very good value. Be sure to check carefully the mileage at the beginning and end of

The hazards of road travel

On most routes it is impossible to average more than 50-60 kph in a car. Journeys are often very long, and can seem an endless succession of horn blowing, unexpected dangers, and unforeseen delays. Villages are often congested – beware of the concealed spine-breaking speed bumps – and cattle, sheep and goats may wander at will across the road.

Directions can also be difficult to find. Drivers frequently don't know the way, maps are often hopelessly inaccurate and map reading is an almost entirely unknown skill. Training in driving is negligible and the test often a farce. There can be real dangers from poor judgement, irresponsible overtaking and a general philosophy of 'might is right'.

the trip. Two- or three-day trips from main towns can also give excellent opportunities for sightseeing off the beaten track in reasonable comfort. Local drivers often know their way much better than drivers from other states, so where possible it is a good idea to get a local driver who speaks the state language, in addition to being able to communicate with you. In the mountains, it is better to use a driver who knows the roads. Drivers may sleep in the car overnight though hotels sometimes provide a bed for them. If you value your driver and your safety, make sure there is a bed for them at the hotel and question hotels who do not provide them. They are responsible for their expenses, including meals. Car (and auto) drivers increase their earnings by taking you to hotels and shops where they get a handsome commission (which you will pay for). If you feel inclined, a tip at the end of the tour of Rs 100 per day in addition to their daily allowance is perfectly acceptable. Check beforehand if fuel and inter-state taxes are included in the hire charge.

Cars can be hired through private companies. International companies such as **Hertz**, **Europcar** and **Budget** operate in some major cities and offer reliable cars; their rates are generally higher than those of local firms (eg **Sai Service**, **Wheels**). The price of an imported car can be three times that of the Ambassador.

Car with driver	Economy Maruti 800 Ambassador	Regular a/c Maruti 800 Contessa	Premium a/c Maruti 1000 Opel	Luxury a/c Esteem Qualis
8 hrs/80 km	Rs 800	Rs 1000	Rs 1400	Rs 1800+
Extra km	Rs 4-7	Rs 9	Rs 13	Rs 18
Extra hour	Rs 40	Rs 50	Rs 70	Rs 100
Out of town				
Per km	Rs 7	Rs 9	Rs 13	Rs 18
Night halt	Rs 100	Rs 200	Rs 250	Rs 250

Car travel tips When booking emphasize the importance of good tyres and general roadworthiness. On main roads across India **petrol stations** are reasonably frequent, but some areas are poorly served. Some service stations only have diesel pumps though they may have small reserves of petrol. Always carry a spare can. Diesel is widely available and normally much cheaper than petrol. Petrol is rarely above 92 octane. Drivers must have third party **insurance**. This may have to be with an Indian insurer, or with a foreign insurer who has a national guarantor. You must also be in possession of an International Driving Permit, issued by a recognized driving authority in your home country (eg the AA in the UK, apply at least six weeks before leaving). **Asking the way** can be very frustrating as you are likely to get widely conflicting advice each time you stop to ask. On the main roads, 'mile' posts periodically appear in English and can help. Elsewhere, it is best to ask directions often and follow the average direction! **Accidents** often produce large and angry crowds very quickly. It is best to leave the scene of the accident and report it to the police as quickly as possible thereafter. Ensure that you have adequate provisions, plenty of food and drink and a basic tool set in the car.

Cycling

Cycling is an excellent way of seeing the quiet byways of India. It is easy to hire bikes in most small towns for about Rs 20-30 per day. Indian bikes are heavy and without gears, but on the flat they offer a good way of exploring comparatively short distances outside towns. In the more prosperous tourist resorts, mountain bikes are now becoming available, but at a higher charge. If you want to tour more extensively and you may want to buy a cycle.

There are shops in every town and the local Hero brand is considered the best, with Atlas and BSA good alternatives; expect to pay around Rs 1200-1500 for a second-hand Indian bike but remember to bargain. At the end of your trip you could sell it easily at half price. Imported bikes have lighter weight and gears, but are more difficult to get repaired and carry the much greater risk of being stolen or damaged. If you wish to take your own, it is quite easy if you dismantle it and pack it in its original shipping carton; be sure to take all essential spares including a pump. It is possible to get Indian spares for 26" wheel cycles. All cyclists should take bungy cords and good lights from home, although cycling at night is not recommended; take care not to leave your bike parked anywhere with your belongings. Bike repair shops are universal and charges are nominal.

It is possible to cover 50-80 km a day quite comfortably. You can even put your bike on a boat for a backwater trip or on top of a bus. If you want to take your bike on the train, allow plenty of time for booking it in on the brake van at the Parcels office and for filling in forms.

It is best to start a journey early in the morning, stopping at midday and then resuming your journey in the late afternoon. Night riding, though cooler, can be hazardous because of lack of lighting and poor road surfaces. Avoid major highways as far as possible. Foreign cyclists are usually greeted with cheers, waves and smiles and truck drivers are sometimes happy to give lifts to cyclists (and their bikes). This is a good way of taking some of the hardship out of cycling round India. For expert advice contact the **Cyclists' Touring Club** ① *T0870- 873 0060, www.ctc.org.uk.*

Hitchhiking

Hitchhiking is uncommon, partly because public transport is so cheap. If you try, you are likely to spend a very long time on the roadside. However, getting a lift on scooters and on trucks in areas with little public transport can be worthwhile, whilst those riding motorbikes or scooters in tourist areas can be expected to pick up the occasional hitchhiking policeman! It is not recommended for women on their own.

Motorcycling

This is a particularly attractive way of getting around. It is easy to buy new Indian-made motorcycles including the 350cc Enfield Bullet and several 100cc Japanese models, including Suzukis and Hondas made in collaboration with Indian firms; Indian Rajdoots are less expensive but have a poor reputation for reliability. Buying new at a fixed price ensures greater ease and reliability. Buying second hand in rupees takes more time but is quite possible (expect to get a 30-40% discount) and repairs are usually easy to arrange and quite cheap. You can get a broker to help with the paperwork involved (certificate of ownership, insurance, etc) for a fee. They charge about Rs 5000 for a No Objection Certificate (NOC), essential for reselling; it's easier to have the bike in your name. Bring your own helmet and an International Driving Permit. Vespa, Kinetic Honda and other makes of scooters in India are slower than motorbikes but comfortable for short hauls of less than 100 km and have the advantage of a 'dicky' (small, lockable box) and a spare tyre.

Rickshaw

Auto-rickshaws (autos) are almost universally available in towns across India and are the cheapest and most convenient way of getting about. It is best to walk a short distance away from a hotel gate before picking up an auto to avoid paying an inflated rate. In addition to using them for short journeys it is often possible to hire them by the hour, or for a half or full day's sightseeing. In some areas younger drivers who speak some English and know their local area well may want to show you around. However, rickshaw drivers are often paid a commission by hotels, restaurants and gift shops so advice is not always impartial. Drivers generally refuse to use a meter, often quote a ridiculous price or may sometimes stop short of your destination. If you have real problems it can help to note down the vehicle license number and threaten to go to the police. Beware of some rickshaw drivers who show the fare chart for taxis. Also, check your change and, when handing over a 100 rupee note, for example, say 'I am giving you 100 rupees', as in a blink of an eye they might have a 10 rupees note in their hand and pretend that you gave it to them. Check this even at pre-paid booths.

Cycle-rickshaws and horse-drawn tongas are more common in the more rustic setting of a small town or the outskirts of a large one. You will need to fix a price by bargaining. The animal attached to a tonga usually looks too undernourished to have the strength to pull the driver, let alone passengers.

Taxi

Yellow-top taxis in cities and large towns are metered, although tariffs change frequently. These changes are shown on a fare chart which should be read in conjunction with the meter reading. Increased night-time rates apply in some cities, but there should not be any extra charge for luggage. Insist on the taxi meter being flagged in your presence. If the driver refuses (he probably will), the official advice is to contact the police. This may not work, but it is worth trying. When a taxi doesn't have a meter, you will need to fix the fare before starting the journey. Ask at your hotel desk for a guide price.

At stations and airports it is often possible to share taxis to a central point. It is worth looking for fellow passengers who may be travelling in your direction and get a pre-paid taxi. At night, always have a clear idea of where you want to go and insist on being taken there. Taxi drivers may try to convince you that the hotel you have chosen 'closed three years ago' or is 'completely full'. Say that you have a reservation.

Maps

For anyone interested in the geography of India, or even simply getting around, trying to buy good maps is a depressing experience. For security reasons it is illegal to sell large-scale maps of areas within 80 km of the coast or national borders, and it is illegal to export any large scale maps.

The **Bartholomew** 1:4 m map sheet of India is the most authoritative, detailed and easy to use map available. It can be bought worldwide. **GeoCenter World Map** 1:2 m, covers India in three regional sections and are clearly printed. **Nelles'** regional maps of India at the scale of 1:1.5 m offer generally clear route maps, though neither the road classifications nor alignments are wholly reliable. The same criticism applies to the attractively produced and easy-to-read **Lonely Planet Travel Atlas of India and Bangladesh** (2001).

State and town plans are published by the **TTK Company**. These are often the best available though they are not wholly reliable. For the larger cities they provide the most compact yet clear map sheets (generally 50 mm by 75 mm format).

The Survey of India publishes large scale 1:10,000 town plans of approximately 70 cities. These detailed plans are the only surveyed town maps in India, and some are over 20 years old. The Survey also has topographic maps at the scale of 1:25,000 and 1:50,000 in addition to its 1:250,000 scale coverage, some of which are as recent as the late 1980s. However, maps are regarded as highly sensitive and it is only possible to buy these from main agents of the Survey of India.

Stanfords ① 12-14 Long Acre, London, WC2, T020-78361321, www.stanfords.co.uk, offers a mail order service.

Sleeping

In larger towns and cities, there are high-quality hotels, offering a full range of personal and business facilities. In small centres hotels are far more variable. In the peak season – October to April – bookings can be extremely heavy in popular destinations. It is sometimes possible to book in advance by telephone, fax or email either from abroad or in India itself. However, double check your reservation, and always try to arrive as early as possible in the day.

Hotels → *See box, opposite, for Sleeping price codes.*

Price categories Individual facilities vary considerably. The most expensive hotels charge in US dollars only. Modest hotels may not have their own restaurant but will often offer 'room service', bringing in food from outside. Many hotels operate a 24-hour checkout system. Make sure that this means that you can stay 24 hours from the time of check-in. Expect to pay more in Delhi for all categories. Prices away from large cities tend to be lower.

Off-season rates Large reductions are often made by hotels in all categories out of season. Always ask. You may also request the 10-15% agent's commission to be deducted from your bill if you book direct. Clarify whether the agreed figure includes all taxes.

Taxes In general most hotel rooms rated at Rs 1200 or above are subject to a tax of 10%. Many states levy an additional luxury tax of between 10 and 25%, and some hotels add a service charge of 10% on top of this. Taxes are not necessarily payable on meals, so it is worth settling your meals bill separately. Most hotels in the **C** category and above accept payment by credit card. Check your final bill carefully. Visitors have complained of incorrect bills, even in the most expensive hotels. The problem particularly afflicts groups, when last-minute extras appear mysteriously on some guests' bills. Check the evening before departure, and keep all receipts.

Hotel facilities You have to be prepared for difficulties that are uncommon in the West. It is best to inspect the room and check that all equipment (air conditioning, TV, water heater, flush) works before checking in at a modest hotel. In some areas **power cuts** are common, or hot water may be restricted to certain times of day. The largest hotels have

Sleeping price codes

LL	over US$200	**B**	US$46-65	**E**	US$12-20
L	US$151-200	**C**	US$31-45	**F**	US$7-11
AL	US$101-150	**D**	US$21-30	**G**	under US$7
A	US$66-100				

Price of a double room in high season, excluding taxes.

their own generators but it is best to carry a good torch. Usually, only category **C** and above have **central air conditioning**. Elsewhere air-conditioned rooms are cooled by individual units and occasionally by large 'air-coolers' which can be noisy and unreliable. When they fail to operate tell the management as it is often possible to get a rapid repair done, or to transfer to a room where the unit is working. During power cuts generators may not be able to cope with providing air conditioning. Fans are provided in all but the cheapest of hotels.

Apart from those in the **A** category and above, 'attached bath' does not necessarily refer to a bathroom with a bathtub. Most will provide a **bathroom** with a toilet, basin and a shower. In the lower priced hotels and outside large towns, a bucket and tap may replace the shower, and an Indian squat toilet instead of a Western WC (squat toilets are often cleaner). Even mid-price hotels, which are clean and pleasant, don't always provide towels, soap and toilet paper.

In some regions **water supply** is rationed periodically. Keep a bucket filled to use for flushing the toilet during water cuts. Occasionally, tap water may be discoloured due to rusty tanks. During the cold weather and in hill stations, hot water will be available at certain times of the day, sometimes in buckets, but is usually very restricted in quantity. Electric water heaters may provide enough for a shower but not enough to fill a bath tub! For details on drinking water, see pages 33 and 45.

At some times of the year and in some places **mosquitoes** can be a real problem, and not all hotels have mosquito-proof rooms or mosquito nets. If you have any doubts check before confirming your room booking. In cheap hotels you need to be prepared for the presence of flies, cockroaches, spiders, ants and geckos (harmless house lizards). Poisonous insects and scorpions are extremely rare in towns. Hotel managements are nearly always prepared with insecticide sprays. Few small hotels in mosquito-prone areas supply nets so it is best for budget travellers to take one from home. An impregnated, wedge-shaped one (for single-point fixing) is preferable, available in all good camping/outdoor shops. Remember to shut windows and doors at dusk. Electrical mats and pellets are now widely available, as are mosquito coils that burn slowly. One traveller recommends Dettol soap to discourage mosquitoes. Dusk and early evening are the worst times for mosquitoes so trousers and long-sleeved shirts are advisable, especially outdoors. At night, fans can be very effective in keeping mosquitoes off; remember to tuck the net under the mattress all round. As well as insects, expect to find spiders larger and hairier than those you see at home; they are mostly harmless and more frightened of you than you are of them!

Hotels close to temples can be very noisy, especially during festivals. Music blares from loudspeakers late at night and from very early in the morning, often making sleep impossible. Mosques call the faithful to prayers at dawn. Ear plugs are invaluable.

Hotels in hill stations often supply wood fires in rooms. Usually there is plenty of ventilation, but ensure that there is always good air circulation, especially when charcoal fires are provided in a basket.

Where staff training is lacking, the person who brings up your cases may proceed to show you light switches, room facilities, TV tuning, and hang around waiting for a **tip**. Room boys may enter your room without knocking or without waiting for a response to a knock. Both for security and privacy, it is a good idea to lock your door when you are in the room. At the higher end, you should expect to tip bellboys a little for every favour.

Palaces, forts and havelis

Several old maharajas' palaces and forts have been privately converted into comfortable and unusual hotels. They retain the inherent character, ambience and interiors of the property but have modernized bathrooms and amenities (eg TV and fridge). Many of these are individual homes where former ruling families still reside. They treat guests as if they were part of a house party. Others are managed by well-known chains while a few (eg Neemrana Fort on the Jaipur–Delhi road) are run by private entrepreneurs. Many merchants' *havelis* (see page 281) and mansions belonging to the *rawals* and *thakurs*, have also been converted into atmospheric hotels with a lot of character. It must be said that the standard of these does vary and, although many are wonderful, some of them fall short of the idyllic experience. Particularly in more remote rural areas you may find facilities remain very simple (eg hot water may come in buckets) and, despite efforts to control them, pests (such as rats) are sometimes found.

The **Heritage Hotels Association** ⓘ *306, Anukampa Tower, Church Rd, Jaipur, T0141-2372 084*, can supply a list of member hotels which are particularly attractive. The following hotel groups specialize in converting heritage properties into well-run luxury accommodation: **Historic Resort Hotels (HRH)** ⓘ *City Palace, Udaipur, T0294-2528016, www.eternalmewar.in*; **Neemrana Hotels** ⓘ *A-20, Feroze Gandhi Marg, Lajpat Nagar-I, New Delhi, T011-4666 1666, www.neemranahotels.com*; **WelcomHeritage** ⓘ *25 Community Shopping Centre, Basant Lok, Vasant Vihar, New Delhi, T011-4603 5500, www.welcomheritagehotels.com*; **Taj Group** ⓘ *www.tajhotels.com, UK T020-78346655, USA T212-515-5889, India T022-66651000.*

Jungle lodges and camps

Accommodation in the national parks and wildlife sanctuaries varies from royal hunting lodges in some (eg **Sawai Madhopur Lodge**, Ranthambhore and **Ramgarh Lodge**, facing Jamwa Ramgarh Lake) and palaces (eg Gajner, Sariska) to spartan rooms often lacking hot water and electricity (eg **Bagha ke Bagh**, Ghanerao, Forestry Department Rest Houses).

Tent resorts and camps are popular in Rajasthan. Some are permanent or semi-permanent camps, self-contained with attached showers, which are situated in orchards or farms and charge about US$100 full board for two. **The Maharaja of Jodhpur Royal Tents** imitate hunting tents used in the 1930s. They are pitched inside forts such as Nagaur and in the grounds of a number of palace properties and have showers and flush toilets. Temporary camps are set up for fairs and festivals by Rajasthan Tourism and private hoteliers, as at Pushkar.

Guesthouses

Guesthouses in towns and cities usually provide basic accommodation, generally with Indian squat toilets and running cold water with hot water brought in buckets, but there are exceptions. Bedding is not always provided; there will always be a sheet on the mattress and usually a pillow, but that may be all. Towels and soap are unlikely to be provided. Those aimed at the backpacker market might have internet facilities on offer, however, as well as basic travel desks.

Paying guest accommodation

Paying guest accommodation varies from rooms in a family home to small hotels. This option can provide a great opportunity to gain an insight into Indian family life. A list is available from the Tourist Reception Centres. Contact Ramesh Jangid at **Alternative Travels** ⓘ *Nawalgarh, Rajasthan, T01594-222 239, www.apanidhani.com*, if you want to experience rural life with home-stays in villages.

Railway and airport retiring rooms

Railway stations often have 'Retiring Rooms' or 'Rest Rooms' which may be hired for periods of between one and 24 hours by anyone holding an onward train ticket. They are cheap and simple, though some stations have a couple of a/c rooms, which are often heavily booked. They are convenient for short stops, though some can be very noisy. Some major airports (eg Delhi) have similar facilities.

Government rest houses

In many areas there are government guesthouses, ranging from 'Dak Bungalows' to 'Circuit Houses', often in attractive locations. The latter are now reserved almost exclusively for travelling government officers, but Dak Bungalows may sometimes be available for overnight stays, particularly in remote areas. They are usually extremely basic, with a caretaker who can sometimes provide a simple meal, given sufficient notice. Travelling officials always take precedence, even over booked guests. Check the room rate in advance as foreigners are sometimes overcharged.

Hostels

The Department of Tourism runs 16 hostels, each with about 50 beds, usually organized into dormitory accommodation. The YHA also have a few sites all over India. Travellers may also stay in religious hostels (*dharamshalas*) for up to three days. These are primarily intended for pilgrims and are sometimes free of charge, though voluntary offerings are always welcome. Usually only vegetarian food is permitted; smoking and alcohol are not.

Eating and drinking

Food → *See box opposite, for Eating price codes.*

When travelling through Rajasthan you will encounter a huge variety of delicous dishes from all over India. Combinations of spices and local produce give each region its distinctive flavour. Rajasthani food varies regionally between the arid desert districts and the greener eastern areas. Typical dishes are *Dal-Bhatti-Choorma*, little breads full of clarified butter roasted over hot coals served with a dry, flaky sweet made of gram flour, and *Ker-Sangri* made with a desert fruit and beans. Millets, lentils and beans are basic ingredients. *Sogra* (thick and rather heavy millet *chapatis*) and *makkai ka roti* (maize flour *chapatis*) are very popular, served with *ghee*. Game (wild boar, fowl) feature in local non-vegetarian dishes. *Sohita* (mutton cooked with millet), *sulla* (mutton *kebabs* which have been marinated in piquant vegetables and cooked over charcoal), *Khud kharghosh* (rabbit), *Ker kumidai saliria* (beans with cumin and chillies) are also favourites. *Mawa-ki-kachori* is a particularly rich dessert consisting of pastry stuffed with nuts and coconut and smothered in syrup. *Halwas* and *kheer* (made with thickened milk) are other favourite sweets.

In many of the tourist centres, European options such as toasted sandwiches, stuffed pancakes, apple pies, crumbles and cheese cakes are readily available. Italian favourites (pizzas, pastas) can be very different from what you are used to. Western confectionery, in general, is disappointing. Ice creams, on the other hand, can be exceptionally good.

For many visitors, with the prevalence of Indian cuisine in the West, eating out in Rajasthan is unlikely to present your first encounter with Indian food. However, if you are unused to spicy food, go slow. Stick to good restaurants that are used to foreign palates, and ease your way in by eating a variety of Indian and mild Western or Chinese meals. Popular local restaurants are obvious from the number of people eating in them, though when applying this rule be aware that Indians tend to eat an hour or two later than you may be used to.

A very cheap way to fill your belly is with a traditional *thali*, which is a complete meal served on a large stainless steel plate. Several preparations, placed in small bowls, surround the central serving of wholewheat *chapati* and rice. A vegetarian *thali* would include *dal* (lentils), two or three curries (which can be quite hot), and crisp papads, although there are regional variations. In restaurants offering an 'unlimited' *thali*, the waiters will continue filling your plate with breads and dal until you beg them to stop. A variety of pickles are offered – mango and lime are two of the most popular. These can be exceptionally hot, and are designed to be taken in minute quantities alongside the main dishes. Plain *dahi* (yoghurt), or *raita*, usually acts as a bland 'cooler'.

India has many delicious tropical fruits. Some are highly seasonal (eg mangoes, pineapples and lychees), while others (eg bananas, grapes, oranges) are available throughout the year. It is safe to eat the ones you can wash and peel.

Eating out

Rajasthan offers a huge variety of eating experiences, from local specialities dished out on street corners – often delicious but care should be taken to ensure freshness – to full-blown luxury restaurants replete with a wine list. Standards of service vary just as widely, with a common complaint being the failure to produce the component parts of a dish at the same time, your toast arriving five minutes after your scrambled eggs for example. Street stalls and *dhabas*, basic local restaurants, can be good places for breakfast, with an *aloo parantha*, flat bread stuffed with potato and chilli, washed down with tea often the favourite choice. South Indian cuisine is less heavy than its Northern and Rajasthani counterparts, and so is a good choice for lunch, with *masala dosa*, a thin crisp pancake folded over a stuffing of curried potato, a perennial favourite. Rajasthani or Punjabi dishes are quite rich, so make a satisfying dinner experience. Some Western dishes are usually offered, but can be a bit of a gamble, even in the major tourist centres; it's generally best to stick to what the chef knows best. The smarter restaurants can appear overstaffed, with a different waiter to take your order, serve food, drinks, etc. There's sometimes even someone standing at your table while you eat; this is not considered intrusive by Indian diners, but rather a sign of attentive service.

The larger hotels, open to non-residents, often offer buffet lunches with Indian, Western and sometimes Chinese dishes. These can be good value (Rs 250-300; but around Rs 450-600 in the top grades) and can provide a welcome, comfortable break in the cool, as well as a good chance to have a look at some stunning interiors without the cost of spending a night. However, the health risks of food kept warm for long periods in metal containers are considerable, especially if turnover at the buffet is slow. We have received several complaints of stomach trouble following a buffet meal, even in five-star hotels.

It is essential to be very careful since food hygiene may be poor, flies abound and refrigeration in the hot weather may be inadequate and intermittent because of power cuts. It is best to eat only freshly prepared food by ordering from the menu (especially meat and fish dishes); avoid salads and cut fruit except in kitchens of known cleanliness; some places use iodinized water to wash their salads, rendering them reasonably safe to eat.

Drink

Drinking water Water from the tap or a well should never be considered safe to drink since public water supplies are often polluted. Bottled water is now widely available although most bottled water is not mineral water, but simply purified water from an urban supply. Buy from a shop or stall, check the seal carefully (some companies now add a second clear plastic seal around the bottle top) and avoid street hawkers; when disposing bottles puncture the neck which prevents misuse but allows recycling for storage. There is growing concern over the mountains of plastic bottles that are collecting and the waste of resources to produce them, so travellers are encouraged to use alternative methods of getting safe drinking water (see box, page 45). Always carry enough drinking water with you when travelling. It is important to use pure water for cleaning teeth.

Hot drinks Tea and coffee are safe and widely available. Both are normally served sweet and with milk. If you wish, say 'no sugar' (*chini nahin*), 'no milk' (*dudh nahin*) when ordering. Alternatively, ask for a pot of tea, and milk and sugar to be brought separately. Freshly brewed coffee is a common drink in South India, but in the North, ordinary city restaurants will usually serve the instant variety. Even in aspiring smart cafés, *Espresso* or *Capuccino* may not turn out quite as one would expect in the West.

Soft drinks Bottled carbonated drinks such as 'Coke', 'Pepsi', 'Limca' and 'Thums Up' are universally available but always check the seal when you buy from a street stall. Fruit juice, including mango, pineapple and apple, is also sold in cartons. Don't add ice cubes as the water source may be contaminated. Take care with fresh fruit juices or *lassis* as ice is often added. Juice stalls often charge an extra rupee for drinks without ice.

Alcohol Indians rarely drink alcohol with a meal. In the past, wines and spirits were generally either imported and extremely expensive, or local and of poor quality. Now, the best Indian whisky, rum and brandy (IMFL or 'Indian Made Foreign Liquor') are widely accepted, as are good Champagneoise and other wines from Maharashtra. If you hanker after a bottle of imported wine, you will only find it in the top restaurants and have to pay at least Rs 800-1000. For the urban elite, refreshing Indian beers are popular when eating out and are widely available and 'pubs' have sprung up in the major cities. Elsewhere in the cities, the seedy, all-male drinking dens are best avoided for women travellers but can make quite an experience otherwise. Smart bars are more or less restricted to major hotels except in cities such as Delhi, which has an increasingly vibrant though scattered nightlife scene.

Because of increased rates of bar licences in Rajasthan, many hotels and restaurants have stopped serving alcohol. You can, however, buy alcoholic drinks from shops and have them in your hotel room. In some heritage hotels, owners 'invite' guests to join them for drinks. Some others will serve beer even if it is not listed and bill you for soft drinks at the price of the beer consumed! For liquor permits, see page 55.

Entertainment

Despite an economic boom in cities like Delhi and Mumbai and the rapid growth of a young business class, India's nightlife has been slow to respond. Until now focused on club discos in the biggest hotels, more and more private clubs and 'lounge bars' are opening up in the bigger cities. More traditional, popular entertainment is widespread across Indian villages in the form of folk drama, dance and music, each region having its own styles, and open-air village performances are common. The hugely popular Hindi film industry comes largely out of this tradition. It's always easy to find a cinema, but prepare for a long sitting, sudden plot changes and a formulaic storyline, the traditional recipe for which, as summarized by the Indian pop-culture blog *Loose News* (www.loosenews.com), runs as follows: "Take two lovers, separate them with strict parents; add villain or two to taste. While cooking plot, put songs in between to add to the flavour. Change clothes and move around trees in slow circular motion. Add fight, one full hero against 40 others. Heat film with heroine in wet sari. Combine hero as good, funny, strong, loving, angry, romantic for audience to swallow easily. Make film long to digest story well."

Festivals and events

India has an extraordinary wealth of festivals with many celebrated nationwide, while others are specific to a particular state or community or even a particular temple. Many festivals fall on different dates each year depending on the Hindu lunar calendar so check with the tourist office. Many religious festivals depend on the phases of the moon. **Full-moon days** are particularly significant and can mean extra crowding and merrymaking in temple towns throughout India, and are sometimes public holidays.

The Hindu calendar → *See also page 323.*
Some major regional festivals are listed below. A few count as national holidays: **26 January**: *Republic Day*; **15 August**: *Independence Day*; **2 October**: *Mahatma Gandhi's Birthday*; **25 December**: *Christmas Day*.

January
New Year's Day (1 Jan) is accepted officially when following the Gregorian calendar but there are regional variations which fall on different dates, often coinciding with spring/harvest time in Mar and Apr.
Makar Sankranti or **Uttarayana**, marks the end of winter and the beginning of the spring harvest, to 'welcome the sun to the northern tropic'. The occasion is celebrated with special fervour in Jaipur (14-15 Jan) as a massive kite-flying festival.
Camel Festival, at Bikaner, organized by Rajasthan Tourism, features camel polo, races, dancing camels and camel obedience competitions. The fire dances of the Siddh Naths are another attraction – 30-31 Dec 2010, 18-19 Jan 2011, 8-9 Jan 2012. Also the relatively new Jaipur Literary Festival, www.jaipurliteraturefestival.org, is held every Jan; 2011 promises speakers such as Alice Walker, Orhan Pamuk and William Dalyrymple.

February
Nagaur Fair is one of the best-known camel and cattle marts in Rajasthan. 10-13 Feb 2011, 30 Jan-2 Feb 2012.
Desert Festival at Jaisalmer is a jamboree of classical and folk performances, desert musicians, folk crafts, camel polo, 'Mr Desert' competition and desert sports. 16-18 Feb 2011, 5-7 Feb 2012.

Baneshwar Fair is one of Rajasthan's largest tribal fairs. **Vagad Festival**, nearby, offers an insight into tribal culture of Dungarpur and Bhenswada districts. 14-18 Feb 2011, 3-7 Feb 2012.
Shekhawati Festival highlights rural dances, rural games, *havelis* and agriculture of the 4 districts of Shekhawati.

March-April
Sivaratri marks the night when Siva danced his celestial dance of destruction (*Tandava*). Celebrated with feasting and fairs at Siva temples, but preceded by a night of devotional readings and hymn singing. Orthodox Saivites fast during the day and offer prayers every 3 hrs. Devotees who remain awake through the night believe they will win the Puranic promise of prosperity and salvation. 3 Mar 2011, 20 Feb 2012.
Elephant Festival, Jaipur. Elephant tug-o-war, elephant polo and richly bedecked elephants steal the show. 19 Mar 2011, 7 Mar 2012.
Holi, the festival of colours, marks the climax of spring. The previous night bonfires are lit in parts of North India symbolizing the end of winter (and conquering of evil). People have fun throwing toxin-laden coloured powder and water at each other, not to mention other pernicious substances, and in the evening some gamble with friends. If you don't mind getting covered in colours you can risk going out – wear your least valuable clothes – but

celebrations can sometimes get rowdy, and women are quite likely to find themselves subject to the wrong kind of attention. Some link the festival to worship of Kama the god of pleasure; some worship Krishna who defeated the demon Putana. Holi is particularly colourful at Jaipur, Jodhpur (where the royal family often celebrates it with guests), Jaisalmer, Udaipur and Bikaner. In rural areas like Daspan and Shekhawati it is more subdued with folk dancing and music. 19 Mar 2011, 8 Mar 2012.

Tilwara Fair, near Balotra, is one of Rajasthan's largest camel and cattle fairs.

Gangaur, at Jaipur, Udaipur and other cities, features colourful processions. At Udaipur, the procession arrives on foot at the Pichola Lake, and continues on boats. In Jodhpur colourfully dressed women carry pots of water to Girdikot. 6-7 Apr 2011, 25-26 Mar 2012.

Hindi New Year and the **Sikh Baisakhi festival** are celebrated mid-Apr.

Mewar Festival, Udaipur, features cultural programs of the region. 6-8 Apr 2011, 25-27 Mar 2012.

Mahavir Jayanti celebrates the birth of the founder of the Jain religion.

Mahaveerji Fair, near Sawai Madhopur, is an important Jain event with prayers. 12-18 Apr 2011, 1-6 Apr 2012.

May

A **Summer festival**, which includes traditional music, dance and crafts, is held at Mt Abu. 15-17 May 2011, 4-6 May 2012.

July-August

Raksha Bandhan (literally 'protection bond') commemorates the wars between Indra (the king of heaven) and the demons, when Indra's wife tied a silk amulet around his wrist to protect him from harm. The full-moon festival symbolizes the bond between brother and sister. A sister says special prayers and ties coloured threads around her brother's wrist while he in turn gives her a gift and promises to protect and care for her.

Teej, a fertility festival, celebrates the reunion of Siva and Parvati at the onset of the monsoon. There is a big procession with ornately dressed elephants. In the villages women wear bright clothes and green striped veils, and sit on swings decorated with flowers, singing songs to welcome the rains. 2-3 Aug 2011, 22-23 Aug 2012. Though Teej festival is celebrated all over Rajasthan, **Kajli Teej of Bundi** has its unique characteristics, focusing on the procession of goddess Teej in a decorated palanquin. There are performances by the artists of the Hadoti region. 15-16 Aug 2011, 4 Aug 2012.

Independence Day is a national secular holiday. In cities it is marked by special events, and in Delhi there is an impressive flag-hoisting ceremony at the Red Fort. 15 Aug.

August-September

Janmashtami, the birth of Krishna, is celebrated at midnight at Krishna temples.

Ganesh Chaturthi was established just over 100 years ago by the Indian nationalist leader Tilak. The elephant-headed god of good omen (also called Ganpati) is shown special reverence. On the last of the 5-day festival after harvest, clay images of the god are taken in procession with dancers and musicians, which are then immersed in the sea, river or pond. The Ganesh temple in Ranthambore receives a large influx of pilgrims on this day.

October-November

Gandhi Jayanti, Mahatma Gandhi's birthday, is remembered with prayer meetings and devotional singing (2 Oct). Many businesses close and it's a dry day.

Navratri in parts of Rajasthan is a colourful 9-night event featuring music and dancing. It is marked by Garba, Dandia-ras and other dances as well as fasting, feasting and religious rites. Shakti temples at Ambaji and Pawagadh are visited by pilgrims in this period as it celebrates 9 goddesses, primarily Durga. 28 Sep 2011, 16 Oct 2012 (start dates). Navratri culminates in **Dasara/Dussehra**.

Various episodes of the Ramayana story or *Ramlila*, are enacted and recited, with particular reference to the battle between the forces of good and evil as in **Rama**'s victory over the demon king **Ravana** of Lanka with the help of loyal **Hanuman**, the Monkey God. Huge effigies of Ravana made of bamboo and paper are burnt on the 10th day of *Dasara* in public parks. Kota is well known for its Dasara fair. 4-6 Oct 2011, 22-24 Oct 2012.

Marwar Festival features folk music and dances of the region at Jodhpur. 10-11 Oct 2011, 28-29 Oct 2012.

Diwali/Deepavali (from the Sanskrit *dipa* lamp) is the festival of lights. Some Hindus celebrate Diwali as Krishna's victory over the demon Narakasura, some Rama's return after his 14 years' exile in the forest when citizens lit his way with earthen oil lamps. *Rangolis* are painted on the floor as a sign of welcome. Fireworks have become an integral part of the celebration. Lakshmi, the Goddess of Wealth (as well as Ganesh) is worshipped by merchants and the business community who start the accounting year on the day. Most people wear new clothes; some play games of chance. 26 Oct 2011, 13 Nov 2012.

Kartik Poornima is one of the most important dates in the Hindu calendar. Several towns including Chandrabhaga (9-11 Nov 2011, 27-29 Nov 2012) and Kolayat hold cattle and camel fairs around this time, but the most famous is at Pushkar, which attracts thousands of traders, pilgrims and tourists. 13-21 Nov 2010, 2-10 Nov 2011, 20-28 Nov 2012.

Muslim holy days

These are celebrated in cities with a significant Muslim population like Ajmer. The dates are fixed according to the lunar calendar, see page 324. According to the Gregorian calendar, they tend to fall 11 days earlier each year, dependent on the sighting of the new moon.

Ramadan, the ninth month of the Islamic year, is a month of fasting. It is a period of atonement and recalls the "sending down of the Quran as a guidance for the people". All Muslims (except young children, the very elderly, the sick, pregnant women and travellers) must abstain from food and drink, from sunrise to sunset. **Id-ul-Fitr** is the three-day festival which marks the end of Ramadan.

Id-ul-Zuha/Bakr-Id is when Muslims commemorate Ibrahim's sacrifice of his son according to God's commandment; the main time of pilgrimage to Mecca (the Hajj). It is marked by the sacrifice of a goat, feasting and alms giving.

Muharram is when the killing of the Prophet's grandson, Hussain, is commemorated by Shi'a Muslims. Decorated *tazias* (replicas of the martyr's tomb) are carried in procession by devout wailing followers who beat their chests to express their grief. Shi'as fast for the 10 days.

Shopping

India excels in producing fine crafts at affordable prices through the tradition of passing down ancestral skills. You can get handicrafts of different states from the government emporia in the major cities which guarantee quality at fixed prices (no bargaining), but many are poorly displayed, not helped by reluctant and unenthusiastic staff. Private upmarket shops and top hotel arcades offer better quality, choice and service, but at a price. Vibrant and colourful local bazars (markets) are often a great experience but you must be prepared to bargain.

Bargaining can be fun and quite satisfying but it is important to get an idea of prices by asking at different stalls before taking the plunge. Some shopkeepers will happily quote twice the actual price to a foreigner showing interest, so you might well start by halving the asking price. On the other hand, it would be inappropriate to do the same in an established shop with price tags, though a plea for the 'best price' or a 'special discount' might reap results even here. Remain good humoured throughout. Walking away slowly might be the test to ascertain whether your custom is sought and you are called back!

The country is a vast market place but there are regional specializations. The larger cities give you the opportunity to see a good selection from all over India. If you are planning to travel widely, wait to find the best places to buy specific items. Export of certain items is controlled or banned, see page 42.

Carpets and dhurries Rajasthan has a tradition of carpet and dhurrie weaving using camel wool and cotton. Weaving of traditional woollen dhurries became associated with prisoners in Bikaner, Jaipur and Ahmedabad jails but today attractive dhurries in pastel colours are produced in small commercial units as a cottage industry. The pile carpets made near Jaipur based on floral and geometrical patterns are of medium quality with around 80 knots per square inch. These are good buys.

Jewellery Rajasthan is famed for cut and uncut gemstones (emeralds, sapphires, rubies and diamonds). *Kundan* work specializes in setting stones in gold; sometimes *meenakari* (enamelling) complements the setting on the reverse side of the pendant, locket or earring. Whether it is chunky tribal silver jewellery or precious gems set in gold, or semi-precious stones in silver, the visitor is drawn to the arcade shop window as much as the way-side stall. It is best to buy from reputable shops (and if in Jaipur get expensive purchases checked by the Gem Testing Laboratory). Make sure your knowledge is up to scratch if considering investing in gems or jewellery, and never be persuaded to buy for an unknown third party.

Paintings Miniature paintings on old paper (they are not real antiques) and new silk, sometimes using natural colours derived from minerals, rocks and vegetables, following old techniques are produced in varying degrees of quality. Sadly the industry is reaching mass production levels in Rajasthan's back alleys, though fine examples can still be found in good crafts shops. Coveted contemporary Indian art is exhibited in modern galleries in the state capitals often at a fraction of London or New York prices.

Stoneware Ornamental pieces of perforated marble *jali* work are produced in Rajasthan. Artisans in Agra inspired by the Taj Mahal continue the tradition of inlaying tiny pieces of gem stones on fine white marble, to produce something for every pocket, from a small coaster to a large table top. Softer soap stone is cheaper.

Pitfalls Taxi and rickshaw drivers and tour guides sometimes insist on recommending certain shops where they expect a commission, but prices there are invariably inflated. Some shops offer to pack and post your purchases but not all can be trusted. Unless you have a specific recommendation from a person that you know, only make such arrangements in government emporia or a large store. Don't enter into any arrangement to help 'export' marble items, jewellery, etc which a shopkeeper may propose by making tempting promises of passing on some of the profits to you. Several visitors have been cheated through misuse of their credit card accounts, and have been left with unwanted purchases. Make sure that credit cards are not run off more than once when making a purchase.

Responsible travel

Customs and culture

Most travellers experience great warmth and hospitality. With it comes an open curiosity about personal matters. You should not be surprised if total strangers ask for details of your job, income and family circumstances or discuss politics and religion.

Conduct Respect for the foreign visitor should be reciprocated by a sensitivity towards local customs and culture. How you dress is how people will judge you; cleanliness, modest clothes and a smile go a long way. Scanty, tight clothing draws unwanted attention. Displays of intimacy are inappropriate in public. You may at times be frustrated by delays, bureaucracy and inefficiency, but displays of anger and rudeness will not achieve anything positive, and often make things worse. People's concept of time and punctuality is also often rather vague so be prepared to be kept waiting.

Courtesy It takes little effort to learn common gestures of courtesy and they are greatly appreciated. The greeting when meeting or parting, used universally among the Hindus across India, is the palms joined together as in prayer, sometimes accompanied with the word *namaste* (North and West) or *namoshkar* (East). Muslims use the greeting *assalām aleikum*, with the response *waleikum assalām*, meaning 'peace be with you'; 'please' is *mehrbani-se*; 'thank you' is often expressed by a smile, or with the somewhat formal *dhannyabad* or *shukriya* (Urdu).

Hands and eating Traditionally, Indians use the right hand for giving, receiving, shaking hands and eating, as the left is considered to be unclean since it is associated with washing after using the toilet. In much of rural India cutlery is alien at the table except for serving spoons, and at most humble restaurants you will be offered only small spoons to eat with. If you visit an ashram or are lucky enough to be invited to a temple feast day, you will almost certainly be expected to eat with your hands. Watch and copy others until the technique becomes familiar.

Women (see also page 56) Indian women in urban and rural areas differ in their social interactions with men. To the Westerner, Indian women may seem to remain in the background and appear shy when approached. Yet you will see them working in public, often in jobs traditionally associated with men in the West, in the fields or on construction sites. It is not considered polite for men to photograph women without their consent, so ask before you start snapping.

Women do not usually shake hands with men as physical contact between the sexes is not acceptable. A westernized city woman, however, may feel free to shake hands with a foreign visitor. In certain, very traditional rural circles, it is still the custom for men to be offered food first, separately, so don't be surprised if you, as foreign guest (man or woman), are awarded this special status when invited to an Indian home.

Visiting religious sites Visitors to all religious places should be dressed in clean, modest clothes; shorts and vests are inappropriate. Always remove shoes before entering (and all leather items in Jain temples). Take thick socks for protection when walking on sun-baked stone floors. Menstruating women are considered 'unclean' and should not enter places of

How big is your footprint?

As well as respecting local cultural sensitivities, travellers can take a number of simple steps to reduce, or even improve, their impact on the local environment. Environmental concern is relatively new in India, but don't be afraid to pressurize businesses by asking about their policies.

Litter Many travellers think that there is little point in disposing of rubbish properly when the tossing of water bottles, plastic cups and other non-biodegradable items out of train windows is already so widespread. You can immediately reduce your impact by refusing plastic bags and other excess packaging when shopping – use a small backpack or cloth bag instead – and if you do collect a few, keep them with you to store other rubbish until you get to a litter bin.

Filtered water versus bottled water Plastic mineral water bottles, an inevitable corollary to poor water hygiene standards, are a major contributor to India's litter mountain. However, many hotels, including nearly all of the upmarket ones, most restaurants and bus and train stations, provide drinking water purified using a combination of ceramic and carbon filters, chlorine and sometimes UV irradiation. Ask for 'filter paani'; if the water tastes at all like a swimming pool it is probably quite safe to drink, though it's worth introducing your body gradually to the new water. See box, page 45, for water purification.

Bucket baths versus showers The biggest issue relating to responsible and sustainable tourism is water. Much of northwest India is afflicted by severe water restrictions, with certain cities in Rajasthan and Gujarat having water supply for as little as 20 minutes a day. The traditional Indian 'bucket bath', in which you wet, soap then rinse off using a small hand-held plastic jug dipped into a large bucket, uses on average around 15 litres of water, as compared to 30-45 for a shower. These are commonly offered except in four- and five-star hotels.

Support responsible tourism Spending your money carefully can have a positive impact. Sleeping, eating and shopping at small, locally owned businesses directly supports communities, while specific community tourism concerns provide an economic motivation for people to stay in remote communities, protect natural areas and revive traditional cultures, rather than exploit the environment or move to the cities for work.

Transport Choose walking, cycling or public transport over fuel-guzzling cars and motorbikes.

worship. It is discourteous to sit with one's back to a temple or shrine. You will be expected to sit cross-legged on the floor – avoid pointing your feet at others when attending prayers at a temple. Walk clockwise around a shrine (keeping it to your right).

Non-Hindus are sometimes excluded from the inner sanctum of **Hindu** temples and occasionally even from the temple itself. Look for signs or ask. In certain temples and on special occasions you may enter only if you wear unstitched clothing such as a *dhoti*.

In **Buddhist** shrines, turn prayer wheels in a clockwise direction. In **Sikh** *gurudwaras*, everyone should cover their head, even if it is with a handkerchief (headscarves are often provided). Tobacco and cigarettes should not be taken in. In **Muslim** mosques, visitors should only have their face, hands and feet exposed; women should also cover their heads. Mosques may be closed to non-Muslims shortly before formal prayers.

Some temples have a register or a receipt book for **donations** which works like an obligatory entry fee. The money is normally used for the upkeep and services of the temple or monastery. In some pilgrimage centres, priests can become unpleasantly persistent. If you wish to leave a donation, put money in the donation box; priests and Buddhist monks often do not handle money. It is also not customary to shake hands with a priest or monk. *Sanyasis* (holy men) and some pilgrims depend on donations.

Guide fees Guides vary considerably in their knowledge and ability. Government licensed guides are covered by specified fees. Local temple and site guides should charge less. Charges for four people for half a day are about Rs 280, for a full day Rs 400; for five to 15 people for half a day Rs 400, for a full day Rs 530. Rs 125 for a language other than English.

Begging and charitable giving Beggars are found in busy street corners in large Indian cities, as well as at bus and train stations where they often target foreigners. Visitors can find this distressing, especially the sight of severely undernourished children or those displaying physical deformity. You may be particularly affected when some persist in making physical contact. In the larger cities, beggars are often exploited by syndicates which cream off most of their takings. Yet those seeking alms near religious sites are another matter, and you may see Indian worshippers giving freely to those less fortunate than themselves, since this is tied up with gaining 'merit'. How you deal with begging is a personal choice but it is perhaps better to give to a recognized charity than to make largely ineffectual handouts to individuals. Young children sometimes offer to do 'jobs' such as call a taxi, carry shopping or pose for a photo. You may want to give a coin in exchange. While travelling, some visitors prefer to hand out fruit to the many open-palmed children they encounter.

A pledge to donate a part of one's holiday budget to a local charity could be an effective formula for 'giving'. Some visitors like to support self-help cooperatives, orphanages, refugee centres, disabled or disadvantaged groups, or international charities such as Oxfam, Save the Children or Christian Aid which work with local partners, by either making a donation or by buying their products. A list of charities is detailed below. Also see information about charities and organizations that welcome volunteers on page 56.

Friends of Tilonia, www.tilonia.com, is a US-based charity that supports The Barefoot College, www.barefootcollege.org, near Ajmer. For over 35 years, the focus has been on sustainability and has had a profound effect on the community.

SOS Children's Villages, Plot No 4, Block C1 Institutional Area, Nelson Mandela Marg, Vasant Kunj, New Delhi 110070, T011-4323 9200, www.soscvindia.org. Over 30 children's projects in India, including a children's village and vocational training in Jaipur.

Save the Children India, A-57, 1st floor, Nizammudin (East), New Delhi , www.save thechildrenindia.org.

The Shakti Project of Rajasthan, Old Sabge market, Pushkar, 305022, www.shakti-streetkids-pushkar.org. Shakti means power. The aim is to empower street children through education.

Photography Many monuments and national parks charge a camera fee ranging from Rs 20-100 for still cameras, and as much as Rs 500 for video cameras (more for professionals). Special permits are needed from the Archaeological Survey of India, New Delhi, for using tripods and artificial lights. When photographing people, it is polite to first ask – they will usually respond warmly with smiles. Visitors often promise to send copies of the photos – don't unless you really mean to do so. Photography of airports, military installations, bridges and in tribal and 'sensitive border areas', is not permitted.

Essentials A-Z

Accident and emergency

Contact the relevant emergency service: **police T100; fire T101; ambulance T102.** Also contact your embassy (see Directory in Delhi, page 106). Make sure you obtain police/medical reports required for insurance claims.

Children

Children of all ages are widely welcomed. However, care should be taken when travelling to remote areas where health services are primitive. It's best to visit in the cooler months since you need to protect children from the sun, heat, dehydration and mosquito bites. Cool showers or baths help; avoid being out during the hottest part of the day. Diarrhoea and vomiting are the most common problems, so take the usual precautions. Breastfeeding is best and most convenient for babies. In the big cities you can get safe baby foods and formula milk. It doesn't harm a baby to eat an unvaried and limited diet of familiar food carried in packets for a few weeks if local dishes are not acceptable, but it may be an idea to give vitamin and mineral supplements. Wet wipes and disposable nappies are difficult to find. The biggest hotels provide babysitting. See also Health, page 44.

Customs and duty free

Duty free
Tourists are allowed to bring in all personal effects 'which may reasonably be required', without charge. The official allowance includes 200 cigarettes, 0.95 litres of alcohol, a camera with 5 rolls of film and a pair of binoculars. Valuable personal effects and professional equipment including jewellery, camera equipment and laptop computers must be declared on a Tourist Baggage Re-Export Form (TBRE) in order for them to be taken back out of the country. These forms require the equipment's serial numbers. Find out the numbers in advance and be ready to show them on the equipment. Details of imported equipment may be entered into your passport. Save time by completing the formalities while waiting for your baggage. Keep these forms to show to the customs when leaving India, otherwise considerable delays are very likely.

Currency regulations
There are no restrictions on the amount of foreign currency or TCs a tourist may bring into India. If you are carrying more than US$5000 in cash or US$10,000 or its equivalent in cash and TCs you need to fill in a currency declaration form. This could change with a relaxation in the currency regulations.

Prohibited items
The import of dangerous drugs, live plants, gold coins, gold and silver bullion and silver coins not in current use is subject to strict regulation. It is illegal to import firearms into India without special permission. Enquire at consular offices abroad for details.

Export restrictions
Export of gold jewellery purchased in India is allowed up to a value of Rs 2000 and other jewellery (including precious stones) up to a value of Rs 10,000. Export of antiquities and art objects over 100 years old is restricted. Ivory, musk, skins of all animals, *toosh* and *pashmina* wool, snake-skin and articles made from them are banned, unless you get permission for export. For further information, contact the Indian High Commission or consulate, or access the Central Board of Excise and Customs website, www.cbec.gov.in/travellers.htm.

Disabled travellers

India is not especially geared up for making provisions for the physically handicapped or wheelchair-bound traveller. Access to buildings, toilets (sometimes squat), pavements, kerbs and public transport can prove frustrating, but it is easy to find people to give a hand to help with lifting and carrying. Provided there is an able-bodied companion to help and you are prepared to pay for at least mid-price accommodation, car hire and taxis, India should be rewarding.

Some travel companies specialize in exciting holidays, tailor-made for individuals depending on their level of disability. **Global Access**, Disabled Travel Network, www.globalaccessnews.com, provides travel information for 'disabled adventurers' and includes a number of reviews and tips. *Nothing Ventured*, edited by Alison Walsh (HarperCollins), gives personal accounts of worldwide journeys by disabled travellers, plus advice and listings. **Accessible Journeys Inc**, 35 West Sellers Av, Ridley Park, PA 19078, T610-521 0339, www.disability travel.com, runs some packages to India. **Responsible Travel.com**, 3rd floor, Pavillion House, 6 Old Steine, Brighton, BN1 1EJ, UK, T01273-600030, www.responsible travel.com, specializes in eco-holidays and has some tailored to the needs of disabled travellers.

See also www.asparkholidays.com, based in New Delhi, for high-end tours designed for less able-bodied people.

Electricity

India supply is 220-240 volts AC. There may be pronounced variations in the voltage, and power cuts are common. Power back-up by generator or inverter is becoming more widespread, though it may not cover a/c. Socket sizes vary so take a universal adaptor; low quality versions are available locally. Many hotels, even in the higher categories, don't have electric razor sockets.

Embassies and consulates

For information on visas and immigration, see page 55. For a complete list of embassies and consulates, see http://meaindia.nic.in/onmouse/mission.htm. Many embassies around the world are now outsourcing the visa process so you do not visit the embassy direct – check their websites for details. It might also take longer to obtain your visa.

Indian embassies abroad

Australia 3-5 Moonah Pl, Yarralumla, Canberra, T02-6273 3999, www.hcindia-au.org; Level 2, 210 Pitt St, Sydney, T02-9223 9500; 15 Munro St, Coburg, Melbourne, T03-9384 0141.
Canada 10 Springfield Rd, Ottawa, K1M 1C9, T613-744 3751, www.hciottawa.ca. Toronto, T416-960 0751, Vancouver, T604-662 8811.
France 15 Rue Alfred Dehodencq, Paris, T01-4050 7070, www.amb-inde.fr.
Germany Tiergartenstrasse 17, 10785 Berlin, T030-257950. Consulates: Bonn T0228-540132; Frankfurt T069-153 0050, Hamburg T040-338036, Munich T089-210 2390, Stuttgart T0711-153 0050.
Ireland 6 Leeson Park, Dublin 6, T01-497 0843, www.indianembassy.ie.
Nepal 336 Kapurdhara Marg, Kathmandu, T+9771-441 0900, www.indianembassy.org.np.
Netherlands Buitenrustweg-2, 2517 KD, The Hague, T070-346 9771, www.indianembassy.nl.
New Zealand 180 Molesworth St, Wellington, T+64-4473 6390, www.hicomind.org.nz.
Singapore India House, 31 Grange Rd, T6737 6777, www.embassyofindia.com.
South Africa 852 Schoeman St, Arcadia, Pretoria 0083, T012-342 5392, www.india.org.za.
Sri Lanka 36-38 Galle Rd, Colombo 3, T+94-1-2327587, www.hcicolombo.org.
Switzerland Kirchenfeldstrasse 28, CH-3005 Bern, T031-351 1130, www.indembassybern.ch.
Thailand, 46 Prasarnmitr, Sukhumvit Soi 23 Bangkok – 10110, T662-258 0300.
UK India House, Aldwych, London, WC2B 4NA, T020-7836 8484, www.hcilondon.in. Visas outsourced – apply online at http://in.vfsglobal.co.uk. Consulates: 20 Augusta St,

Jewellery Quarter, Hockley, Birmingham, B18 6JL, T0121-212 2782, www.cgibirmingham.org; 17 Rutland Sq, Edinburgh, EH1 2BB, T0131-229 2144, www.cgiedinburgh.org. **USA** 2107 Massachusetts Av, Washington DC 20008, T202-939 7000. Consulates: New York, T212-774 8600, San Francisco, T415-668 0662, Chicago, T312-595 0405.

Gay and lesbian travellers

Indian law forbids homosexual acts for men (but not women) and carries a maximum sentence of life imprisonment. Although it is common to see young males holding hands in public, this very rarely indicates a gay relationship and is usually an expression of friendship. Overt displays of affection between homosexuals (and heterosexuals) give offence and should be avoided.

Health

See your GP or travel clinic at least 6 weeks before departure for general advice on travel risks and vaccinations. Try phoning a specialist travel clinic if your own doctor is unfamiliar with health conditions in India. Make sure you have sufficient medical travel insurance, get a dental check, know your own blood group and if you suffer a long-term condition such as diabetes or epilepsy, obtain a Medic Alert bracelet/necklace (www.medicalert.co.uk). If you wear glasses, take a copy of your prescription.

Vaccinations
Confirm your primary courses and boosters are up to date. It is advisable to vaccinate against diphtheria, tetanus, poliomyelitis, hepatitis A and typhoid. Yellow fever is not required in India but you may be asked to show a certificate if you are entering from an area with risk of yellow fever transmission.

Vaccination against rabies is advised for those going to risk areas that will be remote

from a reliable source of vaccine. Even when pre-exposure vaccines have been received urgent medical advice should be sought after any animal bite.

Malaria is a danger in India and, although it has some seasonality, it is too unpredictable to not take prophylaxis. Specialist advice should be taken on the best anti-malarials to use.

Health risks
Altitude sickness can creep up on you as just a mild headache with nausea or lethargy. The more serious disease is caused by fluid collecting in the brain in the enclosed space of the skull and can lead to coma and death. The best cure is to descend as soon as possible. It is essential to get acclimatized before undertaking long treks or arduous activities.

The standard advice for **diarrhoea** prevention is to be careful with water and ice for drinking. If you have any doubts about where the water came from then boil it or filter and treat it. Bottled water is readily available and cheap. Food can also transmit disease. Be wary of salads, re-heated foods or food that has been left out in the sun. There is a simple adage that says: wash it, peel it, boil it or forget it. Also be wary of unpasteurized dairy products as these can transmit a range of diseases. Diarrhoea may be also caused by viruses, bacteria (such as E-coli), protozoal (such as giardia), salmonella and cholera. It may be accompanied by vomiting or by severe abdominal pain. The key treatment with all diarrhoea is rehydration. Try to keep hydrated by taking the right mixture of salt and water. This is available as Oral Rehydration Salts (ORS) in ready-made sachets or can be made up by adding a teaspoon of sugar and a half teaspoon of salt to a litre of clean water. You can also use flat carbonated drinks. If the symptoms persist, consult a doctor.

Mosquitoes are more of a nuisance than a serious hazard but some, of course, are carriers of serious diseases such as malaria,

Water purification

There are various ways of purifying water in order to make it safe to drink. Dirty water should be strained through a filter bag, and then boiled or treated.

Bringing water to a rolling boil at sea level will make water safe for drinking, but at higher altitudes you have to boil the water for longer to ensure that all the microbes are killed.

Various sterilizing methods can be used, with preparations containing chlorine or iodine compounds. Chlorine compounds generally do not kill protozoa (eg giardia). Prolonged usage of iodine compounds may lead to thyroid problems, although this is rare if used for less than a year.

There are a number of water filters now on the market, available both in personal and expedition size. There are two types of water filter, mechanical and chemical. Mechanical filters are usually a combination of carbon, ceramic and paper, although they can be difficult to use. Although cheaper, the disadvantage of mechanical filters is that they do not always remove viruses or protozoa. Chemical filters use a combination of an iodine resin filter and a mechanical filter. The advantage is that according to the manufacturers' claims, everything in the water will be killed. The disadvantage is that the filters need replacing, adding a third to the price.

so it is sensible to avoid being bitten as much as possible. Sleep off the ground and use a mosquito net and some kind of insecticide. Mosquito coils release insecticide as they burn and are available in many shops, as are tablets of insecticide, which are placed on a heated mat plugged into a wall socket.

Rabies is endemic throughout certain parts of India, so avoid dogs that are behaving strangely and cover your toes at night from the vampire bats, which also carry the disease. If you are bitten by a domestic or wild animal, do not leave things to chance: scrub the wound with soap and water and/or disinfectant, try to at least determine the animal's ownership, where possible and seek medical assistance at once. The course of treatment depends on whether you have already been vaccinated against rabies.

The range of visible and invisible **sexually transmitted diseases** is vast. Unprotected sex can spread HIV, hepatitis B and C, gonorrhea (green discharge), chlamydia (nothing to see but may cause painful urination and later female infertility), painful recurrent herpes, syphilis and warts, to name a few. You can cut down the risk by using condoms, a femidom or avoiding sex altogether.

Make sure you protect yourself from the **sun** with high-factor sun screen and don't forget to wear a hat.

If you get sick
Contact your embassy or consulate for a list of doctors and dentists who speak your language, or at least some English. Doctors and health facilities in major cities are also listed in the Directory sections of this book. Make sure you have adequate insurance (see below).

Useful websites
www.btha.org British Travel Health Association.
www.cdc.gov US government site that gives excellent advice on travel health and details of disease outbreaks.
www.fco.gov.uk British Foreign and Commonwealth Office travel site has useful information on each country, people, climate and a list of UK embassies/consulates.
www.fitfortravel.scot.nhs.uk A-Z of vaccine/health advice for each country.

www.numberonehealth.co.uk Travel screening services, vaccine and travel health advice, email/SMS text vaccine reminders and screens returned travellers for tropical diseases.

Insurance

Buying insurance with your air ticket is the most costly way of doing things: better go to an independent. Some banks now offer travel insurance for account holders. See also www.dh.gov.uk.

If you are carrying specialist equipment – expensive cameras, VCRs, laptops – you will probably need to get separate cover for these items (claims for individual items are often limited to £250) unless they are covered by existing home contents insurance. Dig out the receipts for these expensive personal effects. Take photos of the items and note down all serial numbers.

Check exactly what your medical cover includes, eg ambulance, helicopter rescue or emergency flights back home, and check for exclusions: you may find that activities such as mountain biking are not covered. Note that drinking alcohol is likely to invalidate a claim in the event of an accident. Also check the payment protocol. You may have to pay first – known as an excess charge – before the insurance company reimburses you.

Always carry with you the telephone number of your insurer's 24-hr emergency helpline and your insurance policy number.

Most annual policies have a trip limit of around a month. If you plan to be abroad for longer insurers including **Columbus**, **Direct Travel Insurance**, **Flexicover** and **Insure and Go** offer suitable cover. If travelling abroad several times in a year, an annual, worldwide insurance policy will save you money.

Senior travellers should note that some companies will not cover people over 65 years old, or may charge higher premiums.

Internet

In 2007, 21.1 million Indians were online, making it the third largest user in the world, behind only the USA and China. You're never far from an internet café or PCO (public call office), which also offers the service. Note that internet cafés now require you to produce ID.

In small towns there is less internet access and it is recommended to take precautions: write lengthy emails in Word, save frequently, then paste them into your web-based email server rather than risking the loss of missives home when the power fails or the connection goes down. Browsing costs vary dramatically depending on the location: these can be anything from Rs 20-100, with most charging somewhere in between. As a rule, avoid emailing from upmarket hotels as their prices can be exorbitant. Wi-fi is becoming more available too, sometimes you are charged, other times its free. If you intend to stay in India for a while, sign up for member-ship with the internet chain **I-way**.

Language

Hindi, spoken as a mother tongue by over 400 million people, is India's official language. The use of English is also enshrined in the Constitution for a wide range of official purposes, notably communication between Hindi and non-Hindi speaking states. Most of the regional languages have their own scripts. In all there are 15 major and several hundred minor languages and dialects. The principle language in Rajasthan is Rajasthani and is closely related to Hindi. You can get away with pigeon Hindi.

It takes little effort to learn and use common gestures of courtesy but they are greatly appreciated by Indians. For a list of useful words and phrases, see page 342. Most people working in the tourist industry are likely to have a good grasp of English.

Media

International **newspapers** (mainly English language) are sold in the bookshops of top hotels in major cities and occasionally by booksellers elsewhere. India has a large and lively English-language press. They all have extensive analysis of contemporary Indian and some international issues. The major papers now have websites, excellent for keeping daily track on events, news and weather.

The best known are the traditionalist *The Hindu*, www.hinduonline.com/today. *The Hindustan Times*, www.hindustantimes.com, the slightly more tabloid-establishment *Times of India*, www.timesofindia.com/ and *The Statesman*, www.thestatesman.org. *The Economic Times* is good for world coverage. *The Telegraph*, www.telegraphindia.com, has good foreign coverage. *The Indian Express*, www.expressindia.com, stands out as being consistently critical of the Congress Party and the government. *The Asian Age* is now published in the UK and India simultaneously and gives good coverage of Indian and international affairs. Of the news weeklies, some of the most widely read are current affairs *India Today*, *Frontline* and *The Week*, which are journals in the *Time* or *Newsweek* mould. *Business Today* is of course economy-based, while *Outlook* has a broader remit and has good general interest features. There is also *Outlook Traveller*, probably the best of the domestic travel titles.

India's national **radio** and **television** network, *Doordarshan*, broadcasts in national and regional languages but things have moved on. The advent of satellite TV has hit even remote rural areas and there are over 500 local broadcast television stations – each state has its own local-language current affairs broadcaster plus normally at least one other channel for entertainment. The 'Dish' can help travellers keep in touch through Star TV from Hong Kong, accessing BBC World, CNN, etc, VTV (music) and Sport, is now available even in modest hotels in the smallest of towns.

Money

Exchange rates → *US$1=Rs 46; €1=Rs 60; UK£1=Rs 71; AUS$1=Rs 42; NZ$1=Rs 33 (Sep 2010)* Indian currency is the Indian Rupee (Re/Rs). It is **not** possible to purchase these before you arrive. If you want cash on arrival it is best to get it at the airport bank (although exchange rates can be poor). Rupee notes are printed in denominations of Rs 1000, 500, 100, 50, 20, 10. The rupee is divided into 100 paise. Coins are minted in denominations of Rs 5, Rs 2, Rs 1 and 50 paise. Carry money in a money belt worn under clothing. Have a small amount in an accessible place.

Credit cards

Major credit cards are accepted in the main centres, but rarely in smaller cities and towns. Payment by credit card can sometimes be more expensive than payment by cash and some credit card companies charge a premium on cash withdrawals. **Visa** and **MasterCard** have a growing number of ATMs in major cities and several banks offer withdrawal facilities for **Cirrus** and **Maestro**. It is easy to obtain a cash advance against a credit card. Some railway reservation centres are now taking payment for train tickets by Visa, which can be very quick as the queue is short, but they cannot be used for Tourist Quota tickets.

ATMs

By far the most convenient method of accessing money, ATMs are all over India, usually attended by security guards. Banks with ATMs for Cirrus, Maestro, Visa and MasterCard include: **AXIS**, **Bank of Baroda**, **Citibank**, **HDFC**, **HSBC**, **ICICI**, **IDBI**, **Punjab National Bank**, **State Bank of India** (SBI) and **Standard Chartered**. A withdrawal fee is usually charged by the issuing bank on top of the various conversion charges applied by your own bank. Fraud prevention measures may result in travellers having their cards blocked by the bank when unexpected overseas transactions occur; advise your bank of your travel plans before leaving.

Changing money

The State Bank of India and several others in major towns are authorized to deal in foreign exchange. Some give cash against Visa/MasterCard (eg ANZ, Bank of Baroda who print a list of their participating branches, Andhra Bank). The larger cities have licensed money changers with offices usually in the commercial sector. Changing money through unauthorized dealers is illegal. Premiums on the currency black market are very small and highly risky. Large hotels change money 24 hrs a day for guests, but banks often give a much better rate of exchange. It is best to exchange money on arrival at the airport bank or the Thomas Cook counter. You should be given a foreign currency encashment certificate when you change money through a bank or authorized dealer; ask for one if it is not automatically given. It allows you to change Indian rupees back to your own currency on departure. It also enables you to use rupees to pay hotel bills or buy air tickets for which payment in foreign exchange may be required. The certificates are only valid for 3 months.

Transferring money to India

HSBC, Barclays and ANZGrindlays and others can make 'instant' transfers to their offices in India but charge a high fee (about US$30). Standard Chartered Bank issues US$ TCs. Sending a bank draft (up to US$1000) by post (4-7 days by Speedpost) is the cheapest option.

Cost of living

The cost of living in India remains well below that in the West. The average wage per capita is about Rs 34,000 per year (US$800). Manual, unskilled labourers (women are often paid less than men), farmers and others in rural areas earn considerably less. However, thanks to booming global demand for workers who can provide cheaper IT and technology support functions and many Western firms transferring office functions or call centres to India, salaries in certain sectors have sky rocketed. An IT specialist can earn an average

Rs 500,000 per year (US$12,000) and upwards – a rate that is rising by around 15% a year.

Cost of travelling

Most food, accommodation and public transport are exceptionally cheap. Budget travellers sharing a room, using public transport and eating nothing but rice and dhal can get away with a budget of Rs 350-400 (about US$8 or £4) a day. This sum leaps up if you drink booze (about US$2, £1 or Rs 80 for a pint), smoke fags or want to have your own wheels. Those planning to stay in fairly comfortable hotels and use taxis sightseeing should budget at US$30 a day.

Opening hours

Banks Mon-Fri 1030-1430 and Sat 1030-1230. Top hotels sometimes have a 24-hr money changing service. **Post offices** Mon-Fri 1000-1700 and Sat mornings. **Government offices** Mon-Fri 0930-1700, Sat 0930-1300 (some on alternate Sat only). **Shops** Mon-Sat 0930-1800. Bazars keep longer hours.

Post

The post is frequently unreliable, and delays are common. It is best to use a post office where you can hand over mail for franking across the counter, or a top hotel post box. Valuable items should only be sent by registered mail. Government emporia or shops in the larger hotels will send purchases home if the items are difficult to carry. Seamail and Book Post have been on hold since Jan 2008 because of the Somali pirate situation – best to check for availability.

Airmail services to Europe, Africa and Australia take at least a week and a little longer for the Americas. Speed post (which takes about 4 days to the UK) is available from major towns and costs around Rs 675 for the first 250g sent and an extra Rs 75 for each 250g thereafter. Specialist shippers deal with larger items, normally around US$150 per cubic metre. Courier services (eg **DHL**) are available in the larger towns. At some main post offices you can send small packages under 2 kg as **letter post** (rather than parcel post), which is much cheaper at Rs 220. Check that the post office holds necessary customs declaration forms (2-3 copies needed). And now, also passport copies.Write 'No commercial value' if returning used clothes, books etc. **Sea mail**, currently on hold, see above, costs Rs 800 for 10 kg. 'Packers' do necessary cloth covering, sealing etc for Rs 20-50; you address the parcel, obtain stamps from a separate counter; stick stamps and a customs form to the parcel with glue available (the other form/s must be partially sewn on). Post at the Parcels Counter and obtain a registration slip. Cost varies by destination and is normally displayed on a board beside the counter. Sea Mail will eventually be replaced by **SAL** (Surface Air Lifted). The prices are fractionally lower than airmail, Rs 500-600 for the first kg and Rs 150-250 per extra kg. Delivery can take up to 2 months. **Poste restante** facilities are widely available in even quite small towns at the GPO where mail is held for 1 month. Ask for mail to be addressed to you with your surname in capitals and underlined. When asking for mail check under surname as well as christian name.

Safety

Personal security
In general the threats to personal security for travellers are low. In most areas it is possible to travel either individually or in groups without any risk of personal violence. However, care should be taken. Specific advice for women travelling alone is given on page 56.

Theft
Theft is not uncommon. It is best to keep TCs, passports and valuables with you at all times since you can't regard hotel rooms as automatically safe; even hotel safes don't guarantee secure storage. Avoid leaving valuables near open windows even when you are in the room. Use your own padlock in a budget hotel when you go out. **Pickpockets** and other thieves operate in the big cities. Crowded areas are particularly high risk. **Confidence tricksters** are particularly common where people are on the move, notably around railway stations or places where budget tourists gather. A common plea is some sudden and desperate calamity. The demands are likely to increase sharply if sympathy is shown.

Take special care of your belongings when getting on or off **public transport**. It can be difficult to keep an eye on your belongings when travelling. Nothing of value should be left close to open train windows. First-class a/c compartments are self-contained and normally completely secure. Second-class compartments are larger, allowing more movement of passengers, and are not so secure. Most thefts occur in non-a/c Sleeper class carriages (see below). Attendants may take little notice of what is going on, so luggage should be chained to a seat for security overnight. Locks and chains are easily available at main stations and bazars. Some travellers prefer to reserve upper berths which offer some added protection against theft and also have the benefit of allowing daytime sleeping. If you put your bags on the upper berth during the day, beware of fellow passengers climbing up for a 'sleep'. Be guarded with new friends on trains who show particular interest in the contents of your bag, and be extra wary of accepting food or drink from casual acquaintances; travellers have reported being drugged and then robbed.

Police
If you have items stolen, they should be reported to the police as soon as possible. Keep a separate record of vital documents, including passport details and TC numbers.

Larger hotels will be able to assist in contacting and dealing with the police. Dealings with the police can be very difficult. The paperwork involved in reporting losses can be time consuming and irritating, and your own documentation (eg passport and visas) may be demanded. In some places the police themselves demand bribes, though tourists should not assume that if procedures move slowly they are automatically being expected to offer a bribe. If you have to go to a police station, try to take someone with you. If you face really serious problems, for example in connection with a driving accident, you should contact your consular office as quickly as possible. Some towns have introduced special Tourist Police to help the foreign traveller.

Drugs

Certain areas have become associated with foreigners taking drugs. The government takes the misuse of drugs very seriously. Anyone charged with the illegal possession of drugs risks facing a fine of Rs 100,000 and a minimum 10 years imprisonment. Several foreigners have been imprisoned for drugs-related offences in the last decade.

Travel advice

Seek advice from your consulate before you travel. Also contact: **British Foreign & Commonwealth Office**Travel Advice Unit, T0845-850 2829 , www.fco.gov.uk/travel; **US State Department Bureau of Consular Affairs, Overseas Citizens Services**, Room 4800, Department of State, Washington, DC 20520-4818, USA, T202-647-1488, www. travel.state.gov. **Australian Department of Foreign Affairs Canberra**, Australia, T02-6261 3305, www.smarttraveller.gov.au. **Canadian** official advice is on www.voyage.gc.ca.

Senior travellers

Travellers over the age of 60 can take advantage of several discounts on travel, including 30% on train fares and up to 50%

on some air tickets. Ask when booking, as these will not be offered automatically.

Student travellers

Full-time students qualify for an **ISIC (International Student Identity Card)** which is issued by student travel and specialist agencies (eg Usit, Campus, STA) at home. The card allows certain travel benefits such as reduced prices and concessions into certain sites. For details see www.isic.org or contact **STIC** in Imperial Hotel, Janpath, New Delhi, T011-2334 3302. Those intending to study in India may get a year's student visa (see page 55).

Telephone

The international code for India is +91. The IDD prefix for dialling out of India is 00. International Direct Dialling is widely available in privately run call booths, usually labelled on yellow boards with the letters 'PCO-STD-ISD'. You dial the call yourself, and the time and cost are displayed on a screen. Cheap rate is 2100-0600, but expect queues. Calls from hotels are usually much more expensive, though some will allow local calls free of charge. Internet phone booths are the cheapest way of calling overseas.

A double ring repeated means it is ringing. Equal tones with equal pauses means engaged, similar to in the UK.

Due to the tremendous pace of the telecommunications revolution, millions of telephone numbers go out of date every year. Current telephone directories are often out of date and some of the numbers given in this book will have been changed even as we go to press. **The best advice is to put an additional 2 on the front of existing numbers**. Directory enquiries, T197, can be helpful but works only for the local area code.

Mobile phones are for sale everywhere, as are local SIM cards that allow you to make calls within India and overseas at much lower rates than using a 'roaming' service – sometimes for as little as Rs 0.5 per min. Private companies such as **Airtel, Hutch, Tata Indicomand Vodafone** are easy to sign up with. To connect you'll need to complete a form, have a local address (a hotel receipt with your name on should do), and present photocopies of your passport and visa plus 2 passport photos. Most phone dealers will be able to help, and can also sell top-up vouchers. India is divided into a number of 'calling circles' or regions, and if you travel outside the region where your connection is based, you will pay higher charges for calls.

Time

GMT +5½ hrs. India doesn't change its clocks, so from the last Sun in Oct to the last Sun in Mar it is UK time +5½ hrs, and the rest of the year it's +4½ hrs (USA, EST +10½ and +9½ hrs; Australia, EST -5½ and -4½ hrs).

Tipping

A tip of Rs 10 to a luggage porter in a modest hotel (Rs 20 in a higher category) would be appropriate. In upmarket restaurants, a 10% tip is acceptable when service is not already included; in cheaper places round off the bill with small change. Indians don't normally tip taxi drivers but a small extra amount over the fare is welcomed. Porters at airports and railway stations often have a fixed rate displayed but will usually press for more.

Tour operators

UK
Ace, T01223-835055, www.acestudytours. co.uk. Cultural study tours, expert led.
Cox & Kings (Taj Group), T020-78735000, www.coxandkings.co.uk. Palaces, forts, tourist high spots.

Dragoman, T01728-861133, www.dragoman. com. Overland group travel, camping.
Exodus Travels, T020-8675 5550, www.exodus.co.uk. Small group overland and trekking tours. Cycling tours in Rajasthan and desert adventures
Greaves Tours, T020-74879111 (USA T1-800-318-7801), www.greavesindia.com. Innovative itineraries – cities, wildlife, heritage, plus tours to unusual areas.
Indian Explorations, Afex House, Holwell, Burford, Oxfordshire, OX18 4JS, T01553-671371, www.indianexplorations.com. Bespoke holidays and safaris, run by experts.
KE Adventure, T01768-773966 (USA T1-800-497-9675), www.keadventure.com. Has a tigers, temples and Taj trip. Focus on responsible tourism.
Pettitts, T01892-515966, www.pettitts.co.uk. Unusual locations, activities, wildlife. Check the online guide to interesting happenings each month.

Steppes Discovery, T01285-643333, www.steppesdiscovery.co.uk. Wildlife safaris with strong conservation ethic.

Trans Indus, Northumberland House, 11 The Pavement, Popes Lane, London W5 4NG, T020-8566 3739, www.transindus.co.uk. Tailor-made and group tours and holidays.

Western & Oriental, T0845-277 3344, www.westernoriental.com. Upmarket, heritage hotels.

India

Banyan Tours and Travels, T+91-124-456 3800, www.bayantours.com. Pan-Indian operator specializing in bespoke, upmarket travel, with focus on culture, heritage, adventure and wildlife. Funky website.

The Blue Yonder, Bangalore, T+91-80 3290 6620, www.theblueyonder.com. Highly regarded sustainable and community tourism operators, now offering green trips in Rajasthan, with options to learn tie-dye and puppet-making, study frescoes and do your bit with responsible shopping.

Discovery Journeys, Chapri House, 88-Sect HUDA, Gurgaon 17, Haryana, New Delhi, T+91-124-4076965, www.india-discovery.com. Experienced in organizing and leading tours, treks and wildlife holidays across India.

Forts & Palaces Tours, Jaipur, T+91-141-235 4508, www.palaces-tours.com. A friendly outfit offering sightseeing tours, hotel reservations and ticketing.

Ibex Expeditions, 30 Community Centre, East of Kailash, New Delhi, T011-2646 0246, www.ibexexpeditions.com. Award-winning eco-aware tour operator for tours, safaris and treks.

India Beat, T+91-141 651 9797, www.india beat.co.uk. This British team based in Jaipur offers a range of Rajasthani delights.

KOKO India, T+91-963 722 4112, www.koko india.com. British team based in India serving up a masala of boutique trips in Rajasthan,

blending holistic and creative pursuits such as yoga, bellydancing and photography, with a Maharajah's homestay fit for a Queen.

Mountain Adventures, Faridabad, T+91-129-411749, www.mountainindia.com. Trekking, cycling, motorbiking, jeep safaris and cultural tours.

Paradise Holidays, 312 Ansals Classique Tower, Rajouri Garden, New Delhi, T+91-011-4552 0735/36/37/38, www.paradise holidays.com. Wide range of tailor-made tours, from cultural to wildlife.

Parul Tours & Travels, 32 Lal Ghat, Udaipur, T0294-2421697, www.rajasthantravel bycab.com. Tours, travel arrangements, hotel bookings, help with itineraries, etc.

Royal Expeditions, 26 Community Center, East of Kailash, New Delhi, T+91-11-2623 8545, www.royalexpeditions.com. Tailor-made tours, gourmet tours, culture, wildlife and photography. Specializes in easy options for senior travellers.

Services International, IATA Code 14-3 4105 1, 25/8 Guru House, Old Rajinder Nagar, New Delhi, T+91-11-41050560/70/80/90, www.india-travelpackages.com. Tours throughout India.

Shanti Travel, C-66 Okhla, 2nd floor, Okhla Phase 1, New Delhi, T+91-11-4607 7800, www.shantitravel.com. Tailor-made tours throughout India.

Wanderlust, Delhi, T+91-11-4163 6896, www.wanderlustindia.com. Safaris, wildlife, cultural tours, etc.

USA

Adventures Abroad, T0800-665 3998, www.adventures-abroad.com.

Myths & Mountains, 976 Tee Court, Incline Village, Nevada 89451, T0800-670 6984, www.mythsandmountains.com.

Spirit of India, T888-3676147, www.spirit-of-india.com. General and spirituality-focused tours.

Australia and New Zealand
Peregrine Adventures, Australia, T+613 8601 4444, www.peregrineadventures.com. Small group overland and trekking tours.

Tourist information

State tourist offices in the major cities of Rajasthan produce their own tourist literature and supply lists of hotels. The quality of material is improving, though maps are often inadequate. The Tourism Development Corporations run modest hotels and mid-way motels with restaurants that are adequate. They also offer tours of the city, neighbouring sights and overnight and regional packages and have a list of approved guides. The officers can put you in touch with car rental firms but their advice may not always be unbiased.

Note Don't take advice from unofficial Tourist Offices at airports or railway stations.

Tourist offices overseas
Australia 135 King St, Sydney, NSW 2000, T02-92219555. info@indiatourism.com.au.
Canada 60 Bloor St West, Suite No 1003, Toronto, Ontario, T416-9623787, info@indiatourismcanada.ca.
France 11-13 Bis Blvd Hausmann, 75009, Paris T01-45233045, indtourparis@aol.com.
Germany Baserler St 48, 60329, Frankfurt AM-Main 1, T069-2429490, office@india-tourism.com.
Italy Via Albricci 9, Milan 20122, T02-8053506, info@indiatourismmilan.com.
Japan B9F Chiyoda Building, 6-5-12 Ginza, Chuo-Ku, Tokyo 104-0061, T03-35715062, indiatourt@smile.ocn.ne.jp.
The Netherlands Rokin 9-15, 1012 KK Amsterdam, T020-6208991, info@indiatourismamsterdam.com.
Singapore 20 Kramat Lane, 01-01A United House, 228773, Singapore, T62353800, indtour.sing@pacific.net.sg.
South Africa PO Box 412452, Craig Hall 2024, 2000 Johannesburg, T011-3250880, goito@global.co.za.

UK 7 Cork St, London WIS 3LH, T020-74373677, T08700-102183, london5@indiatouristoffice.org.
USA 3550 Wilshire Blvd, Room 204, Los Angeles, California 90010, T213-3808855, goitola@aol.com; Suite 1808, 1270 Av of Americas, New York, NY 10020-1700, T212-5864901, ny@itony.com.

Websites
More and more Rajasthan-specific websites are appearing, some very commercially minded and short on objective information, others which add useful insights into certain aspects of the state. Travel and accommodation are widely covered, with historical/cultural content being harder to track down.
www.123india.com Wide-ranging current affairs and general India site.
www.apanidhani.com Environmentally friendly and socially aware tours and information on the Shekhawati region.
www.downtoearth.org.in Interesting articles on India-wide environmental and social issues. Huge database available for a nominal subscription charge.
www.india.org The Sites on India section contains excellent information on the structure of Indian government. Tourism information is less useful.
www.irctc.co.in Comprehensive train timetable and online booking service.
www.mapsofindia.com/maps/rajasthan Exhaustive collection of high-quality maps.
www.rajasthantourismindia.com The official state government website, less commercial than most if a little chaotically put together.
www.rajasthantravelguide.com Good range of information, tour packages, etc.
www.rajasthanunlimited.com Quirky collection of features and travel advice.
www.tourindia.com The official government promotional site with useful information but no objective evaluation of problems and difficulties. Has separate state entries within it. 'India Travel Online' is informative and issued fortnightly.

www.umaidbhawan.com A hotel website, but click on the travel guide for a comprehensive listing of tour/travel options, as well as some useful tips.
www.wunderground.com An excellent weather site, world wide, city specific and fast.

Visas and immigration

For embassies and consulates, see page 43. Virtually all foreign nationals, including children, require a visa to enter India. Nationals of Bhutan and Nepal only require a suitable means of identification. The rules regarding visas change frequently and arrangements for application and collection also vary from town to town so it is essential to check details and costs with the relevant embassy or consulate. These remain closed on Indian national holidays. Now many consulates and embassies are outsourcing the visa process, it's best to find out in advance how long it will take. For example, in London where you used to be able to get a visa in person in a morning if you were prepared to queue, it now takes 2-3 working days and involves 2 trips to the office.

At other offices, it can be much easier to apply in advance by post, to avoid queues and frustratingly low visa quotas. Postal applications can 15 working days to process.

Visitors from countries with no Indian representation may apply to the resident British representative, or enquire at the **Air India** office. An application on the prescribed form should be accompanied by 2 passport photographs and your passport which should be valid 6 months beyond the period of your visit. Note that visas are valid from the date granted, not from the date of entry. For up-to-date information on visa requirements visit www.india-visa.com or check out your embassy or consulate website.

Currently the following visa rules apply:
Transit For passengers en route to another country (no more than 72 hrs in India).

Tourist 3-6 month visa from the date of issue with multiple entry.
Business 3-6 months or up to 2 years with multiple entry. A letter from the company giving the nature of business is required.
5 year For those of Indian origin only, who have held Indian passports.
Student Valid up to 1 year from the date of issue. Attach a letter of acceptance from Indian institution and an AIDS test certificate. Allow up to 3 months for approval.
Visa extensions Applications should be made to the Foreigners' Regional Registration Offices at New Delhi, or an office of the Superintendent of Police in the District Headquarters. After 6 months, you must leave India and apply for a new visa – the Nepal office is known to be difficult. Anyone staying in India for a period of more than 180 days (6 months) must register at a convenient Foreigners' Registration Office.

Registration
No foreigner needs to register within the 180-day period of their tourist visa. All foreign visitors who stay in India for more than 180 days are required to register at the nearest Foreigners' Registration Office and get an **income tax clearance** exemption certificate from the Foreign Section of the Income Tax Department in Delhi.

Liquor permits
Periodically some Indian states have tried to enforce prohibition, but not Rajasthan. When applying for your visa you can ask for an **All India Liquor Permit**. You can also get the permit from any Government of India Tourist Office in Delhi or the state capitals. Instant 'spot' permits are issued by some hotels.

Weights and measures

The metric system has come into universal use in the cities. In remote areas local measures are sometimes used. One lakh is 100,000 and 1 crore is 10 million.

Women travellers

Independent travel is still largely unheard of for Indian women. Although it is relatively safe for women to travel around India, most people find it an advantage to travel with a companion. Even then, privacy is rarely respected and there can be a lot of hassle, pressure and intrusion on your personal space. Backpackers often meet like-minded travelling companions at budget hotels. Cautious solo travellers recommend dying blonde hair black and wearing wedding rings, but the most important measure is to dress appropriately, in loose-fitting, non-see-through clothes, covering shoulders, arms and legs. Take advantage of the gender segregation on public transport, both to avoid hassle and talk with local women. In mosques women should be covered from head to ankle. **Independent Traveller**, T01628 522772, www.independenttraveller.com, runs women-only tours to India.

'Eve teasing', the euphemism for physical harassment, is an unfortunate result of the sexual repression latent in Indian culture, combined with a young male population whose only access to sex education is via the back corners of dingy cyber cafés. Unaccompanied women are most vulnerable in major cities, crowded bazaars, beach resorts and tourist centres where men may follow them and touch them; festival nights are particularly bad for this. Women have reported that they have been molested while being measured for clothing in tailors' shops. If you are harassed, it can be effective to make a scene. Be firm and clear if you don't wish to speak to someone. The best response to staring is to avert your eyes down and away. This is not the submissive gesture it might seem, but an effective tool to communicate that you have no interest in any further interaction. Aggressively staring back or verbally confronting the starer can be construed as a come-on. It is best to be accompanied at night, especially when travelling by rickshaw or taxi in towns. Be prepared to raise an alarm if anything unpleasant threatens.

Most railway booking offices have separate women's ticket queues or ask women to go to the head of the general queue. Some buses have seats reserved for women. See also page 39.

Working in India

Voluntary work
It is best to arrange voluntary work well in advance with organizations in India; alternatively, contact an organization in your home country. Students may spend part of their year off helping in a school or teaching English. Foreigners should apply to the Indian representative in their own country for the latest information about work permits.

UK
International Voluntary Service (IVS), IVS GB, Thorn House, 5 Rose St, Edinburgh EH2 4BJ, T0131-243 2745, http://ivsgb.org/info/.
i to i, Woodside House, 261 Low Lane, Leeds LS18 5NY, T0800-011 1156, www.i-to-i.com.
Volunteer Work Information Service, PO Box 2759, Lewes BN7 1WU, T01273 479047, www.workingabroad.com.
VSO, 317 Putney Bridge Rd, London SW15 2PN, www.vso.org.uk.

USA
Council for International Programs, 1700 East 13th St, Suite 4ME, Cleveland, Ohio, T216-566-1088, www.cipusa.org.

Australia
The website **www.ampersand.org.au** has links to a variety of volunteer organizations.
Australian Volunteers International, 71 Argyle St, Fitzroy, VIC 3065, T03-9279 1788, www.australianvolunteers.com.

Contents

Delhi & Agra

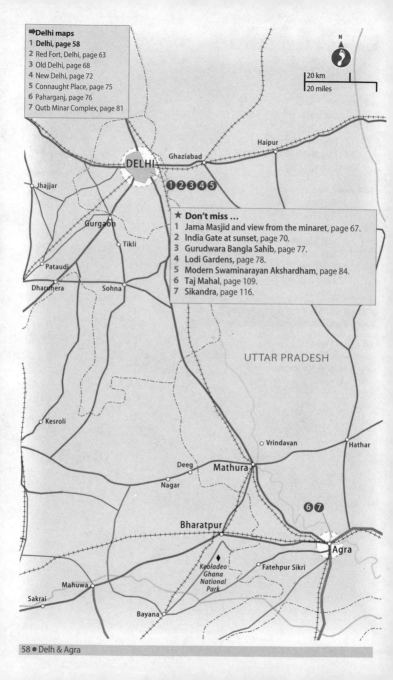

N

20 km
20 miles

Haipur

Ghaziabad

DELHI

Jhajjar

①②③④⑤

Gurgaon

Tikli

★ **Don't miss ...**
1 Jama Masjid and view from the minaret, page 67.
2 India Gate at sunset, page 70.
3 Gurudwara Bangla Sahib, page 77.
4 Lodi Gardens, page 78.
5 Modern Swaminarayan Akshardham, page 84.
6 Taj Mahal, page 109.
7 Sikandra, page 116.

Pataudi

Dharuhera   Sohna

UTTAR PRADESH

Kesroli

Vrindavan   Hathar

Deeg

Mathura

Nagar

⑥⑦

Bharatpur

Agra

Mahuwa

*Keoladeo
Ghana
National
Park*   Fatehpur Sikri

Sakrai

Bayana

Delhi is not so much a city to see as to experience. You'll smell fragrances too exotic to place, odours too familiar to ignore, hear blaring Bhangra and Bryan Adams, taste rich curries and scented sweets. You'll see destiny-driven Hindus, demure Muslims and exuberant Sikhs, playing out a million daily dramas against backdrops that range from the humming chaos of Shahjahanabad's serpentine alleys to the air-conditioned malls of Mehrauli. The multiple-mobile toting, upper-class youth rub gym-honed shoulders with the rag-clad slum dwellers who make up a third of the city's 14 million people. Exclusive housing areas, where hawkers bring every last convenience to doors answered by suppliant servants, lie a stone's throw from the regularly razed slums lining the Yamuna River, a great waterway upon which the city has largely turned its back. The city's history, a study in instability, is reflected in its myriad world-class monuments, temples and mosques. Broad, tree-lined avenues lead directly into teeming alleyways; elegant whitewashed bungalows, surrounded by impossibly green lawns, give way to precarious piles of mismatched masonry. Radical anti-pollution laws mean that all forms of public transport – the heaven-sent new Metro excepted – now run on gas, but the crammed buses still compete for ever-diminishing road space with family-packed cars, rickshaws and bicycles, all watched over with unbending benevolence by the city's true ruling class, its sacrosanct cows.

Like Delhi, Agra stands on the right bank of the Yamuna River. The bustle of the modern-day city only serves to accentuate the serenity of the incomparable Taj Mahal, one of man's most magnificent monuments and now officially a Wonder of the World. The lightness of the Taj's white marble contrasts starkly with the imposing, heavyweight presence of the Red Fort, the transition from defensive solidity to material heartbreak eased by the intervening river.

Ins and outs → *Phone code: 011; dial 1952, then the old number, to get the new phone number. Colour map 5, B2. Population: 12.8 million. Area: 434 sq km. Directory enquiries: T197/1952.*

Getting there

Delhi is served by **Indira Gandhi International (IGI) Airport**, which handles both international and domestic traffic. The Domestic Terminal 1, 15 km from the centre, handles flights from two separate sections: 'A', exclusively for **Indian Airlines** and 'B' for others. The International Terminal 2 is 23 km from the centre. During the day, it can take 30-45 minutes from the Domestic Terminal and 45 minutes to an hour from the International Terminal to get to the centre. A free shuttle runs between the terminals. To get to town take a pre-paid taxi (see Transport, page 102) or an airport coach or ask your hotel to collect you.

The **Inter State Bus Terminus (ISBT)** is at Kashmere Gate, near the Red Fort, about 30 minutes by bus from Connaught Place. Local buses connect it to the other ISBTs.

There are three main railway stations. The busy **New Delhi Station**, a 10-minute walk north of Connaught Place, can be maddeningly chaotic; you need to have all your wits about you. The quieter **Hazrat Nizamuddin** (which has some south-bound trains) is 5 km southeast of Connaught Place. The overpoweringly crowded **Old Delhi Station** (2 km north of Connaught Place) has a few important trains.

Getting around

The new Metro, though still by no means complete, offers a realistic alternative for navigating select parts of the city: it's now possible to get from Connaught Place to Old Delhi in a cool five minutes. For the rest of the city, which is far too spread out to walk, auto-rickshaws and taxis are widely available, though few are prepared to use their meters, especially for foreigners. It's best to use pre-paid stands at stations, airport terminals and at the junction of Radial Road 1 and Connaught Place if possible, otherwise be sure to agree a fare before you get in. The same applies to cycle rickshaws, which ply the streets of Old Delhi. City buses are usually packed and have long queues. Be on your guard from thieves around New Delhi Station. State Entry Road runs from the southern end of Platform 1 to Connaught Place. This is a hassle-free alternative to the main Chelmsford Road during the day (gate closed at night). Fleets of Radio Taxis are the newest additions to the city's transport options. These include: **Mega Cabs**, T011- 4141 4141; **Delhi Cab**, T011-4433 3222; **Easy Cab**, T011-4343 4343; **Quick Cab**, T011- 4533 3333. ▶▶ *See Transport, page 101.*

Orientation

The **Red Fort** and **Jama Masjid** are the focal point of Old Delhi, 2 km northeast of Connaught Place. Chandni Chowk, the main commercial area, heads west from the fort. Around this area are narrow lanes packed to the rafters with all different types of wares for sale. To the southeast are **New Delhi Railway Station** and the main backpackers' area, **Paharganj**, with **Connaught Place**, the notional 'centre' of New Delhi, about 1 km south. Running due south of Connaught Place is **Janpath** with small shops selling craft products, and hotels like the **Imperial**. Janpath is intersected by **Rajpath** with all the major state buildings at its western end. Immediately south is the diplomatic enclave, **Chanakyapuri**. Most of the upmarket hotels are scattered across the wide area between Connaught Place and the airport to the southwest. As Delhi's centre of gravity has shifted southwards, a series of new markets has grown up to serve extensive housing colonies such as **South Extension**, **Greater Kailash** and **Safdarjang Enclave**. This development has brought one of the major historic sites, the **Qutb Minar**, within the limits of the city, about half an hour by taxi south of Connaught Place.

Tourist information

Most tourist offices are open Monday-Friday 1000-1800. **Government of India Tourist Office**① *88 Janpath, T011-2332 0008, Mon-Sat 0900-1800*, helpful, issues permits for visits to Rashtrapati Bhavan and gardens. Also at International Airport. **Delhi Tourism**① *N-36 Connaught Pl, T011-2331 5322* (touts pester you to use one of many imposters; correct office is directly opposite 'Competent House'); **Coffee Home Annexe** ① *Baba Kharak Singh Marg, T011-2336 3607; hotel, transport and tour bookings T011-2462 3782, 0700-2100; also at Airport Terminals;* Inter-State Bus Terminal; **New Delhi Railway Station** ① *T011-2373 2374;* **Nizamuddin Railway Station** ① *T011-2251 1083.* **India Tourism Development Corporation (ITDC)**① *L-1 Connaught Circus, T011-2332 0331.*

Best time to visit

October-March are the best months, but December and January can get quite cold and foggy at night; pollution can affect asthma sufferers. Monsoon lasts from the end of June to mid-September. May and June are very hot and dry.

History

In the modern period, Delhi has only been India's capital since 1911. It is a city of yo-yoing fortunes and has been repeatedly reduced to rubble. There have been at least eight cities founded on the site of modern Delhi.

According to Hindu mythology, Delhi's first avatar was as the site of a dazzlingly wealthy city, Indraprastha, mentioned in the Mahabharata and founded around 2500 BC. The next five cities were to the south of today's Delhi. First was Lalkot, which, from 1206, became the capital of the Delhi Sultanate under the Slave Dynasty. The story of the first Sultan of Delhi, Qutb-ud-din Aybak, is a classic rags-to-riches story. A former slave, he rose through the ranks to become a general, a governor and then Sultan of Delhi. He is responsible for building Qutb Minar, but died before its completion.

The 1300s were a tumultuous time for Delhi, with five cities built during the century. Siri, the first of these, has gruesome roots. Legend has it that the city's founder, Ala-ud-din, buried the heads of infidels in the foundation of the fort. Siri derives its name from the Hindi word for 'head'. After Siri came Tughlaqabad, whose existence came to a sudden end when the Sultan of Delhi, Muhammad Tughlaq, got so angry about a perceived insult from residents, he destroyed the city. The cities of Jahanpanah and Ferozebad followed in quick succession. Delhi's centre of gravity began to move northwards. In the 1500s Dinpanah was constructed by Humayun, whose wonderful tomb (1564-1573) graces Hazrat Nizamuddin. Shahjahanabad, known today as Old Delhi, followed, becoming one of the richest and most populous cities in the world. The Persian emperor Nadir Shah invaded, killing as many as 120,000 residents in a single bloody night and stealing the Kohinoor Diamond (now part of the British royal family's crown jewels).

The next destroyers of Delhi were the British, who ransacked the city in the wake of the Great Uprising/Mutiny of 1857. The resulting bloodbath left bodies piled so high that the victors' horses had to tread on them. For the next 50 years, while the port cities of Calcutta and Bombay thrived under the British, Delhi languished. Then, in 1911, King George, on a visit to India, announced that a new city should be built next to what remained of Delhi, and that this would be the new capital of India. The British architect Edwin Lutyens was brought in to design the city. You could argue that the building hasn't stopped since ...

The central part of New Delhi is an example of Britain's imperial pretensions. The government may have been rather more reticent about moving India's capital, if it had known that in less than 36 years time, the British would no longer be ruling India. Delhi's population swelled after the violence of partition, with refugees flooding to the city. In 10 years the population of Delhi doubled, and many well-known housing colonies were built during this period.

The economic boom that began in the 1990s has lead to an explosion of construction and soaring real estate prices. Delhi is voraciously eating into the surrounding countryside. It is a city changing at such breakneck speed that shops, homes and even airports seem to appear and disappear almost overnight. Go now and witness the changes as they happen.

Delhi

*The sites of interest are grouped in three main areas. In the centre is the British-built capital of New Delhi, with its government buildings and wide avenues. The heart of Shahjahanabad (Old Delhi) is about 2 km north of Connaught Circus. Ten kilometres to the south is the Qutb Minar complex, with the old fortress city of Tughluqabad, 8 km to its east. Across the Yamuna River is the remarkable new Akshardham Temple. You can visit each separately, or link routes together into a day-tour to include the most interesting sites.**➤➤ For listings, see pages 86-106.*

Old Delhi

Shah Jahan (ruled 1628-1658) decided to move back from Agra to Delhi in 1638. Within 10 years the huge city of **Shahjahanabad**, now known as Old Delhi, was built. The plan of Shah Jahan's new city symbolized the link between religious authority enshrined in the Jama Masjid to the west, and political authority represented by the Diwan-i-Am in the Fort, joined by Chandni Chowk, the route used by the emperor. The city was protected by rubble-built walls, some of which still survive. These walls were pierced by 14 main gates. The **Ajmeri Gate**, **Turkman Gate** (often referred to by auto-rickshaw wallahs as 'Truckman Gate'), **Kashmere Gate** and **Delhi Gate** still survive.

Chandni Chowk

Shahjahanabad was laid out in blocks with wide roads, residential quarters, bazars and mosques. Its principal street, Chandni Chowk, had a tree-lined canal flowing down its centre which became renowned throughout Asia. The canal is long gone, but the jumble of shops, alleys crammed with craftsmen's workshops, food stalls, mosques and temples, cause it to retain some of its magic. A cycle rickshaw ride gives you a good feel of the place.

The impressive red sandstone façade of the **Digambar Jain Mandir** (temple) standing at the eastern end of Chandni Chowk, faces the Red Fort. Built in 1656, it contains an image of Adinath. The bird hospital within this compound releases the birds on recovery instead of returning them to their owners; many remain within the temple precincts.

Red Fort (Lal Qila)

ⓘ *Tue-Sun sunrise to sunset, Rs 250 foreigners, Rs 10 Indians, allow 1 hr. The entrance is through the Lahore Gate (nearest the car park) with the admission kiosk opposite; keep your ticket as you will need to show it at the Drum House. The toilets are in Chatta Chowk and near*

Asad Burj but are best avoided. You must remove shoes and cover all exposed flesh from your shoulders to your legs.

Between the new city and the River Yamuna, Shah Jahan built a fort. Most of it was built out of red *lal* (sandstone), hence the name **Lal Qila** (Red Fort), the same as that at Agra on which the Delhi Fort is modelled. Begun in 1639 and completed in 1648, it is said to have cost Rs 10 million, much of which was spent on the opulent marble palaces within. In recent years much effort has been put into improving the fort and gardens, but visitors may be saddened by the neglected state of some of the buildings, and the gun-wielding soldiers lolling around do nothing to improve the ambience. However, despite the modern development of roads and shops and the never-ending traffic, it's an impressive site.

The approach The entrance is by the Lahore Gate. The defensive barbican that juts out in front of it was built by Aurangzeb, see page 294. A common story suggests that Aurangzeb built the curtain wall to save his nobles and visiting dignitaries from having to walk – and bow

☑ **Red Fort, Delhi**

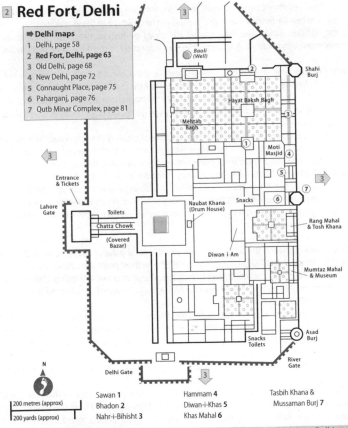

➡ **Delhi maps**
1 Delhi, page 58
2 **Red Fort, Delhi, page 63**
3 Old Delhi, page 68
4 New Delhi, page 72
5 Connaught Place, page 75
6 Paharganj, page 76
7 Qutb Minar Complex, page 81

Baoli (Well)

Shahi Burj

Hayat Baksh Bagh

Mehtab Bagh

Moti Masjid 4

Entrance & Tickets

Lahore Gate

Toilets

Chatta Chowk

(Covered Bazar)

Naubat Khana (Drum House)

Snacks

Diwan i Am

Rang Mahal & Tosh Khana

Mumtaz Mahal & Museum

Asad Burj

Snacks Toilets

River Gate

N

200 metres (approx)
200 yards (approx)

Delhi Gate

Sawan **1**
Bhadon **2**
Nahr-i-Bihisht **3**

Hammam **4**
Diwan-i-Khas **5**
Khas Mahal **6**

Tasbih Khana & Mussaman Burj **7**

A gift from Florence?

There are 318 Florentine pietra dura plaques in the niche behind the throne, showing flowers, birds and lions as well as the central figure of Orpheus, playing to the beasts. In between these Italian panels are Mughal pietra dura works with flowery arabesques and birds. Ebba Koch argues that the techniques employed by the Mughal artisans are exactly the same as the Italian ones, so there must have been a direct connection.

This is not to say that there was no independent development of Mughal inlay craftsmanship. Such a view has been described by Tillotson as the result of wishful thinking by Europeans, eager to claim a stake in the superb work. In fact the Mughals had an equally fine tradition of stone carving and of inlay work on which to draw as the Florentine princes, as can be seen from the work in the Jama Masjid in Ahmadabad, built in 1414.

– the whole length of Chandni Chowk, for no one was allowed to ride in the presence of the emperor. When the emperor sat in the Diwan-i-Am he could see all the way down the Chowk, so the addition must have been greatly welcomed by his courtiers. The new entrance arrangement also made an attacking army more vulnerable to the defenders on the walls.

Chatta Chowk and the Naubat Khana Inside is the 'Covered Bazar', which was quite exceptional in the 17th century. In Shah Jahan's time there were shops on both upper and lower levels. Originally they catered for the Imperial household and carried stocks of silks, brocades, velvets, gold and silverware, jewellery and gems. There were coffee shops too for nobles and courtiers.

The Naubat Khana (Naqqar Khana) (Drum House or music gallery) marked the entrance to the inner apartments of the fort. Here everyone except the princes of the royal family had to dismount and leave their horses or *hathi* (elephants), hence its other name of **Hathi Pol** (Elephant Gate). Five times a day ceremonial music was played on the kettle drum, *shahnais* (a kind of oboe) and cymbals, glorifying the emperor. In 1754 Emperor Ahmad Shah was murdered here. The gateway with four floors is decorated with floral designs. You can still see traces of the original panels painted in gold or other colours on the interior of the gateway.

Diwan-i-Am Between the first inner court and the royal palaces at the heart of the fort, stood the Diwan-i-Am (Hall of Public Audience), the furthest point the normal visitor would reach. It has seen many dramatic events, including the destructive whirlwind of the Persian Nadir Shah in 1739 and of Ahmad Shah the Afghan in 1756, and the trial of the last 'King of Delhi', **Bahadur Shah II** in 1858.

The well-proportioned hall was both a functional building and a showpiece intended to hint at the opulence of the palace itself. In Shah Jahan's time the sandstone was hidden behind a very thin layer of white polished plaster, *chunam*. This was decorated with floral motifs in many colours, especially gilt. Silk carpets and heavy curtains hung from the canopy rings outside the building, such interiors reminders of the Mughals' nomadic origins in Central Asia, where royal durbars were held in tents.

At the back of the hall is a platform for the emperor's throne. Around this was a gold railing, within which stood the princes and great nobles separated from the lesser nobles inside the hall. Behind the throne canopy are 12 marble panels inlaid with motifs of fruiting trees, parrots and cuckoos. Figurative workmanship is very unusual in Islamic buildings, and these panels are the only example in the Red Fort.

As well as matters of official administration, Shah Jahan would listen to accounts of illness, dream interpretations and anecdotes from his ministers and nobles. Wednesday was the day of judgement. Sentences were often swift and brutal and sometimes the punishment of dismemberment, beating or death was carried out on the spot. The executioners were close at hand with axes and whips. On Friday, the Muslim holy day, there would be no business.

☾ *Shah Jahan spent two hours a day in the Diwan-i-Am. According to Bernier, the French traveller, the emperor would enter to a fanfare and mount the throne by a flight of movable steps.*

Inner palace buildings Behind the Diwan-i-Am is the private enclosure of the fort. Along the east wall, overlooking the River Yamuna, Shah Jahan set six small palaces (five survive). Also within this compound are the Harem, the Life-Bestowing Garden and the Nahr-i-Bihisht (Stream of Paradise).

Life-Bestowing Gardens (Hayat Baksh Bagh) The original gardens were landscaped according to the Islamic principles of the Persian *char bagh*, with pavilions, fountains and water courses dividing the garden into various but regular beds. The two pavilions **Sawan** and **Bhadon**, named after the first two months of the rainy season (July-August), reveal something of the character of the garden. The garden used to create the effect of the monsoon and contemporary accounts tell us that in the pavilions, some of which were especially erected for the **Teej** festival, which marks the arrival of the monsoon, the royal ladies would sit in silver swings and watch the rains. Water flowed from the back wall of the pavilion through a slit above the marble shelf and over the niches in the wall. Gold and silver pots of flowers were placed in these alcoves during the day whilst at night candles were lit to create a glistening and colourful effect.

Shahi Burj From the pavilion next to the Shahi Burj (**Royal Tower**) the canal known as the **Nahr-i-Bihisht** (Stream of Paradise) began its journey along the Royal Terrace. The three-storey octagonal tower was seriously damaged in 1857 and is still unsafe. In Shah Jahan's time the Yamuna lapped the walls. Shah Jahan used the tower as his most private office and only his sons and a few senior ministers were allowed with him.

Moti Masjid To the right are the three marble domes of Aurangzeb's 'Pearl Mosque' (shoes must be removed). Bar the cupolas, it is completely hidden behind a wall of red sandstone, now painted white. Built in 1662 of polished white marble, it has some exquisite decoration. All the surfaces are highly decorated in a fashion similar to rococo, which developed at the same time as in Europe. Unusually the prayer hall is on a raised platform with inlaid outlines of individual *musallas* ('prayer mats') in black marble. While the outer walls were aligned to the cardinal points like all the other fort buildings, the inner walls were positioned so that the mosque would correctly face Mecca.

Hammam The **Royal Baths** have three apartments separated by corridors with canals to carry water to each room. The two flanking the entrance, for the royal children, had hot and cold baths. The room furthest away from the door has three basins for rose water fountains.

The peacock throne

In the centre of the Diwan-i-Khas (5) is a marble pedestal on which stood the Peacock Throne that Shah Jahan commissioned on his accession in 1627. It took seven years to make. The throne was designed with two peacocks standing behind with a parrot carved out of a single emerald between them. It was inlaid with a vast number of precious stones – sapphires, rubies, emeralds, pearls and diamonds. Over the top was a gem-encrusted gold canopy edged with pearls, supported by 12 pillars.

The throne was carried off by Nadir Shah, a Turk, who after conquering Persia sacked Delhi in 1739. Soon after his occupation of Delhi a riot broke out in which 900 of his soldiers were killed.

Nadir Shah himself rode through the streets of Delhi to assess the situation when some residents were rash enough to throw stones at him. Enraged, Nadir Shah ordered the entire population of Delhi to be massacred, resulting in 30,000 dead. In the evening the 'Great' Mughal (Mohammad Shah) begged for mercy, and such was Nadir Shah's control over his troops that he was able immediately to halt the carnage. The invaders took with them as much as they could extort from all the nobles. Bahadur Shah later replaced the throne with a poor copy. The Peacock Throne itself was broken up by Nadir Shah's assassins in 1747; some of the jewels are believed to have been incorporated into the late Shah of Iran's throne.

Diwan-i-Khas Beyond is the single-storeyed **Hall of Private Audience**, topped by four Hindu-style *chhattris* and built completely of white marble. The *dado* (lower part of the wall) on the interior was richly decorated with inlaid precious and semi-precious stones. The ceiling was silver but was removed by the Marathas in 1760. Outside, the hall used to have a marble pavement and an arcaded court. Both have gone.

This was the Mughal office of state. Shah Jahan spent two hours here before retiring for a meal, siesta and prayers. In the evening he would return to the hall for more work before going to the harem. The hall's splendour moved the 14th-century poet Amir Khusrau to write the lines inscribed above the corner arches of the north and south walls: *"Agar Firdaus bar rue Zamin-ast/Hamin ast o Hamin ast o Hamin ast"* (If there be a paradise on earth, it is here, it is here, it is here).

Royal palaces Next to the Diwan-i-Khas is the three-roomed **Khas Mahal** (Private Palace). Nearest the Diwan-i-Khas is the **Tasbih Khana** (Chamber for the Telling of Rosaries) where the emperor would worship privately with his rosary of 99 beads, one for each of the mystical names of Allah. In the centre is the Khwabgah (Palace of Dreams) which gives on to the octagonal **Mussaman Burj** tower. Here Shah Jahan would be seen each morning. A balcony was added to the tower in 1809 and here George V and Queen Mary appeared in their Coronation Durbar of 1911. The **Tosh Khana** (Robe Room), to the south, has a beautiful marble screen at its north end, carved with the scales of justice above the filigree grille. If you are standing with your back to the Diwan-i-Khas you will see a host of circulating suns (a symbol of royalty), but if your back is to the next building (the Rang Mahal), you will see moons surrounding the scales. All these rooms were sumptuously decorated with fine silk carpets, rich silk brocade curtains and lavishly decorated walls. After 1857 the British used the Khas Mahal as an officer's mess and sadly it was defaced.

The **Rang Mahal** (Palace of Colours), the residence of the chief *sultana*, was also the place where the emperor ate most of his meals. It was divided into six apartments. Privacy and coolness were ensured by the use of marble *jali* screens. Like the other palaces it was beautifully decorated with a silver ceiling ornamented with golden flowers to reflect the water in the channel running through the building. The north and south apartments were both known as **Sheesh Mahal** (Palace of Mirrors) since into the ceiling were set hundreds of small mirrors. In the evening when candles were lit a starlit effect would be produced.

Through the palace ran the **Life- bestowing Stream** and at its centre is a lotus-shaped marble basin which had an ivory fountain. As might be expected in such a cloistered and cosseted environment, the ladies sometimes got bored. In the 18th century the **Empress of Jahandar Shah** sat gazing out at the river and remarked that she had never seen a boat sink. Shortly afterwards a boat was deliberately capsized so that she could be entertained by the sight of people bobbing up and down in the water crying for help.

The southernmost of the palaces, the **Mumtaz Mahal** (Palace of Jewels) ① *Tue-Sun 1000-1700*, was also used by the harem. The lower half of its walls are of marble and it contains six apartments. After the Mutiny of 1857 it was used as a guardroom and since 1912 it has been a museum with exhibits of textiles, weapons, carpets, jade and metalwork as well as works depicting life in the court. It should not be missed.

Spice market

Outside the Red Fort, cycle rickshaws offer a trip to the spice market, Jama Masjid and back through the bazar. You travel slowly westwards down Chandni Chowk passing the town hall. Dismount at Church Road and follow your guide into the heart of the market on Khari Baoli where wholesalers sell every conceivable spice. Ask to go to the roof for an excellent view over the market and back towards the Red Fort. The ride back through the bazar is equally fascinating – look up at the amazing electricity system. The final excitement is getting back across Netaji Subhash Marg. Panic not, the rickshaw wallahs know what they are doing. Negotiate for one hour and expect to pay about Rs 70. The spice laden air may irritate your throat.

Jama Masjid (Friday Mosque)

① *Visitors welcome from 30 mins after sunrise until 1215; and from 1345 until 30 mins before sunset, free, still or video cameras Rs 150, tower entry Rs 20.*

The magnificent Jama Masjid is the largest mosque in India and the last great architectural work of Shah Jahan, intended to dwarf all mosques that had gone before it. With the fort, it dominates Old Delhi. The mosque is much simpler in its ornamentation than Shah Jahan's secular buildings – a judicious blend of red sandstone and white marble, which are interspersed in the domes, minarets and cusped arches.

The gateways Symbolizing the separation of the sacred and the secular, the threshold is a place of great importance where the worshipper steps to a higher plane. There are three huge gateways, the largest being to the east. This was reserved for the royal family who gathered in a private gallery in its upper storey. Today, the faithful enter through the east gate on Fridays and for **Id-ul-Fitr** and **Id-ul-Adha**. The latter commemorates Abraham's (Ibrahim's) sacrificial offering of his son Ishmael (Ismail). Islam (unlike the Jewish and Christian tradition) believes that Abraham offered to sacrifice Ishmael, Isaac's brother.

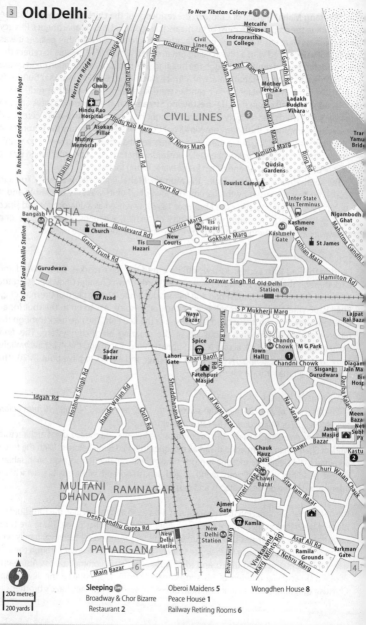

To New Tibetan Colony & 1 8

Metcalfe House

Civil Lines M

Indraprastha College

Underhill Rd

Ridge Rd

Raipur Rd

Chauburja Marg

Sham Nath Marg

Shri Ram Rd

M Gandhi Rd

Pir Ghaib

Northern Ridge

Mother Teresa's

Raj Narain Marg

Ladakh Buddha Vihara

Hindu Rao Hospital

Hindu Rao Marg

CIVIL LINES

5

Asokan Pillar

Mutiny Memorial

Raipur Rd

Raj Niwas Marg

Rani Jhansi Rd

To Roshanara Gardens & Kamla Nagar

Yamuna Marg

Trar Yamu Brid

Court Rd

Ring Rd

Qudsia Gardens

Tourist Camp A

NH1

Pul Bangash M

MOTIA BAGH

Christ Church

(Boulevard Rd)

Qudsia Marg

Tis Hazari

Tis Hazari M

New Courts

Gokhale Marg

Inter State Bus Terminus

Kashmere Gate

Kashmere Gate

Nigambodh Ghat

Mahatma Gandhi

St James

Lothian Marg

Grand Trunk Rd

To Delhi Sarai Rohilla Station

Gurudwara

M Azad

Zorawar Singh Rd

Old Delhi Station 6

(Hamilton Rd)

Naya Bazar

S P Mukherji Marg

Lajpat Rai Baza

Spice

Mission Rd

Church Rd

Town Hall

Chandni Chowk M

M G Park

1

Chandni Chowk

Diagam Jain Ma

Sadar Bazar

Lahori Gate

Khari Baoli

Fatehpuri Masjid

Sisganj Gurudwara

Darba Kalen

Bir Hosp

Idgah Rd

Hotimar Singh Rd

Jhande Walan Rd

Qutb Rd

Shraddhanand Marg

Lal Kuan Bazar

Nai Sarak

Meen Baza

Jama Masjid

Neta Subh Pa

Chauk Hauz Qazi

Chawri Bazar

Chawn

Sita Ram Bazar

Kastu

2

Churi Walan Chauk

MULTANI DHANDA

RAMNAGAR

Ajmeri Gate

Ajmeri Gate Rd

Desh Bandhu Gupta Rd

New Delhi Station

New Delhi Marg M

M Kamla

Asaf Ali Rd

Turkman Gate

PAHARGANJ

N

Main Bazar

6

Bhavbhuti Marg

Vivekananda Marg (Minto Rd)

Ramila Grounds

J Nehru Marg

4

200 metres
200 yards

Sleeping (bed icon)
Broadway & Chor Bizarre
Restaurant 2

Oberoi Maidens 5
Peace House 1
Railway Retiring Rooms 6

Wongdhen House 8

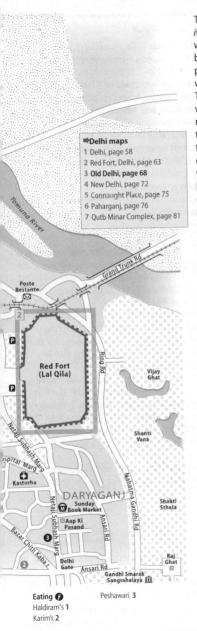

➡ Delhi maps
1 Delhi, page 58
2 Red Fort, Delhi, page 63
3 Old Delhi, page 68
4 New Delhi, page 72
5 Connaught Place, page 75
6 Paharganj, page 76
7 Qutb Minar Complex, page 81

Yomuna River

Grand Trunk Rd

Poste
Restante

Red Fort
(Lal Qila)

Ring Rd

Vijay
Ghat

Netaji Subhash Marg

Shanti
Vana

Hospital Marg

Kasturba

DARYAGANJ

Sunday
Book Market

Aap Ki
Pasand

Bazar Chitli Kabar

Mahatma Gandhi Rd

Ansari Rd

Shakti
Sthala

Delhi
Gate

Ansari Rd

Raj
Ghat

Gandhi Smarak
Sangrahalaya 🏛

Eating 🍴
Haldiram's 1
Karim's 2

Peshawari 3

The courtyard The façade has the main *iwan* (arch), five smaller arches on each side with two flanking minarets and three bulbous domes behind, all perfectly proportioned. The *iwan* draws the worshippers' attention into the building. The minarets have great views from the top; well worth the climb for Rs 10 (women may not be allowed to climb alone). The **hauz**, in the centre of the courtyard, is an ablution tank placed as usual between the inner and outer parts of the building to remind the worshipper that it is through the ritual of baptism that one first enters the community of believers. The **Dikka**, in front of the ablution tank, is a raised platform. Muslim communities grew so rapidly that by the eighth century it sometimes became necessary to introduce a second *muballigh* (prayer leader) who stood on this platform and copied the postures and chants of the *imam* inside to relay them to a much larger congregation. With the introduction of the loudspeaker and amplification, the *dikka* and the *muballigh* became redundant. In the northwest corner of the masjid there is a small shed. For a small fee, the faithful are shown a hair from the beard of the prophet, as well as his sandal and his footprint in rock.

The Kawthar Inscription Set up in 1766, the inscription commemorates the place where a worshipper had a vision of the Prophet standing by the celestial tank in paradise. It is here that the Prophet will stand on Judgment Day. In most Islamic buildings, the inscriptions are passages from the Koran or Sayings of the Prophet. Shah Jahan, however, preferred to have sayings extolling the virtues of the builder and architect as well. The 10 detailed panels on the façade indicate the date of construction (1650-1656), the cost (10 lakhs – one million rupees), the history of the building, the architect (Ustad Khalil) and the builder (Nur Allah Ahmed, probably the son of the man who did most of the work on the Taj Mahal).

Delhi's present position as capital was only confirmed on 12 December 1911, when George V announced at the Delhi Durbar that the capital of India was to move from Calcutta to Delhi. The new city, New Delhi, planned under the leadership of British architect Edwin Lutyens with the assistance of his friend Herbert Baker, was inaugurated on 9 February 1931.

The city was to accommodate 70,000 people and have boundless possibilities for future expansion. The king favoured something in form and flavour similar to the Mughal masterpieces but fretted over the horrendous expense that this would incur. A petition signed by eminent public figures such as Bernard Shaw and Thomas Hardy advocated an Indian style and an Indian master builder. Herbert Baker had made known his own views even before his appointment when he wrote "first and foremost it is the spirit of British sovereignty which must be imprisoned in its stone and bronze". Lutyens himself despised Indian architecture. "Even before he had seen any examples of it", writes architectural historian Giles Tillotson, "he pronounced Mughal architecture to be 'piffle', and seeing it did not disturb that conviction". Yet in the end, Lutyens was forced to settle for the compromise.

India Gate and around

A tour of New Delhi will usually start with a visit to India Gate. This war memorial is situated at the eastern end of **Rajpath**. Designed by Lutyens, it commemorates more than 70,000 Indian soldiers who died in the First World War. Some 13,516 names of British and Indian soldiers killed on the Northwest Frontier and in the Afghan War of 1919 are engraved on the arch and foundations. Under the arch is the Amar Jawan Jyoti, commemorating Indian armed forces' losses in the Indo-Pakistan War of 1971. The arch (43 m high) stands on a base of Bharatpur stone and rises in stages. Similar to the Hindu *chhattri* signifying regality, it is decorated with nautilus shells symbolizing British maritime power. Come at dusk to join the picnicking crowds enjoying the evening. You may even be able to have a pedalo ride if there's water in the canal.

To the northwest of India Gate are two impressive buildings, **Hyderabad House** and **Baroda House**, built as residences for the Nizam of Hyderabad and the Gaekwar of Baroda. Now used as offices, both were carefully placed to indicate the paramountcy of the British Raj over the Princely States. The Nizam, reputed to be the richest man in the world, ruled over an area equal to that of France. The Gaekwar belonged to the top level of Indian princes and both, along with the maharajas of Mysore, Jammu and Kashmir and Gwalior were entitled to receive 21-gun salutes.

Rajpath leads west from India Gate towards **Janpath**. To the north are the Lutyens-designed **National Archives**, formerly the Imperial Record Office. To the south is the National Museum (see below).

National Gallery of Modern Art

① *Jaipur House, near India Gate, T011-2338 4640, www.ngmaindia.gov.in, Tue-Sun 1000-1700, Rs 150 foreigners, Rs 10 Indians.*

The excellent collection is housed in a former residence of the Maharaja of Jaipur. Some of the best exhibits are on the ground floor which is devoted to post-1930 works. To view the collections chronologically, begin on the first floor. Artists include: Amrita Shergil (ground floor): over 100 exhibits, synthesizing the flat treatment of Indian painting with a realistic tone; Rabindranath Tagore (ground floor): examples from a brief but intense spell in the 1930s; The Bombay School or Company School (first floor): includes Western painters who documented their visits to India. Realism is reflected in Indian painting of the early 19th century represented by the schools of Avadh, Patna, Sikkim and Thanjavur; The Bengal School (the late 19th-century Revivalist Movement): artists such as Abanindranath Tagore and Nandalal Bose have their works exhibited here. Western influence was discarded in response to the nationalist movement. Inspiration derived from Indian folk art is evident in the works of Jamini Roy and YD Shukla.

National Museum

① *Janpath, T011-2301 9272, www.national museumindia.gov.in, daily 1000-1700, foreigners Rs 300 (including audio tour), Indians Rs 10, camera Rs 300; free guided tours 1030, 1130, 1200, 1400, films are screened every day (1430), marble squat toilets, but dirty.*

The collection was formed from the nucleus of the Exhibition of Indian Art, London (1947). Now merged with the Asian Antiquities Museum it displays a rich collection of the artistic treasure of Central Asia and India including ethnological objects from prehistoric archaeological finds to the late Medieval period. Replicas of exhibits and books on Indian culture and art are on sale. There is a research library.

Ground floor **Prehistoric**: seals, figurines, toy animals and jewellery from the Harappan civilization (2400-1500 BC). **Maurya Period**: terracottas and stone heads from around the third century BC include the *chaturmukha* (four-faced) *lingam*. **Gandhara School**: stucco heads showing the Graeco Roman influence. **Gupta terracottas** (circa AD 400): include two life-size images of the river goddesses Ganga and Yamuna and the four-armed bust of Vishnu from a temple near Lal Kot. **South Indian sculpture**: from Pallava and early Chola temples and relief panels from Mysore. Bronzes from the Buddhist monastery at Nalanda. Some of Buddha's relics were placed in the Thai pavilion in 1997.

First floor **Illustrated manuscripts**: include the *Babur-i-nama* in the emperor's own hand-writing and an autographed copy of Jahangir's memoirs. **Miniature paintings**: include the 16th-century Jain School, the 18th-century Rajasthani School and the Pahari Schools of Garhwal, Basoli and Kangra. **Aurel Stein Collection** consists of antiquities recovered by him during his explorations of Central Asia and the western borders of China at the turn of the 20th century.

Second floor **Pre-Columbian and Mayan artefacts**: anthropological section devoted to tribal artefacts and folk arts. **Sharad Rani Bakkiwal Gallery of Musical Instruments**: displays over 300 instruments collected by the famous *sarod* player.

The Secretariats

At the Secretariat and Rashtrapati Bhavan gates, the mounted and unmounted troops parade in full uniform on Saturdays at 1030 are worth attending. Standing on either side of Raisina Hill, **North Block** houses the Home and Finance Ministries, **South Block** the Ministry of Foreign Affairs. These long classical buildings topped by Baroque domes, designed by Baker, were derived from Wren's Royal Naval College at Greenwich. The towers were originally designed to be twice the height of the buildings and to act as beacons guarding the way to the inner sanctum. The domes are decorated with lotus motifs and elephants, while the north and south gateways are Mughal in design. On the northern Secretariat building is the imperialistic inscription "Liberty will not descend to a people: a people must raise themselves to liberty. It is a blessing that must be earned before it can be enjoyed".

New Delhi

To KAROL BAGH

DARYAGANJ

PATEL NAGAR EAST

A

Patel Rd

Rajendra Place

Karol Bagh

Desh Bandhu Gupta Rd

Jhandewalan

Pusa Rd

Panchkuin Marg

PAHAR GANJ

New Delhi Station

Jama Masjid

JP Narain

New Delhi Station

GB Pant

700 metres
700 yards

RAJENDRA NAGAR

Lakshmi Narayan Mandir

RK Ashram Marg

Minto Bridge

Connaught Place

Bhagat Singh Marg

Bangla Sahib

Chowk

Rajiv Chowk

Natural History Museum

Bengali

Deen Dayal Rd

Mandir Marg

Buddha Jayanti Park

R M Lohia

Gurudwara Bangla Sahib

Baba Kharak Singh Marg

Barakhamba Rd

Jantar Mantar

Patel Chowk

Nepal Embassy

College

Mandi House

➡ Delhi maps

1 Delhi, page 58
2 Red Fort, Delhi, page 63
3 Old Delhi, page 68
4 New Delhi, page 72
5 Connaught Place, page 75
6 Paharganj, page 76
7 Qutb Minar Complex, page 81

B

Upper Ridge Rd

Talkatora Rd

Ashoka Rd

Baroda House

Prai

Willingdon Cres

North Block Secretariat

Parliament House

Raisina Rd

National Archives

Hyderabad House

Prag
Maid

Dhaula Kuan

Sardar Patel Marg

Kautilya Marg

Panchsheel Marg

Rashtrapati Bhavan

South Block Secretariat

Central Secretariat

Rajpath

National Museum

India Gate

National Gallery of Modern Art

Pura
Qi

C

Teen Murti Mg

Shanti Path

Nehru Museum

Indira Gandhi Museum

Akbar Rd

Aurangzeb Rd

Gandhi Museum

Khan

Bharti Rd

Dr Zakir Husain Marg

Maya Marg

Niti Marg

Santushti Complex

Safdarjung Rd

Prithviraj Rd

Full Circle Book Store

Sujan Singh Park

CHANAKYAPURI

Nehru Park

Vinay

Race Course

Tughlak Rd

Lodi Tombs

Lodi Gardens

Indian Int Centre

Lodi Rd

Safdarjang's Tomb

Jorbagh

Tibet House

India Habitat Centre

D

Ring Rd

Shanti Path

Safdarjang Airport

Bian

Pratap

JOR BAGH

Nehru Stadium

Rao Tularam

Link Rd

SAROJINI NAGAR

Aurobindo Marg

INA

Lodi Estate Rd No 3

R K PURAM

Swamimlai Temple

Dilli Haat

SOUTH EXTENSION I

MG Marg

DEFENCE COLONY

LAJPAT NAGA

Ring Rd

Safdarjang

AIIMS

SOUTH EXTENSION II

Pacific Sports Complex

EAST O
KAILAS

Kath

Olof Palme Marg

VASANT VIHAR

Africa Av

SAFDARJANG ENCLAVE

Yusuf Sarai

Ansal Plaza

Vivekanand Marg

Moth ki Masjid

GREATER KAILASH

E

Priya Cinema

Poorvi Marg

Mandela Marg

Deer Park

Arjun Nagar

Green Park

Siri Fort Marg

Siri Fort Sports Club

Ekasir Vithi Marg

Lala Lajpat Rai Marg

Jawaharlal Nehru University

Gamel Abdul Nasser Marg

Hauz Khas Village

Aurobindo Marg

Asiad Village

SIRI

F

VASANT KUNJ

A Asaf Ali Marg

Indian Institute of Technology

Sri Aurobindo Ashram

Khel Gaon Marg

Bijai Mandal

Panchsheel Marg

PANCHSHEEL SOUTH

Outer Ring Rd

To Anupam Cinema & Qutb Minar

Begumpuri Masjid

To Khirki Masjid & Saket

To

In the **Great Court** between the Secretariats are the four **Dominion Columns**, donated by the governments of Australia, Canada, New Zealand and South Africa – ironically, as it turned out. Each is crowned by a bronze ship sailing east, symbolizing the maritime and mercantile supremacy of the British Empire. In the centre of the court is the Jaipur column of red sandstone topped with a white egg, bronze lotus and six-pointed glass star of India (which has evolved into today's five-pointed star).

Rashtrapati Bhavan and Nehru Memorial Museum

Once the Viceroy's House, Rashtrapati Bhavan is the official residence of the President of India. The Viceroy's House, New Delhi's centrepiece of imperial proportions, was 1 km around the foundations, bigger than Louis XIV's palace at Versailles. It had a colossal dome surmounting a long colonnade and 340 rooms in all. It took nearly 20 years to complete, similar to the time it took to build the Taj Mahal. In the busiest year, 29,000 people were working on the site and buildings began to take shape. The project was surrounded by controversy from beginning to end. Opting for a fundamentally classical structure, both Baker and Lutyens sought to incorporate Indian motifs, many entirely superficial. While some claim that Lutyens achieved a unique synthesis of the two traditions, Tillotson asks whether "the sprinkling of a few simplified and classicized Indian details (especially *chhattris*) over a classical palace" could be called a synthesis. The Durbar Hall, 23 m in diameter, has coloured marble from all parts of India.

To the south is Flagstaff House, formerly the residence of the commander-in-chief. Renamed Teen Murti Bhawan it now houses the **Nehru Memorial Museum** ① *T011-2301 4504, Tue-Sun 1000-1500, planetarium Mon-Sat 1130-1500, library*

Mon-Sat 0900-1900, free. Designed by Robert Tor Russell, in 1948 it became the official residence of India's first prime minister, Jawaharlal Nehru. Converted after his death (1964) into a national memorial, the reception, study and bedroom are intact. A *Jyoti Jawahar* (torch) symbolizes the eternal values he inspired and a granite rock is carved with extracts from his historic speech at midnight on 14 August 1947; an informative and vivid history of the Independence Movement.

The **Martyr's Memorial**, at the junction of Sardar Patel Marg and Willingdon Crescent, is a magnificent 26-m-long, 3-m-high bronze sculpture by DP Roy Chowdhury. The 11 statues of national heroes are headed by Mahatma Gandhi.

Gandhi Museum

ⓘ *Birla House, 5 Tees Jan Marg (near Claridges Hotel), T011-2301 2843, closed Mon and 2nd Sat, 0930-1730, free, film at 1500.*

Gandhi's last place of residence and the site of his assassination, Birla House has been converted into a whizz-bang display of 'interactive' modern technology. Over-attended by young guides eager to demonstrate the next gadget, the museum seems aimed mainly at those with a critically short attention span, and is too rushed to properly convey the story of Gandhi's life. However, a monument in the garden marking where he fell is definitely worth a visit. Other museums in the city related to Gandhi include **National Gandhi Museum** ⓘ *opposite Raj Ghat, T011-2331 1793, www.gandhimuseum.org, Tue-Sat 0930-1730*, with five pavilions – sculpture, photographs and paintings of Gandhi and the history of the *Satyagraha* movement, the philosophy of non-violence; **Gandhi Smarak Sangrahalaya** ⓘ *Raj Ghat, T011-2301 1480, Fri-Wed 0930-1730*, displays some of Gandhi's personal belongings and a small library includes recordings of speeches; **Indira Gandhi Museum** ⓘ *1 Safdarjang Rd, T011-2301 0094, Tue-Sun 0930-1700, free*, charts the phases of her life from childhood to the moment of her death. Fascinating if rather gory exhibits- you can see the blood-stained, bullet-ridden sari she was wearing when assassinated.

Parliament House and around

Northeast of the Viceroy's House is the **Council House**, now **Sansad Bhavan**. Baker designed this based on Lutyens' suggestion that it be circular (173 m diameter). Inside are the library and chambers for the Council of State, Chamber of Princes and Legislative Assembly – the **Lok Sabha**. Just opposite the Council House is the **Rakabganj Gurudwara** in Pandit Pant Marg. This 20th-century white marble shrine, which integrates the late Mughal and Rajasthani styles, marks the spot where the headless body of Guru Tegh Bahadur, the ninth Sikh Guru, was cremated in 1657. West of the Council House is the Cathedral **Church of the Redemption** (1927-1935) and to its north the Italianate Roman Catholic **Church of the Sacred Heart** (1930-1934), both conceived by Henry Medd.

Connaught Place and Connaught Circus

Connaught Place and its outer ring, Connaught Circus (now officially named **Rajiv Chowk** and **Indira Chowk**, but still commonly referred to by their old names), comprise two-storey arcaded buildings, arranged radially around a circular garden that was completed after the Metro line was installed. Designed by Robert Tor Russell, they have become the main commercial and tourist centre of New Delhi. Sadly, the area also attracts bands of insistent touts ready to take advantage of the unwary traveller by getting them into spurious 'official' or 'government' shops and travel agencies. The area (and Palika Bazar, a humid and dingy underground market hidden beneath it) has long been renowned for its shoe-shine tricksters. Large wadges of slime appear mysteriously on shoes and are then pointed out eagerly by attendant boys or men who offer to clean them off at a price. This can just be the start of 'necessary repairs' to the shoes for which bills of over Rs 300 are not unknown.

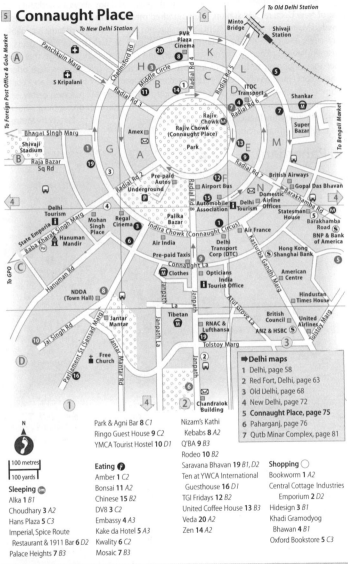

Connaught Place

To Old Delhi Station
To New Delhi Station
Minto Bridge
Shivaji Station
PVR Plaza Cinema
Panchkuin Marg
To Foreign Post Office & Gole Market
Chelmsford Rd
S Kripalani
Middle Circle
Radial Rd 4
K
L
Radial Rd 5
Shankar
ITDC Transport
Radial Rd 6
Bhagat Singh Marg
Amex
Rajiv Chowk
Rajiv Chowk (Connaught Place)
Shivaji Stadium
Raja Bazar Sq Rd
Park
M
Super Bazar
To Bengali Market
Radial Rd 2
Radial Rd 7
British Airways
Pre-paid Autos Underground
Airport Bus
Gopal Das Bhavan
Delhi Tourism
Automobile Association
Domestic Airline Offices
Delhi Tourism
State Emporia
Mohan Singh Place
Regal Cinema
Palika Bazar
Statesman House
Barakhamba Road
Baba Kharak Singh Marg
Hanuman Mandir
Indira Chowk (Connaught Circus)
Air India
Air France
BNP & Bank of America
To GPO
Hanuman Rd
Pre-paid Taxis
Delhi Transport Corp (DTC)
Hong Kong Shanghai Bank
Connaught La
Clothes
Opticians India Tourist Office
Kasturba Gandhi Marg
American Centre
NDDA (Town Hall)
Janpath
Hindustan Times House
Jantar Mantar
Tibetan
British Council
United Airlines
Jai Singh Rd
Janpath La
RNAC & Lufthansa
ANZ & HSBC
Tolstoy Marg
Parliament St (Sansad Marg)
Free Church
Jantar Mantar Rd
Janpath
Chandralok Building

⇒ Delhi maps
1 Delhi, page 58
2 Red Fort, Delhi, page 63
3 Old Delhi, page 68
4 New Delhi, page 72
5 Connaught Place, page 75
6 Paharganj, page 76
7 Qutb Minar Complex, page 81

N

100 metres
100 yards

Sleeping
Alka 1 B1
Choudhary 3 A2
Hans Plaza 5 C3
Imperial, Spice Route Restaurant & 1911 Bar 6 D2
Palace Heights 7 B3

Park & Agni Bar 8 C1
Ringo Guest House 9 C2
YMCA Tourist Hostel 10 D1

Eating
Amber 1 C2
Bonsai 11 A2
Chinese 15 B2
DV8 3 C2
Embassy 4 A3
Kake da Hotel 5 A3
Kwality 6 C2
Mosaic 7 B3

Nizam's Kathi Kebabs 8 A2
Q'BA 9 B3
Rodeo 10 B2
Saravana Bhavan 19 B1, D2
Ten at YWCA International Guesthouse 16 D1
TGI Fridays 12 B2
United Coffee House 13 B3
Veda 20 A2
Zen 14 A2

Shopping
Bookworm 1 A2
Central Cottage Industries Emporium 2 D2
Hidesign 3 B1
Khadi Gramodyog Bhavan 4 B1
Oxford Bookstore 5 C3

If caught – increasingly unlikely as the scammers seem to be on the way out – insist politely but firmly that the dirt is cleaned off free of charge.

Paharganj

Delhi's backpacker ghetto occupies a warren of lanes and dingy alleys immediately to the west of New Delhi railway station, a few hundred metres north of Connaught Circus. The crowded Main Bazar offers an instant immersion into the chaos of which India is capable, as stray cows and cycle rickshaws tangle with a throng of pedestrians, hotel touts, and salesmen hawking knock-off handbags, books and cheap clothing. Though there's little other than shopping to hold your interest, the hundreds of guesthouses here offer the greatest concentration of genuinely cheap accommodation in the city, and the area contains a number of appealing rooftop cafés that provide a respite from the madness below.

Northwest of Paharganj, the grid of streets comprising **Karol Bagh** contains what is, by some definitions, the biggest market in Asia. Conveniently linked to the city by Metro, the area is full of mid-range hotels.

6 Paharganj

➡ **Delhi maps**
1 Delhi, page 58
2 Red Fort, Delhi, page 63
3 Old Delhi, page 68
4 New Delhi, page 72
5 Connaught Place, page 75
6 Paharganj, page 76
7 Qutb Minar Complex, page 81

Sleeping 🛏
Ajay's 1
Ajanta 2
Anoop 3
Gush 19
Hare Krishna 3
Heritage Inn 6
Jyoti Mahal 7
KG Palace 20

Metropolis Tourist Home 18
Namaskar 8
Prince Polonia 17
Railway Retiring Rooms 9
Rak International 11
Shelton 13
Star Palace 14
Vivek 16

Eating 🍴
Appetite 1
Everest Bakery Café 5
Korean Restaurant 8
Madan's 2
Malhotra's 3
Open Hand Café 7
Southern 4
Tadka 6

Lakshmi Narayan Mandir

To the west of Connaught Circus is the Lakshmi Narayan **Birla Temple** in Mandir Marg. Financed by the prominent industrialist Raja Baldeo Birla in 1938, this is one of the most popular Hindu shrines in the city and one of Delhi's few striking examples of Hindu architecture. Dedicated to Lakshmi, the goddess of well-being, it is commonly referred to as **Birla Mandir**. The design is in the Orissan style with tall curved *sikharas* (towers) capped by large *amalakas*. The exterior is faced with red and ochre stone and white marble. Built around a central courtyard, the main shrine has images of Narayan and his consort Lakshmi while two separate cells have icons of Siva (the Destroyer) and Durga (the 10-armed destroyer of demons). The temple is flanked by a *dharamshala* (rest house) and a Buddhist *vihara* (monastery).

Gurudwara Bangla Sahib

ⓘ *Baba Kharak Singh Rd, free.*

This is a fine example of Sikh temple architecture, featuring a large pool reminiscent of Amritsar's Golden Temple. The 24-hour reciting of the faith's holy book adds to the atmosphere, and there's free food on offer, although don't be surprised if you're asked to help out with the washing up! You must remove your shoes and cover your head to enter – suitable scarves are provided if you arrive without.

Further northeast on Baba Kharak Singh Marg is **Hanuman Mandir**. This small temple was built by Maharaja Jai Singh II of Jaipur. **Mangal haat** (Tuesday Fair) is a popular market.

Jantar Mantar

Just to the east of the Hanuman Mandir in Sansad Marg (Parliament Street) is Jai Singh's **observatory** (Jantar Mantar) ⓘ *sunrise to sunset, Rs 100 foreigners, Rs 5 Indians.* The Mughal Emperor Mohammad Shah (ruled 1719-1748) entrusted the renowned astronomer Maharaja Jai Singh II with the task of revising the calendar and correcting the astronomical tables used by contemporary priests. Daily astral observations were made for years before construction began and plastered brick structures were favoured for the site instead of brass instruments. Built in 1725 it is slightly smaller than the later observatory at Jaipur.

Memorial Ghats

Beyond Delhi Gate lies the **Yamuna River**, marked by a series of memorials to India's leaders. The river itself, a kilometre away, is invisible from the road, protected by a low rise and banks of trees. The most prominent memorial, immediately opposite the end of Jawaharlal Nehru Road, is that of Mahatma Gandhi at **Raj Ghat**. To its north is **Shanti Vana** (Forest of Peace), landscaped gardens where Prime Minister Jawaharlal Nehru was cremated in 1964, as were his grandson Sanjay Gandhi in 1980, daughter Indira Gandhi in 1984 and elder grandson, Rajiv, in 1991. To the north again is **Vijay Ghat** (Victory Bank) where Prime Minister Lal Bahadur Shastri was cremated.

South Delhi

South Delhi is often overlooked by travellers. This is a real pity as it houses some of the city's most stunning sites, best accommodation, bars, clubs and restaurants, as well as some of its most tranquil parks. However be warned, South Delhi can be hell during rushhour when the traffic on the endless flyovers comes to a virtual standstill.

Lodi Gardens

These beautiful gardens, with mellow stone tombs of the 15th- and 16th-century Lodi rulers, are popular for gentle strolls and jogging. In the middle of the garden facing the east entrance from Max Mueller Road is **Bara Gumbad** (Big Dome), a mosque built in 1494. The raised courtyard is provided with an imposing gateway and *mehman khana* (guest rooms). The platform in the centre appears to have had a tank for ritual ablutions.

The **Sheesh Bumbad** (Glass Dome, late 15th century) is built on a raised incline north of the Bara Gumbad and was once decorated with glazed blue tiles, painted floral designs and Koranic inscriptions. The façade gives the impression of a two-storeyed building, typical of Lodi architecture. **Mohammad Shah's Tomb** (1450) is that of the third Sayyid ruler. It has sloping buttresses, an octagonal plan, projecting eaves and lotus patterns on the ceiling. **Sikander Lodi's Tomb**, built by his son in 1517, is also an octagonal structure decorated with Hindu motifs. A structural innovation is the double dome which was later refined under the Mughals. The 16th-century **Athpula** (Bridge of Eight Piers), near the northeastern entrance, is attributed to Nawab Bahadur, a nobleman at Akbar's court.

Safdarjang's Tomb

ⓘ *Sunrise to sunset, Rs 100 foreigners, Rs 5 Indians.*

Safdarjang's Tomb, seldom visited, was built by Nawab Shuja-ud-Daulah for his father Mirza Mukhim Abdul Khan, entitled Safdarjang, who was Governor of Oudh (1719-1748), and Wazir of his successor (1748-1754). Safdarjang died in 1754. With its high enclosure walls, *char bagh* layout of gardens, fountain and central domed mausoleum, it follows the tradition of Humayun's tomb. Typically, the real tomb is just below ground level. Flanking the mausoleum are pavilions used by Shuja-ud-Daulah as his family residence. Immediately to its south is the battlefield where Timur and his Mongol horde crushed Mahmud Shah Tughluq on 12 December 1398.

Hazrat Nizamuddin

ⓘ *Dress ultra-modestly if you don't want to feel uncomfortable or cause offence.*

At the east end of the Lodi Road, Hazrat Nizamuddin Dargah (Nizamuddin 'village') now tucked away behind the residential suburb of Nizamuddin West, off Mathura Road, grew up around the shrine of Sheikh Nizamuddin Aulia (1236-1325), a Chishti saint. This is a wonderfully atmospheric place. *Qawwalis* are sung at sunset after *namaaz* (prayers), and are particularly impressive on Thursdays – be prepared for crowds. Highly recommended.

West of the central shrine is the **Jama-at-khana Mosque** (1325). Its decorated arches are typical of the Khalji design also seen at the Ala'i Darwaza at the Qutb Minar. South of the main tomb and behind finely crafted screens is the grave of princess Jahanara, Shah Jahan's eldest and favourite daughter. She shared the emperor's last years when he was imprisoned at Agra Fort. The grave, open to the sky, is in accordance with the epitaph written by her: "Let naught cover my grave save the green grass, for grass suffices as the covering of the lowly". Pilgrims congregate at the shrine twice a year for the **Urs** (fair) held to mark the anniversaries of Hazrat Nizamuddin Aulia and his disciple Amir Khusrau, whose tomb is nearby.

Humayun's Tomb
ⓘ *Sunrise to sunset, Rs 250 foreigners, Rs 10 Indians, video cameras Rs 25, located in Nizamuddin, 15-20 mins by taxi from Connaught Circus, allow 45 mins.*
Eclipsed later by the Taj Mahal and the Jama Masjid, this tomb is the best example in Delhi of the early Mughal style of tomb. Superbly maintained, it is well worth a visit, preferably before visiting the Taj Mahal. Humayun, the second Mughal emperor, was forced into exile in Persia after being heavily defeated by the Afghan Sher Shah in 1540. He returned to India in 1545, finally recapturing Delhi in 1555. The tomb was designed and built by his senior widow and mother of his son Akbar, Hamida Begum. A Persian from Khurasan, after her pilgrimage to Mecca she was known as Haji Begum. She supervised the entire construction of the tomb (1564-1573), camping on the site.

The plan The tomb has an octagonal plan, lofty arches, pillared kiosks and the double dome of Central Asian origin, which appears here for the first time in India. Outside Gujarat, Hindu temples make no use of the dome, but the Indian Muslim dome had until now, been of a flatter shape as opposed to the tall Persian dome rising on a more slender neck. Here also is the first standard example of the garden tomb concept: the **char bagh** (garden divided into quadrants), water channels and fountains. This form culminated in the gardens of the Taj Mahal. However, the tomb also shows a number of distinctively Hindu motifs. Tillotson has pointed out that in Humayun's tomb, Hindu *chhattris* (small domed kiosks), complete with temple columns and *chajjas* (broad eaves), surround the central dome. The bulbous finial on top of the dome and the star motif in the spandrels of the main arches are also Hindu, the latter being a solar symbol.

The approach The tomb enclosure has two high double-storeyed gateways: the entrance to the west and the other to the south. A *baradari* occupies the centre of the east wall, and a bath chamber that of the north wall. Several Moghul princes, princesses and Haji Begum herself lie buried here. During the 1857 Mutiny Bahadur Shah II, the last Moghul emperor of Delhi, took shelter here with his three sons. Over 80, he was seen as a figurehead by Muslims opposing the British. When captured he was transported to Yangon (Rangoon) for the remaining four years of his life. The tomb to the right of the approach is that of Isa Khan, Humayun's barber.

The dome Some 38 m high, the dome does not have the swell of the Taj Mahal and the decoration of the whole edifice is much simpler. It is of red sandstone with some white marble to highlight the lines of the building. There is some attractive inlay work, and some *jalis* in the balcony fence and on some of the recessed keel arch windows. The interior is austere and consists of three storeys of arches rising up to the dome. The emperor's tomb is of white marble and quite plain without any inscription. The overall impression is that of a much bulkier, more squat building than the Taj Mahal. The cavernous space under the main tombs is home to great colonies of bats.

Hauz Khas
ⓘ *1-hr cultural show, 1845, Rs 100 (check with Delhi Tourism, see page 61).*
South of Safdarjang's Tomb, and entered off either Aurobindo Marg on the east side or Africa Avenue on the west side, is Hauz Khas. Ala-ud-din Khalji (ruled 1296-1313) created a

large tank here for the use of the inhabitants of Siri, the second capital city of Delhi founded by him. Fifty years later Firoz Shah Tughluq cleaned up the silted tank and raised several buildings on its east and south banks which are known as Hauz Khas or Royal Tank.

Firoz Shah's austere tomb is found here. The multi-storeyed wings, on the north and west of the tomb, were built by him in 1354 as a *madrasa* (college). The octagonal and square *chhattris* were built as tombs, possibly to the teachers at the college. Hauz Khas is now widely used as a park for early-morning recreation – walking, running and yoga *asanas*. Classical music concerts, dance performances and a *son et lumière* show are held in the evenings when monuments are illuminated by thousands of earthen lamps and torches.

Qutb Minar Complex

ⓘ *Sunrise to sunset, Rs 250 foreigners, Rs 10 Indians. Bus 505 from New Delhi Railway Station (Ajmeri Gate), Super Bazar (east of Connaught Circus) and Cottage Industries Emporium, Janpath. Auto Rs 110, though drivers may be reluctant to take you.*

Muhammad Ghuri conquered northwest India at the very end of the 12th century. The conquest of the Gangetic plain down to Benares (Varanasi) was undertaken by Muhammad's Turkish slave and chief general, Qutb-ud-din-Aibak, whilst another general took Bihar and Bengal. In the process, temples were reduced to rubble, the remaining Buddhist centres were dealt their death blow and their monks slaughtered. When Muhammad was assassinated in 1206, his gains passed to the loyal Qutb-ud-din-Aibak. Thus the first sultans or Muslim kings of Delhi became known as the **Slave Dynasty** (1026-1290). For the next three centuries the Slave Dynasty and the succeeding Khalji (1290-1320), Tughluq (1320-1414), Sayyid (1414-1445) and Lodi (1451-1526) dynasties provided Delhi with fluctuating authority. The legacy of their ambitions survives in the tombs, forts and palaces that litter Delhi Ridge and the surrounding plain. Qutb-ud-din-Aibak died after only four years in power, but he left his mark with the **Qutb Minar** and his **citadel**. Qutb Minar, built to proclaim the victory of Islam over the infidel, dominates the countryside for miles around. Visit the *minar* first.

Qutb Minar (1) In 1199 work began on what was intended to be the most glorious tower of victory in the world and was to be the prototype of all *minars* (towers) in India. Qutb-ud-din-Aibak had probably seen and been influenced by the brick victory pillars in Ghazni in Afghanistan, but this one was also intended to serve as the minaret attached to the Might of Islam Mosque. From here the muezzin could call the faithful to prayer. Later every mosque would incorporate its minaret.

As a mighty reminder of the importance of the ruler as Allah's representative on earth, the Qutb Minar (literally 'axis minaret') stood at the centre of the community. A pivot of Faith, Justice and Righteousness, its name also carried the message of Qutb-ud-din's (Axis of the Faith) own achievements. The inscriptions carved in Kufi script tell that "the tower was erected to cast the shadow of God over both east and west". For Qutb-ud-din-Aibak it marked the eastern limit of the empire of the One God. Its western counterpart is the Giralda Tower built by Yusuf in Seville.

The Qutb Minar is 73 m high and consists of five storeys. The diameter of the base is 14.4 m and 2.7 m at the top. Qutb-ud-din built the first three and his son-in-law Iltutmish embellished these and added a fourth. This is indicated in some of the Persian and Nagari (North Indian) inscriptions which also record that it was twice damaged by lightning in 1326 and 1368. While repairing the damage caused by the second, Firoz Shah Tughluq added a fifth storey and used marble to face the red and buff sandstone. This was the first time contrasting colours were used decoratively, later to become such a feature of Mughal buildings. Firoz's fifth storey was topped by a graceful cupola but this fell down during an earthquake in 1803. A new one was added by a Major Robert Smith in 1829 but was so out of keeping that it was removed in 1848 and now stands in the gardens.

The original storeys are heavily indented with different styles of fluting, alternately round and angular on the bottom, round on the second and angular on the third. The beautifully carved honeycomb detail beneath the balconies is reminiscent of the Alhambra Palace in Spain. The calligraphy bands are verses from the Koran and praises to its patron builder.

Quwwat-ul-Islam Mosque (2) The Quwwat-ul-Islam Mosque (The Might of Islam Mosque), the earliest surviving mosque in India, is to the northwest of the Qutb Minar. It was begun in 1192, immediately after Qutb-ud-din's conquest of Delhi and completed in 1198, using the remains of no fewer than 27 local Hindu and Jain temples.

The architectural style contained elements that Muslims brought from Arabia, including buildings made of mud and brick and decorated with glazed tiles, *squinches* (arches set diagonally across the corners of a square chamber to facilitate the raising of a dome and to effect a transition from a square to a round structure), the pointed arch and the true dome. Finally, Muslim buildings came alive through ornamental calligraphy and

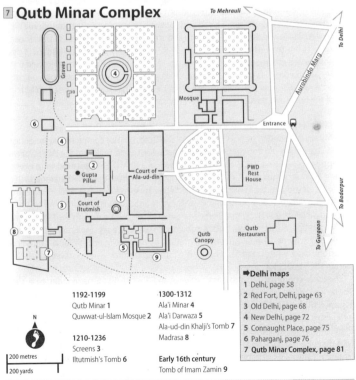

7 Qutb Minar Complex

To Mehrauli
To Delhi
Aurobindo Marg
To Badarpur
To Gurgaon

Graves
Mosque
Entrance
PWD Rest House
Gupta Pillar
Court of Ala-ud-din
Court of Iltutmish
Qutb Canopy
Qutb Restaurant

N
200 metres
200 yards

1192-1199
Qutb Minar **1**
Quwwat-ul-Islam Mosque **2**

1210-1236
Screens **3**
Iltutmish's Tomb **6**

1300-1312
Ala'i Minar **4**
Ala'i Darwaza **5**
Ala-ud-din Khalji's Tomb **7**
Madrasa **8**

Early 16th century
Tomb of Imam Zamin **9**

➡ Delhi maps
1 Delhi, page 58
2 Red Fort, Delhi, page 63
3 Old Delhi, page 68
4 New Delhi, page 72
5 Connaught Place, page 75
6 Paharganj, page 76
7 Qutb Minar Complex, page 81

geometric patterning. This was in marked contrast to indigenous Indian styles of architecture. Hindu, Buddhist and Jain buildings relied on the post-and-beam system in which spaces were traversed by corbelling, ie shaping flat-laid stones to create an arch. The arched screen that runs along the western end of the courtyard beautifully illustrates the fact that it was Hindu methods that still prevailed at this stage, for the 16-m-high arch uses Indian corbelling, the corners being smoothed off to form the curved line.

Screens (3) Qutb-ud-din's screen formed the façade of the mosque and, facing in the direction of Mecca, became the focal point. The sandstone screen is carved in the Indo-Islamic style, lotuses mingling with Koranic calligraphy. The later screenwork and other extensions (1230) are fundamentally Islamic in style, the flowers and leaves having been replaced by more arabesque patterns. Indian builders mainly used stone, which from the fourth century AD had been intricately carved with representations of the gods. In their first buildings in India the Muslim architects designed the buildings and local Indian craftsmen built them and decorated them with typical motifs such as the vase and foliage, tasselled ropes, bells and cows.

Iltutmish's extension The mosque was enlarged twice. In 1230 Qutb-ud-din's son-in-law and successor, Shamsuddin Iltutmish, doubled its size by extending the colonnades and prayer hall – 'Iltutmish's extension'. This accommodated a larger congregation, and in the more stable conditions of Iltutmish's reign, Islam was obviously gaining ground. The arches of the extension are nearer to the true arch and are similar to the Gothic arch that appeared in Europe at this time. The decoration is Islamic. Almost 100 years after Iltutmish's death, the mosque was enlarged again, by Ala-ud-din Khalji. The conductor of tireless and bloody military campaigns, Ala-ud-din proclaimed himself 'God's representative on earth'. His architectural ambitions, however, were not fully realized, because on his death in 1316 only part of the north and east extensions were completed.

Ala'i Minar (4) and the Ala'i Darwaza (5) To the north of the Qutb complex is the 26-m **Ala'i Minar**, intended to surpass the tower of the Qutb, but not completed beyond the first storey. Ala-ud-din did complete the south gateway to the building, the **Ala'i Darwaza**; inscriptions testify that it was built in 1311 (Muslim 710 AH). He benefited from events in Central Asia: since the early 13th century, Mongol hordes from Central Asia fanned out east and west, destroying the civilization of the Seljuk Turks in West Asia, and refugee artists, architects, craftsmen and poets fled east. They brought to India features and techniques that had developed in Byzantine Turkey, some of which can be seen in the Ala'i Darwaza.

The gatehouse is a large sandstone cuboid, into which are set small cusped arches with carved *jali* screens. The lavish ornamentation of geometric and floral designs in red sandstone and white marble produced a dramatic effect when viewed against the surrounding buildings.

The inner chamber, 11 sq m has doorways and, for the first time in India, true arches. Above each doorway is an Arabic inscription with its creator's name and one of his self-assumed titles – 'The Second Alexander'. The north doorway, which is the main entrance, is the most elaborately carved. The dome, raised on squinched arches, is flat and shallow. Of the effects employed, the arches with their 'lotus-bud' fringes are Seljuk, as is the dome with the rounded finial and the façade. These now became trademarks of the **Khalji style**, remaining virtually unchanged until their further development in Humayun's Tomb.

Iltutmish's Tomb (6) Built in 1235, Iltutmish's Tomb lies in the northwest of the compound, midway along the west wall of the mosque. It is the first surviving tomb of a Muslim ruler in India. Two other tombs also stand within the extended Might of Islam Mosque. The idea of a tomb was quite alien to Hindus, who had been practising cremation since around 400 BC. Blending Hindu and Muslim styles, the outside is relatively plain with three arched and decorated doorways. The interior carries reminders of the nomadic origins of the first Muslim rulers. Like a Central Asian *yurt* (tent) in its decoration, it combines the familiar Indian motifs of the wheel, bell, chain and lotus with the equally familiar geometric arabesque patterning. The west wall is inset with three *mihrabs* that indicate the direction of Mecca.

The tomb originally supported a dome resting on *squinches* which you can still see. The dome collapsed (witness the slabs of stone lying around) suggesting that the technique was as yet unrefined. From the corbelled squinches it may be assumed that the dome was corbelled too, as found in contemporary Gujarat and Rajput temples. The blocks of masonry were fixed together using the Indian technology of iron dowels. In later Indo-Islamic buildings lime plaster was used for bonding.

Other tombs To the southwest of the uncompleted Quwwat-ul-Islam mosque, an L-shaped ruin marks the site of **Ala-ud-din Khalji's Tomb (7)** within the confines of a **madrasa** (college) **(8)**. This is the first time in India that a tomb and *madrasa* are found together, another custom inherited from the Seljuks. Immediately to the east of the Ala'i Darwaza stands the **Tomb of Imam Zamin (9)**, an early 16th-century *sufi* 'saint' from Turkestan. It is an octagonal structure with a plastered sandstone dome and has *jali* screens, a characteristic of the Lodi style of decoration.

Tughluqabad

ⓘ *Sunrise to sunset, foreigners Rs 100, Indians Rs 5, video camera Rs 25, allow 1 hr for return rickshaws, turn right at entrance and walk 200 m. The site is often deserted so don't go alone. Take plenty of water.*

Tughluqabad's ruins, 7.5 km east from Qutb Minar, still convey a sense of the power and energy of the newly arrived Muslims in India. From the walls you get a magnificent impression of the strategic advantages of the site. **Ghiyas'ud-Din Tughluq** (ruled 1321-1325), after ascending the throne of Delhi, selected this site for his capital. He built a massive fort around his capital city which stands high on a rocky outcrop of the Delhi Ridge. The fort is roughly octagonal in plan with a circumference of 6.5 km. The vast size, strength and obvious solidity of the whole give it an air of massive grandeur. It was not until Babur (ruled 1526-1530) that dynamite was used in warfare, so this is a very defensible site.

East of the main entrance is the rectangular **citadel**. A wider area immediately to the west and bounded by walls contained the **palaces**. Beyond this to the north lay the **city**. Now marked by the ruins of houses, the streets were laid out in a grid fashion. Inside the citadel enclosure is the **Vijay Mandal tower** and the remains of several halls including a long underground passage. The fort also contained seven tanks.

A causeway connects the fort with the tomb of Ghiyas'ud-Din Tughluq, while a wide embankment near its southeast corner gave access to the fortresses of **Adilabad** about 1 km away, built a little later by Ghiyas'ud-Din's son Muhammad. The tomb is very well preserved and has red sandstone walls with a pronounced slope (the first Muslim building in India to have sloping walls), crowned with a white marble dome. This dome, like that of the Ala'i Darwaza at the Qutb, is crowned by an *amalaka*, a feature of Hindu architecture. Also Hindu is the trabeate arch at the tomb's fortress wall entrance. Inside are three cenotaphs belonging to Ghiyas'ud-Din, his wife and son Muhammad.

Ghiyas'ud-Din Tughluq quickly found that military victories were no guarantee of lengthy rule. When he returned home after a victorious campaign the welcoming pavilion erected by his son and successor, Muhammad-bin Tughluq, was deliberately collapsed over him. Tughluqabad was abandoned shortly afterwards and was thus only inhabited for five years. The Tughluq dynasty continued to hold Delhi until Timur sacked it and slaughtered its inhabitants. For a brief period Tughluq power shifted to Jaunpur near Varanasi, where the Tughluq architectural traditions were carried forward in some superb mosques.

Baha'i Temple (Lotus Temple)
ⓘ *1 Apr-30 Sep 0900-1900, 1 Oct-31 Mar Tue-Sun 0930-1730, free entry and parking, visitors welcome to attend services, at other times the temple is open for silent meditation and prayer. Audio-visual presentations in English are at 1100, 1200, 1400 and 1530, remove shoes before entering. Bus 433 from the centre (Jantar Mantar) goes to Nehru Place, within walking distance (1.5 km) of the temple at Kalkaji, or take a taxi or auto-rickshaw.*

Architecturally the Baha'i Temple is a remarkably striking building. Constructed in 1980-1981, it is built out of white marble and in the characteristic Baha'i temple shape of a lotus flower – 45 lotus petals form the walls – which internally creates a feeling of light and space (34 m high, 70 m in diameter). It is a simple design, brilliantly executed and very elegant in form. All Baha'i temples are nine-sided, symbolizing 'comprehensiveness, oneness and unity'. The Delhi Temple, which seats 1300, is surrounded by nine pools, an attractive feature also helping to keep the building cool. It is particularly attractive when flood-lit. Baha'i temples are "dedicated to the worship of God, for peoples of all races, religions or castes. Only the Holy Scriptures of the Baha'i Faith and earlier revelations are read or recited".

☽ *The Baha'i faith was founded by a Persian, Baha'u'llah (meaning 'glory of God'; 1817-1892), who is believed to be the manifestation of God for this age. His teachings were directed towards the unification of the human race and the establishment of a permanent universal peace.*

East of the Yamuna

Designated as the site of the athletes' village for the 2010 Commonwealth Games, at present East Delhi has just one attraction to draw visitors across the Yamuna.

Swaminarayan Akshardham
ⓘ *www.akshardham.com, Apr-Sep Tue-Sun 1000-1900, Oct-Mar Tue-Sun 0900-1800, temple free, Rs 125 for 'attractions', musical fountain Rs 20, no backpacks, cameras or other electronic items (bag and body searches at entry gate). Packed on Sun; visit early to avoid crowds.*

Opened in November 2005 on the east bank of the Yamuna, the gleaming Akshardham complex represents perhaps the most ambitious construction project in India since the foundation of New Delhi itself. At the centre of a surreal 40-ha 'cultural complex' complete with landscaped gardens, cafés and theme park rides, the temple-monument is dedicated to the 18th-century saint Bhagwan Swaminarayan, who abandoned his home at the age of 11 to embark on a lifelong quest for the spiritual and cultural uplift of Western India. It took 11,000 craftsmen, all volunteers, no less than 300 million hours to complete the temple using traditional building and carving techniques.

If this is the first religious site you visit in India, the security guards and swarms of mooching Indian tourists will hardly prepare you for the typical temple experience. Yet despite this, and the boat rides and animatronic shows which have prompted inevitable comparisons to a 'spiritual Disneyland', most visitors find the Akshardham an inspiring, indeed uplifting, experience, if for no other reason than that the will and ability to build something of its scale and complexity still exist.

The temple You enter the temple complex through a series of intricately carved gates. The Bhakti Dwar (Gate of Devotion), adorned with 208 pairs of gods and their consorts, leads into a hall introducing the life of Swaminarayan and the activities of BAPS (Bochasanwasi Shri Akshar Purushottam Swaminarayan Sanstha), the global Hindu sect-cum-charity which runs Akshardham. The main courtyard is reached through the Mayur Dwar (Peacock Gate), a conglomeration of 869 carved peacocks echoed by an equally florid replica directly facing it.

From here you get your first look at the central monument. Perfectly symmetrical in pink sandstone and white marble, it rests on a plinth encircled by 148 elephants, each sculpted from a 20-tonne stone block, in situations ranging from the literal to the mythological: mortal versions grapple with lions or lug tree trunks, while Airavatha, the eight-trunked mount of Lord Indra, surfs majestically to shore after the churning of the oceans at the dawn of Hindu creation. Above them, carvings of deities, saints and *sadhus* cover every inch of the walls and columns framing the inner sanctum, where a gold-plated *murti* (idol) of Bhagwan Swaminarayan sits attended by avatars of his spiritual successors, beneath a staggeringly intricate marble dome. Around the main dome are eight smaller domes, each carved in hypnotic fractal patterns, while paintings depicting Swaminarayan's life of austerity and service line the walls (explanations in English and Hindi).

Surrounding the temple is a moat of holy water supposedly taken from 151 sacred lakes and rivers visited by Swaminarayan on his seven-year barefoot pilgrimage. 108 bronze *gaumukhs* (cow heads) representing the 108 names of God spout water into the tank, which is itself hemmed in by a 1-km-long *parikrama* (colonnade) of red Rajasthani sandstone.

The exhibition halls and grounds Much of the attention paid to Akshardham revolves around the Disneyesque nature of some of its attractions. Deliberately populist, they aim to instil a sense of pride in the best of Indian values and cultural traditions, and may come across to some as overly flag-waving and patriotic. **Sahajanand Darshan** is an animatronic rendition of Swaminarayan's life, told over a series of rooms through which you are shepherded by an attendant. A beautifully shot Imax movie, *Neelkanth Darshan*, tells the story of the young yogi's seven-year pilgrimage, with dance routines and scenic set pieces worthy of a Bollywood ad campaign. **Sanskruti Vihar** is a 14-minute boat ride along the mythical Saraswati River where visitors are introduced to Indian pioneers in the fields of science, technology, medicine and philosophy.

A similar message imbues the **Cultural Garden**, an avenue of bronze statues extolling the cardinal virtues of prominent figures from Hindu mythology and Indian history. Between the exhibition halls and the main Akshardham is the **Yagnapurush Kund**, an enormous step well (claimed to be the biggest in the world) overlooked by a 9-m bronze statue of Neelkanth. This is the scene for a dramatic and popular musical fountain show each evening.

⊙ Delhi listings

Hotel prices

LL over US$200	**L** US$151-200	**AL** US$101-150	
A US$66-100	**B** US$46-65	**C** US$31-45	
D US$21-30	**E** US$12-20	**F** US$7-11	
G under US$7			

Restaurant prices

🍽🍽🍽 over US$12   🍽🍽 US$6-12   🍽 under US$6

⊜ Sleeping

Avoid hotel touts. Airport taxis may pretend not to know the location of your chosen hotel so give full details and insist on being taken there. Hotel prices in Delhi are significantly higher than in most other parts of the country. Smaller **C-D** guesthouses away from the centre in **South Delhi** (eg Kailash, Safdarjang) or in **Sunder Nagar**, are quieter and often good value but may not provide food. **E-F** accommodation is concentrated around **Janpath** and **Paharganj** (New Delhi), and **Chandni Chowk** (Old Delhi) – well patronized but basic and usually cramped yet good for meeting other backpackers. Some have dormitory beds for less than Rs 100. Some city centre rooms are windowless. Signs in some hotels warn against taking drugs as this is becoming a serious cause for concern. Police raids are frequent.

Old Delhi *p62, map p68*

L-AL Oberoi Maidens, 7 Sham Nath Marg, T011-2397 5464, www.oberoihotels.com. 54 large well-appointed rooms, restaurant (slow), barbecue nights are excellent, coffee shop, old-style bar, attractive colonial style in quiet area, spacious gardens with excellent pool, friendly welcome, personal attention. Recommended.
B Broadway, 4/15A Asaf Ali Rd, T011-4366 3600, www.oldworldhospitality.com. 36 rooms, some wonderfully quirky. The 'coloured' rooms are designed for children, complete with fairy lights, miniature furniture and psychedelic bathroom tiles. Chor Bizarre

restaurant and bar is highly regarded, as is 'Thugs' pub. Easily one of the best options.
C-E Peace House, 20A New Tibetan Colony, Manju-ka-Tilla, T011-2393 9415. Clean, basic rooms in friendly guesthouse.
C-E Wongdhen House, 15A New Tibetan Colony, Manju-ka-Tilla, T011-2381 6689, wongdhenhouse@hotmail.com. Very clean rooms, some with a/c and TV, safe, cosy, convivial, good breakfast and great Tibetan meals, an insight into Tibetan culture, peacefully located by Yamuna River yet 15 mins by auto-rickshaw north of Old Delhi Station. Recommended.

Connaught Place *p74, maps p72 and p75*

LL Imperial, Janpath, T011-2334 1234, www.theimperialindia.com. 230 rooms and beautiful 'deco suites' in supremely elegant Lutyens-designed 1933 hotel. Unparalleled location, great bar, antiques and art everywhere, corridors scented with jasmine oil, gardens with spa and secluded pool, amazing **Spice Route** restaurant, classy and knows it but still quite an experience. Highly recommended.
LL-L Park, 15 Sansad Marg, T011-2374 3000, www.theparkhotels.com. 224 of the best contemporary-style rooms in town, good views, friendly, award-winning restaurant and funky, modern bar, new glass-walled spa overlooking Jantar Mantar. Recommended.
L Hans Plaza, 15 Barakhamba Rd (16th-20th floor), T011-2331 6868, www.hanshotels.com. 67 slightly uninspired rooms, not a 'boutique hotel' as advertised but clean and quiet with superb views. There is very little difference between the 'de luxe' and the 'executive' rooms, so go for the cheapest.
AL-A Palace Heights, D26-28 Connaught Pl, T011-4358 2610, www.hotelpalaceheights.com. Recently given a complete facelift, the bright, modern rooms with good attention to detail, represent the best choice in Connaught Pl in this price bracket. There's also an attractive glass-walled restaurant overlooking the street.

A Hotel Alka, P Block, Connaught Circus, T011-2334 4328, www.hotelalka.com. 21 well-appointed rooms including 2 spotless restaurants but it's nothing special.

C-D YMCA Tourist Hostel, Jai Singh Rd, T011-2336 1915, www.delhiymca.com. 120 rooms, for both sexes, a/c rooms with bath (B-Block, non a/c and shared bath), some reported dirty, common areas have been recently refurbished. Restaurant (breakfast included but disappointing), cybercafé, travel agent, peaceful gardens, tennis, good pool (Rs 200 extra), luggage storage (Rs 10 per day), pay in advance but check bill, reserve ahead, very professional.

D-F Choudhary, H 35/3 Connaught Circus, T011-2332 2043, hkc_guesthouse@hotmail.com. Tucked away but worth seeking out; very clean but basic rooms in a central location with a friendly manager who knows his stuff.

E-F Ringo Guest House, 17 Scindia House (upstairs), off Kasturba Gandhi Marg, T011-2331 0605, ringo_guest_house@yahoo.co.in. Tiny rooms, very basic (some windowless) but no bugs. Hot showers, basic toilets, lockers, courtyard, backpackers' haunt (other hotel touts may try to waylay travellers).

Paharganj *p76, maps p72 and p76*
Paharganj is where backpackers congregate. Its back lanes hide one of Asia's biggest markets for export-quality goods. Sandwiched between the main sights and near the main railway station, it's noisy, dirty and a lot of hassle. Its chief virtues are economy and convenience, with plenty of shops selling souvenirs and cheap clothes, travel agents, budget hotels and cafés catering for Western tastes. For a more sedate, 'authentic' experience, you might like to try elsewhere. Rooms tend to be cheap, often with shared baths. Avoid **Hotel Bright**.

C-D Hotel Ajanta, 36 Arakashan Rd, Ram Nagar (opposite New Delhi railway station), T011-4176 4563, www.ajantahotel.com. A few blocks removed from the madness of Main Bazar, this is a real find, 70 well-maintained rooms, most a/c, good service

and lobby and restaurant. If you make a reservation be sure to stress you want to stay in their main hotel (they have been known to put people in an inferior 'sister' hotel). Enormous suites and family rooms. Spanish quilts, spring mattresses; they stress their use of fabric softener! IATA travel agency on site for tickets and tours.

C-D Jyoti Mahal, 2488 Nalwa St, behind Imperial Cinema, T011-2358 0524, www.jyotimahal.net. An oasis in Paharganj and a glimpse of Rajasthan in the heart of Delhi. A beautiful converted *haveli*, rooms spiral out around a central courtyard with lovely decor, antiquities and a peaceful vibe. Great food in the tented rooftop restaurant.

C-D Metropolis Tourist Home, 1634-35 Main Bazar, Paharganj, T011-2358 5766, www.metropolistravels.com. More expensive rooms have ornate heavy wooden furniture, but walls are grubby throughout. Nice rooftop restaurant, and wonderful wooden expresso bar in the lobby.

C-D Prince Polonia, 2325-26 Tilak Gali (behind Imperial cinema), Paharganj, T011-2358 1930, www.hotelprincepolonia.com. Very unusual for Paharganj in that it has a rooftop pool (small, but good for a cool down). Breezy rooftop café. Attracts a slightly more mature crowd. Safe, clean.

D-E Railway Retiring Rooms, New (and Old) Delhi Railway Station. For 12 hrs and 24 hrs, dorm beds, 10 rooms (6 a/c are usually pre-booked), only for train ticket-holders, basic and noisy, but convenient.

D-F Heritage Inn, 2374 Raj Guru Rd, Chuna Mandi, T011-2358 8222. New building with 20 simple, spotless rooms and friendly staff.

D-F Hotel Gush, 626, Main Bazar, Chowk Bawli, T011-2356 1758, hotelgushinternational@gmail.com. New hotel with same friendly manager as neighbouring **Rak International** (see below). Neetu, runs the hotels with his brothers (they also have the bindi shop on the corner their side street and Main Bazar). Steel and marble themed. Basic, clean rooms.

D-F Rak International, 820 Main Bazar, Chowk Bowli, T011-2358 6508, hotelrakint@

yahoo.co.in. 27 basic but clean rooms in professionally run. Quiet, friendly hotel with a rooftop restaurant and water feature.
D-F Shelton, 5043 Main Bazar, T011-2358 0575. 36 rooms with well-worn sheets in a slightly grander hotel than its neighbours – it even has a lift. Some cleanliness issues (watch out for the occasional cockroach in the bathrooms). Above-average rooftop restaurant does good breakfasts.
D-F Star Palace, 4590 Dal Mandi, off Main Bazar (lane opposite Khalsa Boots), T011-2358 4849, www.stargroupofhotels.com. 31 clean, well-kept rooms (some a/c) with "fantastic showers", quiet, friendly, safe, airport pickup.
D-F Vivek, 1534-1550, Main Bazar, T011-4154 1435, www.vivekhotel.com. 50 adequate rooms which are outshone by the impressive communal areas, pool table, a/c café and nice rooftop restaurant friendly staff, good value, recommended.
D-G Ajay's, 5084A Main Bazar, T011-2358 3125, www.anupamhoteliersltd.com. 48 fairly clean (windowless) rooms with bath, dorm, good bakery, restaurant, friendly, popular backpackers' hangout.
D-G Hotel K G Palace, 1656 Main Bazar, next to Open Hand Café (see Eating). Good size rooms with TV, AC, travel desk and very convenient for Metro station.
F Anoop, 1566 Main Bazar, T011-2358 9366, www.anupamhoteliersltd.com. 43 rooms with bath, some with air-cooler, very clean though basic, noisy at times, safe. Good 24-hr rooftop restaurant shared with

Hare Krishna (see below); waiters can 'forget' to give change.
F-G Hare Krishna, 1572 Main Bazar, T011-4154 1341, www.anupamhoteliersltd.com. 24 clean-ish rooms with bath (some windowless and stuffy), very basic, friendly, travel, good rooftop restaurant.
F-G Namaskar, 917 Chandiwalan, Main Bazar, T011-2358 3456, namaskarhotel@ yahoo.com. Owner is a fount of knowledge, friendly and helpful 32 small basic rooms (2-4 beds), all have showers, clean but some windowless, newer **D** a/c rooms in extension, generator, safe, friendly service, good atmosphere, quiet at night, free luggage storage, car rental, reserve ahead.

Karol Bagh and Rajendra Nagar

West of Pahar Ganj on the Metro line, **Karol Bagh** is full of identikit modern hotels, albeit a degree more upmarket than Paharganj. There are plentiful good eating places, and the area is handy for Sarai Rohilla station. Nearby **Rajendra Nagar**, a residential suburb, has one of Delhi's best homestays.
AL Hotel Clark International, 5/47 WEA, Saraswati Marg, Karol Bagh, T011-4500 5500, www.hotelclarkindia.com. Business hotel with 32 elegant spacious rooms.
A Bajaj Indian Home Stay, 8A/34 WEA, Karol Bagh, T011-2573 6509, www.indianhome stay.com. 10 comfortable rooms, all have a different theme, from gods to holy cities. Mod cons include telephones in all the bathrooms. Homely touches and atmosphere. Tricky

to find – tell the taxi driver, the turn-off is by "Pusa Road metro pillar 122".

A Yatri Paying Guest House, corner of Panchkuin and Mandir Margs, T011-2362 5563, www.yatrihouse.com. A quiet, peaceful oasis with beautiful gardens. 6 large, attractive rooms all with 42-inch televisions, nice bathrooms, Wi-Fi, fridge and a/c. Free airport pickup or drop off. Breakfast, tea/coffee and afternoon snack included.

B Master Guest House, R-500 New Rajendra Nagar (Shankar Rd and GR Hospital Rd crossing), T011-2874 1089, www.masterbedand breakfast.com. 3 clean rooms, a/c, with private bathroom, Wi-Fi, rooftop for breakfast, *thalis*, warm welcome, personal attention, secure, recommended. Each room has the theme of a different god, complete with appropriate colour schemes. Very knowledgeable, caring owners run excellent tours of 'hidden Delhi'.

B Pal's Inn, E Patel Nagar, Karol Bagh, T011-2578 5310, palsinn@del3vsnl.net. 16 rooms clean, full breakfast included, attentive staff, a bit dingy.

South Delhi *p78, map p72*

Most of the city's smartest hotels are located south of Rajpath, in a broad rectangle between Chanakyapuri and Humayun's Tomb. The southern residential suburbs are also peppered with homestays; a list is available from **Delhi Tourism**, BK Singh Marg (see page 61), or arrange with **Metropole** (see Car hire, page 103).

LL Aman New Delhi, Lodhi Rd, T011-4363 3333. This serene and stylish hotel takes luxury to new levels. Come for the suites with private pools, exquisite contemporary design and fantastic spa.

LL Claridges, 12 Aurangzeb Rd, T011-4133 5133, www.claridges.com. 138 refurbished, classy rooms, art deco-style interiors, colonial atmosphere, attractive restaurants (**Jade Garden** is good), slick **Aura** bar, impeccable service, more atmosphere than most. Recommended.

LL Oberoi, Dr Zakir Hussain Marg, T011-2436 3030, www.oberoihotels.com. 300 rooms and extremely luxurious suites overlooking golf club, immaculate, quietly efficient, beautiful touches, eg carved Tree of Life in lobby, all 5-star facilities including 2 pools and spa, superb business centre, good restaurants.

LL Taj Mahal, 1 Mansingh Rd, T011-2302 6162, www.tajhotels.com. 300 attractive rooms, comfortable, new club levels outstanding, excellent restaurants and service (**Haveli** offers wide choice and explanations for the newcomer; **Ming House**'s spicing varies; **Machan** overlooks palm trees and has wildlife library), good Khazana shop, lavishly finished with 'lived-in' feel, friendly 1920s-style bar, good city views but lacks atmosphere.

LL Taj Palace, 2 Sardar Patel Marg, T011-2611 0202, www.tajhotels.com. 421 rooms, renovating to high standard (some still outdated), standard 5-star facilities but well done, purpose-built for business travellers, generally excellent, **Orient Express** restaurant highly recommended (haute French), "service outstanding, food superb", 'Masala Art' Indian restaurant also good.

LL-L Ambassador (Taj), Sujan Singh Park, T011-2463 2600, www.tajhotels.com. 81 rooms in period property, pleasant garden, quirky bar and coffee shop, calm atmosphere, quiet and convenient location.

LL-L ITC Maurya Sheraton, Sardar Patel Marg, T011-2611 2233, www.itcwelcom group.com. 484 rooms, those in ITC block exceptional with private butler, electric massage chairs, excellent decor and service, splendid pool (solar heated), disco (noisy late at night, so avoid rooms nearby), good restaurants.

LL-L Vasant Continental, Vasant Vihar, T011-2614 8800, www.jaypeehotels.com. 110 rooms in recently renovated, contemporary-style hotel, convenient for airports (free transfer), large pool and gardens near Basant Lok Market, good service, interesting range of restaurants. Recommended.

LL-AL Ashok (ITDC), 50-B Chanakyapuri, T011-2611 0101, www.theashok.com.

571 large rooms (some upgraded) in huge property, sunny coffee shop, 24-hr bank, smart new Lebanese restaurant, trendy **Steels** bar, quiet but overpriced.

L Manor, 77 Friends Colony, T011-2692 5151, www.themanordelhi.com. Contemporary boutique hotel with 10 stylish rooms, heavenly beds, polished stone surfaces and chrome, relaxing garden, a haven.

L-AL Jukaso Inn, 50 Sunder Nagar, T011-2435 0308, www.jukasohotels.com. Pleasant, quiet, not much character, friendly staff, restaurant, room service. Not to be confused with cheaper Jukaso Inn Downtown.

AL Amarya Garden C 179 Defense Colony, T011-4656 2735, www.amaryagroup.com. Newer elegant boutique offering from same owners as **Haveli** (see below). Unique, beautifully decorated en suite rooms, with TV, Wi-Fi. Wonderful attention to detail, lovely garden. Plush, modern dining room. Recommended. Book ahead.

AL Amarya Haveli, P5 Hauz Khas Enclave, T011-41759268, www.amaryagroup.com. Luxury, boutique, hip guesthouse, run by 2 Frenchmen. Unique, bright, en suite rooms, with TV, Wi-Fi. Fantastic roof garden. Great home cooked food. Book ahead. Slightly cheaper than their newer hotel. Highly recommended.

AL Diplomat, 9 Sardar Patel Marg, T011-2301 0204, www.thehoteldiplomat.com. 25 rooms, all different. Good attention to detail but a bit overpriced. The delicious **Olive Beach** restaurant (see Eating) is in the garden. No pool, quietly located.

AL Lutyens Bungalow, 39 Prithviraj Rd, T011-2469 4523, www.lutyensbungalow.co.in. Private guesthouse in a bungalow that has been running for over 35 years. Eccentric, rambling property with 15 a/c rooms, a wonderful pool and beautiful gardens. free airport pickup/drop off, full services, used for long-stays by NGOs and foreign consultants.

AL-A La Sagrita, 14 Sunder Nagar, T011-2435 9541, www.lasagrita.com. 24 a/c rooms, some better than others, modern bathrooms, helpful staff, breakfast in garden quiet location. 'Penthouse' rooms share a large balcony.

AL-A Shervani, 11 Sundar Nagar, T011-4250 1000. Swish, business boutique hotel in quiet Sundar Nagar. All mod cons.

A Colonel's Retreat, D 418 Defence Colony, T(0)9999-720024, www.colonelsretreat.com. New B&B. En suite rooms, all mod cons, well located, lively atmosphere.

A Rajdoot, Mathura Rd, T011-2437 6666, www.hotelrajdootdelhi.com. 55 rooms, with pool, convenient location for Hazrat Nizamuddin Station.

A-B K One One, K11, Jangpura Extn, 2nd floor, T011-4359 2583, www.parigold.com. Homely Guesthouse in quiet, central residential area. Run by wonderful ex-TV chef, who also gives cooking lessons. All rooms en suite with ac, minibar, Wi-Fi, some with balconies. Wonderful roof terrace with views of Humayan's Tomb. Rooftop room is lovely. Book ahead.

B '27' Jorbagh, 27 Jorbagh (2 mins from Lodi tombs), T011-2469 4430, www.jorbagh27.com. 20 a/c rooms, car hire, not plush but very quiet hassle free, book ahead.

B Murad Baig, R-block, Hauz Khas Enclave (phone for exact address), T(0)9899-555704. A real find. Just one beautiful bedroom with attached bathroom, leads out onto a large green roof terrace. The owner is an oracle when it comes to Delhi history and his wife, author of 16 cookbooks, gives cookery lessons. They make you part of the family. The room gets booked up, so reserve well ahead.

B On the House B-4/120 Safdarjung Enclave, T011-4602 4897, www.bedandbreakfastnew delhi.com. Popular B&B in quiet, residential area. Colourful en suite rooms, all with a/c, Wi-Fi, TV.

D-F Youth Hostel, 5 Naya Marg, Chanakyapuri, T011-2611 6285, www.yhaindia.org. Wide range of room from a/c doubles to a basic dorm (a/c dorms much better). Meals available at restaurant if ordered in advance. Soulless but clean and comfortable. Great location. You need YHA membership to stay (Rs 250 foreigners, Rs 100 Indians).

Airport

Unless you can afford a 5-star, hotels around the airport are overpriced and best avoided.

LL-L Radisson National Highway 8, T011-2677 9191. Plush, if slightly soulless 5-star, with all mod cons.

L-A Hotel Saptagiri L-322, Mahipalpur Extension, National Highway 8, T011-4616 0000, www.hotelsaptagiri.com. 5-10 mins from the airports. The cheapest rooms have no windows. Suites with balconies overlook the the noisy National Highway. Clean, secure. Wi-fi.

B-C Hotel Star A-288 National Highway 8, Mahipalpur, T011-2678 4092. Clean, a bit musty. All rooms with TV and a/c. 5 mins from the airports.

● Eating

The larger hotel restaurants are often the best for cuisine, decor and ambience. Buffets (lunch or dinner) cost Rs 500 or more. Others may only open around 1930 for dinner; some close on Sun. Alcohol is served in most top hotels, but only in some non-hotel restaurants eg **Amber**, **Ginza** and **Kwality**.

The old-fashioned 'tea on the lawn' is still served at the **Imperial** and in **Claridges** (see Sleeping). **Aapki Pasand**, at 15 Netaji Subhash Marg, offers unusual tea-tasting in classy and extremely professional surroundings; it's quite an experience.

Old Delhi *p62, map p68*

In **Paranthewali Gali**, a side street off Chandni Chowk, stalls sell a variety of fresh *paranthas* including *kaju badam* (stuffed with dry fruits and nuts).

⑪ Chor Bizarre, Broadway Hotel (see Sleeping), T011-2327 3821. Tandoori and Kashmiri cuisine (Wazwan, Rs 500). Fantastic food, quirky decor, including salad bar that was a vintage car. Well worth a visit.

⑪ Haldiram's, 1454/2 Chandni Chowk. Stand-up counter for excellent snacks and sweets on the run (try *dokhla* with coriander chutney from seller just outside), and more elaborate sit-down restaurant upstairs.

⑪ Karim's, Gali Kababiyan (south of Jama Masjid), Mughlai. Authentic, busy, plenty of local colour. The experience, as much as the food, makes this a must. Not a lot to tempt vegetarians though.

⑪ Peshawari, 3707 Subhash Marg, Daryaganj. Closed Tue. Tiny, with tiled walls, serves delicious chicken.

Connaught Place *p74, maps p72 and p75*

⑪⑪⑪ Bonsai, Chorus Hotel, B49 Connaught Pl, T011-4365 2240. Tranquil garden, imaginative, good-value food. Perfect for when you want to escape the noise of CP.

⑪⑪⑪ Rodeo, 12-A, T011-2371 3780. Excellent Mexican, Italian, continental. Fast service, fully stocked bar, Wild West decor.

⑪⑪⑪ Sakura, Hotel Metropolitan Nikko, Bangla Sahib Rd, T011-2334 2000. Top Japanese royal cuisine in classic, uncluttered surroundings. One of the best in the city, priced accordingly.

⑪⑪⑪ Spice Route, Imperial Hotel (see Sleeping). Extraordinary temple-like surroundings (took 7 years to build), Kerala, Thai, Vietnamese cuisines, magical atmosphere but expensive food doesn't always thrill.

⑪⑪⑪ Veda, 27-H, T011-4151 3535. Owned by fashion designer Rohit Bal with appropriately beautiful bordello-style decor, done out like a Rajasthani palace with high-backed leather chairs and candles reflecting from mirror work on ceilings. Food is contemporary Indian. Great atmosphere at night.

⑪⑪⑪ Zen, B-25, T011-2335 7455. Stylish, a little impersonal, but popular, generous portions for Chinese, more expensive Japanese and seafood.

⑪⑪ Amber, N-Block, T011-2331 2092. High-class decor, lightly spiced Mughlai cuisine, beer.

⑪ The Chinese, F14/15, T011-2370 8888. Rivals Q'BA (see below) for the most authentic Chinese food in Connaught Pl, but service is a few degrees better; beers are poured like fine wines.

DV8, 13 Regal Building, T011-2336 3358. International menu, good buffet (Rs 250), club ambience, big screens and loud music, great espresso coffee. Smart, cosy pub below.

Embassy, D-11, T011-2341 7480. International food. Popular with artistic-intellectual-political crowd, good food, long-standing local favourite.

Kwality, 7 Regal Building, near **Park Hotel**, T011-2374 2352. International. Spicy Punjabi dishes with various breads. Try *chhole bhature*.

Mosaic, M 45/1, Outer Circle, T011-2341 6105. This is the place to come to experience food from across India. Pork vindaloo from Goa, *pomfret*-stuffed with prawns from Kerala, fish steamed in banana leaves from Bengal. Good-value imaginative, diverse menu.

Q'BA, E-42 Connaught Pl, T011-4151 2888. Dodgy decor, slow service but attractive menu, excellent Chinese section, and a superb terrace overlooking Connaught Pl (reserve ahead). Live jazz on Sun.

TGI Fridays, F-16, T011-2371 1991. Standard but reliable. 'Happy Hour' 1700-1930.

United Coffee House, E-15 Connaught Pl, T011-2341 1697. Recommended more for the colonial-era cake-icing decor than for the fairly average food. Always attracts a mixed crowd, well worth a visit.

Kake da Hotel, Outer Circle opposite L-block. Famous Punjabi *dhaba*. *Handi* dishes and delicious green masala fish, not the cleanest but very cheap and popular.

Nathu's, and **Bengali Sweet House**, both in Bengali Market (east of Connaught Pl). Sweet shops also serving vegetarian food. Good dosa, *iddli*, *utthapam* and North Indian *chana bathura*, *thalis*, clean, functional. Try *kulfi* (hard blocks of ice cream) with *falooda* (sweet vermicelli noodles).

Nizam's Kathi Kebabs, H-5 Plaza, T011-2371 3078. Very good, tasty filled *parathas*, good value, clean, excellent '3-D toilets' (note the emergency button!).

Saravana Bhavan, P-15/90, near McDonalds, T011-2334 7755; also at 46 Janpath, T011-2331 7755. Chennai-based chain, light and wonderful South Indian, superb chutneys, unmissable *kaju anjeer* ice cream with figs and nuts. Can take hours to get a table at night.

Street stalls, at entrance to Shankar Market. Stalls dish out *rajma chawal* (bean stew and rice) to a vast, appreciative crowd on weekdays.

Paharganj *p76, maps p72 and p76*

The rooftop restaurants at **Hare Krishna** and **Shelton** are great locations for a bite to eat.

Appetite, 1575 Main Bazar, T011-2753 2079. Chinese, Nepali, Italian. Rather grim-looking backpacker den, good bakery items and *lassis*.

Everest Bakery Café, Dal Mandi, near **Star Palace Hotel**. Fantastic *momos*, cakes and pies, green teas, sociable. Recommended.

Korean Restaurant, in the same square as Hotel Rak, above Navrang Guest House. This place is hidden away, opposite the urinals! Rooftop café is a real delight with Korean sushi, spicy kimchi and sizzling pork dishes.

Madan's, 1601 Main Bazar. International. Egg and chips to *thalis*, not special but friendly, popular, good value.

Malhotra's, 1833 Laxmi Narayan St, T011-2358 9371. Good Indian and Chinese, wide choice, a/c section; also takeaway.

Open Hand Café, next to Hotel K G Palace, Main Bazar, near RK Ashram Metro station. An oasis in the midst of the mayhem of Paharganj. Beautiful café serving international portions of cappuccino, carrot cake, salads and sandwiches. A few tables; also mezzanine level of floor cushions. Recommended.

Southern Restaurant, opposite Ajanta, Arakashan Rd. Spartan but clean and very cheap café for excellent fresh *dosas*, friendly Indian clientele, atmosphere better downstairs than in fan-cooled upstairs room.

Tadka, off Main Bazar. Good option for tasty food in this area. Great range of all the usual Indian favourites, with nice decor, friendly staff and good hygiene levels.

South Delhi *p78, map p72*

₩₩₩ **Ai**, MGF Metropolitan Mall, Saket, T011-4065 4567. This glamorous uber-trendy 200-seater restaurant serves top-quality sushi. Stylish decor and great terrace, jazz bar and some fantastic DJ nights. Hang out with the beautiful people.

₩₩₩ **Baci**, 23 Sunder Nagar Market, Near HDFC Bank, T011-4150 7445. Classy, top-quality Italian food, run by gregarious Italian-Indian.

₩₩₩ **Bukhara**, ITC Maurya Sheraton (see Sleeping), T011-2611 2233. Stylish Northwest Frontier cuisine amidst rugged walls draped with rich rugs (but uncomfortable seating). Outstanding meat dishes and dhal. Also tasty vegetable and *paneer* dishes, but vegetarians will miss out on the best dishes.

₩₩₩ **Diva**, M8, M-Block Market, Greater Kailash II, T011-2921 5673. Superb Italian in minimalist space popular with celebrity crowd. Great fish dishes, inventive starters, dedicated vegetarian section, extensive wine list.

₩₩₩ **Dum Phukt**, Maurya Sheraton, T011-2611 2233. North Indian. Slowly steam cooked in sealed *handis* produces excellent melt-in-the-mouth Nawabi dishes. High-quality service and decor. Expensive and a bit pretentious.

₩₩₩ **La Piazza**, Hyatt Regency, Bhikaji Cama Pl, T011-2618 1234. Authentic Italian. Mon-Sat lunch buffet plus smart Sun brunch. Try pizzas from wood-fired oven, excellent pastas, definitely worth the trip.

₩₩₩ **Line of No Control**, Qutab Hotel, Shahid Jeet Singh Marg, T011-4168 8963/62. Well worth braving the outer edges of South Delhi for this blend of Indian and Pakistani cuisine. Sit on the breezy terrace or enjoy the lavish interiors.

₩₩₩ **Lodi**, Lodi Gardens, T011-2465 5054. Continental lunch, Indian dinner menu in pleasant, Mediterranean-style surroundings, nice terrace and garden. Come more for the setting than the food which can be mediocre.

₩₩₩ **Magique**, Gate No 3, Garden of 5 Senses, Mehrauli Badarpur Rd, T011-2953 6767. High-class quality food, in a magical setting. Sit outside among the candles and fairy lights. One of Delhi's most romantic restaurants.

₩₩₩ **Olive Beach**, Diplomat Hotel, 9 Sardar Patel Marg, T011-4604 0404. Top Italian, in a lovely outdoor setting. Book ahead for their legendary blow-out Sun brunches: for Rs 1900 you get open access to a mind-boggling buffet and as many martini's as you can drink.

₩₩₩ **Orient Express**, Taj Palace Hotel, T011-2611 0202. Continental. Recreated luxury of the famous train carriages, formal dress code, expensive but different.

₩₩₩ **Parikrama**, Antariksha Bhavan, Kasturba Gandhi Marg, T011-6630 3399. International. Come for the views and the novelty of this revolving restaurant, rather than for the food which is pretty bad. Book ahead for a window seat.

₩₩₩ **Park Baluchi**, inside Deer Park, Hauz Khas Village, T011-2685 9369. Atmospheric dining in Hauz Khas Deer Park. The lamb wrapped in chicken served on a flaming sword comes highly recommended. Book ahead.

₩₩₩ **Ploof**, 13 Main Market, Lodhi Colony, T011-2464 9026. The place to come for seafood. Very popular. Bright, comfortable restaurant.

₩₩₩ **Smokehouse Bar & Grill**, No 2, VIPPS Centre, Masjid Moth Greater Kailash II, T011-4143 5530. Classy joint, great continental food, fine wines, an enviable cigar selection and a stylish bar. In the same square as Mainland China (see below).

₩₩₩ **Yum Yum Treè**, 1st floor, Friends Colony Community Centre (opposite Nathu Sweets), T011-4260 2020. Excellent Chinese, with an enormous menu. Very popular. Great decor.

₩ **All American Diner**, India Habitat Centre, Lodhi Rd, T011-4366 3333, ext 3162. The place to come if you feel like a shake and a burger. A perfect mock-up of a 1950s diner, in the surreal setting of the Habitat Centre.

₩ **Amici**, Middle Lane, 47 Khan Market, T011-4358 7191. Run by the same team as **Baci** (see Bars and clubs), this has more of a café feel. Fantastic quality, good-value Italian food. Stylish decor, possibly the best coffee in Delhi and a pleasant roof terrace.

₩ **Basil and Thyme**, Santushti Complex, Chanakyapuri, T011-2467 3322. Continental. Pleasant setting, simple decor, a/c, modestly priced Western snacks at lunch, fashionable meeting place (busy 1300-1400).

♥♥ The Big Chill, F-38 East of Kailash (off Lala Lajpat Rai Path near Spring Meadows Hospital), also in Khan Market. 1230 till late. A bright café with a wide range of carefully prepared, wholesome meals of grills, bakes, fresh pasta and home-made desserts.

♥♥ Café Turtle, 5 B, Khan Market, T011-2465 5641/2. Popular café at the top of Full Circle Bookstore. Food is hit and miss, but great cakes, shakes and smoothies and a green roof terrace.

♥♥ Chopsticks, Siri Fort Village, Khel Gaon Marg, T011-2649 2348. Chinese, Thai. Good value, pleasant ambience, bar, weekend buffet lunches.

♥♥ Flavors 52-C, Flyover Complex, Defence Colony, T011-2464 5644. Ignore the bizarre location next to a flyover and enjoy some good Italian food. If you're lucky you may get serenaded by a man with a synthesizer.

♥♥ Le Café N1, N-Block Market, GK1, T011-4173 1935. Stylish café, with wonderful roof garden, hidden on the 3rd floor above **Ravi Bajaj** clothes shop (corner of N-block market).

♥♥ Mainland China, E4 Masjid Moth, Great Kailash II, T011-2922 2123. Excellent Oriental, unusual menu, one of the best in town.

♥♥ Market Café, 2nd floor, Middle Lane, Khan Market, T011-4175 7703. Free Wi-Fi, large menu and a great roof terrace, make this a popular choice.

♥♥ Moti Mahal Deluxe, 20/48 Malcha Marg, Chanakyapuri (near **Diplomat**), T011-2611 8698. Closed Tue. Excellent Mughlai, short on ambience but food makes up for it.

♥♥ Naivedyam, Hauz Khas Village, T011-2696 0426. Very good South Indian, great service and very good value

♥♥ Oh! Calcutta, E-Block, ground floor, International Trade Towers, Nehru Pl, T011-2646 4180. Authentic Bengali cuisine, with excellent vegetarian and fish options, odd location but not far from the Baha'i temple.

♥♥ Punjabi by Nature, 11 Basant Lok, T011-4151 6666. Outstanding food, very popular Punjabi dishes. Nice lounge bar.

♥♥ Swagath, 14 Defence Colony Market, T011-2433 0930. Neighbouring, some say superior rival to the famous **Sagar** (see below), with a variety of cuisines (Chinese, Tamil, Mangalore) and a strong emphasis on seafood.

♥ Andhra Bhavan, near India Gate. Crowded and rushed but atmospheric place for extra-spicy Chettinad (South Indian) food, vegetarian and non-vegetarian options, superb *thalis*.

♥ Colonelz Kebabz, Defence Colony Market. Tandoori. 1000-2200. Excellent tikkas and kebabs. Several others, including **RK Puram**, serving delicious, safe, street food.

♥ Khan Cha Cha, Khan Market, 75 Middle Lane. This no-frills joint serves some of the best kebabs in the city from a window in the middle lane of Khan Market. Fantastic value. You can recognize the place from the crowd clamouring at the counter.

♥ Sagar, 18 Defence Colony Market, T011-2433 3110. Other branches in Vasant Kunj, Malviya Nagar and NOIDA. Excellent South Indian. Cheap and "amazing" *thalis* and coffee, very hectic (frequent queues). One of the best breakfasts in Delhi.

♥ Ten, YWCA International GH, Sansad Marg. Mexican, continental. Cheery café popular with long-stay foreigners, pleasant tree-shaded garden, clean, modern, well run. Recommended.

⊙ Bars and clubs

Many national holidays are 'dry' days. Delhi's bar/club scene has exploded over the last few years. Expect to pay a lot for your drinks and, when in doubt, dress up as some clubs have strict dress codes. Delhi's 'in' crowd is notoriously fickle; city magazines (*Time Out*, *First City*) will point you towards the flavour of the month.

Connaught Place *p74, maps p72 and p75*
1911, Imperial Hotel (see Sleeping). Elegantly styled colonial bar, good snacks.

Agni, Park Hotel (see Sleeping). Terence Conran-style bar, sharply dressed staff, reliable party atmosphere that can descend into bar-top dancing. **Aqua**, in the same hotel, is Delhi's first poolside bar.

South Delhi *p78, map p72*
Baci, ground floor of classy Italian eatery (see Eating). Hosts some stomping DJ nights, especially on Thu.
Bohemia, opposite **Shalom** (see below), T011-2924 3328. Relaxed, contemporary bar, friendly staff plus a good Indian restaurant upstairs.
Café Morrisons, Shop E-12, South Extension Part II, T011-2625 5652. Very popular sticky rock bar. Come for live bands or just for the DJ.
Elevate, 5th floor, Centre Stage Mall, Sector 18, NOIDA, T(0)95120-436 4611, www.elevateindia.com. Attracts a young crowd with its promise of a 0400 finish, but it's a long way out of town.
The F-Bar, Ashok Hotel (see Sleeping), Chanakyapuri, T011-2611 1066. Glitzy, glamorous A-list bar. Generally plays house or electronica. Dress smart. Expensive.
Kuki, E 7, Greater Kailash II, Masjid Moth Commercial Complex, T011-2922 5241. In the same block as **Mainland China** and **Smokehouse Bar & Grill** (see Eating). Sleek, glamorous lounge bar. Dress up.
The Love Hotel, part of **Ai** (see Eating). Super-hip, elegant bar. Some of the best visiting DJs play here.
Ministry of Sound, LSC Sector C, Pocket 6/7, Vasant Kunj, T011-4604 5319. Newly opened in steel-and-glass pyramid, variable crowd and music, large dance floor, expensive entry (Rs 2500 per couple) and drinks, but goes until early hours. The most accessible of the non-hotel clubs.
Pegs-n-Pints, Chanakya Lane, Chanakyapuri (tucked away behind Akbar Bhawan), T011-2687 8320. On Tue evenings it hosts Delhi's only gay club. Western and Indian pop. It gets packed. A lot of fun.
Rick's, Taj Mahal Hotel (see Sleeping). Suave Casablanca-themed bar with long martini list, a long-time fixture on Delhi's social scene.

Shalom, 'N' Block Market, Greater Kailash 1, T011-4163 2280. Comfortable, stylish lounge bar serving Lebanese cuisine; the resident DJ plays ambient music at a pleasantly low volume.
Six Month Story, Daffodil Hotel, Chattapur Rd, New Delhi, T(0)9910-169745. Popular club, with large outdoor area. Hosts some great live acts. Quite a drive.
Smokehouse Bar & Grill (see Eating). Stylish downstairs bar is generally busy, but on a Thu evening it is heaving. Enjoy the bling and some of the most expensive drinks in Delhi.
Stone, Moets Complex, 50 Defence Colony Mkt, T011-4155 0571. Cool and calm bar in busy South Delhi neighbourhood, coffee table books, terrace, decent food, good atmosphere.
Urban Pind, N4, N-block market, GK1, T011-3951 5656. Multi-level bar, with large roof terrace, popular. Hosts a controversial expat/journalist night on Thu with an 'all-you-can-drink' entry fee, unsurprisingly this normally features a lot of drunk foreigners …

⊙ Entertainment

Delhi *p60, maps p58, p68 p72, p75 and p76*
For advance notice of upcoming events see www.delhievents.com. Current listings and reviews can be found in *First City* (monthly, Rs 30), *Time Out* (fortnightly, Rs 30), *Delhi City Info* (fortnightly, free) and *Delhi Diary*(weekly).

Cinema
For programmes see cinema listings in the daily *Delhi Times*.
PVR is a multiplex chain with branches everywhere, mostly screening Hindi movies, including **PVR Plaza** in Connaught Pl.

Music, dance and culture
The Attic, 36 Regal Building, Connaught Pl, T011-5150 3436, www.theatticdelhi.org. Hosts an eclectic range of lectures, films and workshops on art, culture and philosophy.
India Habitat Centre, Lodi Rd, T011-2468 2222. Good programme of lectures, films, exhibitions, concerts, excellent restaurant.

Indian International Centre, 40 Lodhi Estate, Max Mueller Marg, T011-2461 9431, www.iicdelhi.nic.in. Some fantastic debates and performances, well worth checking the 'forthcoming programmes' section of their website.

Triveni Kala Sangam, 205 Tansen Marg (near Mandi House Metro station), T011-2371 8833. Strong programme of photography and art exhibitions, plus an excellent North Indian café.

Son et lumière

Red Fort (see page 62), Apr-Nov 1800-1900 (Hindi), 1930-2030 (English). Entry Rs 50. Tickets available after 1700. Take mosquito cream.

✿ Festivals and events

Delhi p60, maps p58, p68 p72, p75 and p76
For exact dates consult the weekly *Delhi Diary* available at hotels and many shops and offices around town.

Muslim festivals of Ramadan, Id-ul-Fitr, Id-ul-Zuha and Muharram are celebrated according to the lunar calendar.

January
Lohri (13 Jan) The climax of winter, is celebrated with bonfires and singing.
Republic Day Parade (26 Jan) Rajpath. A spectacular fly-past and military march-past, with colourful pageants and tableaux from every state, dances and music. Tickets through travel agents and most hotels, Rs 100. You can see the full dress preview free, usually 2 days before; week-long celebrations during which government buildings are illuminated.
Beating the Retreat (29 Jan) Vijay Chowk, a stirring display by the armed forces' bands marks the end of the Republic Day celebrations.
Martyr's Day (30 Jan) Marks the anniversary of Mahatma Gandhi's death; devotional *bhajans* and Guard of Honour at Raj Ghat.
Kite Flying Festival Makar Sankranti above Palika Bazar, Connaught Pl.

February
Vasant Panchami (2 Feb) Celebrates the first day of spring. The Mughal Gardens are opened to the public for a month.
Delhi Flower Show Purana Qila.
Thyagaraja Festival South Indian music and dance, Vaikunthnath Temple.

March
Basant Ritu Sammelan North Indian music.

April
Amir Khusrau's Birth Anniversary A fair in Nizamuddin celebrates this with prayers and *qawwali* singing.

May
Buddha Jayanti (1st full moon night in May) Marks the birth of the Buddha; prayer meetings are held at Ladakh Buddha Vihara, Ring Rd and Buddha Vihara, Mandir Marg.

August
Janmashtami Celebrates the birth of the Hindu god Krishna. Special *puja*, Lakshmi Narayan Mandir.
Independence Day (15 Aug) Impressive flag-hoisting ceremony and prime ministerial address at the Red Fort.
Vishnu Digambar Sammelan North Indian music and dance festival.

October-November
Gandhi Jayanti (2 Oct) Mahatma Gandhi's birthday; devotional singing at Raj Ghat.
Dasara With over 200 Ramlila performances all over the city recounting the Ramayana story (see page 303).
Ramlila Ballet The ballet, which takes place at Delhi Gate (south of Red Fort) and Ramlila Ground, is performed for a month and is most spectacular. Huge effigies of Ravana are burnt on the 9th night; noisy and flamboyant.
National Drama Festival Shri Ram Centre.
Diwali The festival of lights; lighting of earthen lamps, candles and firework displays.
National Drama Festival Rabindra Bhavan.

December

Christmas (25 Dec) Special Christmas Eve entertainments at major hotels and restaurants; midnight mass and services at all churches.

Ayyappa Temple Festival Ayyappa Swami Temple, Ramakrishnapuram; South Indian music.

New Year's Eve (31 Dec) Celebrated in most hotels and restaurants offering special food and entertainment.

O Shopping

Delhi p60, maps p58, p68 p72, p75 and p76
There are several state emporia around Delhi including the **Cottage Industries Emporium** (CIE), a huge department store of Indian handicrafts, and those along Baba Kharak Singh Marg. It is a convenient way of shopping, as the shelves are packed with a huge choice of goods from all over India, and everything has a fixed price. You may have to pay a little more but it is hassle-free. Shops generally open 1000-1930 (winter 1000-1900). Food stores and chemists stay open later. Most shopping areas are closed on Sun.

Art galleries

Galleries exhibiting contemporary art are listed in *First City*.
Delhi Art Gallery, Hauz Khas Village. A newly expanded gallery with a good range of moderately priced contemporary art.
Espace, 16 Community Centre, New Friends Colony, T011-2683 0499. Group and solo shows by artists from all over India.

Books and music

Hotel booksellers often carry a good selection of imported books about India, though some charge inflated prices. Among those with specialist academic and art books focusing on India are: **Jainson's**, Janpath Hotel; **Krishan**, Claridges; **Khazana**, Taj Mahal and Taj Palace hotels (0900-2000).

Serious bibliophiles should head to the Sun book market in Daryaganj, Old Delhi, when 2 km of pavement are piled high with books – some fantastic bargains to be had.
Bahri & Sons, opposite Main Gate, Khan Market. One among many in the booklovers' heaven of Khan Market. Wide choice.
Bookworm, B-29, Connaught Pl. Wide selection, including art, Indology, fiction.
Central News Agency, P 23/90, Connaught Pl. Carries national and foreign newspapers and journals.
ED Galgotia, 17B, Connaught Pl. Highly recommended.
Full Circle, 5 B, Khan Market, T011-2465 5641. Helpful knowledgeable staff
Jacksons, 5106, Main Bazar, Paharganj, T011-5535 1083. Selection in many languages, mostly second hand at half original price (also buys used books).
Kabaadi Bazaar, Netaji Subhash Marg, Old Delhi. Sun market with thousands of very cheap used books, great for browsing.
Manohar, 4753/23 Ansar Rd, Daryaganj, Old Delhi. A real treasure trove for books on South Asia and India especially, most helpful, knowledgeable staff. Highly recommended.
Motilal Banarsidass, Bungalow Rd, Kamla Nagar (northwest of Old Delhi, opposite Kirorimal College). Far flung, but good for spirituality and Indology.
Munshiram Manoharlal, Nai Sarak, Chandni Chowk. Books on Indology.
Music World, Ansal Plaza (see Malls); also in Plaza PVR, Connaught Pl. Excellent for Indian and Western music, a good place to listen before buying.
New Book Depot, 18B, Connaught Pl. Highly recommended.
Oxford Bookstore, Statesman House, Connaught Pl. Selection of art, Indology, fiction.
People Tree, 8 Regal Building, Parliament St, Connaught Pl. Ecology oriented.
Prabhu & Sons, Hauz Khas Village, well-hidden on 1st-floor balcony down side street, for antiquarian/second-hand books.

Timeless, 46 The Housing Society, 3rd floor and basement, Part 1, South Extension. Full of coffee tables, art books and novels.

Carpets

Carpets can be found in shops in most top hotels and a number round Connaught Pl, not necessarily fixed price. If you are visiting Agra, check out the prices here first.

Clothing

For serious designer-wear that may well break the bank, go to **Lodhi Colony Main Market**. There you'll find: **Bian**, T011-2464 2914, run by New York-based stylist, this is the place to come to ogle at Swarovski crystal-studded saris; and **Pratap**, T011-2463 8788, for sleek designs in an industrial-chic gallery.

For other designer wear, try **Hauz Khas Village, Sunder Nagar Market** near the Oberoi hotel, or the Crescent arcade near the Qutab Minar.

For inexpensive (Western and Indian) clothes, try shops along Janpath and between Sansad Marg and Janpath; you can bargain down 50%.

The **Central Cottage Industries Emporium** (see below) has a good selection of clothing and fabrics. The **Khadi shop** (see Emporia, below) has Indian-style clothing. **Fab India**, 14N-Gt Kailash I (also in B-Block Connaught Pl, Khan Market and Vasant Kunj). Excellent shirts, Nehru jackets, *salwar kameez*, linen, furnishing fabrics and furniture.

Earthenware

Unglazed earthenware *khumba matkas* (water pots) are sold round New Delhi Railway Station (workshops behind main road).

Emporia

Most open 1000-1800 (close 1330-1400). **Central Cottage Industries Emporium**, corner of Janpath and Tolstoy Marg. Offers hassle-free shopping, exchange counter (spend at least 50% of amount to be cashed, take bills to till and use TCs/credit card to

pay), gift wrapping, will pack and post overseas; best if you are short of time. **Dilli Haat**, opposite INA Market. Rs 10, 1100-2200. Well-designed open-air complex with rows of brick alcoves for craft stalls from different states; local craftsmen's outlets (bargaining obligatory), occasional fairs (tribal art, textiles, etc). Also good regional food – hygienic, safe, weighted towards non-vegetarian. Pleasant, quiet, clean (no smoking) and uncrowded, not too much hassle. **Khadi Gramodyog Bhawan**, near the Regal building, Baba Kharak Singh Marg. For inexpensive homespun cotton *kurta pajama* (loose shirt and trousers), cotton/silk waistcoats, fabrics and Jaipuri paintings. **Khazana**, Taj Mahal and Taj Palace hotels (daily 0900-2000). High class. **Santushti**, Chanakyapuri, opposite **Hotel Samrat**. Mon-Sat 1000-1800, some shops close for lunch. Attractive a/c units in a garden setting, hassle free. Shops sell good-quality clothes, crafts, linen, saris, silver, etc. **Basil and Thyme** serves trendy Western snacks.

Food

Aap ki Pasand, opposite Golcha cinema, Netaji Subhash Marg, Old Delhi. Excellent place to taste and buy a variety of Indian teas. **Bhim Sen's**, Bengali Market, end of Tansen Marg, near Connaught Pl. For some of the best, freshest (hence safest) Indian sweets. **Darjeeling Tea Bureau**, Kaka Nagar Market (opposite Delhi Golf Club), nathmulls@goldentipstea.com. Charming, reliable and good selection. Highly recommended. **Haldiram's**, Chandni Chowk near Metro. Wide selection of sweet and salty snack foods. **Khari Baoli**, Chandni Chowk, lined with colourful shops. Spices and dried fruit, etc. MDH, Everest brands are reliable. **Steak House**, Jorbagh Market. Cold meats, cheeses, yoghurts.

Jewellery

Traditional silver and goldsmiths in Dariba Kalan, off Chandni Chowk (north of Jama

Masjid). Cheap bangles and along Janpath; also at Hanuman Mandir, Gt Kailash I, N-Block. Also Sunder Nagar market. Bank St in Karol Bagh is recommended for gold.

Jewel Mine, 12A Palika Bazar. Has silver, beads, semi-precious stones and fair prices.

Silverline, 18 Babar Rd, Bengali Market, T011-2335 0454. Contemporary silver jewellery at wholesale prices.

Leather

Cheap sandals from stalls on Janpath (Rs 100). Yashwant Place Market next to Chanakya Cinema Hall, Chanakyapuri. **Khan Market** (see below) sells leather goods and shoes. **Da Milano**, South Extension and Khan Market. **Hidesign**, G49, Connaught Pl. High class.

Markets and malls

Beware of pickpockets in markets and malls.

Ansal Plaza, HUDCO, Khelgaon Marg (south of South Extension). Delhi's first European-style shopping mall. Very smart, lots of chains.

Basant Lok, Vasant Vihar. Has a few upmarket shops attracting the young.

Hauz Khas village, South Delhi. Authentic, old village houses converted into designer shops selling handicrafts, ceramics, antiques and furniture in addition to luxury wear. Many are expensive, but some are good value. A good place to pick up old Hindi film posters. You will also find art galleries and restaurants.

Jorbagh, Gt Kailash Pt I-M. Western travellers hankering for the familiar, and prepared to pay the price, will find a good range of food and toiletries here.

Khan Market, South Delhi. Great bookshops, cafés, restaurants and boutiques. Full of expats so expect expat prices.

Main Bazar, Paharganj. Good range of food and toiletries for Westerners with enough cash.

Sarojini Nagar, South Delhi. Daily necessities as well as cheap fabric and clothing. Come for incredible bargains. This is where a lot of the Western brands dump their export surplus or end-of-line clothes. Haggle hard.

Select City Walk, Saket. An enormous, glitzy mall for the ultimate in upmarket shopping. Lots of chains, cinemas, etc.

South Extension, South Delhi. Good for clothes, shoes, jewellery, music, etc.

Sunder Nagar, South Delhi. Has a few shops selling Indian handicrafts and jewellery (precious and semi-precious); some quite original.

Tibetan Market, North Delhi. Stalls along Janpath have plenty of curios – most are new but rapidly aged to look authentic.

Tailoring

Small shops charge around Rs 100-150 to copy a dress or shirt; trousers Rs 150-200. **Khan Market** has several tailors and cloth stores. **Shankar Market**, near Connaught Pl, has good suiting, corduroys, denim, etc. **Mohan Singh Place**, Baba Kharak Singh Mg opposite the government emporia. Hundreds of tailors; insist on a good job, and allow 24 hrs for stitching. Nearly all big hotels have upmarket boutiques and also fabric/tailor's shops (some may allow fabric purchased elsewhere).

▲ Activities and tours

Delhi *p60, maps p58, p68 p72, p75 and p76*
Body and soul
Integral Yoga, Sri Aurobindo Ashram, Aurobindo Marg, T011-2656 7863. Regular yoga classes (Tue-Thu and Sat 0645-0745 and 1700-1800) in *asana* (postures), *pranayama* (breathing techniques) and relaxation.

Laughter Club of Delhi, various locations, T011-2721 7164. Simple yogic breathing techniques combined with uproarious laughter. Clubs meet early morning in parks throughout the city – a bright start to the day.

Morarji Desai National Institute of Yoga, 68 Ashoka Rd, T011-2371 8301. Classes run throughout the day, some aimed at particular physical ailments.

Yogalife, Shapur Jat main market,
T(0)9811-863332, www.yogalife.org.
Closed Mon. Bright, friendly centre.

Sport
Delhi Gymkhana Club, 2 Safdarjang Rd,
T011-2301 5533. Mostly for government
and defence personnel, squash, tennis,
swimming, bar and restaurant.
Pacific Sports Complex, next to Central
School, Andrews Ganj, T011-6507 9552. Can
be hard to find – it's near Lady Sri Ram College.
Cheap and cheerful outdoor pool and gym. A
perfect remedy for Delhi's sweltering summers.
Siri Fort Club, August Kranti Marg, New Delhi,
near Siri Fort Auditorium, T011-2649 7482. You
can get temporary membership – wonderful
outdoor swimming pool (summer only), tennis,
squash, basketball, reiki, taekwando, etc.

Tours and tour operators
Local sightseeing tours can be arranged
through approved travel agents and tour
operators. For approved tourist guides/
agencies contact Government of India Tourist
Office and travel agents. There are many small
agents, eg opposite New Delhi Railway Station,
seemingly offer unusual itineraries, but their
standards can't be guaranteed and their
rates are not significantly lower.
Rates Delhi only, half day Rs 90, full day
Rs 160. **India Tourism Development
Corporation (ITDC)** and **Delhi Tourism**
(see page 61) both run city sightseeing tours.
Combining Old and New Delhi tours on
the same day can be very tiring. A/c coaches
are particularly recommended during the
summer months. The price includes transport
and guide services, but all are whistle-stop
tours. Check whether entrance fees to many
sights are included in the price of the tour.
A group of 3 or 4 people could consider
hiring a car and doing the tour at their
own pace. Another alternative is to hire an
auto-rickshaw for the day (around Rs 200).
It will entail visiting gift shops for the driver to
get a commission, but you don't have to buy.

Delhi Tourism tours
Departs from **Delhi Tourism**, Baba
Kharak Singh Mg near State Govt Emporia,
T011-2336 3607, www.delhitourism.nic.in.
Book a day in advance. Check time.
Evening Tour (Tue-Sun 1830-2200): Rajpath,
India Gate, Kotla Firoz Shah, Purana Qila,
son et lumière (Red Fort). Rs 150.
New Delhi Tour (0900-1400): Jantar Mantar,
Qutb Minar, Lakshmi Narayan Temple, Baha'i
Temple (Safdarjang's Tomb on Mon only).
Old Delhi Tour (1415-1715): Jama Masjid,
Red Fort, Raj Ghat, Humayun's Tomb.
Both Rs 100 plus entry fees.

ITDC Tours
Guides are generally good but tours are rushed,
T011-2332 0331. Tickets can be booked from
Hotel Indraprastha, T011-2334 4511.
New Delhi Tour: departs from L-1
Connaught Circus and **Hotel Indraprastha**
(0800-1330), Rs 125 (a/c coach): Jantar
Mantar, Lakshmi Narayan Temple, India
Gate,Nehru Pavilion, Pragati Maidan (closed
Mon), Humayun's Tomb, Qutb Minar.
Old Delhi Tour: departs Hotel Indraprastha.
(1400-1700), Rs 100: Kotla Firoz Shah, Raj Ghat,
Shantivana, Jama Masjid and Red Fort.

Taj Mahal tours
Many companies offer coach tours to Agra
(eg **ITDC**, from L1 Connaught Circus, Sat-Thu
0630-2200, Rs 600, a/c coach). However,
travelling by road is slow and uncomfortable;
by car, allow at least 4 hrs each way. Train is
a better option: either *Shatabdi* or *Taj Express*,
but book early.

Tour operators
There are many operators offering tours,
ticketing, reservations, etc, for travel across
India. Many are around Connaught Circus,
Parharganj, Rajendra Place and Nehru
Place. Most belong to special associations
(IATA, PATA) for complaints.
Capital City Travels and Tours, 36 Arakashan
Rd, Ram Nagar, behind Sheila Cinema,

T011-2956 2097, www.tourism-india.com. Fixed and tailor-made tours throughout India.

Creative Travel, 27-30 Creative Plaza, Nanak Pura, Moti Bagh, T011-2687 2257, www.travel 2india.com. Efficient, reliable, helpful.

Highland, N-29 Middle Circus, Connaught Pl, T011-2331 8236, highlandtravels@usa.net. Friendly, competent and reasonably priced.

Ibex Expeditions, 30 Community Centre East of Kailash, New Delhi, T011-2682 8479, www.ibexexpeditions.com. Offers a wide range of tours and ticketing, etc.

Indebo India, 116-117 Aurobindo Pl, Hauz Khas, New Delhi, www.indebo.com. Customized tours and travel-related services throughout India.

India Tours International, 206 Victoria Cross, 4/54-55 WEA, Saraswati Marg, Karol Bag, New Delhi, T011-2576 2190, www.indiatours web.com. Quality tours, hotels and resorts.

Namaste Voyages Pvt Ltd, I-Block 28G/F South City, 2 Gurgaon, 122001, T0124-221 9330, www.namastevoyages.com. Specializes in tailor-made tours, tribal, treks, theme voyages.

Paradise Holidays, 312 Ansals Classique Tower, Rajouri Garden, New Delhi, T+91-011-4552 0735, www.paradiseholidays.com. Wide range of tailor-made tours, from cultural to wildlife.

Potala Tours & Travels, 101 Antriksh Bhavan, 22 K Ghandi Marg, T011-2373 1620, www.potalatours.com. Excellent staff, car tours, ticketing. Recommended.

Services International, IATA Code 14-3 4105 1, 25/8 Guru House, Old Rajinder Nagar,

New Delhi, T011-41050560/70/80/90, www.india-travelpackages.com. Tours throughout India.

Shanti Travel, F-189/1A Main Rd Savitri Nagar, T011-4607 7800, www.shantitravel.com. Delhi-based travel agency specializing in tailor-made tours throughout India.

Wanderlust Travels Pvt Ltd, G-18, 2nd floor, Masjid Moth, Greater Kailash Part-II, T011- 4053 7116, www.wanderlustindia.com. Tailor-made tours throughout India, groups and individuals.

Walking tours

Chor Bizarre, Hotel Broadway, T011-2327 3821. Special walking tours of Old Delhi, with good lunch, 0930-1330, 1300-1630, Rs 350 each, Rs 400 for both.

Master Guest House (see Sleeping, page 89). Highly recommended walking tours for a more intimate experience of Delhi.

Salaam Baalak Trust, T(0)9873-130383, www.salaambaalaktrust.com. NGO-run tours of New Delhi station and the streets around it, guided by Javed, himself a former street child. Your Rs 200 goes to support the charity's work with street children.

⊖ Transport

Delhi *p60, maps p58, p68 p72, p75 and p76*
Air
All flights arrive at **Indira Gandhi International Airport**, 20 km south of Connaught Pl. Terminal 1 (Domestic) enquiries T011-2567

5126; Terminal 2 (International) T011-2565 2011. At check-in, be sure to tag your hand luggage, and make sure it is stamped after security check.

The domestic air industry is in a period of massive growth, so check a 3rd-party site such as www.flightraja.com for the latest flight schedules and prices. Delhi has connections (many direct) with the following domestic destinations:

Daily flights Ahmedabad; Amritsar; Bagdogra (for Darjeeling); Bengaluru (Bangalore); Bhopal; Bhubaneshwar; Kolkata; Chandigarh; Chennai (Madras); Cochin; Goa; Guwahati; Hyderabad; Jaipur; Jammu; Kathmandu; Khajuraho; Kullu; Lucknow; Mumbai (Bombay); Nagpur; Patna; Pune; Raipur; Rajkot; Ranchi; Srinagar; Trivandrum; Udaipur; Vadodara; Varanasi.

Non-daily flights Aurangabad; Dhaka; Dibrugarh; Gwalior; Indore; Imphal; Jodhpur; Leh; Lucknow; Paro; Shimla; Udaipur.

The most extensive networks are with **Indian Airlines,** T140/T011-2562 2220, www.indianairlines.in; **Jet Airways,** T011-3989 3333, airport T011-2567 5404, www.jetairways.com; and **Air Deccan,** T011-3900 8888, www.airdeccan.net. Other budget airlines fly to the most popular destinations. Many domestic airlines have their offices in N-Block, Connaught Pl, including: **Jet Airways, Air Deccan, Kingfisher,** T011-2844 7700, www.flykingfisher.com, and **Spicejet,** T(0)9871-803333, www.spicejet.com. Other airlines serving Delhi include **Go Air,** T(0)9223-222111, and **Jagsons,** T011-2372 1593, for select Himalayan airports.

For a complete list of international airline offices see *First City* magazine.

Transport to and from the airport

There is a booth just outside 'Arrivals' at the International and Domestic terminals for the **bus** services. It is a safe, economical option. A free **shuttle** runs between the 2 terminals every 30 mins during the day. Some hotel buses leave from the Domestic terminal.

Bus 780 runs between the **airport** and New Delhi Railway Station.

The International and Domestic terminals have **pre-paid taxi** counters outside the baggage hall (3 price categories) which ensure that you pay the right amount (give your name, exact destination and number of items of luggage). Most expensive are white 'DLZ' **limousines** and then white 'DLY' **luxury taxis.** Cheapest are 'DLT' **ordinary Delhi taxis** (black with yellow top Ambassador/Fiat cars and vans, often very old). 'DLY' taxis charge 3 times the DLT price. A 'Welcome' desk by the baggage reclamation offers expensive taxis only. Take your receipt to the ticket counter outside to find your taxi and give it to the driver when you reach the destination; you don't need to tip, although they will ask. From the International terminal DLT taxis charge about Rs 240 for the town centre (Connaught Pl area); night charges double 2300-0500. Rates from the Domestic terminal are slightly lower.

Bus
Local

The city bus service run by the **Delhi Transport Corporation** (DTC) connects all important points in the city and has more than 300 routes. Information is available at www.dtc.nic.in, at DTC assistance booths and at all major bus stops. Don't be afraid to ask conductors or fellow passengers. Buses are often hopelessly overcrowded so only use off-peak.

Long distance

Delhi is linked to most major centres in North India. Services are provided by **Delhi Transport Corporation** (DTC) and State Roadways of neighbouring states from various **Inter-State Bus Termini** (ISBT). Allow at least 30 mins for buying a ticket and finding the right bus.

Kashmere Gate, north of Old Delhi, T011-2296 0290 (general enquiries), is the main terminus, with a restaurant, left luggage, bank (Mon-Fri 1000-1400; Sat 1000-1200), post office (Mon-Sat 0800-

1700) and telephones (includes international calls). The following operators run services to neighbouring states from here: **Delhi Transport Corp**, T011-2386 5181. **Haryana Roadways**, T011-2296 1262; daily to **Agra** (5-6 hrs, quicker by rail), **Chandigarh** (5 hrs), **Jaipur** (Rs 150, 6½ hrs), **Mathura**, etc. **Himachal Roadways**, T011-2296 6725; twice daily to **Dharamshala** (12 hrs), **Manali** (15 hrs), **Shimla** (10 hrs), etc. **J&K Roadways**, T011-2332 4511; **Punjab Roadways**, T011-2296 7892, to **Amritsar**, **Chandigarh**, **Jammu**, **Pathankot**. **UP Roadways**, T011-2296 8709, city office at Ajmeri Gate, T011-2323 5367; to **Almora** (5 hrs), **Dehradun**, **Haridwar**, **Mussoorie**, **Gorakhpur**, **Kanpur**, **Jhansi**, **Lucknow**, **Nainital**, **Varanasi**.

Sarai Kale Khan Ring Rd, smaller terminal near Nizamuddin Railway Station, T011-2469 8343 (general enquiries), for buses to Haryana, Rajasthan and UP: **Haryana Roadways**, T011-2435 1084. **Rajasthan Roadways**, T011-2435 3731. For **Agra**, **Mathura** and **Vrindavan**; **Ajmer**; **Alwar**; **Bharatpur** (5 hrs); **Bikaner** (11 hrs); **Gwalior**; **Jaipur**; **Jodhpur**; **Pushkar**; **Udaipur**, etc.

Anand Vihar, east side of Yamuna River, T011-2214 8097, for buses to Uttar Pradesh, Uttarakhand and Himachal Pradesh.

Bikaner House, Pandara Rd (south of India Gate), T011-2338 1884; for several 'De luxe' a/c buses to **Jaipur** (6 hrs, Rs 300); ask for 'direct' bus (some buses stop at Amber for a tour of the fort). Also to **Udaipur** via **Ajmer**, and to **Jodhpur**.

HPTDC, Chandralok Bldg, 36 Janpath, T011-2332 5320, hptdcdelhi@hub.nic.in, runs a/c Volvo and Sleeper buses to **Manali** and **Dharamshala**. Of the myriad private bus operators, **Raj National Express** has by far the best buses, and highest prices.

To Nepal See also page 110. Direct private buses run to **Kathmandu**, though the 36-hr journey is quite exhausting. A much shorter route to Nepal is to the Indian border town of **Banbassa** via Tanakpur or Khatima (more relaxed, good hotels) and crossing to the western Nepal border town of Mahendranagar. UP Roadways and private buses for Banbessa leave daily from Anand Vihar bus station and take around 9 hrs (but check details carefully). The onward journey to Kathmandu is about 20 hrs; it is best done via Royal Bardia National Park or Nepalganj.

To Pakistan A direct 'Friendship' bus to **Lahore** runs on Tue, Wed, Fri and Sat at 0600, departing from Ambedkar Stadium terminal, near Delhi Gate, Old Delhi (reserve ahead, T011-2331 8180 (14 hrs, Rs 1250), for Indians with valid visas and relations in Pakistan, and for Pakistanis.

Car hire
The main roads out of Delhi are very heavily congested; the best time to leave is in the very early morning.

Hiring a car is an excellent way of getting about town either for sightseeing or if you have several journeys to make during the day.

Full day local use with driver (non a/c) is about Rs 700-800, 80 km/8 hrs, driver overnight *bata* Rs 150 per day; self-drive 24 hrs/150 km Rs 1200. Airport to city centre Rs 400-500. To Jaipur, about Rs 3000; return Rs 5400. The **Tourist Office**, 88 Janpath, has a list of approved agents.
Cozy Travels, N1 BMC House, Middle Circle, Connaught Pl, T011-2331 1593, cozytravels@vsnl.net.com. For Ambassador or similar, Rs 650 non a/c, Rs 850 a/c.
Metropole Tourist Service, 244 Defence Flyover Market, T011-2431 2212, T(0)9810-277699, www.metrovista.co.in. Car/jeep (US$30-40 per day), safe, reliable and recommended, also hotel bookings and can help arrange homestays around Delhi.
Mohindra Tourist Taxis, Vasant Vihar Block D, T011-2614 3188. "Excellent service, safe driving".
Western Court Tourist Taxis, 36 Janpath, Hotel Imperial, T011-2336 8036. Helpful.

Taxi tips

First-time visitors can be vulnerable to exploitation by taxi drivers at the airport. If arriving at night, you are very strongly advised to have a destination in mind and get a pre-paid taxi. Be firm about being dropped at the hotel of your choice and insist that you have a reservation; you can always change hotels the next day if you are unhappy. Don't admit to being a first-time visitor.

If you don't take a pre-paid taxi, the driver will demand an inflated fare.

He may insist that the hotel you want to go to has closed or is full and will suggest one where he will get a commission (and you will be overcharged).

Some travellers have been told that the city was unsafe with street fighting, police barricades and curfews and have then been taken to Agra or Jaipur. In the event of taxi trouble, be seen to note down the licence plate number and threaten to report the driver to the police; if you need to do this, the number is T011-2331 9334.

Metro

The sparkling new Metro system (T011-2436 5202, www.delhimetrorail.com), though still some way from providing a full city-wide network, is set to revolutionize transport within Delhi. So far 3 lines are operating:
Line 1 (Red) Running northwest to east, of limited use to visitors;
Line 2 (Yellow) Running north-south through the centre from Vishwavidyalaya to Central Secretariat via Kashmere Gate, Chandni Chowk, New Delhi Station and Connaught Pl (Rajiv Chowk); and
Line 3 (Blue) Intersecting with Line 2 at Rajiv Chowk and running west through Paharganj (RK Ashram station) and Karol Bagh.

Trains run 0600-2200. Fares are charged by distance: tokens for individual journeys cost Rs 6-19. **Smart Cards**, Rs 100, Rs 200 and Rs 500, save queuing and money. **Tourist Cards** valid for 1 or 3 days (Rs 70/200) are useful if you plan to make many journeys. Luggage is limited to 15 kg; guards may not allow big backpacks on board. There's a Rs 50 fine for riding on the roof.

Motorcycle hire

Chawla Motorcycles, 1770, Shri Kissan Dass Marg, Naiwali Gali, is very reliable, trustworthy, highly recommended for restoring classic bikes.

Ess Aar Motors, Jhandewalan Extn, west of Paharganj, T011-2367 8836; and **Nanna Motors**, 112 Press Rd (east of Connaught Circus), T011-2335 1769. Both recommended for buying Enfields, very helpful.

Rickshaw

Auto-rickshaws Widely available at about half the cost of taxis (Rs 4 per km). Normal capacity for foreigners is 2 people (3rd person extra); very few will use meter so agree fare in advance; see www.delhigovt.nic.in for a 'fare calculator' – slightly out of date. Expect to pay Rs 20 for the shortest journeys. Allow Rs 120 for 2 hrs' sightseeing/shopping. It is best to walk away from hotels and tourist centres to look for an auto.

Cycle-rickshaws Available in the Old City. Be prepared to bargain: Chandni Chowk Metro to Red Fort Rs 8-10. They are not allowed into Connaught Pl.

Taxi

Yellow-top taxis, which run on compressed natural gas, are readily available at taxi stands or you can hail one on the road. Meters should start at Rs 13; ask for the conversion card. Add 25% at night (2300-0500) plus Rs 5 for each piece of luggage over 20 kg. **Easy Cabs**, T011-4343 4343. Runs clean a/c cars and claim to pick up anywhere within 15 mins; Rs 15 per km.

Train

Delhi stations from which trains originate have codes: **OD** – Old Delhi, **ND** – New Delhi, **HN** – Hazrat Nizamuddin, **DSR** – Delhi Sarai Rohilla. The publication *Trains at a Glance'* (Rs 30) lists important trains across India, available at some stations, book shops and newsagents,

New Delhi Railway Station and **Hazrat Nizamuddin Station** (500 m north and 5 km southeast of Connaught Pl respectively) connect Delhi with most major destinations. The latter has many important southbound trains. **Old Delhi Station**, 6 km north of the centre, has broad and metre-gauge trains. **Delhi Sarai Rohilla**, northeast of CP, serves Rajasthan.

Train enquiries T131. Reservations T1330. Each station has a computerized reservation counter where you can book any Mail or Express train in India. Allow time (1-2 hrs) and be prepared to be very patient as it can be a nightmare. Have your train's name and number ready and, if necessary, politely muscle your way in to get a reservation form before lining up. Separate queues for ladies and for credit card payments can save barging. Smaller suburban booking offices (eg Sarojini Nagar) are less fraught and worth the detour; alternatively, you can use a recommended travel agent for tickets and pay Rs 50-100 fee.

International Tourist Bureau (ITB), 1st floor, Main Building, New Delhi Station, T011-2340 5156, Mon-Fri 0930-1630, Sat 0930-1430, provides assistance with planning and booking journeys, for foreigners only; efficient and helpful if slow. You need your passport; pay in US$, or rupees (with an encashment certificate/ATM receipt). Those with **Indrail** passes should confirm bookings here. At the time of writing the station was under renovation, so the layout may change, but be wary of rickshaw drivers/travel agents who tell you the ITB has closed or moved elsewhere. (There are also counters for foreigners and NRIs at **Delhi Tourism**, N-36 Connaught Pl, 1000-1700, Mon-Sat, and at the airport; quick and efficient.)

New Delhi and Hazrat Nizamuddin stations have pre-paid taxi and rickshaw counters with official rates per km posted: expect to pay around Rs 30 for up to 4 km. Authorized *coolies* (porters), wear red shirts and white *dhotis;* agree the charge, around Rs 20 per bag, before engaging one. For left luggage, you need a secure lock and chain.

Some principal services are: **Agra**: *Shatabdi Exp 2002*, ND 0615, 2 hrs; *Taj Exp 2280*, HN, 0715, 2¾ hrs. **Ahmedabad**: *Rajdhani Exp 2958, ND, 1935*, Wed-Mon, 14½ hrs. **Amritsar**: *Shatabdi Exp, 2013*, ND, 1630, 6 hrs; *New Delhi-Amritsar Exp 2459*, ND, 1340, 8 hrs; *Shan-e-Punjab Exp 2497*, ND, 0650, 7½ hrs. **Bengaluru (Bangalore)**: *Rajdhani Exp 2430*, Mon, Tue, Fri, Sat, HN, 2050, 34 hrs; **Bhubaneswar**: *Rajdhani Exp 2422*, ND, 1715, 24 hrs. **Bhopal**: *Shatabdi Exp 2002*, ND, 0615, 8¾ hrs. **Bikaner**: *Bikaner Exp 2463*, Wed, Fri, Sun, DSR, 0835, 10¼ hrs. **Chandigarh**: *Shatabdi Exp 2011*, ND, 0740, 3½ hrs; *Shatabdi Exp 2005*, ND, 1715, 3 hrs. **Chennai**: *Rajdhani Exp, 2434*, Wed, Fri, HN, 1600, 29 hrs; *GT Exp 2616*, ND, 1840, 36¼ hrs; *Tamil Nadu Exp 2622*, ND, 2230, 33¼ hrs. **Dehradun**: *Shatabdi Exp 2017*, ND, 0655, 5¾ hrs. **Goa**: see Madgaon, below. **Guwahati**: *Rajdhani Exp 2424*, ND, Mon, Tue, Wed, Fri, Sat, 1400, 28 hrs; *Rajdhani Exp 2436*, ND, Thu, Sun, 0930, 32 hrs. **Gwalior**: *Shatabdi Exp 2002*, ND, 0615, 3¼ hrs. **Haridwar**: *Shatabdi Exp 2017*, ND, 0655, 4¼ hrs; *Mussoorie Exp 4041*, DSR, 2110, 8¾ hrs. **Jabalpur**: *Gondwana Exp 2412*, HN, 1525, 16 hrs. **Jaipur**: *Shatabdi Exp 2015*, Thu-Tue, ND, 0610, 4¾ hrs; *Ashram Exp 2916*, OD, 1505, 5 hrs. **Jammu**: *Rajdhani Exp 2425*, ND, Fri, 2100, 9½ hrs. **Jhansi**: *Shatabdi Exp 2002*, ND, 0615, 4½ hrs; *Lakshadweep Exp 2618*, HN, 0920, 6 hrs. **Jodhpur**: *Mandore Exp 2461*, OD, 2045, 11 hrs. **Kalka**: see Shimla, below. **Kanpur**: *Shatabdi Exp 2004*, ND, 0615, 5 hrs. **Kolkata**: *Rajdhani Exp 2302*, ND, 1700, 17½ hrs (via Gaya; except Fri, *2306* via Patna, 19½ hrs); *Kalka-Howrah Mail 2312*,

OD, 0730, 24 hrs. **Lucknow**: *Shatabdi Exp 2004*, ND, 0615, 6½ hrs. **Madgaon** (Goa): *Rajdhani Exp 2432*, Tue, Sun, HN, 1105, 26 hrs. **Mathura**: *Taj Exp 2280*, HN, 0715, 2 hrs. **Mumbai** (**Central**): *Rajdhani Exp 2952*, ND, 1630, 16 hrs; *Paschim Exp 2926*, ND, 1655, 22 hrs; *Golden Temple Mail 2904*, ND, 0750, 22 hrs. **New Jalpaiguri** (for **Darjeeling**): *Rajdhani Exp 2424*, Mon-Wed, Fri, Sat, ND, 1400, 21½ hrs. **Patna**: *NE Exp 5622*, ND, 0640, 17 hrs. **Secunderabad** *Rajdhani Exp 2430*, Mon, Tue, Fri, Sat (2438 Sun), HN, 2050, 22 hrs. **Shimla**: to Kalka on *Himalayan Queen 4095*, ND, 0600, 5¼ hrs, or *Shatabdi Exp 2011*, ND, 0740, 4¼ hrs; change to narrow gauge *255*, 1210, total 12 hrs. **Thiruvanantapuram**: *Rajdhani Exp 2432*, Sun, Tue, HN, 1105, 31 hrs. **Udaipur**: *Mewar Exp 2963*, HN, 1900, 12 hrs. **Varanasi** (take extra care with possessions): *Poorva Exp 2382*, Mon, Tue, Fri, ND, 1625, 12¼ hrs; *Farakka Exp 3414*, Mon, Wed, Sat (*3484* other days), OD, 12145, 18 hrs.

◐ Directory

Delhi *p60, maps p58, p68 p72, p75 and p76*
Banks Open Mon-Fri 1000-1400, Sat 1000-1200. It is usually quicker to change foreign cash and TCs at hotels. ATMs for International Visa/ Plus/Cirrus/Maestro card-holders at HDFC, HSBC, Standard Chartered, UTI, State Bank of India, ICICI and Citibank all over Delhi. Foreign banks and money changers include: American Express, A-Block Connaught Pl, excellent; small branch in Paharganj; Standard Chartered Grindlays, 15 K Gandhi Marg; Thomas Cook, Hotel Imperial, Janpath; New Delhi Railway station (24 hrs). Indian banks (dealing in foreign exchange) open 24 hrs: Central Bank of India, Ashok Hotel, State Bank of India, Palam Airport. Swift transfers from overseas through Western Union, SITA, F-12, Connaught Pl.
Embassies and consulates Most are in the diplomatic enclave/ Chanakyapuri.

Australia, 1/50-G Shantipath, T011-4139 9900. Canada, 7-8 Shantipath, T011-4178 2000. France, 2/50-E Shantipath, T011-2419 6100. Ireland, 230 Jor Bagh, T011-2462 6733. Netherlands, 6/50F Shantipath, T011-2419 7600. New Zealand, 50-N Nyaya Marg, T011-688 3170. South Africa, B/18 Vasant Marg, T011-2614 4911. UK, Shantipath, T011-2419 2100. USA, Shantipath, T011-2419 8000.
Medical services Ambulance (24 hrs): T102. Hospitals: Embassies and high commissions have lists of recommended doctors and dentists. Doctors approved by IAMAT (International Association for Medical Assistance to Travellers) are listed in a directory. Casualty and emergency wards in both private and government hospitals are open 24 hrs. Ram Manohar Lohia, Willingdon Crescent, T011-2336 5525, 24-hr A&E. Bara Hindu Rao, Sabzi Mandi, T011-2391 9476. JP Narayan, J Nehru Marg, Delhi Gate, T011-2323 2400. Safdarjang General, Sri Aurobindo Marg, T011-2616 5060. S Kripalani, Panchkuin Rd, T011-2336 3728. Chemists: Many hospitals have 24-hr services: Hindu Rao Hospital, Sabzi Mandi; Ram Manohar Lohia Hospital, Willingdon Crescent; S Kripalani Hospital, Panchkuin Rd. In Connaught Pl: Nath Brothers, G-2, off Marina Arcade; Chemico, H-45.
Post Stamps are often available from the reception in the larger hotels. Speedpost from 36 centres. Head post offices at Sansad Marg, Mon-Sat 1000-1830, Eastern Court, Janpath, 24 hrs, Connaught Pl, A-Block, Mon-Sat 1000-1700 (parcel packing service outside). New Delhi GPO at Ashoka Place, southwest of Connaught Pl, 24 hrs, poste restante available; make sure senders specify 'New Delhi 110001'; collect from the counter behind sorting office, Mon-Fri 0900-1700, Sat 0900-1300. Take your passport.
Useful contacts Fire: T101. Foreigners' Registration Office: East Block-VIII, Level 2, Sector 1, RK Puram, T011-2671 1443. Police: T100.

Agra and around

→ *Colour map 5, C3. Phone code: 0562. Population: 1.3 million.*

The romance of what is arguably the world's most famous building still astonishes in its power. In addition to the Taj Mahal, Agra also houses the great monuments of the Red Fort and the I'timad-ud-Daulah, but to experience their beauty you have to endure the less attractive sides of one of India's least prepossessing towns. A big industrial city, the monuments are often covered in a haze of polluted air, while visitors may be subjected to a barrage of high-power selling. Despite it all, the experience is unmissable. The city is also the convenient gateway to the wonderful, abandoned capital of Fatehpur Sikri and some of Hinduism's most holy sites.▸▸ *For listings, see pages 125-130.*

Ins and outs

Getting there By far the best way to arrive is by the *Shatubdi Express* train from Delhi, which is much faster than travelling by car and infinitely more comfortable than the frequent 'express' buses, which can take five tiring hours.

Getting around Buses run a regular service between the station, bus stands and the main sites. See Entrances, page 110. Cycle-rickshaws, autos and taxis can be hired to venture further afield, or hire bike if it's not too hot.▸▸ *See Transport, page 129.*

Tourist information **Government of India tourist office** ① *191 The Mall, T0562-222 6378.* Guides available (Rs 100), helpful and friendly. **UPTDC**① *64 Taj Rd, T0562-222 6431, also at Agra Cantt, T0562-242 1204,* and **Tourist Bungalow** ① *Raja-ki-Mandi, T0562-285 0120.* **UP Tours**① *Taj Khema, Taj East Gate, T0562-233 0140.*

Note that there is an **Agra Development Authority Tax** of Rs 500 levied on each day you visit the Taj Mahal, with lesser fees for the Red Fort, Fatehpur Sikri and other attractions. This is in addition to the individual entry fees.

Climate The best time to visit is between November and March.

History

With minor interruptions Agra alternated with Delhi as the capital of the Mughal Empire. **Sikander Lodi** seized it from a rebellious governor and made it his capital in 1501. He died in Agra but is buried in Delhi (see page 78). Agra was Babur's capital. He is believed to have laid out a pleasure garden on the east bank of the River Yamuna and his son Humayun built a mosque here in 1530. **Akbar** lived in Agra in the early years of his reign. Ralph Fitch, the English Elizabethan traveller, described a "magnificent city, with broad streets and tall buildings". He also saw Akbar's new capital at Fatehpur Sikri, 40 km west, describing a route lined all the way with stalls and markets. Akbar moved his capital again to Lahore, before returning to Agra in 1599, where he spent the last six years of his life. **Jahangir** left Agra for Kashmir in 1618 and never returned. Despite modifying the Red Fort and building the Taj Mahal, **Shah Jahan** also moved away in 1638 to his new city Shah Jahanabad in Delhi, though he returned in 1650, taken prisoner by his son Aurangzeb and left to spend his last days in the Red Fort. It was **Aurangzeb**, the last of the Great Mughals, who moved the seat of government permanently to Delhi. In the 18th century Agra suffered at the hands of the Jats, was taken, lost and retaken by the Marathas who, in turn, were ousted by the British in 1803. It was the centre of much fighting in the 'Uprising' and was the administrative centre of the Northwest Provinces and Oudh until that too was transferred to Allahabad in 1877.

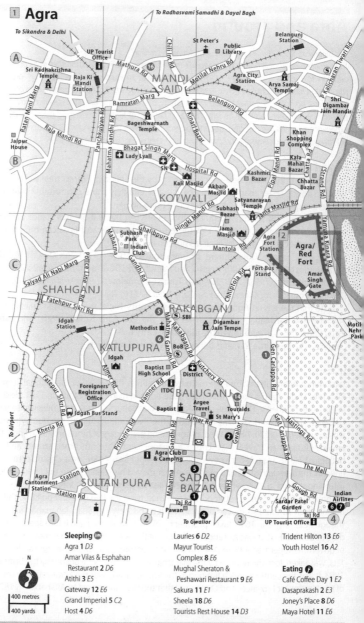

1 Agra

To Radhasvami Samadhi & Dayal Bagh

To Sikandra & Delhi

St Peter's
Public Library

Belangunj Station

UP Tourist Office

Sri Radhakrishna Temple

Raja Ki Mandi Station

MANDI SAID

Agra City Station

Arya Samaj Temple

Shri Digambar Jain Mandir

Ramratan Marg

Belangunj Rd

Bageshwarnath Temple

Khan Shopping Complex

Jaipur House

Raja Mandi Rd

Bhagat Singh Marg

Lady Lyall

SN

Hospital Rd

Kali Masjid

Akbari Masjid

Kashmiri Bazar

Kala Mahal Bazar

Chhatta Bazar

KOTWALI

Satyanarayan Temple

Subhash Bazar

Jama Masjid Rd

Ghalibpura Rd

Subhash Park

Indian Club

Jama Masjid

Mantola

Agra Fort Station

2 Agra/ Red Fort

Amar Singh Gate

Yamuna Kinara Rd

SHAHGANJ

Saiyad Ali Nabi Marg

Fatehpur Sikri Rd

Fort Bus Stand

Idgah Station

RAKABGANJ

SBI

Methodist

Digambar Jain Tempe

Motil Nehr Park

Idgah

KATLUPURA

BoB

Baptist High School

Foreigners' Registration Office

Idgah Bus Stand

District

ITDC

BALUGANJ

Argee Travel

Touraids

Baptist

St Mary's

Kheria Rd

Agra Club & Camping

The Mall

Agra Cantonment Station

Station Rd

SULTAN PURA

SADAR BAZAR

Gough Rd

Sardar Patel Garden

Indian Airlines

Taj Rd

Pawan

To Gwalior

UP Tourist Office

N

400 metres

400 yards

➡ **Agra maps**
1 Agra, page 108
2 Agra Fort, page 113

To Ram Bagh, Battis Khamba, Radhasvami & Samadhi

To Shikohabad

Chini Ka Rauza

Aligarh Rd

Kanpur Rd

I'timad-ud-Daulah

Yamuna Bridge Station

Taj Viewing Point (Mehtab Bagh)

Yamuna River

Taj Mahal

Yamuna Kinara Rd

Local

Shahjahan Park

Fatehabad Rd

Taj Rd

To 2 & Fatehabad

PURANI MANDI

TAJ GANJ

Fatehabad Rd

Dr Siyamlal Marg

Taj Rd

Mirza Fatehabad Rd

ATM

Travel Bureau

TELIPARA

To 1 & Fatehabad

VIBHAVNAGAR

IA, Jet Airways & Touraids

Taj Mahal

ⓘ *Sat-Thu 0600-1930 (last entry 1800), foreigners Rs 750 (including Development Tax), Indians Rs 20, cash only, includes still camera, video cameras, tripods, other electronic items eg mobile phones not allowed, lockers at East and West Gates Rs 1. No photos inside the tomb (instant fines). Allow at least 1 hr. Full moon viewing 2 nights either side of full moon (see www.stardate.org/nightsky/moon for full moon dates), 2030-0030, separate entry fee of foreigners Rs 750, Indians Rs 510, book tickets day before at Architectural Survey of India, 22 The Mall, T0562-222 7261.*

Of all the world's great monuments, the Taj Mahal is one of the most written about, photographed, televised and talked about. To India's Nobel Laureate poet, Tagore, the Taj was a "tear drop on the face of humanity", a building to echo the cry "I have not forgotten, I have not forgotten, O beloved" and its mesmerizing power is such that despite the hype, no one comes away disappointed.

Shah Jahan, the fifth of the Great Mughals, was so devoted to his favourite wife, Mumtaz Mahal (Jewel of the Palace) that he could not bear to be parted from her and insisted that she always travel with him, in all states of health. While accompanying him on a military campaign, she died at the age of 39 giving birth to their 14th child. On her deathbed, it is said, she asked the emperor to show the world how much they loved one another.

The grief-stricken emperor went into mourning for two years. He turned away from the business of running the empire and dedicated himself to architecture, resolving to build his wife the most magnificent memorial on earth. On the right bank of the River Yamuna in full view of his fortress palace, it was to be known as the Taj-i-Mahal (Crown of the Palace).

According to the French traveller Tavnier, work on the Taj commenced in 1632 and took 22 years to complete, employing a workforce of 20,000. The red sandstone was available locally but the white marble was quarried at Makrana in Rajasthan and transported 300 km by a fleet of 1000 elephants. Semi-precious stones for the inlay came from far and wide: red carnelian from Baghdad; red, yellow and brown jasper from the Punjab; green jade and crystal from China; blue lapis lazuli from Ceylon and Afghanistan; turquoise from Tibet; chrysolite from Egypt; amethyst from Persia; agates from the Yemen; dark green malachite from Russia; diamonds from Central India and mother-of-pearl from the Indian Ocean. A 3-km ramp was used to lift material up to the dome and, because of the sheer weight of the building; boreholes were filled with metal coins and fragments to provide suitable foundations. The resemblance of the exquisite double dome to a huge pearl is not coincidental; a saying of the Prophet describes the throne of God as a dome of white pearl supported by white pillars.

Myths and controversy surround the Taj Mahal. On its completion it is said that the emperor ordered the chief mason's right hand to be cut off to prevent him from repeating his masterpiece. Another legend suggests that Shah Jahan intended to build a replica for himself in black marble on the other side of the river, connected to the Taj Mahal by a bridge built with alternate blocks of black and white marble. Some have asserted that architects responsible for designing this mausoleum must have come from Turkey, Persia or even Europe (because of the pietra dura work on the tomb). In fact, no one knows who drew the plans. What is certain is that in the Taj Mahal, the traditions of Indian Hindu and Persian Muslim architecture were fused together into a completely distinct and perfect art form.

Viewing

The white marble of the Taj is extraordinarily luminescent and even on dull days seems bright. The whole building appears to change its hue according to the light in the sky. In winter (December to February), it is worth being there at sunrise. Then the mists that often lie over the River Yamuna lift as the sun rises and casts its golden rays over the pearl-white tomb. Beautifully lit in the soft light, the Taj appears to float on air. At sunset, the view from across the river is equally wonderful. The **Archaeological Survey of India** explicitly asks visitors not to make donations to anyone including custodians in the tomb.

 Visit at sunrise and sunset to avoid crowds and take photographs in peace (early morning can be misty). Hiring a guide isn't necessary.

Entrances

To reduce damage to the marble by the polluted atmosphere, local industries are having to comply with strict rules now and vehicles emitting noxious fumes are not allowed within 2 km of the monument. People are increasingly using horse-drawn carriages or walking. You can approach the Taj from three directions. The western entrance is usually used by those arriving from the fort and is an easy 10-minute walk along a pleasant garden road. At the eastern entrance, rickshaws and camel drivers offer to take visitors to the gate for up to Rs 100 each; however, an official battery bus ferries visitors from the car park to the gate for Rs 2 each.

The approach

In the unique beauty of the Taj, subtlety is blended with grandeur and a massive overall design is matched with immaculately intricate execution. You will already have seen the dome of the tomb in the distance, looking almost like a miniature, but as you go into the open square, the Taj itself is so well hidden that you almost wonder where it can be. The glorious surprise is kept until the last moment, for wholly concealing it is the massive red sandstone gateway of the entrance, symbolizing the divide between the secular world and paradise.

The gateway was completed in 1648, though the huge brass door is recent. The original doors (plundered by the Jats) were solid silver and decorated with 1100 nails whose heads were contemporary silver coins. Although the gateway is remarkable in itself, one of its functions is to prevent you getting any glimpse of the tomb inside until you are right in the doorway itself. From here only the tomb is visible, stunning in its nearness, but as you move forward the minarets come into view.

The four minarets at each corner of the plinth provide balance to the tomb – see how each slants outwards. Familiar with the disastrous effects of earthquakes on mosques in Gujarat, the architects deliberately designed the minarets so they would fall away from the tomb, not onto it.

The garden

The Taj garden, well kept though it is nowadays, is nothing compared with its former glory. The guiding principle is one of symmetry. The *char bagh*, separated by the watercourses (rivers of heaven) originating from the central, raised pool, were divided into 16 flower beds, making a total of 64. The trees, all carefully planted to maintain the symmetry, were either cypress (signifying death) or fruit trees (life). The channels were stocked with colourful fish and the gardens with beautiful birds. It is well worth wandering along the side avenues for not only is it much more peaceful but also good for framing photos of the tomb with foliage. You may see bullocks pulling the lawnmowers around.

The mosque and its jawab

On the east and west sides of the tomb are identical red sandstone buildings. On the west (left-hand side) is a mosque. It is common in Islam to build one next to a tomb. It sanctifies the area and provides a place for worship. The replica on the other side is known as the **Jawab** (answer). This can't be used for prayer as it faces away from Mecca.

The tomb

There is only one point of access to the **plinth** and tomb, where shoes must be removed (socks can be kept on; remember the white marble gets very hot) or cloth overshoes worn (Rs 2, though strictly free).

The **tomb** is square with bevelled corners. At each corner smaller domes rise while in the centre is the main dome topped by a brass finial. The dome is actually a double dome and this device, Central Asian in origin, was used to gain height. The resemblance of the dome to a huge pearl is not coincidental. The exterior ornamentation is calligraphy (verses of the Koran), beautifully carved panels in bas relief and superb inlay work.

The **interior** of the mausoleum comprises a lofty central chamber, a *maqbara* (crypt) immediately below this, and four octagonal corner rooms. The central chamber contains replica tombs, the real ones being in the crypt. The public tomb was originally surrounded by a jewel-encrusted silver screen. Aurangzeb removed this, fearing it might be stolen, and replaced it with an octagonal screen of marble carved from one block of marble and inlaid with precious stones. It is an incredible piece of workmanship. This chamber is open at sunrise, but may close during the day.

Above the tombs is a **Cairene lamp** whose flame is supposed never to go out. This one was given by Lord Curzon, Governor General of India (1899-1905), to replace the original which was stolen by Jats. The tomb of Mumtaz with the 'female' slate, rests immediately beneath the dome. If you look from behind it, you can see how it lines up centrally with the main entrance. Shah Jahan's tomb is larger and to the side, marked by a 'male' pen-box, the sign of a cultured or noble person. Not originally intended to be placed there but squeezed in by Aurangzeb, this flaws the otherwise perfect symmetry of the whole complex. Finally, the acoustics of the building are superb, the domed ceiling being designed to echo chants from the Koran and musicians' melodies.

The **museum** ⓘ *above the entrance, Sat-Thu 1000-1700*, has a small collection of Mughal memorabilia, photographs and miniatures of the Taj through the ages but has no textual information. Sadly, the lights do not always work.

Agra Fort (Red Fort)

ⓘ *0600-1800, foreigners Rs 300 (Rs 250 if you've been to the Taj on the same day), Indians Rs 15, video Rs 25; allow a minimum of 1½ hrs for a visit. The best route round is to start with the building on your right before going through the gate at the top of the broad 100 m ramp; the gentle incline made it suitable for elephants.*

On the west bank of the River Yamuna, Akbar's magnificent fort dominates the centre of the city. Akbar erected the walls and gates and the first buildings inside. **Shah Jahan** built the impressive imperial quarters and mosque, while Aurangzeb added the outer ramparts. The outer walls, just over 20 m high and faced with red sandstone, tower above the outer moat. The fort is crescent-shaped with a long, nearly straight wall facing the river, punctuated at regular intervals by bastions. The main entrance used to be in the centre of the west wall, the **Delhi Gate**, facing the bazar. It led to the Jami Masjid in the city but is now permanently closed. You can only enter now from the **Amar Singh Gate** in the south. Although only the southern third of the fort is open to the public, this includes nearly all the buildings of interest. At the gate you will have to contend with vendors of cheap soapstone boxes and knick-knacks. If you want to buy something, bargain hard. Guides will offer their services – most are not particularly good.

Fortifications

The fortifications tower above the 9-m-wide, 10-m-deep moat (still evident but containing stagnant water) formerly filled with water from the Yamuna River. There is an outer wall on the riverside and an imposing 22-m-high inner, main wall, giving a feeling of great defensive power. Although it served as a model for Shah Jahan's Red Fort in Delhi, its own model was the Rajput fort built by Raja Man Singh Tomar of Gwalior in 1500. If an aggressor managed to get through the outer gate they would have to make a right-hand turn and thereby expose their flank to the defenders on the inner wall. The inner gate is solidly powerful but has been attractively decorated with tiles. The similarities with Islamic patterns of the tilework are obvious, though the Persian blue was also used in the Gwalior Fort and may well have been imitated from that example. The incline up to this point and beyond was suitable for elephants and as you walk past the last gate and up the broad brick-lined ramp with ridged slabs, it is easy to imagine arriving on elephant back. At the top of this 100-m ramp is a gate with a map and description board on your left.

Jahangiri Mahal (1) Despite its name, this was built by Akbar (circa 1570) as women's quarters. It is all that survives of his original palace buildings. In front is a large **stone bowl**, with steps both inside and outside, which was probably filled with fragrant rose water for bathing. Almost 75 m sq, the palace has a simple stone exterior. Tillotson has pointed out that the blind arcade of pointed arches inlaid with white marble which decorate the façade is copied from 14th-century monuments of the Khaljis and Tughluqs in Delhi. He notes that they are complemented by some features derived from Hindu architecture, including the *jarokhas* (balconies) protruding from the central section, the sloping dripstone in place of *chajja* (eaves) along the top of the façade, and the domed *chhattris* at its ends. The presence of distinctively Hindu features does not indicate a synthesis of architectural styles at this early stage of Mughal architecture, as can be seen much more clearly from inside the

2 Agra Fort

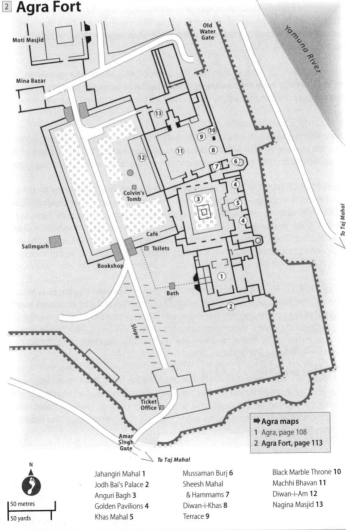

Moti Masjid

Old Water Gate

Yamuna River

Mina Bazar

13

9 10

11

12 8

7 6

Colvin's Tomb

3

4

5

4

Salimgarh

Café

Toilets

Bookshop

Slope

Bath

1

2

To Taj Mahal

Ticket Office

→ Agra maps
1 Agra, page 108
2 Agra Fort, page 113

Amar Singh Gate

To Taj Mahal

N

50 metres
50 yards

Jahangiri Mahal **1**
Jodh Bai's Palace **2**
Anguri Bagh **3**
Golden Pavilions **4**
Khas Mahal **5**

Mussaman Burj **6**
Sheesh Mahal
& Hammams **7**
Diwan-i-Khas **8**
Terrace **9**

Black Marble Throne **10**
Machhi Bhavan **11**
Diwan-i-Am **12**
Nagina Masjid **13**

Jahangiri Mahal. Here most of the features are straightforwardly Hindu; square-headed arches and extraordinarily carved capitals and brackets illustrate the vivid work of local Hindu craftsmen employed by Akbar without any attempt either to curb their enthusiasm for florid decoration and mythical animals nor to produce a fusion of Hindu and Islamic ideas. Tillotson argues that the central courtyard is essentially Hindu, in significant contrast with most earlier Indo-Islamic buildings. In these, an Islamic scheme was modified by Hindu touches. He suggests, therefore, that the Jahangiri Mahal marks the start of a more fundamental kind of Hinduization, typical of several projects during Akbar's middle period of rule, including the palace complex in Fatehpur Sikri. However, it did not represent a real fusion of ideas – something that only came under Shah Jahan – simply a juxtaposition of sharply contrasting styles.

Jodh Bai's Palace (2) On the south side, this is named after one of Jahangir's wives. On the east the hall court leads onto a more open yard by the inner wall of the fort. In contrast to other palaces in the fort, this is quite simple. Through the slits in the wall you can see the Taj.

Shah Jahan's palace buildings

Turn left through to Shah Jahan's Khas Mahal (1636). The open tower allows you to view the walls and see to your left the decorated Mussaman Burj tower. The use of white marble transforms the atmosphere, contributing to the new sense of grace and light.

Anguri Bagh (3) (Vine Garden) The formal, 85-m-sq, geometric gardens are on the left. In Shah Jahan's time the geometric patterns were enhanced by decorative flower beds. In the middle of the white marble platform wall in front is a decorative water slide. From the pool with its bays for seating and its fountains, water would drain off along channels decorated to mimic a stream. The surface was scalloped to produce a rippling waterfall, or inlaid to create a shimmering stream bed. Behind vertical water drops, there are little cusped arch niches into which flowers would be placed during the day and lamps at night. The effect was magical.

Golden Pavilions (4) The curved *chala* roofs of the small pavilions by the Khas Mahal are based on the roof shape of Bengali village huts constructed out of curved bamboo, designed to keep off heavy rain. The shape was first expressed in stone by the Sultans of Bengal. Originally gilded, these were probably ladies' bedrooms, with hiding places for jewellery in the walls. These pavilions are traditionally associated with Shah Jahan's daughters, Roshanara and Jahanara.

Khas Mahal (5) This was the model for the Diwan-i-Khas at the Red Fort in Delhi. Some of the original interior decoration has been restored (1895) and gives an impression of how splendid the painted ceiling must have been. The metal rings were probably used for *punkhas*. Underneath are cool rooms used to escape the summer heat. The Khas Mahal illustrates Shahs' original architectural contribution.

The buildings retain distinctively Islamic Persian features – the geometrical planning of the pavilions and the formal layout of the gardens, for example. Tillotson points out that here "Hindu motifs are treated in a new manner, which is less directly imitative of the Hindu antecedents. The temple columns and corbel capitals have been stripped of their rich carving and turned into simpler, smoother forms ... the *chhattris* have Islamic domes. Through these subtle changes the indigenous motifs have lost their specifically Hindu identity; they therefore contrast less strongly with the Islamic components, and are bound with them into a new style. The unity is assisted by the use of the cusped arch and the *Bangladar* roof". Seen in this light, the Khas Mahal achieves a true synthesis which eluded Akbar's designs.

Mussaman Burj (6) On the left of the Khas Mahal is the Mussaman Burj (Octagonal Tower, though sometimes corrupted into Saman Burj, then translated as Jasmine Tower). It is a beautiful octagonal tower with an open pavilion. With its openness, elevation and the benefit of cooling evening breezes blowing in off the Yamuna River, this could well have been used as the emperor's bedroom. It has been suggested that this is where Shah Jahan lay on his deathbed, gazing at the Taj. Access to this tower is through a magnificently decorated and intimate apartment with a scalloped fountain in the centre. The inlay work here is exquisite, especially above the pillars. In front of the fountain is a sunken courtyard which could be filled by water carriers, to work the fountains in the pool.

Sheesh Mahal (7) (Mirror Palace) Here are further examples of decorative water engineering in the *hammams*; the water here may have been warmed by lamps. The mirrors, which were more precious than marble, were set into the walls, often specially chiselled to accommodate their crooked shape. The defensive qualities of the site and the fortifications are obvious. In the area between the outer rampart and the inner wall gladiatorial battles were staged pitting man against tiger, or elephant against elephant. The tower was the emperor's grandstand seat.

Diwan-i-Khas (8) (Hall of Private Audience, 1637) This is next to the Mussaman Burj, approached on this route by a staircase which brings you out at the side. The interior of the Diwan-i-Khas, a three-sided pavilion with a terrace of fine proportions, would have been richly decorated with tapestries and carpets. The double columns in marble inlaid with semi-precious stones in delightful floral patterns in pietra dura have finely carved capitals.

Terrace and Machhi Bhavan
In front of the Diwan-i-Khas are two throne 'platforms' on a **terrace (9)**. Gascoigne recounts how Shah Jahan tried to trick a haughty Persian ambassador into bowing low as he approached the throne by erecting a fence with a small wicket gate so that his visitor would have to enter on hands and knees. The ambassador did so, but entered backwards, thus presenting his bottom first to the Emperor. The **black marble throne (10)** at the rear of the terrace was used by Jahangir when claiming to be Emperor at Allahabad. The emperor sat on the white marble platform facing the **Machhi Bhavan (11)** (Fish Enclosure), which once contained pools and fountains, waiting to meet visiting dignitaries.

Diwan-i-Am (12) Go down an internal staircase and you enter the Diwan-i-Am from the side. The clever positioning of the pillars gives the visitor arriving through the gates in the right- and left-hand walls of the courtyard an uninterrupted view of the throne. On the back wall of the pavilion are *jali* screens to enable the women of the court to watch without being seen. The open-sided, cusped arched hall built of plaster on red stone, is very impressive. The throne alcove of richly decorated white marble completed in 1634 after seven years' work used to house the Peacock Throne. Its decoration made it extraordinary: "the canopy was carved in enamel work and studded with individual gems, its interior was thickly encrusted with rubies, garnets and diamonds, and it was supported on 12 emerald covered columns" writes Tillotson. When Shah Jahan moved his capital to Delhi he took the throne with him to the Red Fort, only for it to be taken back to Persia as loot by Nadir Shah in 1739.

Nagina Masjid (13) From the corner opposite the Diwan-i-Khas two doorways lead to a view over the small courtyards of the *zenana* (harem). Further round in the next corner is the Nagina Masjid. Shoes must be removed at the doorway. Built by Shah Jahan, this was the private mosque of the ladies of the court. Beneath it was a *mina* bazar for the ladies to make purchases from the marble balcony above. Looking out of the Diwan-i-Am you can see the domes of the **Moti Masjid** (Pearl Mosque, 1646-1653), an extremely fine building closed to visitors because of structural problems. Opposite the Diwan-i-Am are the barracks and **Mina Bazar**, also closed to the public. In the paved area in front of the Diwan-i-Am is a large well and the **tomb of Mr John Russell Colvin**, the Lieutenant Governor of the Northwest Provinces who died here during the 1857 'Uprising'. Stylistically it is sadly out of place. The yellow buildings date from the British period.

Jama Masjid

The mosque built in 1648, near the fort railway, no longer connected to the fort, is attributed to Shah Jahan's dutiful elder daughter Jahanara. In need of repair and not comparable to buildings within the fort, its symmetry has suffered since a small minaret fell in the 1980s. The fine marble steps and bold geometric patterns on the domes are quite striking.

I'timad-ud-Daulah and Sikandra

I'timad-ud-Daulah

ⓘ *0630-1830 (last entry 1700), foreigners Rs 100 plus Rs 10 tax, Indians Rs 10, video Rs 25.*
The tomb of I'timad-ud-Daulah (or 'Baby Taj'), set a startling precedent as the first Mughal building to be faced with white marble inlaid with contrasting stones. Unlike the Taj it is small, intimate and has a gentle serenity, but is just as ornate. The tomb was built for **Ghiyas Beg**, a Persian who had obtained service in Akbar's court, and his wife, see page 293. On Jahangir's succession in 1605 he became *Wazir* (chief minister). Jahangir fell in love with his daughter, **Mehrunissa**, who at the time was married to a Persian. When her husband died in 1607, she entered Jahangir's court as a lady-in-waiting. Four years later Jahangir married her. Thereafter she was known first as **Nur Mahal** (Light of the Palace), later being promoted to **Nur Jahan** (Light of the World). Her niece Mumtaz married Shah Jahan.

Nur Jahan built the tomb for her father in the *char bagh* that he himself had laid out. It is beautifully conceived in white marble, mosaic and lattice. There is a good view from the roof of the entrance. Marble screens of geometric lattice work permit soft lighting of the inner chamber. The yellow marble caskets appear to have been carved out of wood. On the engraved walls of the chamber is the recurring theme of a wine flask with snakes as handles – perhaps a reference by Nur Jahan, the tomb's creator, to her husband Jahangir's excessive drinking. Stylistically, the tomb marks a change from the sturdy and manly buildings of Akbar's reign to softer, more feminine lines. The main chamber, richly decorated in pietra dura with mosaics and semi-precious stones inlaid in the white marble, contains the tomb of I'timad-ud-Daulah (Pillar of the Goverment) and his wife. Some have argued that the concept and skill must have travelled from its European home of 16th-century Florence to India. However, Florentine pietra dura is figurative whereas the Indian version is essentially decorative and can be seen as a refinement of its Indian predecessor, the patterned mosaic.

Sikandra

ⓘ *Sunrise-sunset, foreigners Rs 110, Indians Rs 10, includes camera, video Rs 25. Morning is the quietest time to visit.*

Following the Timurid tradition, Akbar (ruled 1556-1605) had started to build his own tomb at Sikandra. He died during its construction and his son **Jahangir** completed it in 1613. The result is an impressive, large but architecturally confused tomb. A huge gateway, the **Buland Darwaza**, leads to the great garden enclosure, where spotted deer run free on the immaculate lawns. The decoration on the gateway is strikingly bold, with its large mosaic patterns, a forerunner of the pietra dura technique. The white minarets atop the entrance were an innovation which reappear, almost unchanged, at the Taj Mahal. The walled garden enclosure is laid out in the *char bagh* style, with the mausoleum at the centre.

A broad paved path leads to the 22.5-m-high tomb with four storeys. The lowest storey, nearly 100 m sq and 9 m high, contains massive cloisters. The entrance on the south side leads to the tomb chamber. Shoes must be removed or cloth overshoes worn (hire Rs 2). In a niche opposite the entrance is an alabaster tablet inscribed with the 99 divine names of Allah. The sepulchre is in the centre of the room, whose velvety darkness is pierced by a single slanting shaft of light from a high window. The custodian, in expectation of a donation, makes "Akbaaarrrr" echo around the chamber.

Some 4 km south of Sikandra, near the high gateway of the ancient **Kach ki Sarai** building, is a sculptured horse, believed to mark the spot where Akbar's favourite horse died. There are also *kos minars* (marking a *kos*, about 4 km) and several other tombs on the way.

Mathura → *For listings, see pages 125-130. Colour map 5, C3. Phone code: 0565. Population: 300,000.*

Mathura, 50 km from Agra on the west bank of the Yamuna, is one of the most sacred cities of Hinduism dating back to 600 BC. For Vaishnavites, it is perhaps the supremely sacred city of India, being the reputed birthplace of **Krishna**, the most human aspect of Vishnu. Krishna is widely seen as the embodiment of the ideal lover, soldier, statesman, as well as the adorable baby, or wayward child. Many places around are associated with episodes in his life. Mathura's ancient structures were mostly destroyed by Muslims but its religious association draws thousands of pilgrims. Today, it is also an important industrial city with much evidence of modernizing on the approach from the highway. The opening of a big oil refinery on the outskirts of the city in 1975 caused great concern among environmentalists that atmospheric pollution would irreversibly damage the Taj Mahal, only 50 km away. UPTDC ① *near Old Bus Stand, T0565-250 5351.*

History

Ptolemy mentioned the town and it assumed the importance of a capital city during the first to second century **Kushan Empire**. When the Chinese traveller Hiuen Tsang visited it in AD 634 it was an important Buddhist centre with several monasteries. However, **Mahmud of Ghazni** sacked the city and desecrated its temples in 1017, followed by **Sikander Lodi** in 1500, whilst the Mughal **Emperor Aurangzeb** used a local revolt in which his governor was killed as an excuse to destroy the main temples. Jats and Marathas fought over the city as the Mughal Empire declined, but at the beginning of the 19th century it came under British control. They laid out a cantonment in the south and left a cemetery and the Roman Catholic Sacred Heart Cathedral (1870).

Sights

There are no pre-Muslim monuments of any significance, and some of the finest buildings have been badly scarred by decay, neglect and misuse. You enter Mathura by the finely carved **Holi Gate** and in the centre of the bustling old city is the **Jami Masjid** (1660-1661) with four minarets, which was built by Abd-un-Nadi, Aurangzeb's governor. It has a raised courtyard, and above the façade, which was once covered with brightly coloured enamel tiles, are the 99 names of Allah.

The **Katra** (500 m) contains a mosque built by Aurangzeb. This stands over the ruins of one of Mathura's most famous temples, the **Kesava Deo Mandir** which in turn had been built on the ruins of a Buddhist monastery of the Kushan period. This is considered to be **Sri Krishna Janmabhumi** (Krishna's birthplace). The main statues are particularly serene and attractive but there may at times be difficulty in entering due to extra security. At the rear of the enclosure is a newer **Temple of Kesava**, built by Bir Singh of Orchha. Nearby is the impressive **Potara Kund**, a stepped tank in which Krishna's baby clothes were washed. It is faced in the familiar local red sandstone with access for cattle and horses.

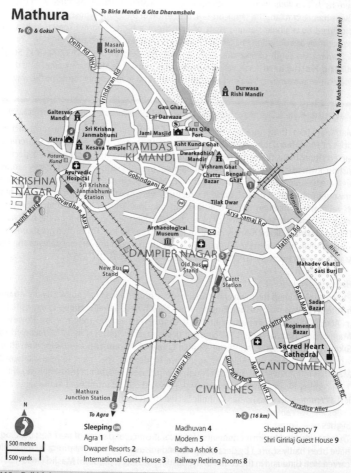

Mathura

Sleeping
Agra 1
Dwaper Resorts 2
International Guest House 3

Madhuvan 4
Modern 5
Radha Ashok 6
Railway Retiring Rooms 8

Sheetal Regency 7
Shri Giririaj Guest House 9

The river and its ghats are the focal point for Hindu pilgrims. A paved street runs their length, but recent developments have made the area very congested, and the two industrial-looking bridges which cross the river close to the ghats have taken away some of the charm. **Vishram Ghat** (rebuilt in 1814) is where Krishna rested after killing Kamsa. Cows, monkeys and turtles are fed when the *Arati* ceremony is performed in the morning and evening; best seen from a boat.

The **Sati Burj** (late 16th century), on the river, is a square, four-storey red sandstone tower with a plastered dome said to commemorate the *sati* by the wife of Rajbihari Mal of Amber. The **Kans Qila** fort was built by Raja Man Singh of Amber and was rebuilt by Akbar but only the foundations remain.

Archaeological museum ① *Dampier Nagar, T0565-250 0847, Tue-Sun 1030-1630, foreigners Rs 25, Indians Rs 5, camera Rs 20*, has an extensive and impressive collection of sculptures, terracottas, bronzes and coins housed in an octagonal red sandstone building. Also exhibited is the fifth-century 'Standing Buddha', numerous Gupta figures, a first-century headless Buddha, and Kushana sculptures and Gandhara pieces.

Around Mathura

Gokul, 2 km away, is approached by a long flight of steps from the river. It is associated with very early Hindu legends, where Vishnu first appeared as Krishna. It is the headquarters of the Vallabhacharya Sect who built some large temples.

Mahaban, 9 km southeast of Mathura on the east bank of the Yamuna, means 'a great forest'. There is no forest now but in 1634 Shah Jahan is recorded as having killed four tigers in a hunt here. The town was sacked by Mahmud of Ghazni in the 11th century. Each year in August Vaishnavite pilgrims come to the **Nanda Krishna Palace** where Krishna was believed to have been secretly raised. His cradle stands in the hall, the hole in the wall is where the *gopis* hid his flute, and the place where his mother stood churning butter is marked by a polished pillar.

Baradari of Sikander Lodi, 28 km south of Mathura, is the 12 pillared pavilion of Sikander Lodi, one time King of Delhi, built in 1495, and the 1611 **tomb of Mariam uz Zamani**, Akbar's Hindu Rajput wife who is said to have been converted to Christianity, though there is little supporting evidence. There are beautiful carvings on the red sandstone structure.

Govardhan, 26 km west of Mathura, lies in the narrow range of the Girraj Hills. In legend, when Indra caused a tremendous flood, Krishna raised these hills up above the flood for seven days so that people could escape. The **Harideva Temple**, by the Manasi Ganga River, was built by Raja Bhagwan Das in the reign of Akbar. On the opposite bank are the *chhattris* of Ranjit Singh and Balwant Singh, both rulers of Bharatpur. There are stone ghats on all sides, built in 1817. Krishna is believed to have ritually bathed at the temple to purify himself after killing the demon bull Arishta.

Vrindavan → *For listings, see pages 125-130. Colour map 5, C3. Phone code: 0565.*

① *The temples are open morning and evening usually 0900-1200 and 1800-2100 when visitors are welcome to attend worship.*

Vrindavan – 'Forest of Tulsi (basil) Plants' – is the most famous of the holy sites around Mathura. In Vrindavan, Krishna played with the *gopis* (cowgirls), stealing their clothes while they bathed. You are entering perhaps the most sacred region of India for Vaishnavite Hindus, where many of the stories surrounding Krishna are set. The town retains a tranquil, welcoming atmosphere, and offers an interesting mix of stunning temples, narrow medieval alleyways and beautiful river scenes, observed by an equally interesting mix of local Sadhus and international devotees of Hare Krishna.

At the entrance to the town is the 16th-century **temple of Gobind Dev** (1590), the 'Divine Cowherd', Krishna. Built by Man Singh of Jaipur during Akbar's reign, it was severely damaged by the less tolerant Aurangzeb. Nearby there is a Dravidian-style temple dedicated to **Sri Ranganathji** (Vishnu), with three *gopura*, each nearly 30 m high. There is an annual 10-day **Rath** (car) **festival** in March/April. The 16th-century **Madan Mohan temple** stands above a ghat on an arm of the river; there is a pavilion decorated with cobra carvings. Siva is believed to have struck Devi here and made it a place for curing snake bites. The octagonal tower is similar to the one on the 16th-century **Jagat Krishna temple**.

Other temples include **Jugal Kishor** (reputedly 1027) near Kesi Ghat, **Banke Behari** near Purana Bazar and **Radha Ballabh**, partly demolished by Aurangzeb, close by. **International Society for Krishna Consciousness (ISKCON)** with the Shri Krishna Balaram Temple, has a modern marble memorial.

Vrindavan

Sleeping 🛏
Ananda Krishna Van **1**
International Rest House **2**
MVT Guest House **3**
Shri Shri Radhashyam Palace **4**

The red sandstone capital of Emperor Akbar, one of his architectural achievements, spreads along a ridge. The great mosque and palace buildings, deserted after only 14 years are still a vivid reminder of his power and vision. Perfectly preserved, it conjures up the lifestyle of the Mughals at the height of their glory.

History

The first two Great Mughals, Babur (ruled 1526-1530) and his son Humayun (ruled 1530-1540, 1555-1556) both won (in Humayun's case, won back) Hindustan at the end of their lives, and they left an essentially alien rule. Akbar, the third and greatest of the Mughals changed that. By marrying a Hindu princess, forging alliances with the Rajput leaders and making the administration of India a partnership with Hindu nobles and princes rather than armed foreign minority rule, Akbar consolidated his ancestors' gains, and won widespread loyalty and respect. Akbar had enormous magnetism. Though illiterate, he had great wisdom and learning as well as undoubted administrative and military skills. Fatehpur Sikri is testimony to this remarkable character.

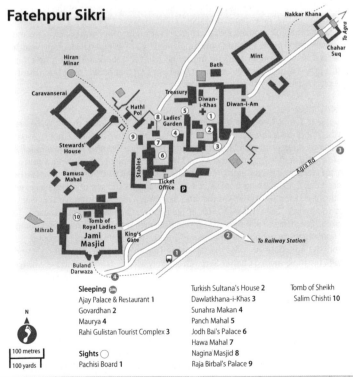

Fatehpur Sikri

N

100 metres
100 yards

Sleeping 🛏
Ajay Palace & Restaurant **1**
Govardhan **2**
Maurya **4**
Rahi Gulistan Tourist Complex **3**

Sights ◯
Pachisi Board **1**

Turkish Sultana's House **2**
Dawlatkhana-i-Khas **3**
Sunahra Makan **4**
Panch Mahal **5**
Jodh Bai's Palace **6**
Hawa Mahal **7**
Nagina Masjid **8**
Raja Birbal's Palace **9**

Tomb of Sheikh
Salim Chishti **10**

Although he had many wives, the 26-year-old Akbar had no living heir; the children born to him had all died in infancy. He visited holy men to enlist their prayers for a son and heir. **Sheikh Salim Chishti**, living at Sikri, a village 37 km southwest of Agra, told the emperor that he would have three sons. Soon after, one of his wives, the daughter of the Raja of Amber, became pregnant, so Akbar sent her to live near the sage. A son Salim was born, later to be known as **Jahangir**. The prophecy was fulfilled when in 1570 another wife gave birth to Murad and in 1572, to Daniyal. Salim Chishti's tomb is here.

Akbar, so impressed by this sequence of events, resolved to build an entirely new capital at Sikri in honour of the saint. The holy man had set up his hermitage on a low hill of hard reddish sandstone, an ideal building material, easy to work and yet very durable. The building techniques used imitated carvings in wood, as well as canvas from the Mughal camp (eg awnings). During the next 14 years a new city appeared on this hill – 'Fatehpur' (town of victory) added to the name of the old village, 'Sikri'. Later additions and alterations were made and debate continues over the function and dates of the various buildings. It is over 400 years old and yet perfectly preserved, thanks to careful conservation work carried out by the Archaeological Survey of India at the turn of the century. There are three sections to the city: the 'Royal Palace', 'Outside the Royal Palace' and the 'Jami Masjid'.

When Akbar left, it was slowly abandoned to become ruined and deserted by the early 1600s. Some believe the emperor's decision was precipitated by the failure of the water supply, whilst local folklore claims the decision was due to the loss of the court singer Tansen, one of the 'nine gems' of Akbar's court. However, there may well have been political and strategic motives. Akbar's change in attitude towards orthodox Islam and his earlier veneration of the Chishti saints supplanted by a new imperial ideology, may have influenced his decision. In 1585 he moved his court to Lahore and when he returned south again, it was to Agra. But it was at Fatehpur Sikri that Akbar spent the richest and most productive years of his 49-year reign.

The entrance

ⓘ *Sunrise to sunset, foreigners US$5/Rs 250, Indians Rs 5. It is best to visit early, before the crowds. Official guides are good (about Rs 100; Rs 30 off season) but avoid others. Avoid the main entrance (lots of hawkers); instead, take the right-hand fork after passing through Agra gate to the hassle-free 2nd entrance. Allow 3 hrs and carry plenty of drinking water.*

Entry to Fatehpur Sikri is through the **Agra Gate**. The straight road from Agra was laid out in Akbar's time. If approaching from Bharatpur you will pass the site of a large lake, which provided one defensive barrier. On the other sides was a massive defensive wall with nine gates (clockwise): Delhi, Lal, Agra, Bir or Suraj (Sun), Chandar (Moon), Gwaliori, Tehra (Crooked), Chor (Thief's) and Ajmeri. Sadly there are men with 'performing' bears along the road from Agra – they should be discouraged – avoid stopping to photograph or tip.

From the Agra Gate you pass the sandstone **Tansen's Baradari** on your right and go through the triple-arched **Chahar Suq** with a gallery with two *chhattris* above which may have been a **Nakkar khana** (Drum House). The road inside the main city wall leading to the entrance would have been lined with bazars. Next on your right is the square, shallow-domed **Mint** with artisans' workshops or animal shelters, around a courtyard. Workmen still chip away at blocks of stone in the dimly lit interior.

Royal Palace

The **Diwan-i-Am** (Hall of Public Audience) was also used for celebrations and public prayers. It has cloisters on three sides of a rectangular courtyard and to the west, a pavilion with the emperor's throne, with *jali* screens on either side separating the court ladies. Some scholars suggest that the west orientation may have had the added significance of Akbar's vision of himself playing a semi-divine role.

This backed onto the private palace. In the centre of the courtyard behind the throne is the **Pachisi Board (1)** or Chaupar. It is said that Akbar had slave girls dressed in yellow, blue and red, moved around as 'pieces'!

The **Diwan-i-Khas** (Hall of Private Audience) to your right, is a two-storey building with corner kiosks. It is a single room with a unique circular throne platform. Here Akbar would spend long hours in discussion with Christians, Jains, Buddhists, Hindus and Parsis. They would sit along the walls of the balcony connected to the **Throne Pillar** by screened 'bridges', while courtiers could listen to the discussions from the ground floor. Decorative techniques and metaphysical labels are incorporated here – the pillar is lotus shaped (a Hindu and Buddhist motif), the Royal Umbrella (*chhattri*) is Hindu, and the Tree of Life, Islamic. The bottom of the pillar is carved in four tiers; Muslim, Hindu, Christian and Buddhist designs. The Throne Pillar can be approached by steps from the outside although there is no access to the upper floor. The design of the Hall deliberately followed the archaic universal pattern of establishing a hallowed spot from which spiritual influence could radiate. In his later years, Akbar developed a mystical cult around himself that saw him as being semi-divine.

An Archaeological Survey of India team recently discovered an 'air-conditioned palace' built for Akbar, while digging up steps leading down to a water tank set in the middle of the main palace complex. The subterranean chambers were found under the small quadrangle in sandstone, set in the middle of a water tank and connected on all four sides by narrow corridors. It's not yet open to the public.

In the **Treasury** in the northwest corner of the courtyard is the **Ankh Michauli** (Blind Man's Buff), possibly used for playing the game, comprising three rooms each protected by a narrow corridor with guards. The *makaras* on brackets are mythical sea creatures who guard the treasures under the sea. Just in front of the Treasury is the **Astrologer's Seat**, a small kiosk with elaborate carvings on the Gujarati 'caterpillar' struts which may have been used by the court astrologer or treasurer.

The **Turkish Sultana's House (2)** or Anup Talao Pavilion is directly opposite, beyond the Pachisi Board. Sultana Ruqayya Begum was Akbar's favourite and her 'house', with a balcony on each side, is exquisitely carved with Islamic decorations. Scholars suggest this may have been a pleasure pavilion. The geometrical pattern on the ceiling is reminiscent of Central Asian carvings in wood while the walls may have been set originally with reflecting glass to create a Sheesh Mahal (Mirror Palace). In the centre of this smaller south courtyard is the **Anup Talao** where the Emperor may have sat on the platform, surrounded by perfumed water. The *Akbarnama* mentions the emperor's show of charity when he filled the Talao with copper, silver and gold coins and distributed them over three years.

Dawlatkhana-i-Khas (3), the emperor's private chambers, are next to the rose-water fountain in the corner. There are two main rooms on the ground floor. One housed his library – the recesses in the walls were for manuscripts. Although unable to read or write himself, Akbar enjoyed having books read to him. Wherever he went, his library of 50,000 manuscripts accompanied him. The larger room behind was his resting area. On the first floor is the **Khwabgah** (Palace of Dreams) which would have had rich carpets, hangings and cushions. This too was decorated with gold and ultramarine paintings. The southern window (Jharokha Darshan) was where the emperor showed himself to his people every morning.

Leaving the Dawlatkhana-i-Khas you enter another courtyard which contained the **Ladies' garden** for the *zenana*, and the **Sunahra Makan (4)** or the Christian wife

Maryam's House, a two-storeyed affair for the emperor's mother, which was embellished with golden murals in the Persian style. The inscriptions on the beams are verses by Fazl, Akbar's poet laureate, one of the *'Navaratna'* (Nine Jewels) of the Court.

The **Panch Mahal (5)** is an elegant, airy five-storeyed pavilion just north of this, each floor smaller than the one below, rising to a single domed kiosk on top. The horizontal line of this terraced building is emphasized by wide overhanging eaves (for providing shade), parapets broken by the supporting pillars of which there are 84 on the ground floor (the magic number of seven planets multiplied by 12 signs of the zodiac). The 56 carved columns on the second floor are all different and show Hindu influence. Originally dampened scented *khuss* (grass screens) which were hung in the open spaces, provided protection from the heat and sun, as well as privacy for the women who used the pavilion.

Jodh Bai, the daughter of the Maharaja of Amber, lived in Raniwas. The spacious **palace (6)** in the centre, assured of privacy and security by high walls and a 9-m-high guarded gate to the east. Outside the north wall is the 'hanging' **Hawa Mahal (7)** (Palace of Winds) with beautiful *jali* screens facing the *zenana* garden which was once enclosed, and the bridge (a later addition) led to the Hathipol. Through the arch is the small **Nagina Masjid (8)**, the mosque for the ladies of the court. The *hammams* (baths) are to the south of the palace. The centre of the building is a quadrangle around which were the harem quarters, each section self-contained with roof terraces. The style, a blend of Hindu and Muslim (the lotus, chain and bell designs being Hindu, the black domes Muslim), is strongly reminiscent of Gujarati temples, possibly owing to the craftsmen brought in (see *jarokha* windows, niches, pillars and brackets). The upper pavilions north and south have interesting ceiling structure (imitating the bamboo and thatch roof of huts), here covered with blue glazed tiles, adding colour to the buildings of red sandstone favoured by Akbar. Jodh Bai's vegetarian kitchen opposite the palace has attractive chevron patterns.

Raja Birbal's Palace (9) is a highly ornamented house to the northwest of Jodh Bai's Palace. It has two storeys – four rooms and two porches with pyramidal roofs below, and two rooms with cupolas and screened terraces above. Birbal, Akbar's Hindu prime minister, was the brightest of Akbar's 'Nine Jewels'. Again the building combines Hindu and Islamic elements (note the brackets, eaves, *jarokhas*). Of particular interest is the insulating effect of the double-domed structure of the roofs and cupolas which kept the rooms cool, and the diagonal positioning of the upper rooms which ensured a shady terrace. Some scholars believe that this building, *Mahal-i-Ilahi*, was not for Birbal, but for Akbar's senior queens.

South of the Raja's house are the **stables**, a long courtyard surrounded by cells which probably housed zenana servants rather than the emperor's camels and horses, though the rings suggest animals may have been tied there.

Jami Masjid

Leaving the Royal Palace you proceed across a car park to the Jami Masjid and the sacred section of Fatehpur Sikri. The oldest place of worship here was the **Stone Cutters' Mosque** (circa 1565) to the west of the Jami Masjid. It was built near Sheikh Salim Chishti's cell which was later incorporated into it by stonecutters who settled on the ridge when quarrying for the Agra Fort began. It has carved monolithic 'S' brackets to support the wide sloping eaves.

The **Badshahi Darwaza** (King's Gate) is the entrance Akbar used. Shoes must be left at the gate but there are strips of carpet cross the courtyard to save burning your feet. The porch is packed with aggressive salesmen. The two other gates on the south and north walls were altered by subsequent additions. Built in 1571-1572, this is one of the largest mosques in India. Inside is the congregational courtyard (132 m by 111 m). To your right in the corner is the **Jamaat Khana Hall** and next to this the **Tomb of the Royal Ladies** on the north wall. The square nave carries the principal dome painted in the Persian style, with pillared aisles leading to side chapels carrying subsidiary domes. The **mihrab** in the centre of the west wall orientates worshippers towards Mecca. The sanctuary is adorned with carving, inlay work and painting.

The **Tomb of Sheikh Salim Chishti (10)**, a masterpiece in brilliant white marble, dominates the northern half of the courtyard. The Gujarati-style serpentine 'S' struts, infilled with *jali*, are highly decorative while the carved pillar bases and lattice screens are stunning pieces of craftsmanship. The canopy over the tomb is inlaid with mother of pearl. On the cenotaph is the date of the saint's death (1571) and the date of the building's completion (1580); the superb marble screens enclosing the veranda were added by Jahangir's foster brother in 1606. Around the entrance are inscribed the names of God, the Prophet and the four Caliphs of Islam. The shrine inside, on the spot of the saint's hermitage, originally had a red sandstone dome, which was marble veneered around 1806. Both Hindu and Muslim women pray at the shrine, tying cotton threads, hoping for the miracle of parenthood that Akbar was blessed with.

Next to it, in the courtyard, is the larger, red, sandstone tomb of **Nawab Islam Khan**, Sheikh Salim's grandson, and other members of the family.

Buland Darwaza (Triumphal Gate) dominates the south wall but it is a bit out of place. Built to celebrate Akbar's brilliant conquest of Gujarat (circa 1576), it sets the style for later gateways. The high gate is approached from the outside by a flight of steps which adds to its grandeur. The decoration shows Hindu influence, but is severe and restrained, emphasizing the lines of its arches with plain surfaces.

Outside the Royal Palace

Between the Royal Palace and the Jami Masjid, a paved pathway to the northwest leads to the **Hathipol** (Elephant Gate). This was the ceremonial entrance to the palace quarters, guarded by stone elephants, with its *nakkar khana* and bazar alongside. Nearby are the **waterworks**, with a deep well which had an ingenious mechanism for raising water to the aqueducts above ridge height. The **caravanserai** around a large courtyard fits on the ridge side, and was probably one of a series built to accommodate travellers, tradesmen and guards. Down a ramp immediately beyond is the **Hiran Minar**, an unusual tower studded with stone tusks, thought to commemorate Akbar's favourite elephant, Hiran. However, it was probably an *Akash Diya* (lamp to light the sky) or the 'zero point' for marking road distances in *kos*. You can climb up the spiral staircase inside it but take care as the top has no guard rail. This part of Fatehpur Sikri is off the main tourist track, and though less well preserved it is worth the detour to get the 'lost city' feeling, away from the crowds.

◉ Agra and around listings

For Sleeping and Eating price codes and other relevant information, see Essentials pages 28-33.

◉ Sleeping

Agra *p107, map p108*
The most atmospheric place to stay is in the busy lanes of **Taj Ganj**, where the basic hotels

are clustered. Most of the upscale hotels are along **Fatehabad Rd**, a rather charmless strip of pricey restaurants, international fast-food outlets and handicrafts emporia.
LL Amar Vilas, near Taj East Gate, T0562-223 1515, www.amarvilas.com. 105 rooms, all Taj-facing. The modern-day equivalent of the most luxurious of maharaja's palaces,

designed in strict adherence to the Mughal style. Stunning swimming pool, superb rooms, extraordinary ambience. Guests are entertained at sunset with traditional dancing and musicians. Expensive, but a magical experience.

LL-L Mughal Sheraton, Fatehabad Rd, T0562-233 1701, www.itcwelcomgroup.in. 285 rooms. Stunning suites, a palatial spa and beautiful gardens. Low-rise construction means only rooftop observatory offers good views of the Taj. Excellent restaurant.

LL-AL Gateway Hotel (formerly Taj View), Fatehabad Rd, T0562-223 2400, www.the gatewayhotels.com. 100 rooms. Tasteful Mughal-style interiors, large pool surrounded by lovely gardens, comfortable rooms some Taj facing. Friendly staff, good restaurant Jhankar.

LL-AL Trident Hilton, Fatehabad Rd, T0562-233 1818, www.tridenthotels.com. 138 very comfortable rooms, good pool, beautiful gardens, lovely zen minimalist foyer which has recently been renovated. Kids' club with splash pool and activities. Friendly staff. Good restaurant. Recommended.

L Grand Imperial, Mahatma Gandhi Rd, T0562-225 1190, www.hotelgrand imperial.com. Agra's first bid at a genuine heritage hotel, with 30 pretty rooms, some still displaying their original red brickwork, arcaded around a pleasant lawn in a 100-year-old neoclassical mansion, all modern facilities, smart international restaurant. Swimming pool and small spa. The only drawback is the distance from the Taj and the proximity to a loud main road.

B-C Atithi, Fatehabad Rd, T0562-223 0040, www.hotelatithiagra.com. 44 a/c rooms in reasonable condition, pool not always kept clean, friendly staff, and better value than others in the area.

C-D Mayur Tourist Complex, Fatehabad Rd, T0562-233 2302, www.mayurcomplex.com. 24 a/c rooms in slightly run-down bungalows. The complex has a campground feel with bucket showers and children's park. Built in

1970s, decor unchanged since. Internet. Restaurant, beer-only bar, large pool, garden.

D Agra Hotel, 165 FM Cariappa Rd, T0562-236 3331, agrahotel@yahoo.com. Backpacker hotel away from the main hub. 18 rooms in 1926 'British-time' bungalow. Basic, old-fashioned, good food, pleasant garden. Very friendly family-run hotel. Views from the terrace.

D Lauries, Mahatma Gandhi Rd, T0562-242 1447, lauries hotel@hotmail.com. 28 rooms in 1880 building rich in history, including a 1961 visit from Queen Elizabeth II. An elegant air, and is set in beautiful surroundings with lovely gardens. Rooms are clean with the deepest baths in all of India. Fantastic budget hotel. Recommended.

D-E Sakura, 49 Old Idgah Colony, T0562-242 0169, ashu_sakura@yahoo.com. No-frills rooms on noisy street, but handy for train station and Jaipur buses (leave outside the door). Manager is also a tour guide who has lots of tips. Hotel provides free pickup from train or bus station.

E-F Sheela, East Gate, 2 mins' walk from Taj, T0562-233 1194, www.hotelsheelaagra.com. 25 decent rooms with bath, pleasant garden, good restaurant, clean, peaceful, reliable laundry, secure (ask for gates to be unlocked for sunrise), very helpful manager. Good location in low pollution area. May be moved to sister hotel **Sheela Inn**, which is a 10-min bicycle rickshaw ride away if the hotel is full. (no commission to rickshaws), reserve ahead.

E-F Tourists Rest House, 4/62 Kutchery Rd, Balugunj, T0562-246 3961, www.dontworry chickencurry.com. 28 basic but reasonably clean rooms, bucket baths some a/c, vegetarian restaurant, knowledgeable manager, often full. Runs popular 2-week trips to Rajasthan.

F-G Host,West Gate, T(0)9219-143409. 15 spartan but spacious and quite clean rooms with bath and hot water, rooftop restaurant with great view of Taj, some rooms have no windows but very good location.

G Youth Hostel, Sanjay Pl, Mahatma Gandhi Rd, T0562-215 4462. 4 double rooms, 2 singles, 6 dorms. Clean if a little drab, good value but a long way from the Taj. Usual YHA rules apply.

Mathura *p117, map p118*

Hotels serve vegetarian food only. No alcohol.

A-B Radha Ashok (Best Western), Masani By-pass Rd, Chatikara, 4 km north of centre, T0565-329 8427, www.bestwestern.com. 21 comfortable, spacious rooms (freezing a/c) in modern if bland hotel, good restaurant, pool.

B Sheetal Regency, near Krishna Janma-bhoomi, Deeg Gate, Masani Rd, T0565-240 4401, www.hotelsheetalregency.com. 28 passable rooms in friendly, modern hotel. Also changes money.

C Madhuvan, Krishna Nagar, T0565-242 0064, madhuvanhotel@indiatimes.com. 28 clean, fragrant rooms, some a/c with bath, restaurant, exchange, travel, pool, a little gloomy but friendly.

C-D Dwaper Resorts, Km 162 marker, NH2, 17 km south of Mathura on the Agra Rd, T0565-248 0092. Restaurant, bar, attractive gardens, convenient rest stop but the rooms are in poor condition.

D-F Agra, near Bengali Ghat, T0565-240 3318. 15 clean, basic rooms, some a/c, traditional, friendly, well-run.

E Shri Giriraj Guest House, near Potra Kund, Shri Krishna Janma Bhumi, T0565-242 3545. 11 basic rooms in quieter location than most.

F-G International Guest House, Katra Keshav Deo, T0565-242 3888. Some air-cooled rooms, interesting place to stay.

F-G Modern, near Old Bus Stand, T0565-240 4747. Basic rooms plus bar and restaurant.

G Railway Retiring Rooms, at Cantt and Junction stations.

Vrindavan *p119, map p120*

B Ananda Krishna Van, Parikrama Marg, near ISKCON, T0565-329 8855, www.ananda krishna van.com. Sprawling new construction complete with waterfall, bathing pool, temple and restaurants, many rooms taken on timeshare basis, but some 4 bed a/c rooms available to visitors, remarkable undertaking.

D-E MVT Guest House, next to ISKCON, T0565-320 7578, www.mvtindia.com. Comfortable rooms, some a/c, set around pleasant gardens. Highly rated restaurant.

E International Rest House (ISKCON), Raman Reti, T0565-254 0022. Clean rooms, good, reasonably priced vegetarian restaurant, very popular, book well ahead.

E Shri Shri Radheshyam Palace, signposted behind ISKCON, T0565-254 0729. 22 clean rooms in friendly, well-located hotel.

Fatehpur Sikri *p121, map p121*

It is worth spending a night here to make an early start.

D-E Rahi Gulistan Tourist Complex (UP Tourism), Agra Rd, 1 km from bus stand, T05613-282490, www.up tourism.com. Reasonable rooms with modern facilities, Campground feel, quiet, pleasant grounds, restaurant, bar.

D-F Govardhan, Buland Darwaza Rd Crossing, T05613-882643, www.hotelfatehpur sikriviews.com. Clean shared bathroom, air-cooled suites with fridge, camping (Rs 20), 20% student discount, garden restaurant, pool, badminton, well maintained, lively and conscientious owner. Recommended.

E-F Ajay Palace, near bus stand, T05613-282950. Clean rooms in busy location over-looking market, nice view from rooftop restaurant. Luggage storage facilities.

🍴 Eating

Agra *p107, map p108*

🍴🍴🍴 **Esphahan**, Amar Vilas (see Sleeping). Outstanding, rich Avadhi food in high-class setting, but non-residents will find it hard to get a table.

🍴🍴🍴 **Jhanka**, Gateway Hotel (see Sleeping). Tasty Indian food, pleasant surroundings and good service.

🍴🍴🍴 **Mughal Room**, Hotel Clarks Shiraz, 54 Taj Rd. Pretty standard 5-star fare, rich and meaty, mainly distinguished by glassed-in rooftop setting with great views over the city.

🍴🍴🍴 **Peshawari**, Mughal Sheraton (see Sleeping). Regarded as the city's best, refined North Indian cuisine, smart surroundings, vegetarian offerings less inspired.

Dasaprakash, Meher Theatre Complex, 1 Gwalior Rd, T0562-236 3535. Comprehensive range of South Indian offerings, *thalis* and *dosas* a speciality, slightly sterile chain-style interior but good hygiene and service.

Only, 45 Taj Rd, T0562-236 4333. Interesting menu, attractive outside seating, popular with tour groups, live entertainment.

Riao, next to **Clarks Shiraz**, 44 Taj Rd, T0562-329 9663. Good North Indian food, puppet shows and live music, great garden and atmosphere.

Sonam, 51 Taj Rd. Indian, Chinese. A/c, good food, well-stocked bar, large garden, popular with locals.

Joney's Place, near South Gate, Taj Ganj. The original and, despite numerous similarly named imitators, still the best. Tiny place but the food is consistently good. Can produce Israeli and Korean specialities. Recommended.

Maya, 18 Purani Mandi Circle, Fatehabad Rd. Varied menu, good Punjabi *thalis*, pasta, 'special tea', friendly, prompt service, hygienic, tasty, Moroccan-style decor. Recommended.

Shankara Vegis, Taj Ganj. Vegetarian food prepared in reassuringly clean, open kitchen. Rooftop seats have obscured view of Taj, vies with **Joney's Place** for the best *lassis* in Agra.

Shivam, Raj Hotel, near Taj south gate. Quality Indian, clean.

Yash Café. Indian/Western menu, cheap but freshly prepared, *malai kofta* very tasty.

Zorba the Buddha, E-19 Sadar Bazaar, T0562-222 6091, zorbaevergreen@yahoo.com. 1200-1500, 1800-2100. Run by disciples of Osho, one of India's more popular, and most libidinous gurus. Unusual menu (in a good way), naan breads a speciality, very clean, undersize furniture gives doll's house feel, an enjoyably quirky experience.

Cafés

Café Coffee Day, A7 Sadar Bazaar. Part of nationwide chain, good coffee and Western snacks, nice escape.

Park, Taj Rd, Sadar Bazaar. Standard North Indian menu, decor and service above average.

⊛ Festivals and events

Agra *p107, map p108*

18-27 Feb Taj Mahotsav, a celebration of the region's arts, crafts, culture and cuisine.
Aug/Sep A fair at Kailash (14 km away). A temple marks the spot where Siva is believed to have appeared in the form of a stone lingam.

Mathura *p117, map p118*

Mar Rang Gulal, the colourful Holi festival. Similar festivities at Janmashtami.
Aug/Sep Banjatra (Forest Pilgrimage). During the monsoon, episodes from Krishna's life are enacted.

⊙ Shopping

Agra *p107, map p108*

Agra specializes in jewellery, inlaid and carved marble, carpets and clothes. The main shopping areas are Sadar Bazar (closed Tue), Kinari Bazar, Gwalior Rd, Mahatma Gandhi Rd and Pratap Pura. Beware, you may order a carpet or an inlaid marble piece and have it sent later but it may not be what you ordered. Never agree to any export 'deals' and take great care with credit card slips (scams reported). Many rickshaws, taxi drivers and guides earn up to 40% commission by taking tourists to shops. Insist on not being rushed away from sights and shop independently. To get a good price you have to bargain hard anyway.

Carpets

Silk/cotton/wool mix hand-knotted carpets and woven *dhurries* are all made in Agra. High quality and cheaper than in Delhi.
Kanu Carpet Factory, Purani Mandi, Fatehabad Rd, T0562-233 0167. A reliable source.
Mughal Arts Emporium, Shamshabad Rd. Also has marble. Artificial silk is sometimes passed off as pure silk.

Handlooms and handicrafts

Government emporia in Taj. UP Handlooms and UPICA, Sanjay Place, Hari Parbat.

Marble

Delicately inlaid marble work is a speciality. Sometimes cheaper alabaster and soapstone is used and quality varies.

Akbar International, Fatehabad Rd. Good selection, inlay demonstration, fair prices.
Handicrafts Inn, 3 Garg Niketan, Fatehabad Rd, Taj Ganj.
Krafts Palace, 506 The Mall. Watch craftsmen working here.
UP Handicrafts Palace, 49 Bansal Nagar. Wide selection from table tops to coasters, high quality and good value.

▲ Activities and tours

Agra *p107, map p108*
Tour operators
Aargee, Fatehabad Rd, T0562-272 0914.
Mercury, Hotel Clarks Shiraz, 54 Taj Rd, T/F0562-222 6531. Helpful and reliable.
Travel Bureau, near Taj View Hotel, T0562-233 0245, www.travelbureauagra.com. Long-established local company, highly experienced (handle ground arrangements for most foreign travel agents), helpful, can arrange anything. Reliable and recommended.
UP Tours, Taj Khema (5 mins' walk from Taj East Gate), T0562-233 0140, tajkhema@up-tourism.com. Coach tours: Fatehpur Sikri-Taj Mahal-Agra Fort (full day) 1030-1830, Rs 1700 (Indian Rs 400) including guide and entry fees; half-day Fatehpur Sikri tour ends at 1300 which only gives 45 mins at the site, not worthwhile, better take a taxi if you can afford it. Sikandra–Fatehpur Sikri (half day) 0930-1400, Rs 100 (excludes entry fees); Sikandra–Fatehpur Sikri–Taj Mahal–Agra Fort (full day), 1030-1830. Tours start and finish at Agra Cantt Railway Station and tie in with arrival/departure of *Taj Express* (see Transport); check times. Pickup also possible from India Tourism office on The Mall (advance notice).
World Ways, Taj East Gate, T(0)9358-499616, worldways@mail.com. Arrangements for budget travellers.

⊖ Transport

Agra *p107, map p108*
Air
Kheria airport is 7 km from city centre. At the time of writing all flights are suspended. Several airlines have offices in Clarks Shiraz Hotel, including **Indian**, T0562-222 6801, and **Jet Airways**, T0562-222 6529.

Bus
Local City Bus Service covers most areas and main sights. Plenty leave from the Taj Mahal area and the **Fort Bus Stand**.
Long distance Most long-distance services leave from the **Idgah Bus Stand**, T0562-242 0324, including to: **Delhi** (4-5 hrs) via **Mathura** (1 hr); **Fatehpur Sikri** (40 km, 1 hr); **Bharatpur** (2 hrs); **Khajuraho** (10 hrs). Agra Fort Stand, T0526-236 4557, has additional buses to **Delhi**, **Lucknow** (10 hrs) and **Haridwar** (minimum 12 hrs). De luxe buses for **Jaipur** arrive and depart from a stop near **Hotel Sakura**: closer to most hotels and where there is less hassle from touts. **Delhi** from tourist office, 0700, 1445, de luxe, 4 hrs.

Motorbike/bicycle hire
Firoz Motorcycle House, Cariappa Rd, Enfield Bullets Rs 500 per day. Bike hire from Sadar Bazar, near police station and near Tourist Rest House, Rs 30-40 per day.

Rickshaw
Auto rickshaw Prepaid stand at Agra Cantt Station has prices clearly listed for point-to-point rates and sightseeing. Expect to pay Rs 60-70 to Fatehabad Rd or Taj Ganj, or Rs 300 for a full day.
Cycle rickshaw Negotiate (pay more to avoid visiting shops); Taj Ganj to Fort Rs 20; Rs 80-120 for visiting sights; Rs 150 for 10 hrs.

Taxi/car hire
Tourist taxis from travel agents, remarkably good value for visiting nearby sights. Non-a/c car Rs 5 per km, full day Rs 800 (100 km),

half day Rs 400 (45 km); a/c rates double; to Fatehpur Sikri Rs 1200 return). **Travel Bureau**, T0562-233 0230; **UP Tours**, T0562-233 0140.

Train

From Delhi train is the quickest and most reliable way. Most trains use **Agra Cantonment Railway Station**, 5 km west of Taj Mahal, enquiries T131, reservations T0562-242 1039, open 0800-2000. Foreigners' queue at Window 1. Pre-paid taxi/auto-rickshaw kiosk outside the station. Some trains to Rajasthan from quieter **Agra Fort Station**, T132, T0562-236 9590. Trains mentioned arrive and depart from **Agra Cantt** unless specified. To **Delhi**: *Shatabdi Exp 2001*, (**ND**), 2040, 2½ hrs; *Taj Exp 2279* (**HN**), 1855, 3¼ hrs (CC/II); *Intercity Exp 1103* (**HN**), 0600, 3½ hrs (2nd class only). To **Jaipur**: *Intercity Exp 2307*, 1645, 6 hrs (from Agra Fort); *Marudhar Exp 4853/63*, 0715, 6¾ hrs. **Jhansi** (via **Gwalior**): *Taj Express 2280*, 1015, 3 hrs, (Gwalior 1¾ hrs), **Mumbai** (**CST**): *Punjab Mail 2138*, 0855, 23¼ hrs. **Sawai Madhopur** (for Ranthambore) at 0600, 0900, 1800.

Mathura *p117, map p118*

Bus Frequent service to **Delhi**, **Jaipur** and neighbouring towns from the **New Bus Stand** opposite Hotel Nepal. Buses to **Govardhan** and **Agra** from Old Bus Stand near the railway station, T0565-240 6468.

Taxi From opposite District Hospital. Also, buses, auto and cycle rickshaws.

Train Mathura Junction is the main station, T0565-240 5830. Cantt Station is at Bahadurganj (metre gauge). **Sri Krishna Janmabhumi** is at Bhuteshwar. For Delhi and Agra, the best is to **Agra Cantt**: *Taj Exp 2280*, 0900, 47 mins. **New Delhi** (**HN**): *Taj Exp 2279*, 1930, 2¼ hrs. **Sawai Madhopur**: *Golden Temple Mail 2904*, 1025, 3 hrs; *Bandra Exp 9020*, 0140, 3½ hrs; *Janata Exp 9024*, 1735, 4 hrs. **Vrindavan**: see below.

Vrindavan *p119, map p120*

Bus/taxi Buses, *tempos* and rickshaws to and from **Mathura**.

Train Services from Mathura Junction at 0627, 0850, 1457, 1655, 1925, takes 35 mins; returns from **Vrindavan** at 0725, 0940, 1610, 1740, 2015.

Fatehpur Sikri *p121, map p121*

Bus Frequent buses from Agra Idgah Bus Stand (1 hr) Rs 17.

Taxi Taxis from **Agra** include the trip in a day's sightseeing (about Rs 1200 return).

● Directory

Agra *p107, map p108*

Banks Several ATMs on Fatehabad Rd (Cirrus, Maestro, Visa cards, etc). Andhra Bank, Taj Rd, opposite **Kwality's** gives cash against card. **Thomas Cook**, Crystal Tower, Fatehabad Rd, TCs and cash against card. **Internet** The Mall (24 hrs). Many in Taj Ganj and around hotel areas, Rs 40-50/hr. **Khurana Cyber Café**, 805 Sadar Bazar, opposite Cantt Hospital. **Medical services** Ambulance: T102. **District Hospital**, Chhipitola Rd/ Mahatma Gandhi Rd, T0562-236 2043. Dr VN, Kaushal, opposite Imperial Cinema, T0562-236 3550. Recommended. **Post** GPO opposite India Tourist Office, with Poste Restante. **Useful contacts** Fire: T101. Police: T100.

Mathura *p117, map p118*

Medical services District Hospital, near Agra Rd, T0565-240 3006. Methodist Hospital, Vrindavan Rd, T0565-273 0043.

Contents

Footprint features

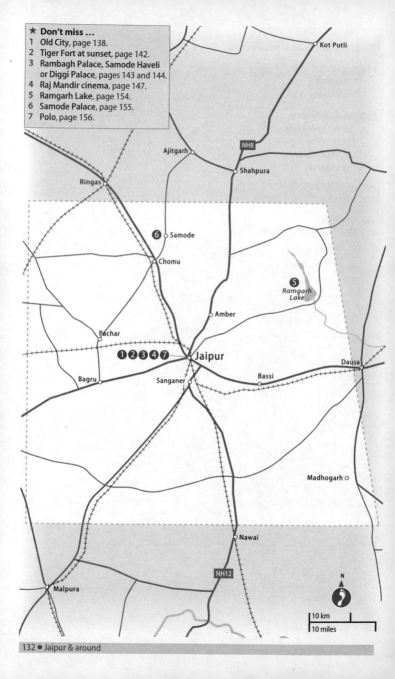

★ **Don't miss ...**
1 Old City, page 138.
2 Tiger Fort at sunset, page 142.
3 Rambagh Palace, Samode Haveli or Diggi Palace, pages 143 and 144.
4 Raj Mandir cinema, page 147.
5 Ramgarh Lake, page 154.
6 Samode Palace, page 155.
7 Polo, page 156.

Kot Putli

Ajitgarh

NH8

Shahpura

Ringas

6 Samode

Chomu

5 *Ramgarh Lake*

Amber

Pachar

1 2 3 4 7 Jaipur

Dausa

Bagru

Sanganer

Bassi

Madhogarh

Nawai

NH12

Malpura

N

10 km

10 miles

The bustle of Jaipur, the capital of Rajasthan and the state's most visited city, is at stark contrast to the tranquillity of the area surrounding it. Jaipur has much to offer, but can be something of an assault on your defences; touts preying on new arrivals make visiting the city's attractions sometimes as much an exercise in refusal as perusal.

Indeed, defence against unwelcome advances is a tradition built into Jaipur's landscape. The fortifications which stride across the arid ridges above the city, including the stunningly situated Amber Fort, are a reminder of the fiercely contested political history of northern Rajasthan. Yet alongside its status as a battleground, its dry hills and sometimes fertile valleys have also seen great prosperity, reflected in the palaces and country houses of the maharajas, and in vividly painted *havelis* such as the inimitable Samode Palace, rich with living reminders of past wealth and culture.

Having savoured Jaipur's historical sights, you might appreciate the opportunity to escape the city, and won't need to go far to find places that are equipped to refresh and revive the sated sightseer. Indeed, at times it can seem as though every palace, fort and hunting lodge for miles around has been sumptuously restored into a sybaritic bolthole, bestowing upon its (invariably well-heeled) guests the generous and almost manically attentive hospitality for which Rajasthan is fast becoming renowned.

Jaipur

→ *Colour map 4, C6. Phone code: 0141. Population: 2,600,000.*

The 'pink city', gateway to the state, is on the popular 'Golden Triangle' route (Delhi–Agra–Jaipur–Delhi), which, for many short-haul visitors, is their only experience of Rajasthan. The steady stream of tourists means the city has to make little effort to attract visitors; as a result its pastel-hued buildings are not what they used to be and many of the sights are poorly maintained. Nonetheless it's a worthwhile stopover in itself, as well as a staging post for the surrounding area. The old city, with its bazars, palaces and havelis, along with a couple of forts and the ancient city of Amber nearby, are well worth a wander. Knotted, narrow streets hold cupboard-sized workshops where elderly women dash out clothes on rusty Singers; men energetically stuff mattresses with piles of rags; boys mend bicycles next to old men rolling pellets of paste into sweets; whole families carve table legs or hammer bed headboards out of sheet metal; and 'gold men' leave the old city's textile houses sprinkled with metallic pigment from a day's work rubbing the powder into fabric patterned with resin glue. Escape the bustle and head up to the Tiger Fort (Nahargarh) for sunset, where proud peacocks pick among the ruins and monkeys scamper about in the twilight against the backdrop of Man Sagar Lake and its Jal Mahal (Water Palace). ▸▸ *For listings, see pages 143-151.*

Ins and outs

Getting there Sanganer Airport, 15 km south of town, has flights from Ahmedabad, Chennai, Delhi, Jodhpur, Mumbai, Rajkot and Udaipur. Airport buses, taxis and auto-rickshaws take 30 minutes to the centre. The railway station has links with most major cities. The Main Bus Terminal at Sindhi Camp is used by state and private buses. Buses from Delhi use the dramatically improved NH8; the journey now takes under four hours by car. The alternative Gurgaon–Alwar–Jaipur route is more interesting but much slower. Most hotels are a short auto-rickshaw ride away from the station and bus terminal.

Getting around The walled Old City, to the northeast of town, holds most of the sights and the bazar. Take a rickshaw to the area, then explore on foot. What few attractions the new town holds are spread out so it's best explored by rickshaw, bus or taxi. ▸▸ *See Transport, page 150.*

Tourist information Government of India Tourism ⓘ *Hotel Khasa Kothi, T0141-237 2200, Rajasthan, Paryatan Bhavan, Tourist Hotel, Mirza Ismail Rd, T0141-511 0598*, also has counters at the **Railway Station** ⓘ *T0141-231 5714*, and **Central Bus Stand** ⓘ *T0141-506 4102*. Guides for four to eight hours cost Rs 250-400 (Rs 100 extra for French, German, Japanese, Spanish). *'Jaipur for Aliens'*, a free miniature guidebook created by the owner of the **Pearl Palace Hotel**, has regularly updated information on transport and attractions; available at the hotel (see Sleeping, page 145).

History

Jaipur ('City of Victory') was founded in 1727 by **Maharaja Jai Singh II**, a Kachhawaha Rajput, who ruled from 1699 to 1744. He had inherited a kingdom under threat not only from the last great Mughal Emperor Aurangzeb, but also from the Maratha armies of Gujarat and Maharashtra. Victories over the Marathas and diplomacy with Aurangzeb won back the favour of the ageing Mughal, so that the political stability that Maharaja Jai Singh was instrumental in creating was protected, allowing him to pursue his scientific and cultural interests. Jaipur is very much a product of his intellect and talent. A story relates an encounter between the **Emperor Aurangzeb** and the 10-year-old Rajput prince. When asked what punishment he deserved for his family's hostility and resistance to the Mughals, the boy answered "Your Majesty, when the groom takes the bride's hand, he confers lifelong protection. Now that the Emperor has taken my hand, what have I to fear?" Impressed by his tact and intelligence, Aurangzeb bestowed the title of *Sawai* (one and a quarter) on him, signifying that he would be a leader.

Jai Singh loved mathematics and science, and was a keen student of astronomy, via Sanskrit translations of Ptolemy and Euclid. A brilliant Brahmin scholar from Bengal, Vidyadhar Bhattacharya, helped him to design the city. Work began in 1727 and it took four years to build the main palaces, central square and principal roads. The layout of streets was based on a mathematical grid of nine squares representing the ancient Hindu map of the universe, with the sacred Mount Meru, home of Siva, occupying the central square. In Jaipur the royal palace is at the centre. The three-by-three square grid was modified by relocating the northwest square in the southeast, allowing the hill fort of Nahargarh (Tiger Fort) to overlook and protect the capital. At the southeast and southwest corners of the city were squares with pavilions and ornamental fountains. Water for these was provided by an underground aqueduct with outlets for public use along the streets. The main streets are 33 yards wide (33 is auspicious in Hinduism). The pavements were deliberately wide to promote the free flow of pedestrian traffic and the shops were also a standard size. Built with ancient Hindu rules of town planning in mind, Jaipur was advanced for its time. Yet many of its buildings suggest a decline in architectural power and originality. The architectural historian Giles Tillotson argues that the "traditional architectural details lack vigour and depth and are also flattened so that they become relief sculpture on the building's surface, and sometimes they are simply drawn on in white outline".

In addition to its original buildings, Jaipur has a number of examples of late 19th-century buildings which marked an attempt to revive Indian architectural skills. A key figure in this movement was Sir Samuel Swinton Jacob. A school of art was founded in 1866 by a group of English officers employed by Maharaja Sawai Madho Singh II to encourage an interest in Indian tradition and its development. In February 1876 the Prince of Wales visited Jaipur, and work on the Albert Hall, now the Central Museum, was begun to a design of Jacob. It was the first of a number of construction projects in which Indian craftsmen and designers were employed in both building and design. This ensured that the Albert Hall was an extremely striking building in its own right. The opportunities for training provided under Jacob's auspices encouraged a new school of Indian architects and builders. One of the best examples of their work is the Mubarak Mahal (1900), now Palace Museum, designed by Lala Chiman Lal.

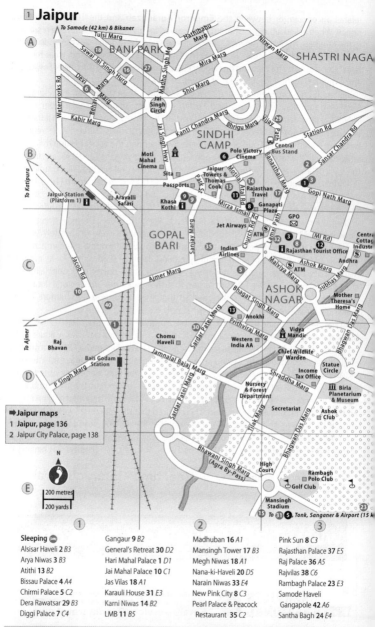

Jaipur

To Samode (42 km) & Bikaner
Tulsi Marg
Hathibabu Marg

BANI PARK

SHASTRI NAGA

Sawai Jai Singh Hurg
Devi Marg
Behari Marg
Kabir Marg

Mira Marg
Nirwan Marg

Madho Singh Mg
Shiv Marg

Jai Singh Circle

Kanti Chandra Marg
Bhrigu Marg

SINDHI CAMP

Vijay Path
Station Rd
Sansar Chandra Rd

Moti Mahal Cinema

Jai Singh Hwy

Jaipur Towers & Thomas Cook

Polo Victory Cinema

Central Bus Stand

Banasthali Marg

Jaipur Station (Platform 1)

Aravalli Safari

Sita

Passports

Khasa Kothi

Park St

Motilal Atal Rd

Rajasthan Travel

Gopi Nath Marg

Mirza Ismail Rd

Ganapati Plaza

GPO

To Katipura

GOPAL BARI

Jet Airways

Sanjay Marg

Indian Airlines

Church Marg

Tonk Path

ATM

Rajasthan Tourist Office

(MI Rd)

Central Cottage Industr

Andhra

Malviya Marg

Ashok Marg

ATM

Subhash Marg

To Ajmer

Jacob Rd

Ajmer Marg

Bhagat Singh Marg

ASHOK NAGAR

Bhagwan Das Marg

Mother Theresa's Home

Anokhi

Prithviraj Marg

Vidya Mandir

Raj Bhavan

Bais Godam Station

P Singh Marg

Chomu Haveli

Sardar Patel Marg

Jamnalal Bajaj Marg

Western India AA

Chief Wildlife Warden

Income Tax Office

Statue Circle

To Ajmer

Bhawani Singh Marg (Agra By-Pass)

Nursery & Forest Department

Secretariat

Shraddha Marg

Tilak Marg

Ashok Club

Birla Planetarium & Museum

➡ **Jaipur maps**
1 Jaipur, page 136
2 Jaipur City Palace, page 138

N

200 metres
200 yards

High Court

Rambagh Polo Club

Golf Club

Mansingh Stadium

To Tonk, Sanganer & Airport (15 k

Sleeping 🛏

Alsisar Haveli **2** *B3*	Gangaur **9** *B2*	Madhuban **16** *A1*	Pink Sun **8** *C3*
Arya Niwas **3** *B3*	General's Retreat **30** *D2*	Mansingh Tower **17** *B3*	Rajasthan Palace **37** *E5*
Atithi **13** *B2*	Hari Mahal Palace **1** *D1*	Megh Niwas **18** *A1*	Raj Palace **36** *A5*
Bissau Palace **4** *A4*	Jai Mahal Palace **10** *C1*	Nana-ki-Haveli **20** *D5*	Rajvilas **8** *C6*
Chirmi Palace **5** *C2*	Jas Vilas **18** *A1*	Narain Niwas **33** *E4*	Rambagh Palace **23** *E3*
Dera Rawatsar **29** *B3*	Karauli House **31** *E3*	New Pink City **8** *C3*	Samode Haveli
Diggi Palace **7** *C4*	Karni Niwas **14** *B2*	Pearl Palace & Peacock	Gangapole **42** *A6*
	LMB **11** *B5*	Restaurant **35** *C2*	Santha Bagh **24** *E4*

Shahar Palace **40** *C1*
Shahpura House **6** *A1*
Tourist **32** *C3*
Umaid Bhawan **27** *A2*
Umaid Mahal **16** *A1*
Youth Hostel **15** *E2*

Eating 🍴
BMB **2** *C5*
Chaitanya **1** *B3*
Chokhi Dhani **5** *E2*
Copper Chimney **3** *C3*
Dasaprakash **12** *C3*
Four Seasons **13** *C2*
Handi **3** *C3*

Kanji **6** *B2*
Lassiwala **4** *C4*
Mohan **11** *B2*
Natraj **10** *C4*
Niros & Book Corner **7** *C4*
Suriya India **8** *B2*
Surya Mahal **10** *C4*

Bars & clubs 🍸
Sheesha **9** *B2*

Hawa Mahal

ⓘ *Enter from Tripolia Bazar, Sat-Thu 0900-1630, Rs 5, cameras Rs 30, video Rs 70; for the best views accept invitations from shop owners on upper floors across the street.*

The 'Palace of the Winds' (circa 1799) forms part of the east wall of the City Palace complex and is best seen from the street outside. Possibly Jaipur's most famous building, this pink sandstone façade of the palace was built for the ladies of the harem by Sawai Pratap Singh. The five storeys stand on a high podium with an entrance from the west. The elaborate façade contains 953 small casements in a huge curve, each with a balcony and crowning arch. The windows enabled *hawa* (cool air) to circulate and allowed the women who were secluded in the *zenana* to watch processions below without being seen. The museum has second-century BC utensils and old sculpture

City Palace (1728-1732)

ⓘ *0930-1700 (last entry 1630). Foreigners Rs 300 (includes still camera and a good audio guide), Indians Rs 35 (camera Rs 50 extra); includes Sawai Man Singh II Museum and Jaigarh Fort, valid for 1 week. Video (unnecessary) Rs 200; doorkeepers expect tips when photographed. Photography in galleries prohibited.*

The City Palace occupies the centre of Jaipur, covers one seventh of its area and is surrounded by a high wall – the *Sarahad*. Its style differs from conventional Rajput fort palaces in its separation of the palace from its fortifications, which in other Rajput buildings are integrated in one massive interconnected structure. In contrast the Jaipur Palace has much more in common with Mughal models, with its main buildings scattered in a fortified campus. To find the main entrance, from the Hawa Mahal go north about 250 m along the Sireh Deori Bazar past the Town Hall (Vidhan Sabha) and turn left through an arch – the *Sireh Deori* (boundary gate). Pass under a second arch – the *Naqqar* Darwaza (drum gate) –

2 **Jaipur City Palace**

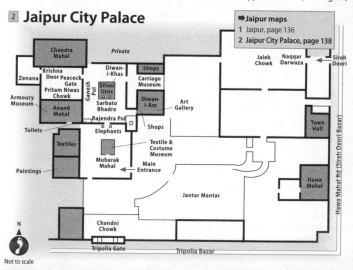

➡ **Jaipur maps**
1 Jaipur, page 136
2 Jaipur City Palace, page 138

Devotion across the seas

The present maharaja's grandfather was an extremely devout Hindu. Any physical contact with a non-Hindu was deemed to be ritually defiling, so contact with the British carried awkward ritual problems. Whenever required to meet a British official, including the viceroy, the maharaja would wear white gloves, and after any meeting would ritually purify himself in a bath of Ganga water and have the clothes he wore burnt. When he went to England to celebrate Queen Victoria's Diamond Jubilee, Sawai Madho Singh had a P&O liner refitted to include a Krishna temple and carried with him sufficient Ganga water to last the trip. The two 309-kg silver urns he used, the largest in the world, are currently on display in Jaipur's City Palace.

into Jaleb Chowk, the courtyard which formerly housed the palace guard. Today it is where coaches park. This is surrounded by residential quarters which were modified in the 19th century under Sawai Ram Singh II. A gateway to the south leads to the Jantar Mantar, the main palace buildings and museum and the Hawa Mahal.

Mubarak Mahal The main entrance leads into a large courtyard at the centre of which is the Mubarak Mahal, faced in white marble. Built in 1890, originally as a guesthouse for the Maharaja, the Mubarak Mahal is a small but immaculately conceived two-storeyed building, designed on the same cosmological plan in miniature as the city itself – a square divided into a three by three square grid.

The **Textile and Costume Museum** on the first floor has fine examples of fabrics and costumes from all over India, including some spectacular wedding outfits, as well as musical instruments and toys from the royal nursery. In the northwest corner of the courtyard is the **Armoury Museum** containing an impressive array of weaponry – pistols, blunderbusses, flintlocks, swords, rifles and daggers, as well as some fascinating paintings on the way in. This was originally the common room of the harem. From the north-facing first-floor windows you can get a view of the Chandra Mahal (see below). Just outside the Armoury Museum is **Rajendra Pol**, a gate flanked by two elephants, each carved from a single block of marble, which leads to the inner courtyard. There are beautifully carved alcoves with delicate arches and *jali* screens and a fine pair of patterned brass doors.

Diwan-i-Khas (Sarbato Bhadra) The gateway leads to the courtyard known variously as the Diwan-i-Am, the Sarbato Bhadra or the Diwan-i-Khas Chowk. Today, the building in its centre is known as the Diwan-i-Khas (circa 1730). Originally the Diwan-i-Am, it was reduced to the hall of private audience (Diwan-i-Khas) when the new Diwan-i-Am was built to its southeast at the end of the 18th century. The courtyard itself reflects the overwhelming influence of Mughal style, despite the presence of some Hindu designs, a result of the movement of Mughal-trained craftsmen from further north in search of opportunities to practise their skills. In the Diwan-i-Khas (now known by the Sanskrit name Sarbato Bhadra) are two huge silver urns – ratified by Guinness as being the largest pieces of silver in the world – used by Sawai Madho Singh for carrying Ganga water to England, see box, above.

Diwan-i-Am (Diwan Khana) Art Gallery With its entrance in the southeast corner of the Diwan-i-Am courtyard, the 'new' Hall of Public Audience built by Maharaja Sawai Pratap

Singh (1778-1803) today houses a fine collection of Persian and Indian miniatures, some of the carpets the maharajas had made for them and an equally fine collection of manuscripts. To its north is the **Carriage Museum**, housed in a modern building. In the middle of the west wall of the Diwan-i-Am courtyard, opposite the art gallery, is the **Ganesh Pol**, which leads via a narrow passage and the Peacock Gate into **Pritam Niwas Chowk**. This courtyard has the original palace building 'Chandra Mahal' to its north, the *zenana* on its northwest, and the Anand Mahal to its south. Several extremely attractive doors, rich and vivid in their colours, have small marble Hindu gods watching over them.

Chandra Mahal Built between 1727 and 1734 the Moon Palace is the earliest building of the palace complex. Externally it appears to have seven storeys, though inside the first and second floors are actually one high-ceilinged hall. The top two floors give superb views of the city and Tiger Fort. On the ground floor (north) a wide veranda – the **Pritam Niwas** (House of the Beloved) – with Italian wall paintings, faces the formal Jai Niwas garden. The main section of the ground floor is an Audience Hall. The palace is not always open to visitors.

The hall on the first and second floors, the **Sukh Niwas** (House of Pleasure), underwent a Victorian reconstruction. Above it are the **Rang Mandir** and the **Sobha Niwas**, built to the same plan. The two top storeys are much smaller, with the mirror palace of the **Chavi Niwas** succeeded by the small open marble pavilion which crowns the structure, the **Mukat Niwas**.

In the northeast corner of the Pritam Niwas Chowk, leading into the *zenana*, is the **Krishna door**, its surface embossed with scenes of the deity's life. The door is sealed in the traditional way with a rope sealed with wax over the lock.

Govind Deo Temple and beyond North of the Chandra Mahal, the early 18th-century Govind Deo Temple, which was probably built as a residence, has been restored by an ancient technique using molasses, curd, coconut water, fenugreek, rope fibres and lime, but is again not always open to visitors. The furniture is European – Bohemian glass chandeliers – the decoration Indian. Following the steps around you will see a *mandala* (circular diagram of the cosmos), made from rifles around the royal crest of Jaipur. The ceiling of this hall is in finely worked gold. Further on are the beautiful Mughal-style fountains and the **Jai Niwas gardens** (1727), laid out as a *char bagh*, the **Badal Mahal** (circa 1750) and the **Tal Katora** tank. The view extends across to the maharaja's private Krishna temple and beyond the compound walls to the Nahargarh (Tiger Fort) on the hills beyond.

Jantar Mantar (Observatory)

① *1000-1630, foreigners Rs 100, Indians Rs 10, camera Rs 50, video Rs 100 (stills better).*
Literally 'Instruments for measuring the harmony of the heavens', the Jantar Mantar was built between 1728 and 1734. Jai Singh wanted things on a grand scale and chose stone with a marble facing on the important planes. Each instrument serves a particular function and each gives an accurate reading. Hindus believe that their fated souls move to the rhythms of the universe, and the matching of horoscopes is still an essential part in the selection of partners for marriage. Astrologers occupy an important place in daily life and are consulted for all important occasions and decision-making. The observatory is fascinating. We recommend you hire a guide to explain the functions of the instruments. There is little shade so avoid the middle of the day. Moving clockwise the *yantras* (instruments) are as follows: **Small 'Samrat'** is a large sundial (the triangular structure) with flanking quadrants marked off in hours and minutes. The arc on your left shows the time from sunrise to midday, the one on the right midday to sundown. Read the time where the shadow is

sharpest. The dial gives solar time, so to adjust it to Indian Standard Time (measured from Allahabad) between one minute 15 seconds and 32 minutes must be added according to the time of year and solar position as shown on the board.

'Dhruva' locates the position of the Pole Star at night and those of the 12 zodiac signs. The graduation and lettering in Hindi follows the traditional unit of measurement based on the human breath, calculated to last six seconds. Thus: four breaths = one *pala* (24 seconds), 60 *palas* = one *gati* (24 minutes), 60 *gatis* = one day (24 hours).

'Narivalya' has two dials: south facing for when the sun is in the southern hemisphere (21 September-21 March) and north facing for the rest of the year. At noon the sun falls on the north-south line.

The Observer's Seat was intended for Jai Singh.

Small 'Kranti' is used to measure the longitude and latitude of celestial bodies.

'Raj' (King of Instruments) is used once a year to calculate the Hindu calendar, which is based on the Jaipur Standard as it has been for 270 years. A telescope is attached over the central hole. The bar at the back is used for sighting, while the plain disk is used as a blackboard to record observations.

'Unnathamsa' is used for finding the altitudes of the celestial bodies. Round-the-clock observations can be made and the sunken steps allow any part of the dial to be read.

'Disha' points to the north.

'Dakshina', a wall aligned north-south, is used for observing the position and movement of heavenly bodies when passing over the meridian.

Large 'Samrat' is similar to the small one (see above) but 10 times larger and thus accurate to two seconds instead of 20 seconds. The sundial is 27.4 m high. It is used on a particularly holy full moon in July/August, to predict the length and heaviness of the monsoon for the local area.

'Rashivalayas' has 12 sundials for the signs of the zodiac and is similar to the Samrat yantras. The five at the back (north to south), are Gemini, Taurus, Cancer, Virgo and Leo. In front of them are Aries and Libra, and then in the front, again (north-south), Aquarius, Pisces, Capricorn, Scorpio and Sagittarius. The instruments enable readings to be made at the instant each zodiacal sign crosses the meridian.

'Jai Prakash' acts as a double check on all the other instruments. It measures the rotation of the sun, and the two hemispheres together form a map of the heavens. The small iron plate strung between crosswires shows the sun's longitude and latitude and which zodiacal sign it is passing through.

Small 'Ram' is a smaller version of the Jai Prakash Yantra (see above).

Large 'Ram Yantra' Similarly, this finds the altitude and the azimuth (arc of the celestial circle from Zenith to horizon).

'Diganta' also measures the azimuth of any celestial body.

Large 'Kranti' is similar to the smaller Kranti (see above).

Gatore Ki Chhatriyan (Royal Gaitor)
ⓘ *Foreigners Rs 30, Indians Rs 20, camera Rs20.*

The gaitor is a complex of temples and tombs in the foothills of the the Nahargarh (Tiger Fort), see below. It has a dramatic rocky setting and good views of the crenellated city wall snaking up and over the dusty hills behind. Creamy marble domes with interiors of beautiful stonework encrusted with carvings of elephants, battle scenes and wild flowers. The site is barely maintained and the lawns are parched lawns, but endearingly so. It's a very peaceful, restful spot.

Nahargarh (Tiger Fort)

ⓘ *1000-1630, foreigners Rs 30, Indians Rs 5, camera Rs 30, video Rs 70. Rickshaw for sunset Rs 300-400 return. Snacks and drinks are available at the Durg Café.*

The small fort with its immense walls and bastions stands on a sheer rock face. The city at its foot was designed to give access to the fort in case of attack. To get there on foot you have to first walk through some quiet and attractive streets at the base of the hill, then 2 km up a steep, rough winding path to reach the top. Alternatively, it can also be reached by road via Jaigarh Fort. Beautifully floodlit at night, it dominates the skyline by day. Much of the original fort (1734) is in ruins but the walls and 19th-century additions survive, including rooms furnished for maharajas. This is a 'real fort', quiet and unrushed, and well worth visiting for the breathtaking views, to look inside the buildings and to walk around the battlements. However, it is an active fort used as a training ground for soldiers; women alone may feel quite vulnerable here. You can combine this visit with Jaigarh Fort (see page 154), 7 km away along the flat-topped hill, which is part of the same defensive network.

Central Museum and Modern Art Gallery

ⓘ *Museum Sat-Thu 1000-1630, Rs 30 (Mon free); gallery 1000-1700, free, closed 2nd Sat of month and Sun; garden 0900-1700, foreigners Rs 100, Indians Rs 10.*

Within the Ram Niwas Gardens you can visit the museum, gallery and a zoological garden. Housed in the beautiful Albert Hall is the **Central Museum**, displaying mainly excellent decorative metalware, miniature portraits and other art pieces. It also features Rajasthani village life – including some gruesome torture techniques – displayed through costumes, pottery, woodwork, brassware, etc. The first-floor displays are covered in dust and poorly labelled. **Modern Art Gallery**, Ravindra Rang Manch, has an interesting collection of contemporary Rajasthani art. Finally, in the gardens is the **Zoological Garden** containing lions, tigers, panthers, bears, crocodiles and deer, plus a bird park opposite.

SRC Museum of Indology

ⓘ *24 Gangwal Park, 0800-1600, foreigners Rs 40, Indians Rs 20.*

Further south, along J Nehru Marg, is the extraordinarily eclectic, and not a little quirky, SRC Museum of Indology. It houses a collection of folk and tantric art including all manner of manuscripts, textiles, paintings, Hindi written on a grain of rice, Sanskrit on a rabbit hair, fossils, medals, weapons and so on.

Birla Mandir

Something of an architectural curiosity, the modern temple built by the Birla family in the southeast of the city is impressive in scale and in the eclecticism of its religious art. The quality of the marble used can be seen in its near transparency.

Surya Mandir

ⓘ *Galta Pol can be reached by taking a bus or by walking 2 km east from the Hawa Mahal; from there it is about 600 m uphill and then downhill. A rickshaw costs Rs 200-250 return.*

From Galta Pol take a walk to the 'Valley of the Monkeys' to get a view of the city from the Surya Mandir (Sun Temple), which is especially impressive at sunset. It is not on the tourist circuit and so you are less likely to get hassled here. There are plenty of monkeys on the way up to the temple and you can buy bags of nuts to feed them. Walk down the steps from the top of the ridge to the five old temples, with impressive wall paintings, dedicated to Rama-Sita and Radha-Krishna. Hundreds of monkeys can be seen playing in the water tank below.

For Sleeping and Eating price codes and other relevant information, see Essentials pages 28-33.

● Sleeping

Jaipur *p134, map p136*

The city's popularity has meant that foreigners are targeted by hotel and shop touts, many of whom drive rickshaws, so be on your guard.

LL Jai Mahal Palace (Taj), Jacob Rd, Civil Lines, T0141-222 3636, www.tajhotels.com. 100 rooms in 250-year-old palace that has managed to maintain a real sense of authenticity. Bathrooms not as good as some but rooms are tastefully decorated and set in very attractive, peaceful gardens. Attentive staff. Pool is lovely.

LL Raj Palace (GKV Heritage), Chomu Haveli, Zorawar Singh Gate, Amer Rd, T0141-263 4077, www.rajpalace.com. 25 spacious suites with modern baths (extra bed US$15), 5-storeyed *haveli* (1728) with character carefully restored, traditional courtyard, Darbar Hall, garden, well managed, friendly service.

LL Rajvilas (Oberoi), 8 km from town on Goner Rd, T0141-268 0101, www.oberoi hotels.com. This award-winning hotel is housed in a low-lying recreated fort-palace within large, exquisitely landscaped gardens with orchards, pools and fountains. There are 71 rooms including 13 'tents' and 3 private villas with their own pools. Room interiors are not especially imaginative, but the safari-style 'tents' in a desert garden area are delightful. Bathrooms are impressive. There is also an Ayurvedic spa in a restored *haveli*. Indulgent and atmospheric, but slightly lacking in buzz.

LL Rambagh Palace (Taj), Bhawani Singh Rd, T0141-221 1919, www.tajhotels.com. 90 luxuriously appointed rooms and extraordinary suites arranged around a courtyard in the former maharaja's palace, still feels like the real thing. Set in 19 ha of beautifully maintained garden, larger groups are invited to participate in elephant polo on the back lawn! Stunning indoor pool and a new tented spa, but the real pièce de résistance is the spectacular dining hall, reminiscent of Buckingham Palace. Pleasant, relaxed atmosphere, good food and friendly staff. Extremely pricey but unforgettable.

LL-L Samode Haveli Gangapole, T0141-263 2407, www.samode.com. 150-year-old, beautifully restored *haveli* with a leafy courtyard and gardens. 30 rooms and 2 suites (the spectacular Maharaja and Maharani suites have original mirrored mosaics, faded wall paintings, pillars, lamp-lit alcoves, cushions and carved wooden beds). Evening meals are served in the peaceful, atmospheric courtyard or in the magnificent, somewhat over-the-top dining room. Large pool with bar. Excellent food, including a good Western selection, huge wine list.

L Mansingh Tower, Sansar Chandra Rd, T0141-237 8771, www.mansinghhotels.com. 45 rooms in modern business hotel, tastefully and imaginatively designed. A good option if palaces don't appeal.

A Alsisar Haveli, Sansar Chandra Rd, T0141-236 8290, www.alsisarhaveli.com. 36 intricately painted a/c rooms, modern frescoes, excellent conversion of 1890s character home, attractive courtyards, beautiful pool, but average food and below par service can be frustrating (try nearby **Chaitanya**, see Eating, below), village safaris available.

A Narain Niwas, Kanota Bagh, Narain Singh Rd, T0141-256 1291, www.hotelnarain niwas.com. The well-presented rooms pale in comparison to the suites in this characterful old mansion. There's a great dining room and lounge area, and clean pool in beautiful gardens, with lots of room to sit around the pool (which is rare). Patchy reports on food and service. The beautiful boutique **Hot Pink** is in the grounds and offers designer names.

A-B Bissau Palace, outside Chandpol Gate, T0141-230 4371, www.bissaupalace.com. 45 a/c rooms, some charming, in the home of the Rawal of Bissau (built 1919) with library and royal museum, interesting 'memorabilia' and antiques, bookshop, pleasant garden, good views from terrace of city and nearby forts, tours, excellent camel safaris, exchange, etc, from **Karwan Tours**, but temple music may irritate. Good summer discounts.

A-B Shahpura House, Devi Marg, Bani Park, T0141-220 2293, www.shahpurahouse.com. The only genuine 'heritage' option in the area, this 1950s maharaja's residence is still run by the family and has with many original features including mirrored *thekri* ceilings, comfortable individually decorated suites, old-fashioned bathrooms, lovely canopied rooftop restaurant (pricey meals), and a pool.

A-C Dera Rawatsar, D-194/C, Vijay Path, behind Sindhi Camp Bus Station, T0141-236 0717, www.derarawatsar.com. Beautiful rooms and **A-B** suites in smart new premises, all kept to a high standard. Outside areas are more understated than others in the area so has a more relaxed, family-run vibe.

A-C Hari Mahal Palace, Jacob Rd, Civil Lines, T0141-222 1399, www.harimahalpalace.com. 11 large, quirky rooms with big bath tubs, period furniture in old mansion, large lawn, old world feel.

B Jas Vilas, next to **Megh Niwas**, C-9 Sawai Jai Singh Highway, Bani Park, T0141-220 4638, www.jasvilas.com. A charming family-run hotel. 12 a/c rooms with bath (tub, power shower), internet, delicious home-cooked meals, very pretty pool surrounded by a lawn, friendly family. Their suite has a particularly amazing tiled bathtub. Recommended.

B Karauli House, New Sanganer Rd, Sodala (towards the airport), T0141-229 0763, www.karauli.com. 6 rooms in a family 'retreat', large garden, pool, personal attention, home-cooked meals.

B LMB, Johari Bazar, Old City, T0141-256 5844, www.hotellmb.com. Centrally a/c rooms above a famous restaurant/sweet shop, recently renovated, comfortable but dingy rooms with traffic noise, but certainly at the heart of everything and in walking distance of major sites.

B-C Diggi Palace, SMS Hospital Rd, T0141-237 3091, www.hoteldiggipalace.com.

43 attractive rooms in charming 125-year-old building. Not as glitzy as some but effortlessly chic with large range of rooms, Rs 500 category particularly good value. Lovely open restaurant, great home-grown food, peaceful garden, enthusiastic, helpful owners who host the Jaipur Literature and Heritage Festival. Calming atmosphere; you can really feel at home here. Highly recommended.

B-C Madhuban, D237 Behari Marg, Bani Park, T0141-220 0033, www.madhuban.net. Elegant, characterful hotel, 25 beautifully furnished rooms, small courtyard pool, pleasant garden, helpful staff, good food. Recommended.

B-C Megh Niwas, C-9 Jai Singh Highway, Bani Park, T0141-220 2034, www.meghniwas.com. 27 tastefully decorated, comfortable rooms, run by charming, knowledgeable family, good pool, excellent food.

B-C Nana-ki-Haveli, Fateh Tiba, Moti Dungri Rd, near Old City, T0141-261 5502, nanakihavelijaipur@yahoo.com. 12 spacious a/c rooms in a modernized 1918 garden house, the grounds are not as nice as others in this range, very hospitable, friendly family, excellent home cooking.

B-C Umaid Bhawan, D1-2A Bani Park, T0141-231 6184, www.umaidbhawan.com. 28 beautifully decorated and ornately furnished rooms, many with balconies, one of the most charming *haveli*-style guest houses with a lovely pool and friendly, knowledgeable owners. Highly recommended.

B-C Umaid Mahal, B2 Bihari Marg, Bani Park, T0141-220 1954, www.umaidmahal.com. A new heritage-style development with good modern facilities and stunning architectural features. Beautiful courtyard pool and Wi-Fi.

C General's Retreat, 9 Sardar Patel Rd, T0141-237 7134, www.generalsretreat.com. 8 rooms with bath, some with kitchenettes, attractive bungalow of a retired general, airy rooms, pleasant gardens and nice communal areas, restaurant.

C Santha Bagh, Kalyan Path, Narain Singh Rd, T0141-256 6790. 12 simple, comfortable rooms (a/c or air-cooled), very friendly, helpful and charming staff, excellent meals, lawn, quiet location. Recommended.

C-E Chirmi Palace, Dhuleshwar Garden, Sardar Patel Marg, T0141-236 5063, www.chirmi.com. 23 spacious but variable a/c rooms in 150-year-old *haveli* conversion. Traditional Rajasthani decor, attractive dining room, lawns, pool (summer only), email, gentle staff, slightly run-down but pleasant overall.

C-E Rajasthan Palace, 3 Peelwa Gardens, 1 km from Sanganeri Gate, Moti Dungri Rd, T0141-261 1542, rajasthanmotel@yahoo.co.in. 40 rooms, some old-fashioned and wacky, others modern and clean, plus budget rooms with shared bathroom, around pleasant gardens and small pool. In a city of palaces, this isn't in the same league.

C-E Shahar Palace, Barwada Colony, Civil Lines, T0141-222 1861, www.shahar palace.com. 9 rooms in a separate annexe of a residential home. Well-maintained gardens, home-cooked food and friendly but discreet staff make this a soothing retreat. Recommended.

D Arya Niwas, Sansar Chandra Rd (behind Amber Tower), T0141-237 2456, www.aryaniwas.com. 95 very clean, simple rooms but not always quiet, modernized and smart, good very cheap vegetarian food, pleasant lounge, travel desk, tranquil lawn, friendly, helpful, impressive management, book ahead (arrive by 1800), great value.

D Gangaur (RTDC), Mirza Ismail Rd, T0141-237 1641. 63 rooms, some a/c, restaurant, coffee shop, in need of a lick of paint and an airing, but convenient for bus/railway stations.

D-E Atithi, 1 Park House Scheme, T0141-237 8679, atithijaipur@hotmail.com. 24 rooms, being upgraded at time of writing, wonderful hot showers, relaxing roof terrace, internet, good vegetarian food, helpful, friendly staff. Recommended.

D-E Karni Niwas, C-5 Motilal Rd, T0141-236 5433, www.hotelkarniniwas.com. Ever-expanding place with a variety of rooms, some large with a/c, some with balconies, poor standard at time of writing, you can find better at this price range, breakfast and snacks available, and internet.

E Tiger Fort, T0141-236 0238. For an atmospheric stay. Here, you'll find 2 simple rooms with bath. Enquire at the Durg Café (see page 142).

E-F Pearl Palace, Hathroi Fort, Ajmer Rd, T0141-237 3700, www.hotelpearlpalace.com. A real gem. Rooms are quirky and all slightly different with art pieces gathered or designed by the charming owner, modern, comfortable, some with a/c, Wi-Fi, lots of character. The pinnacle is the Peacock restaurant on the roof serving excellent food with great views of Jaipur, surrounded by plants. Money exchange at good rates. The owner will also soon be opening a heritage-style property close by – www.pearlpalaceheritage.com. Wholeheartedly recommended.

F Hotel Pink Sun, Mirza Ismail Rd, opposite GPO, behind Kamal & Co, T0141-236 3774. Basic, clean rooms with bath, set around beautiful gardens. Access is through an alleyway; not ideal for solo women.

F New Pink City, Chameliwala market, off Mirza Ismail Rd, T0141-237 6753. Clean, simple rooms in busy location, right at the heart of things, good for doing business in the market. Good rooftop restaurant. New floor being built, so more rooms soon.

F Shakuntalam, D-157 Durga Marg, Bani Park, T0141-220 3225. 16 adequate rooms, family-run, attentive service, meals available.

F Tourist Hotel (RTDC), Mirza Ismail Rd, same building as tourist office, T0141-236 0238. 47 simple rooms with bath, dorm (Rs 50), little atmosphere, beer bar, tours, well located.

G Youth Hostel, near the SMS Stadium, out of town, T0141-274 1130. 8 clean double rooms plus 3 dorms (Rs 40), renovated, good value. Discounts for YHA members.

Paying guests

Good home-cooked meals are a big bonus.

E Mandap Homestays, 1 Bhilwa Garden, Moti Dungri Rd, T0141-261 4389. Friendly home of former ruling family with 10 rooms and more under construction.

E Shri Sai Nath, 1233 Mali Colony, outside Chandpol Gate, T0141-230 497. 10 clean, quiet rooms, meals on request, very hospitable, helpful and warm.

❷ Eating

Jaipur p134, map p136

† † † **Jai Mahal Palace** (see Sleeping). International cuisine in beautiful surroundings, buffet breakfast and dinner recommended; but snack bar inadequate.

† † † **Rambagh Palace** (see Sleeping). Royal Indian cuisine from 4 regions in the beautiful *Suvarna Mahal* restaurant, attractive light-filled coffee shop, popular for lunch, pricey (Rs 2500 minimum for non-residents) but generous.

† † † - † **Chokhi Dhani**, 19 km south on Tonk Rd, T0141-277 0555, www.chokhidhani.com. 2 options in an enjoyable 'village' theme park with camel rides, dancing and puppet shows: the posh **Bindola**, multi-cuisine with live ghazals, or the fun but very crowded **Sangari**, where you sit on the floor and eat Rajasthani food with your fingers. The latter is included in Rs 250 per person entry fee. A taxi will cost around Rs 400 return. There's also good accommodation, *haveli*-style or in huts, and a pool.

† † **Chaitanya**, Sansar Ch Rd, 100 m from **Alsisar Haveli** (see Sleeping), in shopping complex on opposite side of road. Excellent vegetarian in civilized surroundings. Extensive menu includes Rajasthani, Italian and Mexican specialities.

† † **Copper Chimney**, Mirza Ismail Rd, T0141-237 2275. Open for lunch and dinner. A/c, quality international food, large non-vegetarian selection including seafood from Sep to Mar. Incessant *muzak*.

† † **Dasaprakash**, Mirza Ismail Rd. Upmarket and modern South Indian chain restaurant, serving first-rate *utthapam* and *upma* alongside the usual range of dosas. A/c can be a bit fierce.

† † **Four Seasons**, D-43A2 Subhash Mg, C-Scheme, T0141-227 5450. High-quality

vegetarian Indian and Chinese, with an extensive menu, pleasantly smart ambience and good staff. A worthwhile detour.

† † **Handi**, back of Maya Mansion on Mirza Ismail Rd, T0141-236 4839. Indian. Partly open-air, simple canteen style.

† † **LMB**, Johari Bazar. Rajasthani vegetarian in slightly confused contemporary interior matched by upbeat dance tunes. Tasty (if a little overpriced) *thalis*; (*panchmela saag* particularly good). Popular sweet shop and egg-free bakery attached. During *Diwali*, this is a feast for the senses.

† † **Natraj**, Mirza Ismail Rd. Rajasthani, some Chinese, vegetarian only. A/c, much smarter inside than out. Good range of *thalis* and sweets, Western classical on stereo.

† † **Niros**, Mirza Ismail Rd, T0141-2374493. International. With its bland decor you could be anywhere, but there's a good choice of Indian, Chinese and continental dishes, all set to blasting a/c and *popzak*.

† † **Suriya India**, B Ganpati Plaza, Motilal Atal Rd, T0141-360749. Good selection of pure vegetarian North Indian, live music.

† † **Surya Mahal**, Mirza Ismail Rd, T0141-236 9840. East meets west in chaotic clash of interiors. Wide variety including Mexican and pizzas, food far superior to music.

† **BMB**, Sanganeri Gate. Excellent value dosas and snacks on the edge of the Old City; dingy but clean a/c section upstairs. Good sweets too.

† **Kanji**, opposite Polo Victory Cinema, Station Rd. Clean and extremely popular sweets-and-snacks joint, a good place to experiment with exotica such as *Raj kachori* or *aloo tikki*, both of which come smothered in yoghurt and mild sweet chutney. Stand-up counters downstairs, a/c seating upstairs.

† **Lassiwala**, Mirza Ismail Rd, opposite Niro's. The unrivalled best *lassis* in the city, served in rough clay cups and topped off with a crispy portion of milk skin. Of the 3 'original' Lassiwalas parked next to each other, the genuine one is on the left, next to the alley. Come early; they run out by afternoon.

† **Mohan**, Motilal Atal Rd, opposite **Neelam Hotel**. Simple restaurant with good

pan-Indian food accompanied by Punjabi prayer music, *thalis* recommended.

♉ **Peacock**, on roof of **Pearl Palace** (see Sleeping). Excellent Indian and continental dishes plus backpacker fare, with vegetarian and non-vegetarian food prepared in separate kitchens. Superb views by day and night, eclectic collection of quirky furniture designed by the owner watched over by a giant peacock. Worth seeking out if you're not staying.

☊ Bars and clubs

Jaipur *p134, map p136*
Nawabganj Safari, Crystal Palm Mall, Level 3, Sardar Patel Parg. A little bit like a Disney jungle ride with moving plastic animals and with bar stools designed on the rear ends of zebra and ostriches (which can make for very unflattering photographs) this bar is a sight to behold, Grab a cocktail and enjoy your safari.
Sheesha, City Pearl, near Khasa Kothi, M I Rd. Get giddy with great views and cocktails at this vibey bar spread over 4 levels (outdoor and indoor seating).

⊕ Entertainment

Jaipur *p134, map p136*
Raj Mandir Cinema, off Mirza Ismail Rd. 'Experience' a Hindi film in shell pink interior.
Ravindra Rang Manch, Ram Niwas Garden. Hosts cultural programmes and music shows.

⊛ Festivals and events

Jaipur *p134, map p136*
See page 35 for nationwide festivals.
14 Jan Makar Sankranti The kite-flying festival is spectacular. Everything closes down in the afternoon and kites are flown from every rooftop, street and even from bicycles. The object is to bring down other kites to the deafening cheers of huge crowds.

Late Jan Jaipur Literary Festival. Started in 2006, this is an exciting gathering of writers and musicians with readings, workshops and performances. Speakers have included Vikram Seth, Pico Iyer, Hanif Kureshi and Simon Shama.
Feb/Mar Elephant Festival (28 Feb 2010, 19 Mar 2011) at Chaugan Stadium, procession, elephant polo, etc.
Mar/Apr Gangaur Fair (18-19 Mar 2010, 19 Mar 2011) about a fortnight after **Holi**, when a colourful procession of women starts from the City Palace with the idol of Goddess Gauri. They travel from the Tripolia Gate to Talkatora, and these areas of the city are closed to traffic during the festival.
Jul/Aug Teej (12-13 Aug 2010, 2-3 Aug 2011). The special celebrations in Jaipur have elephants, camels and dancers joining in the processions.

⊙ Shopping

Jaipur *p134, map p136*
Jaipur specializes in printed cotton, handicrafts, carpets and *durries* (thick handloomed rugs); also embroidered leather footwear and blue pottery. You may find better bargains in other cities in Rajasthan.

Antiques and art
Art Palace, Chomu Haveli. Specializes in 'ageing' newly crafted items – alternatives to antiques. Also found around Hawa Mahal.
Manglam Arts, Amer Rd. Sells modern miniature paintings and silver.
Mohan Yadav, 9 Khandela House, behind Amber Gauer, SC Rd, T0141-378 009. Visit the workshop to see high-quality miniatures produced by the family.
Royale Treasure, 5 Jacob Rd, Civil Lines, www.royaletreasure.com. If you are inspired to redecorate, **Royale Treasure** offers up an eclectic mix of hand-painted cabinets, decorative lamps, jewellery boxes, textiles and wall hangings. A day out in itself.

Bazars

Traditional bazars and small shops in the Old City are worth a visit; cheaper than Mirza Ismail Rd shops but may not accept credit cards. Most open Mon-Sat 1030-1930.
Bapu Bazar specializes in printed cloth.
Chaupar and **Nehru Bazars** for textiles.
Johari Bazar for jewellery.
Khajanewalon-ka-Rasta, off Chandpol bazar, for marble and stoneware.
Maniharon-ka-Rasta for lac bangles which the city is famous for.
Ramganj Bazar has leather footwear while opposite Hawa Mahal you will find the famous featherweight Jaipuri *rezais* (quilts).
Tripolia Bazar (3 gates), inexpensive jewellery.

Blue pottery

Blue Pottery Art Centre, Amer Rd, near Jain Mandir. For unusual pots.
Kripal Kumbha, B-18, Shiv Marg, Bani Park, T0141-220 0127. Gives lessons by appointment. Recommended.

Books

Book Corner, Mirza Ismail Rd, by Niros Restaurant (see Eating). Good selection.
Bookwise, Rajputana Sheraton Hotel, also in Mall 21 opposite Rajmandir Cinema. Vast range, excellent service, fair price.
City Books and Art Palace, just inside gate at City Palace, T0141-261 0970. Wide range of reference and coffee-table books on Rajasthan.
Photo Service, Rambagh Palace Hotel (see Sleeping), T0141-238 5030, bookshop506@hotmail.com. Has old and obscure Rajasthani titles as well as typical holiday reading.

Carpets

Channi Carpets and Textiles, Mount Rd opposite Ramgarh Rd. Factory shop, watch carpets being hand-knotted, then washed, cut and quality checked with a blow lamp.
Maharaja, Chandpol (near **Samode Haveli**). Watch carpet weavers and craftsmen, good-value carpets and printed cotton.
The Reject Shop, Bhawani Singh Rd. For 'Shyam Ahuja' *durrie* collections.

Fabrics

Chirag International, 771 Khawasji ka Rasta, Hawa Mahal Rd. Wholesale warehouse, with a corresponding vast selection.
Ridhi Sidhi Textiles, 9 East Govind Nagar, Amber Rd.

Handicrafts

Anokhi, 2nd floor, KK Sq, Yudhistra Marg, opposite Udyog Bhawan. Well-crafted, attractive block- printed clothing, linen, etc. Recommended.
Gems & Silver Palace, G11 Amber Tower, Sansar Ch Rd. Good choice of 'old' textiles, reasonable prices, helpful owners.
Handloom Haveli, Lalpura House, Sansar Ch Rd.
Handloom House, Rituraj Building, Mirza Ismail Rd (near **Tourist Hostel**).
Rajasthali, Government Handicrafts, Mirza Ismail Rd, 500 m west of Ajmeri Gate.
Rajasthan Fabrics & Arts, near City Palace gate. Exquisite textiles.

Clothing and lifestyle

Hot Pink, Narain Niwas (see Sleeping) T0141-510 8932, www.hotpinkindia.com. Beautiful boutique in the grounds of Narain Niwas Palace in the south of city with pieces from Indian designers including Manish Arora (the master of kitsch chic), Abraham & Thakore (for true elegance) and Tarun Tahliani (for Bollywood style). Homeware also available.

Jewellery

Jaipur is famous for gold, jewellery and gem stones (particularly emeralds, rubies, sapphires and diamonds, but diamonds require special certification for export). Semi-precious stones set in silver are more affordable (but check for loose settings, catches and cracked stones); sterling silver items are rare in India and the content varies widely. Johari Bazar is the scene of many surreptitious gem deals, and has backstreet factories where you may be able to see craftsmen at work. Bargaining is easier on your own so avoid being taken by a 'guide'. For about Rs 40 you can have gems authenticated and valued at the **Gem Testing Laboratory**, off Mirza Ismail Rd near New Gate, T0141-256 8221 (reputable jewellers should not object).

Do not use credit cards to buy these goods and never agree to 'help to export' jewellery. There have been reports of misuse of credit card accounts at **Apache Indian Jewellers** (also operating as **Krishna Gems** or **Ashirwad Gems & Art**) opposite Samodia Complex, Loha Mandi, SC Rd; and **Monopoli Gems**, opposite Sarga Sooli, Kishore Niwas (1st floor) Tripolia Bazar.

Reputable places include **Beg Gems**, Mehdi-ka-Chowk, near Hawa Mahal. **Bhuramal Rajmal Surana**, 1st floor, between Nos 264 and 268, Haldiyon-ka-Rasta. Highly recommended. **Dwarka's**, H2O Bhagat Singh Marg. Crafts high-quality gemstones in silver, gold and platinum in modern and traditional designs. **Ornaments**, 32 Sudharma Arcade, Chameliwala Market, opposite GPO (turn left, first right and right again). Recommended for stones and silver (wholesale prices; made up in 24 hrs).

Photography
Sentosa Colour Lab, Ganpati Plaza, Mirza Ismail Rd. Good fast printing service and limited range of supplies.

Silverware
Amrapali Silver Shop, corner of Mirza Ismail and Mahavir Marg, opposite Thomas Cook and Natraj.
Arun's Emporium, Mirza Ismail Rd.
Mona Lisa, Hawa Mahal Rd.
Nawalgarh Haveli, near Amber Fort bus stop.

▲▲ Activities and tours

Jaipur *p134, map p136*
Some hotels (such as the **Rambagh Palace**, see Sleeping) will arrange golf, tennis, squash, or elephant polo.

Body and soul
Kerala Ayurveda Kendra, T0141-510 6743, www.keralaayurvedakendra.com. Ayurvedic treatments, clean and hygienic, recommended for massages, also constitution analysis, Panchkarma, classes in Ayurveda. Phone for free pickup.
Vipasana Centre, Dhammathali, Galta, 3 km east of centre, T0141-268 0220. Meditation courses for new and experienced students.

City tours
RTDC City Sightseeing Half day: 0800-1300, Rs 150; Central Museum, City Palace, Amber Fort and Palace, Gaitore, Laxmi Narayan Temple, Jantar Mantar, Jal Mahal, Hawa Mahal.

Full day: 0900-1800, Rs 200; including places above, plus Jaigarh Fort, Nahargarh Fort, Birla Planetarium, Birla Temple and Kanak Vrindavan. **Pink City by Night**: 1830-2230, Rs 250. Includes views of Jai Mahal, Amber Fort, etc, plus dinner at Nahargarh Fort. Call T0141-220 3531 or book at railway station, **Gangaur Hotel** or **Tourist Hotel** (see Sleeping).

Other operators also offer city sightseeing: half/full day, Rs 100-150. The tours are worthwhile, but may miss out promised sights claiming they are closed. Some may find the guides' English difficult to follow and the obligatory shopping trips tedious.

General tours

Aravalli Safari, opposite **Rajputana Palace Hotel**, Palace Rd, T0141-236 5344, aravalli2@datainfosys.net. Very professional. **Chetan**, 17 Muktanand Nagar, Gopalpura Bypass, Tonk Rd, T0141-254 5302. Experienced, reliable car tours. **Forts & Palaces Tours Ltd**, S-1, Prabhakar Apartment No 8, Vaishali Nagar, T0141-235 4508, www.palaces-tours.com. A very friendly, knowledgeable outfit offering camel safaris, sightseeing tours, hotel reservations, etc. **Karwan Tours**, Bissau Palace Hotel, Chandpol Gate, T0141-230 8103, karwantours@mailcity.com. For camel safaris, tours, taxis, ticketing, exchange; very helpful. **Rajasthan Travel**, 52 Ganpati Plaza, Mirza Ismail Rd, T0141-236 5408, rtsjaipur@bhaskarmail.com. Ticketing, reliable guides. Recommended.

❸ Transport

Jaipur *p134, map p136*
Air
Sanganer Airport, T0141-272 1333, has good facilities. Transport to town: taxi, 30 mins, Rs 250-300; auto-rickshaw Rs 150. Indian Airlines, Nehru Pl, Tonk Rd, T0141-274 3324; airport, T0141-272 1519, flies to **Delhi, Mumbai, Udaipur, Ahmedabad, Kolkata, Dubai**. Jet Airways, T0141-511 2222; airport

T0141-255 1352, flies to **Delhi, Mumbai** and **Udaipur**. Go Air, T0141-650 0801, flies to **Delhi** and **Mumbai**. Spicejet, T18000-180 3333, to **Ahmedabad, Chennai, Hyderabad** and **Mumbai**. Air Deccan, T3900 8888, to **Bengaluru (Bangalore)** and **Mumbai**. Kingfisher, T0141-272 3485 or T1800-180 0101 to **Goa, Hyderabad, Kolkata** and **Mumbai**.

Bus
Local Unless you have plenty of time and a very limited budget, the best way to get around the city is by auto-rickshaw. To **Amber**, buses originate from Ajmeri Gate, junction with Mirza Ismail Rd, so get on there if you want a seat.
Long distance Central Bus Stand, Sindhi Camp, Station Rd. Enquiries: *De luxe*, Platform 3, T0141-511 6031, *Express*, T0141-511 6044 (24 hrs). Left luggage, Rs 10 per item per day. When arriving, particularly from Agra, you may be told to get off at Narain Singh Chowk, a bus stand some distance south of the centre; to avoid paying an inflated auto-rickshaw fare, insist on staying on until you reach the bus stand. Private buses will drop you on Station Rd but are not allowed inside the terminal. State and private *De luxe* buses are very popular so book 2 days in advance. To **Agra** 12 buses a day 0600-2400, 6½ hrs with 1 hr stop, a/c buses at 0800 and 1415, Rs 194/316, a/c, pay when seat number is written on ticket; (230 km, 5 hrs, via Bharatpur) – get off at the 2nd (last) stop to avoid being hassled by rickshaw drivers; **Ajmer** (131 km, regular service 0400-2330, 3 hrs, Rs 94/135 for a/c); **Bharatpur** 5 buses a day, but all de luxe and a/c buses to Agra go through Bharatpur but you have to pay Agra fare Rs 119; **Delhi** (261 km, ½ hourly, 5½ hrs, almost hourly service with de luxe, Pink Line and Volvo buses running Rs 300/500 for a/c; **Jaisalmer** (654 km, 2145, 13 hrs via Jodhpur, Rs 391). **Jodhpur** (332 km, frequent, 7 hrs, Rs 219/322); **Udaipur** (374 km, 12 hrs, Rs 267 for a/c, 4 a/c and sleeper buses Rs 419 for a/c and sleeper); **Kota** via **Bundi** (7 daily, 4-5 hrs);

Chittaurgarh (de luxe, 1200, 2115, 2400). One daily to **Shimla** (2000) and **Haridwar** (2200) – mixed reports on Shimla and Haridwar service, often you have to change in Delhi and pay again.

Rickshaw
Auto-rickshaw Avoid hotel touts and use the pre-paid auto-rickshaw counter to get to your hotel. Persistent auto-rickshaw drivers at railway station may quote Rs 10 to anywhere in town, then overcharge for city tour.

From city centre hotel, about Rs 30; sightseeing (3-4 hrs) Rs 200, 6-7 hrs, Rs 360. From railway and bus stations, drivers (who expect to take you to shops for commission) offer whole-day hire including Amber for Rs 150; have your list of sights planned and refuse to go to shops.

Cycle rickshaw (Often rickety) station to central hotels, Rs 15-20; full day Rs 100.

Taxi
Unmetered taxis; 4 hrs costs Rs 450 (40 km), 8 hrs costs Rs 750 (city and Amber). Extra hill charge for Amber, Raigarh, Nahargarh. Out of city Rs 5-8 per km; **Marudhar Tours** (see Activities and tours) recommended; or try RTDC, T0141-220 3531. Also **Pink City Taxis**, T0141-511 5100, excellent radio cab service.

Train
Enquiry, T131, T0141-220 4536, reservation T135. Computerized booking office in separate building to front and left of station; separate queue for foreigners. Use pre-paid rickshaw counter. **Abu Rd** (for **Mount Abu**) *Ahmedabad Mail 9106*, 0455, 8½ hrs; *Aravali Exp 9708* (goes on to Mumbai), 0835, 8 hrs; **Agra Cantt**: *Marudhar Exp 4854/4864*, 1550, 7 hrs. **Ahmedabad**: *Aravali Exp 9708*, 0845, 14 hrs; *Ashram Exp 2916*, 2045, 11½ hrs. *Rajdhani Exp 2958*, not Tue 0045, 9 hrs. **Ajmer**: *Aravali Exp 9708*, 0845, 2½ hrs; **Bikaner**: *Bikaner Exp 4737*, 2210, 10 hrs; *Intercity Exp 2468*, 1550, 7 hrs. **Chittaurgarh**: *Chittaurgarh Exp 9769*, 1200, 7½ hrs; *Chetak Exp 4715*, 1945, 8½ hrs. **Delhi**: *Shatabdi 2016*, 1745, 4 hrs

25 mins, Jaipur JAT Exp 2413, 1635, 5½ hrs; *Haridwar Mail 9105*, 2310, 5½ hrs. **Indore**: *Jaipur Indore Exp 2974*, Fri and Sun 2115, 9½ hrs; **Jodhpur**: *Ranthambhore Exp 2465*, 1705, 5½ hrs; *Intercity Exp 2465*, 1740, 5½ hrs. **Mumbai (C)**: *Jaipur BCT Superfast 2956*, 1410, 18½ hrs; **Udaipur** : *Udaipur City Exp 2965*, 2240, 10 hrs. **Varanasi** via **Lucknow**: *Marudhar Exp 4864*, 1540, 20 hrs.

Directory

Jaipur p134, map p136
Banks Several on Mirza Ismail Rd and Ashok Marg. Open 1030-1430, 1530-1630; most change money and have ATMs. ATMs also scattered along Johari Bazar and in C scheme **Thomas Cook**, Jaipur Towers, 1st floor, Mirza Ismail Rd (500 m from railway station, T0141-236 0801, 0930-1800, open Sun). No commission on own TCs, Rs 20 for others. Recommended. Often easier to use hotels, eg Pearl Palace (24-hr, fast, good rates). **Karwan Tours**, Bissau Palace (sunrise until late). Jewellery shops opposite Hawa Mahal often hold exchange licences but travellers report misuse of credit cards at some.
Internet Most hotels have a computer or 2. Handy new facility at railway station near platform ticket office, plus many others scattered around city, eg Ganpati Plaza basement, Re 1 per min; Mirza Ismail Rd opposite Niro's, Rs 25-30/hr; **Mewar**, near Central Bus Stand, 24 hrs, also has faxing.
Medical services Ambulance: I102. Santokba Durlabhji Hospital, Bhawani Singh Rd, T0141-256 6251. **SMS Hospital**, Sawai Ram Singh Marg, T0141-256 0291.
Post GPO, Mirza Ismail Rd. Excellent parcel service. Take parcels to Customs counter upstairs for quick dispatch. Parcel-wallah to left of gate stitches packages, Rs 50-150.
Useful contacts Fire: T101. Police: T100. Directory enquiries T197. Foreigners' Registration Office: Hazari Garden, behind Hawa Mahal.

Around Jaipur

Amber Fort is one of Jaipur's biggest draws, with an elephant ride to the top a priority on many people's 'to do' list. It's still an impressive building but has been poorly maintained in recent years. Sanganer and Bagru offer good opportunities to see handicrafts in production, while Samode is perhaps the last word in elegant living. ▶▶ For listings, see pages 155-156.

Amber (Amer) → *For listings, see pages 155-156. Colour map 4, C6.*

Today there is no town to speak of in Amber, just the palace clinging to the side of the rocky hill, overlooked by the small fort above, with a small village at its base. In the high season this is one of India's most popular tourist sites, with a continuous train of colourfully decorated elephants walking up and down the ramp to the palace. One penalty of its popularity is the persistence of the vendors.

History
Amber, which takes its name from Ambarisha, a king of the once-famous royal city of Ayodhya, was the site of a Hindu temple built by the Mina tribes as early as the 10th century. Two centuries later the Kachhawaha Rajputs made it their capital, which it remained until Sawai Jai Singh II moved to his newly planned city of Jaipur in 1727. Its location made Amber strategically crucial for the Mughal emperors as they moved south, and the Maharajahs of Amber took care to establish close relations with successive Mughal rulers. The building of the fort palace was begun in 1600 by Raja Man Singh, a noted Rajput general in Akbar's army, and Mughal influence was strong in much of the subsequent building.

The approach
ⓘ *Around Rs 550 per elephant carrying 4, no need to tip, though the driver will probably ask, takes 10 mins. Jeeps Rs 100 each way, or Rs 10 per seat. It can be quite a long wait in a small garden with little shade and you will be at the mercy of the hawkers. If you do want to buy, wait until you reach the steps when the price will drop dramatically.*

From the start of the ramp you can either walk or ride by elephant; the walk is quite easy and mainly on a separate path. Elephants carry up to four people on a padded seat. The ride can be somewhat unnerving when the elephant comes close to the edge of the road, but it is generally perfectly safe. You have to buy a 'return ticket' even if you wish to walk down later. The elephants get bad tempered as the day wears on. If you are interested in finding out more about the welfare of Amber's elephants, or indeed any of Jaipur's street animals, you should contact an organization called **Help in Suffering** ⓘ *T0141-276 0803, www.his-india.org.au.*

The Palace
ⓘ *0900-1630 (it's worth arriving at 0900), foreigners Rs 100, Indians Rs 10, camera Rs 75, video Rs 150 (tickets in the Chowk, below the steps up to Shila Mata). Take the green bus from the Hawa Mahal, Rs 5. Auto-rickshaw Rs 80 (Rs 200 for return, including the wait). Guides are worth hiring, Rs 400 for a half day (group of 4), find one with a government guide licence.*

After passing through a series of five defensive gates, you reach the first courtyard of the **Raj Mahal** built by Man Singh I in 1600, entered through the **Suraj Pol** (Sun Gate). Here you can get a short ride around the courtyard on an elephant, but bargain very hard. There are some toilets near the dismounting platform. On the south side of this Jaleb Chowk with the flower beds, is a flight of steps leading up to the **Singh Pol** (Lion Gate) entrance to the upper courtyard of the palace.

A separate staircase to the right leads to the green marble-pillared **Shila Mata Temple** (to Kali as Goddess of War), which opens at certain times of the day and then only allows a limited number of visitors at a time (so ask before joining the queue). The temple contains a black marble image of the goddess that Man Singh I brought back from Jessore (now in Bangladesh; the chief priest has always been Bengali). The silver doors with images of Durga and Saraswati were added by his successor.

In the left-hand corner of the courtyard, the **Diwan-i-Am** (Hall of Public Audience) was built by Raja Jai Singh I in 1639. Originally, it was an open pavilion with cream marble

Amber Palace

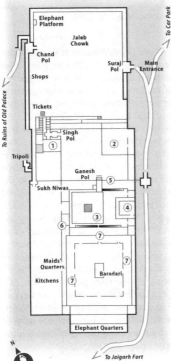

Not to scale

Shila Mata Temple **1**
Diwan-i-Am **2**
Jai Singh I Garden **3**

To Jaigarh Fort
Jai Mandir (Jas Mandir,
1st floor) **4**
Sohag Mandir (1st floor) **5**
Palace of Man Singh I
(1st floor) **6**
Zenana **7**

pillars supporting an unusual striped canopy-shaped ceiling, with a portico on double red sandstone columns. The room on the east was added by Sawai Ram Singh II. **Ganesh Pol** (circa 1700-1725), south of the chowk, colourfully painted and with mosaic decoration, takes its name from the prominent figure of Ganesh above the door. It separates the private from the public areas.

This leads onto the **Jai Singh I** court with a formal garden. To the east is the two-storeyed cream-coloured marble pavilion – **Jai Mandir** (Diwan-i-Khas or Hall of Private Audience) below and **Jas Mandir** (1635-1640) with a curved Bengali roof, on the terrace above. The former, with its marble columns and painted ceiling, has lovely views across the lake. The latter has colourful mosaics, mirrors and marble *jali* screens which let in cooling breezes. Both have **Shish Mahals** (Mirror Palaces) faced with mirrors, seen to full effect when lit by a match. To the west of the chowk is the **Sukh Niwas**, a pleasure palace with a marble water course to cool the air, and doors inlaid with ivory and sandalwood. The Mughal influence is quite apparent in this chowk.

Above the Ganesh Pol is the **Sohag Mandir**, a rectangular chamber with beautiful latticed windows and octagonal rooms to each side. From the rooftop there are stunning views over the palace across the town of Amber, the long curtain wall surrounding the town and further north, through the 'V' shaped entrance in the hills, to the plains beyond. Beyond this courtyard is the **Palace of Man Singh I**. A high wall separates it from the Jai Singh Palace. In the centre of the chowk which was once open is a *baradari* (12-arched pavilion), combining Mughal and Hindu influences. The surrounding palace, a complex warren of passages and staircases, was turned into *zenana* quarters when the newer palaces were built by Jai Singh. Children find it great fun to explore this part.

Old Palace and nearby temples

Old Palace of Amber (1216) lies at the base of Jaigarh Fort. A stone path (currently being restored) from the Chand Pol in the first courtyard of Amber Palace leads to the ruins. Though there is little interest today, nearby are several worthwhile temples. These include the **Jagatsiromani Temple** dedicated to Krishna, with carvings and paintings; it is associated with Mira Bai. Close by is the old temple to Narasinghji and **Panna Mian-ki-Baoli** (step well). Some of the *chhatris* on Delhi Road still retain evidence of paintings.

North of Jaipur → *For listings, see pages 155-156. Colour map 4, C6.*

Jaigarh Fort

ⓘ *0900-1630. Foreigners Rs 35, Indians Rs 20, free with City Palace entry ticket (use within 48 hrs), still camera Rs 40, video Rs150, vehicle entry Rs 50. To reach the fort, from Amber Palace turn right out of the Suraj Pol and follow a stone road past the old elephant quarters. This is the start of the ascent – a steady climb of about 25 mins, or take a taxi. What appears at first to be 2 adjoining forts is in fact all part of the same structure. There is also a good road from the Jaipur–Amber road which goes straight to Jaigarh Fort and on to Nahargarh.*

Above the palace on the hill top stands the gigantic bulk of Jaigarh, impressively lit at night; its *parkotas* (walls), bastions, gateways and watchtowers a testimony of the power of the Jaipur rulers. It is well worth a visit. The forbidding medieval fort was never captured and so has survived virtually intact which makes it particularly interesting. In the 16th-century cannon foundry you can see the pit where the barrels were cast, the capstan-powered lathe which bored out the cannon and the iron-workers' drills, taps and dies. The armoury has a large collection of swords and small arms, their use in the many successful campaigns having been carefully logged. There is an interesting photograph collection and a small café outside the armoury. There are gardens, a granary, open and closed reservoirs; the ancient temples of Ram Harihar (10th century) and Kal Bhairava (12th century) are within the fort. You can explore a warren of complicated dark passageways among the palaces. Many of the apartments are open and you can see the collections of coins and puppets (shows on demand). The other part of the fort, at a slightly higher elevation, has a tall watch tower. From here there are tremendous views of the surrounding hills. The massive 50-tonne **Jai Ban cannon** stands on top of one tower. Allegedly the largest cannon on wheels in the world, with an 8-m barrel, it had a range of around 20 km, but it was never used. Some 7 km further along the top of the hill is the smaller Nahargarh Fort overlooking Jaipur itself (see page 142).

Ramgarh Lake and Jamwa Sanctuary → *30 km northeast of Jaipur.*

The 15-sq-km lake of Jamwa Ramgarh attracts large flocks of waterfowl in winter, and lies within a game sanctuary with good boating and birdwatching. Built to supply Jaipur with water, it now provides less than 1% of the city's needs and in years of severe drought may dry up completely. The 300-sq-km Jamwa Sanctuary, which once provided the Jaipur royal family with game, still has some panthers, nilgai and small game. Contact the tourist office in Jaipur (see page 134) for details of public buses. It is about a 45-minute drive.

Samode → *Colour map 4, C6. Phone code: 01423. 42 km northwest of Jaipur.*

At the head of the enclosed valley in the dry rugged hills of the northern Aravallis, Samode stands on a former caravan route. The sleepy village, with its local artisans producing printed cloth and glass bangles, nestles within a ring of old walls. The painted *havelis* are still full of character. Samode is well worth the visit from Jaipur, and makes a good stop en route to the painted towns of Shekhawati (see page 279). Both the palace and the *bagh* are wonderful, peaceful places to spend a night.

The **palace** ① *now a heritage hotel, entry Rs 500 for non-residents includes tea/coffee*, which dominates the village, is fabulously decorated with 300-year-old wall paintings (hunting scenes, floral motifs, etc) which still look almost new. Around the first floor of the Darbar Hall are magnificent alcoves, decorated with mirrors like *shish mahal* and *jali* screens through which the royal ladies would have looked down into the grand jewel-like Darbar Hall.

Towering immediately above the palace is **Samode Fort**, the maharajah's former residence, reached in times of trouble by an underground passage. The old stone zigzag path has been replaced by 300 steps. Though dilapidated, there are excellent views from the ramparts; a caretaker has the keys. The main fort gate is the starting point of some enticing walks into the Aravallis. A paved path leads to a shrine about 3 km away. There are two other powerful forts you can walk to, forming a circular walk ending back in Samode. Allow three hours, wear good shoes, a hat and carry water.

Samode Bagh, a large 400-year-old Mughal-style formal garden with fountains and pavilions, has been beautifully restored. It is 3 km southeast of Samode, towards the main Jaipur–Agra road. Within the grounds are modest-sized but elaborately decorated tents.

South of Jaipur → *For listings, see pages 155-156.*

Madhogarh → *Colur map 5, C1. 45 km southeast of Jaipur, off the Jaipur–Agra Rd.*

Madhogarh is a small but impressive fort, with a strong medieval flavour, and a pleasant place to break your journey between Jaipur and Ranthambore if you have your own transport. It is located on a hillock, and has huge walls, bastions, wells and turrets. The Rajput-Maratha battle of Tunga was fought at the nearby village, with the Jaipur army based at Madhogarh, during the mid-18th century.

⊙ Around Jaipur listings

For Sleeping and Eating price codes and other relevant information, see Essentials pages 28-33.

⊜ Sleeping

Ramgarh Lake and Jamwa Sanctuary *p154*
LL-L Ramgarh Lodge (Taj), overlooking the lake, T01426-252217, www.tajhotels.com. 18 elegant a/c rooms (3 enormous suites)

in the former royal hunting lodge with a museum and library, furnished appropriately, hunting trophies, limited restaurant, delightful walks, fishing and boating plus ruins of old Kachhawaha fort nearby. **AL** in summer.
E-F Jheel Tourist Village (RTDC), Mandawa Choraha, T01426-252170. Pleasant surroundings for 10 not especially well-maintained rustic huts.

Samode p155
LL-L Samode Palace, T01423-240014, www.samode.com. Reservations essential. Half price 1 May-30 Sep. Contact Samode Haveli, T0141-263 2407, to reserve and arrange taxi (Rs 950) from Jaipur. 42 a/c rooms, tastefully modernized without losing any of the charm, magnificent setting with gardens and beautiful secluded pool with plenty of space to lounge, courtyard and modern indoor restaurants (international menu), also buffets for groups, shop with good textiles, camel rides around village and to Samode Bagh (but some animals are in poor condition). Really remarkable for its setting and atmosphere and generally friendly, but some reports of impersonal, disappointing service (tip-seeking). Well worth a visit even if not staying. Highly recommended.
L-AL Samode Bagh, 3 km from the palace T01423-240235, www.samode.com. 44 luxury a/c tents decorated in the Mughal-style, each with a beautiful modern bath room and its own veranda. *Darbar* tent, al fresco meals, pool with slide, tennis, volleyball, badminton, lovely setting in peaceful walled Mughal gardens, plenty of birdwatching, safaris to sand dunes, amazing. Reservations essential. Recommended.
B-C Maharaja Palace, modern hotel. 18 rooms (some a/c) in mock *haveli*, restaurant, garden with village-style huts.

Madhogarh p155
C Fort Madhogarh, T01428-281141, www.fortmadhogarh.in. A **Rajput Special Hotels** with 25 quaint rooms (some in the tower) with views of the countryside. Good (though rather spicy) food, interesting temples nearby, family-run, recently converted so still finding its feet. Great atmosphere on the ramparts in the evening when the family and guests enjoy tea.

○ Shopping

Amber p152
Near the *baoli* and temples, you can see demonstrations of block printing and other handicrafts, simple snacks, shops selling gems, jewellery, textiles, handicrafts and 'antiques' (objects up to 90 years old; genuine 100-year-old antiques may not be exported). Amber is a tax holiday zone, and products manufactured by industries here are 10-15% cheaper than at Jaipur (though the benefit may not be passed on to the customer).

Samode p155
A small artists' colony in the village produces good-quality miniature paintings on old paper. Contact Krishan Kumar Khari, often found at the hotel entrance.

▲ Activities and tours

Ramgarh Lake and Jamwa Sanctuary p154
Polo can be played at **Ramgarh Resort** (HRH), T0294-252 8016, www.hrhindia.com. An exclusive facility for polo enthusiasts with a full-size polo field near the lake, occasional matches and polo training camps run by World Cup Indian captain Lokendra Singh. **A** de luxe tented accommodation for participants, restaurant, pool and riding stable.

Samode p155
Contact **Samode Bagh** (see Sleeping), for activities around this Moghul garden/hotel. See also **Samode Palace** for camel safaris. Birdwatching around this area is good.

⊖ Transport

Samode p155
Samode is a 1-hr drive from **Jaipur**. Buses from Chandpol Gate go to Chomu where you can pick up a local bus to Samode. Taxi Rs 950.

Contents

Footprint features

Eastern Rajasthan

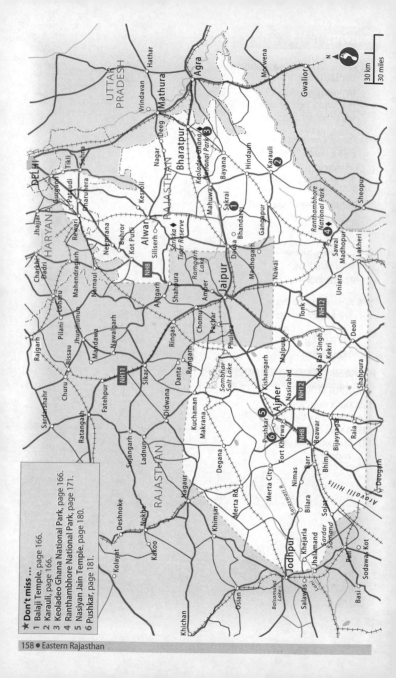

★ Don't miss ...
1 Balaji Temple, page 166.
2 Karauli, page 166.
3 Keoladeo Ghana National Park, page 171.
4 Ranthambhore National Park, page 171.
5 Nasiyan Jain Temple, page 180.
6 Pushkar, page 181.

This is one of the most visited regions of Rajasthan, lying as it does on the well-trodden 'Golden Triangle' route of Delhi-Agra-Jaipur, but it retains some hidden treasures. Primary among these are a handful of delightful, sensitively restored heritage hotels, essentially ex-maharaja's palaces, including those at Neemrana and Kesroli, and the quirky charms of Bhanwar Vilas Palace in Karauli.

From the bustling pilgrimage centre of Ajmer in the south and its laid-back neighbour, Pushkar, renowned for its holy lake and extraordinary November camel fair, to the utterly unspoilt towns of Alwar and Deeg in the north, there's an amazing variety of human habitats to choose from; and all are within easy reach of Delhi.

The towns and villages of Eastern Rajasthan are surrounded by a natural world in which wild animals and birds continue to find a protected home in sanctuaries and wildlife parks. Rajasthan's finest wildlife reserves are here, including the peaceful Keoladeo Ghana National Park, still theoretically a stop on the migratory route of the highly endangered Siberian crane (and a great place for an early-morning cycle ride), and the incomparable Ranthambhore National Park, one of the world's top venues for tiger-spotting and a beautiful landscape to explore even when the big cats don't show.

Alwar, Sariska and around

Alwar has fascinating monuments including the Bala Quilla fort, overlooking the town, and the Moti Doongri fort, in a garden. The former, which was never taken by direct assault, has relics of the early Rajput rulers, the founders of the fort, who had their capital near Alwar. Over the centuries it was home to the Khanzadas, Mughals, Pathans, Jats and finally the Rajputs. There are also palaces and colonial period parks and gardens. The town itself is very untouristy and spread over a large area, making navigation difficult at times, but is generally very welcoming.

The 480-sq-km Sariska reserve is a dry deciduous forest set in a valley surrounded by the barren Aravalli hills. The princely shooting reserve of the Maharajah of Alwar was declared a sanctuary in 1955. Exactly 50 years later it acquired the dubious honour of being the first Project Tiger reserve to be declared free of tigers, the last ones presumably having been poached to feed the Chinese demand for erectile function in old age. Nevertheless, the park still holds some wildlife, and a certain rugged appeal. ⟩⟩ *For listings, see pages 162-163.*

Ins and outs

Getting there and around Alwar is well connected to both Delhi and Jaipur by bus and train, and is only a three-hour drive from Delhi, or 1½ hours from Jaipur. Sariska is an easy 35-km drive from Alwar. ⟩⟩ *See Transport, page 163.*

Tourist information Rajashtan Tourist Reception Centre ⓘ *Nehru Marg, opposite railway station, Alwar, T0144-234 7348, closed weekends.*

Background

As Mughal power crumbled Rao Pratap Singhji of Macheri founded Alwar as his capital in 1771. He shook off Jat power over the region and rebelled against Jaipur suzerainty making Alwar an independent state. His successors lent military assistance to the British in their battles against the Marathas in AD 1803, and in consequence gained the support of the colonial power. The Alwar royals were flamboyant and kept a fleet of custom-made cars (including a throne car and a golden limousine), and collected solid silver furniture and attractive walking sticks.

Alwar → *For listings, see pages 162-163. Colour map 5, C1. Phone code: 0144. Population: 211,000.*

Alwar is protected by the hilltop **Bala Quilla** which has the remains of palaces, temples and 10 tanks built by the first rulers of Alwar. It stands 308 m above the town, to the northwest, and is reached by a steep 4WD track (with permission from the police station). There are splendid views.

The City Palace, **Vinai Vilas Mahal** (1840) ⓘ *closed Fri, 1000-1630, free, museum Rs 3,* with intricate *jali* work, ornate *jarokha* balconies and courtyards, houses government offices on the ground floor, and a fine museum upstairs. The palace is impressive but is poorly maintained, with dusty galleries (you may find children playing cricket in the courtyard). The Darbar Room is closed, and the throne, miniatures and gilt-edged mirrors can only be viewed through the glass doors and windows or by prior permission of the royal family (not easily obtained). The museum is interesting, housing local miniature paintings, as well as some of the Mughal, Bundi and other schools, an array of swords, shields, daggers, guns and armour, sandalwood carvings, ivory objects, jade art, musical instruments and princely relics. Next to the city palace are the lake and royal cenotaphs.

On the south side of the tank is the Cenotaph of Maharaja Bakhtawar Singh (1781-1815) which is of marble on a red sandstone base. The gardens are alive with peacocks and other birds. To the right of the main entrance to the palace is a two-storey processional elephant carriage designed to carry 50 people and be pulled by four elephants.

The **Yeshwant Niwas**, built by Maharaja Jai Singh in the Italianate style, is also worth seeing. Apparently on its completion he disliked it and never lived in it. Instead he built the **Vijay Mandir** in 1918, a 105-room palace beside Vijay Sagar, 10 km from Alwar. Part of it is open with prior permission from the royal family or their secretary, but even without it is worth seeing from the road, with its façade resembling an anchored ship. When not in Delhi, the royal family now live in Phool Bagh, a small 1960s mansion opposite the New Stadium.

Alwar to Sariska → For listings, see pages 162-163. Colour map 5, C1.

At **Siliserh**, 15 km to the west, runs an aqueduct which supplies the city with water. The lake, a local picnic spot, has boats for hire. **Kesroli**, 10 km northeast, has a seven-turreted 16th-century fort atop a rocky hillock, now sympathetically restored into a hotel. It is a three-hour drive from Delhi and convenient for an overnight halt. Turn left off the NH8 at Dharuhera for Alwar Road and you will find it. **Kushalgarh Fort** is en route to Sariska. Near Kushalgarh is the temple complex of **Talbraksha** (or Talvriksh) with a large population of rhesus macaque monkeys. Guides report panthers having been seen near the **Cafeteria Taal** here, probably on the prowl for monkeys near the canteen.

Sariska Tiger Reserve → For listings, see pages 162-163. Colour map 5, C1. Phone code: 0144.

ⓘ *Rs 200 including still camera, Indians Rs 10, video Rs 200; vehicle Rs 125 per trip. Early-morning jeep trips from Sariska Palace Hotel or Tiger Den (see Sleeping, page 162) venture into the park as far as the Monkey Temple, where you can get a cup of tea and watch monkeys and peacocks. Jeep hire for non-standard trips in the reserve, Rs 800 for 3 hrs, excluding entry fees.*

Despite the lack of tigers, Sariska provides plenty of opportunities to see wildlife. The main rhesus monkey population lives at Talvriksh near Kushalgarh, while at Bhartri-Hari you will see many langurs. The chowsingha, or four-horned antelope, is found here, as are other deer including chital and sambar. You may see nilgai, wild boar, jackals, hyenas, hares and porcupines; leopards are present but rarely seen since the reserve is closed at night to visitors. During the monsoons many animals move to higher ground, but the place is alive with birds. There are ground birds such as peafowl, jungle fowl, spur fowl and grey partridge. Babblers, bulbuls and treepies are common round the lodges.

The park is open all year round. During the monsoon travel through the forest may be difficult. The best season to visit is between November and April. In the dry season, when the streams disappear, the animals become dependant on man-made water holes at Kalighatti, Salopka and Pandhupol.

Sariska, the gateway for Sariska National Park, is a pleasant, quiet place to stay and relax. Excursions by jeep are possible to forts and temples nearby. The **Kankwari Fort** (2 km), where Emperor Aurangzeb is believed to have imprisoned his brother **Dara Shikoh**, the rightful heir to the Mughal throne, is within the park. The old **Bhartrihari** temple (6 km) has a fair and six-hour dance-drama in September to October. **Neelkanth** (33 km) has a complex of sixth- to 10th-century carved temples.

Bhangarh (55 km), on the outskirts of the reserve, is a deserted city of some 10,000 dwellings established in 1631. It was abandoned 300 years ago, supposedly after it was cursed by a magician.

◉ Alwar, Sariska and around listings

For Sleeping and Eating price codes and other relevant information, see Essentials pages 28-33.

● Sleeping

Alwar p160

A-F Aravali, Nehru Marg, near the train station, T0144-233 2883. An eclectic range of rooms, from suites to dorms, plus a restaurant and bar. There's a pool, but even guests have to pay to use it. 50% discount to YHA members.
B-C Kothi Rao, 31 Moti Dungri, T0144-270 0741, kothirao@yahoo.com. 9 a/c rooms in extremely homely hotel, reminiscent of an English B&B, run by polite, welcoming family.
C Alwar, 26 Manu Marg, T0144-270 0012, www.hotelalwar.com. Set off the road in an attractive garden, 16 rooms, 7 in new block, attached baths (hot showers), TV, fridge, phone, restaurant, use of pool and tennis courts at nearby club, efficient service, popular.
C-E New Tourist, 2 Manu Marg, T0144-270 0897. Keen and friendly management, 20 rooms of a higher standard than most here, beer bar, homely. Recommended.
D-F Ankur, Manu Marg, T0144-233 3025. The same hotel occupies 2 buildings on opposite sides of square. The 27 rooms (10 a/c) in the motel-style block closest to the Imperial Hotel are significantly better than the 19 rooms opposite; the pick of the nearby options.
D-F Atlantic, Manu Marg, T0144-234 3181. 15 rooms with attached baths, only **D** a/c and de luxe rooms have Western toilets.
D-G Ashoka, Manu Marg, T0144-234 6780. 30 rooms, clean and comfortable, de luxe rooms have TV, running hot water and Western toilets, cheaper rooms have Indian toilets and hot water in buckets,

restaurant (Rs 35 *thalis*), good value.
E Meenal (RTDC), near Circuit House, T0144-234 7352. 6 rooms with bath (2 a/c), restaurant, bar, quiet location.
E Saroop Vilas Palace, near Moti Doongri, T0144-233 1218. Renovated royal mansion taken over by private entrepreneur, 4 rooms with attached baths (Western toilets), vegetarian restaurant serving reasonable Chinese and South Indian fare.

Alwar to Sariska p161

AL-B Hill Fort Kesroli (Heritage Hotel), Alwar Rd, Kesroli, T01468-289352, www.neemranahotels.com. Comfortable, if eccentric, airy rooms and plush suites, set around a courtyard, reasonable restaurant and service, relaxing, and in a lovely isolated rural location.

Sariska Tiger Reserve p161

AL Sariska Palace, 40 km from Alwar railway station, T0144-284 1325, www.thesariska palace.in. 100 refurbished a/c rooms (annexe lacks the charm of the lodge) in an enormous converted royal hunting lodge, restaurant and bar (generally only open for residents), gym, pool, new Ayurvedic and yoga centre, tours, built in 1898, full of photographs and stuffed tigers, set in expansive and well-maintained gardens. Rs 500 entry fee for non-residents, offset against restaurant bill.
A-C Lake Palace (RTDC), Siliserh, T0144-288 6322. 10 rooms, 5 a/c, restaurant, modest but superb location. Includes all meals.
A-C Tiger Den (RTDC), in the sanctuary, T0144-284 1342. Superbly located tourist bungalow with views of hill and park, 30 rooms with attached baths (hot showers) but shabby, dirty public areas, vegetarian restaurant (Indian buffets Rs 130-150), bar (no snacks, carry your own to have

with beer/drinks) shop sells cards and souvenirs, nice garden, friendly management.
C Baba Resorts, T0144-288 5231, next door to **Sariska Tiger Camp** (see below), and similar. Both are good options for the price.
C Sariska Tiger Camp, 19 km towards Alwar on main road, T0144-288 5311. Looks better from inside than out. 8 mud-walled but classy rooms in pleasant surroundings, plus 20 luxury tents during the winter season.
D Forest Rest House, Main Rd, opposite turning to Kushalgarh. 3 simple rooms, only open during the winter season.

🍴 Eating

Alwar *p160*
🍴 **Narulas**, Kashiram Circle, T0144-233 3966. Indian/Chinese/continental. A/c restaurant, popular for Punjabi non-vegetarian and vegetarian dishes.
🍴 **Baba**, Hope Circle. Popular for *kalakand*

('milk cake') and other Rajasthani sweets.
🍴 **Imperial Guest House**, 1 Manu Marg, T0144-270 1730. Rooms disappointing but South Indian restaurant is popular and good value.
🍴 **Moti Doongri Park** has a number of stalls selling cheap South Indian snacks in the evening. Some Chinese and North Indian.

⊖ Transport

Alwar *p160*
Bus Regular buses to/from **Delhi** (4½-5 hrs) and **Jaipur**. Frequent service to **Bharatpur** (2½ hrs), **Deeg** (1½ hrs) and **Sariska** (1 hr).
Train New Delhi: *Shatabdi Exp 2016*, not Sun, 1941, 2½ hrs. **Delhi**: *Jodhpur Delhi Exp 4860*, 0835, 3 hrs; *Jaipur-JAT Exp 2413*, 1900, 3 hrs.

Sariska Tiger Reserve *p161*
Train The nearest station is at Alwar (36 km), with buses to the sanctuary.

Deeg, Bharatpur and around

For a typical dusty and hot North Indian market town, Deeg gained the somewhat surprising reputation as the summer resort of the Raja of Bharatpur. Located on the plains just northwest of Agra, the raja decided to develop his palace to take full advantage of the monsoon rains. The fort and the 'monsoon' pleasure palace have ingenious fountains and are of major architectural importance, their serenity in stark contrast to the barely controlled chaos of the rest of the town. One of the most popular halting places on the 'Golden Triangle', Bharatpur is best known for its Keoladeo Ghana Bird Sanctuary. Once the hunting estate of the Maharajas of Bharatpur, with daily shoots recorded of up to 4000 birds, the 29-sq-km piece of marshland, with over 360 species, is potentially one of the finest bird sanctuaries in the world, but has suffered badly in recent years from water deprivation. Lesser visited are the sights off the road which connects Agra to Jaipur, NH11, which sees huge volumes of tourist traffic. The Balaji temple is particularly remarkable. ▶▶ For listings, see pages 168-170.

Ins and outs
There are regular bus services from both Mathura and Bharatpur to Deeg, with the road from Bharatpur being by far the smoother of the two. Bharatpur, 40 km south of Deeg, has good bus and train connections from Agra, Jaipur and Delhi. Keoladeo Ghana National Park is 4 km south of Bharatpur town.

Deeg → For listings, see pages 168-170. Colour map 5, C2. Phone code: 05641. Population: 38,000.

The rubble and mud walls of the square **fort** are strengthened by 12 bastions and a wide, shallow moat. It has a run-down *haveli* within, but is otherwise abandoned. The entrance is over a narrow bridge across the moat, through a gate studded with anti-elephant spikes. Negotiating the undergrowth, you can climb the ramparts which rise 20 m above the moat; some cannons are still in place on their rusty carriages. You can walk right around along the wide path on top of the walls and climb the stairs to the roof of the citadel for good views.

The **palaces** ① *opposite the fort, Sat-Thu 0930-1730, Rs 200*, are flanked by two reservoirs, Gopal (west) and Rup Sagar (east), and set around a beautifully proportioned central formal garden in the style of a Mughal *char bagh*. The main entrance is from the north, through the ornamental, though unfinished, Singh (Lion) Pol; the other gates are Suraj (Sun) Pol (southwest) and Nanga Pol (northeast). The impressive main palace **Gopal Bhavan** (1763), bordering Gopal Sagar, is flanked by Sawon and Bhadon pavilions (1760), named after the monsoon months (mid-July to mid-September). Water was directed over the roof lines to create the effect of sheets of monsoon rain. The palace still retains many of the original furnishings, including scent and cigarette cases made from elephant's feet and even a dartboard. There are vegetarian and non-vegetarian dining rooms, the former particularly elegant, with floor seating around a low-slung horseshoe-shaped marble table. Outside, overlooking the formal garden, is a beautiful white marble *hindola* (swing) which was brought as booty with two marble thrones (black and white) after Suraj Mal attacked Delhi.

To the south, bordering the central garden, is the single-storey marble **Suraj Bhavan** (circa 1760), a temple, and **Kishan Bhavan** with its decorated façade, five arches and fountains. The water reservoir to its west was built at a height to operate the fountains and cascades effectively; it held enough water to work all the fountains for a few hours, though it took a week to fill from four wells with bullocks drawing water up in leather buckets. Now, the 500 or so fountains are turned on once a year for the **Monsoon festival** in August. All these are gravity fed from huge holding tanks on the palace roof, with each fountain jet having its own numbered pipe leading from the tank. Coloured dyes are inserted into individual pipes to create a spectacular effect. The (old) **Purana Mahal** beyond, with a curved roof and some fine architectural points, was begun by Badan Singh in 1722. It now houses government offices but the simple wall paintings in the entrance chamber of the inner court are worth seeing.

Keshav Bhavan, a *baradari* or garden pavilion, stands between the central garden and Rup Sagar with the **Sheesh Mahal** (Mirror Palace, 1725) in the southeast corner. **Nand Bhavan** (circa 1760), north of the central garden, is a large hall 45 m long, 24 m wide and 6 m high, raised on a terrace and enclosed by an arcade of seven arches. There are frescoes inside but it has a deserted feel. The pavilion's ingenious double-roof design took the monsoon theme further: water was channelled through hollow pillars to rotate heavy stone balls, mimicking the sound of thunder!

Bhandarej to Bharatpur → *For listings, see pages 168-170. Colour map 5, C1-C3.*

Bhandarej, 62 km from Jaipur, south of NH11 after Dausa, is a relaxing place to stop for the night. From here the NH11 goes through a series of small towns and villages to **Şakrai** (77 km) which has a good roadside RTDC restaurant. Some 15 km after Sakrai is the turning

1 Bharatpur

➡ Bharatpur maps
1 Bharatpur, page 165
2 Keoladeo Ghana National Park, page 167

Sleeping 🛏
Bagh 4
Laxmi Vilas Palace 1

Shagun Guest House 2

for Balaji, home to the truly extraordinary **Balaji Temple**. People who believe themselves to have been possessed by demons come here, to have the evil spirits exorcized. The scenes on the first floor in particular are not for the faint-hearted; methods of restraining the worst afflicted include chaining them to the walls and placing them under large rocks. Most exorcisms take place on Tuesdays and Saturdays, when there are long queues to get in. From **Mahuwa** a road south leads through Hindaun to Karauli (64 km).

Noted for its pale red sandstone, **Karauli** (1348), was the seat of a small princely state which played a prominent part in support of the Mughal emperors. The impressive **City Palace** has some fine wall paintings, stone carvings and a fine Darbar Hall. Fairs are held at nearby temples lasting a week to a fortnight (see Festivals and events, page 170). Mahavirji, associated with the 24th Tirthankar Mahavir, is an important Jain pilgrimage centre.

Bharatpur → *For listings, see pages 168-170. Colour map 5, C1-C3. Phone code: 05644.*

Built by Suraj Mal, the **Lohagarh Fort**, which occupies the island at the centre of Bharatpur village, appears impregnable, but the British, initially repulsed in 1803, finally took it in 1825. There are double ramparts, a 46-m-wide moat and an inner moat around the palace. Much of the wall has been demolished but there are the remains of some of the gateways. Inside the fort are three palaces (circa 1730) and Jewel House and Court to their north. The **museum** ① *1000-1630, closed Fri, Rs 3,* in the Kachhari Kalan exhibits archaeological finds from villages nearby, dating from the first to 19th centuries as well as paintings and artefacts; the armoury is upstairs.

Peharsar ① *23 km away, Rs 30 to 'headman' secures a tour,* with a carpet weaving community, makes a very interesting excursion from Bharatpur.

Keoladeo Ghana National Park → *For listings, see pages 168-170. Colour map 5, C3.*

① *www.knpark.org, Rs 200, video Rs 200, professional video Rs 1500, payable each time you enter. Park closed May and Jun. Cafés inside, or ask your hotel to provide a packed lunch.*
The late Maharaja Brajendra Singh converted his hunting estate into a bird sanctuary in 1956 and devoted many of his retired years to establishing it. He had inherited both his title and an interest in wildlife from his deposed father, Kishan Singh, who grossly overspent his budget – 30 Rolls Royces, a private jazz band and some extremely costly wild animals including "dozens of lions, elephants, leopards and tigers" – for Bharatpur's jungles. It has been designated a World Heritage Site, and can only be entered by bicycle or cycle rickshaw, thus maintaining the peaceful calm of the park's interior.

Tragically, at the end of 2004 the state government bowed to pressure from local farmers and diverted 97% of the park's water supply for irrigation projects. The catastrophic damage to its wetlands has resulted in the loss of many of the migratory birds on which Bharatpur's reputation depends. At some future time the supply may be at least partially restored; in the meantime, birdwatchers may go away disappointed.

Ins and outs
Getting around Good naturalist guides cost Rs 70-100 per hour (depending on group size) at entrance, or contact **Nature Bureau** ① *Haveli SVP Shastri, Neemda Gate, T/F05644-225498.* Official cycle-rickshaws at the entrance are numbered and work in rotation, Rs 50 per hour for two people (drivers may be reluctant to take more than one). This is well worthwhile as some rickshaw-wallahs are very knowledgeable and can help identify birds

(and know their location): a small tip is appropriate. The narrower paths are not recommended as the rough surface makes rickshaws too noisy. It is equally feasible to just walk or hire a bike, particularly once you're familiar with the park. If there's any water, a boat ride is highly recommended for viewing.

2 Keoladeo Ghana National Park

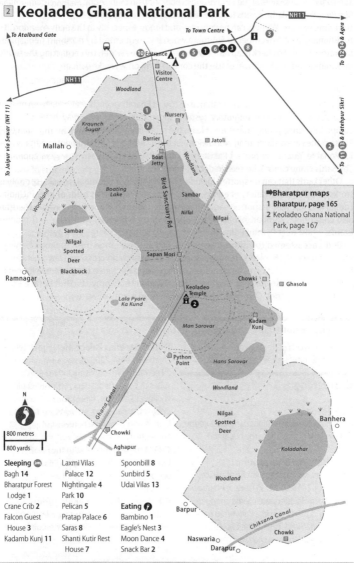

→Bharatpur maps
1 Bharatpur, page 165
2 Keoladeo Ghana National Park, page 167

N

800 metres
800 yards

Sleeping
Bagh **14**
Bharatpur Forest Lodge **1**
Crane Crib **2**
Falcon Guest House **3**
Kadamb Kunj **11**

Laxmi Vilas Palace **12**
Nightingale **4**
Park **10**
Pelican **5**
Pratap Palace **6**
Saras **8**
Shanti Kutir Rest House **7**

Spoonbill **8**
Sunbird **5**
Udai Vilas **13**

Eating
Bambino **1**
Eagle's Nest **3**
Moon Dance **4**
Snack Bar **2**

Tourist information **RTDC** ⓘ *Hotel Saras, T05644-222542*, and **Wildlife Office** ⓘ *Forest Rest House, T05644-222777*. Guides available. For tours contact **GTA** ⓘ *near Tourist Lodge, Gol Bagh Rd, T05644-228188, vfauzdar@yahoo.com*. Knowledgeable English-speaking guides, Rs 300 for two hours. It is worth buying the well-illustrated *Collins Handguide to the Birds of the Indian Sub-continent* (available at the reserve and in bookshops in Delhi, Agra, Jaipur, etc). *Bharatpur: Bird Paradise* by Martin Ewans (Lustre Press, Delhi) is extremely good.

Best time to visit Winters can be very cold and foggy, especially in the early morning. It is traditionally best November to February when it is frequented by northern hemisphere migratory birds. To check in advance whether there is any water, try contacting the tourist information numbers above, or use the contact form on www.knpark.org.

Sights

The handful of rare Siberian cranes that used to visit Bharatpur each year have been missing since 2003. The ancient migratory system, some 1500 years old, may have been lost completely, since young cranes must learn the route from older birds (it is not instinctive). These cranes are disappearing worldwide – eaten by Afghans and sometimes employed as fashionable 'guards' to protect Pakistani homes (they call out when strangers approach). The Sarus crane can still be seen in decent numbers.

Other birds that can be spotted include Asian openbills, Ferruginous ducks, spoonbills, storks, kingfishers, a variety of egrets, ducks and coots, as well as birds of prey including Laggar falcon, greater-spotted eagle, marsh harrier, Scops owl and Pallas' eagle. There are also chital deer, sambar, nilgai, feral cattle, wild cats, hyenas, wild boar and monitor lizards, whilst near Python Point, there are usually some very large rock pythons.

Birds, accustomed to visitors, can be watched at close range from the road between the boat jetty and Keoladeo temple, especially at Sapan Mori crossing. Dawn (which can be very cold) and dusk are the best times; trees around Keoladeo temple are favoured by birds for roosting, so are particularly rewarding. Midday may prove too hot so take a book and find a shady spot. Carry a sun hat, binoculars and plenty of water.

◉ Deeg, Bharatpur and around listings

For Sleeping and Eating price codes and other relevant information, see Essentials pages 28-33.

🛏 Sleeping

Deeg *p164*
If you have to spend a night there are a couple of very basic options near the bus stand.

Bhandarej to Bharatpur *p165*
B Bhadrawati Palace, 5 km from palace, Bhandarej, T01427-283351, www.bhadrawati palace.com. 35 adequate rooms arranged around a central lawn in a converted palace, extensive gardens, pool, wide choice in beautiful restaurant; orchard with camping.

B Bhanwar Vilas Palace (Heritage Hotel), Karauli, T07464-220024, www.karauli.com. 29 comfortable rooms, including 4 a/c suites in converted palace, most air-cooled, cheaper in cottage, Rajasthani restaurant, pool, tours, camping, amazingly ornate lounge and dining halls, real air of authenticity. Recommended.
C-D Manglam Inn, next to the Balaji turn-off on the NH11, Balaji. The closest option, 10 clean, good-sized rooms, 3 a/c, friendly.
E-F Motel (RTDC), Mahuwa, T07461-240260. With 5 simple rooms, a fast-food restaurant, toilets, basic motor repair facilities.

Bharatpur *p166, map p165*

Most of Bharatpur's accommodation is out of town, close to the bird sanctuary. However, there is a great budget choice in the old city.
B Chandra Mahal, Peharsar, Jaipur–Agra Rd, Nadbai, Peharsar, T05643-264336, www.chandramahalhaveli.com. 23 rooms in simply furnished, 19th-century Shia Muslim *haveli* with character, quality set meals (from Rs 250), jeep hire and good service.
F Shagun Guest House, just inside Mathura Gate, T05644-232455. Has 6 basic rooms, 1 with attached bathroom, all under Rs 100, bicycle and binocular hire. Friendly, welcoming and knowledgeable manager.

Keoladeo Ghana National Park
p166, map p167

Some budget hotels have tents. The NH11 past the park is being widened, affecting the hotels near the park entrance, some of which will have to be partly demolished; prepare for a degree of construction/traffic disturbance.

Inside the park
B Bharatpur Forest Lodge (Ashok), 2.5 km from gate, 8 km from railway and bus stand, T05644-222760, itdchba@sancharnet.in, book in advance. 17 comfortable a/c rooms with balconies, pricey restaurant and bar, very friendly staff, peaceful, boats for birdwatching, animals (eg wild boar) wander into the compound. Entry fee each time you enter park.
E Shanti Kutir Rest House, near boat jetty. 5 clean rooms in old hunting lodge, mostly used by guests of the park director.

Outside the park
LL-A Udai Vilas, Fatehpur Sikri Rd, 3 km from park, T05644-233161, www.udaivilaspalace.com. Contemporary rooms plus 10 luxurious suites in impressively run hotel, excellent restaurant, pleasant gardens. Recommended.
L-AL The Bagh, Agra Rd, 4 km from town, T05644-225515, www.thebagh.com. 14 classy, well decorated, centrally a/c rooms with outstanding bathrooms in upmarket garden retreat. Attractive dining

room, pool and coffee shop planned, beautiful 200-year-old gardens, some may find facilities rather spread out.
A Laxmi Vilas Palace (Heritage Hotel), Kakaji ki Kothi, Agra Rd, 2.5 km from town (auto-rickshaws outside), T05644-223523, www.laxmivilas.com. 30 elegant, a/c rooms around a lovely central courtyard, good food and service, attractive 19th-century hunting lodge decorated in period style, pleasant old fashioned, welcoming staff, exceptional pool and jacuzzi. Recommended.
B Kadamb Kunj, Fatehpur Sikri Rd, 3 km from park, T022-2404 2211, www.nivalink.com/kadambkunj. 16 modern, a/c rooms, well-kept lawns, good gift shop and restaurant.
B-C Park Regency, opposite park, T05644-224232, hotelparkregency@yahoo.co.uk. 8 large, modern, clean rooms, 24-hr room service, lawns, friendly, good value.
B-E Crane Crib, Fatehpur Sikri Rd, 3 km from park, T05644-222224. Attractive sandstone building, 25 rooms of wide-ranging standards and tariffs, all reasonable value. Small cinema where wildlife films are shown nightly, bonfires on the lawn during winter and welcoming staff. Recommended.
C The Park, opposite park gate, T05644-233192, bansal39@sancharnet.in. 10 large, clean rooms plus an atypically light restaurant and well-maintained lawn.
D Sunbird, near park gate, T05644-225701, www.hotelsunbird.com. Clean rooms with hot shower, better on 1st floor, pleasant restaurant, friendly staff, bike hire, good value, well maintained. Highly recommended.
D-F Pratap Palace, near park gate, T05644-224245, www.hotelpratappalace.net. 30 rooms (10 a/c) with bath, whole place feels slightly run-down, mediocre restaurant but helpful management, good value.
D-G Nightingale and Tented Camp, near park gate, T05644-227022. De luxe 2-bed tents with bath, others with shared bath, good food, open during the winter.
E Saras (RTDC), Fatehpur Sikri Rd, T05644-223700. Hotel with 25 simple clean rooms, some a/c (limited hot water), dorm (Rs 50),

restaurant (indifferent food), lawns, camping, dull, but helpful tourist information.

E-F Falcon Guest House, near Saras, T05644-223815. 10 clean, well-kept rooms, some a/c with bath, owned by naturalist, good information, bike hire, quiet, very helpful, warm welcome, off-season discount.

E-G Kiran Guest House, 364 Rajendra Nagar, 300 m from park gate, T05644-223845. 5 clean rooms, excellent meals in rooftop restaurant, peaceful, safe, homely, helpful, knowledgeable family, free station pick ups. Recommended.

F-G Pelican, near park gate, T05644-224221. 9 clean rooms with fan, best No 8 with hot (salty!) shower, quite modern with tiny balcony, restaurant, friendly, bike hire (Rs 40 per day), good information.

F-G Spoonbill, near Saras, T05644-223 571, hotelspoonbill@rediffmail.com. Good-value rooms with shared facility (hot water in buckets), dorm (Rs 60), run by charming ex-army officer, courteous and friendly service, good food, bike hire, also 4 more good-size rooms in 'New Spoonbill' down the road.

● Eating

Keoladeo Ghana National Park
p166, map p167
Inside the park
ψψψ Forest Lodge, overpriced buffets feeding the many tour groups.
ψ Snack Bar, dirty, serving drinks and biscuits.

Outside the park
All restaurants offer Indian and Western dishes.
ψψψ Laxmi Vilas, wide choice but some find it disappointing, standard fare for Westerners.
ψψ Eagle's Nest, new 100-seater restaurant with the promise of a/c to come.
ψψ Moon Dance tent, near **Pratap Palace**. Good food, lively atmosphere, beer.
ψ Bambino, open-air dining in a garden.
ψ Pelican, good choice, chicken, vegetarian, Israeli dishes, 'Westernized'.
ψ Spoonbill, good food, obliging (beer and special *kheer* on request). Recommended.

⊛ Festivals and events

Bhandarej to Bharatpur *p165*
Feb/Mar In Karauli, Sivaratri.
Mar/Apr Kaila Devi (12 Mar 2010, 31 Mar 2011). Held in Karauli.

Bharatpur *p166, map p165*
2-4 Feb Brij Festival, honours lord Krishna with folk dances and drama relating the love story of Radha-Krishna.

⊖ Transport

Bhandarej to Bharatpur *p165*
Train Nearly all trains on the main Delhi–Mumbai line stop at Gangapur City, 30 km from Karauli.

Bharatpur *p166, map p165*
Air The nearest airport is at Jaipur (175 km).
Bus Buses to Bharatpur tend to get very crowded but give an insight into Indian rural life. The main stand is at Anah Gate just off NH11 (east of town). To **Agra** (55 km, 1½ hrs), **Deeg**; **Delhi**, 185 km, 6 hrs; and **Jaipur** 175 km, 5 hrs.
Train From: **Delhi (ND)**: *Paschim Exp 2925*, 0635, 4 hrs; *Golden Temple Mail 2903*, 1513, 3½ hrs; *Mumbai-Firozepur Janata Exp 9023*, 0805, 5½ hrs. **Sawai Madhopur**: *Paschim Exp 2926*, 1945, 2½ hrs; *Golden Temple Mail 2904*, 1045, 2½ hrs.
An auto-rickshaw from train station (6 km) to park Rs 50; from bus stand (4 km), Rs 20.

Keoladeo Ghana National Park
p166, map p167
Cycle There are bikes for hire near Saras or ask at your hotel; Rs 40 per day; hire on previous evening for an early start next day.

● Directory

Bharatpur *p166, map p165*
Banks SBBJ, near Binarayan Gate, may ask for proof of purchase, or refuse to change TCs.

Ranthambhore National Park

→ *Colour map 3, A4. Phone code: 07462.*
The park is one of the finest tiger reserves in the country, although even here their numbers have dwindled due to poachers. Most visitors spending a couple of nights here are likely to spot one of these wonderful animals, although many leave disappointed. Set in dry deciduous forest, some trees trailing matted vines, the park's rocky hills and open valleys are dotted with small pools and fruit trees. The reserve covers 410 sq km between the Aravalli and Vindhya hills. Scrubby hillsides surrounding Ranthambhore village are pleasantly peaceful, their miniature temples and shrines glowing pink in the evening sun before they become silhouetted nodules against the night sky. Once the private tiger reserve of the Maharajah of Jaipur, in 1972 the sanctuary came under the Project Tiger scheme following the government Wildlife Protection Act. By 1979, 12 villages inside the park had been 'resettled' into the surrounding area, leaving only a scattering of people still living within the park's boundaries. Should the tigers evade you, as you pass along misty dust tracks as the crisp morning air disperses with the sunrise, you may well spot leopard, hyena, jackal, marsh crocodile, wild boar, langur monkey, bear, and many species of deer and birdlife. The park's 10th-century fort, proudly flanked by two impressive gateways, makes a good afternoon excursion after a morning drive.▶▶ *For listings, see pages 174-175.*

Ins and outs

Getting there and around The national park is 10 km east of Sawai Madhopur, with the approach along a narrow valley; the main gate is 4 km from the boundary. The park has good roads and tracks. Entry is by park jeep (gypsy) or open bus (canter) on four-hour tours; 16 jeeps and 20 canters are allowed in at any one time to minimize disturbance. You can book online. Some lodges can organize trips for you or there are a couple of jeeps and canters reserved for same-day bookings, which involves a queue and elbows and you may get gazumped by hotels paying over the odds for a private jeep. Jeeps are better but must be booked in advance so request one at the time of booking your lodge (passport number and personal details required) or try online. Visitors are picked up from their hotels.

The park is open 1 October-30 June for two sessions a day: winter 0630-1030, 1400-1800; summer 0600-1000, 1430-1830, but check as times change. Jeep hire: Rs 800-1200 per person for up to five passengers; jeep entry Rs 125; guide Rs 150. A seat in a canter, Rs 500-550, can often be arranged on arrival, bookings start at 0600 and 1330 for same-day tours; advance bookings from 1000-1330. Individual entry fees are extra: foreigners Rs 200, Indians Rs 25, camera free, video Rs 200.▶▶ *See Transport, page 175.*

Tourist information **Rajasthan Tourism** ⓘ *Hotel Vinayak, T07462-220808.* Conservator of Forests/Field Director, *T07462-220223.* **Forest Officer** ⓘ *T07462-221142.* A very informative background with photography tips is available on www.ranthambhore.com.

Climate Best from November to April, though vegetation dies down in April exposing tigers. Maximum temperatures from 28-49°C. It can be very cold at dawn in winter.

History

Much of the credit for Ranthambhore's present position as one of the world's leading wildlife resorts goes to India's most famous 'tiger man', Mr Fateh Singh Rathore. His enthusiasm for all things wild has been passed on to his son, Dr Goverdhan Singh Rathore, who set up the Prakratik Society in 1994. This charitable foundation was formed in response to the increasing human encroachment on the tiger's natural forest habitat; in

1973 there were 70,000 people living around Ranthambhore Park, a figure which has now increased to 200,000.

The human population's rapidly increasing firewood requirements were leading to ever-more damaging deforestation, and the founders of the Prakratik Society soon realized that something needed to be done. Their solution was as brilliant as it was simple; enter the 'biogas digester'. This intriguingly named device, of which 225 have so far been installed, uses cow dung as a raw material, and produces both gas for cooking, negating the need for firewood, and organic fertilizer, which has seen crop yields increase by 25%. The overwhelming success of this venture was recognized in June 2004, when the Prakratik Society was presented with the prestigious Ashden Award for Sustainable Energy in London.

Wildlife

Tiger sightings are recorded almost daily, usually in the early morning, especially from November to April. Travellers report the tigers seem "totally unconcerned, ambling past only 30 ft (10 m) away". Sadly, poaching is prevalent: between 2003 and 2005, 22 tigers were taken out of the park by poachers operating from surrounding villages, a wildlife scandal that spotlighted official negligence in Ranthambhore. Since then the population

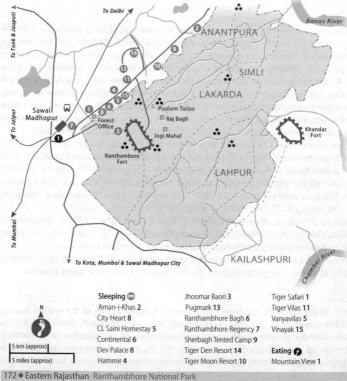

Ranthambhore National Park

Sleeping
Aman-i-Khas **2**
City Heart **8**
CL Saini Homestay **5**
Continental **6**
Dev Palace **8**
Hammir **4**

Jhoomar Baori **3**
Pugmark **13**
Ranthambhore Bagh **6**
Ranthambhore Regency **7**
Sherbagh Tented Camp **9**
Tiger Den Resort **14**
Tiger Moon Resort **10**

Tiger Safari **1**
Tiger Vilas **11**
Vanyavilas **5**
Vinayak **15**

Eating
Mountain View **1**

N

5 km (approx)
5 miles (approx)

Wildlife for the future

Travel Operators for Tigers (TOFT), www.toftigers.org, was established in 2002 to promote responsible wildlife tourism across India. In partnership with **Global Tiger Patrol**, www.globaltiger patrol.org, TOFT counts accommodation providers and international and domestic tour operators among its members, and works across Rajasthan, Madhya Pradesh and Uttarakhand. Funded through a small levy imposed by participating operators, TOFT aims to reverse the decline in tiger numbers, to support the park's efforts against poaching, to assist local community employment, as well as to cover the costs of running park tours.

To ensure such tourism is sustainable, there are 'best practice' guidelines for tour operators, service providers and visitors. Visitors are urged to book lodges and tours with TOFT members and to abide by a code of conduct when visiting conservation areas. TOFT also seeks to empower and inspire local communities to become involved in wildlife tourism projects to benefit themselves and to help park conservation. Also among the organization's initiatives are waste and water management, trade cooperatives and fair wage plans. The inaugural TOFT Wildlife Tourism Awards were held in Delhi in April 2009.

has recovered somewhat, with six cubs born in 2008. The lakeside woods and grassland provide an ideal habitat for herds of chital and sambar deer and sounders of wild boar. Nilgai antelope and chinkara gazelles prefer the drier areas of the park. Langur monkeys, mongoose and hare are prolific. There are also sloth bear, a few leopards, and the occasional rare caracal. Crocodiles bask by the lakes, and some rocky ponds have freshwater turtles. Extensive birdlife includes spurfowl, jungle fowl, partridges, quails, crested serpent eagle, woodpeckers, flycatchers, etc. There are also water birds like storks, ducks and geese at the lakes and waterholes. Padam Talao by the Jogi Mahal is a favourite water source; there are also water holes at Raj Bagh and Milak.

Ranthambhore Fort
ⓘ *The entrance to the fort is before the gate to the park. Open from dawn to dusk, though the Park Interpretation Centre near the small car park may not be open. Free entry.*
There is believed to have been a settlement here in the eighth century. The earliest historic record is of it being wrested by the Chauhans in the 10th century. In the 11th century, after Ajmer was lost to Ghori, the Chauhans made it their capital. Hamir Chauhan, the ruler of Ranthambhore in the 14th century, gave shelter to enemies of the Delhi sultanate, resulting in a massive siege and the Afghan conquest of the fort. The fort was later surrendered to Emperor Akbar in the 16th century when Ranthambhore's commander saw resistance was useless, finally passing to the rulers of Jaipur. The forests of Ranthambhore historically guarded the fort from invasions but with peace under the Raj they became a hunting preserve of the Jaipur royal family. The fort wall runs round the summit and has a number of semi-circular bastions, some with sheer drops of over 65 m and stunning views. Inside the fort you can see a Siva temple – where Rana Hamir beheaded himself rather than face being humiliated by the conquering Delhi army – ruined palaces, pavilions and tanks. Mineral water, tea and soft drinks are sold at the foot of the climb to the fort and next to the Ganesh temple near the tanks.

⊚ Ranthambhore National Park listings

For Sleeping and Eating price codes and other relevant information, see Essentials pages 28-33.

⊛ Sleeping

Ranthambhore National Park
p171, map p172

Book well ahead. Hotels tend to be overpriced, with dusty rooms and erratic electricity. Take a torch. Most **B** category and above are geared for tour groups so may neglect independent travellers. Heavy discounts are offered May-Jun. Sawai Madhopur has a few seedy hotels in the market area, but little else going for it.
LL Aman-i-Khas, close to park, T07462-252052, www.amanresorts.com. 6 super luxury a/c tents in beautiful surroundings, minimum 3-night stay on all-inclusive basis.
LL Dev Vilas Village Khilchipur, Ranthambhore Rd, Sawai Madhopur, T07462-252168, www.devvilas.com. 21 rooms and 7 a/c tents. Tiger safaris, 5-min drive to park entrance. Nice pool, lawns, large bedrooms. Meals included. Evening buffet hit and miss. Very friendly and attentive. Member of **TOFT** (see box, page 173).
LL Sherbagh Tented Camp, Sherpur-Khiljipur, T07462-252120, www.sherbagh.com. Open 1 Oct-30 Mar. Award-winning eco-camp with luxury tents and hot showers, bar, dinner around fire, lake trips for birders, stunning grounds and seated areas for quiet contemplation, jungle ambience, well organized. All meals included. Beautiful shop on site. Highly recommended.
LL Vanyavilas (Oberoi), T07462-223999, www.oberoihotels.com. Very upmarket 8-ha garden resort set around a recreated *haveli* with fantastic frescoes. 25 unbelievably luxurious a/c tents (wooden floors, marble baths), billiards, elephant rides, wildlife lectures, dance shows in open-air auditorium, "fabulous spa", friendly and professional. Elephants greet you at the door.
LL-L The Pugmark, Khilchipur, T07462-252205, www.thepugmark.net. 22 luxury a/c cottages (one with its own pool), in an entertainingly over-the-top resort. Defining feature is the "imaginatively landscaped" garden, replete

with waterways, illuminations and plastic rocks. Rooms are modern and uninspiring.
L Tiger Moon Resort, near Sherpur on the edge of the park, 12 km from railway, T07462-252284, www.indianadventures.com. 32 stone (25 a/c), and 5 simple bamboo cottages, all with modern fittings, hot water, some tents are added in the peak season, buffet meals, bar, library, pool, pleasant "jungle ambience". All meals and 2 safaris included.
AL Ranthambhore Regency, T07462-223456, www.ranthambhor.com. 39 a/c rooms in cottages in swanky modern surroundings. Very clean pool and huge, 100-cover dining hall, plus evening folk performances.
AL Tiger Den Resort, 6 km from park, Khilchipur, Ranthambhore Rd, T07462-252070, www.tigerdenresort.com. 40 modern a/c rooms in brick cottages around a well-kept lawn, evening meals (Indian buffet) seated around braziers, surrounded by farmland and guava groves. Lacks character. Meals included.
A-B Jhoomar Baori (RTDC), Ranthombore Rd, T07462-220495. Set high on a hillside, this former hunting lodge is an interesting building and offers fantastic views of the area. 12 quirky rooms, varying in size, plus a small bar, reasonable restaurant and beautifully decorated communal lounges on each floor.
B Ranthambore Bagh, Ranthambhore Rd, T07462-221728, www.ranthambhore.com. 12 luxury tents and 12 simple but attractive rooms in this pleasantly laid-back property owned by a professional photographer. Family-run, pride has been taken in every detail; the public areas and dining hall are particularly well done. Fantastic food including traditional Rajasthani and atmospheric suppers around the campfire. Highly recommended.
B-C Tiger Vilas, Ranthambore Rd, T07462-221121, aranyaresort@rediffmail.com. 10 clean, modern rooms in convenient location for park, beautiful decor, reasonably priced veggie food.
C-D Hammir, T07462-220562. One of the oldest hotels, in interesting building fresh from much-needed renovation, forgettable

rooms (some a/c) plus a new pool and a
friendly, cheerful manager. Nice vibe.
C-E Tiger Safari, T07462-221137, www.tiger
safariresort.com. 14 cosy rooms, 4 attractive a/c
cottages, very clean, hot shower, quiet, jeep/
bus to park, very helpful, good value, ordinary
food but few other options. Recommended.
D-E Vinayak (RTDC), Ranthambhore Rd,
close to park, T07462-221333. Good location.
14 adequate rooms, including 5 a/c, bit
institutional, but pleasant lawns. Gloomy
restaurant serves fantastic vegetarian *thalis*.
E C L Saini Homestay, Ranthambhore Rd.
T(0)9828-214049, op_ranthambhore@yahoo
co.in. Ranthambhore's first homestay – decent
size rooms with hot water, garden and rooftop
views of the forest and food served on request.
E-G City Heart, Ranthambhore Rd, 100 m
from Ranthambhore Bagh, T07462-223402.
Good, clean rooms, some with TV.
E-G Continental, set back from Ranthambhore
Rd, next to Ranthambhore Bagh, T(0)9414-
727157. Beautiful gardens with 4 simple but
big rooms and 2 rooftop tents. Pretty, good
home-cooked food; great reports from guests.
F-G Dev Palace, Ranthambhore Rd, near City
Heart, T(0)9413-023628, ranthambhoresafari@
rediffmail.com. Only 4 rooms, but one of the
cheapest options; simple but sweet. Friendly.
F-G Rajeev Resort, 16 Indira Colony, Civil Lines,
Sawai Madhopur, T07462-221413. 12 fairly
decent rooms, 2 a/c (some with Western toilets),
and larger 4-bed rooms, simple meals to order.
F-G Vishal, Main Bazar, opposite SBI, Sawai
Madhopur, T07462-220695. 7 passable
rooms some with bath (hot water in buckets).

🍴 Eating

Ranthambhore National Park
p171, map p172
🍴 **Mountain View Restaurant**, Ranthambhore Rd. Standard menu but pleasant lawns
to sit out on and a friendly welcome.
🍴 **Asha**, T07462-220803. Don't be put off by
uninviting exterior, this is a great little eatery,
friendly, fast service, cheap and scrumptious.

🛍 Shopping

Ranthambhore National Park
p171, map p172
Dastkar, the original women's collective
shop is near Sherbagh, with another branch
on Ranthambhore Rd near Ranthambhore
Regency. Many locals have jumped on the
'Women's Collective Crafts' bandwagon
but **Dastkar** is the only genuine one. The
collective empowers women by making
them self sufficient. They started with just
6 women, but now employ 360 women to
do quilting, patchwork, block printing and
sequin embroidery based on traditional local
skills that were dying out. Beautiful fabrics,
clothes, toys and collectibles are sold at
extremely fair prices. Highly recommended.

⊖ Transport

Ranthambhore National Park
p171, map p172
Bus Stand is 500 m from Sawai Madhopur
Railway Station. Buses go to **Kota** and **Jaipur**,
but trains are quicker and more pleasant.
Train The railway station at Sawai Madhopur,
T07462-220222, is on the main Delhi–Mumbai
line. To **Jaipur**: *Mumbai-Jaipur Exp 2955*, 1045,
2 hrs. From Jaipur to **Mumbai**: *Jaipur-Mumbai
Exp 2956*, 1410, 2 hrs. **Jodhpur**: *Ranthambore
Exp 2465*, 1435. **Mumbai** via **Kota**: *Jaipur
Mumbai Exp 2956*, 1610, 16 hrs; *Paschim Exp
2926*, 2205, 17¼ hrs; *Golden Temple Mail 2904*,
1310, 15 hrs (Kota 1½ hrs). **New Delhi** (via
Bharatpur and Mathura) *Golden Temple Mail
2903*, 1240, 6 hrs; *Dehra Dun Exp 9019*, 2130, 8 hrs.

🛈 Directory

Ranthambhore National Park
p171, map p172
Internet Cyber Café on Ranthambhore
Rd near to Ankur Resort. **Useful contacts**
Police, T07462-220456. Tiger Watch,
T07462-220811.

Ajmer and Pushkar

Although geographically close, these towns could hardly be more different. Situated in a basin at the foot of Taragarh Hill (870 m), Ajmer is surrounded by a stone wall with five gateways. Renowned throughout the Muslim world as the burial place of Mu'inuddin Chishti, who claimed descent from the son-in-law of Mohammad, seven pilgrimages to Ajmer are believed to equal one to Mecca. Every year, especially during the annual Islamic festivals of Id and Muharram, thousands of pilgrims converge on this ancient town on the banks of Ana Sagar Lake. Many visitors are discouraged by the frantic hustle of Ajmer on first arrival, but it's worth taking time to explore this underrated city.

Separated from Ajmer by Nag Pahar (Snake Mountain), Pushkar lies in a narrow valley over-shadowed by rocky hills, which offer spectacular views of the desert at sunset. The lake at its heart, almost magically beautiful at dawn and dusk, is one of India's most sacred. The village is transformed during the celebrated camel fair into a colourful week of heightened activity, but a visit outside this annual extravaganza is also worthwhile.

The village has been markedly changed in recent years by the year-round presence of large numbers of foreigners originally drawn by the Pushkar Fair, but there are still plenty of chances for an unhurried stroll around the lake that uncovers a very holy site: ghats dotted with shrines to the elephant-god Ganesh; little alcoves filled with candles, flowers and burning incense; here and there a wild-haired, spindly sadhu sits in repose by a tiny charcoal fire, knees brought up to his chin …

Dozens of hotels, restaurants, cafés and shops cater to Western tastes and many travellers find it hard to drag themselves away from such creature comforts. The village's main bazar, though busy, has banned rickshaws so is relieved of revving engines and touting drivers. Take the short trek up to the Savitri Temple (3 km along a sandy track and jagged stone steps cut into the mountain), and you can swap village activity for open swathes of valley and fringes of desert beyond. From on high, the houses crowd the lake's edges as if it's a plug-hole down which all of Pushkar is slowly being drawn. Come the evening, groups of women promenade the bazars, the clashing colours of their saris all flowing together. Men dry their turbans in the evening sun after washing them in the lake, wafting the metres of filmy fabric in the breeze or draping it on nearby trees. Note that Pushkar is not to everybody's taste as there is a high hassle factor from cash-seeking ubiquitous Brahmin 'priests' requesting a donation receipt for the 'Pushkar Passport' (a red string tied around the wrist as part of a puja/blessing). A huge cleaning project is currently underway, which will involve draining the lake and could take up to two years, but should create a healthier, cleaner environment. ▸▸ *For listings, see pages 182-188.*

Ins and outs

Getting there Pushkar has relatively few direct buses, but Ajmer is well connected by bus and train to the main towns and cities. The station is in the centre, while the main bus stand is 2 km east. Buses to Pushkar leave from the State Bus Stand, and also from a general area 1 km northwest of the station, near the Jain temple. In Pushkar, most buses arrive at the Central (Marwar) Bus Stand, to the usual gauntlet of touts; others pull in at a separate stand 10 minutes' walk east of the lake.

Getting around The main sights and congested bazars of Ajmer, which can be seen in a day at a pinch, are within 15 to 20 minutes' walk of the railway station but you'll need a rickshaw to get to Ana Sagar. Pushkar is small enough to explore on foot. Hire a bike to venture further. ▸▸ *See Transport, page 187.*

Tourist information In Ajmer, there are offices at the railway station and next to **Khadim Hotel** ① *T0145-262 7426, tourismajmer@rediffmail.com, Mon-Sat 0800-1800, closed 2nd Sat of the month*. Both are very helpful. In Pushkar, at the **Sarovar Hotel** ① *T0145-277 2040*.

Sambhar Lake → *Colour map 4, C5.*

The salt lake, one of the largest of its kind in India, until recently attracted thousands of flamingos and an abundance of cranes, pelicans, ducks and other waterfowl; some 120 species of bird have been recorded. However, the poor monsoons of recent years have caused the lake to dry up leaving only a few marshy patches. Check the situation before visiting. Nilgai, fox and hare are spotted around the lake. The saline marshes are used for the production of salt. **Sakambari Temple**, nearby, dedicated to the ancestral deity of the Chauhans, is believed to date from the sixth century.

Kuchaman

Kuchaman is a large village with temples and relics. Many visitors stop here for tea and snacks between Shekhawati and Ajmer. If you do stop, make time for a visit to the fort; it is a unique experience. Before the eighth century, Kuchaman lay on the highly profitable Central Asian caravan route. Here Gurjar Pratiharas built the massive **cliff-top fort** with 10 gates leading up from the Meena bazar in the village to the royal living quarters. The Chauhans drove the Pratiharas out of the area and for some time it was ruled by the Gaurs. From 1400, it has been in the hands of the Rathores who embellished it with mirrors, mural and gold work in superb palaces and pavilions such as the golden Sunheri Burj and the mirrored Sheesh Mahal, both in sharp contrast to the fort's exterior austerity. The Sariska Palace Group have restored and renovated the fort at enormous cost. You can also visit the **Krishna temple** with a 2000-year-old image, and the **Kalimata ka Mandir** which has an eighth-century black stone deity and you can shop in the **Meena Bazar** or watch local village crafts people.

Kishangarh → *Colour map 3, A2. Population: 22,000.*

Enormous blocks of marble in raw, polished and sculpted forms line the road into Kishangarh, the former capital of a small princely state founded by Kishan Singh in 1603, with a fort facing Lake Gundalao. Local artists – known for their depiction of the Krishna legend and other Hindu themes – were given refuge here by the royal family during the reign of the Mughal emperor, Aurangzeb, who, turning his back on the liberal views of earlier emperors, pursued an increasingly zealous Islamic purity. Under their patronage the artists reached a high standard of excellence and they continue the tradition of painting Kishangarh miniatures which are noted for sharp facial features and elongated almond-shaped eyes. Most of those available are cheap copies on old paper using water colours instead of the mineral pigments of the originals. The town has a bustling charm, and is an interesting place to wander around.

The fort palace stands on the shores of Lake Gundalao. Its **Hathi Pol** (Elephant Gate) has walls decorated with fine murals and, though partly in ruins, you can see battlements, courtyards with gardens, shady balconies, brass doors and windows with coloured panes of glass. The temple has a fine collection of miniatures.

Roopangarh

About 20 km from Kishangarh, Roopangarh was an important fort of the Kishangarh rulers founded in AD 1649 on the old caravan route along the Sambhar Lake. The fort stands above the village which is a centre for craft industries – leather embroidery, block printing, pottery and handloom weaving can all be seen. The Sunday market features at least 100 cobblers making and repairing *mojdi* footwear.

The **Dargah of Khwaja Mu'inuddin Chishti** (1143-1235) is the tomb of the Sufi saint (also called 'The Sun of the Realm') which was begun by Iltutmish and completed by Humayun. Set in the heart of the old town, the main gate is reached on foot or by *tonga* or auto-rickshaw through the bazar. The Emperor Akbar first made a pilgrimage to the shrine to give thanks for conquering Chittor in 1567, and the second for the birth of his son Prince Salim. From 1570 to 1580 Akbar made almost annual pilgrimages to Ajmer on foot from Agra, and the *kos minars* (brick marking pillars at about two-mile intervals) along the road from Agra are witness of the popularity of the pilgrimage route. It is

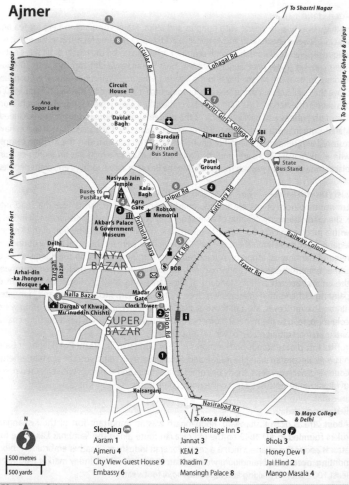

Ajmer

Sleeping
Aaram 1
Ajmeru 4
City View Guest House 9
Embassy 6
Haveli Heritage Inn 5
Jannat 3
KEM 2
Khadim 7
Mansingh Palace 8

Eating
Bhola 3
Honey Dew 1
Jai Hind 2
Mango Masala 4

A saint of the people

Khwaja Mu'inuddin Chishti probably came to India before the Turkish conquests which brought Islam sweeping across Northern India. A sufi, unlike the Muslim invaders, he came in peace. He devoted his life to the poor people of Ajmer and its region. He was strongly influenced by the Upanishads; some reports claim that he married the daughter of a Hindu raja.

His influence during his lifetime was enormous, but continued through the establishment of the Chishti school or *silsila*, which flourished "because it produced respected spiritualists and propounded catholic doctrines". Hindus were attracted to the movement but did not have to renounce their faith, and Sufi khanqah (a form of hospice) were accessible to all.

Almost immediately after his death Khwaja Mu'innuddin Chishti's followers carried on his mission. The present structure was built by Ghiyasuddin Khalji of Malwa, but the embellishment of the shrine to its present ornate character is still seen as far less important than the spiritual nature of the Saint it commemorates.

considered the second holiest site after Mecca. On their first visit, rich Muslims pay for a feast of rice, ghee, sugar, almonds, raisins and spices to be cooked in one of the huge pots in the courtyard inside the high gateway. These are still in regular use. On the right is the Akbar Masjid (circa 1570); to the left, an assembly hall for the poor. In the inner courtyard is the white marble Shah Jahan Masjid (circa 1650), 33 m long with 11 arches and a carved balustrade on three sides. In the inner court is the square *dargah* (tomb), also white marble, with a domed roof and two entrances. The ceiling is gold-embossed velvet, and silver rails and gates enclose the tomb. At festival times the tomb is packed with pilgrims, many coming from abroad, and the crush of people can be overpowering.

The whole complex has a unique atmosphere. The areas around the tomb have a real feeling of community; there is a hospital and a school on the grounds, as well as numerous shops. As you approach the tomb the feeling of religious fervour increases – as does the barrage of demands for 'donations' – often heightened by the music being played outside the tomb's ornate entrance. For many visitors, stepping into the tomb itself is the culmination of a lifetime's ambition, reflected in the ardour of their offerings.

Nearby is the **Mazar** (tomb) of Bibi Hafiz Jamal, daughter of the saint, a small enclosure with marble latticework. Close by is that of Chimni Begum, daughter of Shah Jahan. She never married, refusing to leave her father during the seven years he was held captive by Aurangzeb in Agra Fort. She spent her last days in Ajmer, as did another daughter who probably died of tuberculosis. At the south end of the Dargah is the **Jhalra** (tank).

The **Arhai-din-ka Jhonpra Mosque** ('Hut of Two and a Half Days') lies beyond the Dargah in a narrow valley. Originally a Jain college built in 1153, it was partially destroyed by Muhammad of Ghori in 1192, and in 1210 turned into a mosque by **Qutb-ud-din-Aibak** who built a massive screen of seven arches in front of the pillared halls, allegedly in 2½ days (hence its name). The temple pillars which were incorporated in the building are all different. The mosque measures 79 m by 17 m with 10 domes supported by 124 columns and incorporates Hindu and Jain masonry. Much of it is in ruins though restoration work was undertaken at the turn of the century; only part of the 67-m screen and the prayer hall remain.

Akbar's Palace, built in 1570 and restored in 1905, is in the city centre near the east wall. It is a large rectangular building with a fine gate. Today it houses the **Government Museum** ① *Sat-Thu 1000-1630, Rs 3, no photography*, which has a dimly presented collection of fine sculpture from sixth to 17th centuries, paintings and old Rajput and Mughal armour and coins.

The ornate **Nasiyan Jain Temple (Red Temple)** ① *Prithviraj Marg, 0800-1700, Rs 5*, has a remarkable museum alongside the Jain shrine, which itself is open only to Jains. It is well worth visiting. Ajmer has a large Jain population (about 25% of the city's total). The Shri Siddhkut Chaityalaya was founded in 1864 in honour of the first Jain Tirthankar, Rishabdeo, by a Jain diamond merchant, Raj Bahadur Seth Moolchand Nemichand Soni (hence its alternative name, the Soni temple). The opening was celebrated in 1895. Behind a wholly unimposing exterior, on its first floor the Svarna Nagari Hall houses an astonishing reconstruction of the Jain conception of the universe, with gold-plated replicas of every Jain shrine in India. Over 1000 kg of gold is estimated to have been used, and at one end of the gallery diamonds have been paced behind decorative coloured glass to give an appearance of backlighting. It took 20 people 30 years to build. The holy mountain, Sumeru, is at the centre of the continent, and around it are such holy sites as Ayodhya, the birthplace of the Tirthankar, recreated in gold plate, and a remarkable collection of model temples. Suspended from the ceiling are *vimanas* (airships of the gods) and silver balls. On the ground floor, beneath the model, are the various items taken on procession around the town on the Jain festival day of 23 November each year. The trustees of the temple are continuing to maintain and embellish it.

☽ *From Station Road, a walk through the bazars, either to Dargah/Masjid area or to Akbar's Palace/Nasiyan Temple area, is interesting.*

Excursions from Ajmer

Mayo College (1873), only 4 km from the centre, was founded to provide young Indian princes with a liberal education, one of two genuinely Indo-Saracenic buildings designed by De Fabeck in Ajmer, the other being the **Mayo Hospital** (1870). The college was known as the 'Eton of Rajputana' and was run along the lines of an English public school. Access is no longer restricted to Rajput princes.

Ana Sagar, an artificial lake (circa 1150), was further enhanced by emperors Jahangir and Shah Jahan who added the baradari and pavilions. The **Foy Sagar**, 5 km away, another artificial lake, was a famine relief project.

Taragarh (Star Fort), built by Ajaipal Chauhan in 1100 with massive 4.5-m-thick walls, stands on the hilltop overlooking the town. There are great views of the city but the walk up the winding bridle path is tiring. A road accessible by road has reduced the climb on foot and made access easier. Jeeps charge Rs 500 for the trip. Along the way is a graveyard of Muslim 'martyrs' who died storming the fort.

Pushkar → *For listings, see pages 182-188. Colour map 3, A2. Phone code: 0145. Population: 15,000.*

ⓘ *There are dozens of temples here, most of which are open 0500-1200, 1600-2200.*

Pushkar Lake is one of India's most sacred lakes. It is believed to mark the spot where a lotus thrown by Brahma landed. Fa Hien, the Chinese traveller who visited Pushkar in the fifth century AD, commented on the number of pilgrims, and although several of the older temples were subsequently destroyed by Aurangzeb, many remain. Ghats lead down to the water to enable pilgrims to bathe, cows to drink, and the town's young folk to wash off after the riotous Holi celebrations. They also provide a hunting ground for Brahmin 'priests', who press a flower into the hand of any passing foreigner and offer – even demand – to perform *puja* (worship) in return for a sum of money. If this hard-sell version of spirituality appeals, agree your price in advance – Rs 50 should be quite sufficient – and be aware that a proportion of so-called priests are no such thing.

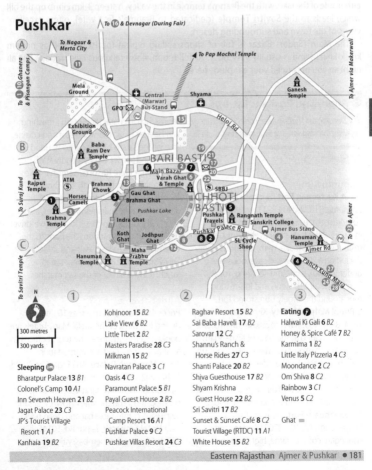

Sleeping 🛏
Bharatpur Palace **13** *B1*
Colonel's Camp **10** *A1*
Inn Seventh Heaven **21** *B1*
Jagat Palace **23** *C3*
JP's Tourist Village
  Resort **1** *A1*
Kanhaia **19** *B2*

Kohinoor **15** *B2*
Lake View **6** *B2*
Little Tibet **2** *B2*
Masters Paradise **28** *C3*
Milkman **15** *B2*
Navratan Palace **3** *C1*
Oasis **4** *C3*
Paramount Palace **5** *B1*
Payal Guest House **2** *B2*
Peacock International
  Camp Resort **16** *A1*
Pushkar Palace **9** *C2*
Pushkar Villas Resort **24** *C3*

Raghav Resort **15** *B2*
Sai Baba Haveli **17** *B2*
Sarovar **12** *C2*
Shannu's Ranch &
  Horse Rides **27** *C3*
Shanti Palace **20** *B2*
Shiva Guesthouse **17** *B2*
Shyam Krishna
  Guest House **22** *B2*
Sri Savitri **17** *B2*
Sunset & Sunset Café **8** *C2*
Tourist Village (RTDC) **11** *A1*
White House **15** *B2*

Eating 🍴
Halwai Ki Gali **6** *B2*
Honey & Spice Café **7** *B2*
Karmima **1** *B2*
Little Italy Pizzeria **4** *C3*
Moondance **2** *C2*
Om Shiva **8** *C2*
Rainbow **3** *C1*
Venus **5** *C2*

Ghat ═

The **Brahma temple** ⓘ *0600-1330, 1500-2100 (changes seasonally)*, beyond the western end of the lake, is a particularly holy shrine and draws pilgrims throughout the year. Although it isn't the only Brahma temple in India, as people claim, it is the only major pilgrim place for followers of the Hindu God of Creation. It is said that when Brahma needed a marital partner for a ritual, and his consort Saraswati (Savitri) took a long time to come, he married a cow-girl, Gayatri, after giving her the powers of a goddess (Gayatri because she was purified by the mouth of a cow or *gau*). His wife learnt of this and put a curse on him – that he would only be worshipped in Pushkar.

There are 52 ghats around the lake, of which the Brahma Ghat, Gan Ghat and Varah Ghat are the most sacred. The medieval **Varah Temple** is dedicated to the boar incarnation of Vishnu. It is said the idol was broken by Emperor Jahangir as it resembled a pig. The **Mahadev Temple** is said to date from 12th century while the **Julelal Temple** is modern and jazzy. Interestingly enough the two wives of Brahma have hilltop temples on either side of the lake, with the Brahma temple in the valley. A steep 3-km climb up the hill which leads to the **Savitri Temple** (dedicated to Brahma's first wife), offers excellent views of the town and surrounding desert.

The **Main (Sadar) Bazar** is full of shops selling typical tourist, as well as pilgrim knick-knacks and is usually very busy. At full moon, noisy religious celebrations last all night so you may need your ear plugs here.

◉ Ajmer and Pushkar listings

For Sleeping and Eating price codes and other relevant information, see Essentials pages 28-33.

● Sleeping

Jaipur to Ajmer *p177*
AL-A Kuchaman Fort (Heritage Hotel), Kuchaman, T022-2404 2211, www.nivalink. com/kuchaman. 35 distinctive a/c rooms in a part of the fort, attractively furnished, restaurant, bar, jacuzzi, gym, luxurious pools (including a 200-year-old cavernous one underground), camel/horse riding, royal hospitality, superb views and interesting tour around the largely unrestored fort.
B Phool Mahal Old City, Kishangarh, T01463-247405, www.royalkishangarh.com. Superbly located at the base of Kishangarh Fort on the banks of Gundalao lake (dries up in summer), this 1870 garden palace has 21 well-maintained a/c rooms, as well as an elegant lounge and dining room, all with period furnishings and marble floors.
B Roopangarh Fort (Heritage Hotel), Roopangarh, T01497-220217, www.royal kishangarh.com. 20 large, high-ceilinged

rooms, rich in character though furnishing can be a bit basic. Marwar decor and cuisine, free village safaris plus excursions, good sunrise and sunset views, friendly staff.
D Sambhar Lake Resorts, Sambhar Lake. 6 cottage rooms, bath with hot showers, friendly staff, camel rides and jeep safaris across the saline marshes and dunes, also short rail journey on diesel locomotive-driven trolleys that carry salt from the pans to the towns. Price includes meals and safaris. Day visit (Rs 500) includes vegetarian lunch, tea and a tour of the salt marshes.

Ajmer *p178, map p178*
Prices rise sharply, as much as 10 times, during the week of the **mela**. Many hotels are booked well in advance. The tourist office has a list of Paying Guest accommodation.
AL-A Mansingh Palace, Ana Sagar Circular Rd, T0145-242 5702, www.mansinghhotels.com. 54 rooms in attractive sandstone modern building, most comfortable in town. Pleasant restaurant, comfortable bar and clean pool.
B-D Hotel Embassy, Jaipur Rd, T0145-262 3859, www.hotelembassyajmer.com.

31 smart a/c rooms in building newly renovated to 3-star standard. Enthusiastic, professional staff, elegant restaurant.

C-E Khadim (RTDC), Savitri Girls' College Rd, near bus station, T0145-262 7490. Pleasant setting 55 rooms, some a/c (**C** suites), best are the uncarpeted, renovated rooms, dorm (Rs 50), gloomy restaurant, bar, tourist information, car hire, usual RTDC service.

C-F Haveli Heritage Inn, Kutchery Rd, T0145-262 1607. 12 good-sized, clean, comfortable rooms in homely 125-year-old building, no hot water in cheaper rooms. Rooms are quite expensive for what you get. Family-run, good home cooking, located on busy main road but set back with a pleasant courtyard, very charming owner.

D-F Aaram, off Ana Sagar Circular Rd, opposite Mansingh, T0145-242 5250. 22 slightly grubby rooms, some a/c, restaurant, small garden, friendly manager.

D-F Hotel Ajmeru, Khailand Market, near Akbar Fort, T0145-243 1103, www.hotel ajmeru.com. 12 very clean, light, modern rooms, 8 a/c, in relatively quiet location.

E-F Hotel Jannat, very close to Durgah, T0145-243 2494, www.ajmerhotel jannat. com. 36 clean, modern rooms in great location, find yourself in labyrinthine alleys, friendly staff, a/c restaurant, all mod cons.

E-G KEM, Station Rd, T0145-242 9936. 45 rooms in period building near the railway station, 1st-class rooms are clean and acceptable, 2nd-class ones are less so. Service practically non-existent. Attached bath.

G City View Guest House, 133/17 Nalla Bazar, T0145-263 0958. Very basic but charmingly run guesthouse in warrens of the Old City, Indian toilets, atmospheric building, friendly hosts.

Northwest of Ajmer
There are 2 good options on the road towards Nagaur.

D Fort Khejarla, Khejarla, T02930-258311, madhoniwas@satyam.net.in. A Rajput Special Hotels. Simple rooms in the old part the fort, meals (Rs 180), excursions to Raika and Bishnoi tribal villages. Contact Curvet India, Delhi, T011-2684 0037.

D Raj Palace Motel, Merta Rd, T01590-220202. 25 clean rooms with bath, 6 a/c, friendly family. Recommended.

Pushkar *p181, map p181*
The town suffers from early-morning temple bells. During the fair, hotel charges can be 10 times the normal rate. Booking in advance is essential for the better places. Some budget hotels offer views of the lake from communal rooftops; however, local authorities periodically threaten to close down all commercial properties within 100 m of the lake, including hotels and restaurants. To escape the noise of the Main Bazar, choose one in a back street of Bari Basti or near Ajmer Bus Stand.

L-A Pushkar Palace (WelcomHeritage), on lakeside, T0145-277 2001, www.hotelpushkar palace.com. 52 overpriced rooms including 25 suites overlooking the lake, in beautifully renovated old palace, attractive gardens. It looks good but is rather uncomfortable and lakeside rooms have very small windows. Alas, too the terrace restaurant is now closed, so the restaurant is in the courtyard with no lake view.

A Jagat Palace (WelcomHeritage), Ajmer Rd, T0145-277 2953, www.jagatpalace.co.in. Rooms of various sizes in new building made to resemble a Rajput fort, colourful, naturally lit interiors, beautiful pool and gardens, a bit lacking in atmosphere.

B-C Master Paradise, Panch Kund Rd, T0145-277 3933, www.pushkarmasterparadise.com. Newly built with spacious modern rooms, some suites, slightly extravagant decor, nice pool with seating area.

C-E JP's Tourist Village Resort, Ganhera, 2 km from town, T0145-277 2067, www.pushkarhotelbooking.com. 30 very rustic, basic rooms built in traditional style with mud walls, quirky feel, great gardens with dusty pool, outside town so a popular retreat for those seeking non-vegetarian food and a tipple.

C-F Inn Seventh Heaven, next to Mali ka Mandir, T0145-510 5455, www.inn-seventh-heaven.com. 12 beautiful rooms in a fantastically well-restored 100-year-old *haveli*, plus a handful of ascetic but much cheaper rooms in neighbouring building. Lots of seating areas dotted throughout the 3-storey building, even some lovely swinging diwans. Also some new de luxe chic rooms available in a new building. Very friendly, informal, excellent rooftop restaurant (baked potatoes from open coal fire in winter), charming owner and a sociable atmosphere. Fair trade shop, **Water Chocolate Biscuit**, downstairs sells clothes and fabrics from collectives like Peoples' Tree and Sadhna. Highly recommended.

D-E Navratan Palace, near Brahma temple, T0145-277 2145. Comfortable though not particularly attractive. 33 clean rooms, some a/c with hot showers (Rs 300-600), clean pool, small garden with views, well kept.

D-E Pushkar Villas Resort, Panch Kund Rd, T0145-277 2689, arajoria@hotmail.com. Newish place which feels a little unfinished, strange vibe, very popular with tourist taxi drivers. 14 good-sized rooms (7 a/c) around pleasant gardens and a well-maintained pool.

D-E Sarovar (RTDC), on lakeside, T0145-277 2040. 38 clean rooms (best with amazing lake view, in old part), some a/c with bath, new rooms good but no atmosphere, cheap 6-bed dorm, set around courtyard in former lakeside palace, indifferent vegetarian restaurant, attractive gardens.

D-F Sunset, on the lake, T0145-277 2382, hotelsunset@hotmail.com. 20 plain, clean rooms, 3 a/c, around a lovely garden, lots of flowers and papaya trees. Well located close to lake, plus access to **Sunset Café**.

E-G Oasis, near Ajmer Bus Stand, T0145-277 2100, www.hoteloasispushkar.com. 34 clean motel-style rooms with bath, some a/c, garden, courtyard pool, no seating area.

E-G Paramount Palace, Bari Basti, T0145-277 2428, hotelparamountpalace@hotmail.com. 16 clean, basic rooms, some

with bath, best with balcony, elevated site with splendid views from rooftop, highest in Pushkar. Very friendly host.

F-G Bharatpur Palace, lakeside, T0145-277 2320. Exceptional views of the ghats, one very simple room practically hangs over the ghat, 18 unusually decorated rooms, clean bathrooms.

F-G Kanhaia, near Mali Mandir, T0145-277 2146. Friendly staff, good value, 14 small rooms with more coming, recently renovated, best has sofa, with good bathrooms.

F-G Lake View, lakefront, Sadar Bazar, T0145-277 2106. Basic rooms some with shared bath, but great views and relaxed atmosphere perched right on the lake. Restaurant serves up the usual fare, but lovely view.

F-G Milkman, near White House, T0145-277 3452, Mostly cheap and basic rooms, some bigger. Very sociable.

F-G Payal Guest House, opposite Municipality, Sadar Bazar, T0145-277 2163. Pushkar standard room fare but with great view from rooftop and great Tibetan restaurant in the courtyard.

F-G Raghav Resort, Panday Nursery Farm, T0145-277 2207, www.lakeviewpushkar.com. 14 reasonable rooms surrounded by beautiful nursery gardens, attractive outdoor restaurant, a peaceful retreat.

F-G Sai Baba Haveli, near market post office, T0145-510 5161, lola_singh_modiano@hotmail.com. Nice big rooms around a central courtyard, lots of greenery and hanging plants, lots of potential but needs a lick of paint.

F-G Shannu's Ranch, Panch Kund Rd, T0145-277 2043. On the edge of town, with nice quirky, 'rustique' cottages in a garden, owned by French-Canadian riding instructor, good for a longer stay but could get cold in winter.

G Shanti Palace, near Varah temple, T(0)9414-415351, shantipalace@hotmail.com. 12 basic rooms in very peaceful surroundings, plus a friendly owner and good views of town.

G Shiva Guest house, near market post office, T0145-277 2120. Basic but clean rooms in calm environment enhanced by free-range tortoises in central courtyard, 7 of them at last count

G Sri Savitri, near market post office, T0145-277 2631. Hotel with 7 slightly ramshackle but characterful rooms. Highly recommended by frequent visitors, not least for the friendly owner.

G Shyam Krishna Guest House, Chhoti Basti, T0145-277 2461. Part of 200-year-old temple complex with 25 rooms around a courtyard, some with *jali* work on upper floor, run by friendly Brahmin family, bit difficult to find.

G Tulsi Palace, VIP Rd, Holika Chowk, T0145-277 3409, tulsi_palace@yahoo.com. Basic guesthouse. Helpful family hosts live on ground floor. Very basic food served on terrace. Quiet. 5-min walk from main bazar so good respite from strolling crowds. Attached bathrooms moderately clean.

G White House, in narrow alley near Marwar Bus Stand, T0145-277 2147, hotelwhitehouse@hotmail.com. Very clean, impressively white rooms in well-maintained building overlooking nursery gardens. Good views from pleasant rooftop restaurant with excellent food, free and very tasty mango tea. Also nice cheaper rooms available at their sister guesthouse, **Kohinoor**. Recommended.

During the fair

It is best to visit early in the week when toilets are still reasonably clean.

Tourist village Erected by RTDC, this is a remarkable feat, accommodating 100,000 people. Conveniently placed with de luxe/super de luxe tents (Rs 6000-6500 with meals), ordinary/dorm tents (Rs 300 per bed), 30 'cottages', some de luxe (Rs 4000-5000). Beds and blankets, some running water, Indian toilets are standard. Meals are served in a separate tent (or eat cheap, delicious local food at the tribal tented villages near the show ground). Reservation with payment, essential (open 12 months ahead);

contact RTDC in Jaipur, T0141-220 3531, www.rajasthantourism.gov.in.

Private camps Privately run camps charge about US$150-250 including meals for Regular and 'Swiss' double tent. They might be some distance from fair ground and may lack security:

Colonel's Camp, Motisar Rd, Ghanera, T0141-220 2034, www.meghniwas.com. 120 de luxe tents with toilet and shower in attractive gardens.

Peacock International Camp Resort, at Devnagar (2 km from Mela Ground), T0145-277 2689. Common facilities for the 25 tents among orchards with pool, free transport.

Pushkar Palace (see page 183). Sets up 50 'Swiss' tents and 50 de luxe.

Royal Tents Camp, www.welcomheritage. com, T0291-257 2321. Comfortable tents with veranda, flush toilet, hot water in buckets or shower of sorts, Rajasthani cuisine, very well organized.

Wanderlust Desert Camp, T011-2467 9059, www.wanderlustindia.cim. 120 Swiss tents with bath, electricity, varied meals.

❶ Eating

Ajmer *p178, map p178*
Son halwa, a local sweet speciality, is sold near the Dargah and at the market. Delicious street snacks can be found in the back lanes between Delhi and Agra gates.

❛❛❛ Mansingh Palace, Ana Sagar Circular Rd. International. Pricey, unexciting food, popular with meat-seeking Pushkaris.

❛❛ Mango Masala, Sandar Patel Marg, T0145-242 2100. American diner-styled place with wide-ranging menu including pizzas, sizzlers, Indian and sundaes. Standard is high, portions large and service outstanding.

❛❛ Silver Leaf, Hotel Embassy (see Sleeping). Good range of multi-cuisine choices in sophisticated surroundings.

❛ Bhola, Agra Gate. Good vegetarian food, no nonsense service.

¶ **Honey Dew**, Station Rd. Indian, continental. Pleasant shady garden, good Indian snacks all day, disappointing Western.

¶ **Jai Hind**, in alley by clock tower, opposite railway station. Best for Indian vegetarian. Delicious, cheap meals.

¶ **Madeen**, opposite station. Simple but tasty.

Pushkar *p181, map p181*

No meat, fish or eggs are served in this temple town, and alcohol is banned, as are 'narcotics' – in theory. Take special care during the fair: eat only freshly cooked food and drink bottled water. Long-stay budget travellers have resulted in an increase of Western and Israeli favourites like falafel, granola and apple pie, while Nepali and Tibetan immigrants have brought their own specialities. Roadside vendors offer cheap, filling *thalis* close to Ajmer Bus Stand.

¶¶¶ **Little Italy Pizzeria**, Panch Kund Rd. High-quality Italian dishes plus Israeli and Indian specialities, pleasant garden setting.

¶¶¶ **Moondance**, just by the turning to Pushkar Palace. Western food. Highly rated café run by friendly Nepalese, popular and occasionally slow, but the food hits the mark. Recommended.

¶ **Halwai ki gali** (alley off Main Bazar). Sweet shops sell *malpura* (syrupy pancake), as well as other Rajasthani/Bengali sweets.

¶ **Karmima**, and other small places opposite Ashish-Manish Riding. Home-cooked *thalis* (Rs 15/20) and excellent fresh, orange/sweet lime juice.

¶ **Little Tibet Garden Restaurant**, Sadar Bazar, **Payal Guest House** (see Sleeping). Very good Tibetan food and a bit of everything else. Pretty courtyard restaurant. Very popular. Recommended.

¶ **Om Shiva**, Pushkar Palace Rd. Garden buffet place, hygienic if uninspired breakfasts (brown bread, garlic cheese, pancakes, fruit), also à la carte for lunch and dinner.

¶ **Rainbow**, near Brahma Ghat. Wide choice (pizzas, jacket potatoes, enchiladas, humous, falafel, Indian dishes), tasty muesli, fruit crumble with choc sauce and ice cream, long climb but good lake view.

¶ **Sunset Café** by Pushkar Palace. Particularly atmospheric in the evening when crowds gather to listen to music and watch sunset, lacklustre food. Recommended for ambience.

¶ **Venus**, Ajmer Rd. Mixed menu. A la carte (good sizzlers) in the garden, also *thalis* (Rs 40), on the attractive rooftop.

✿ Festivals and events

Ajmer *p178, map p178*

Urs Festival, commemorating Khwaja Mu'inuddin Chishti's death in 1235, is celebrated with 6 days of almost continuous music, and devotees from all over India and the Middle East make the pilgrimage. Qawwalis and other Urdu music developed in the courts of rulers can be heard. Roses cover the tomb. The festival starts on sighting the new moon in Rajab, the 7th month of the Islamic year. The peak is reached on the night between the 5th and 6th days when tens of thousands of pilgrims pack the shrine. At 1100 on the last morning, pilgrims and visitors are banned from the dargah, as the khadims, who are responsible through the year for the maintenance of worship at the shrine, dressed in their best clothes, approach the shrine with flowers and sweets. On the final day, women wash the tomb with their hair, then squeeze the rose water into bottles as medicine for the sick.

Pushkar *p181, map p181*

Oct/Nov Kartik Purnima is marked by a vast **cattle and camel fair** (13-21 Nov 2010, 2-10 Nov 2011), see box opposite. Pilgrims bathe in the lake – the night of the full moon being the most auspicious time – and float 'boats' of marigold and rose petals in the moonlight. Camel traders often arrive a few days early to engage in the serious business of buying and selling and most of the animals disappear before the official

The pull of the cattle and camels

The huge **Mela** is Pushkar's biggest draw. Over 200,000 visitors and pilgrims and hordes of cattle and camels with their semi-nomadic tribal drivers, crowd into the town. Farmers, breeders and camel traders buy and sell. Sales in leather whips, shoes, embroidered animal covers soar while women bargain over clay pots, bangles, necklaces and printed cloth.

Events begin four to five days before the full moon in November. There are horse and camel races and betting is heavy. In the **Ladhu Umt** race teams of up to 10 men cling to camels, and one another, in a hilarious and often chaotic spectacle. The Tug-of-War between Rajasthanis and foreigners is usually won by the local favourites. There are also sideshows with jugglers, acrobats, magicians and folk dancers. At nightfall there is music and dancing outside the tents, around friendly fires – an unforgettable experience despite its increasingly touristy nature, even including a laser show. The cattle trading itself actually takes place during the week before the fair; some travellers have reported arriving during the fair and there being no animals left!

starting date. Arrive 3 days ahead if you don't want to miss this part of the fair. The all-night drumming and singing in the Mela Ground can get tiring, but the fair is a unique spectacle. Travellers warn of pickpockets.

O Shopping

Ajmer *p178, map p178*
Fine local silver jewellery, tie-dye textiles and camel hide articles are best buys. The shopping areas are Madar Gate, Station Rd, Purani Mandi, Naya Bazar and Kaisarganj. Some alleys in the old town have good shopping.

Pushkar *p181, map p181*
There is plenty to attract the Western eye; check quality and bargain hard. Miniatures on silk and old paper are everywhere.
Essar, shop 6, Sadar Bazar, opposite Narad Kunj. Excellent tailoring (jacket Rs 250-300 including fabric).
Harish, Brahma Temple Rd. For lightweight razai quilts, bedsheets, cloth bags.
JP Dhabai's, opposite Shiva Cloth Store near Payal Guest House, Main Bazar. Offers fine quality (painted with a single squirrel hair!) miniatures at a price. Recommended.

▲ Activities and tours

Pushkar *p181, map p181*
Horse and camel safaris
Hiring a horse costs Rs 1500 per day, camels around Rs 400 per day, at most hotels and near the Brahma temple. **Ashish-Manish**, opposite Brahma Temple, T0145-277 2584, or **Shannu's Riding School**, owned by a French Canadian, Panch Kund Rd, T0145-277 2043. For lessons, Rs 150 per hr (minimum 10 hrs over 5 days).

Swimming
Sarovar, Oasis, Navratan hotels, non-residents pay Rs 40-50.

Tour operators
Pushkar Travels, Pushkar Palace Rd, T0145-277 2437. Tours, excellent service, good buses, ticketing Rs 75.

⊖ Transport

Jaipur to Ajmer *p177*
Train and jeep
For **Sambhar Lake** take the train to **Phulera**, 7 km from Sambhar village, 9 km from the lake. Jeeps charge Rs 50 for the transfer.

Kishangarh is an important railway junction between Jaipur and Ajmer, with regular trains from both places.

Ajmer *p178, map p178*
Bus
The **State Bus Stand** is 2 km east of centre, enquiries T0145-242 9398. Buses to **Agra**, 9 hrs; **Delhi**, 9 hrs; **Jaipur**, 2½ hrs; **Jodhpur**, 5 hrs; **Bikaner**, 7 hrs; **Chittaurgarh**, 5 hrs; **Udaipur**, 7 hrs via Chittaurgarh; **Kota** via Bundi; **Pushkar**, 45 mins, frequent. Private buses for **Pushkar** leave from near the Jain Temple.

Train
Ajmer Station is seemingly overrun with rats and is not a great place to wait for a night train. Taxis outside the station charge Rs 200-250 to **Pushkar**.

Reservations, T0145-243 2535, 0830-1330, 1400-1630, enquiries, T131/132. **Ahmedabad**: *Aravali Exp 9708*, 1125, 11½ hrs; *Ahmedabad Mail 9106*, 0740, 10 hrs; *Ashram Exp 2916*, 2320, 8½ hrs. **Jaipur**: *Ajmer Jaipur Exp 9652*, 0640, 3 hrs. *Aravali Exp 9707*, 1733, 2½ hrs; *Shatabdi Exp 2016*, 1530, not Sun, 2 hrs. **Delhi** (all via **Jaipur**): *Ahmedabad Delhi Mail 9105*, 2028, 9 hrs; *Shatabdi Exp 2016* not Sun, 1550, 6½ hrs; (**OD**) *Ashram Exp 2915*, 0155, 8 hrs.

Pushkar *p181, map p181*
Bicycle/car/motorbike hire
Rs 10 entry 'tax' per vehicle. **Michael Cycle SL Cycles**, Ajmer Bus Stand Rd, very helpful, Rs 30 per day; also from the market. **Hotel Oasis** has Vespa scooters, Rs 300 per day.

Enfield Ashram, near Hotel Oasis, Rs 400 per day for an Enfield.

Bus
Frequent service to/from **Ajmer**, Rs 10. Long-distance buses are more frequent from Ajmer, and tickets bought in Pushkar may involve a change. Direct buses to **Jaipur**, **Jodhpur** via Merta (8 hrs), **Bikaner**, and **Haridwar**. Sleeper bus to **Delhi**, Rs 250, 1930 (11 hrs); **Agra**, Rs 250, 1930 (11 hrs); **Jaisalmer** Rs 450, 2200 (11 hrs), **Udaipur**, Rs 250, 2200 (8 hrs) and 2300 (8 hrs). Many agents in Pushkar have times displayed. **Pushkar Travels**, T0145-277 2437, reliable for bookings.

ⓘ Directory

Ajmer *p178, map p178*
Banks ATMs are on Station Rd but can run out on weekends. **Bank of Baroda**, opposite GPO, accepts Visa, MasterCard; **State Bank of India** near bus stand, changes cash, TCs. Government-approved money changers in Kavandas Pura main market.

Pushkar *p181, map p181*
Banks ATM near Brahma temple, accepts some overseas cards. **SBBJ** changes TCs; **Hotels Peacock** and **Oasis** offer exchange for a small commission. **Internet** All over town, Rs 30-40. **Inn Seventh Heaven** rooftop café for wireless. **Medical services** Shyama Hospital, Heloj Rd, T0145-277 2029. **Post** One at the Chowk with a very helpful postmaster, east end of Main Bazar.

Contents

Footprint features

Southern Rajasthan

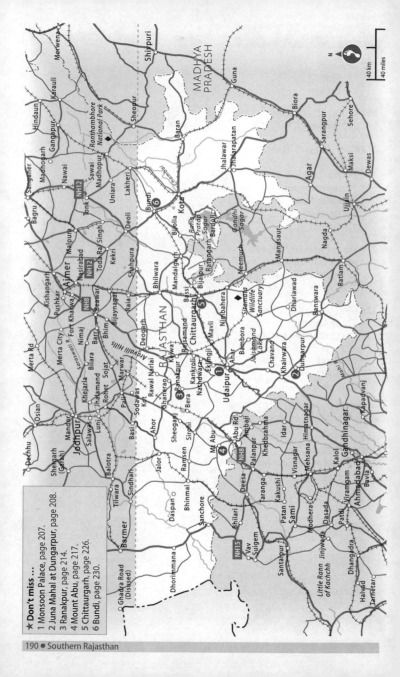

★ **Don't miss ...**
1 Monsoon Palace, page 207.
2 Juna Mahal at Dungarpur, page 208.
3 Ranakpur, page 214.
4 Mount Abu, page 217.
5 Chittaurgarh, page 226.
6 Bundi, page 230.

Possibly the most varied region in Rajasthan, the southern part of the state boasts a wide array of sights, sounds and experiences. The main draw is incomparable Udaipur, with its Lake Palace gleaming like a marble lotus amid the shimmering waters of Lake Pichola, and the City Palace – home to the legendary Ranas of Mewar, the world's oldest ruling dynasty – forming a massive curtain of golden stone behind it. Many regard this as India's most romantic city, and as the sun sets on the lake and the white buildings soften in the warm light, it is hard to disagree.

The rest of the area is equally appealing, from time-warped, untouristy Bundi and Chittaurgarh in the east to the quirky charms of Mount Abu, Rajasthan's only hill station and a great escape from the heat of the summer, in the west. To the south lie delightful Dungarpur and a range of small heritage hotels dotted around the countryside, perfect places to unwind away from the tourist fray. The area to the north boasts majestic Kumbhalgarh Fort, its mammoth walls so vast they're visible from space, and the exquisite Jain temples at Ranakpur, comparable to those in Mount Abu but in a far more tranquil setting. Fascinating drives through the surprisingly green Aravalli hills link one place to the other, passing through picturesque rural villages and agricultural areas unlike those anywhere else in Rajasthan along the way.

Udaipur

→ *Colour map 3, B1. Phone code: 0294. Population: 500,000.*

Enchanting Udaipur, set in the Girwa Valley in the Aravalli Hills of south Rajasthan, must be one of the most romantic cities in India, with white marble palaces, placid blue lakes, attractive gardens and green hills that are a world away from the surrounding desert. High above the lake towers the massive palace of the Maharanas. From its rooftop gardens and balconies, you can look over Lake Pichola, the Lake Palace "adrift like a snowflake" in its centre. The monsoons that deserted the city earlier in the decade have returned – though water shortage remains a threat – to replenish the lakes and ghats, where women gently thrash wet heaps of washing with wooden clubs, helped by splashing children. The houses and temples of the old city stretch out in a pale honeycomb, making Udaipur an oasis of colour in a stark and arid region. Sunset only intensifies the city's beauty, turning the city palace's pale walls to gold, setting the lake to shimmer in silvery swathes against it, while mynah birds break out into a noisy twilight chorus. Ochre and orange skies line the rim of the westernmost hills while countless roof terraces light up and the lake's islands appear to float on waters dancing in the evening breeze and turning purple in the fading light. ▶▶ *For listings, see pages 199-206.*

Ins and outs

Getting there The airport, about 30-45 minutes by taxi or city bus, is well connected. The main bus stand is east of Udai Pol, 2-3 km from most hotels, while Udaipur City Railway Station is another 1 km south. Both have auto-rickshaw stands outside as well as pushy hotel touts.

Getting around The touristy area around the Jagdish temple and the City Palace, the main focus of interest, is best explored on foot but there are several sights further afield. Buses, shared tempos, auto-rickshaws and taxis cover the city and surrounding area; some travellers prefer to hire a scooter or bike. ▶▶ *See Transport, page 205.*

Tourist information Be prepared for crowds, dirt and pollution and persistent hotel touts who descend on new arrivals. It is best to reserve a hotel ahead or ask for a particular street or area of town. Travellers risk being befriended by someone claiming to show you the city for free. If you accept, you run the risk of visiting one shop after another with your 'friend'. **Rajasthan Tourism Development Corporation (RTDC)** ① *Tourist Reception Centre, Fateh Memorial, Suraj Pol, T0294-241 1535, 1000-1700, guides 4-8 hrs, Rs 250-400.*

History

The legendary **Ranas of Mewar** who traced their ancestry back to the Sun, first ruled the region from their seventh-century stronghold Chittaurgarh. The title 'Rana', peculiar to the rulers of **Mewar**, was supposedly first used by Hammir who reoccupied Mewar in 1326. In 1568, **Maharana Udai Singh** founded a new capital on the shores of Lake Pichola and named it Udaipur (the city of sunrise) having selected the spot in 1559. On the advice of an ascetic who interrupted his rabbit hunt, Udai Singh had a temple built above the lake and then constructed his palace around it.

In contrast to the house of Jaipur, the rulers of Udaipur prided themselves on being independent from other more powerful regional neighbours, particularly the Mughals. In a piece of local princely one-upmanship, **Maharana Pratap Singh**, heir apparent to the throne of Udaipur, invited Raja Man Singh of Jaipur to a lakeside picnic. Afterwards he had the ground on which his guest had trodden washed with sacred Ganga water and insisted that his generals take purificatory baths. Man Singh reaped appropriate revenge by preventing Pratap Singh from acceding to his throne. Udaipur, for all its individuality,

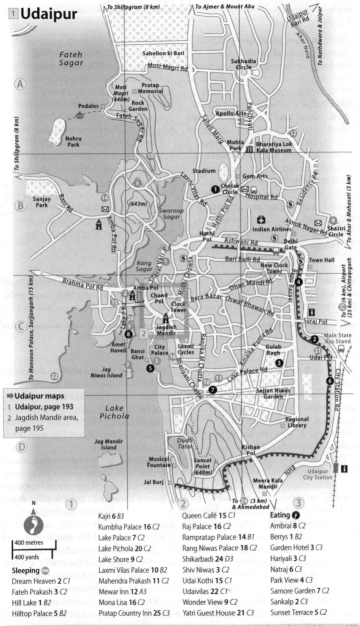

Udaipur

Udaipur maps
1 Udaipur, page 193
2 Jagdish Mandir area, page 195

N

400 metres
400 yards

Sleeping
Dream Heaven 2 C1
Fateh Prakash 3 C2
Hill Lake 1 B2
Hilltop Palace 5 B2
Kajri 6 B3
Kumbha Palace 16 C2
Lake Palace 7 C2
Lake Pichola 20 C2
Lake Shore 9 C2
Laxmi Vilas Palace 10 B2
Mahendra Prakash 11 C2
Mewar Inn 12 A3
Mona Lisa 16 C2
Pratap Country Inn 25 C3
Queen Café 15 C1
Raj Palace 16 C2
Rampratap Palace 14 B1
Rang Niwas Palace 18 C2
Shikarbadi 24 D3
Shiv Niwas 3 C2
Udai Kothi 15 C1
Udaivilas 22 C1
Wonder View 9 C2
Yatri Guest House 21 C3

Eating
Ambrai 8 C2
Berrys 1 B2
Garden Hotel 3 C3
Hariyali 3 C3
Natraj 6 C3
Park View 4 C3
Samore Garden 7 C2
Sankalp 2 C3
Sunset Terrace 5 C2

Eco-Udaipur

"Save Lakes, Save Water, Save Udaipur", reads a sign painted on the wall on Gangaur Ghat. Increased environmental awareness in the city in the past few years has centred around Udaipur's glorious lakes, both as a water supply and tourist draw. **Udaipur Lake Conservation Society** (Jheel Sanrakshan Samiti, see http://green ingindia.net/content/view/23/43) was formed in 1992 by a group of volunteers in order to protect the city's six large lakes and more than 100 smaller ones.

Waste from residential areas and hotels located on the sloping land around the lake, can easily drain into it, threatening the quality of drinking water and spreading waterborne disease. For the city's population, the lake is a convenient means of rubbish disposal, religious rituals, bathing, ablutions, washing clothing, and even washing vehicles, but the resulting pollution, water shortage and eutrophication endanger not only the lakes' ecosystems but threaten their existence altogether.

As a result of the campaign, the JSS has become a leading NGO on water conservation in India. Working alongside the **Global Water Partnership**, regular rallies, seminars and street demonstrations bring its message to city residents. Government-backed plans include the transferal of water from other nearby lakes and basins.

remained one of the poorer princely states in Rajasthan, a consequence of being almost constantly at war. In 1818, Mewar, the Kingdom of the Udaipur Maharanas, came under British political control but still managed to avoid almost all British cultural influence.

Sights

Old City

Udaipur is a traditionally planned fortified city. Its bastioned rampart walls are pierced by massive gates, each studded with iron spikes as protection against enemy war elephants. The five remaining gates are: **Hathi Pol** (Elephant Gate – north), **Chand Pol** (Moon Gate – west), **Kishan Pol** (south), the main entrance **Suraj Pol** (Sun Gate – east) and **Delhi Gate** (northeast). On the west side, the city is bounded by the beautiful Pichola Lake and to the east and north, by moats. To the south is the fortified hill of Eklingigarh. The main street leads from the Hathi Pol to the massive City Palace on the lake side.

The walled city is a maze of narrow winding lanes flanked by tall whitewashed houses with doorways decorated with Mewar folk art, windows with stained glass or *jali* screens, majestic *havelis* with spacious inner courtyards and shops. Many of the houses here were given by the Maharana to retainers – barbers, priests, traders and artisans while many rural landholders (titled jagirdars), had a *haveli* conveniently located near the palace.

The **Jagdish Mandir** ① *150 m north of the palace, 0500-1400, 1600-2200*, was built by Maharana Jagat Singh in 1651. The temple is a fine example of the Nagari style, and contrasts with the serenity of Udaipur's predominantly white-washed buildings, surrounded as it often is by chanting Sadhus, gambolling monkeys and the smell of incense. A shrine with a brass Garuda stands outside and stone elephants flank the entrance steps; within is a black stone image of Vishnu as Jagannath, the Lord of the Universe.

A quiet, slightly eccentric museum, including what they claim is the world's largest turban, now lies in the lovely 18th-century **Bagore ki Haveli** ① *1000-1900, Rs 25, camera Rs 10*, has

130 rooms and was built as a miniature of the City Palace. There are cool shady courtyards containing some peacock mosaics and fretwork, and carved pillars made from granite, marble and the local blueish-grey stone. A slightly forlorn but funny puppet show plays several times a day on the ground floor.

City Palace

① *0930-1730, last entry 1630. From Ganesh Deori Gate: Rs 50 (more from near Lake Palace Ghat). Camera Rs 100, video Rs 300. From 'Maharajah's gallery', you can get a pass for Fateh Prakash Palace, Shiv Niwas and Shambu Niwas, Rs 75. Guided tour, 1 hr, Rs 100 each. Guides hang around the entrance; standards vary wildly and they can cause a scene if you already have hired a guide. Ask at the ticket office. Rs 25 gets you access to the complex and a nice walk down to the jetty.*

This impressive complex of several palaces is a blend of Rajput and Mughal influences. Half of it, with a great plaster façade, is still occupied by the royal family. Between the **Bari Pol** (Great Gate, 1608, men traditionally had to cover their heads with a turban from this point on) to the north, and the **Tripolia Gate** (1713), are eight *toranas* (arches), under which the rulers were weighed against gold and silver on their birthdays, which was then distributed to the poor. One of the two domes on top of the Tripolia originally housed a water clock; a glass sphere with a small hole at the base was filled with water and would take exactly one hour to empty, at which point a gong would be struck and the process repeated. The gate has three arches to allow the royal family their private entrance, through the middle, and then a public entry and exit gate to either side. Note the elephant to the far left (eastern) end of the gate structure; they were seen as bringers of good fortune and appear all over the palace complex. The Tripolia leads in to the **Manak Chowk**, originally a large courtyard which was converted in to a garden only in 1992. The row of lumps in the surface to the left are original, and demarcate elephant parking bays! Claiming descent from Rama, and therefore the sun, the Mewars always insured that there was an image of the sun available for worship even on a cloudy day, thus the beautiful example set in to the exterior wall of the palace. The large step in front of the main entrance was for mounting horses, while those to the left were for elephants. The family crest above the door depicts a Rajput warrior and one of the Bhil tribesmen from

2 Jagdish Mandir area

Chand Pol 2
Bara Bazar
Clock Tower
Ganesh Chowk
Shreeji Sari Centre
Gangaur Ghat
Jagdish Mandir
Mewar International
Motorbike Hire
Gangaur Ghat
Bagore-ki-Haveli
Lal Ghat
Lake Pichola
Sai Books
To City Palace
To City Palace

N
100 metres
100 yards

➡ **Udaipur maps**
1 Udaipur, page 193
2 Jagdish Mandir area, page 195

Nayee Haveli 4
Nukkad Guest House 9
Poonam Haveli 12
Pratap Bhawan 10
Rana Castle 8
The Tiger 11
Udai Niwas 13

Sleeping 🛏
Anjani 5
Badi Haveli 1
Jagat Niwas 6
Jaiwana Haveli 2
Jheel Guest House 7
Kankarwa Haveli 6
Lake Ghat 8
Lalghat Guest House 3
Lehar 1
Minerva 14

Eating 🍴
Café Edelweiss 1
Mayur 3
Savage Garden 2

the local area whose renowned archery skills were much used in the defence of the Mewar household. The motto translates as 'God protects those who stand firm in upholding righteousness'.

As you enter the main door, a set of stairs to the right leads down to an armoury which includes an impressive selection of swords, some of which incorporate pistols in to their handles. Most people then enter the main museum to the right, although it is possible to access the government museum from here (see below). The entrance is known as **Ganesh Dori**, meaning 'Ganesh's turn'; the image of the elephant God in the wall as the steps start to turn has been there since 1620. Note the tiles underneath which were imported from Japan in the 1930s and give even the Hindu deities an Oriental look to their eyes. The second image is of Laxmi, bringer of good fortune and wealth.

The stairs lead in to **Rai Angan**, 'Royal Court' (1559). The temple to the left is to the sage who first advised that the royal palace be built on this side. Opposite is a display of some of Maharana Pratap Singh's weapons, used in some of his many battles with the Mughals, as well as his legendary horse, Chetak. The Mughals fought on elephants, the Mewars on horses; the elephant trunk fitted to Chetak's nose was to fool the Mughal elephants in to thinking that the Mewar horses were baby elephants, and so not to be attacked. A fuller version of this nosepiece can be seen in one of the paintings on the walls, as indeed can an elephant wielding a sword in its trunk during battle.

The stairs to the left of the temple lead up to **Chandra Mahal**, featuring a large bowl where gold and silver coins were kept for distribution to the needy. Note that the intricately carved walls are made not from marble but a combination of limestone powder, gum Arabic, sugar cane juice and white lentils. From here steps lead up in to **Bari Mahal** (1699-1711), situated on top the hill chosen as the palace site; the design has incorporated the original trees. The cloisters' cusped arches have wide eaves and are raised above the ground to protect the covered spaces from heavy monsoon rain. This was an intimate 'playground' where the royal family amused themselves and were entertained. The painting opposite the entrance is an aerial view of the palace; the effect from the wall facing it is impressive. The chair on display was meant for Maharana Fateh Singh's use at the Delhi Darbar, an event which he famously refused to attend. The chair was sent on and has still never been used.

The picture on the wall of two elephants fighting shows the area that can be seen through the window to the left; there is a low wall running from the Tripolia Gate to the main palace building. An elephant was placed either side of the wall, and then each had to try to pull the other until their opponent's legs touched the wall, making them the victor.

The next room is known as **Dil Kushal Mahal** ('love entertainment room'), a kind of mirrored love nest. This leads on to a series of incredibly intricate paintings depicting the story of life in the palace, painted 1782-1828. The **Shiv Vilas Chini ki Chatar Sali** incorporates a large number of Chinese and Dutch tiles in to its decoration, as well as an early petrol-powered fan. Next is the Moti Mahal, the ladies' portion of the men's palace, featuring a changing room lined with mirrors and two game boards incorporated into the design of the floor.

Pritam Niwas was last lived in by Maharana Gopal Singh, who died in 1955 having been disabled by polio at a young age. His wheel armchair and even his commode are on display here. This leads on to **Surya Chopar**, which features a beautiful gold-leaf image of the sun; note the 3D relief painting below. The attractive **Mor Chowk** court, intended for ceremonial darbars, was added in the mid-17th century, and features beautiful late 19th-century peacock mosaics. The throne room is to its south, the **Surya Chopar**, from which the Rana (who claimed descent from the Sun) paid homage to his divine ancestor. The **Manak Mahal** (Ruby Palace) was filled with figures of porcelain and glass in the mid-19th century. To the north, the **Bari Mahal** or Amar Vilas (1699-1711) was added on top of a low hill. It has a pleasant garden with full grown trees around a square water tank in the central court.

A plain, narrow corridor leads in to the **Queen's Palace**, featuring a series of paintings, lithographs and photographs, and leading out in to **Laxmi Chowk**, featuring two cages meant for trapping tigers and leopards. The entrance to the **government museum** ① *Sat-Thu 1000-1600, Rs 3*, is from this courtyard. The rather uncared for display includes second century BC inscriptions, fifth- to eighth-century sculptures and 9000 miniature paintings of 17th- and 19th-century Mewar schools of art but also a stuffed kangaroo and Siamese twin deer.

On the west side of the Tripolia are the **Karan Vilas** (1620-1628) and **Khush Mahal**, a rather grotesque pleasure palace for European guests, whilst to the south lies the **Shambhu Niwas Palace** the present residence of the Maharana.

Maharana Fateh Singh added to this the opulent **Shiv Niwas** with a beautiful courtyard and public rooms, and the **Fateh Prakash Palace**. Here the Darbar Hall's royal portrait gallery displays swords still oiled and sharp. The Bohemian chandeliers (1880s) are reflected by Venetian mirrors, the larger ones made in India of lead crystal. Both, now exclusive hotels (see Sleeping, below), are worth visiting.

On the first floor is the **Crystal Gallery** ① *0900-2000, Rs 500 for a guided tour with a talk on the history of Mewar, followed by a cup of tea (overpriced with a cold reception according to some; avoid the cream tea as the scones are so hard they will crack your teeth)*. The gallery has an extensive collection of cut-crystal furniture, vases, etc, made in Birmingham, England in the 1870s, supplemented by velvet, rich 'zardozi' brocade, objects in gold and silver and a precious stone-studded throne.

'The Legacy of honour', outlining the history of the Mewar dynasty, is a good **Son et Lumière**, the first privately funded one in India. There are two shows daily at 1930 and 2030, Rs 100 for ground seating, Rs 300 on terrace; book at the City Palace ticket office.

Lake Pichola

Fringed with hills, gardens, *havelis*, ghats and temples, Lake Pichola is the scenic focus of Udaipur though parts get covered periodically with vegetation, and the water level drops considerably during the summer. Set in it are the Jag Niwas (Lake Palace) and the Jag Mandir Palaces.

Jag Mandir, built on an island in the south of the lake, is notable for the Gul Mahal, a domed pavilion started by Karan Singh (1620-1628) and completed by Jagat Singh (1628-1652). It is built of yellow sandstone inlaid with marble around an attractive courtyard. Maharajah Karan Singh gave the young Prince Khurram (later Shah Jahan), refuge here when he was in revolt against his father Jahangir in 1623, cementing a friendly relationship between the Mewar Maharaja and the future Mughal Emperor. Refugee European ladies and children were also given sanctuary here by Maharana Sarap Singh during the Mutiny. There is a lovely pavilion with four stone elephants on each side (some of the broken trunks have been replaced with polystyrene!). You get superb views from the balconies. It's possible to take an enjoyable **boat trip** ⓘ *Apr-Sep 0800-1100, 1500-1800, Oct-Mar 1000-1700, on the hour, Rs 300 for 1 hr landing on Jag Mandir, Rs 200 for boat ride without stop*, from Rameshwar Ghat, south of City Palace complex. It's especially attractive in the late afternoon light. Rates from the boat stand at Lal Ghat may be slightly cheaper. There is a pricey bar/restaurant on the island but it's worth stopping for the stunning views.

Jag Niwas Island (Lake Palace) ⓘ *for non-residents boat ticket from Bansi Ghat jetty with lunch or dinner, Rs 2500-3500, T0294-252 8800; tour operators make block bookings so book in advance, or try your luck at the jetty*, has the Dilaram and Bari Mahal Palaces. They were built by **Maharana Jagat Singh II** in 1746 and cover the whole island. Once the royal summer residences and now converted into a hotel, they seem to float like a dream ship on the blue waters of the lake. The courtly atmosphere, elegance and opulence of princely times, the painted ceilings, antique furniture combined with the truly magical setting make it one of the most romantic buildings in India. There are, of course, superb views.

Jal Burj is on the water's edge, south of the town. From the small **Dudh Talai** nearby, there is an attractive walk alongside the main lake (especially pleasant in the evening; large fruit bats can also often be seen). A left turn up a new road leads to **Manikya Lal Verma Park** ⓘ *Rs 5 during the day, Rs 10 evening*, which has great lake views and a delightfully kitsch 'musical fountain', switched on in the evening – a favourite with Indian families.

On the hill immediately to the east of Dudh Talai, a pleasant two-hour walk to the south of the city, is **Sunset Point** which has excellent free views over the city. The path past the café (good for breakfast) leads to the gardens on the wall; a pleasant place to relax. Although it looks steep it is only a 30-minute climb from the café.

Fateh Sagar and around

This lake, north of Lake Pichola, was constructed in 1678 during the reign of Maharana Jai Singh and modified by Maharana Fateh Singh. There is a pleasant lakeside drive along the east bank but, overall, it lacks the charm of the Pichola. **Nehru Park** on an island (accessible by ferry) has a restaurant.

Overlooking the Fateh Sagar is the **Moti Magri (Pearl Hill)** ⓘ *0900-1800, Rs 20, camera free*. There are several statues of local heroes in the attractive rock gardens including one of Maharana Pratap on his horse Chetak, to which he owed his life. Local guides claim that Chetak jumped an abyss of extraordinary width in the heat of the battle of Haldighati (1576) even after losing one leg. To find out more look at *Hero of Haldighati*.

Sahelion ki Bari (Garden of the Maids of Honour) ⓘ *0900-1800, Rs 10, plus Rs 2 for 'fountain show'*, a little north from Moti Magri, is an ornamental pleasure garden; a great spot, both attractive and restful. There are many fountains including trick ones along the edge of the path which are operated by the guide clapping his hands! In a pavilion in the first courtyard, opposite the entrance, a children's museum has curious exhibits including a pickled scorpion, a human skeleton and busts of Einstein and Archimedes. Beautiful black marble kiosks decorate the corners of a square pool. An elegant round lotus pond has four marble elephants spouting water. To the north is a rose garden with over 100 varieties.

At **Ahar** (3 km east) are the remains of the ancient city which have some Jain *chhatris* set on high plinths in the Mahasati (royal cremation ground). A small **museum** ⓘ *1000-1700, closed Fri and holidays, Rs 3*, contains pottery shards and terracotta toys from the first century BC and 10th-century sculptures. Nearby are the temples of Mira Bai (10th century), Adinatha (11th century) and Mahavira (15th century).

◉ Udaipur listings

For Sleeping and Eating price codes and other relevant information, see Essentials pages 28-33.

● Sleeping

Udaipur *p192, map p193 and p195*
Frenzied building work continues to provide more hotels while restaurants compete to offer the best views from the highest rooftop. The area around the lake is undeniably the most romantic place to stay, but also the most congested. The hotels on Lake Palace Rd and on the hilltop above Fateh Sagar Lake offer more peaceful surroundings, while Swaroop Sagar offers a good compromise between calmness and convenience. **Tourist Reception Centre**, Fateh Memorial, has a list of accommodation.
LL Fateh Prakash (HRH), City Palace, T0294-252 8016, www.hrhindia.com. Well-appointed lake-facing rooms in modern 'Dovecote' wing and 7 superb suites in main palace building. Original period furniture, great views from Sunset Terrace restaurant, facilities of Shiv Niwas, good service (residents may ask for a pass at City Palace entrance for a short cut to hotel).
LL Lake Palace (Taj), Lake Pichola, T0294-252 8800, www.tajhotels.com. 84 rooms, most with lake view, in one of the world's most spectacularly located hotels. Standard rooms are tasteful but unremarkable, suites are outstanding and priced to match, spa and small pool, quite an experience, service can be slightly abrupt. Location for the 1980s Bond film *Octopussy*.

LL Laxmi Vilas Palace, on hillock above Fateh Sagar, 5 km from station, T0294-252 9711, www.thegrandhotels.net. Extremely posh and expensive suites in the palace, plus 54 rooms situated in the royal guesthouse (built in 1911), which while still atmospheric and comfortable, have less character. Good pool (non-residents, Rs 175), tennis.
LL Udaivilas (Oberoi), Lake Pichola, T0294-243 3300, www.oberoihotels.com. The elegant but monochrome exterior of this latter-day palace does nothing to prepare you for the opulence within; the stunning entry courtyard sets the scene for staggeringly beautiful interiors. The 87 rooms are the last word in indulgence; some have one of the hotel's 9 swimming pools running alongside their private balcony. The setting on the lake, overlooking both the lake and city palaces, is superb, as are the food and service. Outstanding.
LL-L Shiv Niwas (HRH), City Palace (turn right after entrance), T0294-252 8016, www.hrhindia.com. 19 tasteful rooms, 17 luxurious suites including those stayed in by Queen Elizabeth II and Roger Moore, some with superb lake views, very comfortable, good restaurant, very pleasant outdoor seating for all meals around a lovely marble pool (non-residents pay Rs 300 to swim), tennis, squash, excellent service, beautiful surroundings, reserve ahead in season. Recommended.
L-AL Shikarbadi (HRH), Govardhan Vilas, Ahmedabad Rd, 5 km from centre, T0294-258 3201, www.hrhindia.com. 26 good,

refurbished a/c rooms, pool, horse riding, attractive 100-year-old royal hunting lodge and stud farm with lake, lovely gardens, deer park, charming and peaceful.

A Hilltop Palace, 5 Ambavgarh near Fateh Sagar, T0294-243 2245, www.hotelhilltop palace.net. Above Fateh Sagar lake, 62 pleasant but unremarkable rooms (large rooms upstairs with balcony), restaurant (visit for a view from the roof), bar, exchange, pool, good food, friendly and efficient service.

A The Tiger, 33 Gangaur Ghat, T0294-242 0430, www.thetigerudaipur.com. Stylish new rooms, funky decor and vibe. Fantastic in-house spa with steam room, sauna, jacuzzi and traditional massage. Great sunset view from rooftop restaurant. Recommended.

A Udai Kothi, Hanuman Ghat, T0294-243 2810, www.udaikothi.com. 24 attractive rooms and Udaipur's only rooftop pool! Great restaurant; book the poolside table for maximum romance. A real treat.

A-C Rampratap Palace (Rajpur Special Hotel), Fateh Sagar, T0294-243 1701, www.hotel rpp.com. Smart rooms, some a/c, most with views of Fateh Sagar lake in new attractive hotel, lawns, on busy road but friendly.

A-D Anjani Hotel, 77 Gangour Ghat, T0294-242 1770, www.anjanihotel.com. Plush Rajasthani-themed rooms – nice artwork and stained-glass features. Small courtyard swimming pool to cool off in. Good views from rooftop restaurant.

A-D Jagat Niwas, 24-25 Lal Ghat, T0294-242 0133, www.jagatniwaspalace.com. 30 individual, very clean rooms in beautifully restored 17th-century 'fairy tale' *haveli*, good restaurant (see Eating), helpful staff, good travel desk, excellent service. Lots of groups, though, so book well in advance. Recommended.

A-E Kankarwa Haveli, 26 Lal Ghat, T0294-241 1457, khaveli@yahoo.com. Wide range of rooms in renovated 250-year-old *haveli* on lake shore, some with views and some with beautiful original artwork and features – each room is unique. Quiet, breakfast and snacks available with impressive views on the roof

terrace, meals on request, family-run, lots of cosy nooks to sit in with owner's massive magazine collection. Highly recommended.

B-E Rang Niwas Palace, Lake Palace Rd, T0294-252 3890, www.rangniwaspalace.com. 20 beautifully renovated a/c rooms in 200-year-old building, some with charming balconies facing garden, some with beautiful window seats, old-world charm, restaurant, pool, pretty gardens, helpful staff, good location, but some road noise. Recommended.

C Hotel Hill Lake, Purohit Ji Ka Khurra, inside Chandpole, T0294-241 9412, www.hotel hilllake.com. Stylish rooms in new build, but with exceptional views across both Fateh Sagar lake and across to City Palace and Lake Pichola from atmospheric rooftop restaurant.

C Lake Pichola, Hanuman Ghat, overlooking lake, T0294-243 1197, www.lakepichola hotel.com. 32 rooms, some a/c, fantastic views from some rooms with lots of beautiful window seats sitting over lake, boat rides, friendly, relatively cheap food.

C-D Jaiwana Haveli, 14 Lal Ghat, T0294-252 1103, hjaiwanahaveli@yahoo.com. 18 clean, modern rooms, in a part mid-18th-century *haveli*, some with great views, particularly good from rooftop restaurant and great food to boot with some traditional Rajasthani dishes; cheaper rooms are dank and viewless.

C-D Raj Palace, 103 Bhatiyani Chotta, T0294-241 0364, raj palaceudr@yahoo.com. 26 beautiful rooms arranged around pleasant courtyard garden, lovely rooftop restaurant, excellent service with views of City Palace.

C-D Wonder View, 6 Panch Dewari Marg, near **Lake Pichola Hotel**, T0294-243 2494. Good views but rather lacklustre and musty rooms. Fabulous views from rooftop restaurant (food arrives slowly from ground-floor kitchen), friendly, excellent taxis, peaceful and relaxed part of town.

C-E Jheel Guest House, 56 Gangaur Ghat (behind temple), T0294-242 1352. Friendly owner and fantastic views. Don't be deceived by the unremarkable entrance, one room in particular practically hangs over the ghats with a spectacular view all the way towards the **Lake Palace** hotel. New extension has 6 pleasant rooms with bath and hot water; 8 rooms in older part, good rooftop restaurant. Recommended.

C-E Mahendra Prakash, Lake Palace Rd, T0294-241 9811, udai99@hotmail.com. 20 large, spotless, well-furnished rooms in an attractive mansion, some a/c, pleasant patio garden, excellent pool and poolside restaurant, plus pool table. Owner/manager is of the Maharana's family, friendly, excellent service.

C-F Gangaur Palace, 339 'Ashoka Haveli' Gangaur Rd, T0294-242 2303, www.ashokahaveli.com. Attractive, clean rooms around an interesting courtyard – nice design features, although most lake views have been obscured by new hotels. Good rooftop restaurant, but pretty café downstairs is blighted by traffic noise. Recommended.

D Pratap Country Inn, Airport Rd, Titadhia Village, T0294-258 3138. 20 rooms, few a/c, restaurant, horse and camel safaris, riding, pool (sometimes empty), old royal country house in attractive grounds, 6 km from centre (free transfer from railway station).

D-E Kajri (RTDC), Shastri Circle, T0294-241 0501. 53 rooms, some a/c, and dorm, typical institutional RTDC feel, money is better spent elsewhere, restaurant (dull food), bar, travel, Tourist Reception Centre.

D-E Lake Ghat, 4/13 Lalghat, 150 m behind Jagdish Mandir, T0294-252 1636. 13 atmospheric, well-decorated rooms, friendly, lots of greenery cascading down inner staircase, light and airy great views from terraces, good food.

D-E Pratap Bhawan, 12 Lal Ghat, T0294-256 0566, pratapbhawan@yahoo.co.in. 10 large, very clean rooms with a bit of a Raj feel, lake-facing terrace restaurant, excellent, home-cooked meals, warm welcome from retired army colonel and his wife.

D-F Minerva, 5/13 Gadiya Devra, Gangaur Ghat (behind temple), T0294-252 3471. Good range of rooms for many budgets, decorative touches. Atmospheric rooftop restaurant. Good, speedy internet.

D-G Udai Niwas, near Jagdish Temple, Gangaur Marg, T0294-512 0789, www.hotel udainiwas.com. 14 renovated rooms in friendly hotel with a pleasant rooftop and good views, new 'penthouse' with lake view with 4-poster bed, all are well decorated with Rajasthani touches. Recommended.

E Poonam Haveli, 39 Lal Ghat, T0294-241 0303, poonamhaveli@hotmail.com. 16 modern, attractive, clean rooms all with nice touches of Rajasthani decor, plus large roof terrace.

E-F Yatri Guest House, 3/4 Panchkuin Rd, Udaipol, near the bus stand, T0294-242 1959. 13 simple rooms, helpful, knowledgeable owner, best option in area.

E-G Dream Heaven, just over Chandpol, on the edge of the lake, T0294-243 1038, deep_rg@yahoo.co.uk. 6 clean, simple rooms with bath, family-run, no frills but excellent rooftop restaurant – exceptional overflowing *thalis* and very good lasagne. Great views.

F Badi Haveli, near Jagdish Temple, T0294-241 2588, hotelbadahaveli@hotmail.com. 8 recently renovated rooms with bath, some good, restaurant, travel services, terraces with lake view, pleasant atmosphere, very friendly owner.

F-G Kumbha Palace, 104 Bhatiyani Chotta, T0294-242 2702. Run by Dutch-Indian family. 9 clean and quiet rooms with quality linen, good but not particularly busy rooftop restaurant (see Eating), a little way from the heart of things, horse riding arranged.

F-G Lake Shore, by Lake Pichola, near Lake Palace Rd, T0294-243 2480. Good views of ghats, 7 funkily decorated rooms, superb terrace, garden, very relaxing, friendly owner.

F-G Lalghat Guest House, 33 Lal Ghat, T0294-252 5301. The best dorm in town (good clean beds with curtains). Some of the 24 rooms have lake views. Spotless baths, breakfast, snacks, drinks, great views from terraces, very relaxed and sociable but indifferent management, reports that you often show up and the great room with a view you were promised has already been taken.

G Gangaur Palace, Gangaur Ghat Marg, T0294-242 2303, www.ashokahaveli.com. Rooms set around the courtyard of a large, slightly shabby *haveli*. Most rooms charmingly painted, some with window seats. Some cleaner than others. Coffee shop on the ground floor, off noisy street. Rooftop restaurant (Indian food is good, Western food dodgy) has good sunset views over lake. Gallery on ground floor offers drawing lessons. 1-min walk to Gangaur Ghat, good lake-viewing point, or 5 mins to Lal Ghat for best sunset spot.

G Lehar, 86 Gangaur Ghat, T0294-241 7651. 5 small rooms with bath, best with lake view. Run by a charming lady.

G Mewar Inn, 42 Residency Rd (pleasantly away from centre), T0294-241 1590, mewarinn@hotmail.com. 27 spotless rooms, some with hot shower, street side very noisy, no commission to rickshaws (if they refuse to go try a horse carriage), **Osho** vegetarian restaurant, good cheap bike hire, rickshaw to town Rs 30, very friendly, YHA discounts. Cheap but very out of the way.

G Mona Lisa, 104 Bhatiyani Chotta, T0294-256 1562. Pleasant and quiet, 8 rooms, some air-cooled, with bath, good breakfast, garden, newspaper, cooking lessons, beauty parlour, family-run, good value.

G Nayee Haveli, 55 Gangaur Marg, T(0)9828-045109, nayee.haveli.udaipur@newyork.com. 5 clean, basic rooms in friendly family home, home-cooked food. Recommended.

G Nukkad Guest House, 56 Ganesh Chowk (signposted from Jagdish Temple), T0294-241 1403, nukkad_raju@yahoo.com. 10 small, simple rooms, some with bath, in typical family house, home-cooked meals, rooftop, very friendly and helpful, clean.

G Queen Café, 14 Bajrang Marg (from Gangaur Ghat cross footbridge, then continue until the first proper street to find the hotel on your right), T0294-243 0875. 2 decent rooms, shared bath, roof terrace with good views, home-cooked meals (including continental Swiss), informal,

welcoming family. Meenu teaches cooking and Hindi. Highly recommended.
G Rana Castle, 4, Lal Ghat, T0294-241 3666. 8 well-maintained rooms, particularly charming lower down, cheap but with character. Disappointing food in restaurant.

⑦ Eating

Udaipur *p192, map p193 and p195*
The local belly-buster to try is *dhal-bhatti-choorma*. Plush heritage hotels have expensive menus, but the non-vegetarian buffet food can be kept warm for long periods and can therefore be risky. Many of the budget places are attached to hotels in the Lal Ghat area; the usual fare includes pancakes, macaroni, falafel, etc, for the homesick visitor, and an amazing number still wheel out the TV for a nightly showing of *Octopussy*. Those near Jagdish Mandir do not serve alcohol.

₸₸₸ Ambrai, Lake Pichola Rd. Delightful garden restaurant with tables under trees by lake shore, superb views of City Palace, good at sunset.

₸₸₸ Gallery Restaurant, Fateh Prakash (see Sleeping). Beautiful restaurant, superb views but pretty tasteless continental food, English cream teas.

₸₸₸ Lake Palace, see Sleeping. Buffet lunch 1230-1430, dinner 1930-2030 often preceded by puppet show at 1800. Expensive drinks (check bill), best way for non-residents to experience this unique palace.

₸₸₸ Shiv Niwas, see Sleeping. Wonderful buffet followed by disappointing desserts, eat in the bar, or dine in luxury by the pool listening to live Indian classical music; bar expensive but the grand surroundings are worth a drink.

₸₸₸ Sunset Terrace, Bansi Ghat, Lake Pichola. Very pleasant, superb views of City Palace Complex and lake, good à la carte selection.

₸₸ Bagore-ki-Haveli, Gangaur Ghat, T0294-242 3610. Multi-cuisine menu including some local specialities in fantastic setting by lake. Recommended.

♔ **Berrys**, near Chetak Circle, T0294-242 9027. Open 0900-2300. International cuisine. Standard menu, comfortable, friendly, beer available, worthwhile if you're in the area.

♔ **Jagat Niwas** (see Sleeping). Mainly Indian food. Jarokha rooftop restaurant with fabulous lake views, excellent meals, breakfast, ice cream. Fluorescent lighting can be a mood-killer at night.

♔ **Park View**, opposite Town Hall, City Station Rd. Good North Indian. Comfortable.

♔ **Sankalp**, outside Suraj Pol, City Station Rd, T0294-510 2686. Upmarket South Indian, modern, great range of chutneys.

♔ **Savage Garden**, up alley near east end of Chandpol bridge. Good in the evenings: striking blue interior and superior food including Indian-style pasta dishes, risottos and great mezze.

♔ **Café Edelweiss**, 73 Gangaur Ghat, opposite The Tiger. Hallelujah – great coffee! Small patisserie – sometimes you just have to sit on the side of the road – but the coffee is that good. Recommended.

♔ **Dream Heaven** (see Sleeping). Excellent, never-ending *thalis* on rooftop "watch the sun go down over the lake listening to the drums from the Jagdish Mandir".

♔ **Garden Hotel**, opposite Gulab Bagh, Excellent Gujarati/Rajasthani vegetarian *thalis*, Rs 50, served in the former royal garage of the Maharanas of Mewar, an interesting circular building. The original fuel pumps can still be seen in the forecourt where 19 cars from the ancestral fleet have been displayed. Packed at lunch, less so for dinner, elderly Laurel-and-Hardyesque waiters shout at each other and forget things, food may arrive cold, but worth it for the experience. Recommended.

♔ **Gokul**, on roof of **Minerva Hotel** (see Sleeping). Good range of international cuisines, decent burgers and Israeli food, well-run and good views. Great divans for lounging. Recommended.

♔ **Hariyali**, near Gulab Bagh. Good North Indian food in a pleasant garden setting.

♔ **Kumbha Palace** (see Sleeping), T0294-242 2702. Closed 1500-1800. Excellent Indian and Western food (chocolate cake, baked potato, pizzas, milk shakes) on rooftop from where you can sneak a distant view of the City Palace sound-and-light show, friendly, helpful.

♔ **Mayur**, Mothi Chowtha, opposite Jagdish Temple. Mainly Indian. Pleasant for vegetarian *thali* (Rs 45) snacks and *Octopussy*, but slow service, also exchange after-hours, internet.

♔ **Natraj**, near Town Hall. Rajasthani. Excellent *thalis* in family-run simple dining hall, very welcoming.

♔ **Queen Café**, 14 Bajrang Marg. Fantastic menu of unusual curries (mango, pumpkin and irresistible chocolate balls. Also offers cooking lessons. Highly recommended.

♔ **Samore Garden**, opposite Rang Niwas Palace, Lake Palace Rd. Wide international menu, open later than most, no beer.

☻ Entertainment

Udaipur *p192, map p193 and p195*
Bagore-ki-Haveli, T0294-242 3610 (after 1700). Daily cultural shows 1900-2000. Enjoyable music and dance performances, including traditional dances with women balancing pots of fire on their heads. No need to book.

Bharatiya Lok Kala Museum, T0294-252 5077. The 20-min puppet demonstrations during the day are good fun. Evening puppet show and folk dancing Sep-Mar 1800-1900, Rs 30, camera Rs 50. Recommended.

Meera Kala Mandir, south of railway station, T0294-258 3176. Mon-Sat 1900-2000, Rs 60; cultural programme, a bit touristy and amateurish.

☻ Festivals and events

Udaipur *p192, map p193 and p195*
Mar/Apr Mewar Festival (18-20 Mar 2010, 6-8 Apr 2011). See page 35 for state-wide festivals.

O Shopping

Udaipur *p192, map p193 and p195*
The local handicrafts are wooden toys, colourful portable temples (*kavad*), Bandhani tie-dye fabrics, embroidery and Pichchwai paintings. Paintings are of 3 types: miniatures in the classical style of courtly Mewar; phads or folk art; and pichchwais or religious art (see Nathdwara, page 209). The more expensive ones are 'old' – 20-30 years – and are in beautiful dusky colours; the cheaper ones are brighter.

The main shopping centres are Chetak Circle, Bapu Bazar, Hathipol, Palace Rd, clock tower, Nehru Bazar, Shastri Circle, Delhi Gate, Sindhi Bazar, Bada Bazar.

Books
BA Photo and Books, 708 Palace Rd. Very good selection in several languages, also has internet access.
Mewar International, 35 Lalghat. A wide selection of English books, exchange, films.
Pustak Sadan (Hindi sign), Bapu Bazar, near Town Hall. Good for Rajasthani history.
Sai, 168 City Palace Rd, 100 m from palace gate. Good English books (new and second-hand), internet, exchange, travel services.
Suresh, Hospital Rd. Good fiction, non-fiction and academic books.

Fabric and tailoring
Ashoka, opposite entrance to Shiv Niwas. Good quality but very expensive.
Monsoon Collection, 55 Bhatiyani Chotta. Quick, quality tailoring. Recommended.
Shree Ji Saree Centre, Mothi Chowtha, 200 m from temple. Good value, very helpful owner. Recommended.
Udaipur New Tailors, inside Hathipol. Gents tailoring, reasonably priced, excellent service.

Handicrafts and paintings
Some shops sell old pieces of embroidery turned into bags, cushion covers, etc. Others may pass off recent work as antique.

Apollo Arts, 28 Panchwati; **Ashoka Arts** and **Uday Arts** on Lake Palace Rd, for paintings on marble paper and 'silk'; bargain hard. Hathipol shop has good silk scarves (watch batik work in progress).
Gallery Pristine, Kalapi House, Bhatiyani Chotta, Palace Rd, T0294-242 3916. Good collection of contemporary art, including original 'white on brown' paintings, pleasant ambience. Recommended.
Ganesh Handicraft Emporium, City Palace Rd, ganeshemporium@yahoo.com. Through the dull entrance of Ganesh on the main road, you disappear down an alley and come out at a huge old *haveli* spilling with traditional Udaipur and Gujarati embroideries, wooden horses and all manner of textiles. Maybe not the cheapest place, but great selection and ask for a tour of the building.
Gangour, Mothi Chowtha. Quality miniature paintings.
KK Kasara, opposite Nami Gali, 139 Mothi Chowtha. Good religious statues, jewellery.
Sadhna Women's Collective , Jagdish Temple Rd. www.sadhna.org. Sadhna started in 1988 with 15 women and has grown to include the work of 600 women today as artisans and co-owners. On offer is a beautiful variety of clothes, *kurtas* and scarves as well as a homeware range with traditional appliqué, tanka and patchwork. The patterns incorporated in the pieces reflect rural life in Rajasthan.
Shivam Ayurvedic, Lake Palace Rd. Also art store, interesting, knowledgeable owner.
Sisodia Handicrafts, entrance of Shiv Niwas Palace. Miniature 'needle paintings' of high quality – see the artists at work, no hard sell.

▲ Activities and tours

Udaipur *p192, map p193 and p195*
Art, cooking and Hindi classes
Ashoka Arts, 339 'Ashoka Haveli' Gangaur Ghat. In the courtyard of Gangaur Palace, art classes are available.

Hare Krishna Arts, City Palace Rd, T0294-242 0304. Rs 450 per 2-hr art lesson, miniature techniques a speciality. Cooking classes, too.
Queen Café, 14 Bajrang Marg, T0294-243 0875. Rs 2000 for 5-hr introductory class in basics of Indian cooking: tiny kitchen but very good class. Also Hindi lessons. Both are highly recommended.

Body and soul
Bharti Guesthouse, Lake Pichola Rd, T0294-243 3469. Therapeutic, Swedish-style massage.
Jiva Spas, Taj Hotel, www.tajhotels.com/JivaSpa/JivaSpa, Udaipur/boat.htm. Jiva Spas run a spa boat on Lake Pichola – it doesn't get much more fabulous than this!
The Tiger, 33 Gangaur Ghat. T0294-242 0430. Great spa, with real sauna and steam rooms, jacuzzi and a range of traditional massages on offer. Recommended.

Elephant, camel and horse riding
Travel agencies (eg **Namaskar**, **Parul** in Lalghat) arrange elephant and camel rides, Rs 200 per hr but need sufficient notice. Horse riding through **Pratap Country Inn**, or **Princess Trains**, T(0)9829-042 012, www.princesstrails.com, a German-Indian company that offers Marwari horses for 3 trips from 2 hrs to 8 days.

Sightseeing tours
Offered by **RTDC Fateh Memorial**, Suraj Pol. City sightseeing: half day (0830-1300) Rs 90 (reported as poor). Excursion: half day (1400-1900), Haldighati, Nathdwara, Eklingji, Rs 130. Chittaurgarh (0830-1800), Rs 350 (with lunch); Ranakpur, Kumbhalgarh (0830-1900) Rs 330; Jagat–Jaisamand–Chavand–Rishabdeo (0830-1900) Rs 330 (with lunch).
  In addition to sightseeing tours, some of the following tour operators offer accommodation bookings and travel tickets.
Aravalli Safari, 1 Sheetla Marg, Lake Palace Rd, T0294-242 0282, F242 0121. Very professional. Recommended.
Parul, Jagat Niwas Hotel, Lalghat, T0294-242 1697, parul_tour@rediffmail.com.

Air/train, palace hotels, car hire, exchange. Highly recommended.
People & Places, 34-35 Shrimal Bhawan, Garden Rd, T0294-241 7359, www.palaces-tours.com.
Tourist Assistance Centre, 3 Paneri House, Bhatiyani Chotta, T0294-252 8169. Government guides charge Rs 350-400 per day for a group of 1-4 people.

Swimming
Some hotel pools are open to non-residents: Lakshmi Vilas (Rs 175); Mahendra Prakash (Rs 125); Rang Niwas (Rs 100); Shiv Niwas (Rs 300). Also at Shilipgram Craft Village, Rs 100.

◎ Transport

Udaipur *p192, map p193 and p195*
Air
Dabok airport is 25 km east, T0294-265 5453. Security check is thorough; no batteries allowed in hand luggage. Transport to town: taxis, Rs 190. **Indian Airlines**, Delhi Gate, T0294-241 0999, open 1000-1315, 1400-1700; airport, T0294-265 5453, enquiry T142. Reserve well ahead. **Indian Airlines** flights to **Delhi**, via **Jodhpur** and **Jaipur**; **Mumbai**. Jet Airways, T0294-256 1105, airport T0294-265 6192: **Delhi** via **Jaipur**, **Mumbai**; Kingfisher/Air Deccan, T0294-510 2468: **Jodhpur** via **Jaisalmer**, **Aurangabad**, and **Agra**.

Bicycle
Laxmi Bicycles, halfway down Bhatiyani Chotta, charges Rs 30 per day for hire, well maintained and comfortable. Also shops near Kajri Hotel, Lalghat and Hanuman Ghat area, which also have scooters (Rs 200 per day).

Bus
Long distance Main State Bus Stand, near railway line opposite Udai Pol, T0294-248 4191; reservations 0700-2100. State RTC buses to **Agra**, 15 hrs; **Ahmedabad**, 252 km, 6 hrs; **Ajmer**, 274 km, 7 hrs; **Bhopal**,

765 km, 15 hrs; **Bikaner**, 500 km, 13 hrs; **Chittaurgarh**, 2½ hrs; **Delhi**, 635 km, 17 hrs; **Indore**, 373 km, 12 hrs; **Jaipur**, 405 km, 9 hrs; **Jaisalmer**, 14 hrs; **Jodhpur**, 8 hrs (uncomfortable, poorly maintained but scenic road); **Mount Abu**, 270 km, 0500-1030, 6 hrs; **Mumbai**, 802 km, very tiring, 16 hrs; **Pushkar**, tourist bus, 7 hrs; **Ujjain**, 7 hrs. Private buses and luxury coaches run mostly at night; ticket offices offices on City Station Rd, from where most buses depart. **Ahmedabad** with Bonney Travels, Paldi, Ahmedabad, has a/c coaches with reclining seats (contact Shobha Travels, City Station Rd), departs 1400 (5½ hrs), Rs 325, with drink/snack stops every 2 hrs. Highly recommended. **Shrinath**, T0294-242 2204, and Punjab Travels have non a/c buses to **Ahmedabad** and **Mount Abu**. **Jaipur**: several 'de luxe' buses (computerized booking) with reclining seats, more expensive but better. For **Jaisalmer**: change at Jodhpur. **Jodhpur**: several options but best to book a good seat, a day ahead, Rs 180. Tour operators have taxis for **Kumbhalgarh** and **Ranakpur**.

Motorbike
Scooters and bikes can be hired from Heera Tours & Travels in a small courtyard behind Badi Haveli (Jagdish Temple area), Rs 250-500 per day depending on size of machine.

Rickshaw
Auto-rickshaw Agree rates: about Rs 40 from bus stand to Jagdish Mandir.

Taxi
RTDC taxis from Fateh Memorial, Suraj Pol. Private taxis from airport, railway station, bus stands and major hotels; negotiate rates. Taxi Stand, Chetak Circle, T0294-252 5112. Tourist Taxi Service, Lake Palace Rd, T0294-252 4169.

Train
Udaipur City station, 4 km southeast of centre, T0294-252 7390, T131, reservations T135. **Ahmedabad**: *Ahmedabad Exp 9943*, 1945, 8½ hrs. **Chittaurgarh**: 5 local trains daily. **Delhi (HN)**: *Mewar Exp 2964*, 1835, 12 hrs, via Chittaurgarh, Kota and Bharatpur. **Jaipur**: *Jaipur Exp 2966*, 2220, 9½ hrs, and on to **Agra** (12 hrs) and **Gwalior** (14 hrs) via **Kota** (5 hrs) and **Sawai Madhopur** (7 hrs); **Mumbai**: *Jaipur Exp 2966*,

⊙ Directory

Udaipur *p192, map p193 and p195*
Banks Many ATMs on Town Hall Rd. Chetak circle and around Bapu Bazar. Foreign exchange at Andhra Bank, Shakti Nagar. Cash advance against Visa/MasterCard, efficient. Bank of Baroda, Bapu Bazar. For Amex. Thomas Cook, Lake Palace Rd. Poor rates. Trade Wings, Polo Ground Rd, Vijaya Bank, City Palace entrance. **Internet** Many options around Jagdish Mandir and Hanuman Ghat, Rs 30-50/hr. Wireless at Whistling Teal, next to Raj Palace Hotel, pleasant garden cafe but poor service, overpriced. **Medical services** Ambulance: T102. General Hospital, Chetak Circle. Aravali Hospital (private), 332 Ambamata Main Rd, opposite Charak Hostel, T0294-243 0222, very clean, professional. Recommended. Chemist on Hospital Rd. **Post** The GPO is at Chetak Circle. Posting a parcel can be a nightmare. Poste Restante: Shastri Circle Post Office. **Useful contacts** Fire: T0294-227 111. Police: T100. Tourist Assistance Force: T0294-241 1535.

Around Udaipur

The area around Udaipur is dotted with a wide range of attractions, from some of the grandest of Rajasthan's heritage hotels to some of its cosiest castles, from secluded forest lakes, surrounded by wildlife, to one of the largest reservoirs in Asia. It's also home to some ancient temples and perhaps the most evocative of Rajasthan's plentiful palaces, the Juna Mahal near Dungarpur. ▶▶ *For listings, see pages 210-211.*

Ins and outs

Most of the sights in this area are a little isolated and so not well connected by train. However, the quality of the region's roads has greatly improved recently, making travel either by bus or taxi both quick and convenient. ▶▶ *See Transport, page 211.*

Monsoon Palace

ⓘ *15 km west. Foreigners Rs 80 plus Rs 65 road toll. Taxis minimum Rs 250 (tourist taxis Rs 450 including toll), auto-rickshaws Rs 200 return including toll. Allow about 3 hrs for the round trip.*
There are good views from this deserted palace on a hilltop. The unfinished building on **Sajjangarh**, at an altitude of 335 m, which looks picturesque from the west-facing battlements, was named after Sajjan Singh (1874-1884) and was planned to be high enough to see his ancestral home, Chittaurgarh. Normally, you need a permit from the police in town to enter, though many find a tip to the gateman suffices. It offers panoramic views of Udaipur (though the highest roof is spoilt by radio antennas); the windows of the Lake Palace can be seen reflecting the setting sun. The palace itself is very run down but the views from the hill top are just as good. A visit in the late afternoon is recommended; take binoculars.

Jaisamand Lake → *Colour map 3, B/C1. 52 km southeast of Udaipur.*

Before the building of huge modern dams in India, Jaisamand was the second largest artificial lake in Asia, 15 km by 10 km. Dating from the late 17th century, it is surrounded by the summer palaces of the Ranis of Udaipur. The two highest surrounding hills are topped by the **Hawa Mahal** and **Ruti Rani palaces**, now empty but worth visiting for the architecture and views. A small sanctuary nearby has deer, antelope and panther. Tribals still inhabit some islands on the lake while crocodiles, keelback water snakes and turtles bask on others.

Bambora → *Colour map 3, B1. 45 minutes' drive southeast of Udaipur.*

The imposing 18th-century hilltop fortress of Bambora has been converted to a heritage hotel by the royal family of Sodawas at an enormous restoration cost yet retaining its ancient character. The impressive fort is in Mewari style with domes, turrets and arches. To get here from Udaipur, go 12 km east along the airport road and take the right turn towards Jaisamand Lake passing the 11th-century Jagat Temple (38 km) before reaching Bambora.

Sitamata Wildlife Sanctuary → *Colour map 3, B2. 117 km from Udaipur.*

The reserve of dense deciduous forests covers over 400 sq km and has extensive birdlife (woodpeckers, tree pies, blue jays, jungle fowl). It is one of the few sanctuaries between the Himalaya and the Nilgiris where giant brown flying squirrels have been reported. Visitors have seen hordes of langur monkey, nilgai in groups of six or seven, four-horned antelope, jackal and even panther and hyena, but the thick forests make sighting difficult. There are crocodiles in the reservoirs.

Rishabdeo → Colour map 3, C1. 63 km south of Udaipur along the NH8.

Rishabdeo, off the highway, has a remarkable 14th-century Jain temple with intricate white marble carving and black marble statuary, though these are not as fine as at Dilwara or Ranakpur. Dedicated to the first Jain Tirthankar, Adinath or Rishabdev, Hindus, Bhils as well as Jains worship there. An attractive bazar street leads to the temple, which is rarely visited by tourists. Special worship is conducted several times daily when Adinath, regarded as the principal focus of worship, is bathed with saffron water or milk. The priests are friendly; a small donation (Rs 10-20) is appreciated.

Dungarpur → Colour map 3, C1. Phone code: 02964. Population 50,000.

Dungarpur (City of Hills) dates from the 13th century. The district is the main home of the Bhil tribal people. It is also renowned for its stone masons, who in recent years have been employed to build Hindu temples as far afield as London. The attractive and friendly village has one of the most richly decorated and best-preserved palaces in Rajasthan, the Juna Mahal. Surrounded on three sides by Lake Gaibsagar and backed by picturesque hills, the more recent **Udai Bilas Palace** (now a heritage hotel, see page 210) was built by Maharawal Udai Singhji in the 19th century and extended in 1943. The huge courtyard surrounds a 'pleasure pool' from the centre of which rises a four-storeyed pavilion with a beautifully carved wooden chamber.

The **Juna Mahal**, above the village, dates from the 13th century when members of the Mewar clan at Chittaur moved south to found a new kingdom after a family split. It is open to guests staying at Udai Bilas and by ticket (Rs 150) for non-residents, obtainable at the hotel. The seven-storeyed fortress-like structure with turrets, narrow entrances and tiny windows has colourful and vibrant rooms profusely decorated over several centuries with miniature wall paintings (among the best in Rajasthan), and glass and mirror inlay work. There are some fine *jarokha* balconies and sculpted panels illustrating musicians and dancers in the local green-grey parava stone which are strikingly set against the plain white walls of the palace to great effect. The steep narrow staircases lead to a series of seven floors giving access to public halls, supported on decorated columns, and to intimate private chambers. There is a jewel of a Sheesh Mahal and a cupboard in the Maharawal's bedroom on the top floor covered in miniatures illustrating some 50 scenes from the Kama Sutra. Windows and balconies open to the breeze command lovely views over the town below. Perhaps nowhere else in Rajasthan gives as good an impression of how these palaces must have been hundreds of years ago; it is completely unspoilt and hugely impressive.

Some interesting temples nearby include the 12th-century Siva temple at **Deo Somnath**, 12 km away, and the splendid complex of temple ruins profusely decorated with stone sculptures.

🌙 *Dungarpur is a birdwatchers' paradise with lots of ducks, moorhens, waders, ibises at the lake, tropical green pigeons and grey hornbills in the woods.*

Khempur

This small, attractive village is conveniently located midway between Udaipur and Chittaurgarh. To find it turn off the highway, 9 km south of Mavli and about 50 km from Udaipur. The main reason for visiting is to eat or stay in the charming heritage hotel, see Sleeping, page 211.

Eklingji and Nagda → *Colour map 3, B1. 22 km north of Udaipur.*
① *0400-0700, 1000-1300 and 1700-1900. No photography.*
The white marble **Eklingji Temple** has a two-storey mandapa to Siva, the family deity of the Mewars. It dates from AD 734 but was rebuilt in the 15th century. There is a silver door and screen and a silver Nandi facing the black marble Siva. The evenings draw crowds of worshippers and few tourists. Many smaller temples surround the main one and are also worth seeing. Nearby is the large but simple **Lakulisa Temple** (AD 972), and other ruined semi-submerged temples. The back-street shops sell miniature paintings. It is a peaceful spot attracting many waterbirds. Occasional buses go from Udaipur to Eklingji and Nagda which are set in a deep ravine containing the Eklingji Lake. The **RTDC** (see page 192) run tours from Udaipur, 1400-1900.

At Nagda, are three temples: the ruined 11th-century Jain temple of **Adbhutji** and the **Vaishnavite Sas-Bahu** (Mother-in-law/Daughter-in-law) temples. The complex, though comparatively small, has some very intricate carving on pillars, ceiling and mandapa walls. You can hire bicycles in Eklingji to visit them. There are four 14th-century Jain Temples at **Delwara** about 5 km from Eklingji, which also boast the **Devi Garh**, one of India's most luxurious hotels.

Nathdwara → *Colour map 3, B1. 48 km from Udaipur.*
This is a centre of the Krishna worshipping community of Gujarati merchants who are followers of Vallabhacharya (15th century). Non-Hindus are not allowed inside the temple, which contains a black marble Krishna image, but the outside has interesting paintings. **Shrinathji Temple** is one of the richest Hindu temples in India. At one time only high caste Hindus (Brahmins, Kshatriyas) were allowed inside, and the *pichhwais* (temple hangings) were placed outside, for those castes and communities who were not allowed into the sanctum sanctorum, to experience the events in the temple courtyard and learn about the life of lord Krishna. You can watch the 400-year-old tradition of *pichhwai* painting which originated here. The artists had accompanied the Maharana of Mewar, one of the few Rajput princes who still resisted the Mughals, who settled here when seeking refuge from Aurangzeb's attacks. Their carriage carrying the idol of Shrinathji was stuck at Nathdwara in Mewar, 60 km short of the capital Udaipur. Taking this as a sign that this was where God willed to have his home, they developed this into a pilgrim centre for the worship of lord Krishna's manifestation, Shrinathji. Their paintings, *pichhwais*, depict Lord Krishna as Shrinathji in different moods according to the season. The figures of lord Krishna and the *gopis* (milkmaids) are frozen on a backdrop of lush trees and deep skies. The bazar sells *pichhwais* painted on homespun cloth with mineral and organic colour often fixed with starch.

Rajsamand Lake → *Colour map 3, B1. 56 km north of Udaipur.*
At **Kankroli** is the Rajsamand Lake. The **Nauchoki Bund**, the embankment which contains it, is over 335 m long and 13 m high, with ornamental pavilions and *toranas*, all of marble and exquisitely carved. Behind the masonry bund is an 11-m-wide earthen embankment, erected in 1660 by Rana Raj Singh who had defeated Aurangzeb on several occasions. He also commissioned the longest inscription in the world, "Raj Prashasthi Maha Kavyam", which tells the story of Mewar on 24 granite slabs in Sanskrit. Kankroli and its beautiful temple are on the southeast side of the lake.

Deogarh → *Colour map 3, B1. 2 km off the NH8. Altitude: 700 m.*

Deogarh (Devgarh) is an excellent place to break journey between Udaipur and Jaipur or Pushkar. It is a very pleasant, little frequented town with a dusty but interesting bazar (if you are interested in textiles, visit **Vastra Bhandar** ① *T02904-252187*, for reasonably priced and good-quality textiles). Its elevation makes it relatively cool and the country-side and surrounding hills are good for gentle treks. There is an old fort on a hill as well as a magnificent palace on a hillock in the centre with murals illustrating the fine local school of miniature painting. **Raghosagar Lake**, which is very pleasant to walk around, has an island with a romantic ruined temple and centotaphs (poor monsoons leave the lake dry). It attracts numerous migratory birds and is an attractive setting for the charming 200-year-old palace, **Gokal Vilas**, the home of the present Rawat Saheb Nahar Singhji and the Ranisahiba. Their two sons have opened the renovated 17th-century **Deogarh Mahal Palace** to guests, see Sleeping, page 211. The Rawat, a knowledgeable historian and art connoisseur, has a private collection of over 50 paintings which guests may view, advance notice required. The shop at the hotel has good modern examples to buy. There is plenty to do here including an excellent 45-minute train journey from Deogarh to Phulud which winds down through the Aravalli hills to the plain below through tunnels and bridges.

◉ Around Udaipur listings

For Sleeping and Eating price codes and other relevant information, see Essentials pages 28-33.

◉ Sleeping

Jaisamand Lake *p207*

A Jaisamand Island Resort, Baba Island on Jaisamand Lake, T02906-234723, http://jaisamand.com. 40 well-equipped a/c rooms in an unsubtle concrete castle, pool, garden, excellent location, great views, restaurant (international menu), mixed reports on food and service.

Bambora *p207*

AL-A Karni Fort, Bambora, T0291-2512101, www.karnihotels.com. Heritage hotel with 30 beautifully decorated rooms (circular beds) in large, imposing fort, marble bathrooms, modern facilities, impressive interiors, enthusiastic and friendly manager, exceptional marble pool, folk concerts, great beer bar, delicious food, hugely enjoyable. Recommended.

Sitamata Wildlife Sanctuary *p207*

B-C Fort Dhariyawad, at the sanctuary, T02950-220050. 14 rooms and 4 suites in restored and converted, mid-16th century fort (founded by one of Maharana Pratap's sons) and some in contemporary cottage cluster, meals (international menu), period decor, medieval flavour, great location by sanctuary (flying squirrels, langur monkeys in garden, crocodiles in reservoir), tribal village tours, jeeps to park, horse safaris, treks.

D Forest Lodge, at the sanctuary, Dhariyawad, contact District Forest Officer, Chittorgarh, T01472-244915. Rather expensive considering lack of amenities, but fantastic location and views, a paradise for birders.

Dungarpur *p208*

A Udai Bilas Palace, 2 km from Dungarpur, T02964-230808, www.udaibilas palace.com. 22 unique a/c rooms (including 16 suites of which 6 are vast 'grand suites') mirror mosaics, some dated with art deco furniture, marble bathrooms, some with modern furniture in old guesthouse, all with either a

lake or garden view, good food (lunch Rs 380) a 'country house' style hotel (guests dine together at one table), somewhat inappropriate tiger heads line walls, Harshvardhan Singh is a charming host, beautiful new pool, boating, credit cards accepted, idyllic setting, very relaxing. Highly recommended.
E-F Vaibhav, Saghwara Rd, T02964-230244. Simple rooms, tea stall/restaurant, owner very friendly and helpful.

Khempur *p208*
C Ravla Khempur, T02955-237154, www.ravlakhempur.com. The former home of the village chieftain, this is a charming, small-scale heritage property. The rooms have been sensitively renovated with modern bathrooms, pleasant lawns, horse rides a speciality.

Eklingji and Nagda *p209*
LL Devi Garh, Delwara, 5 km from Eklingji, T02953-289211, www.deviresorts.com. For the ultimate in luxury. It specializes in letting all 30 individually decorated suites for fabulous weddings or parties.
A Heritage Resort, Lake Bagela, Eklingji, T(0)9829-252507, www.heritageresort.com. Fabulously located by the lake and ringed by hills. 30 excellent a/c rooms, contemporary building in traditional design, good food (organic vegetarian grown on property, pool, jacuzzi, boating, riding, good walking and cycling. Recommended.

Nathdwara *p209*
E Gokul (RTDC), near Lalbagh, 2 km from bus stand, Nathdwara, T02953-230917. 6 rooms and dorm (Rs 50), restaurant.
F Yatrika Mangla (RTDC), Nathdwara, T02953-231119. Hotel with 5 rooms and dorm (Rs 50).

Deogarh *p210*
AL-B Deogarh Mahal, T02904-252777, www.deogarhmahal.com. 50 rooms in superb old fort built in 1617, including

atmospheric suites furnished in traditional style with good views, best have balconies with private jacuzzis, but not all are up to the same standard. Fabulous keyhole-shaped pool, Keralan massage, Mewari meals, home-grown produce (room service 50% extra), bar, good gift shop, log fires, folk entertainment, boating, birdwatching, jeep safaris, talks on art history, hospitable and delightful hosts. Outstanding hotel; highly recommended. Reserve well ahead. The family have also renovated the **Singh Sagar** fort, 5 km from Deogarh, with 4 superbly decorated suites. It is in the middle of a small lake (sadly dry) and is an ideal hideaway. Prices start at US$350 per night.

⊛ Festivals and events

Dungarpur *p208*
Feb Baneshwar Fair (usually in Feb, in 2010 it falls 26-30 Jan; in 2011 14-18 Feb). The tribal festival at the Baneshwar Temple, 70 km from Dungarpur, is one of Rajasthan's largest tribal fairs when Bhils gather at the temple in large numbers for ritual bathing at the confluence of rivers. There are direct buses to Baneshwar during the fair. The temporary camp during the fair is best avoided. **Vagad Festival** in Dungarpur offers an insight into local tribal culture. Both are uncommercialized and authentic. Details from **Udai Bilas Palace**, see Sleeping, page 210.

⊖ Transport

Around Udaipur *p207*
Bus For **Nathdwara**, several buses from Udaipur from early morning. Buses also go to **Nagda**, **Eklingji** and **Rajsamand**. Private transport only for Khempur and Deogarh. From Dungarpur buses travel to/from **Udaipur** (110 km), 2 hrs, **Ahmedabad** (170 km), 4 hrs. You will need to hire a taxi to get to the other destinations.

Kumbhalgarh, Ranakpur and around

Little-known Kumbhalgarh is one of the finest examples of defensive fortification in Rajasthan. You can wander around the palace, the many temples and along the walls – 36 km long in all – to savour the great panoramic views. It is two hours north (63 km) of Udaipur through the attractive Rajasthani countryside. The small fields are well kept and Persian wheels and 'tanks' are dotted across the landscape. In winter, wheat and mustard grow in the fields, and the journey there and back is as magical as the fort.

The temples of Ranakpur are incredibly ornate and amazingly unspoilt by tourism, having preserved a dignified air which is enhanced by the thick green forests that surround them. There are a number of interesting villages and palaces in the nearby area; if time allows this is a great region to explore at leisure, soaking in the unrushed, rural way of life. ▶ *For listings, see pages 214-216.*

Kumbhalgarh → *For listings, see pages 214-216. Colour map 3, B1.*

Kumbhalgarh Fort → *Phone code: 02954. Altitude: 1087m. 63 km from Udaipur.*
ⓘ *Foreigners Rs 100, Indians Rs 5.*

Kumbhalgarh Fort, off the beaten tourist track, was the second most important fort of the Mewar Kingdom after Chittaurgarh. Built mostly by Maharana Kumbha (circa 1485), it is situated on a west-facing ridge of the Aravalli hills, commanding a great strategic position on the border between the Rajput kingdoms of Udaipur (Mewar) and Jodhpur (Marwar). It is accessible enough to make a visit practicable and getting there is half the fun. There are superb views over the lower land to the northwest, standing over 200 m above the pass leading via Ghanerao towards Udaipur.

The approach Passing though charming villages and hilly terrain, the route to the fort is very picturesque. The final dramatic approach is across deep ravines and through thick scrub jungle. Seven gates guarded the approaches while seven ramparts were reinforced by semicircular bastions and towers. The 36-km-long black walls with curious bulbous towers exude a feeling of power as they snake their way up and down impossibly steep terrain. They were built to defy scaling and their width enabled rapid deployment of forces – six horses could walk along them side by side. The walls enclose a large plateau containing the smaller Katargarh Fort with the decaying palace of Fateh Singh, a garrison, 365 temples and shrines, and a village. The occupants (reputedly 30,000) could be self-sufficient in food and water, with enough storage to last a year. The fort's dominant location enabled defenders to see aggressors approaching from a great distance. Kumbhalgarh is believed to have been taken only once and that was because the water in the ponds was poisoned by enemy Mughals during the reign of Rana Pratap.

The gates The first gate **Arait Pol** is some distance from the main fort; the area was once thick jungle harbouring tigers and wild boar. Signals would be flashed by mirror in times of emergency. **Hulla Pol** (Gate of Disturbance) is named after the point reached by invading Mughal armies in 1567. **Hanuman Pol** contains a shrine and temple. The **Bhairava Pol** records the 19th-century chief minister who was exiled. The fifth gate, the **Paghra (Stirrup) Pol** is where the cavalry assembled; the Star tower nearby has walls 8 m thick. The Top-Khana (Cannon Gate) is alleged to have a secret escape tunnel. The last, **Nimbu (Lemon) Pol** has the Chamundi temple beside it.

The palace It is a 30-minute walk (fairly steep in parts) from the car park to the roof of the Maharana's darbar hall. Tiers of inner ramparts rise to the summit like a fairytale castle, up to the appropriately named Badal Mahal (19th century) or 'palace in the clouds', with the interior painted in pastel colours. Most of the empty palace is usually unlocked (a *chaukidar* holds the keys). The views over the walls to the jungle-covered hillsides (now a wildlife reserve) and across the deserts of Marwar towards Jodhpur, are stunning. The palace rooms are decorated in a 19th-century style and some have attractive coloured friezes, but are unfurnished. After the maze-like palace at Udaipur, this is very compact. The Maharana's palace has a remarkable blue darbar hall with floral motifs on the ceiling. Polished *chunar* (lime) is used on walls and window sills, but the steel ceiling girders give away its late 19th-century age. A gap separated the *mardana* (men's) palace from the *zenana* (women's) palace. Some of the rooms in the *zenana* have an attractive painted frieze with elephants, crocodiles and camels. A circular Ganesh temple is in the corner of the *zenana* courtyard. A striking feature of the toilets was the ventilation system which allowed fresh air into the room while the toilet was in use.

Kumbhalgarh Wildlife Sanctuary

① *Foreigners Rs 100, Indians Rs 10, car Rs 65, open sunrise to sunset.*

The sanctuary to the west of the fort covering about 600 sq km has a sizeable wildlife population but you have to be extremely lucky to spot any big game in the thick undergrowth. Some visitors have seen bear, panther, wolf and hyena but most have to be contented with seeing nilgai, sambhar deer, wild boar, jackal, jungle cat and birds. Crocodiles and water fowl can be seen at **Thandi Beri Lake**. Jeep and horse safaris can be organized from hotels in the vicinity including **Aodhi**, **Ranakpur**, **Ghanerao** and **Narlai** (see Sleeping, pages 214 and 215). The rides can be quite demanding as the tracks are very rough. There is a 4WD jeep track and a trekking trail through the safari area can be arranged through **Shivika Lake Hotel**, Ranakpur (see page 215).

The tribal Bhils and Garasias – the latter found only in this belt – can be seen here, living in their traditional huts. The Forest Department may permit an overnight stay in their **Rest House** in **Kelwara**, the closest town, 6 km from sanctuary. With steep, narrow streets devoid of cars it is an attractive little place.

Ghanerao and Rawla Narlai → *For listings, see pages 214-216. Colour map 3, B1.*

Ghanerao was founded in 1606 by Gopal Das Rathore of the Mertia clan, and has a number of red sandstone *havelis* as well as several old temples, *baolis* and marble *chhatris*, 5 km beyond the reserve. The village lay at the entrance to one of the few passes through the Aravallis between the territories held by the Rajput princes of Jodhpur and Udaipur. The beautiful 1606 **royal castle** has marble pavilions, courtyards, paintings, wells, elephant stables and walls marked with canon balls. The present Thakur Sajjan Singh has opened his castle to guests (see Sleeping, page 215), and organizes two- to three-day treks to Kumbhalgarh Fort, 50 km by road accessible to jeep, and Ranakpur.

The **Mahavir Jain Temple**, 5 km away, is a beautiful little 10th-century temple. It is a delightful place to experience an unspoiled rural environment.

Rawla Narlai, 25 km from Kumbhalgarh Fort, and an hour's drive from Ranakpur, is a Hindu and Jain religious centre. It has a 17th-century fort with interesting architecture, right in the heart of the village, which is ideal for a stopover.

Ranakpur → *For listings, see pages 214-216. Colour map 3, B1. Phone code: 02934. 90 km Udaipur, 25 km Kumbhalgarh.*

ⓘ *Daily; non-Jains are only allowed to visit the Adinatha 1200-1700, free. Photos with permission from Kalyanji Anandji Trust office next to the temple, camera Rs 50, video Rs 150, photography of the principal Adinatha image is prohibited. Shoes and socks must be removed at the entrance. Black clothing and shorts are not permitted. No tips, though unofficial 'guides' may ask for baksheesh.*

One of five holy Jain sites and a popular pilgrimage centre, it has one of the best-known Jain temple complexes in the country. Though not comparable in grandeur to the Dilwara temples in Mount Abu, it has very fine ornamentation and is in a wonderful setting with peacocks, langurs and numerous birds. The semi-enclosed deer park with spotted deer, nilgai and good birdlife next to the temple, attracts the occasional panther! You can approach Ranakpur from Kumbhalgarh through the wildlife reserve in 1½ hours although you will need to arrange transport from the Sanctuary entrance. A visit is highly recommended.

The **Adinatha** (1439), the most noteworthy of the three main temples here, is dedicated to the first Tirthankar. Of the 1444 engraved pillars, in Jain tradition, no two are the same, each individually carved. The sanctuary is symmetrically planned around the central shrine and is within a 100-sq-m raised terrace enclosed in a high wall with 66 subsidiary shrines lining it, each with a spire; the gateways consist of triple-storey porches. The sanctuary with a clustered centre tower contains a *chaumukha* (four-fold) marble image of Adinatha. The whole complex, including the extraordinary array of engraved pillars, carved ceilings and arches are intricately decorated, often with images of Jain saints, friezes of scenes from their lives and holy sites. The lace-like interiors of the corbelled domes are a superb example of western Indian temple style. The **Parsvanatha** and **Neminath** are two smaller Jain temples facing this, the former with a black image of Parsvanatha in the sanctuary and erotic carvings outside. The star-shaped **Surya Narayana Temple** (mid-15th century) is nearby.

There is a beautiful 3.7-km trek around the wildlife sanctuary, best attempted from November to March, contact sanctuary office next to temples for information.

◉ Kumbhalgarh, Ranakpur and around listings

For Sleeping and Eating price codes and other relevant information, see Essentials pages 28-33.

◉ Sleeping

Kumbhalgarh *p212*
AL Aodhi (HRH), 2 km from fort gate, T02954-242341, www.hrhindia.com. Closest place to fort, great location set in to the rock face. 27 rooms in modern stone 'cottages' decorated in colonial style to good effect with attached modern bathrooms. Beautiful restaurant and coffee shop, pool, relaxing atmosphere, very helpful staff, fabulous views, very quiet, superb horse safaris

(US$200 per night), trekking, tribal village tours. Highly recommended.
A-B Kumbhalgarh Fort, Kelwara–Kumbhalgarh Rd, T02954-242058, hilltop@bppl.net.in. 21 a/c rooms in attractively designed stone building, superb location with hill, lake and valley views, garden, restaurant, bar, lovely pool, cycle hire, riding, friendly staff.
C Kumbhal Castle, Khelwara Kumbhalgarh Rd, T02954-242171, www.kumbhal castle.com. 12 simply decorated rooms, some a/c, in new construction which feels a little unfinished. Basic restaurant, good views.

C-E Ratnadeep, Kelwara, in the middle of a bustling village, T02954-242217, hotelratnadeep@yahoo.co.in. 14 reasonably clean rooms, some de luxe with cooler and marble floors, Western toilets, small lawn, restaurant, camel, horse and jeep safaris, friendly, well run.

E Forest Department Guest House, near the Parsram Temple, about 3 km from **Aodhi** by road then 3 km by 4WD jeep or on foot. Basic facilities but fantastic views over the Kumbalgarh sanctuary towards the drylands of Marwar.

G Lucky, 2 km from fort at bottom of hill by Kelwara turn-off, T02593-513965. Simple, quite new guesthouse, some rooms with shared bath, good cheap food in generous portions, friendly and keen owner.

Ghanerao and Rawla Narlai p213

AL Fort Rawla Narlai, Rawla Narlai, T02934-282425. 20 rooms (11 a/c) individually decorated with antiques in the renovated fort, new showers, plus 5 luxurious, well-appointed 'tents', good simple meals under the stars, helpful, friendly staff, attractive garden setting, good riding, overlooked by huge granite boulder; temple on top can be reached via 700 steps.

B Kotri Raola, Ghanerao, T02934-240224, www.kotriraola.com. 8 rooms, 2 suites in 18th-century royal 'bungalow', excellent horse safaris run by Thakur Mahendra Singh, an expert on Marwari horses and his son, a well-known polo player.

B-C Ghanerao Royal Castle, see page 213, reservations, T022-404 2211 (Mumbai), www.nivalink.com/ghanerao. Suites and a restaurant serving simple food, slightly run-down but has nostalgic appeal of faded glory, charming hosts, expensive local guide (bargain hard if buying paintings), jeeps and camping arranged.

C Bagha-ka-Bagh (Tiger's Den), Ghanerao. Spartan hunting lodge among tall grass jungle near wildlife sanctuary gate. 8 basic rooms, 5 with bucket hot water, dorm, generator for electricity, breathtaking location, wildlife

(including panther, nilgai), rich in birdlife, 5-day treks including Kumbhalgarh, Ranakpur. Contact **North West Safaris**, T079-2630 8031, ssibal@ad1.vsnl.net.in.

Ranakpur p214

AL Fateh Bagh Palace (HRH), on the highway near the temple, T02934-286186, www.hrhindia.com. A 200-year-old fort was dismantled in to 65,000 pieces and transported here from its original site 50 km away in order to make this palace. The result is a beautiful property, cleverly combining old and new. There are 20 tastefully decorated, well-appointed rooms, including 4 suites, the best of which have attached jacuzzis. Good pool, friendly staff.

A Maharani Bagh (WelcomHeritage), Ranakpur Rd, T02934-285105, www.marudharhotels.com. 18 well-furnished modern bungalows with baths in lovely 19th-century walled orchard of Jodhpur royal family, full of bougainvillea and mangos, outdoor Rajasthani restaurant (traditional Marwari meals Rs 300), pool, jeep safaris, horse riding.

C Ranakpur Hill Resort, Ranakpur Rd, T02934-286411, www.ranakpurhillresort.com. 16 good-sized, well-appointed rooms, 5 a/c, in new construction, pleasant dining room, clean pool, friendly owner.

C Shivika Lake Hotel, T02934-285078, www.shivikalakehotel.com. A **Rajput Special Hotel** bordering the lake in pleasant jungle setting. 9 simple but comfortable a/c rooms with bath, hot water, 5 tents with shared bath, delicious Rajasthani food in basic dining room, swimming pool overlooks lake and wooded hills. Thakur Devi Singh Ji Bhenswara organizes treks, excellent jeep safaris with spotter guide in Kumbhalgarh sanctuary (he is the honorary warden), camping trips, personal attention, friendly hosts. Recommended.

D-F Roopam, Ranakpur Rd, T02934-285321, www.roopamresort.com. 12 well-maintained rooms, some a/c, pleasant restaurant, attractive lawns.

E-F Shilpi (RTDC), T02934-285074.
12 clean-ish rooms, best with hot water
and a/c, dorm (dirty), vegetarian meals.
F Dharamshala, T02934-285119. Some
comfortable rooms, simple and extremely
cheap vegetarian meals.

🍴 Eating

Kumbhalgarh *p212*
Aodhi (see Sleeping). Thatched restaurant
with central barbecue area. Good Indian (try
laal maas, a mutton dish), authentic 7-course
Mewari meal but service can be very slow.
Ratnadeep, à la carte vegetarian menu.

Ranakpur *p214*
There are no eateries near the temple, only
a tea stall, but the *dharamshala* serves very
good cheap food at lunchtime and sunset.
Roopam, Ranakpur–Maharani Bagh Rd,
near Shivika. Good Rajasthani food. Pleasant
village theme setting, modern, popular.
Shivika Lake, part open-air restaurant
by lake with hill views. Delicious Rajasthani
lunches, non-spicy curries possible,
barbecued chicken, excellent breakfasts,
tea by the lake, family-run, clean.

⊖ Transport

While most of the places in this section do
have bus links, a private car is indispensable
and makes the most of the scenic drives on
offer. A round-trip from Udaipur could also
take in Eklingji, Nagda and Nathdwara.

Kumbhalgarh *p212*
Bus and taxi For the fort: buses (irregular
times) from Chetak Circle, Udaipur go to
Kelwara, Rs 20, 3 hrs (cars take 2 hrs); from
there a local bus (Rs 6) can take you a further
4 km up to a car park; the final 2-km climb
is on foot; the return is a pleasant downhill
walk of 1 hr. Jeep taxis charge Rs 50-100
from Kelwara to the fort (and say there are
no buses). Return buses to Udaipur from
Kelwara until 1730. Buses to **Saira** (for
Ranakpur, see below) leave in the afternoon.
   From Udaipur, a taxi for 4, Rs 1200,
can cover the fort and Ranakpur in
11 hrs; very worthwhile.

Ranakpur *p214*
Bus From Udaipur, there are 6 buses daily
(0530-1600), slow, 3 hrs. Also buses from
Jodhpur and **Mount Abu**. To get to
Kumbhalgarh, take Udaipur bus as far as
Saira (20 km, 45 mins), then catch a bus
or minibus to the Kumbhalgarh turn-off
(32 km, 1 hr). The nearest railway line is Falna
Junction on the Ajmer–Mount Abu line,
39 km away. For taxi options, see above.

Footprint Mini Atlas
Rajasthan

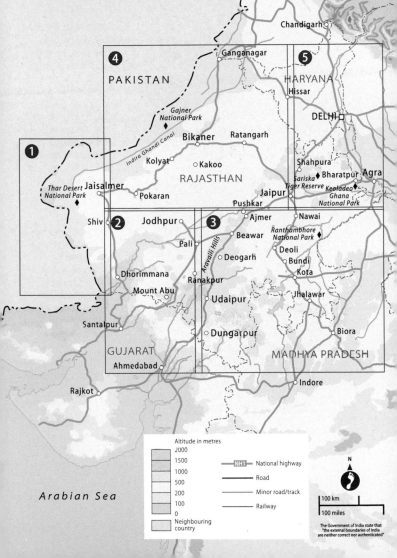

❹ PAKISTAN

❺

Chandigarh

Ganganagar

HARYANA

Hissar

DELHI

Gajner National Park

Indira Ghandi Canal

Bikaner

Ratangarh

Shahpura

❶

Kolyat

Kakoo

RAJASTHAN

Sariska Tiger Reserve

Bharatpur

Agra

Thar Desert National Park

Jaisalmer

Pokaran

Jaipur

Pushkar

Keoladeo Ghana National Park

Shiv

❷ Jodhpur

❸ Ajmer

Nawai

Pali

Beawar

Ranthambhore National Park

Aravalli Hills

Deogarh

Deoli

Bundi

Dhorimanna

Ranakpur

Kota

Mount Abu

Udaipur

Jhalawar

Santalpur

GUJARAT

Dungarpur

MADHYA PRADESH

Biora

Ahmedabad

Indore

Rajkot

Arabian Sea

Altitude in metres

2000	
1500	
1000	
500	
200	
100	
0	

Neighbouring country

NH1 — National highway

—— Road

—— Minor road/track

—— Railway

N

100 km
100 miles

The Government of India state that "the external boundaries of India are neither correct nor authenticated"

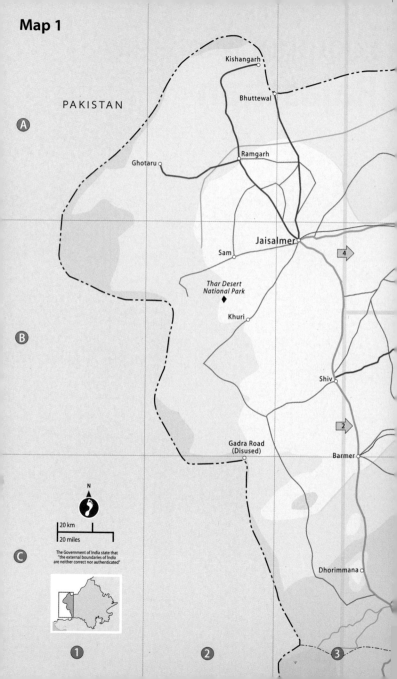

Map 1

PAKISTAN

Ⓐ

Kishangarh

Bhuttewal

Ramgarh

Ghotaru

Jaisalmer

Sam

→ 4

Thar Desert National Park ◆

Khuri

Ⓑ

Shiv

→ 2

Gadra Road (Disused)

Barmer

N ▲

20 km
20 miles

The Government of India state that "the external boundaries of India are neither correct nor authenticated"

Ⓒ

Dhorimmana

① ② ③

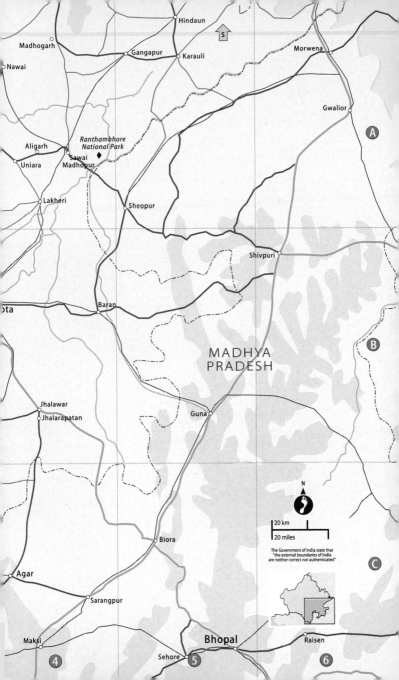

Map 4

N

20 km
20 miles

The Government of India state that "the external boundaries of India are neither correct nor authenticated"

PAKISTAN

Anupgarh
Kaliba

Gajner
National Park

Indira Gandhi Canal

Bikaner

Kolayat

Deshnoke

Nokha
Kakoo

Bap

Phalodi Khichan

aisalmer

Pokaran

Khimsar

Dechhu

Osian

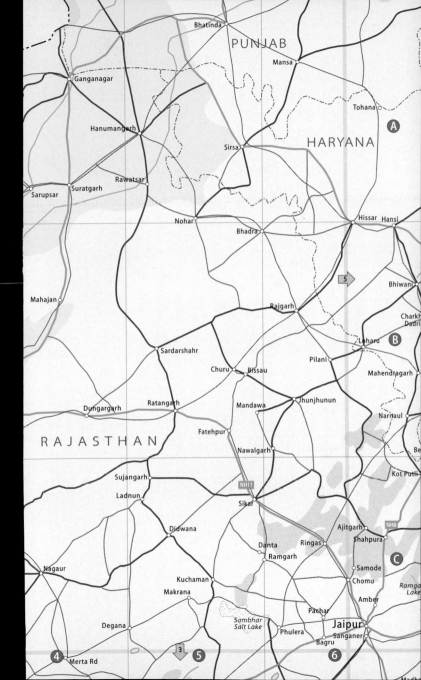

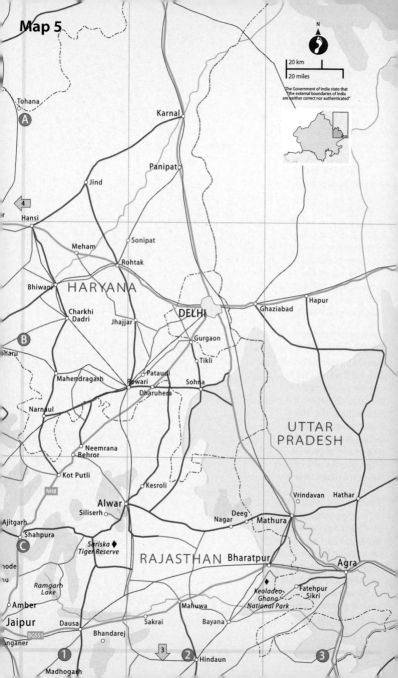

Map 5

N

20 km
20 miles

Tohana

A

Karnal

Panipat

Jind

4

Hansi

Meham

Sonipat

Bhiwani

Rohtak

HARYANA

Charkhi
Dadri

Jhajjar

DELHI

Ghaziabad

Hapur

B

Gurgaon

aru

Tikli

Mahendragarh

Pataudi

Rewari

Sohna

Dharuhera

**UTTAR
PRADESH**

Narnaul

Neemrana
Behror

Kot Putli

NH8

Kesroli

Vrindavan

Hathar

Alwar

Siliserh

Deeg

Ajitgarh

Nagar

Mathura

C

Shahpura

Sariska ◆
Tiger Reserve

RAJASTHAN

Bharatpur

Agra

node

Ramgarh
Lake

Keoladeo
Ghana
National Park

Fatehpur
Sikri

u

Amber

Mahuwa

Jaipur

BG551

Dausa

Bhandarej

Sakrai

Bayana

anganer

Madhogarh

1

3

2

Hindaun

3

Mount Abu and around

Mount Abu, Rajasthan's only hill resort, stretches along a 20-km plateau. Away from the congestion and traffic of the tourist centres on the plains, Mount Abu is surrounded by well-wooded countryside filled with flowering trees, numerous orchids during the monsoon and a good variety of bird and animal life. Many of the rulers from surrounding princely states had summer houses built here and today it draws visitors from Rajasthan and neighbouring Gujarat who come to escape the searing heat of summer (and Gujarat's alcohol prohibition) and also to see the exquisite Dilwara Jain temples. Alas it is a bit like Margate with softy ice creams, pedalos on Nakki Lake and portrait sketches, but is great for a birds' eye view of Indians at play – it is overrun in the hot months between April and June and around Diwali when hotel prices can triple. There are some fabulous heritage hotels in the area, well off the beaten track and worthwhile experiences in themselves. ▸▸ *For listings, see pages 222-225.*

Ins and outs

Getting there and around The nearest railway station is at Abu Road, 27 km away. It is usually quicker to take a bus directly to Mount Abu, instead of going to Abu Road by train and then taking a bus up the hill. The compact area by Nakki Lake, with hotels, restaurants and shops, is pedestrianized. Taxis are available at a stand nearby. A form of transport unique to Mount Abu is the *baba gari*, a small trolley generally used to pull small children up the steepest of Mount Abu's hills. ▸▸ *See Transport, page 225.*

Tourist information **RTDC** ⓘ *opposite the bus stand, T02974-235151, 0800-1100, 1600-2000.* Guides available, four to eight hours, Rs 250-400.

Mount Abu → *For listings, see pages 222-225. Colour map 2, B2. Phone code: 02974. Altitude: 1720 m.*

Mount Abu was the home of the legendary sage Vasishtha. One day Nandini, his precious wish-fulfilling cow, fell into a great lake. Vasishtha requested the gods in the Himalaya to save her so they sent Arbuda, a cobra, who carried a rock on his head and dropped it into the lake, displacing the water, and so saved Nandini. The place became known as Arbudachala, the 'Hill of Arbuda'. Vasishtha also created the four powerful 'fire-born' Rajput tribes, including the houses of Jaipur and Udaipur at a ritual fire ceremony on the mount. Nakki Talao (Lake), sacred to Hindus, was, in legend, scooped out by the *nakki* (fingernails) of gods attempting to escape the wrath of a demon. Abu was leased by the British government from the Maharao of Sirohi and was used as the headquarters for the Resident of Rajputana until 1947, and as a sanatorium for troops.

Dilwara Jain Temples

ⓘ *Free (no photography), shoes and cameras, mobile phones, leather items and backpacks (Rs 1 per item) are left outside, tip expected; 1200-1800 for non-Jains; some guides are excellent, it's a 1-hr uphill walk from town, or share a jeep, Rs 5 each.*

Set in beautiful surroundings of mango trees and wooded hills, 5 km from the town centre, the temples have superb marble carvings. The complex of five principal temples is surrounded by a high wall, dazzling white in the sunlight. There is a resthouse for pilgrims on the approach road, which is also lined with stalls selling a collection of tourist kitsch lending a carnival atmosphere to the sanctity of the temples. It would be beautiful and serene here, but noisy guides and visitors break the sanctity of the magnificent temples.

Chaumukha Temple The grey sandstone building is approached through the entrance on your left. Combining 13th- and 15th-century styles, it is generally regarded as inferior to the two main temples. The colonnaded hall (ground floor) contains four-faced images of the Tirthankar Parsvanatha (hence *chaumukha*), and figures of *dikpalas* and *yakshis*.

Adinatha Temple (Vimala Shah Temple) This temple lies directly ahead; the oldest and most famous of the Dilwara group. Immediately outside the entrance to the temple is a small

① Mount Abu

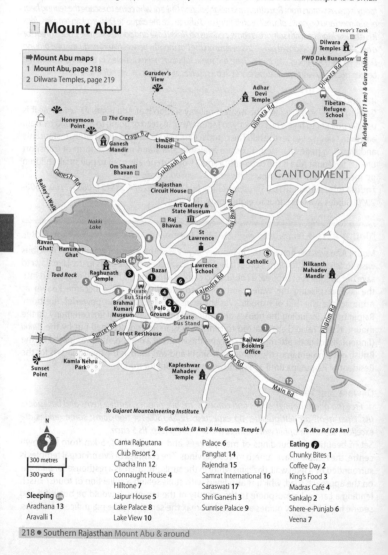

➡ **Mount Abu maps**
1 Mount Abu, page 218
2 Dilwara Temples, page 219

Sleeping 🛏
Aradhana 13
Aravalli 1
Cama Rajputana
Club Resort 2
Chacha Inn 12
Connaught House 4
Hilltone 7
Jaipur House 5
Lake Palace 8
Lake View 10
Palace 6
Panghat 14
Rajendra 15
Samrat International 16
Saraswati 17
Shri Ganesh 3
Sunrise Palace 9

Eating 🍴
Chunky Bites 1
Coffee Day 2
King's Food 3
Madras Café 4
Sankalp 2
Shere-e-Punjab 6
Veena 7

portico known as the Hastishala (elephant hall), built by Prithvipal in 1147-1159 which contains a figure of the patron, Vimala Shah, the Chief Minister of the Solanki King, on horseback. Vimala Shah commissioned the temple, dedicated to Adinatha, in 1031-1032. The riders on the 10 beautifully carved elephants that surround him were removed during Alauddin Khilji's reign. Dilwara belonged to Saivite Hindus who were unwilling to part with it until Vimala Shah could prove that it had once belonged to a Jain community. In a dream, the goddess Ambika (Ambadevi or Durga) instructed him to dig under a champak tree where he found a huge image of Adinatha and so won the land. To the southwest, behind the hall, is a small shrine to Ambika, once the premier deity. In common with many Jain temples the plain exterior conceals a wonderful ornately carved interior, remarkably well preserved given its age. It is an early example of the Jain style in West India, set within a rectangular court lined with small shrines and a double colonnade. The white marble of which the entire temple is built was brought not from Makrana, as other guidebooks suggest, but from the relatively nearby marble quarries of Ambaji in Gujarat, 25 km south of Abu Road. Hardly a surface is left unadorned. Makaras guard the entrance, and below them are conches. The cusped arches and ornate capitals are beautifully designed and superbly made.

Lining the walls of the main hall are 57 shrines. Architecturally, it is suggested that these are related to the cells which surround the walls of Buddhist monasteries, but in the Jain temple are reduced in size to house simple images of a seated Jain saint. Although the carving of the images themselves is simple, the ceiling panels in front of the saints' cells are astonishingly ornate. Going clockwise round the cells, some of the more important ceiling sculptures illustrate: cell 1, lions, dancers and musicians; cells 2-7, people bringing offerings, birds, music-making; cell 8, Jain teacher preaching; cell 9, the major auspicious events in the life of the Tirthankars; and cell 10, Neminath's life, including his marriage, and playing with

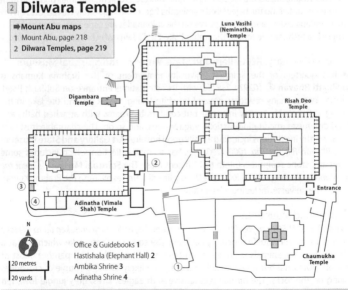

2 Dilwara Temples

➡ Mount Abu maps
1 Mount Abu, page 218
2 Dilwara Temples, page 219

Luna Vasihi (Neminatha) Temple

Digambara Temple

Risah Deo Temple

Adinatha (Vimala Shah) Temple

Entrance

Chaumukha Temple

N

20 metres
20 yards

Office & Guidebooks 1
Hastishala (Elephant Hall) 2
Ambika Shrine 3
Adinatha Shrine 4

Krishna and the *gopis*. In the southeast corner of the temple between cells 22 and 23 is a large black idol of Adinath, reputedly installed by Vimal Shah in 1031.

Cell 32 shows Krishna subduing Kaliya Nag, half human and half snake, and other Krishna scenes; cell 38, the 16-armed goddess Vidyadevi (goddess of knowledge); cells 46-48, 16-armed goddesses, including the goddess of smallpox, Shitala Mata; and cell 49, Narasimha, the 'man-lion' tearing open the stomach of the demon Hiranya-Kashyapa, surrounded by an opening lotus.

As in Gujarati Hindu temples, the main hall focuses on the sanctum which contains the 2.5-m image of Adinatha, the first Tirthankar. The sanctum with a pyramidal roof has a vestibule with entrances on three sides. To its east is the Mandapa, a form of octagonal nave nearly 8 m in diameter. Its 6-m-wide dome is supported by eight slender columns; the exquisite lotus ceiling carved from a single block of marble, rises in 11 concentric circles, carved with elaborately repeated figures. Superimposed across the lower rings are 16 brackets carved in the form of the goddesses of knowledge.

Risah Deo Temple Opposite the Vimala Visahi, this temple is unfinished. It encloses a huge brass Tirthankar image weighing 4.3 tonnes and made of *panchadhatu* (five metals) – gold, silver, copper, brass and zinc. The temple was commenced in the late 13th century by Brahma Shah, the Mewari Maharana Pratap's chief minister. Building activity was curtailed by war with Gujarat and never completed.

Luna Vasihi or Neminatha Temple (1231) To the north of the Adinatha Temple, this one was erected by two wealthy merchants Vastupala and Tejapala, and dedicated to the 22nd Tirthankar; they also built a similar temple at Girnar. The attractive niches on either side of the sanctum's entrance were for their wives. The craftsmanship in this temple is comparable to the Vimala Vasihi; the decorative carving and *jali* work are excellent. The small domes in front of the shrine containing the bejewelled Neminatha figure, the exquisitely carved lotus on the sabhamandapa ceiling and the sculptures on the colonnades are especially noteworthy.

There is a fifth temple for the Digambar ('Sky-Clad') Jains which is far more austere.

Spiritual University, Art Gallery and State Museum and Spiritual Museum
The headquarters of the Spiritual University movement of the Brahma Kumaris is **Om Shanti Bhavan** ⓘ *T02974-238268*, with its ostentatious entrance on Subhash Road. You may notice many residents dressed in white taking a walk around the lake in the evening. It is possible to stay in simple but comfortable rooms with attached baths and attend discourses, meditation sessions, yoga lessons, and so on. The charitable trust runs several worthy institutions including a really good hospital. **Art Gallery and State Museum** ⓘ *Raj Bhavan Rd, Sat-Thu 1000-1700, free*, has a small collection which includes some textiles and stone sculptures (ninth to 10th centuries). The **Spiritual Museum** ⓘ *near the pony stand by the lake, 0800-2000*, has a Disney-like diorama explaining the Brahma Kumari vision of the universe, including a laser show.

Walks around Mount Abu
Trevor's Tank ⓘ *50 m beyond the Dilwara Jain temples, Rs 5, car/jeep taken up to the lake Rs 125*, is the small wildlife sanctuary covering 289 sq km with the lake which acts as a watering hole for animals including sloth bear, sambhar, wild boar, panther. Most of these are nocturnal but on your walk you are quite likely to see a couple of crocodiles basking on the rocks. The birdlife is extensive with eagles, kites, grey jungle fowl, red

spurfowl, francolin, flycatchers, bulbuls and more seen during walks on the trails in the sanctuary. There are superb views from the trails.

Adhar Devi, 3 km from town, is a 15th-century Durga temple carved out of a rock and approached by 220 steep steps. There are steep treks to Anandra point or to a Mahadev temple nearby for great views.

Around Nakki Lake **Honeymoon Point** and **Sunset Point** to the west, afford superb views across the plains. They can both be reached by a pleasant walk from the bus stand (about 2 km). You can continue from Honeymoon Point to **Limbdi House**. If you have another 1½ hours, walk up to **Jai Gurudev's meditation eyrie**. If you want to avoid the crowds at Sunset Point, take the **Bailey's Walk** from the **Hanuman Temple** near Honeymoon Point to **Valley View Point**, which joins up with the Sunset Point walk. You can also walk from the Ganesh temple to the Crags for some great views. The owner of **Shri Ganesh Guest House** advises his guests only to do this walk, and others in the area, when there are other people around as attacks by animals and robberies do occur.

Excursions from Mount Abu

The Aravalli hills, part of the subcontinent's oldest mountain range, look more like rocky outcrops, in places quite barren save for date palms and thorny acacias. From Mount Abu it is possible to make day-treks to nearby spots.

Achalgarh, 11 km away, has superb views. The picturesque **Achaleshwar Temple** (ninth century) is believed to have Siva's toeprint, a brass Nandi and a deep hole claimed to reach into the underworld. On the side of **Mandakini tank** near the car park is an image of Adi Pal, the Paramara king and three large stone buffaloes pierced with arrows. In legend, the tank was once filled with ghee and the buffaloes (really demons in disguise) came every night to drink from it until they were shot by Adi Pal. A path leads up to a group of carved Jain temples (10 minutes' climb).

Guru Shikhar is the highest peak in the area (1720 m) with a road almost to the top. It is 15 km from Mount Abu; taxis take about an hour. To get to the small Vishnu temple you must climb 300 steps or hire a palanquin. Good views especially at dawn.

Gaumukh (Cow's Mouth), 8 km southeast, is on the way to Abu Road. A small stream flows from the mouth of a marble cow. There is also a Nandi bull, and the tank is believed to be the site of Vasishtha's fire from which the four great Rajput clans were created. An image of the sage is flanked by ones of Rama and Krishna.

The **Arbuda Devi Temple** carved out of the rocky hillside is also worth walking to for the superb views over the hills.

Around Mount Abu → *For listings, see pages 222-225. Colour map 2, B2.*

Bera → *34 km from Sirohi.*
The large panther population in the surrounding hills of Bera and the Jawai River area draws wildlife photographers. Antelopes and jackals also inhabit the area. Visit the **Jawai Dam**, 150 km from Mount Abu towards Jodhpur, to see historic embankments, numerous birds and basking marsh crocodiles. A bed for the night is provided by **Leopard's Lair** in a colourful Raika village near the lake and jungle (see Sleeping, page 223).

Jalor → *160 km north of Mount Abu.*
Jalor is a historic citadel. In the early 14th century, during court intrigues, the Afghani Diwan of Marwar, Alauddin Khilji, took over the town and set up his own kingdom. Later,

the Mughal emperor Akbar captured it and returned the principality to his allies, the Rathores of Marwar by means of a peaceful message to the Jalori Nawabs, who moved south to Palanpur in Gujarat. The medieval fort straddles a hill near the main bazar and encloses Muslim, Hindu and Jain shrines. It is a steep climb up but the views from the fort are rewarding. The old Topkhana at the bottom of the fortified hill has a mosque built by Alauddin Khilji using sculptures from a Hindu temple. Of particular interest are the scores of domes in different shapes and sizes, the symmetry of the columns and the delicate arches. Jalor bazar is good for handicrafts, silver jewellery and textiles, and is still relatively unaffected by tourist pricing.

Bhenswara → 16 km east of Jalor.

Bhenswara is a small, colourful village on the Jawai River. It has another Rajput country estate whose 'castle' has been converted into an attractive hotel. The jungles and the impressive granite Esrana hills nearby have leopard, nilgai, chinkara, blackbuck, jungle cat, porcupines, jackals and spiny-tailed lizards. It's a good place to stay for a couple of nights.

Bhinmal → 95 km northwest of Mount Abu.

Bhinmal has some important archaeological ruins, notably one of the few shrines in the country to Varaha Vishnu. It is also noted for the quality of its leather embroidered *mojdis*. Nearby, at **Vandhara**, is one of the few marble *baolis* (step wells) in India, while the historic **Soondha Mata Temple** is at a picturesque site where the green hills and barren sand dunes meet at a freshwater spring fed by a cascading stream.

Daspan → 25 km north of Bhinmal.

Daspan is a small village where the restored 19th-century castle built on the ruins of an old fort provides a break between Mount Abu and Jaisalmer.

◉ Mount Abu and around listings

For Sleeping and Eating price codes and other relevant information, see Essentials pages 28-33.

● Sleeping

Mount Abu p217, map p218
Touts can be a nuisance to budget travellers at the bus stand. Prices shoot up during Diwali, Christmas week and summer (20 Apr-20 Jun) when many **D-F** hotels triple their rates; meals, ponies and jeeps cost a lot more too. Off-season discounts of 30-50% are usual, sometimes up to 70% in mid-winter (when it can get very cold). For a list of families receiving paying guests visit the tourist office.
A Cama Rajputana Club Resort, Adhar Devi Rd, T02974-238205, www.camahotels india.com. Refurbished old club house (1895)

for Mt Abu's royal and British residents, guests become temporary members, 42 rooms in split-level cottages with views and modern decor, 2 period suites, lounge with fireplaces and old club furniture, average restaurant, eco-friendly (recycled water, alternative energy, drip irrigation), beautifully landscaped gardens, billiards, tennis, etc, efficient service, immaculate pool.
A Connaught House (WelcomHeritage), Rajendra Marg, take track uphill opposite the bus stand, T02974-238560, www.welcom heritage.com. British Resident of Jodhpur's colonial bungalow, 5 good, old-fashioned rooms (royal memorabilia), good bathrooms, 8 modern a/c rooms in quieter new cottage, comfortable, restaurant (average à la carte, good Rajasthani meals), trekking with guide (Rs 2000 plus), beautiful gardens filled with

birds, interesting old retainer of the Jodhpur family, efficient management. Recommended.
A The Jaipur House, above Nakki Lake, T02974-235176, www.royalfamilyjaipur.com. 9 elegant rooms and 14 new cottages in the Maharaja of Jaipur's former summer palace, unparalleled hilltop location, fantastic views, especially from terrace restaurant, friendly, professional staff. Recommended.
A Palace Hotel, Bikaner House, Dilwara Rd, 3 km from centre, T02974-235121, www.palace hotelbikanerhouse.com. 33 large renovated rooms with period and reproduction furniture in Swinton Jacob's imposing 1894 hunting lodge, also a new annexe, atmospheric public rooms, grand dining hall (good English breakfast, Rajasthani meals, memorable à la carte, expensive set menu), tennis, etc, civilized but average service, very quiet, set in sprawling grounds and backdrop of hills.
A-B Hilltone, set back from road near petrol pump, T02974-238391, www.hotel hilltone. com. 66 tastefully decorated rooms (most a/c), attractive Handi (a style of cooking using baking/steaming in covered pots) restaurant, pool, garden, quiet, most stylish of Mt Abu's hotels, helpful staff. Recommended.
B-C Aravalli, Main Rd, T02974-235316. 40 rooms (12 in cottages, 10 in new wing) on different levels, good restaurant, very well maintained, landscaped garden, pool, gym, good off-season discount, very helpful staff.
B-C Sunrise Palace, Bharatpur Kothi, T02974-235573, www.sunrisepalace-mtabu.co.in. 20 large, sparsely furnished rooms, great bathrooms, in a grand, slightly unloved converted mansion, good small restaurant, open-air BBQ, elevated with excellent views from the restaurant.
B-D Aradhana, St Mary's Rd, T02974-237227, T(0)9829-827755. Modern rooms, some a/c, large terraces, pleasant atmosphere, 10 mins' walk from town.
B-D Samrat International, near bus stand, T02974-235173, www.mountabu.com. 50 comfortable rooms with some incredibly kitsch suites, Bollywood restaurant, and terraces. Noise from the road can be irritating.

C Chacha Inn, Main Rd (2 km from centre), T02974-235374, www.mountabu.com. Attractive though a bit brash, with lots of artefacts on display, 22 good a/c rooms with modern facilities, some with balconies offering hill views, restaurant, bar, garden really good fun; dining lawns with magic and puppet shows, dancing and music.
C-E Lake Palace, facing lake, T02974-237154, www.savshantihotels.com. 13 rooms (some a/c), garden restaurant, beautifully situated with great lake views from terrace, rear access to hill road for Dilwara, well run and maintained. Recommended.
E-F Saraswati, west of Polo Ground, T02974-238887. Best of many options in area, 36 rooms (some with balconies), better in annexe, good views from upstairs, simple, clean, large rooms with bath and hot water, smart restaurant (Gujarati *thalis* only).
E-G Lake View, on a slope facing the lake, T02974-238659. Beautiful location, 15 basic rooms, Indian WC, helpful staff.
F Krishna, Raj Bhawan Rd, T02974-238045. 12 clean, simple rooms, quiet and homely.
F Rajendra, Rajendra Rd, T02974-238174. Well-designed, clean rooms with bucket hot water, *thalis*, huge balcony, friendly.
F-G Panghat, overlooking Nakki Lake, T02974-238 886. Great location, 10 small but adequate rooms and friendly staff.
F-G Shri Ganesh, west of the polo ground, uphill behind Brahma Kumari, T02974-237292, lalit_ganesh@yahoo.co.in. 23 clean, simple rooms, plenty of solar-heated hot water, very quiet, cookery classes, wildlife walks in morning and afternoon (Rs 100), one of the few places catering specifically for foreigners, 16 years' experience shows in the service, recommended. Ring ahead for free pickup.

Around Mount Abu *p221*
A Leopard's Lair, in a colourful Raika village, Bera, T02933-243478. Well-designed stone cottages, 6 a/c rooms modern amenities, delicious meals included (fresh fish from lake), bar, pool, garden, riding, birdwatching, panther-viewing 'safaris' with owner.

C Rawla Bhenswara (Rajput Special Hotel), Bhenswara, T02978-22080. Reservations from **North West Safaris**, T079-2630 8031 (Gujarat), ssibal@ad1.vsnl. net.in. 20 rooms with bath, painted exterior, inspired decor ('Badal Mahal' with cloud patterns, 'Hawa Mahal' with breezy terrace, etc), breakfast treats of masala cheese toast or vegetarian *parathas*, delicious Marwari meals. Courtyard lawns. Walk to parakeet-filled orchards and pool at the nearby Madho Bagh. Hospitable family are very knowledgeable and enterprising. Visits to Rabari herdsmen, Bhil tribal hamlets, night safaris for leopards, camping safaris including the Tilwara cattle fair or even treks to Mt Abu. Highly recommended.

D Castle Durjan Niwas, Daspan, T0141-222 6126 (Jaipur). Pleasant sitting areas, 11 rooms, folk entertainment, knowledgeable owners, camel rides (Rs 200 per hr; Rs 800 per day).

🍴 Eating

Mount Abu *p217, map p218*
Small roadside stalls sell tasty local vegetarian food. You can also get good *thalis* (Rs 30-40) at simple restaurants.

₩₩₩ Handi, Hilltone Hotel (see Sleeping). 0900-2300. Gujarati, Punjabi, Western. Plenty of choice, very comfortable but pricey. Has a bar.

₩₩ Sankalp, opposite **Samrat International** (see Sleeping), excellent South Indian chain restaurant with amazing chutneys.

₩₩ Shere-e-Punjab, near the taxi stand. One of the best in town for vegetarian/non-vegetarian Indian (some Chinese/Western).

₩ Chunky Bites, on main drag. Good selection of Punjabi, pizza, pasta and *chaat*.

₩ Coffee Day, next to **Sankalp** (see above). Coffee chain but best coffee in town.

₩ King's Food, near MK, Nakki Lake Rd. Very popular for North Indian vegetarian (Rs 40); Chinese, South Indian and Western snacks.

₩ Madras Café, Nakki Lake Rd. Indian. vegetarian 'hot dog', *thalis*, juices, real coffee and milk shakes in a garden, meals indoors.

₩ Maharaja, near bus stand. Gujarati. Simple, clean, produces excellent value *thalis*.

₩ Veena, near taxi stand. Brews real coffee, serves traditional Indian meals and a few Western favourites, very clean, outdoors, loud music, best of many on same strip.

🎉 Festivals and events

Mount Abu *p217, map p218*
Diwali is especially colourful here.
May An annual **Summer Festival** (26-28 May 2010, 15-17 May 2011) features folk music, dancing, fireworks, etc.
29-31 Dec Winter Festival.

Around Mount Abu *p221*
Sep The **Navratri Festival** is held in Bhinmal. Despan also holds special Navratri celebrations.

🛍 Shopping

Mount Abu *p217, map p218*
Shopping is less hassle here than in the tourist towns; most places are open daily 0900-2100. Ready-made Indian clothing and silver jewellery are particularly good value. For Garasia tribal jewellery try stalls near the GPO.
Chacha Museum, good metal, wood, stone crafts, paintings and odd curios (fixed price but may give a discount).
Khadi Gramudyog, by pony hire. Handloom fabric, carved agate boxes, marble figures.
Roopali, near Nakki Lake. Silver jewellery.
Saurashtra and **Rajasthan Emporia**, Raj Bhavan Rd, opposite the bus stand, sell a good selection.

⛰ Activities and tours

Mount Abu *p217, map p218*
Mountain sports
For rock climbing and rapelling, contact the **Mountaineering Institute**, near Gujarat Bhawan Hostel. Equipment and guide/instructors are available.

Polo

Occasional matches and tournaments have begun to take place at the long-abandoned polo ground in the town centre. Entry is free, with local investors keen to generate income from 'polo tourism'. Ask the tourist office for information on upcoming matches.

Swimming, tennis and billiards

Non-residents can use facilities at the **Cama Rajputana** and **Bikaner House Palace** hotels.

Tour operators

RTDC, and **Rajasthan SRTC**, run daily tours to Dilwara, Achalgarh, Guru Shikhar, Nakki Lake, Sunset Point, Adhar Devi and Om Shanti Bhavan, 0830-1300, 1330-1900, Rs 80. **Gujarat, Maharajah, Shobha** (T02974-238302) and **Green Travels** also offer similar tours for Rs 40-60; Ambaji-Kumbhairyaji tours Rs 120.

A wildlife guide who comes very highly recommended is **Charles**, T(0)9414-154854, mahendradan@yahoo.com, also contactable through **Lake Palace Hotel**. He offers a wide range of treks from 3- to 4-hr excursions at Rs 150 per person to longer overnight camping trips, very knowledgeable.

☉ Transport

Mount Abu p217, map p218

Toll on entering town, Rs 10 per head. Frequent rockfalls during the monsoon makes the road from Mount Abu hazardous; avoid night journeys. The nearest airport is Udaipur.
Bus Local buses go to **Dilwara** and **Achalgarh** at 1100 and 1500, go early if doing a day-trip. **State Bus Stand**, Main Rd (opposite tourist office, T02974-235434); **Private Bus Stand**, south of Govt Bus Stand on Petrol Pump road. Many 'direct' long distance buses involve a change at Abu Rd bus stand, T02974-222323. To **Abu Rd**: every 30 mins (45 mins-1 hr) Rs 20. **Ahmedabad**: several (7 hrs, Rs 200) via Palanpur (3 hrs, change here for Bhuj); **Delhi**: overnight. **Jaipur** (overnight, 9 hrs), **Jodhpur** morning

and afternoon (7 hrs). **Mumbai**, **Pune**: early morning (18 hrs). **Udaipur**: 0830, 1500, 2200 (5-6 hrs, Rs 80). **Vadodara**: 0930, 1930 (5 hrs). **Shobha**, T02974-235302, and **Gujarat Travels**, T02974-235564, run private buses.

Taxi and jeep Posted fares for sightseeing in a jeep; about Rs 800 per day, but open to negotiation; anywhere in town Rs 40; to Sunset Point Rs 70. Taxi (for sharing) Abu Rd Rs 300; shared taxis for Jain Temples from Dilwara stand near the bazar opposite Chacha Museum (from Rs 5).

Train Western Railway Out Agency, Tourist Reception Centre, has a small reservation quota, Mon-Sat 0900-1600, Sun 0900-1230. Book well in advance; you may have to wait 2-3 days even in the off-season. Abu Rd, T02974-222222, is the railhead with frequent buses to Mt Abu. To **Ahmedabad**: *Ashram Exp 2916*, 0355, 3½ hrs; *Ahmedabad Mail 9106*, 1248, 5 hrs; *Aravalli Exp 9708*, 1710, 5 hrs (continues to **Mumbai**, further 8½ hrs). **Jaipur**: *Aravalli Exp 9707*, 0958, 9 hrs, via **Ajmer**, 6 hrs; *Ahmedabad-Delhi Mail 9105*, 1405, 9 hrs. **Jodhpur**: *Ranakpur Exp 4708*, 0427, 5½ hrs; *Surya Nagari Exp 2480*, 0122, 5½ hrs. **Delhi**: *Ahmedabad Delhi Mail 9105*, 1405, 15¾ hrs; *Ashram Exp 2915*, 2120, 13¾ hrs; **Margao Goa** *BKN TVC Express 6311* on Wednesdays, There are additional trains at Diwali and New Year.

Around Mount Abu p221
Train/bus To Bera from **Mumbai** and **Ajmer** via Abu Rd (*Aravalli* and *Ranakpur Exp*) stop at Jawai Dam and Mori Bera. For **Bhenswada**, trains and buses from Abu Rd. For **Bhinmal**, trains from **Jodhpur**. From **Ahmedabad**, 2130 (12 hrs); to Ahmedabad, 1940.

☉ Directory

Mount Abu p217, map p218

Internet Yanj-Ya, Hotel Mount Winds, Raj Bhavan Rd. Friendly place with free chai.

Chittaurgarh and around

This is a relatively undiscovered corner of Rajasthan but is home to some of the state's oldest and most interesting treasures. Chittaurgarh's 'Tower of Victory' has become well known in recent years, but the whole of this ancient, historically important city is worth exploring. Kota and the area around Jhalawar contain some of the oldest and most impressive temples and cave paintings in India, while nowhere takes you back in time as far as Bundi, seemingly untouched for centuries. There are limited rail connections in this area, but a new highway has now been completed across the whole of southern Rajasthan which will improve travel in this region. Limited transport links mean that a visit to this region does require a little more time and effort than to other areas in Rajasthan, but also that the region has remained uncrowded, unspoilt and hugely hospitable. ▸▸ *For listings, see pages 233-236.*

Ins and outs

Getting there All of the region's major towns are served by the railway, but often by branch lines some way off the main routes. Buses starting from all the major cities surrounding the area give quick access to the main towns; from Udaipur to Chittaurgarh takes 2½ hours.

Getting around Most of the principal sights are fairly close together, making travel by road a convenient option. Frequent buses criss-cross the area, but a private taxi might be worth considering as some of the sights and most interesting places to stay are somewhat off the beaten track. ▸▸ *See Transport, page 236.*

Tourist infortmation **Tourist office** ① *Janta Avas Grih, Station Rd, T01472-241089.*

Chittaurgarh → *For listings, see pages 233-236. Colour map 3, B2. Phone code: 01472.*

The hugely imposing Chittaurgarh Fort stands on a 152-m-high rocky hill, rising abruptly above the surrounding plain. The walls, 5 km long, enclose the fascinating ruins of an ancient civilization, while the slopes are covered with scrub jungle. The modern town lies at the foot of the hill with access across a limestone bridge of 10 arches over the Gambheri River.

History

One of the oldest cities in Rajasthan, Chittaurgarh was founded formally in 728 by Bappu Rawal, who according to legend was reared by the Bhil tribe. However, two sites near the River Berach have shown stone tools dating from half a million years ago and Buddhist relics from a few centuries BC. From the 12th century it became the centre of Mewar. Excavations in the Mahasati area of the fort have shown four shrines with ashes and charred bones, the earliest dating from about the 11th century AD. This is where the young Udai Singh was saved by his nurse Panna Dai; she sacrificed her own son by substituting him for the baby prince when, as heir to the throne, Udai Singh's life was threatened.

Chittaurgarh Fort

① *0600-1800, entry Rs 100/US$2. Visiting the fort on foot means a circuit of 7 km; allow 4 hrs. The views from the battlements and towers are worth the effort.*

The fort dominates the city. Until 1568 the town was situated within the walls. Today the lower town sprawls to the west of the fort. The winding 1.5-km ascent is defended by seven impressive gates: the **Padal Pol** is where Rawat Bagh Singh, the Rajput leader, fell during the second siege; the Bhairon or **Tuta Pol** (broken gate) where Jaimal, one of the heroes of the third siege, was killed by Akbar in 1567 (*chhatris* to Jaimal and Patta); the

Hanuman Pol and Ganesh Pol; the Jorla (or Joined) Gate whose upper arch is connected to the Lakshman Pol; finally the **Ram Pol** (1459) which is the main gate. Inside the walls is a village and ruined palaces, towers and temples, most of which are out in the open and so easy to explore.

Rana Kumbha's Palace, on the right immediately inside the fort, are the ruins of this palace (1433-1468), originally built of dressed stone with a stucco covering. It is approached by two gateways, the large Badi Pol and the three-bay deep Tripolia. Once there were elephant and horse stables, *zenanas* (recognized by the *jali* screen), and a Siva

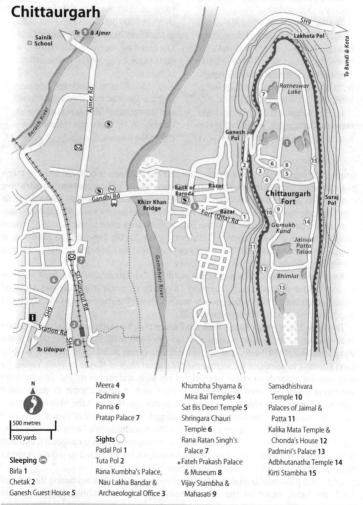

Chittaurgarh

500 metres
500 yards

N

Sleeping 🛌
Birla **1**
Chetak **2**
Ganesh Guest House **5**

Meera **4**
Padmini **9**
Panna **6**
Pratap Palace **7**

Sights ○
Padal Pol **1**
Tuta Pol **2**
Rana Kumbha's Palace,
Nau Lakha Bandar &
Archaeological Office **3**

Khumbha Shyama &
Mira Bai Temples **4**
Sat Bis Deori Temple **5**
Shringara Chauri
Temple **6**
Rana Ratan Singh's
Palace **7**
✦Fateh Prakash Palace
& Museum **8**
Vijay Stambha &
Mahasati **9**

Samadhishvara
Temple **10**
Palaces of Jaimal &
Patta **11**
Kalika Mata Temple &
Chonda's House **12**
Padmini's Palace **13**
Adbhutanatha Temple **14**
Kirti Stambha **15**

The jauhar – Rajput chivalry

On three occasions during Chittaurgarh's history its inhabitants preferred death to surrender, the women marching en masse into the flames of a funeral pyre in a form of ritual suicide known as *jauhar* before the men threw open the gates and charged towards an overwhelming enemy and annihilation.

The first was in 1303 when Ala-ud-din Khalji, the King of Delhi, laid claim to the beautiful Padmini, wife of the Rana's uncle. When she refused, he laid siege to the fort. The women committed *jauhar*, Padmini entering last, and over 50,000 men were killed. The fort was retaken in 1313.

In 1535 Bahadur Shah of Gujarat laid claim to Chittaurgarh. Every Rajput clan lost its leader in the battle in which over 32,000 lives were lost, and 13,000 women and children died in the sacred *jauhar* which preceded the final charge.

The third and final sack of Chittaurgarh occurred only 32 years later when Akbar stormed the fort. Again, the women and children committed themselves to the flames, and again all the clans lost their chiefs as 8000 defenders burst out of the gates. When Akbar entered the city and saw that it had been transformed into a mass grave, he ordered the destruction of the buildings.

In 1567 after this bloody episode in Chittaurgarh's history, it was abandoned and the capital of Mewar was moved to Udaipur. In 1615 Jahangir restored the city to the Rajputs.

temple. The *jauhar* committed by Padmini and her followers is believed to have taken place beneath the courtyard. The north frontage of the palace contains an attractive combination of canopied balconies. Across from the palace is the Nau Lakha Bhandar (The Treasury; nau lakha – 900,000). The temple to Rana Kumbha's wife **Mira Bai** who was a renowned poetess is visible from the palace and stands close to the Kumbha Shyama Temple (both circa 1440). The older 11th-century Jain **Sat Bis Deori** with its 27 shrines, is nearby. The **Shringara Chauri Temple** (circa 1456), near the fort entrance, has sculptured panels of musicians, warriors and Jain deities.

Rana Ratan Singh's Palace is to the north by the Ratneshwar Lake. Built in stone around 1530 it too had stucco covering. Originally rectangular in plan and enclosed within a high wall, it was subsequently much altered. The main gate to the south still stands as an example of the style employed.

The early 20th-century **Fateh Prakash Palace** built by Maharana Fateh Singh (died 1930) houses an interesting **museum** ① *Sat-Thu 0800-1630, Rs 3*. To the south is the **Vijay Stambha** (1458-1468), one of the most interesting buildings in the fort, built by Rana Kumbha to celebrate his victory over Mahmud Khilji of Malwa in 1440. Visible for miles around, it stands on a base 14 sq m and 3 m high, and rises 37 m. The nine-storeyed sandstone tower has been restored; the upper section retains some of the original sculpture. For no extra charge you can climb to the top. Nearby is the Mahasati terrace where the ranas were cremated when Chittaurgarh was the capital of Mewar. There are also numerous *sati* stones. Just to the south is the **Samdhishvara Temple** to Siva (11th and 15th centuries), which still attracts many worshippers and has some good sculptured friezes. Steps down lead to the deep Gomukh Kund, where the sacred spring water enters through a stone carved as a cow's mouth (hence its name).

Of the two palaces of **Jaimal and Patta**, renowned for their actions during the siege of 1567, the latter, based on the *zenana* building of Rana Kumbha's Palace, is more interesting. You then pass the Bhimtal before seeing the **Kalika Mata Temple** (originally an eighth-century Surya temple, rebuilt mid-16th) with exterior carvings and the ruins of Chonda's House with its three-storey domed tower. Chonda did not claim the title when his father, Rana Lakha, died in 1421.

Padmini's Palace (late 13th century, rebuilt end of the 19th) is sited in the middle of the lake surrounded by pretty gardens. Ala-ud-din Khilji is said to have seen Padmini's beautiful reflection in the water through a mirror on the palace wall. This striking vision convinced him that she had to be his.

You pass the deer park on your way round to the **Suraj Pol** (Sun Gate) and pass the **Adbhutanatha Temple** to Siva before reaching the second tower, the **Kirti Stambha**, a Tower of Fame (13th and 15th centuries). Smaller than the Vijay Stambha (23 m) with only seven storeys, but just as elegant, it is dedicated to Adinath, the first Jain Tirthankar. Naked figures of Tirthankars are repeated several hundred times on the face of the tower. A narrow internal staircase goes to the top.

Of particular interest are the number of tanks and wells in the fort that have survived the centuries. Water, from both natural and artificial sources, was harnessed to provide an uninterrupted supply to the people.

Chittaurgarh to Kota → For listings, see pages 233-236. Colour map 3, B2/3/4.

Bassi, 28 km from Chittaurgarh, is famous for handicrafts and miniature wooden temples painted with scenes from the epics. The palace, a massive 16th-century fort, has been opened as a hotel (see Sleeping, page 234).

Bijaipur is a feudal village with a 16th-century **castle**, set among the Vindhya hills and now open as a hotel (see Sleeping, page 233). It has a splendid location near the **Bassi-Bijaipur wildlife sanctuary**, which is home to panther, antelope and other wildlife. The forests are interspersed with lakes, reservoirs, streams and waterfalls with good birdlife in the winter months. The ruined **Pannagarh Fort** facing a lily covered lake is believed to be one of the oldest in Rajasthan.

Menal, further east, has a cluster of Siva temples believed to date from the time of the Guptas. They are associated with the Chauhans and other Rajput dynasties. Though neglected the temples have some fine carvings and a panel of erotic sculptures somewhat similar to those at Khajuraho in Madhya Pradesh. Behind is a deep, wooded ravine with a seasonal waterfall.

Kota → Colour map 3, B4.

Kota's attractive riverside location and decent hotels make it a comfortable place to stay. The town itself is of no special appeal, but can be used as a base from which to visit nearby Bundi if you're short on time. There's a **tourist office** ① *Hotel Chambal (see Sleeping), T0744-232 7695.*

At the south end of the town, near the barrage, is the vast, strongly fortified **City Palace** (1625) which you enter by the south gate having driven through the bustling but quite charming old city. There are some striking buildings with delicate ornamental stonework on the balconies and façade, though parts are decaying. The best-preserved murals and carved marble panels are in the chambers upstairs and in the Arjun Mahal. These murals feature motifs characteristic of the Kota School of Art, including portraiture (especially profiles), hunting scenes, festivals and the Krishna Lila.

Flower power

Crossing the high plateau between Bundi and Chittaurgarh the landscape is suddenly dotted with tiny patches of papery white flowers. These two Rajasthani districts, along with the neighbouring districts of Madhya Pradesh, are India's opium poppy growing belt, accounting for over 90% of production. As early as the 15th century this region produced opium for trade with China. Today the whole process is tightly monitored by the government. Licences to grow are hard won and easily lost. No farmer can grow more than half a *bigha* of opium poppy (less than one-twentieth of a hectare), and each must produce at least 6 kg of opium for sale to the government.

Failure to reach this tough target results in the loss of the licence to grow. Laying out the field, actual cultivation and sale are all government controlled. Between late February and early April the farmers harvest the crop by incising fine lines in one quarter of each poppy head in the evening, and collecting the sap first thing in the morning. The harvesting has to be so precise that each evening a different quarter of the seed head will be cut on a different face – north, south, east or west. Finally the government announces the collection point for the harvested opium just two or three days in advance, and farmers have to travel miles to the centre selected for weighing and final payment.

The 15th-century **Kishore Sagar** tank between the station and the palace occasionally has boats for hire. **Jag Mandir Island Palace**, closed to visitors, is in the centre of the lake. The **Chambal Gardens** by Amar Niwas, south of the fort, is a pleasant place for a view of the river, although the rare fish-eating gharial crocodiles with which the pond was stocked are rarely seen these days. A variety of birds, occasionally including flamingos, can be seen at the river and in nearby ponds.

The **Umed Bhawan** (1904), 1 km north of town, was built for the Maharao Umaid Singh II and designed by Sir Samuel Swinton Jacob in collaboration with Indian designers. The buff-coloured stone exterior with a stucco finish has typical Rajput detail. The interior, however, is Edwardian with a fine drawing-room, banquet hall and garden. It has now been converted into a heritage hotel (see Sleeping, page 234).

Bundi → *For listings, see pages 233-236. Colour map 3, B3. Phone code: 0747. Population: 100,000.*

Bundi lies in a beautiful narrow valley with Taragarh Fort towering above. The drive into the town is lovely as the road runs along the hillside overlooking the valley opposite the fort. You might feel 'forted out' by the time you reach Bundi, but this beautiful old town nestles under the palace and fort and offers spectacular views and a unique charm. Much less developed than the other fort towns, Bundi is starting to blossom – now more classic *havelis* are being 'boutiqued', and there are plenty of more down-home family guest houses springing up too. Popular with backpackers and now increasingly tour buses, Bundi is relaxed and friendly and still a long way off the bazar bustle of Pushkar and the speed and hustle of the more developed fort towns of Jodhpur and Jaisalmer, but good cafés serving cappuccinos cannot be too far along the line. It is well worth spending a day or two here to soak in the atmosphere. Bundi is especially colourful and interesting during the many festivals, see page 236. **Tourist office** ① *Circuit House, near Raniji ki Baori, T0747-244 3697.*

History

Formerly a small state founded in 1342, Bundi's fortunes varied inversely with those of its more powerful neighbours. Neither wealthy nor powerful, it nevertheless ranked high in the Rajput hierarchy since the founding family belonged to the specially blessed Hada Chauhan clan. After Prithviraj Chauhan was defeated by Muhammad Ghuri in 1193, the rulers sought refuge in Mewar. However, adventurous clan members overran the Bhils and Minas in the Chambal valley and established the kingdom of Hadavati or **Hadoti**

Bundi

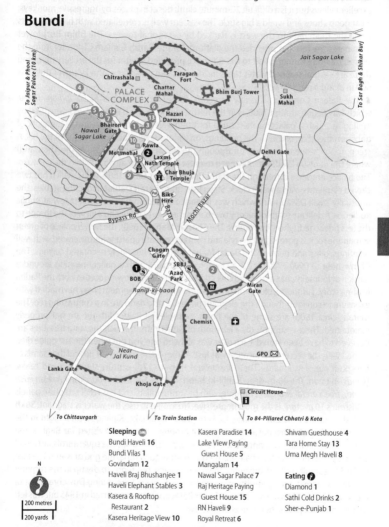

Sleeping
Bundi Haveli **16**
Bundi Vilas **1**
Govindam **12**
Haveli Braj Bhushanjee **1**
Haveli Elephant Stables **3**
Kasera & Rooftop
 Restaurant **2**
Kasera Heritage View **10**

Kasera Paradise **14**
Lake View Paying
 Guest House **5**
Mangalam **14**
Nawal Sagar Palace **7**
Raj Heritage Paying
 Guest House **15**
RN Haveli **9**
Royal Retreat **6**

Shivam Guesthouse **4**
Tara Home Stay **13**
Uma Megh Haveli **8**

Eating
Diamond **1**
Sathi Cold Drinks **2**
Sher-e-Punjab **1**

which covers the area around Bundi, Kota and Jhalawar in southeastern Rajasthan. It prospered under the guidance of the able 19th-century ruler Zalim Singh, but then declined on his death. The British reunited the territory in 1894.

Sights

Taragarh Fort (1342) ① *0600-1800, foreigners Rs 50, Indians Rs 20, camera Rs 50, video Rs 100,* stands in sombre contrast to the beauty of the town and the lakes below. There are excellent views but it is a difficult 20-minute climb beset in places by aggressive monkeys; wear good shoes and wield a big stick. The eastern wall is crenellated with high ramparts while the main gate to the west is flanked by octagonal towers. The **Bhim Burj** tower dominates the fort and provided the platform for the Garbh Ganjam ('Thunder from the Womb'), a huge cannon. A pit to the side once provided shelter for the artillery men, and there are several stepped water tanks inside. Cars can go as far as the TV tower then it is 600 m along a rough track.

The **Palace Complex** ① *below Taragarh, 0900-1700, foreigners Rs 50, Indians Rs 20,* which was begun around 1600, is at the northern end of the bazar, and was described by Kipling as "such a palace as men build for themselves in uneasy dreams – the work of goblins rather than of men". The buildings, on various levels, follow the shape of the hill. A steep, rough stone ramp leads up through the **Hazari Darwaza** (Gate of the Thousand) where the garrison lived; you may need to enter through a small door within the *darwaza*. The palace entrance is through the **Hathi Pol** (Elephant Gate, 1607-1631), which has two carved elephants with a water clock. Steps lead up to **Ratan Daulat** above the stables, the unusually small Diwan-i-Am which was intended to accommodate a select few at public audience. A delicate marble balcony overhangs the courtyard giving a view of the throne to the less privileged, who stood below. The **Chattar Mahal** (1660), the newer palace of green serpentine rock, is pure Rajput in style and contains private apartments decorated with wall paintings, glass and mirrors. The **Badal Mahal** bedroom has finely decorated ceilings. The **Chitrashala** ① *0900-1700, Rs 20,* a cloistered courtyard with a gallery running around a garden of fountains, has a splendid collection of miniatures showing scenes from the Radha Krishna story. Turquoise, blues and greens dominate (other pigments may have faded with exposure to sunlight) though the elephant panels on the dado are in a contrasting red. The murals (circa 1800) are some of the finest examples of Rajput art but are not properly maintained. There is supposedly a labyrinth of catacombs in which the state treasures are believed to have been stored. Each ruler was allowed one visit but when the last guide died in the 1940s the secret of its location was lost. At night, the palace is lit up and thousands of bats pour out of its innards. There are several 16th- to 17th-century step wells and 'tanks' (*kunds*) in town. The 46-m-deep **Raniji-ki-baori** ① *Mon-Sat 1000-1700, closed 2nd Sat each month, free, caretaker unlocks the gate,* with beautiful pillars and bas relief sculpture panels of Vishnu's 10 *avatars,* is the most impressive. No longer in use, the water is stagnant. **Sukh Mahal**, a summer pleasure palace, faces the **Jait Sagar** lake; Kipling spent a night in the original pavilion. Further out are the 66 royal memorials at the rarely visited **Sar Bagh**, some of which have beautiful carvings. The caretaker expects Rs 10 tip. The square artificial **Nawal Sagar** lake has in its centre a half-submerged temple to Varuna, the god of water. The lake surface beautifully reflects the entire town and palace, but tends to dry up in the summer months. A dramatic tongue-slitting ceremony takes place here during Dussehra. West of the Nawal Sagar, 10 km away, is **Phool Sagar Palace**, which was started in 1945 but was left unfinished. Prior permission is needed to view.

South of Kota → For listings, see pages 233-236. *Colour map 3, B4.*

Jhalawar, 85 km southeast of Kota, was the capital of the princely state of the Jhalas, which was separated from Kota by the British in 1838. It lies in a thickly forested area on the edge of the Malwa plateau with some interesting local forts, temples and ancient cave sites nearby. The **Garh Palace** in the town centre, now housing government offices, has some fine wall paintings which can be seen with permission. The **museum** ① *Sat-Thu 1000-1630, Rs 3*, established in 1915, has a worthwhile collection of sculptures, paintings and manuscripts. **Bhawani Natyashala** (1921) was known for its performances ranging from Shakespearean plays to Shakuntala dramas. The stage with a subterranean driveway allowed horses and chariots to be brought on stage during performances. The **tourist office** ① *T07432-230081*, is at the **Hotel Chandravati**.

The small walled town of **Jhalarapatan**, 7 km south of Jhalawar, has several fine 11th-century Hindu temples, the **Padmanath Sun Temple** on the main road being the best. The **Shantinath Jain** temple has an entrance flanked by marble elephants. There are some fine carvings on the rear façade and silver polished idols inside the shrines.

About 7 km away, **Chandrawati**, on the banks of the Chandrabhaga River, has the ruins of some seventh-century Hindu temples with fragments of fine sculpture.

◉ Chittaurgarh and around listings

For Sleeping and Eating price codes and other relevant information, see Essentials pages 28-33.

● Sleeping

Chittaurgarh *p226, map p227*
C-D Pratap Palace (Rajput Special Hotels), Sri Gurukul Rd, near GPO, T01472-240099, hpratapp@hotmail.com. Clean, well-maintained rooms, some a/c, 2 with ornately painted walls good fun, good food in restaurant or in the pleasant garden, jeep and horse safaris visiting villages. Recommended.
C-E Padmini, Chanderiya Rd, near Sainik School, T01472-241718, hotel_padmini@rediffmail.com. 46 clean, modern rooms, 30 a/c, Indian-style furniture, gloomy restaurant, quiet, airport transfer from Udaipur.
D-E Panna (RTDC), Udaipur Rd, near railway station, T01472-241238. Indian business hotel, popular with those visiting quarries/mines. 31 simple rooms, some a/c, best with fort view, dorm (Rs 50), vegetarian dining hall, bar, run-down but attentive service.
D-F Meera, near railway station, Neemuch Rd, T01472-240266. Modern, 24 a/c and non-a/c rooms with TV and phone, Gujarati/Punjabi

restaurant, bar, laundry, car rental, travel assistance, internet, characterless but efficient.
F Chetak, opposite railway station, T01472-241589. Modern, 23 clean, fairly pleasant rooms, 'de luxe' have Western toilets and hot showers.
F-G Ganesh Guest House, New Fort Rd, opposite Sukhadiya Park, T01472-248240. 20 basic and yet still overpriced rooms, Indian and Western toilets.
G Birla, near the Kirti Stambh in the fort, T01472-246939. Has been opened by the dharamshala group. 17-room guesthouse, very basic but only Rs 50 per double, great location, water a problem in the summer.

Chittaurgarh to Kota *p229*
B Castle Bijaipur (Rajput Special Hotels), Bijaipur, T01472-240099, hpratapp@hotmail.com. 25 simple rooms in traditional style with comfortable furniture and modern bathrooms in castle and a new wing, lawns and gardens, hill views from breezy terrace, superb pool, delicious Rajasthani meals, also tea on medieval bastion, jeep/horse safaris with camping, jungle trekking. You may find yoga groups bedding down and bending here.

C Bassi Fort Palace, Bassi, T01472-225321, www.bassifortpalace.com. 16 unpretentious rooms in a family-run 16th-century fort. Same family has an abandoned fort on top of the nearby hill (where dinner can be arranged) and a hunting lodge 6 km away accessible by boat or horse. Safaris to this lodge and local tribal villages can be arranged. Refreshingly informal. Recommended.

E-F Menal Motel, Menal. One simple room – handy for a cup of tea or a simple meal.

Kota *p229*

Kota has a good selection of mid-range hotels, but little for budget travellers; there's a far better choice in Bundi. Budget hotels (**G**) near the bus station can be noisy and dirty.

B Umed Bhawan (WelcomHeritage), Palace Rd, T0744-232 5262, www.welcom heritage.com. 32 large, comfortable rooms, sympathetic conversion, interesting memora-bilia and state rooms, elegant dining room, great beer bar, sunny terraces, behind woods (langurs, deer, parakeets, peacocks), billiards, tennis, attentive staff. Recommended.

B-C Brijraj Bhawan Palace, Civil Lines, T022-2404 2211 (Mumbai), www.indianheritage hotels.com. 7 spacious a/c rooms with verandas, fixed Indian meals, old British Residency with character, stately drawing and dining rooms (regal memorabilia), superb location overlooking river, immaculate gardens, croquet, tennis, very civilized.

C Palkiya Haveli, Mokha Para (in walled city), near Suraj Pol, T0744-238 7497, www.alsisarhaveli.com. 6 traditionally furnished a/c rooms with bath (tubs), well restored, carved wood furniture, exquisite murals, very good fixed meals, peaceful courtyard garden (full of birds), family-run.

C-D Navrang, Collectorate Circle, Civil Lines, T0744-232 3294. Much more ornate inside than out, 25 rooms, de luxe much better than standard, air-cooled or a/c, TV, **C** suites, new a/c vegetarian restaurant, well managed.

C-D Sukhdham Kothi, Civil Lines, T0744-232 0081, www.indianheritagehotels.com. 15 elegant rooms (size varies), 10 a/c, in a

19th-century British residence with sand-stone balconies and screens, good fixed meals, large, private garden well set back from road, family-run, friendly. Recommended.

E Chambal (RTDC), Nayapura, T0744-232 6527. 12 rooms, nothing special but clean, friendly staff, well located close to old city.

Bundi *p230, map p231*

A-E Haveli Braj Bhushanjee, below the fort, opposite Ayurvedic Hospital, T0747-244 2322, www.kiplingsbundi.com. 16 quaint rooms with clean bath (hot showers), in 19th-century 4-storey *haveli* covered in frescos, plenty of atmosphere and memorabilia but a bit stuffy and overpriced. Home-cooked vegetarian meals (no alcohol), pleasant terrace, good fort views, pickup from station on request, good craft shop below, mixed reports on service. Also modern rooms in attached, newly restored 17th-century Badi Haveli.

B Bundi Haveli, 107 Balchand Parra, near Naval Sagar Lake, T0747-244 7861, www.hotel bundihaveli.com. Chic and beautiful rooms around a central courtyard in restored *haveli*. Large rooms with beautiful furniture, divans and fantastic artwork. Good shop of collectibles and fabrics in courtyard.

B Bundi Vilas, below palace, behind Haveli Braj Bhushanjee, T(0)9414-175280, www.bundivilas.com. Newly restored sumptuous *haveli*. Stylish decor, beautifully furnished with good views from rooftop.

C-D Royal Retreat, inside fort, T0747-244 4426, www.royalretreatbundi.com. Looks run-down but quite clean and well kept inside, open courts, 5 largish rooms most with bath, family-run, good vegetarian restaurant, café, rooftop dining with views, good craft shop, internet, overpriced but in a fabulous location.

C-F Nawal Sagar Palace Balchandpada, T0747-230 0644, nawalsagarpalace@ hotmail.com. Through an imposing door, you find charming, comfortable rooms. Beautifully decorated. New restaurant planned in adjacent wing. Friendly owner, friendly dog.

E-F Kasera Heritage View, below palace, T0747-244 4679, www.kaseraheritageview.com.

Good rooms with attached bathrooms and some with good views, enjoy the rooftop restaurant for a beer and a good view of the palace, but poor reports on the food. Same family owns Kasera and **B-D Kasera Paradise**, with 10 a/c rooms, marble bathrooms and a rooftop restaurant 5 storeys up in an old *haveli*.
E-F R N Haveli, behind Laxmi Nath Temple, T0747-512 0098, rnhavelibundi@yahoo.co.in. 5 rooms in a friendly family home run exclusively by 'woman power', a little persistent but the home cooking is excellent. Recommended.
F-G Haveli Elephant Stables, at base of palace near gate, T(0)9928-154064, elephant stable_guesthouse@hotmail.com. Formerly used to house royal elephants, the 4 simple but huge rooms have mosquito nets and basic Indian toilets, beneath a huge peepal tree in a dusty courtyard. Good home cooking, relaxed.
F-G Lake View Paying Guest House, Bohra Meghwan Ji Ki Haveli, Balchand Para, below the palace, by Nawal Sagar, T0747-244 2326, lakeviewbundi@yahoo.com. 7 simple clean rooms (3 in separate, basic garden annexe with shared bath) in 150-year-old *haveli* with wall paintings, private terrace shared with monkeys and peacocks, lovely views from rooftop, warm welcome, popular, very friendly hosts.
F-G Shivam Guesthouse, outside the walls near the Nawal Sagar, T0747-244 7892, shivam_pg@yahoo.com. Simple, comfortable rooms around a shaded blue courtyard, exceptionally friendly, good home cooking, come for food even if you're not staying.
F-G Uma Megh Haveli, Balchand Para, T0747-244 2191. Very atmospheric, 11 unrestored rooms, 7 with basic attached bathrooms, plus a pleasant garden and restaurant.
G Govindam, opposite Nawal Sagar Palace, T(0)9887-332761. Basic rooms. Friendly family.
G Mangalam, next to Kasera Paradise, T0747-244 2555, mangalam_bundi@yahoo.com. Basic clean rooms, family-run, good reports on food and service.
G Raj Heritage Paying Guest House, Nahar Ka Couhatta, opposite Sathi Cold Drinks, T(0)9251-506925. Backpacker hangout with basic rooms with more being built.

G Tara Home Stay, near Elephant Stables, T(0)9829-718554, tarahomestay@gmail.com, Only a couple of rooms, but exceptional views of the palace.

South of Kota *p233*
E Purvaj, centre of Jhalawar. A delightful old *haveli*, owned by an interesting family, delicious and simple home-cooked meals.

🍴 Eating

Chittaurgarh *p226, map p227*
For the best places to eat, visit the hotels. There are several cheap options near the bus stand.
🍴 **Pratap Palace** (see Sleeping). Tasty Indian in pleasant surroundings.
🍴 **RTDC Café**, near the Vijay Stambha. Handy for visitors to the fort.

Kota *p229*
The best places to eat are the hotels; those listed below offer cheaper alternatives. Good *kulfis* and home-made ices in Sindhi shops.
🍴 **Payal**, Nayapura. Good Indian. Also some Chinese, and Indian-style continental.
🍴 **Venue**, Civil Lines. A/c, good but very spicy Indian, disappointing Western.
🍴 **Hariyali**, Bundi Rd. Good Punjabi, some Chinese/continental. Pleasant garden restaurant, outdoors or under a small shelter, very popular but some way out of town.
🍴 **Jodhpur Sweets**, Ghumanpura Market. Saffron *lassis* and flavoured milks.
🍴 **Palace View**, outdoor meals/snacks. Handy for visitors to the City Palace.
🍴 **Priya**, Nayapura. Popular Indian vegetarian.

Bundi *p230, map p231*
Several of the hotels have pleasant rooftop restaurants, see Sleeping.
🍴 **Diamond**, Suryamahal Chowk. Very popular locally for cheap vegetarian meals, handy when visiting step wells.
🍴 **Sathi Cold Drinks**, Palace Rd. Excellent *lassis* (saffron, spices, pistachio and fruit), pleasant.
🍴 **Sher-e-Punjab**, near Diamond. Non-vegetarian.

☀ Festivals and events

Chittaurgarh *p226, map p227*
Oct/Nov Mira Utsav, 2 days of cultural evening programmes and religious songs in the fort's Mira temple.

Kota *p229*
Mar/Apr Colourful **Gangaur** (18-19 Mar 2010, 6-7 Apr 2011).
Jul/Aug Teej (12-13 Aug 2010, 2-3 Aug 2011).
Sep/Oct Dasara Mela (15-17 Oct 2010, 4-6 Oct 2011). Great atmosphere, with shows in lit up palace grounds.

Bundi *p230, map p231*
Aug Kajli Teej (26-27 Aug 2010, 15-16 Aug 2011), and Bundi Utsav, which takes place 3 days after the Pushkar fair has finished, see box, page 187.
Nov Jhalawar sees the **Chandrabhaga Fair** (20-22 Nov 2010, 9-11 Nov 2011) a cattle and camel fair with all the colour and authenticity of Pushkar but less commercialization. Animals are traded in large numbers, pilgrims come to bathe in the river as the temples become the centre of religious activity and the town is abuzz with all manner of vendors.

⊖ Transport

Chittaurgarh *p226, map p227*
Bicycle hire By railway station, Rs 5 per hr.
Bus Enquiries, T01472-241177. Daily buses to **Bundi** (4 hrs), **Kota** (5 hrs), **Ajmer** (5 hrs) and frequent buses to **Udaipur**.
Train Enquiries, T01472-240131. A 117-km branch line runs from Chittaurgarh to **Udaipur**. At **Mavli Junction** (72 km) another branch runs down the Aravalli scarp to **Marwar Junction** (150 km). The views along this line are very picturesque, though trains are slow, with hard seats. By taking this route you can visit Udaipur, Ajmer and Jodhpur in a circular journey. Call for times as services have been scaled back in recent years. **Jaipur**: *Jaipur Exp*

9770, 0515, 8½ hrs; *Chetak Exp 9616*, 2200, 8½ hrs; both call at **Ajmer** (4½-5 hrs).

Kota *p229*
Bus At least hourly to **Bundi** (45 mins) and a few daily to **Ajmer**, **Chittaurgarh**, **Jhalarapatan** (2½ hrs) and Udaipur; also to **Gwalior**, **Sawai Madhopur** and **Ujjain**.
Train From Kota Junction: **Bharatpur**: *Golden Temple Mail 2903*, 1125, 4 hrs (continues to **Mathura**, 5 hrs). **Mumbai** (**Central**): *Rajdhani Exp 2952*, 2105, 11¾ hrs; *Paschim Exp 2926*, 2345, 15½ hrs; *Golden Temple Mail 2904*, 1440, 15¼ hrs. **New Delhi**: *Rajdhani Exp 2951*, 0330, 5½ hrs; *Golden Temple Mail 2903*, 1125, 7½ hrs; *Dehra Dun Exp 9019*, 1945, 10½ hrs, all via **Sawai Madhopur**, 1½ hrs.

Bundi *p230, map p231*
Bus Enquiries: T0747-244 5422. To **Ajmer** (165 km), 5 hrs; **Jaipur**, several daily, 4 de luxe, 4-5 hrs; **Kota** (37 km), 45 mins; **Chittaurgarh** (157 km), 5 hrs; **Udaipur** (120 km), 3 hrs. For **Jhalarapatan** catch a bus from **Kota** to **Jhalawar**; then auto-rickshaw or local bus for sights. The Ujjain–Jhalawar road is appalling.
Train Enquiries: T0747-244 3582. The station south of town has a train each way between **Kota** and **Neemuch** via **Chittaurgarh**. A direct Delhi service may be running, but involves hours waiting in Kota; better to take the bus to Kota and board trains there.

❶ Directory

Kota *p229*
Internet Acme, 2nd floor, Kalawati Paliwal Market, Gumantpura. **Medical services** MBS Hospital, T0744-232 3261. **Police** T0744-245 0066.

Bundi *p230, map p231*
Banks Exchange can be a problem; try Bank of Baroda, T0747-244 3706. **Internet** Dotted around town. **Medical services** City Hospital, T0747-244 2333.

Contents

Western Rajasthan

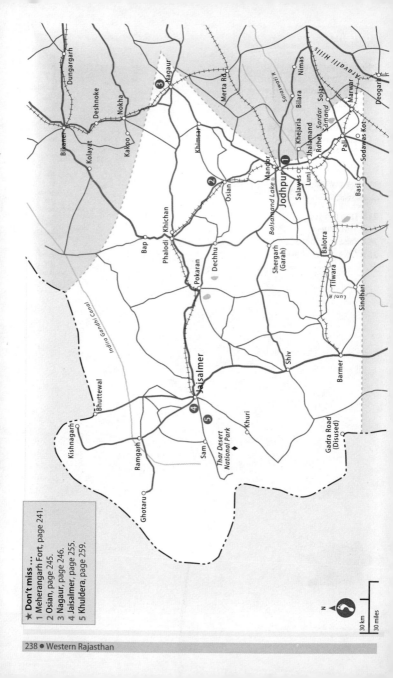

★ Don't miss ...
1 Meherangarh Fort, page 241.
2 Osian, page 245.
3 Nagaur, page 246.
4 Jaisalmer, page 255.
5 Khuldera, page 259.

Bikaner
Dungargarh
Deshnoke
Kolayat
Nokha
Kakoo

Nagaur
Merta Rd
Saraswati R
Nimaj
Bilara
Khejarla
Jhalamand
Rohet
Sardar Samand
Sojat
Marwar
Deogarh
ARAVALLI HILLS

Khinsar
Osian
Jodhpur
Mandor
Luni
Salawas
Pali
Sodawas Kot
Basi

Balsamand Lake

Khichan
Bap
Phalodi
Dechhu
Shergarh (Garah)
Balotra
Tilwara
Luni R
Sindhari

Pokaran

India Gandhi Canal

Jaisalmer
Shiv
Barmer

Bhuttewal
Khuri
Gadra Road (Disused)

Kishnagarh
Ramgarh
Sam
Thar Desert National Park

Ghotaru

N

30 km
30 miles

The desertified West is the Rajasthan conjured by the imagination, a land of formidable clifftop fortresses, camels swaying across windswept sand dunes, and colourful tribes coexisting with the stark landscape, according to Dalrymple, "as if they are growing almost organically out of the dust".

Jaisalmer is perhaps the ultimate expression of these romantic desert images. The amazing, almost painfully picturesque fort crowns a rocky outcrop surrounded by sand dunes that seem to roll away to infinity in the dusty haze. However, no fort in Rajasthan exudes authority as forcefully as Jodhpur's Meherangarh, which looms monstrously over the bluewalled city like a stone battleship borne aloft on a great tidal wave of red rock.

There are interesting excursions from both of these cities; the area south of Jodhpur is dotted with Bishnoi tribal villages, and some of the state's most secluded heritage hotels, while to the north lie the utterly authentic attractions of Nagaur and Osian. Jaisalmer serves as the gateway to desert culture, although you can expect to journey some way beyond its walls before encountering anything remotely untouristy.

Proximity to the Pakistan border makes this a key strategic region for the Indian Army, which from a visitor's point of view means that the roads are exceptionally well maintained, and journeys therefore less bone-jarring than elsewhere in the State. Nevertheless, if it all starts feeling too comfortable, there are plenty of opportunities to hop on a camel's back and shake yourself senseless in good old-fashioned discomfort.

Jodhpur and around

→ *Colour map 2, A3. Phone code: 0291.*

Rajasthan's second largest city, Jodhpur is entirely dominated by its spectacular Meherangarh fort, towering over proceedings below with absolute authority. You could spend most of a day wandering this grand stone edifice on its plinth of red rock, pausing in the warm shafts of sunlight in its honey-coloured courtyards and strolling its chunky, cannon-lined ramparts high above the moat of blue buildings which make up the old city. Up there, birds of prey circle on the thermals, close to eye level, while the city hums below, its rickshaw horns and occasional calls to prayer still audible. Jodhpur's fascinating old city is a hive of activity, the colourful bazars, narrow lanes, and bustling Sardar Market frequented by equally colourful tribal people from the surrounding areas. South of the railway line things are altogether more serene, and nowhere more so than the impressive Umaid Bhawan Palace, its classic exterior belying the art deco extravaganza within. There are also some remarkable sights around Jodhpur: the temples of Osian and Nagaur are well worth a visit and there are some great heritage hotels set in quiet nearby villages. ➤➤ *For listings, see pages 248-254.*

Ins and outs

Getting there Jodhpur has good air, rail and road links with the other major cities of Rajasthan as well as Delhi and Mumbai. Many visitors stop here either on the way to or from Jaisalmer, or on their way down to Udaipur.

Getting around The train and bus stations are conveniently located close to the old city, with most hotels a Rs 20-30 rickshaw ride away, while the airport is 5 km south of town. The old city is small enough to walk around, although many people find a rented bicycle the best way to get about. ➤➤ *See Transport, page 254.*

Tourist information The government tourist office is on the grounds of the **RTDC** ① *Hotel Ghoomar, High Court Rd, T0291-254 5083.* As well as the usual supply of maps and pamphlets, it also organize half-day city tours and village safaris. Also, **Tourist Assistance Force** has a presence at the railway station bus stand and clock tower.

History

The **Rathore** Rajputs had moved to **Marwar** – the 'region of death' – in 1211, after their defeat at Kanauj by Muhammad Ghori. In 1459 Rao Jodha, forced to leave the Rathore capital at Mandore, 8 km to the north, chose this place as his capital because of its strategic location on the edge of the Thar Desert. The Rathores subsequently controlled wide areas of Rajasthan. Rao Udai Singh of Jodhpur (died 1581) received the title of Raja from Akbar, and his son, Sawai Raja Sur Singh (died 1595), conquered Gujarat and part of the Deccan for the emperor. Maharaja Jaswant Singh (died 1678), having supported Shah Jahan in the Mughal struggle for succession in 1658, had a problematic relationship with the subsequent Mughal rule of Aurangzeb, and his son Ajit Singh was only able to succeed him after Aurangzeb's own death in 1707. In addition to driving the Mughals out of Ajmer he added substantially to the Meherangarh Fort in Jodhpur. His successor, Maharaja Abhai Singh (died 1749) captured Ahmedabad, and the state came into treaty relations with the British in 1818.

Jodhpur lies on the once strategic Delhi–Gujarat trading route and the Marwaris managed and benefited from the traffic of opium, copper, silk, sandalwood, dates, coffee and much more besides.

The Old City

The Old City is surrounded by a huge 9.5-km-long wall which has 101 bastions and seven gates, above which are inscribed the names of the places to which the roads underneath them lead. It comprises a labyrinthine maze of narrow streets and lively markets, a great place to wander round and get lost. Some of the houses and temples are of richly carved stone, in particular the red sandstone buildings of the Siré (Sardar) Bazar. Here the **Taleti Mahal** (early 17th century), one of three concubines' palaces in Jodhpur, has the unique feature of *jarokhas* decorated with temple columns.

Meherangarh

① *T0291-254 8790, 0900-1700, foreigners Rs 250, students Rs 200, Indians Rs 20, includes excellent MP3 audio guide and camera fee, video Rs 200, allow at least 2 hrs, there is a pleasant restaurant on the terrace near the ticket office.*

The 'Majestic Fort' sprawls along the top of a steep escarpment with a sheer drop to the south. Originally started by Rao Jodha in 1459, it has walls up to 36 m high and 21 m wide, towering above the plains. Most of what stands today is from the period of Maharajah Jaswant Singh (1638-1678). On his death in 1678, Aurangzeb occupied the fort. However, after Aurangzeb's death Meherangarh returned to Jaswant Singh's son Ajit Singh and remained the royal residence until the Umaid Bhavan was completed in 1943. It is now perhaps the best preserved and presented palace in Rajasthan, an excellent example which the others will hopefully follow.

The summit has three areas: the palace (northwest), a wide terrace to the east of the palace, and the strongly fortified area to the south. There are extensive views from the top. One approach is by a winding path up the west side, possible by rickshaw, but the main approach and car park is from the east. The climb is quite stiff; those with walking difficulties may use the elevator (Rs 15 each way).

◗ *The fort is used for film shoots and adverts, and hosts the Rajasthan Folk Music Festival which is patronized by Mick Jagger. The 2008 event was cancelled in memory of the 249 people killed in the stampede at Chamunda Devi temple in the fort complex who were gathered for Navratra.*

The gateways There were originally seven gateways. The first, the **Fateh Gate**, is heavily fortified with spikes and a barbican that forces a 45° turn. The smaller **Gopal Gate** is followed by the **Bhairon Gate**, with large guardrooms. The fourth, **Toati Gate**, is now missing but the fifth, **Dodhkangra Gate**, marked with cannon shots, stands over a turn in the path and has loopholed battlements for easy defence. Next is the **Marti Gate**, a long passage flanked by guardrooms. The last, **Loha (Iron) Gate**, controls the final turn into the fort and has handprints (31 on one side and five on the other) of royal *satis*, the wives of maharajas. It is said that six queens and 58 concubines became *satis* on Ajit Singh's funeral pyre in 1724. *Satis* carried the Bhagavad Gita with them into the flames and legend has it that the holy book would never perish. The main entrance is through the **Jay (Victory) Pol**.

The palaces From the Loha Gate the ramp leads up to the Suraj (Sun) Pol, which opens onto the Singar Choki Chowk, the main entrance to the museum, see below. Used for royal ceremonies such as the anointing of rajas, the north, west and southwest sides of the Singar Choki Chowk date from the period immediately before the Mughal occupation in 1678. The upper storeys of the chowk were part of the *zenana*, and from the **Jhanki Mahal**

Jodhpur

N

300 metres
300 yards

Sleeping
Bal Samand Palace **1** A3
Blue House **27** B1
Chauhan's Guest House **4** A2
Cosy Guest House **5** A1
Devi Bhavan **6** C2
Durag Niwas Guest
  House **7** B2
Durag Vilas **7** B2
Ghoomar **10** B2
Govind **11** B1
Hare Krishna Guest
  House **9** A1
Haveli **28** A1
Haveli Inn Pal **29** A1
Inn Season **17** C1
Karni Bhawan **12** C3
Krishna Prakash Haveli **9** A1
Madho Niwas **3** C3
Newton's Manor **13** C3
Nora Villa **16** C3
Pal Haveli **29** A1
Raman Palace **15** B2
Ranbanka **2** B2
Ratan Vilas **24** C1
Saji Sanwri **18** B1
Shahi Guest House **8** B1
Singhvi's Haveli **25** B1
Sun City Guest House **23** C2
Umaid Bhawan Palace **20** B3
Yogi's Guest House **5** A1
Youth Hostel **22** C2

Eating
Ajit Bhawan **11** B2
Café Sheesh Mahal **12** A1
Gypsy **8** C1
Hotel Priya **5** B1
Jodhpur Coffee House **10** B1
Kalinga **3** B1
Mishrilal **4** B1
New Jodhpur Lodge **9** B1
On the Rocks **11** B2
Poonam **2** B2
Sankalp **7** C1
Shandar **6** B1
Softy & Softy **2** B2
Uttam **1** B1

(Glimpse Palace) on the upper floor of the north wing the women could look down on the activities of the courtyard. Thus the chowk below has the features characteristic of much of the rest of the *zenana*, *jarokhas* surmounted by the distinctive Bengali-style eaves and beautifully ornate *jali* screens. These allowed cooling breezes to ventilate rooms and corridors in the often stiflingly hot desert summers.

Also typical of Mughal buildings was the use of material hung from rings below the eaves to provide roof covering, as in the columned halls of the **Daulat Khana** and the **Sileh Khana** (armoury), which date from Ajit Singh's reign. The collection of Indian weapons in the armoury is unequalled, with remarkable swords and daggers, often beautifully decorated with calligraphy. Shah Jahan's red silk and velvet tent, lavishly embroidered with gold thread and used in the Imperial Mughal campaign, is in the **Tent Room**. The **Jewel House** has a wonderful collection of jewellery, including diamond eyebrows held by hooks over the ears. There are also palanquins, howdahs and ornate royal cradles, all marvellously well preserved.

The **Phool Mahal** (Flower Palace), above the Sileh Khana, was built by Abhai Singh (1724-1749) as a hall of private audience. The stone *jali* screens are original and there are striking portraits of former rulers, a lavishly gilded ceiling and the Jodhpur coat of arms displayed above the royal couch; the murals of the 36 musical modes are a late 19th-century addition.

The **Umaid Vilas**, which houses Rajput miniatures, is linked to the **Sheesh Mahal** (Mirror Palace), built by Ajit Singh between 1707 and 1724. The room has characteristic large and regularly sized mirror work, unlike Mughal 'mirror palaces'. Immediately to its south, and above the Sardar Vilas, is the **Takhat Vilas**. Added by Maharajah Takhat Singh (1843-1873), it has wall murals of dancing girls, love legends and Krishna Lila, while its ceiling has two unusual features: massive wooden beams to provide support and the curious use of colourful Belgian Christmas tree balls.

The **Ajit Vilas** has a fascinating collection of musical instruments and costumes. On the ground floor of the Takhat Vilas is **Sardar Vilas**, and to its south the **Khabka** and **Chandan Mahals** (sleeping quarters). The **Moti Vilas** wings to the north, east and south of the Moti Mahal Chowk, date from Jaswant Singh's reign. The women could watch proceedings in the courtyard below through the *jali* screens of the surrounding wings. Tillotson suggests that the **Moti Mahal** (Pearl Palace) ① *Rs 150 for 15 mins*, to the west, although placed in the *zenana* of the fort, was such a magnificent building that it could only have served the purpose of a Diwan-i-Am (Hall of Public Audience). The Moti Mahal is fronted by excellently carved 19th-century woodwork, while inside waist-level niches housed oil lamps whose light would have shimmered from the mirrored ceiling. A palmist reads your fortune at Moti Mahal Chowk (museum area).

Meherangarh Fort Palace Museum is in a series of palaces with beautifully designed and decorated windows and walls. It has a magnificent collection of the maharajas' memorabilia – superbly maintained and presented.

Jaswant Thada ⓘ *off the road leading up to the fort, 0900-1700, Rs 30*, is the cremation ground of the former rulers with distinctive memorials in white marble which commemorate Jaswant Singh II (1899) and successive rulers of Marwar. It is situated in pleasant and well-maintained gardens and is definitely worth visiting on the way back from the fort.

The new city

The new city beyond the walls is also of interest. Overlooking the Umaid Sagar is the **Umaid Bhawan Palace** on Chittar Hill. Building started in 1929 as a famine relief exercise when the monsoon failed for the third year running. Over 3000 people worked for 14 years, building this vast 347-room palace of sandstone and marble. The hand-hewn blocks are interlocked into position, and use no mortar. It was designed by HV Lanchester, with the most modern furnishing and facilities in mind, and completed in 1943. The interior decoration was left to the artist JS Norblin, a refugee from Poland; he painted the frescoes in the Throne Room (East Wing). For the architectural historian, Tillotson, it is "the finest example of Indo-Deco. The forms are crisp and precise, and the bland monochrome of the stone makes the eye concentrate on their carved shapes". The royal family still occupy part of the palace.

The **Umaid Bhawan Palace Museum** ⓘ *T0291-251 0101, 0900-1700, Rs 50*, includes the Darbar Hall with its elegantly flaking murals plus a good collection of miniatures, armour and quirky old clocks as well as a bizarre range of household paraphernalia; if it was fashionable in the 1930s, expensive and not available in India, it's in here. Many visitors find the tour and the museum in general disappointing with not much to see (most of the china and glassware you could see in your grandma's cabinets). The palace hotel which occupies the majority of the building has been beautifully restored, but is officially inaccessible to non-residents; try sneaking in for a cold drink and a look at the magnificent domed interior, a remarkable separation from the Indian environment in which it is set (see Sleeping, page 248).

Government Museum ⓘ *Umaid Park, Sat-Thu 1000-1630, Rs 3*, is a time-capsule from the British Raj, little added since Independence, with some moth-eaten stuffed animals and featherless birds, images of Jain Tirthankars, miniature portraits and antiquities. A small zoo in the gardens has a few rare exotic species.

Just southeast of Raikabagh Station are the **Raikabagh Palace** and the **Jubilee Buildings**, public offices designed by Sir Samuel Swinton Jacob in the Indo-Saracenic style. On the Mandore Road, 2 km to the north, is the large **Mahamandir Temple**.

☾ *In 1886, before steam engines were acquired, the Jodhpur Railway introduced camel-drawn trains. The maharaja's luxurious personal saloons (1926) are beautifully finished with inlaid wood and silver fittings and are on display near the Umaid Bhawan Palace.*

Excursions from Jodhpur

A village safari visiting a **Bishnoi village** is recommended, although they have naturally become more touristy over the years. Most tours include the hamlets of **Guda**, famous for wildlife, **Khejarali**, a well-known Bishnoi village, **Raika** cameleers' settlement and **Salawas**, see page 247.

The small, semi-rural village of **Jhalamand**, 12 km south of Jodhpur, is a good alternative to staying in the city, particularly if you have your own transport. It works especially well as a base from which to explore the Bishnoi and Raika communities.

Marwar, 8 km north of Jodhpur, is the old 14th-century capital of Mandore, situated on a plateau. Set around the old cremation ground with the red sandstone *chhatris* of the Rathore rulers, the gardens are usually crowded with Indian tourists at weekends. The **Shrine of the 33 Crore Gods** is a hall containing huge painted rock-cut figures of heroes and gods, although some of the workmanship is a little crude. The largest deval, a combination of temple and cenotaph, is Ajit Singh's (died 1724); worth a closer look but is unkempt. The remains of an eighth-century Hindu temple is on a hilltop nearby.

Bal Samand Lake is the oldest artificial lake in Rajasthan, 5 km north. Dating from 1159, it is surrounded by parkland laid out in 1936 where the 19th-century **Hawa Mahal** was turned into a royal summer palace. Although the interior is European in style, it has entirely traditional red sandstone filigree windows and beautifully carved balconies. The peaceful and well-maintained grounds exude calm and tranquillity, while the views over the lake are simply majestic.

Around Jodhpur → *For listings, see pages 248-254.*

The temples of Osian are remarkable as much for their location in the middle of the desert as their architecture, while Nagaur is one of Rajasthan's busiest but most unaffected cities. The area south of Jodhpur is refreshingly green and fertile compared to the desert landscapes of most of Western Rajasthan (although it can be very dry from March until the monsoon). Leaving the city, the landscape soon becomes agricultural, punctuated by small, friendly villages, some housing stunning heritage hotels.

Osian → *Colour map 4, A3.*

Surrounded by sand dunes, this ancient town north of Jodhpur in the Thar Desert contains the largest group of eighth- to 10th-century Hindu and Jain temples in Rajasthan. The typical Pratihara Dynasty **temple complex** is set on a terrace whose walls are finely decorated with mouldings and miniatures. The sanctuary walls have central projections with carved panels' and above these rise curved towers. The doorways are usually decorated with river goddesses, serpents and scrollwork. The 23 temples are grouped in several sites north, west and south of the town. The western group contains a mixture of Hindu temples, including the **Surya Temple** (early eighth century) with beautifully carved pillars. The Jain **Mahavira Temple** (eighth to 10th centuries) the best preserved, 200 m further on a hillock, rises above the town, and boasts a fantastically gaudy interior. The 11th- to 12th-century **Sachiya Mata Temple** is a living temple of the Golden Durga. Osian is well worth visiting.

Khimsar → *Colour map 2, C3.*

On the edge of the desert, 80 km northeast of Jodhpur, Khimsar was founded by the Jain saint Mahavir 2500 years ago. The isolated, battle scarred, 16th-century moated castle of which a section remains, had a *zenana* added in the mid-18th century and a regal wing added in the 1940s. See Sleeping, page 250, for one of the best hotels in the state.

Nagaur → *Colour map 4, C4.*
ⓘ *Foreigners Rs 50, Indians Rs 10, camera Rs 25, video Rs 50.*

Nagaur, 137 km north of Jodhpur, was a centre of Chishti Sufis. It attracts interest as it preserves some fine examples of pre-Mughal and Mughal architecture. The dull stretch of desert is enlivened by Nagaur's fort palace, temples and *havelis*. The city walls are said to date from the 11th- to 12th-century Chauhan period. Akbar built the mosque here and there is a shrine of the disciple of Mu'inuddin Chishti of Ajmer, see page 178. **Ahhichatragarh Fort**, which dominates the city, is absolutely vast, contains palaces of the Mughal emperors and of the Marwars, and is being restored with help from the Paul Getty Foundation. The Akbar Mahal is stunningly elegant and perfectly proportioned. The fort also has excellent wall paintings and interesting ancient systems of rainwater conservation and storage, ably explained by a very knowledgeable curator. It was awarded a UNESCO Heritage Award in 2000.

Khichan → *Colour map 4, C2.*
Four kilometres from Phalodi, southwest of Bikaner just off the NH15, is a lovely, picturesque village with superb red sandstone *havelis* of the Oswal Jains. Beyond the village are sand dunes and mustard fields, and a lake which attracts ducks and other waterfowl. The once small quiet village has grown into a bustling agricultural centre and a prominent bird-feeding station. Jain villagers put out grain behind the village for winter visitors; up to 8000 demoiselle cranes and occasionally common eastern cranes can be seen in December and January on the feeding grounds. At present you can go along and watch without charge.

Pokaran → *Colour map 4, C2.*
Pokaran, between Jaisalmer and Jodhpur, stands on the edge of the great desert with dunes stretching 100 km west to the Pakistan border. It provides tourists with a mid-way stopover between Bikaner/Jodhpur and Jaisalmer as it did for royal and merchant caravans in the past. The impressive 16th-century yellow sandstone **Pokaran Fort** ⓘ *foreigners Rs 50, Indians Rs 10, camera Rs 50*, overlooking a confusion of streets in the town below, has a small museum with an interesting collection of medieval weapons, costumes and paintings. There are good views from the ramparts. Pokaran is also well known for its potters who make red-and-white pottery and terracotta horses/elephants. **Ramdeora**, the Hindu and Jain pilgrim centre nearby, has Bishnoi hamlets and a preserve for blackbuck antelope, Indian gazelle, bustards and sand grouse. **Ramdeora Fair** (September) is an important religious event with cattle trading.

   Khetolai, about 25 km northwest of Pokaran, is the site of India's first nuclear test explosion held underground on 18 March 1974, and of further tests in May 1998.

Balotra and around → *Colour map 2, A2.*
The small textile town, 100 km southwest of Jodhpur, is known for its traditional weaving using pit looms and block prints, although many are now mechanized causing pollution of the Luni River. Nearby is the beautiful Jain temple with elephant murals at **Nakoda**. **Kanana**, near Balotra, celebrates **Holi** with stage shows and other entertainment. There is a *dharamshala* at Nakoda and guesthouses at Balotra. At **Tilwara**, 127 km from Jodhpur, the annual Mallinathji **cattle fair** is a major event, which takes place just after **Holi** on the dry Luni riverbed. Over 50,000 animals are brought (although this has declined in recent years due to the drought), including Kapila (Krishna's) cows and Kathiawari horses,

making it Rajasthan's largest. Few tourists make it this far as so it is much less commercial than Pushkar. Try and go with a Rajasthani-speaking guide as the farmers and traders are very happy to allow you in on the negotiations as well as describing the key things to look for when buying a camel (the front legs should not rub against its belly, for instance). There are some interesting trade stalls including sword makers.

Salawas
Salawas, about 30 minutes' drive south from Jodhpur, is well known for its pit loom weaving. The village produces *durries*, carpets, rugs, bed covers and tents using camel hair, goat hair, wool and cotton in colourful and interesting patterns. You can visit the weavers' co-operatives such as **Roopraj** and **Salawas Durry Udhyog** (anyone on a Bishnoi village tour is normally frogmarched into one of them), where you can buy authentic village crafts, but watch out for high prices and pushy salesmen.

Luni → Colour map 2, A3.
The tiny bustling village of Luni, 40 km from Jodhpur, sits in the shadow of the 19th-century red sandstone Fort Chanwa which has been converted to a hotel. With its complex of courtyards, water wheels, and intricately carved façades, the fort and its village offer an attractive and peaceful alternative to the crowds of Jodhpur. The village of **Sanchean**, which you will pass through on the way, is worth exploring.

Rohet and Sardar Samand → Colour map 2, A3.
Rohet, 50 km north of Jodhpur, was once a picturesque hamlet settled by the Bishnoi community. It is now a busy highway village although it has a busy bazar and is pleasant to wander around. At the end of the village a lake attracts numerous winter migrants in addition to resident birds. Here also are the family cenotaphs. Rohetgarh, a small 'castle' beside the lake, which has been converted to a hotel, has a collection of antique hunting weapons. The hotel will organize trips to the local Bishnoi villages. It is quite usual to see blue bull, black buck and other antelopes in the fields. Village life can be very hard in this arid environment but the Bishnoi are a dignified people who delight in explaining their customs. You can take part in the opium tea ceremony which is quite fun and somewhat akin to having a pint with the locals down at the pub.

The lake nearby is a beautiful setting for the royal 1933 art deco hunting lodge, **Sardar Samand Palace**, see page 251. The lake attracts pelicans, flamingos, cranes, egrets and kingfishers and the wildlife sanctuary has blackbuck, gazelle and nilgai, but the water level drops substantially during summer; the lake has actually dried up from April to June in recent years. Sardar Samand is 60 km southeast of Jodhpur.

Nimaj → Colour map 3, A1.
A small feudal town 110 km east of Jodhpur on the way to the Jaipur–Udaipur highway, the real attraction is the artificial lake, **Chhatra Sagar**, 4 km away. The ex-ruling family have recreated a 1920s-style tented hunting lodge on the lake's dam, which offers amazing views over the water and a genuine family welcome (see Sleeping, page 251).

For Sleeping and Eating price codes and other relevant information, see Essentials pages 28-33.

⊜ Sleeping

Jodhpur *p241, map p242*

Certain budget hotels, including some of those listed below, may quote low room prices that depend on you booking a tour or camel safari with them; some have been known to raise the price dramatically or even evict guests who refuse. Confirm any such conditions before checking in.

LL Umaid Bhawan Palace, T0291-251 0101, www.tajhotels.com. Freshly renovated in stunning contemporary art deco, with 36 rooms and 40 beautifully appointed suites, best with garden-view balconies and unforgettable marble bathrooms, rather cool and masculine, far removed from the typical Rajasthani colour-fest, soaring domed lobbies, formal gardens and an extraordinary underground swimming pool with smart new spa treatment rooms to one side. Good for once-in-a-lifetime indulgence (this is where Liz Hurley tied the knot), but money perhaps better spent elsewhere.

AL Ranbanka, Circuit House Rd, T(0)9811-892683, www.ranbankahotels.com. 31 stylish rooms and beautiful suites in period property, communal areas a little unloved but staff are charming, lovely pool, large garden, nice lounge areas adjoining the restaurant. Popular with groups. New shopping centre with cinema and cafés next door is coming soon.

A-C Inn Season, PWD Rd, T0291-261 6400, www.innseasonjodhpur.com. 11 classy a/c rooms with interesting layout and private areas in , well-run hotel, good pool in beautiful gardens, a definite cut above.

A-C Karni Bhawan, Palace Rd, T0291-251 2101, www.karnihotels.com. 30 clean, simple, classy rooms (20 a/c), each with a different theme and period furniture to match, in 1940s sandstone 'colonial bungalow' (on

3 floors). Village-theme restaurant, peaceful lawns, clean pool, unhurried helpful staff. More expensive and lacking the charm of its neighbour **Devi Bhavan** (see below).

B-C Pal Haveli, behind clock tower in the middle of town, T0291-329 3328, www.palhaveli.com. 20 chic and atmospheric rooms in authentic 200-year-old *haveli* with stylishly decorated drawing room/mini-museum, attractive courtyard dining area plus good views from roof bar/restaurant of both the fort and clock tower. Occasional theme nights are held. Massage available, friendly staff and chilled vibe.   Recommended.

B-D Krishna Prakash Haveli, Killikhana, T0291-320 0254, www.kpheritage.com. Pleasant and spacious rooms with bath in 100-year-old building, "heartfully decorated" with repro antique furniture, some facing fort, slightly less inspired ones in recently added block, quite close to base of fort so impressive views from stylish shaded rooftop restaurant. One extra special suite with a swimming pool size bathtub and 3 rooms.

C Nora Villa, 37 Central School Scheme, south of Panch Batti Circle, T0291-309 4439, noravilla@sify.com. Indian facsimile of a British B&B, without the awkward silences at breakfast, in a far-flung but pleasantly lived-in house with board games and lots of Hindi movies in a comfy living room. Unremarkable but pleasant rooms, a different atmosphere.

C-D Devi Bhavan, 1 Ratanada Circle, T0291-251 1067, www.devibhawan.com. Beautiful rooms with bath and most with a/c, delightful shady garden with lovely new pool, excellent Indian dinner (set timings), Rajput family home. Popular with independent travellers. Recommended.

C-D Haveli Inn Pal, T0291-261 2519, www.haveliinnpal.com. Quirkily designed rooms, some with huge windows over-looking fort, some with lake views and unusual marble shower troughs, others with beds you need a ladder to get into, fantastic furniture, rooftop restaurant with commanding views and a rare patch of lawn, pleasant, Recommended.

C-D Madho Niwas, New Airport Rd, Ratanada, T0291-251 2486, madhoniwas@satyam.net.in.16 simple rooms in art deco 1920s bungalow. Thakur Dalvir Singh oversees excellent Marwari meals in garden, small plunge pool. His family at Bhenswar and Ranakpur can organize excellent safaris, treks, etc.

C-D Ratan Vilas, Loco Shed Rd, Ratanada, T0291-261 4418, www.ratanvilas.com. 15 rooms, some a/c, arranged around beautiful courtyard in elegant period property. Peaceful as no TVs. Very well maintained, lovely gardens with seated areas, friendly family. Recommended.

C-E Hotel Ghoomar (RTDC), High Court Rd, T0291-254 4010. Most rooms not worth considering, but 'super-de luxe' a/c rooms have been renovated to a high standard.

C-E Shahi Guest House, City Police, Gandhi St, opposite Narsingh Temple, T0291-262 3802, www.shahiguesthouse.com. Enchanting 350-year-old mughal-style *haveli* with 6 quirky rooms (4 a/c, 2 with air-coolers) set around central courtyard. The building was traditionally the *janana dodi*, or women's area, of Rajput officers' quarters. The Queen's Palace room and Honeymoon Suite are particularly lovely. Friendly family and little rooftop restaurant with beautiful views of the old city and the fort. Charming young family hosts.

C-E Sun City Guest House, 1/C High Court Colony, Ratanada, T0291-262 5880. 8 good-sized, clean, basic rooms run by very enthusiastic and friendly family.

C-F Hotel Haveli (formerly **Haveli Guest House**), Makaran Mohalla, opposite Turjika Jhalra, T0291-261 4615, www.haveliguest house.com. Attractive sandstone building with 22 simple, clean rooms, prices vary according to view, cheerful decor, breezy roof terrace with vegetarian restaurant and great views of fort, particularly atmospheric

in the evening with trickling fountains, comfy lounges and nightly live music and dance.

C-G Singhvi's Haveli, Navchokiya, Ramdevjika Chowk, T0291-262 4293, singhvi15adhaveli@hotmail.com. 11 rooms in charming, 500-year-old *haveli* (one of the oldest), tastefully decorated, friendly family. New extra-special suite with mirror-work ceiling reminiscent of the fort that towers above. Nice chill-out area. Recommended.

D Newton's Manor, 86 Jawahar Colony, Central School Rd, T0291-267 0986, www.newtonsmanor.com. 5 quaintly kitsch a/c rooms, touches of Victoriana plus stuffed animals, breakfast and dinner on request, a break from the norm.

D-F Saji Sanwri, Gandhi St, near City Police Station, T0291-244 0305, www.saji sanwri.com. Hugely varied choice of interestingly furnished rooms in old building with roof café and friendly if slightly batty lady owner, who has big plans to add more rooms and an internet café. No commission.

D-G Blue House, Sumer Bhawan, Moti Chowk, T0291-262 1396, bluehouse36@hotmail.com. 11 clean rooms with bath (hot water all day), home-cooked meals, great views from rooftop restaurant, mixed reports on food and service. Be wary of trips to cousin's overpriced handicrafts shop.

D-G Yogi's Guest House, Raj Purohit Ji Ki Haveli, Manak Chowk, old town, T0291-264 3436, yogiguesthouse@hotmail.com. 12 rooms, most in 500-year-old *haveli*, clean, modern bathrooms, camel/jeep safaris, experienced management. Lovely atmosphere.

E Durag Vilas, 1 Old Public Park, near Circuit House, T0291-251 2298. Family-run, friendly, and helpful, with 10 quiet, air-cooled rooms with shower, lacks atmosphere, travel bookings, desert safaris, free lift from station/airport.

E-G Cosy Guest House, Novechokiya Rd, in Brahm Puri, a narrow lane full of cheap guesthouses just west of the fort, T0291-261 2066, www.cosyguesthouse.com.

6 clean and simple little rooms, good if slightly pricey home-cooked meals (other restaurants 15-min walk), outstanding roof-top views of old city, sociable atmosphere, can be good for meeting other travellers.

E-G Govind, Station Rd, opposite GPO, T0291-262 2758, www.govindhotel.com. 12 cleanish rooms, recently smartened up, some a/c, good rooftop vegetarian restaurant with real coffee, fort views, camel safaris, bus and rail ticketing, luggage storage, internet, friendly, very helpful owner but noisy location.

E-G Hare Krishna Guest House, Killi Khana, Mehron Ka Chowk, T0291-265 4367, harekrishnaguesthouse@hotmail.com. 7 small, clean, characterful and airy rooms in Brahmin family home, plus 6 newer rooms with fort and city views, very welcoming.

E-G Raman Palace, opposite Keshar Bagh, Shiv Rd, T0291-251 3980. Family atmosphere, 20 clean though simply furnished rooms with bath (hot water) in nice building made of Jaisalmer sandstone, 3 with a/c, traditional meals, quiet area, pleasant rooftop, friendly and efficient owner.

F Durag Niwas Guest House, Old Public Park Lane, near Circuit House, T0291-251 2385, www.durag-niwas.com. Cheaper and more character than **Durag Vilas** next door. Runs a women's craft collective 'Sambhali' on-site.

F Youth Hostel, Bhatia Circle, Ratanada, T0291-251 0160. Attractive, well-located building with 5 rooms and 6 dorms. Friendly staff, camping.

F-G Chauhan's Guest House, Fort Rd, T0291-254 1497. Quirky homestay offering courses in Hindi, yoga, music, painting, relaxing café, family-run, set above large art shop where you can watch painters at work, book exchange.

Excursions from Jodhpur *p244*
A Bal Samand Palace (WelcomHeritage), T0291-257 2321, www.welcomheritage.com. In extensive grounds on the lake, 9 attractively furnished suites in an atmospheric palace and 26 rooms in the imaginatively renovated stables, restaurant (mainly buffet), lovely pool, boating, pleasant orchards which attract nilgai, jackals and peacocks, has a calming, tranquil atmosphere.

B Jhalamand Garh, Jhalamand, T0291-272 0481, www.heritagehotelsindia.com. 17 comfortable rooms in whitewashed, family-run period property. Good local dishes, atmospheric dining hall, jeep, horse and camel safaris arranged, perhaps not the most professional set up but charming.

Osian *p245*

Also some **E** and **F** guesthouses in town.
L Camel Camp, on the highest sand dunes, T0291-243 7023, www.camelcamposian.com. A beautiful complex of 50 double-bedded luxury tents with modern conveniences (attached baths, hot showers), superb restaurant and bar plus an amazing pool – quite a sight at the top of a sand dune! Tariff inclusive of meals and camel safaris, ask in advance for jeep/camel transfers to avoid a steep climb up the dunes. Recommended.

Khimsar *p245*

AL Khimsar Fort, T01585-262 345, www.khimsarfort.com. 48 large, comfortable a/c rooms, good restaurant on breezy rooftop with lovely views, fabulous pool, yoga, gym, beautiful large gardens, fire dances at the illuminated medieval fort, award-winning heritage hotel, one of the best in Rajasthan.

AL Khimsar Sand Dunes Village, 6 km from the fort, contact fort as above. 16 ethnically styled luxury huts in the heart of the dunes around a small lake, unbeatable setting, 'safaris' by camel cart.

Nagaur *p246*

AL Royal Camp, T0291-257 2321, www.marudharhotels.com. Operates during the camel fair (when the price rises to **L**) and Oct-Mar. 20 delightful 2-bed furnished tents (hot water bottles, heaters, etc), flush toilets, hot water in buckets, dining tent for buffets, all inside fort walls. An experience.

D-F Mahaveer International, Vijay Vallabh Chowk, near bus stand, T01582-243158. 15 reasonable rooms, 7 a/c, huge dining hall, friendly knowledgeable manager.
E Shree Aditya, Ajmer Rd, near Vyas petrol pump, T01582-245438. Brand new building with 24 modern rooms, 12 a/c.

Pokaran p246
A Tented Resort, 61 km from Pokaran, Manwar, 2.5 km away on a sand dune. Good 2-bed tents with hot showers, flush toilets, meals, camel, jeep safaris and visits to Bishnoi villages.
A-B Fort Pokaran, T02994-222274, www.fortpokaran.com. 19 quaint, quirky rooms with bath (some run-down), old 4-posters, some carved columns, good hot lunches Rs 200-250 (order ahead if passing through town), service a little detached.
B-C Manwar Desert Camp, 61 km from Pokaran in Manwar, has beautifully designed cottages with attractive interiors, some a/c, restaurant (a good lunch stop), handicrafts.
E Motel Pokaran (RTDC), on NH15, T02994-222275. A ramshackle building with 8 sparse rooms, plus 5 passable garden cottages.

Luni p247
A Fort Chanwa, T02931-284 216, www.fort chanwa.com. 47 good rooms in 200-year-old fort, not large but well furnished, individually designed, excellent Rajasthani meals in impressive dining room, pleasant lawn for drinks, excellent pool and well managed.

Rohet and Sardar Samand p247
A Rohetgarh, Rohet, T0291-243 1161, www.rohetgarh.com. 34 pleasant rooms, some cramped, attached baths (avoid rooms near outdoor restaurant), in 1622 fort. Fine Rajasthani food, ordinary architecture but in beautiful environment, pleasant lake view terraces, lovely pool, health club, riding and safaris to Bishnoi, Raika and artisans' villages, boating on the lake, a relaxing getaway.
A Sardar Samand Palace, Sardar Samand, T02960-245001, www.marudharhotels.com. 19 colonial-style rooms (11 a/c), in a slightly

forbidding-looking building. Built in 1933 as a hunting lodge, much of the furniture is original, and lends a very un-Indian feel. Safaris and boating trips arranged in the season, Nov best time for birdwatching on the lake, good pool and tennis court, isolated but atmospheric.

Nimaj p247
LL Chhatra Sagar, 4 km from Nimaj, T02939-230118, www.chhatrasagar.com. Open 1 Oct-31 Mar. 11 beautiful colonial-style tents on the banks of a very picturesque reservoir. The ex-rulers of Nimaj have recreated the hunting lodge of their forefathers to great effect, and still live on the lake themselves, so a very convivial family atmosphere. Safaris arranged, all meals included in the tariff. Recommended.

Eating

Jodhpur p241, map p242
The best restaurants are in hotels; reserve ahead. Rooftop restaurants in most budget and mid-range hotels welcome non-residents. For *Daal-bhatti, lassi* and *kachoris* head for Jalori and Sojati gates. Great food at **Pal Haveli** and **Hotel Haveli** (see Sleeping).
¶¶¶ Ajit Bhawan, Airport Rd, T0291-251 1410. Evening buffet, excellent meal in garden on a warm evening with entertainment, but poor atmosphere if eating indoors in winter.
¶¶¶ Umaid Bhavan, T0291-251 0101. Fabulous setting and fine food make it a great place for dinner. **Pillars**, a tiny garden restaurant, can be hired for one couple for Rs 2000, the most romantic setting in town.
¶¶ Gypsy, PWD Colony, T0291-510 3888. 1130-1530 and 1900-2300. Good range of Indian, continental and Mexican dishes, choice of indoor or outdoor seating, swanky place popular with well-off locals.
¶¶ Kalinga, opposite station. Western and Indian. A/c, good food (try butter chicken and aubergine dishes), friendly service, music may not please, breakfast good value.

¶¶ **On the Rocks**, near **Ajit Bhavan**, T0291-510 2701. Good mix of Indian and continental, plus a relaxing bar, patisserie, ice cream parlour and lovely gardens.
¶¶ **Sankalp**, 12th Rd (west of city centre), 1030-2300. Upmarket a/c South Indian, dosas come with a fantastic range of chutneys, good service. Recommended.
¶ **Café Sheesh Mahal**, behind clock tower and next to **Pal Haveli**. Great cappuccino and macchiato in stylish coffee lounge.
¶ **Hotel Priya**, 181 Nai Sarak. Fantastic special *thalis* for Rs 55 and extra quick service.
¶ **Jodhpur Coffee House**, Sojati Gate. Good South Indian snacks and *thalis*.
¶ **Mishrilal**, High Court Rd. Probably the best *lassis* in town.
¶ **New Jodhpur Lodge**, a real challenge to find, ask for Golion ki Haveli in Tripoliya Bazar in the old city, T0291-261 3340. A family home which offers good, basic *thalis* for Rs 30 in a shaded courtyard, quite an experience.
¶ **Poonam**, High Court Rd. Pure vegetarian Indian. "Gorgeous 4-ft masala dosas".
¶ **Shandar**, Jalori Gate. Indian vegetarian. Good food and sweets.
¶ **Softy and Softy**, High Court Rd. Excellent sweets and *namkeen*, thick shakes, fun for people-watching.
¶ **Uttam**, High Court Rd, near Sojati Gate. Good a/c *thali* restaurant friendly, fast service.

⊛ Festivals and events

Jodhpur *p241, map p242*
Jul/Aug Nag Panchami, when Naga (*naag*), the cobra, is worshipped. The day is dedicated to Sesha, the 1000-headed god or *Anant* (infinite) Vishnu, who is often depicted reclining on a bed of serpents. In Jodhpur, snake charmers gather for a colourful fair in Mandore.
Oct Marwar Festival (21-22 Oct 2010, 10-11 Oct 2011), held at full moon, includes music, puppet shows, turban-tying competitions, camel polo and ends with a fire dance on the dunes at Osian.

Oct Jodhpur Music Festival. Coinciding with Kartik Purnima, the brightest full moon of the year, Jodhpur's Rajasthan International Folk Festival (RIFF) is an eclectic mix of master musicians from local Rajasthan communities, acts from around the world and cutting-edge global dance music at Club Mehran. There are workshops and interactive daytime sessions for visitors. Some performances are around the city, while the main stage and club are in the stunning Mehrangahr Fort itself. See www.jodhpurfolkfestivadeluxel.org for dates.

Nagaur *p246*
Jan/Feb The popular **Cattle and Camel Fair** (22-25 Jan 2010, 10-13 Feb 2011) is held just outside the town. There are camel races, cock fights, folk dancing and music. The fields become full of encampments of pastoral communities, tribal people and livestock dealers with their cattle, camels, sheep, goats and other animals.

⚙ Shopping

Jodhpur *p241, map p242*
Jodhpur is famous for its once-popular riding breeches although it is pricey to get a pair made these days, tie-dye fabrics, lacquer work and leather shoes. Export of items over 100 years old is prohibited. The main areas are: **Sojati Gate** for gifts; **Station Rd** and Sarafa Bazar for jewellery; **Tripolia Bazar** for handicrafts; **Khanda Falsa** and Kapra Bazar for tie-dye; **Lakhara Bazar** for lac bangles. **Raj Rani** has a nice selection of more unusual designed clothes (probably from Pushkar) at Makrana Mohalla, near clock tower. Shoes are made in **Mochi Bazar**, **Sardarpura** and **Clock Tower**, *bandhanas* in **Bambamola**, and around **Siwanchi** and **Jalori Gates**. *Durries* are woven at **Salawas**, 18 km away. In most places you'll need to bargain.

Antiques

Shops on road between Umaid and Ajit Bhawans, flourishing trade though pricey. **Kirti Art Collection**, T0291-251 2136. Has a good selection. Recommended.

Clothing and lifestyle

New parade of shops next to Ajit Bhawan (Circuit House Rd) including beautiful designer jewellery shop **Amrapali**, clothes and prints from Anokhi and Pahnava. Also new shopping centre coming next to Ranbanka Palace on the same road with cinema and cafés.

Handloom and handicrafts

Chauhan's (see Sleeping). Great range of artworks and miniatures at fair prices. You can also watch artists at work.
Krishna Arts and Crafts, by Tija Mata temple on main road running west from clock tower. Interesting shop, fixed prices.
Marasthaly, High Court Rd.
Marwar Heritage Art School, 116 Kamal, T0291-5132187. Among many shops keeping the miniature painting tradition alive.
Rajasthan Khadi Sangathan, BK ka Bagh.
Shriganesham, 1st floor, outside **Pal Haveli**, behind clock tower. Wide selection.

Jewellery

Amrapali, near Ajit Bhawan, Circuit House Rd. Beautiful designer jewellery in gold and silver with a range of traditional pieces. Recommended.
Gems & Art Plaza, Circuit House Rd. As patronized by Angelina Jolie. Some nice pieces in Kundan and Minakari styles, gaudy rings.

Spices

Mohanlal Verhomal Spices, 209-B, Kirana Merchant Vegetable Market (inside the market to the left of clock tower), T0291-261 5846, www.mvspices.com. Sought after for hand-mixed spices, but quality assured and is simply the best spice outlet in the city. Usha, along with her 6 sisters and mother,

runs the shop. Insist your guide takes you here as many have tried to pass themselves off as her shop.

Pokaran *p246*

Kashida, just outside town, Jaisalmer–Bikaner Rd, T02994-222 511. Excellent handwoven crafts from the desert region, clean, well laid out, reasonably priced, profits help local self-help projects, part of the URMUL trust (see box, page 272).

▲ Activities and tours

Jodhpur *p240, map p242*
Body and soul

Ayurvedic massages are offered by **Khimsar Fort**, page 250, **Pal Haveli** (see Sleeping) and **Ajit Bhawan**, page 251.

Tour operators

Many of the hotels organize village safaris, as does the tourist office, which charges Rs 1100 for 4 people including car, guide and tips given to villagers. City sightseeing, starts from tourist office at **Ghoomar Hotel**, T0291-254 5083: half day (0830-1300, 1400-1800). Fort and palaces, Jaswant Thada, Mandore Gardens, Government Museum, bazar around Old City Clock Tower.
Aravalli Safari, 4 Kuchaman House Area, Airport Rd, T0291-262 6799.
Exclusive India, Kishan Villas, Police Line Rd, Ratanada, T0291-342006, exclinjdh@ datainfosys.net. Ask for Rajendra Singh Rathore who is very knowledgeable and an excellent companion.
Forts & Palaces, 15 Old Public Park, T0291-251 1207, www.palaces-tours.com.
Marwar Eco-Cultural Tours, Makrana Mohalla near **Haveli Guest House**, T0291-513 2409, www.nativeplanet.org/tours/india. NGO-run tours into tribal country, connecting with a mix of settled and nomadic tribes. Profits divided between the NGO and communities.

⊖ Transport

Jodhpur *p241, map p242*
Air
Transport to town: by taxi, Rs 300; auto-rickshaw, Rs 150. **Indian Airlines**, near Bhati crossroads, T0291-2510757, 1000-1300, 1400-1700; airport enquiries T0291-251 2617, flies to **Delhi, Jaipur, Mumbai, Udaipur.** **Jet Airways**, T0291-510 2222, airport T0291-251 5551, to **Delhi** and **Mumbai.**

Bus
Local Minibuses cover most of the city except Fort and Umaid Bhavan Palace. For **Mandore**, frequent buses leave from Paota Bus Stand. Also several daily buses to **Salawas, Luni** (40 km), **Rohet** (450 km) and **Osian** (65km).
Long distance RST Bus Stand, near Raikabagh Railway Station, T0291-254 4989. 1000-1700; bookings also at tourist office. A convenient bus route links Jodhpur with **Ghanerao** and **Ranakpur, Kumbhalgarh** and **Udaipur.** Other daily services include: **Abu Rd**, 6 hrs; **Ahmedabad**, 10 hrs; **Ajmer**, 5 hrs; **Jaipur**, frequent, 8 hrs; **Jaisalmer**, 0530 (depart Jaisalmer, 1400), 5-6 hrs; faster than train but scenically tedious; **Pali**, 1 hr; **Udaipur**, 7 hrs by rough road, best to book a good seat a day ahead.
Private operators arrive at Barakuttulah Stadium west of town, to a scrum of rickshaw drivers: pay around Rs 30 to the old city. Some companies have offices opposite railway station, eg **HR Travels, Sun City Tours**, and **Sethi Yatra**, or book at **Govind Hotel** (see Sleeping, page 250).

Car and taxi
Car hire from tourist office, **Ghoomar Hotel**, whole day about Rs 900; half day Rs 500. For a taxi, T0291-262 0238.

Rickshaw
Railway station to fort should be about Rs 25 (may demand Rs 50; try walking away).

Train
Jodhpur Station enquiries: T131. Open 0800-2400. Reservations: T0291-263 6407. Open 0900-1300, 1330-1600. Advance reservations, next to GPO. Tourist Bureau, T0291-254 5083 (0500-2300). **International tourist waiting room** for passengers in transit (ground floor), with big sofas and showers; clean Indian toilets in 2nd-class waiting room on the 1st floor of the station foyer.

To: **Agra**: *Jodhpur-Howrah Exp 2308*, 1945, 12¾ hrs, continues via **Varanasi** to **Kolkata.** **Ahmedabad** via **Abu Rd (Mount Abu)**: *Ranakpur Exp 4707*, 1510, 5½ hrs; *Surya Nagari Exp 2479*, 1845, 9½ hrs (Abu Rd 4½-5½ hrs), both continue to **Mumbai** (17 hrs). **Barmer**: *Barmer Exp 4059*, 0645, 3½ hrs. **Delhi**: *Mandore Exp 2462*, 1930, 11 hrs (OD); *Jodhpur Delhi Exp 4060*, 2230, 12½ hrs (OD). **Kalka/Haridwar** via **Bikaner**: *Kalka Exp 4888/ Link Exp 4888A*, 1045, 23 hrs; **Jaipur**: *Inter-City Exp 2467*, 0500, 6 hrs; *Mandore Exp 2462*, 1930, 5 hrs; *Marudhar Exp 4854/4864*, 0915, 5 hrs. **Jaisalmer (via Osian)**: *Jodhpur Jaisalmer Exp*, and *Jaisalmer Exp 4059*, 0645, 6½ hrs; *Jaisalmer Exp 4810*, 2330, 6½ hrs. **Varanasi** via Agra and Lucknow: *Marudhar Exp 4854/ 4864*, 0915, 12 hrs (**Agra**) 19 hrs (**Lucknow**), 26 hrs (**Varanasi**).

⊙ Directory

Jodhpur *p241, map p242*
Banks 1030-1400. Plenty of ATMs around Sojati Gate. For TC: **State Bank of India**, High Court Rd (inside High Court complex). Currency and TCs. **Internet** Sify i-Way, Ratanada Rd behind Raman Guest House and behind clock tower, near Café Sheesh Mahal. Also at **Ghoomar Hotel** and most guesthouses. **Medical services** Ambulance: T102. MG Hospital, T0291-636437. Dispensary: Paota, Residency. Mon-Sat 0800-1200, 1700-1900, Sun 0800-1200. **Post** GPO, south of railway station, 1000-2000, Sat 1000-1600. **Useful contacts** Fire: T101. Police: T100.

Jaisalmer and around

→ *Phone code: 02992. Population: 80,000.*

The approach to Jaisalmer is magical as the city rises out of the vast barren desert like an approaching ship. With its crenellated sandstone walls and narrow streets lined with exquisitely carved buildings, through which camel carts trundle leisurely, it has an extraordinarily medieval feel and an incredible atmosphere. The fort inside, perched on its hilltop, contains some gems of Jain temple building, while beautifully decorated merchants' havelis are scattered through the town. Once inside the fort walls looking out to the desert, it's easy to imagine caravans and camels sweeping across towards you in a dream of Arabian nights, but what you actually see are growing legions of windmills flanking the dunes in the distance. Unlike the other forts you visit in Rajasthan, Jaisalmer's is fully alive with shops, restaurants and guesthouses inside its walls and labyrinthine alleyways. It's beautiful to wander the tiny streets always finding a new nook or a great view.

All this has not failed to attract the attention of mass tourism, and at times Jaisalmer can feel overrun with package tourists, being swept from one shop to the next in a whirlwind of rapid consumption by insistent guides. Over the years, increased development of guesthouses and businesses within the walls has put pressure on the sewage, drainage and foundations of the fort. Three of the 99 bastions crumbled a couple of years ago and several people were killed. These bastions have now been replaced, but if you look at the fort bastions from the outside you can see signs of water discolouration (see box, page 257).

If you find Jaisalmer's magic diminished there's always the romantic desolation of the Thar Desert, easily accessible beyond the edge of the city. Many of the settlements close to the city have become well used to tourists, so it's worth venturing a little further out to get an idea of life in the desert. Highlights include the remarkable ghost city of Khuldera and, of course, the chance to take it all in from on top of a camel. ▸▸ *For listings, see pages 262-266.*

Ins and outs

Getting there The nearest airport is at Jodhpur, 275 km away, which is connected to Jaisalmer by buses and several daily trains. Most long-distance buses arrive at the bus stand, a 15-minute walk from the fort. Your hotel may offer a pickup. If not, have a place in mind and prepare for a barrage of competing touts.

Getting around Unmetered jeeps and auto-rickshaws can be hired at the station but they are no help inside the fort so you may have to carry your luggage some distance uphill if you choose a fort hotel. Rickshaws are allowed into the fort at certain times. You can hire a bike from Gopa Chowk (Rs 30) though the town is best explored on foot. Most hotels and restaurants are found around the two chowks and inside the fort. ▸▸ *See Transport, page 266.*

Tourist information RTDC ① *near TRC, Station Rd, Gadi Sagar Pol, T02992-252406, 0800-1200, 1500-1800.* Counter at railway station.

Background

Founded by Prince Jaisal in 1156, Jaisalmer grew to be a major staging post on the trade route across the forbidding Thar Desert from India to the West. The merchants prospered and invested part of their wealth in building beautiful houses and temples with the local sandstone. The growth of maritime trade between India and the West caused a decline in trade across the desert which ceased altogether in 1947. However, the wars with Pakistan (1965 and 1971) resulted in the Indian government developing the transport facilities to the border to improve troop movement. This has also helped visitors to gain access. Today, the army and tourism are mainstays of the local economy; hotel touts and pushy shopkeepers have become a problem in recent years.

Jaisalmer → *For listings, see pages 262-266. Colour map 1, B3.*

The fort
ⓘ *Best light for photography is late afternoon.*
On the roughly triangular-shaped Trikuta Hill, the fort stands 76 m above the town, enclosed by a 9-km wall with 99 bastions (mostly 1633-1647). Often called the Golden Fort because of the colour of its sandstone walls, it dominates the town. You enter the fort from the east from Gopa Chowk. The inner, higher fort wall and the old gates up the ramp (Suraj Pol, Ganesh Pol, Hawa Pol and Rang Pol) provided further defences. The Suraj Pol (1594), once an outer gate, is flanked by heavy bastions and has bands of decoration which imitate local textile designs. Take a walk through the narrow streets within the fort, often blocked by the odd goat or cow, and see how even today about 1000 of the town's people live in tiny houses inside the fort often with beautiful carvings on doors and balconies. It is not difficult to get lost.

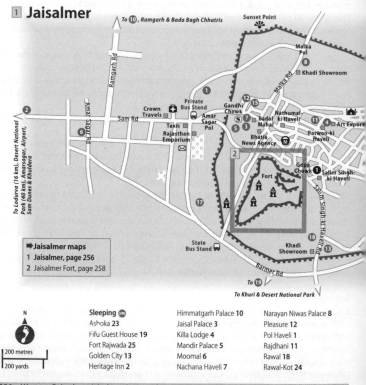

1 Jaisalmer

→Jaisalmer maps
1 Jaisalmer, page 256
2 Jaisalmer Fort, page 258

N
200 metres
200 yards

Sleeping	Himmatgarh Palace 10	Narayan Niwas Palace 8
Ashoka 23	Jaisal Palace 3	Pleasure 12
Fifu Guest House 19	Killa Lodge 4	Pol Haveli 1
Fort Rajwada 25	Mandir Palace 5	Rajdhani 11
Golden City 13	Moomal 6	Rawal 18
Heritage Inn 2	Nachana Haveli 7	Rawal-Kot 24

Jaisalmer in jeopardy

Jaisalmer in Jeopardy is a UK-based charity fighting to preserve the unique historical architecture of the city. Through raising awareness and funds, it has achieved the restoration of buildings such as the Rajput Palace and Rani-ka Mahal (Maharani's Palace) and helped ensure that Jaisalmer Fort is listed on the World Monuments Fund '100 Most Endangered Sites in the World'.

Some visitors feel that it is unethical to stay in the fort guesthouses and add to the problems of water consumption and waste disposal. As far back as the late 1990s guesthouses inside the fort were offered incentives to start their businesses in new locations outside the walls, although only one, Shahi Palace Guest House, took up the offer. Nowadays, thanks to greater awareness, there are many beautiful guesthouses both within the walls of the fort and outside gazing up at the fairytale. Jaisalmer in Jeopardy want to ensure that the Jaisalmer Fort can be enjoyed for another 400 years. Check out www.jaisalmer-in-jeopardy.org and www.intach.org (Indian National Trust for Art and Cultural Heritage) for further information.

Residency Centre Point **11**
Shahi Palace **17**
Star Haveli &
Oasis Haveli **17**
Swastika **15**

Eating 🍴
Natraj **1**

As with many other Rajput forts, within the massive defences are a series of palaces, the product of successive generations of rulers' flights of fancy. The local stone is relatively easy to carve and the dry climate has meant that the fineness of detail has been preserved through the centuries. The *jali* work and delicately ornamented balconies and windows with wide eaves break the solidity of the thick walls, giving protection from the heat, while the high plinths of the buildings keep out the sand. '**Sunset Point**', just north of the fort, is popular at sundown for views over Jaisalmer.

The entire **Fort Palace Museum and Heritage Centre** ① *0800-1800 summer, 0900-1800 winter, foreigners Rs 250 includes an excellent audio guide and camera, Indians Rs 10, video Rs 150,* has been renovated and an interesting series of displays established, including sculpture, weapons, paintings and well-presented cultural information. The view from the roof, the highest point inside the fort, is second to none. The **Juna Mahal** (circa 1500) of the seven-storey palace with its *jali* screens is one of the oldest Rajasthani palaces. The rather plain *zenana* block to its west, facing the *chauhata* (square) is decorated with false *jalis*. Next to it is the *mardana* (men's quarters) including the Rang Mahal above the Hawa Pol, built during the reign of Mulraj II (1762-1820), which has highly detailed murals and mirror decoration. **Sarvotam Vilas** built by Akhai Singh (1722-1762) is ornamented with blue tiles and glass mosaics. The adjacent **Gaj Vilas** (1884) stands on a high plinth. Mulraj II's **Moti Mahal** has floral decoration and carved doors.

The open square beyond the gates has a platform reached by climbing some steps; this is where court was held or royal visitors entertained. There are also fascinating **Jain temples** (12th-16th centuries) ① *0700-1200, Rs 10, camera Rs 50, video Rs 100, leather shoes not permitted*, within the fort. Whilst the Rajputs were devout Hindus they permitted the practice of Jainism. The **Parsvanatha** (1417) has a fine gateway, an ornate porch and 52 subsidiary shrines surrounding the main structure. The brackets are elaborately carved as maidens and dancers. The exterior of the **Rishbhanatha** (1479) has more than 600 images as decoration whilst clusters of towers form the roof of the **Shantinatha** built at the same time. **Ashtapadi** (16th century) incorporates the Hindu deities of Vishnu, Kali and Lakshmi into its decoration. The **Mahavir Temple** ① *view 1000-1100*, has an emerald statue. The **Sambhavanatha** (1431) ① *1000-1100*, has vaults beneath it that were used for document storage. The **Gyan Bhandar** here is famous for its ancient manuscripts.

Havelis

There are many exceptional *havelis* (see box, page 281) in the fort and in the walled town. Many have beautifully carved façades, *jali* screens and oriel windows overhanging the streets below. The ground floor is raised above the dusty streets and each has an inner courtyard surrounded by richly decorated apartments. An unofficial 'guide' will usually show you the way for about Rs 20. When the *havelis* are occupied, you may be allowed in on a polite request, otherwise, your 'guide' will help you gain access for a small fee (though this may just get you as far as the shops in the courtyard!).

Inside Amar Sagar Pol, the former ruler's 20th-century palace **Badal Mahal** with a five-storeyed tower, has fine carvings. Near the fort entrance, the 17th-century **Salim Singh-ki Haveli** ① *0800-1800, Rs 10, good carvings but is being poorly restored, over-long guided tour*, is especially attractive with peacock brackets; it is often referred to as the 'Ship Palace' because of its distinctive and decorative upper portion. **Nathumal-ki Haveli** (1885), nearer Gandhi Chowk, was built for the prime minister. Partly carved out of rock by two craftsmen, each undertaking one half of the house, it has a highly decorative façade with an attractive front door guarded by two elephants. Inside is a wealth of decoration; notice the tiny horse-drawn carriage and a locomotive showing European influence.

2 Jaisalmer Fort

➡Jaisalmer maps
1 Jaisalmer, page 256
2 Jaisalmer Fort, page 258

100 metres
100 yards

N

Simla **8**
Suraj **10**
Temple View **7**

Eating 🍴
8th July **1**
Kanchan Shree **5**
La Purezza **3**
Little Tibet **2**
Palace View **6**
Vyas **4**

Sleeping 🛏
Desert Boy's Guest House **1**
Desert Haveli **9**
Jaisal Castle **3**
Killa Bhawan **2**

Further east, **Patwon-ki Haveli** (1805) ⓘ *1030-1700, Rs 50 to view the gold ceilings and enjoy the view from the rooftop*, is a group of five *havelis* built for five brothers. Possibly the finest in town, they have beautiful murals and carved pillars. A profusion of balconies cover the front wall and the inner courtyard is surrounded by richly decorated apartments; parts have been well restored. The main courtyard and some roofs are now used as shops.

Desert Cultural Centre
ⓘ *Gadisar Circle, T02992-252 188, 1000-1700, Rs 10.*
The Desert Cultural Centre was established in 1997 with the aim of preserving the culture of the desert. The museum contains a varied display of fossils, paintings, instruments, costumes and textiles which give an interesting glimpse in to life in the desert. The charismatic founder, Mr Sharma, is a fount of information and has written several books on Jaisalmer.

Gadi Sagar tank
The Gadi Sagar (Gadisar or Gharisar) tank, southeast of the city walls, was the oasis which led Prince Jaisal to settle here. Now connected by a pipe to the Indira Gandhi Canal, it has water all year. It attracts migratory birds and has many small shrines around it and is well worth visiting, especially in the late afternoon. The delightful archway is said to have been constructed by a distinguished courtesan who built a temple on top to prevent the king destroying the gate. Pedalos are available for trips round the lake from Rs 50 for half an hour.

Around Jaisalmer → *For listings, see pages 262-266.*

Amar Sagar and Lodurva
Amar Sagar ⓘ *5 km northwest of Jaisalmer, foreigners Rs 30, Indians free, camera Rs 50, video Rs 100*, was once a formal garden with a pleasure palace of Amar Singh (1661-1703) on the bank of a lake which dries up during the hot season. The Jain temple there has been restored.

A further 10 km away is **Lodurva** ⓘ *0630-1930, foreigners Rs 20, Indians free, camera Rs 50, video Rs 100*, which contains a number of Jain temples that are the only remains of a once-flourishing Marwar capital. They are beautifully carved with *jali* outside and are well maintained and worth visiting. The road beyond Lodurva is unsealed.

Khuldera
This is a fascinating ghost town, and well worth stopping at on the way to Sam. The story goes that 400 or so years ago, Salim Singh, the then prime minister of Jaisalmer, took a

distinct shine to a Paliwal girl from this village. The rest of the Paliwal people did not want this beautiful girl taken away from them, and so after intense pressure from the prime minister decided to abandon the village one night, with everyone dispersing in different directions, never to return. It is remarkably well preserved, and best visited with a guide who can point out the most interesting buildings from the many still standing. **Khabha**, just south of here, is also recommended.

Sam dunes (Sain) → *Colour map 1, B2.*
① *Rs 10, car Rs 20 (camera fees may be introduced), camel rates start at Rs 50 per hr but can be bargained down.*
Sam dunes, 40 km west of Jaisalmer, is popular for sunset camel rides. It's not a remote spot in the middle of the desert but the only real large stretch of sand near town; the dunes only cover a small area, yet they are quite impressive. Right in the middle of the dunes, **Sunset View** is like a fairground, slightly tacky with lots of day-trippers – as many as 500 in the high season; the only escape from this and the camel men is to walk quite a way away.

Khuri → *Colour map 1, B2.*
① *Rs 10, car Rs 20, buses from Jaisalmer take 1½ hrs, jeep for 4 people Rs 450 for a sunset tour.*
Khuri, 40 km southwest of Jaisalmer, is a small picturesque desert village of decorated mud-thatched buildings which was ruled by the Sodha clan for four centuries. Visitors are attracted by shifting sand dunes, some 80 m high, but the peace of the village has been spoilt by the growing number of huts, tents and guesthouses which have opened along the road and near the dunes. Persistent hotel and camel agents board all buses bound for Khuri. The best months to visit are from November to February.

Thar Desert National Park → *Colour map 1, B2.*
① *Rs 150 per person; car permits Rs 500; permits are required, apply 2 days in advance to Forest Department, T02992-252489, or through travel agents.*
The Thar Desert National Park is near Khuri, the core being about 60 km from Jaisalmer (the road between Sam and Khuri is passable with a high-clearance vehicle). The park was created to protect 3000 sq km of the Thar Desert, the habitat for drought resistant, endangered and rare species which have adjusted to the unique and inhospitable conditions of extreme temperatures. The desert has undulating dunes and vast expanses of flat land where the trees are leafless, thorny and have long roots. Fascinating for birdwatching, it is one of the few places in India where the **great Indian bustard** is proliferating (it can weigh up to 14 kg and reach a height of 40 cm). In winter it also attracts the migratory **houbara bustard**. You can see imperial black-bellied and common Indian sand grouse, five species of vulture, six of eagle, falcons, and flocks of larks at Sudasari, in the core of the park, 60 km from Jaisalmer. Chinkaras are a common sight, as are desert and Indian foxes. Blackbuck and desert cat can be seen at times. Close to sunset, you can spot desert hare in the bushes.

While most hotels will try to sell you a tour by 4WD vehicle, this is no longer necessary. You can hire any jeep or high-clearance car (Ambassador, Sumo) for the trip to the park. Off-the-road journeys are by camel or camel cart (park tour Rs 50 and Rs 150 respectively).

Barmer → *Colour map 1, B/C3.*
This dusty desert town, 153 km south of Jaisalmer, is surrounded by sand dunes and scrublands. It is a major centre for wood carving, *durrie* rug weaving, embroidery and block

On a camel's back

Camel safaris draw many visitors to Jaisalmer. They allow an insight into otherwise inaccessible desert interiors and a chance to see rural life, desert flora and wildlife. The 'safari' is not a major expedition into the middle of nowhere. Instead, it is often along tracks, stopping off for sightseeing at temples and villages along the way. The camel driver/owner usually drives the camel or rides alongside (avoid one sharing your camel), usually for two hours in the morning and three hours in the afternoon, with a long lunch stop in between. There is usually jeep or camel cart backup with tents and 'kitchen' close by, though thankfully out of sight. It can be fun, especially if you are with companions and have a knowledgeable camel driver.

Camel safaris vary greatly in quality with prices ranging from around Rs 350 per night for the simplest (sleeping in the open, vegetarian meals) to those costing Rs 4500 (deluxe double-bedded tents with attached Western baths). Bear in mind that it is practically impossible for any safari organizer to cover his costs at anything less than Rs 350 – if you're offered cheaper tours, assume they'll be planning to get their money back by other means, ie shopping/drug selling along the way. Safaris charging Rs 500-1000 can be adequate (tents, mattresses, linen, cook, jeep support, but no toilets). It's important to ascertain what is included in the price and what are extras.

The popular 'Around Jaisalmer' route includes Bada Bagh, Ramkunda, Moolsagar, Sam dunes, Lodurva and Amar Sagar with three nights in the desert. Some routes now include Kuldhara's medieval ruins and the colourful Kahla village, as well as Deda, Jaseri lake (good birdlife) and Khaba ruins with a permit. Most visitors prefer to take a two days/one night or three days/two nights camel safari, with jeep transfer back to Jaisalmer. A more comfortable alternative is to be jeeped to a tented/hut camp in the desert as a base for a night and enjoy a camel trek during the day without losing out on the evening's entertainment under the stars. A short camel ride in town up to Sunset Point (or at Sam/Khuri) is one alternative to a 'safari' before deciding on a long haul, and also offers great views of upper levels of *havelis* – but watch out for low-slung electric wires! Pre-paid camel rides have now been introduced – Rs 80 for a 30-minute ride. For some, "half an hour is enough on a tick-ridden animal". For a selection of tour operators offering camel safaris, see page 265.

Make sure you cover up all exposed skin and use sunscreen to avoid getting burnt.

printing (you can watch printers in Khatriyon ki galli). The 10th- to 11th-century Kiradu temples, though badly damaged, are interesting. **Someshvara** (1020), the most intact, has some intricate carving but the dome and the tower have collapsed. The town itself is surprisingly industrial and not especially charming; those interested in seeking out handicrafts are well advised to locate **Gulla**, the town's only guide. He can normally be contacted at the **KK Hotel** (see Sleeping, page 264), or emailed in advance on gulla_guide@ yahoo.com. The small number of visitors to Barmer means that he doesn't get too many opportunities to practice his profession; be sure to explain exactly what you would like to see, and try to fix a price before starting the tour.

Dhorimmana → *Colour map 1, C3.*

The area further south of Barmer has some of the most colourful and traditional Bishnoi villages and a large population of *chinkaras* and desert fauna. The village women wear a lot of attractive jewellery but may be reluctant to be photographed so it is best to ask first. **PWD Rest house** has clean and comfortable rooms.

◉ Jaisalmer and around listings

For Sleeping and Eating price codes and other relevant information, see Essentials pages 28-33.

● Sleeping

Jaisalmer *p256, maps p256 and p258*
Some hotels close in Apr-Jun. Very low room prices may be conditional on taking the hotel's camel safari – check; refusal may mean having to move out. Some budget places allow travellers to sleep on the roof for Rs 30-50. The tourist office has a Paying Guest list. Negative reports on **Himalayan Guest House** and **Peacock Hotel**.

LL-AL Fort Rajwada, 1 Hotel Complex, Jodhpur Rd, T02992-253533, www.fort rajwada.com. 65 top-class, central a/c rooms and 4 **LL** suites conceived by an opera set designer, in a modern luxury hotel, deceptively old looking from the outside, built in strict accordance to the principles of *vaastu*, India's answer to feng shui. Architectural features have been recovered from crumbling local *havelis* and incorporated in to the stylish interior, which houses all the expected mod cons, of which the exquisite bar is particularly worthy of mention. Friendly management, eager staff.

L-A Heritage Inn, Hotel Complex, Sam Rd, T02992-250901, www.carnivalhotels.com. 15 uninspired rooms plus 40 more attractive cottages, single-storey sandstone desert architecture, restaurant, bar, pleasant interior, garden, pool, well-managed, although slightly lacking in atmosphere.

L-A Killa Bhawan, Kotri Para, T02992-251204, www.killabhawan.com. 7 rooms, 2 a/c, in characterful old building, beautiful interiors, classiest place in fort by some margin.

AL Rawal-Kot (Taj), Jodhpur Rd, T02992-252638, www.tajhotels.com. 31 large a/c

rooms, attractively furnished, good restaurants, modern yet medieval atmosphere, good views of fort from beautiful pool, friendly.

AL-A Narayan Niwas Palace, opposite Jain Temple, Malka Rd, T02992-252408, www.narayanniwas.com. A converted caravanserai with 51 disappointing dingy rooms; rest of property is far more impressive and could be amazing if better maintained. Pillared indoor pool is remarkable, and views from rooftop restaurant exceptional. Good reports on entertainment provided.

A Himmatgarh Palace, 1 Ramgarh Rd, 2.5 km from town, T02992-252002, himmatgarh@sancharnet.in. 40 a/c rooms and cottages in attractive, quirky sandstone building, great views from garden and pool.

A Mandir Palace, T02992-252788, www.welcomheritagehotels.com. Well-maintained a/c rooms and beautiful atmospheric suites in exclusive location inside royal palace. Not very well run but an experience.

B Killa Lodge, opposite Patwon-ki Haveli, T02992-253833, www.killabhawan.com. Small boutique hotel with only 6 rooms run by the same team as **Killa Bhawan** in the fort. Good style, but pricey. Great location opposite beautiful *haveli*. Lovely café on top and bookshop downstairs.

B-C Nachana Haveli, Gandhi Chowk, T02992-252 110, nachana_haveli@yahoo.com. Converted 18th-century Rajput *haveli* with carved balconies and period artefacts. Rooms are stylishly done with great bathrooms, particularly upstairs suites. Rooftop restaurant in the season, has very authentic feel overall. Friendly family. Highly recommended.

C-D Desert Boy's Guest House, Vyasa Para in fort, T02992-253091, desert_p@yahoo.com. 14 jauntily furnished rooms in attractive property that feels quite new, good if pricey Italian rooftop restaurant with seating on the floor, camel safaris have a good reputation.

C-D Jaisal Castle, in fort, T02992-252362, www,naryanniwas.com. 11 quirky rooms in rambling, characterful old *haveli*. Room 101 is particularly lovely, ironically. Beautiful communal areas.

C-E Moomal (RTDC), Amar Sagar Rd, T02992-252492. Better than RTDC average but still has institutional air. 60 rooms (17 a/c), could be cleaner, mediocre restaurant, bar, tours, friendly and helpful. 12 tribal-style circular huts offer a great alternative although in slightly scrubby grounds – they have a lot more character.

C-F Hotel Pol Haveli (RTDC), near Geeta Ashram, Dedansar Rd, T02992-250131. New *haveli*-style building with stylish decor and chilled-out vibe. Beautiful furnishings, especially the beds. Run by same family as **Shahi Palace**. Slightly odd area as it feels you are staying in a dusty village, but it is just a short walk from Gandhi Chowk and the heart of things. Good views of sunset point and the fort in the distance.

D-E Fifu Guest House, opposite Nagarpalika (1 km out of town), T02992-254317, www.fifutravel.com. 8 well-decorated rooms in modern building with excellent rooftop views. Location slightly inconvenient but hosts are charming and free bike hire for guests. Ring ahead for free pickup.

D-E Jaisal Palace, near Gandhi Chowk, behind SBI, T02992-252717, www.hoteljaisal palace.com. 14 clean, simple rooms with bath, 6 a/c, 8 air-cooled, 1st-floor balconies with views, Rajasthani food on roof terrace in season, train/bus bookings.

D-E Rawal, Salim Singh-ki Haveli Marg, Dibba Para, T02992-252570. Pleasant and relaxed with 20 large, clean albeit a bit dreary rooms, all with attached bathrooms, Indian restaurant, good views from rooftop.

D-E Suraj, behind Jain Temple, T02992-251623, hotelsurajjaisalmer@hotmail.com. Suraj boasts 6 beautiful rooms in this 530-year-old *haveli* overlooking the Jain temple and has appeared in Italian *Marie*

Claire Décor. Gets quite chilly in winter, but very atmospheric. Also 4 newer rooms in annexe opposite, standard equally high.

D-F Shahi Palace, near Government Bus Stand, T02992-255920, www.shahipalace hotel.com. 16 super stylish rooms in a beautiful sandstone building with outstanding bathrooms. The team of 4 brothers here work hard to make everyone feel at home. Beautiful chic rooftop restaurant with lots or archways and even a wooden boat from Karnataka masquerading as a flowerpot. There are also 2 new *haveli*-style buildings adjacent offering up more of the same vibe but a little quieter – **Star** and **Oasis**. Good camel safaris and small Thar crafts shop offering up traditional pieces at fair prices underneath **Oasis Haveli**. Wholeheartedly recommended.

D-F Simla, Kund Para, T02992-253061, simla haveli@yahoo.co.in. 5 clean rooms in thought-fully renovated 550-year-old *haveli*, attractive wall hangings, 1 large with bath, others tiny with bath downstairs, no safari pressure, friendly management, a cut above the norm.

E-F Golden City, Dibba Para, T02992-251664, hotelgoldencity@hotmail.com. Clean comfortable air-cooled rooms with hot shower, 3 **D** a/c, rooftop restaurant with good views, free station transfer, exchange, internet, family atmosphere with pool (open to non-residents). Away from the heart of things.

E-G The Desert Haveli, near Jain Temple, T02992-251555, desert_haveli@yahoo.com. 7 characterful rooms in charming, 400-year-old *haveli*, honest, friendly owner. Very atmospheric. Recommended.

F-G Pleasure, Gandhi Chowk, T02992-252323, hotelpleasure@rediffmail.com. 5 clean rooms in homely establishment with innovative facilities including free washing machine and filtered drinking water.

F-G Swastika, Chainpura St, T02992-252483. 9 clean, well-kept rooms, all with bath, reasonable view, free tea and pickups.

F-G Temple View, next to Jain Temple, T02992-252 832, jaisalmertempleview@ hotmail.com. 7 well-decorated rooms, 3 with attached bath, attention to detail, great view of temples from roof, entertaining owner.

G Ashoka, opposite railway station, T02992-256021. 20 cleanish rooms, in quiet location, good option as close to the station.
G Rajdhani, near Patwon-ki Haveli, T02992-252746. Great view from rooftop, 7 clean rooms some with strange statues and decor, hot shower, friendly staff, calm atmosphere.
G Residency Centre Point, near Patwon-ki Haveli, T02992-252883. Quiet family-run hotel with 5 basic but characterful rooms, good views from roof.

Sam dunes *p260*
D Sam Dhani (RTDC), T02992-252392. 8 huts facing the dunes, very busy in late afternoon and sunset but very pleasant at night and early morning. Includes all meals.

Khuri *p260*
E-F Khuri Guest House, reservations T022-240 42211, www.nivalink.com/khuri. Simple rooms or huts, friendly management. Recommended.
E-F Mama's, T01304-274 023. Cool, thatched huts, tasty meals. Recommended.

Thar Desert National Park *p260*
F Rest Huts, facing the park. Adequate. Contact Park Director on T02992-252489.

Barmer *p260*
E-F KK Hotel, Station Rd, T02982-230038. 24 reasonable rooms, some a/c, very similar to Krishna nearby.
E-F Krishna, Station Rd, a few mins' walk from station, T02982-220785. The biggest and best in town with 32 decent rooms, some a/c, but no restaurant.

🍴 Eating

Jaisalmer *p256, maps p256 and p258*
♥♥ **8th July**, just inside fort (another opposite Fort Gate). Vegetarian. Pleasant rooftop seating – popular for breakfast, pizzas, food average, 'famous' apple pie a letdown, pleasant for evening drink, mixed reports on service.

♥♥ **La Purezza**, Vyas Para. Excellent salads, Italian cheese veggies and other unusual offerings. Has another outlet in Manali.
♥♥ **Little Tibet**, beyond the palace chowk. Momos and much more of travellers' choice, generous, hygienic, enthusiastic staff, popular.
♥♥ **Nachana Haveli** (see Sleeping), another hotel with great views of fort at night. Beautiful decor, lovely food and relaxed vibe.
♥♥ **Natraj**, next to Salim Singh-ki Haveli near the entrance to the fort. Spacious rooftop with good views and a/c room, bar, wide choice (meat dishes Rs 80-100), average Indian and Chinese, clean toilet, pleasant spot.
♥♥ **Shahi Palace** (see Sleeping). Great food from this beautiful rooftop restaurant with amazing views of fort. Try traditional Rajasthani meals like *kej sangari* (desert beans) and *kadi pakoda* (yoghurt turmeric curry) and, if they're not busy, you can go in the kitchen and watch how they make it.
♥ **Little Italy**, in the main fort gate: charming, cool interiors with windows looking up the pathway to the fort: excellent bruschetta and a great meeting point before or after fort walks.
♥ **Palace View Restaurant**, Gandhi Chowk, near Jain Temples. Varied selection but main attraction is the home-made apple pie.
♥ **Vyas**, Fort. Simple, good vegetarian *thalis* (Rs 20-30), pleasant staff.

Snacks and drinks
Chai stalls at **Gopa Chowk** make good masala tea before 1730. Hot and crisp *kachoris* and samosas opposite Jain temples near **Narayan Niwas**, are great for breakfast or tea.
Dhanraj Bhatia, scrumptious Indian sweets including Jaisalmeri delights (try *godwa*).
Doodh bhandars, in Hanuman Chauraya. Sells a delicious mix of creamy milk, cardamom and sugar, whipped up with a flourish, between sunset and midnight.
Kanchan Shree, Gopa Chowk, 250 m from Salim Singh-ki Haveli. *Lassis* (19 varieties) and ice cream floats, as well as cheap, tasty *thalis*. Many recommendations for this place.
Mohan Juice Centre, near Sunil Bhatia Rest House. Delicious *lassis*, good breakfasts.

⊙ Entertainment

Jaisalmer *p256, maps p256 and p258*
The more expensive hotels have bars.
Desert Cultural Centre, Gadisar Circle.
2 puppet shows every evening, at 1830 and
1930, Rs 30 entry, Rs 20 camera, Rs 50 video.

❀ Festivals and events

Jaisalmer *p256, maps p256 and p258*
Feb/Mar Holi is especially colourful but
gets riotous.

Sam dunes *p260*
Feb 3-day **Desert Festival** (28-30 Jan 2010,
16-18 Feb 2011) with *son et lumière* amid the
sand dunes at Sam, folk dancing, puppet
shows and camel races, camel polo and
camel acrobatics, Mr Desert competition.
You can also watch craftsmen at work.
Rail and hotel reservations can be difficult.

Barmer *p260*
Mar Thar Festiva highlights desert culture
and handicrafts.

○ Shopping

Jaisalmer *p256, maps p256 and p258*
Shops open 1000-1330 and 1500-1900.
Jaisalmer is famous for its handicrafts –
stone-carved statues, leather ware, brass
enamel engraving, shawls, tie-dye work,
embroidered and block printed fabrics, but
garments are often poorly finished. Look in
Siré Bazar, **Sonaron-ka-Bas** and shops in the
narrow lanes of the old city including **Kamal
Handicrafts**, **Ganpati Art Home**, and **Damodar**
in the fort. In Gandhi Chowk: **Rajasthali**, closed
Tue; the good, fairly priced selection at **Khadi
Emporium** at the end of the courtyard just
above Narayan Niwas Hotel. **Jaisalmer Art
Export**, behind Patwon-ki Haveli has
high-quality textiles. Good shopping at **Thar
Crafts**, under Oasis Haveli near Shahi Palace

Hotel. For textiles try **Amrit Handprint Factory**,
just inside Sagar Gate on the left. **Geeta
Jewellers** on Aasni Rd near Fort Gate is
recommended, good value and no hard sell.
    For tailors try **Mr Durga**, small shop near
fort entrance on Kacheri Rd, Bansari Bazar,
"beware imitations". Excellent Western-style
tailoring. Shirts made to measure, around
Rs 200. Also **Nagpur**, Koba Chowk, and
Raju, Kachari Rd, outside Amar Sagar Pol,
for Western-style tailoring.

▲ Activities and tours

Jaisalmer *p256, maps p256 and p258*
Camel safaris
Thar Safaris, T02992-252722, www.dera
jaisalmer.com, charges Rs 950). Upscale
options include: **Safari Tours**, T02992- 251058.
10 'desert huts' with shared facilities and 10
tents with private bathrooms, about 8 km from
Sam; **Rajasthan Desert Safaris**, T(0)9414-
140109, Swiss-cottage tents with attached
toilets near the dunes, Rs 4500 per night.
Ganesh Travels, T02992-252538, and **Trotters'
Independent Travels**, Gopa Chowk, near
Bhang Shop, T(0)9414-469292, www.trotters
camelsafari jaisalmer.com, well recommended
for less fancy safaris. Also: **Sahara Travels**, run
by local identity "Mr Desert" (see Tour
operators, below); **Comfort Tours** (Gorbandh
Palace); **Travel Plan**. Less upmarket, but still
reliable options include those from **Shahi
Palace**, **Fifu Guesthouse** and **Desert Haveli**.

Cooking
Karuna, Ishar Palace, in the fort near the
Laxminath Temple, T02992-253062,
karunaacharya@yahoo.com. Learn Indian
cookery with Karuna, Courses of any length
can be arranged. Highly recommended.

Music
Anyone interested in learning to play a
Rajasthani musical instrument, or to hear a
performance, should contact Kamru Deen
on T02992-254181, arbamusic@yahoo.co.in.

Paragliding

SPS Kaushik, T94143-05121. Paragliding in the desert, with participants being towed behind a jeep for Rs 750 a go. An unusual way to see the desert, but "best to fly backwards if you want to keep the sand out of your eyes"!

Swimming

Gorbandh Palace (non-residents Rs 350); also **Heritage Inn** (meal plus swim deals) and **Fort Rajwada**.

Tour operators

Aravalli Safari, near Patwon-ki Gali, T02992-252 632. Professional. Recommended.
Rajasthan Tourism, T02992-252 406. City sightseeing: half day, 0900-1200. Fort, *havelis*, Gadisagar Lake. Sam sand dunes: half day, 1500-1900.
Royal Desert Safaries, Nachna Haveli, Gandhi Chowk, T02992-252 538, www.palaces-tours.com. Experienced and efficient.
Sahara Travels, Gopa Chowk, right of the 1st Fort gate, T02992-252609. Mr (Desert) Bissa's reliable camel safaris with good food.
Thar Safari, Gandhi Chowk, near **Trio**, T02992-252722. Reliable tours.

☺ Transport

Jaisalmer *p256, maps p256 and p258*
Jaisalmer is on NH15 (Pathankot–Samakhiali). Transport to town from train and bus station is by auto-rickshaws or jeeps; police are on duty so less harassment.

Bus

Touts may board buses outside town to press you to take their jeep; it is better to walk 10-15 mins from Amar Sagar Pol and choose a hotel.
  State Roadways buses, from near the station, T02992-251541, and at SBBJ Bank Government Bus Stop. Services to **Ajmer**, **Barmer**, **Bikaner** (330 km on good road, 8 hrs, Rs 160), **Jaipur** (638 km); Abu Rd for **Mount Abu**. **Jodhpur** (285 km, 0500, 0600, 0630, 0730 and 2230, 5 hrs, Rs 130). **Udaipur** (663 km, a tiring 14 hrs). **Bikaner** 0600 and 2130 from Hanuman Chowk; Private de luxe coaches from outside Amar Sagar Pol or Airforce Circle, to a similar range of destinations. Most hotels can reserve bus tickets. Operators: **Marudhara Travels**, Station Rd, T02992-252351. **National Tours**, Hanuman Choraha, T02992-252348.

Train

The military presence can make getting tickets slow; book in advance if possible. Foreign Tourist Bureau with waiting room, T02992-252354, booking office T02992-251301. *Jaisalmer Delhi Exp 4060*, to **Jodhpur** (6 hrs) and **Delhi** (19 hrs). *Jodhpur Exp 4809*, 2315, 7 hrs. Can get very cold (and dusty) try and book 3AC where bedding is provided.

Barmer *p260*
From Barmer, the hot and dusty bus journey to **Jaisalmer** takes 4 hrs; **Mt Abu**, 6 hrs.

☺ Directory

Jaisalmer *p256, maps p256 and p258*
Banks Mon-Fri 1030-1430, Sat 1030-1230. On Gandhi Chowk: **Bank of Baroda** with ATM and **SBBJ** with ATM, TCs and cash against credit cards; **State of Bank of India**, Nachna Haveli, currency only. There is also an ATM which accepts international cards close to Hanuman Chowk on the road which leads to Sam and one opposite Government Hospital. **Internet** Slow, expensive dial-up connections are the norm in the fort. **Joshi Travel**, opposite PO, Central Market, Gopa Chowk, T02992-250455, joshitravel@hotmail.com. Cybercafé, modern equipment, also STD, fax, etc. **Desert Cyber Inn**, inside fort close to Little Tibet restaurant. **Medical services** Maheshwan Hospital, Barmer Rd, T02992-250024. **Post** The GPO is near Police Station, T02992-252407. With Poste Restante. **Useful contacts** Fire: T02992-252352. Police: T02992-252668.

Contents

Northern Rajasthan

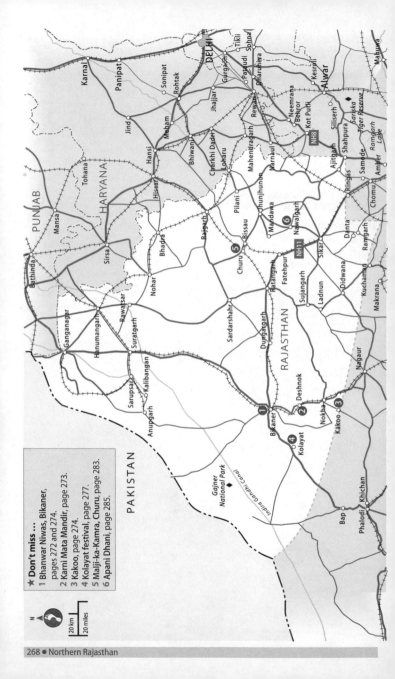

★ Don't miss …
1 Bhanwar Niwas, Bikaner,
  pages 272 and 274.
2 Karni Mata Mandir, page 273.
3 Kakoo, page 274.
4 Kolayat festival, page 277.
5 Malji-ka-Kamra, Churu, page 283.
6 Apani Dhani, page 285.

N

20 km
20 miles

PAKISTAN

PUNJAB

HARYANA

RAJASTHAN

DELHI

Tikli
Sohna

Karnal
Panipat
Sonipat
Rohtak
Gurgaon
Papudi
Bhiwadi

Kessroli
Alwar
Mahuwa

Jind
Meham
Jhajjar
Rewari
Neemrana
Behror
Kot Putli
Shahpura
Siliserh
Sariska
Tiger Reserve
Ramgarh
Lake

Hansi
Bhiwani
Charkhi Dadri
Loharu
Mahendragarh
Narnaul
Ajitgarh
Samode
Amber

NH8

Tohana
Hisar
Pilani
Jhunjhunun
Mandawa
Nawalgarh
Ringas
Chomu

Mansa
Bhadra
Bargarh
Bissau
6
Danta
Ramgarh

Bathinda
Sirsa
Nohar
Churu
Ratangarh
Fatehpur
Sikar
Didwana
Kuchaman
Makrana

5

NH11

Ganganagar
Hanumangarh
Rawatsar
Sardarshahr
Dungargarh
Sujangarh
Ladnun
Nagaur

Suratgarh

Kalibangan

Sarupsar
Anupgarh

Deshnok
Nokha
3
Kakoo

2

Gajner
National Park

1
Bikaner
4
Kolayat

Indira Gandhi Canal

Bap
Phalodi
Khichan

This is one of the less-visited regions of Rajasthan, but is well worth passing through on your way to the better known areas. Bikaner, perhaps the least touristy big city in Rajasthan, has traditionally been somewhat overshadowed by the state's other cities, but is gaining popularity both as an interesting place to visit in its own right, and as a place to go for a camel safari; as scenic as Jaisalmer but far less commercial. Even further off the beaten track, desert villages such as Kakoo offer an accessible insight in to rural desert life, while wildlife enthusiasts will find plenty of interest in both Gajner National Park and Tal Chappar Wildlife Sanctuary.

Shekhawati has its own quirky charm; still largely undeveloped, its outdoor treasures sit as silent testimony to an illustrious past, strangely at odds with the day to day bustle on their doorsteps. The region's boom days, when the indigenous Marwari businessmen were trading with the four corners of the globe, constantly vying to out do each other in the elaborateness of their *haveli* homes, are long gone. Marwari traders still enjoy a reputation as astute businessmen, but today operate in India's major business centres, many of their *havelis* having fallen in to disrepair, yet still intact enough to give a fascinating glimpse of a time gone by. It's an area which should be experienced rather than glimpsed at; the numerous horse, camel and bicycle safaris on offer represent the perfect pace of travel in this unrushed region.

Bikaner and around

Bikaner is something of a dusty oasis town among the scrub and sand dunes of northwest Rajasthan. Its rocky outcrops in a barren landscape provide a dramatic setting for the Junagarh Fort, one of the finest in western Rajasthan. The old walled city retains a medieval air, and is home to over 300 havelis, while outside the walls some stunning palaces survive. Well off the usual tourist trail, Bikaner is en route to Jaisalmer from Jaipur or Shekhawati, and is well worth a visit. ▸▸ For listings, see pages 274-278.

Ins and outs → *Phone code: 0151. Population: 530,000.*

Getting there Bikaner is a full day's drive from Jaipur so it may be worth stopping a night in Samode or the Shekhawati region (see pages 155 and 279). The railway station is central and has services from Delhi (Sarai Rohilla), Jaipur and Jodhpur. The New Bus Stand is 3 km to the north, so if arriving from the south you can ask to be dropped in town. There are regular bus services to Desnok, but to get to Gajner, Kakoo or Tal Chappar you'll need to hire private transport. ▸▸ *See Transport, page 277.*

Getting around The fort and the Old City are within easy walking distance from the station. Auto- and cycle-rickshaws transfer passengers between the station and the New Bus Stand. Taxis can be difficult to get from the Lalgarh Palace area at night.

Tourist information **Dhola-Maru Tourist Bungalow** ⓘ *Poonam Singh Circle, T0151-252 9621, Oct-Mar 0800-1800.* As well as information, car hire is available.

Bikaner → *For listings, see pages 274-278. Colour map 4, B3.*

Junagarh Fort

ⓘ *1000-1630 (last entry), Rs 100 foreigners, Rs 10 Indians; camera Rs 30, video Rs 100 (limited permission), guided tours in Hindi and English, private guides near the gate offer better 'in-depth' tours; Rs 100 for 4 people, 2 hrs.*

This is one of the finest examples in Rajasthan of the paradox between medieval military architecture and beautiful interior decoration. Started in 1588 by Raja Rai Singh (1571-1611), a strong ally of the Mughal Empire, who led Akbar's army in numerous battles, it had palaces added for the next three centuries.

You enter the superbly preserved fort by the yellow sandstone **Suraj Prole** (Sun Gate, 1593) to the east. The pale red sandstone perimeter wall is surrounded by a moat (the lake no longer exists) while the Chowks have beautifully designed palaces with balconies, kiosks and fine *jali* screens. The interiors are beautifully decorated with shell-work, lime plaster, mirror-and-glass inlays, gold leaf, carving, carpets and lacquer work. The ramparts offer good views of the elephant and horse stables and temples, the old city with the desert beyond, and the relatively more recent city areas around the medieval walls. The walls of the **Lal Niwas**, which are the oldest, are elaborately decorated in red and gold. Karan Singh commemorated a victory over Aurangzeb by building the **Karan Mahal** (1631-1639) across the Chowk. Successive rulers added the **Gaj Mandir** (1745-1787) with its mirrored Shish Mahal, and the **Chattra Niwas** (1872-1887) with its pitched roof and English 'field sport' plates decorating the walls. The magnificent **Coronation Hall**, adorned with plaster work, lacquer, mirror and glass, is in Maharaja Surat Singh's **Anup Mahal** (1788-1828). The decorative façades around the Anup Mahal Chowk, though painted white, are in fact of stone. The fort also includes the **Chetar Mahal** and **Chini Burj** of Dungar Singh (1872-1887) and **Ganga Niwas** of Ganga Singh (1898-1943), who did much to modernize his state and also built the Lalgarh Palace to the north. Mirror work, carving and marble decorate the ornate **Chandra Mahal** (Moon Palace) and the **Phul Mahal** (Flower Palace), built by Maharaja Gaj Singh. These last two, the best rooms, are shown to foreigners at the end as a 'special tour' when the guide expects an extra tip. The royal chamber in the Chandra Mahal has strategically placed mirrors so that any intruder entering could be seen by the maharaja from his bed. The fort **museum** has Sanskrit and Persian manuscripts, miniature paintings, jewels, enamelware, silver, weapons, palanquins, howdahs and war drums. **Har Mandir**, the royal temple where birth and wedding ceremonies were celebrated, is still used for Gangaur and other festivities. The well nearby is reputedly over 130 m deep. **Prachina Museum** ① *1000-1700, foreigners Rs 50 (guided tour), Indians Rs10, camera Rs 20, small clean café outside is open-air but shady*, in the grounds, exhibits beautifully crafted costumes, carpets and ornamental objects.

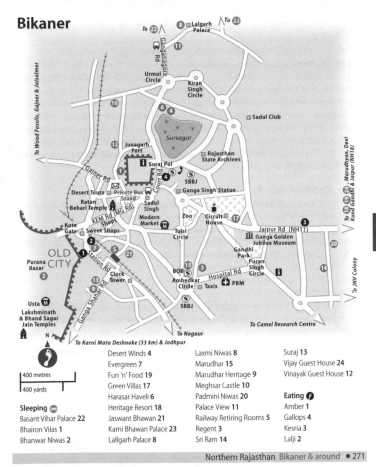

Bikaner

	Desert Winds **4**	Laxmi Niwas **8**
	Evergreen **7**	Marudhar **15**
	Fun 'n' Food **19**	Marudhar Heritage **9**
	Green Villas **17**	Meghsar Castle **10**
	Harasar Haveli **6**	Padmini Niwas **20**
Sleeping	Heritage Resort **18**	Palace View **11**
Basant Vihar Palace **22**	Jaswant Bhawan **21**	Railway Retiring Rooms **5**
Bhairon Vilas **1**	Karni Bhawan Palace **23**	Regent **3**
Bhanwar Niwas **2**	Lallgarh Palace **8**	Sri Ram **14**

Suraj **13**
Vijay Guest House **24**
Vinayak Guest House **12**
Eating ⑦
Amber **1**
Gallops **4**
Kesria **3**
Lalji **2**

Life after the rains

When in Bikaner, drop in at URMUL's showroom, **Abhiviyakyi**, opposite the New Bus Stand. A fair trade NGO, URMUL works with the marginalised tribespeople of the Thar Desert. The droughts of the 1980s made farming, the traditional source of livelihood for the majority of these people, no longer a viable option. URMUL was formed in 1991 with the aim to teach people new skills which could bring them the income that the absent rains had taken away. As the range of products on offer testifies, the project has been a huge success. All the items on sale, including clothing, tablecloths, bed linen, shoes and bags, have been made by the project's participants, and are of a quality previously unseen in the often all-too-amateur 'craft' sector. Visit the shop before agreeing to go with rickshaw drivers or touts to a 'URMUL' village; scams are not unknown.

Lalgarh Palace

ⓘ *Palace Thu-Tue, museum Mon-Sat 1000-1700, Rs 40 (museum extra Rs 20).*

The red sandstone palace stands in huge grounds to the north of the city, surrounded by rocks and sand dunes. Designed by Sir Swinton Jacob in 1902, the palace complex, with extensions over the next few decades, has attractive courtyards overlooked by intricate *zenana* screen windows and *jarokha* balconies, columned corridors and period furnishings. The banquet hall is full of hunting trophies and photographs. His Highness Doctor Karni Singh of Bikaner was well known for his shooting expertise – both with a camera and with a gun. The bougainvillea, parakeets and peacocks add to the attraction of the gardens in which the Bikaner State Railway Carriage is preserved. The Lalgarh complex has several hotels (see Sleeping, page 275).

Rampuria Street and the Purana Bazar

There are some exquisite *havelis* in Bikaner belonging to the Rampuria, Kothari, Vaid and Daga merchant families. The sandstone carvings combine traditional Rajasthani *haveli* architecture with colonial influence. Around Rampuria Street and the Purana Bazar you can wander through lanes lined with fine façades. Among them is **Bhanwar Niwas** which has been converted into a heritage hotel (see Sleeping, page 274).

Ganga Golden Jubilee Museum

ⓘ *Public Park, 1000-1630, Rs 3.*

This museum has a fine small collection of pottery, massive paintings, stuffed tigers, carpets, costumes and weapons. There are also some excellent examples of Bikaner miniature paintings which are specially prized because of their very fine quality.

Around Bikaner → *For listings, see pages 274-278.*

Bhand Sagar

ⓘ *Free but caretakers may charge Rs 10 for cameras.*

Some 5 km southwest of Bikaner, Bhand Sagar has a group of Hindu and Jain temples which are believed to be the oldest extant structures of Bikaner, dating from the days when it was just a desert trading outpost of Jodhpur. The white-painted sandstone **Bandeshwar Temple** with a towering *shikhara* roof and painted sculptures, murals and mirrorwork inside, is the most interesting. The **Sandeshwar Temple**, dedicated to Neminath, has gold-leaf painting, *meenakari* work and marble sculptures. They are hard to find and difficult to approach by car but rickshaw wallahs know the way. There are numerous steps but wonderful views.

Camel Research Centre
ⓘ *10 km from Bikaner in Jorbeer, 1500-1730, foreigners Rs 50, Indians Rs 5, camera Rs 20.*
This 800-ha facility is dedicated to scientific research into various aspects of the camel, with the aim of producing disease-resistant animals that can walk further and carry more while consuming less water. As well as genetically increasing the camel's tolerances, researchers are investigating the nutritional benefits of drinking camel milk; camel ice cream is for sale if you want to test for yourself – and coming soon are camel milk moisturizers! It's particularly worth being here between 1530 and 1600, when the camels return to the centre for the evening: the spectacle of 100 or more camels ambling out of the desert towards you is quite unforgettable.

On the way to the Camel Research Centre, you will find the **Museum of Turbans and Cooking Utensils** ⓘ *near Shiv Bari Temple, Camel Farm Rd, T(0)9829-867323*, run by a French NGO. This quirky museum contains traditional musical instruments, cooking utensils and turbans for every occasion – you can even learn to tie one.

Gajner National Park → *Colour map 4, B2.*
Now part of a palace hotel, this park, 30 km west of Bikaner, used to be a private preserve which provided the royal family of Bikaner with game. It is a birder's paradise surrounded by 13,000 ha of scrub forest which also harbours large colonies of nilgai, chinkara, blackbuck, wild boar and desert reptiles. Throughout the day, a train of antelope, gazelle and pigs can be seen arriving to drink at the lake. Winter migratory birds include the Imperial black-bellied sand grouse, cranes and migratory ducks. Some visitors have spotted great Indian bustard at the water's edge. It is worth stopping for an hour's mini-safari if you are in the vicinity.

Kolayat → *Colour map 4, B3.*
Some 50 km southwest via Gajner road, Kolayat is regarded as one of the 58 most important Hindu pilgrimage centres. It is situated around a sacred lake with 52 ghats and a group of five temples built by Ganga Singhji (none of which is architecturally significant). The oasis village comes alive at the November full moon when a three-day festival draws thousands of pilgrims who take part in ritual bathing.

Karni Mata Mandir
ⓘ *Closed 1200-1600, free, camera Rs 40.*
This 17th-century temple, 33 km south of Bikaner at Deshnoke, has massive silver gates and beautiful white marble carvings on the façade. These were added by Ganga Singh (1898-1943) who dedicated the temple to a 15th-century female mystic Karniji, worshipped as an incarnation of Durga. A gallery describes her life. Mice and rats, revered and fed with sweets and milk in the belief that they are reincarnated saints, swarm over the temple around your feet; spotting the white rat is supposed to bring good luck. Take socks as the floor is dirty, but note that the rats are far less widespread than they are made out to be. Sensationalised accounts give the impression of a sea of rats through which the visitor is obliged to walk barefoot, whereas in reality, while there are a good number of

rats, they generally scurry around the outskirts of the temple courtyard – you're very unlikely to tread on one. The temple itself is beautiful, and would be well worth visiting even without the novelty of the rats.

Kakoo → *Colour map 4, C3.*
This picturesque village, 75 km south of Bikaner, with attractive huts and surrounded by sand dunes, is the starting point for desert camel safaris costing Rs 1500 per day with tented facilities. Staying here makes a fantastic introduction to the practicalities of life in the desert; this is probably the most authentic desert settlement in this area that can be easily reached by road. Good trips to Kakoo are organized by Mr Bhagwan Singh T(0)9829-218237, www.kakusafari.com. You can travel to Kakoo by bus changing at Nokhamandi (62 km) from Bikaner.

Kalibangan and Harappan sites → *Colour map 4, A3.*
One of North India's most important early settlement regions stretches from the Shimla hills down past the important Harappan sites of **Hanumangarh** and **Kalibangan**, north of Bikaner. Late Harappan sites have been explored by archaeologists, notably A Ghosh, since 1962. They were identified in the upper part of the valley, the easternmost region of the Indus Valley civilization. Across the border in Pakistan are the premier sites of Harappa (200 km) and Moenjo Daro (450 km). Here, the most impressive of the sites today is that of Kalibangan (west off the NH15 at Suratgarh). On the south bank of the Ghaggar River it was a heavily fortified citadel mound, rising about 10 m above the level of the plain. There were several pre-Harappan phases. Allchin and Allchin record that the bricks of the early phase were already standardized, though not to the same size as later Harappan bricks. The ramparts were made of mud brick and a range of pottery and ornaments have been found. The early pottery is especially interesting, predominantly red or pink with black painting.

◉ Bikaner and around listings

For Sleeping and Eating price codes and other relevant information, see Essentials pages 28-33.

● Sleeping

Bikaner *p270, map p271*
Budget hotel rooms usually have shared bath; often serve Indian vegetarian food only. The tourist office has a list of Paying Guest hotels.
LL-AL Laxmi Niwas, Lallgarh Palace Complex, T0151-2252 1188, www.laxmi niwaspalace.com. 60 large rooms and suites which once formed Maharaja Ganga Singh's personal residence, with fabulous carvings and beautifully painted ceilings, all arranged around the stunningly ornate courtyard. Superb bar, restaurant and lounge, discreet but attentive service, absolutely one-off.

Recommended. You can also pay Rs 100 to have a tour if you are not staying here.
AL-A Bhanwar Niwas, Rampuria St, Old City (500 m from Kote Gate), ask for Rampuria Haveli, T0151-252 9323, www.bhanwar niwas.com. 26 beautifully decorated rooms (all different) around a fantastic courtyard in an exquisite early 20th-century *haveli*. Original decor has been painstakingly restored to stunning effect, takes you back to another era, great service. Highly recommended.
AL-A Karni Bhawan Palace (HRH), Gandhi Colony behind Lallgarh Palace, T0151-252 4701, www.hrhindia.com. 12 comfortable a/c rooms and spacious suites in original art deco mansion. Elegant furniture, modern fittings, good restaurant, large garden, peaceful, attentive service, feels like the original inhabitants have just stepped out for a while.

AL-B Lalgarh Palace, 3 km from the railway, T0151-254 0201, www.lallgarhpalace.com. Large a/c rooms in beautiful and authentic surroundings (see page 272), magnificent indoor pool, atmospheric dining hall, mixed reports on food but quite an experience.

A Heritage Resort, along the Jaipur highway, '9 km' post, T0151-275 2393, www.carnival hotels.com. 36 modern, well-appointed cottage rooms in a pleasant location. Attractive gardens, outdoor coffee shop, pool, 3-hole golf course, friendly.

C Basant Vihar Palace, Ganganagar Rd, T0151-225 0675, www.basantvihar palace.com. Rooms in attractive early 20th-century palatial sandstone mansion built by Maharajah Ganga Singhji albeit a little faded today, magnificent darbar hall, pool, large gardens, old lily ponds.

C Fun 'n' Food, NH11, 8 km from town, T0151-752 589, www.realbikaner.com. Good option for families; reasonable rooms plus 2 pools, fairground rides and a boating lake.

C-D Bhairon Vilas, near fort, T0151-254 4751, www.hotelbaironvilas.tripod.com. Restored 1800s aristocratic *haveli*, great atmosphere, 18 eclectic rooms decorated with flair – you can spend hours simply exploring the antiquities in your own room, excellent rooftop restaurant (musicians, dancers), great views across the city and fort, funky boutique shop, lawn, and a new restaurant planned. Kitsch chic, wholeheartedly recommended.

C-D Palace View, near Lalgarh Palace, T0151-2543625. 15 clean, comfortable rooms (some a/c), good views of palace and gardens, food to order, small garden, courteous, hospitable family.

C-E Meghsar Castle, 9 Gajner Rd, T0151-252 7315, www.hotelmeghsarcastle.com. 16 air-cooled rooms in modern hotel built in traditional Rajput sandstone style, some bigger family rooms, attractive garden, friendly manager and dalmatian.

C-F Harasar Haveli, opposite Karni Singh Stadium, T0151-220 9891, www.hotel harasarhaveli.com. Notorious for paying hefty commissions to rickshaw drivers; often full when others empty. Otherwise nice enough; rooms in converted mansion, some with verandas and good views, TVs, dining room with period memorabilia, plus great rooftop restaurant, garden, internet, clean, friendly.

D-E Desert Winds, opposite Karni Stadium, next to Harasar Haveli, T0151-254 2202. 22 clean, comfortable rooms with TV, good food, pleasant balcony and garden, friendly family. Run by knowledgable ex-tourist officer.

D-E Jaswant Bhawan, Alakh Sagar Rd, near railway station, T0151-254 8848, jaswantbhawan@yahoo.co.in.15 rooms in a charming old building, quiet location, restaurant, lawn, good value. Recommended.

D-F Marudhar Heritage, Bhagwan Mahaveer Marg, near Station Rd, T0151-252 2524, hmheritage20000@yahoo.co.in. 27 variable rooms, air-cooled or a/c, bath with hot showers (am), TV, clean and comfortable, generous *thalis* (Rs 50), friendly owner.

D-F Sri Ram, A-228, Sadul Ganj, T0151-252 2651, www.hotelsriram.com. A hotel, guesthouse and youth hostel in one. 20 rooms, all clean and well-maintained, some a/c, run by a knowledgeable, entertaining ex-army man and family, free pickups. More rooms being built. Recommended.

E Marudhar, Ambedkar Circle, T0151-220 4853, hotelmarudhar@yahoo.com. 26 clean, well maintained rooms, 9 a/c, friendly staff. Better than **Thar** and **Ashoka** next door.

E Padmini Niwas, 148 Sadul Ganj, T0151-252 2794, padmini_hotel@rediffmail.com. Clean, basic, comfy rooms (some a/c) in laid-back bungalow in quiet location, only outdoor pool in town, pleasant lawn, includes 1 hr free internet, free pickup. Recommended.

E-F Hotel Regent, Sadul Colony, near PBM Hospital, T0151-254 1598, bituharisingh@ yahoo.com. 11 modern, clean, comfortable rooms, 4 a/c, in quiet area. Excellent home-cooked meals, owner Hari is a most hospitable and knowledgeable host, good value, recommended. Camel safaris also arranged.

E-F Suraj Hotel, near railway station, Rani Bazar, T0151-252 1902, surajhotel@vsnl.com. 20 rooms in modern building, well run, slightly shabby but good value. Attached vegetarian restaurant recommended.

F Railway Retiring Rooms and dorm are good value.

F-G Evergreen, Station Rd, T0151-254 2061. Once-excellent hotel, but deeply in need of a facelift with musty, unattractively stained rooms. However, the downstairs restaurant is clean and gets very favourable reviews.

F-G Green Villas, behind Raj Vilas, T0151-252 1877. A friendly homestay with 3 simple, clean rooms, home-cooked meals great value.

F-G Vijay Guest House, opposite Sophia School, Jaipur Rd, T0151-223 1244, www.camelman.com. 6 clean rooms with attached bathrooms, plus 2 with common bath. Slightly distant location compensated for by free use of bicycles or scooter, free pickups from bus/train, Rs 5 in shared rickshaw to town. Delicious home-cooked meals, pleasant garden, quiet, very hospitable (free tea and rum plus evening parties on lawn), knowledgeable host, great value. Good camel safaris. Recommended.

F-G Vinayak Guest House, near Junagarh fort, Hanuman Temple, Old Ginani, T0151-220 2634, vinayakguesthouse@gmail.com. Friendly homestay run by manager of URMUL shop and his wildlife expert son who cannot do enough for you, excellent home cooking and cooking lessons, also runs camel safaris, photography classes, village and wildlife tours. Highly recommended.

Around Bikaner *p272*

L-A Gajner Palace, Gajner National Park, T01534-275061, www.hrhindia.com. 44 a/c rooms in the elegant palace and its wings, set by a beautiful lake. Rooms in main building full of character (Edwardian Raj nostalgia), those in wings well maintained but very middle England. Sumptuous lounge bar and restaurant overlooking lake, magnificent gardens, boating, good walking,

pleasantly unfrequented and atmospheric, friendly manager and staff, no pool. Visitors are welcome 0800-1730, Rs 100.

E Dr Karni Singh's Rest House, adjoining the home of his forefathers, Kakoo, T01532-253006. Resthouse with 6 simple rooms and 4 rustic huts with attached baths, hot water in buckets, a great experience. Good camel safaris arranged, with the advantage of getting straight in to the desert rather than having to get out of town first as in Jaisalmer/Bikaner.

F Yatri Niwas, near Karni Mata Mandir. Simple rooms.

● Eating

Bikaner *p270, map p271*
You can dine in style at several of the hotels. Try the local specialities – *Bikaneri bhujia/sev/namkeen* – savoury snacks made from dough. Purana Bazar sells ice-cold *lassis* by day, hot milk, sugar and cream at night.

♨ Amber, Station Rd. Indian, some Western dishes. Popular, vegetarian *thali* is exceptional but some reports of falling standards.

♨ Bhairon Vilas (see Sleeping). Breezy rooftop for Rajasthani meals, atmospheric, order ahead.

♨ Bhanwar Niwas (see Sleeping). Amazingly ornate dining hall, good way of having a look around if you're not staying there.

♨ Gallops, Court Rd. Excellent views of the fort, but overpriced and disappointing food but good for a rest after exploring the fort.

♨ Kesria, Jaipur Rd. Pleasant countryside location, popular on breezy summer evenings but disappointing food.

♨ Padmini Niwas (see Sleeping). An average hotel restaurant, but eating here buys you the right to use the swimming pool.

♨ Lalji, Station Rd near Evergreen. Popular local joint serving good dosas and sweets.

♨ Vijay Guest House (see Sleeping). Delicious home-cooked vegetarian *thalis*, non-vegetarian set menu (Rs 60-100).

😊 Festivals and events

Bikaner *p270, map p271*
Both the following are especially spectacular in Junagarh Fort in the Old City near Kote Gate and some smaller palaces.
Oct/Nov Diwali.
Dec/Jan Camel Fair (Although usually in Jan, the 2009 fair is 30-31 Dec and so none in 2010, but then 18-19 Jan 2011 and 8-9 Jan 2012).

Around Bikaner *p272*
Oct/Nov In Kolayat, the **Cattle and Camel Fair** (17-26 Nov 2010) is very colourful and authentic but it can get quite riotous after dark. Since facilities are minimal, it is best to arrive before the festival to find a local family with space to spare, or ask a travel agent in Bikaner.

🛍 Shopping

Bikaner *p270, map p271*
Bikaner is famous for *Usta* work including footwear, purses and cushions. Local carpets and woodwork available too. Main shopping centres are on KEM (MG) Rd and around Kote Gate in the Old City, Modern Market.
Abhivyakti, URMUL Desert Craft, Sri Ganga nagar Rd, next to New Bus Stand, T0151-252 2139. Run by **URMUL** trust, see box, page 272.
Kalakar Arts, Sardar Hall, Lalgarh Palace Rd, T0151-220 4477. Good selection of silver jewellery and other artefacts.

🏔 Activities and tours

Bikaner *p270, map p271*
Camel safaris must be arranged through private operators. Budget tours (Rs 500-600 per day) for groups of 4 or more; bring water.
Aravalli Tours, opposite Municipal Council Hall, Junagarh Rd, T0151-220 1124. Rs 1800 per person (toilet tent shared

between 10 people) for upmarket experience. Other tours too.
Camel Man, Vijay Guest House, Jaipur Rd, T0151-223 1244, www.camelman.com. Good value, reliable, friendly and professional safaris, jeep tours, cycling. Lightweight 'igloo' tents, clean mattresses, sheets, good food and guidance. Safaris to see antelopes, colourful villages and potters at work; from 1- to 2-hr rides to 5-day trips; Rs 800-1000 per person per day.
Thar Desert Safari, Ganganagar Rd, behind New Bus Stand, T0151-252 1661, www.thar desertsafari.com. Honest, unpretentious outfit offering simple, no frills camel tours.
Vinayak Desert Safari, T(0)9414-430948, vinayakguesthouse@gmail.com. Eco-friendly camel trekking with Jitu Solanki who has a Masters degree in wildlife and specializes in the study of reptiles. Offer camel, jeep and wildlife safaris and village homestays. Highly informed and friendly guide.
Vino Desert Safari, Gangashahar, T0151-227 0445, www.vinodesertsafari.com. Good-value low-key safaris, including some longer distance 'inter-city' treks, eg 12-day Bikaner-Osian.

➡ Transport

Bikaner *p270, map p271*
Bus
The New Bus Stand is 3 km north of town. Private buses leave from south of the fort.
Rajasthan Roadways, enquiries, T0151-252 3800; daily de luxe buses to **Ajmer**, **Jodhpur**, **Jaisalmer** (8 hrs), **Udaipur**. 2 daily to **Delhi** via Hissar (12 hrs).

Rickshaw/taxi
Autos between station and bus stand or Lallgarh Palace, Rs 25. Taxis are unmetered. Shared *tempos* run on set routes, Rs 5.

Train
Enquiries, T0151-220 0131, reservations, Mon-Sat 0800-1400, 1415-2000, Sun 0800-1400. For tourist quota (when trains are full)

apply to Manager's Office by Radio Tower near **Jaswant Bhawan Hotel**. There are 2 direct trains to **Delhi**: *Assam Awadh Express 5610*, 2000 (12 hrs) arrives Old Delhi station; *Sampark Kranti Express 2464*, 1720 (12 hrs Tue, Thu, Sat) or take a train to Rewari and change. **Rewari**: *Link Exp 4710*, 1750, 8 hrs; *Rewari Mail 4792*, 1955, 8 hrs; *Rewari Exp 4790*, 0835, 8½ hrs. **Jaipur**: *Intercity Exp 2467*, 0500, 6½ hrs. **Jodhpur**: *Ranakpur Exp 4707*, 0945, 5½ hrs, continues to **Ahmedabad**, 16 hrs, and **Mumbai** (Bandra), 27 hrs.

Around Bikaner *p272*
Bus
For **Karni Mata Mandir**, buses leave from Bikaner New Bus Stand, Rs 15, or on Ganga Shahar Rd and at Ambedkar Circle. Taxis charge around Rs 300 return. For **Kalibangan** catch a bus to **Suratgarh** then change; this junction town also has connections to Hanumangarh, Sirsa (Haryana) or Mandi Dabwali (Punjab).

Train
The broad-gauge train line from Suratgarh to **Anupgarh**, about 15 km from the Pakistan border, calls at Raghunathgarh, the closest station to Kalibangan; travel from there to Kalibangan is difficult (check at Suratgarh). Trains from Suratgarh: **Anupgarh**: Passenger, 0755, 2¼ hrs. **Bikaner** (Lalgarh Junction): *Chandigarh Exp 4887*, 0835, 3¼ hrs. **Bhatinda**: *Chandigarh Exp 4888*, 1955, 3¼ hrs.

◑ Directory

Bikaner *p270, map p271*
Banks Bank of Baroda, Ambedkar Circle, cash against Visa; **State Bank of Bikaner & Jaipur**, Ambedkar Circle; also near fort's Suraj Pol. Changes TCs but may charge up to 10% commission. Harasar Haveli Hotel charges 1%. **Internet** Meghsar Castle, Hotel Sagar and **Harasar Haveli**, Rs 2 per min; others at Sadulganj, Sagar Rd, Jaipur Rd and near the fort. **Medical services** PBM Hospital, Hospital Rd, T0151-252 5312. **Post** GPO: behind Junagarh Fort. **Useful contacts** Police: T100/T0151-252 2225.

Shekhawati

Covering an area of about 300 sq km on the often arid and rock-studded plains to the northwest of the Aravalli mountain range, Shekhawati is the homeland of the Marwari community. The area is particularly rich in painted havelis; Sikar district in the southwest and Jhunjhunun in the northeast form an 'open-air art gallery' of paintings dating from the mid-19th century. Although a day trip gives you an idea of its treasures, it is better to spend two or three nights in Shekhawati to see the temples, frescoed forts, chhatris and step wells at leisure. There are other diversions laid on such as horse or camel safaris and treks into the hills. Shekhawati sees far fewer visitors than the better-known areas of Rajasthan, and as such retains something of a 'one pen/rupee' attitude to tourists. This is generally quite innocent and should not be a deterrent to potential visitors.

Ramgarh has the highest concentration of painted havelis, though they are not as well maintained as those of Nawalgarh which has the second largest selection. It is easier to visit havelis in towns that have hotels, such as Nawalgarh, Mandawa, Dundlod, Mukundgarh, Mahansar, Fatehpur, Baggar and Jhunjunun, and where the caretakers are used to visitors, though towns like Bissau, Alsisar, Malsisar and Churu have attractive havelis as well.➤➤ *For listings, see pages 283-286.*

Ins and outs

Getting there You can get to the principal Shekhawati towns by train but road access is easier. A car comes in handy, though there are crowded buses from Delhi, Jaipur and Bikaner to some towns. Buses leave every 30 minutes from 0500-2000 from Jaipur's Main Bus Station and take three hours.➤➤ *See Transport, page 286.*

Getting around You can get from one Shekhawati town to another by local bus, which run every 15 to 20 minutes. Within each town it is best to enlist the help of a local person (possibly from the hotels listed below) to direct you to the best *havelis*, as it can be very difficult to find your way around.

The *havelis* are often occupied by the family or retainers who will happily show you around, either for free or for a fee of about Rs 20. Many *havelis* are in a poor state of repair with fading paintings which may appear monotonously alike to some.

Tourist information **RTDC** ① *Mandawa Circle, Jhunjhunun, T01592-232909*. Recommended reading includes *The painted towns of Shekhawati*, by Ilay Cooper, a great Shekhawati enthusiast, with photos and maps.

History

The 'Garden of Shekha' was named after Rao Shekhaji of Amarsar (1433-1488) who challenged the Kachhawahas, refusing to pay tribute to the rulers at Amber. These Rajput barons made inroads into Muslim territory even during Mughal rule, and declared Shekhawati independent from the Jaipur suzerainty until 1738. During this period the merchants lavishly decorated their houses with paintings on religious, folk and historical themes. As Mughal power collapsed Shekhawati became a region of lawless banditry. In the early 19th century the British East India Company brought it under their control, bringing peace but also imposing taxes and tolls on trade which the Marwaris resented. Many of the merchants migrated to other parts of the country to seek their fortune and those who flourished returned their wealth to their homeland and took over as patrons of the arts.

Sikar

The late 17th-century fort was built when Sikar was an important trading centre and the wealthiest *thikana* (feudatory) under Jaipur. It now has a population of 148,000. You can visit the old quarter and see the Wedgwood blue 'Biyani' (1920) and 'Mahal' (1845), Murarka and Somani *havelis* and murals and carvings in Gopinath, Raghunath and Madan Mohan temples. From Jaipur take the NH11 to Ringas (63 km) and Sikar (48 km).

Laksmangarh

Founded early 19th century, the town plan was based on Jaipur's model; this can be seen by climbing up to the imposing old fort which has now been renovated by the Jhunjhunwala family. The fine *havelis* include one of the area's grandest – Ganeriwala with *char chowks* (four courtyards). Others include the 'Rathi' *haveli* near the clock tower in the market, and several in the Chowkhani.

Pachar

This is a little town west of Jaipur in the middle of the sand dunes with a golden sandstone castle scenically situated on a lakeshore. A road north from Bagru on the NH8 also gives access.

Ramgarh

Ramgarh was settled by the Poddars in the late 18th century. In addition to their many *havelis* and that of the Ruias, visit the *chhatris* with painted entrances near the bus stand, as well as the temples to Shani (with mirror decoration) and to Ganga. Ramgarh has the highest concentration of painted *havelis*, though they are not as well maintained as those of Nawalgarh which has the second largest assemblage. The town has a pleasantly laid-back feel. Look for handicrafts here.

Danta

Originally a part of Marwar, Danta was given to Thakur Amar Singhji in the mid-17th century. It is well off the beaten track and as such is completely unspoilt. Two empty *kilas* (forts) and the residential wing (early 18th-century) combine Mughal and Rajput art and architectural styles.

Mukundgarh

The market for textiles and brass betel cutters, Mukundgarh lies 10 km south of Jhunjhunun. The Ganeriwala *havelis* (1860s and 1870s) are worth visiting as well as the Jhunjhunwala (1859) *haveli* with Krishna stories and Sukhdev *haveli* (circa 1880).

Nawalgarh

Some 25 km southeast of Mandawa, Nawalgarh was founded in 1737 by Thakur Nawal Singh. There are numerous fine *havelis* worth visiting here. The town has a colourful bazar – though lone tourists have been harassed here – and two forts (circa 1730). **Nawalgarh fort** has fine examples of maps and plans of Shekhawati and Jaipur. The **Bala Kila**, which has a kiosk with beautiful ceiling paintings, is approached via the fruit market in the town centre and entered

Fit for a merchant

The *havelis* in Shekhawati were usually built around two courtyards – one for general use, and the other a *zenana* courtyard for the women. The latter was also used for laundry and so often had a well and occasionally a play area for children. Security was a prime concern so a *haveli* was typically entered by a solid gate with a smaller door in it for regular use by residents. Watchmen had rooms on either side of the entrance. The *baithak* (reception room) had mattresses and bolsters for sitting on the floor while others were set aside for sleeping or storage. The *havelis* were enlarged as the families grew larger or wealthier, and with the onset of peaceful times, they became more palatial and lavished with decoration.

The *haveli* was made from brick or local stone. It was plastered in two layers with decorations on the second layer – a polished lime plaster finish often set with agate and other semi-precious stones. Murals were either painted on dry surfaces or on wet plaster. Mineral colours were derived from indigo, ochre, lead, copper, lapis lazuli, lime and even gold. Synthetic blue was imported and only the wealthiest could afford strong blue tones on their *havelis*. Some of the finest frescoes were near the door separating the courtyard from the main chambers and these were often restored or repainted during weddings and festivals. The subject of the paintings varied. The 10 avatars of Vishnu were popular, especially scenes from *Krishna Lila* and the *Ramayana*. The *Mahabharata*, the *Ragamala* (depicting musical modes of different seasons), folk tales, historic events, daily life in Shekhawati and floral and faunal themes were also popular, and there was a fascination for portraying the British and their curious ways.

through the **Hotel Radha**. It also has the **Roop Niwas Palace** (now a hotel) and some 18th-century temples with 19th- and early 20th-century paintings. There are other interesting temples in town including Ganga Mai near Nansa Gate.

The **Anandilal Poddar Haveli**, now converted to the **Poddar Haveli Museum** ⓘ *foreigners Rs 100, includes camera and guide*, is perhaps the best restored *haveli* of Shekhawati. The 1920s *haveli* has around 700 frescoes including a Gangaur procession, scenes from the Mahabharata, trains, cars, the avatars of Vishnu, bathing scenes and British characters. Exceptionally well restored throughout, some of the best paintings frame the doors leading from the courtyard to the rooms. The upper storey of the *haveli* is now a school but the ground floor has been opened as a museum. The photo-gallery records the life of congressman and freedom fighter Anandilal Poddar, and the merchant-turned-industrialist Poddar family. There is a diorama of costumes of various Rajasthani tribes and communities, special bridal attires and a gallery of musical instruments.

Other remarkable Murarka *havelis* include the 19th-century **Kesardev Murarka**, which has a finely painted façade and the early 20th-century **Radheshyam Murarka**. The latter portrays processions, scenes from folk tales and various Hindu and Christian religious themes, sometimes interspersed with mirror-work. Other fine *havelis* are those of the Bhagat, Chokhani, Goenka, Patodia, Kedwal, Sangerneria, Saraogi, Jhunjhunwala, Saha and Chhauchuria families. The paintings here depict anything from European women having a bath to Hindu religious themes and Jesus Christ. Some of the *havelis* are complexes of several buildings which include a temple, dharamshala, cenotaph and a well). Most charge Rs 15-20 for viewing.

Parasarampura

About 12 km southeast of Nawalgarh, Parasarampura has a decorated *chhatri* to Sardul Singh (1750) and the adjacent **Gopinath** temple (1742); these are the earliest examples of Shekhawati frescoes painted with natural pigments (the caretaker has the keys, and will point things out with a peacock feather).

Dundlod

West of Nawalgarh, the best of Dundlod's murals are in the **castle** (1750) ① *Darbar Hall, Rs 20 for non-residents*, now a heritage hotel. You enter the moated castle by the **Suraj Pol** and proceed through the **Bichla Darwaza** and **Uttar Pol** (north) before arriving at the courtyard. Steps lead up to the majestic **Diwan Khana**, furnished with period furniture, portraits and hangings; there is a library with a collection of rare books of Indian history and the *duchatta* above, which allowed the ladies in *purdah* to watch court ceremonies unobserved. Ask for the key to the painted family *chhatris* nearby. The **Goenk** *haveli* near the fort has three painted courtyards, and the **Satyanarayan temple** has religious paintings but both these may be closed in the low season. The interesting deep step well now has an electric pump. The **Polo Centre** provides an opportunity to see camel, horse and bicycle polo, tent pegging, etc. Mukundgarh is the nearest station, from where you can take a jeep or taxi.

Jhunjhunun

A stronghold of the Kayamkhani Nawabs, Jhunjhunun was defeated by the Hindu Sardul Singh in 1730. The Mohanlal **Iswardas Modi** (1896), **Tibriwala** (1883) and the Muslim **Nuruddin Farooqi Haveli** (which is devoid of figures) and the *maqbara* are all worth seeing. The *Chhe* Haveli complex, Khetri Mahal (1760) and the Biharilal temple (1776), which has attractive frescoes (closed during lunch time), are also interesting. The **Rani Sati** temple commemorates Narayana Devi who is believed to have become a *sati*; her stone is venerated by many of the wealthy *bania* community and an annual Marwari fair is held (protesting women's groups feel it glorifies the practice of *sati*). Since 1947, 29 cases of *sati* have been recorded in Jhunjhunun and its two neighbouring districts.

Baggar

The grand *haveli* of the **Makharias**, 10 km north east of Jhunjhunun, has rooms along open corridors around grassy courtyards; worth seeing if only for the wall paintings of gods and angels being transported in motor cars.

Mahansar

Founded in the mid-18th century, Mahansar, 30 km northeast of Jhunjhunun, has a distinctly medieval feel. It has the Poddar *haveli* of **Son Chand**, the **Rama Temple** (ask for the key to the Golden Room; expensive at Rs 100 but very well preserved) and the large **Raghunath Temple** with some of the finest paintings of the region. The fort (1768) has palaces and a *baradari* which were added later.

Churu

Set in semi-desert countryside, Churu, northwest of Baggar, was believed to have been a Jat stronghold in the 16th century. In the 18th century it was an important town of Bikaner state and its fort dates from this period. The town thrived during the days of overland desert trade. The town has some interesting 1870s Oswal Jain *havelis* like those of the Kotharis and the Suranas. Also worth a look are the **Banthia** (early 20th century), **Bagla** (1880), **Khemka** (1800s), **Poddar** and **Bajranglal Mantri** *havelis*. The main attraction, however, is the extraordinary '**Malji-ka-Kamra**', a crumbling, colonnaded *haveli* which houses some amazing interior scenes.

Tal Chappar

A possible day excursion from one of the castle hotels is a visit to **Tal Chappar Wildlife Sanctuary** near Sujjangarh covering 71 sq km of desert scrubland with ponds and salt flats. It has some of the largest herds of Blackbuck antelope in India (easily seen at the watering point near the park gate itself during the dry season), besides chinkara gazelle, desert cat, desert fox and other dryland wildlife. Huge flocks of demoiselle and common cranes can be seen at nearby lakes and wetlands during the winter months (September to March) where they feed on tubers and ground vegetation. Some 175 different species of bird visit the park over the course of a year, including sandgrouse, quails, bar-headed geese and cream-coloured desert courser.

Ins and outs The best time to visit is just after the rainy season, generally August and September. The enthusiastic and charming forest guard, Brij Dansamor, is a good guide to the area. A local NGO, **Krishna Mirg**, is active in tree plantation and in fundraising for the eco-development of Tal Chappar, providing support fodder during dry months to blackbuck and cranes. **Forest Department Rest House** has five basic but adequate rooms at Rs 300 per double. To book ahead call the head office in Churu on T01562-250938. Try **Hanuman** tea stall for delicious *chai* and the local sweet, *malai laddoo*. the drive to Tal Chappar can be long and tiring. If you are travelling between Bikaner and Shekhawati in a jeep, it is worth making a detour.

◉ Shekhawati listings

For Sleeping and Eating price codes and other relevant information, see Essentials pages 28-33.

◯ Sleeping

Sikar District *p280*
B-C Ashirwad Palace, Churu Bypass, NH11, 2 km from Fatehpur, T01571-222635. 12 rooms around a small lawn.
B-C Castle Pachar, Pachar, T0141-222 6920 (Jaipur office) www.castlepachar.com. 16 well-decorated rooms in a fascinating old property with portraits, paintings and weaponry, delicious if very rich food, charming hosts, swimming pool under construction. Recommended.
C Dera, off the high street, Danta, T01577-270 041. Open 1 Oct-31 Mar. 14 large, characterful rooms in residential wing

below the 2 old forts, good restaurant (meals Rs 160), peacocks at dawn, camel rides (Rs 350 per hr, Rs 6050 for 3 hrs), horse safaris, jeep safaris (minimum 4 people), Rs 1400 each per day.
D-E Hotel Niros, Station Rd, Sikar, T01572-241 0060. An upmarket establishment with 31 rooms including an a/c restaurant boasting some unusual water features.
E-F Haveli (RTDC), Sikar Rd, 500 m south of bus stand, Fatehpur, T01571-230293. 8 clean rooms, some a/c with bath, pleasant building, dull restaurant, best bet in town.
F Aravalli Resort, NH11, Sikar. Simple and shabby with 2 air-cooled rooms with bath, inexpensive Indian restaurant.
F Shekhaji Resort, opposite Asirwad Palace, Fatehpur. Hotel with 4 basic rooms plus an airy restaurant.

Jhunjhunun District *p280*

AL-A Castle Mandawa, Mandawa, T0141-237 1194 (Jaipur office), www.mandawahotels.com. Huge castle with lots of character but parts rather run-down. 68 a/c rooms, some in tower, complete with swing, most with 4-posters and period trappings but rooms vary and beds can be hard so select with care, excellent views, atmospheric but a bit overpriced, mixed reports, some disappointed with meals (Rs 450-500).

AL-A Desert Resort, 1 km south of Mandawa, T0141-237 1194 (Jaipur office), www.mandawahotels.com. 60 rooms in 3 wings including a *haveli*, modern amenities, pricey restaurant (Rs 250-500 and only buffets for tour groups), pool, shady garden, good views of countryside, camel rides. Again lacks warmth, very business-like.

AL-A Grand Haveli, Bawari Gate, Nawalgarh, T01594 225301, www.grandhaveli.com. Stunning newly restored *haveli* with 19 de luxe rooms and several suites and duplexes. This impressive building is ornately decorated with frescoes and each room has its own *jhakora* with diwan and stained glass windows. Beautiful restaurant and cocktail bar. A swimming pool and spa are in the making.

A-B Dundlod Fort (Heritage Hotel), in village centre, Dundlod, T01594-252519, www.dundlod.com. 42 rooms. Upgraded rooms particularly good, good state rooms with period furniture, suites with terraces, good food (Rs 180-220), power cuts can be a problem but full of atmosphere and interesting murals, pool, library, tours, horse safaris a speciality, warm welcome, very hospitable and helpful. Recommended.

B Mukundgarh Fort (Heritage Hotel), T01594-252397, www.crosscountry.co.in. 45 rooms in converted mid-18th-century fort with frescoes along wide corridors, slightly musty but authentic interiors, modern bathrooms, restaurant, bar and pool, friendly management, slightly run-down.

B Roop Vilas Palace, Rawal Sab Ki Kothi, T01594-224321, www.roopvilas.com.

Elegant heritage-style hotel with 21 rooms and 3 luxury tents. Beautifully set around an open courtyard, stylish rooms, and good locally grown food.

B-C Mandawa Haveli, near Sonthaliya Gate, Mandawa, T01592-223088, http://hotelmandawa.free.fr. 18 stunning rooms with modernized baths in a 3-storeyed, characterful *haveli* with original 19th-century frescoes in courtyard, every aspect is beautiful inside and out, great Rajasthani meals, museum and library. Friendly staff, authentic feel. Recommended.

B-C Piramal Haveli, Baggar, T0159-221220, www.neemranahotels.com. 100-year-old home, restored sensitively, excellent vegetarian meals and attentive service, quirky original frescoes, simple but over-priced, less atmosphere than castle hotels.

B-C Roop Niwas Kothi, 1 km north of Nawalgarh, T01594-222008, www.roopniwaskothi.com. 25 rooms in sunny colonial-style buildings. Beautiful grounds with peacocks, Good food, large gardens with peacocks, pool, horse safaris are highly recommended, qualified guides, good food but service is disappointing.

B-D Heritage Mandawa, off Mukundgarh Rd, 200 m from the main bazar street and the bus stand, Mandawa, T01592-223742, www.hotelheritagemandawa.com. 13 rooms with local 'ethnic' furnishings in an opulent, fresco-covered *haveli*, attached baths, dining hall, clean and pleasant, manager and staff very friendly and accommodating (good discounts in the low-season), camel rides, guides, taxis. Camping possible in grounds.

B-D Jamuna Resort, Baggar Rd, Jhunjhunun, T01592-232871, www.shivshekawati.com. 14 a/c cottage rooms with attractive mirror work and murals, 'Golden Room' with painted ceiling "like a jewel box", frescos, open-air Rajasthani vegetarian/non-vegetarian restaurant serving delicious food, gardens, pool (open to hotel/restaurant guests only), local guided tours. Recommended.

C-D Hotel Shekhawati Heritage, off Station Rd, Jhunjhunun, T01592-237134,

www.hotelshekhawatiheritage.com.
22 rooms, 10 a/c, certainly not heritage
but clean and friendly, quiet location.
C-D Narayan Niwas Castle, near bus stand,
Mehansar, T01565-264322, www.mehansar
castle.com. Rooms in the fort, converted
by Thakur Tejpal Singh. Only 16 rooms are
open (out of a total of 500); Nos 1 and 5 are
really exceptional. Attractive wall paintings,
pleasingly unspoilt but poor bathrooms.
Delicious meals (cooked by Mrs Singh),
home-made liqueurs, charming owners,
a *Fawlty Towers* experience.
C-D Thikana, T01594-222152, www.heritage
thikana.com. Comfortable rooms in attractive
building. Family-run and welcoming, good
locally grown food.
D Apani Dhani, Jhunjhunu Rd, 1 km from
railway station, 500 m north of bus stand,
Nawal garh, T01594-222239, www.apani
dhani.com. 8 environmentally friendly huts
and 3 beautiful tents on an ecological farm
run by the charming and authoritative
Ramesh Jangid. Attractive, comfortable,
solar-lit thatched cottages traditionally built
using mud and straw, modern bathrooms
(some with 'footprint' toilets), home-grown
vegetarian, immaculately presented, relaxing
atmosphere. Accommodation and education
in one enticing package. Cooking lessons
also possible. Very special place. No alcohol
permitted and modest respectful dress
requested. Recommended.
D-E Natraj Hotel, Churu, T01562-257245.
28 clean, modern rooms, best bet in town.
D-F Shiv Shekhawati, Muni Ashram,
Khemi Sati Rd, Jhunjhunun, I0159-223 2651,
www.shivshekhawati.com. 20 simple clean
rooms, 8 a/c, bath and hot water, good
vegetarian restaurant, tourist office
(guides). Same owner as **Jamuna
Resort** (see above). Friendly.
E Shekawati Guest House, near Roop Niwas,
Nawalgarh, T01594-224 658, www.shekawati
restaurant.com. 6 clean, well-presented

rooms and also now a circle of simple, yet
beautiful thatched cottages, as well as an
attractive thatched restaurant run by the
friendly qualified cook Kalpana Singh. The
food is exceptional and cooking classes can
be arranged, as can local tours. Check out
their organic garden. Recommended.
E Tourist Pension, behind Maur Hospital,
Nawalgarh, T01594-224060, www.apani
dhani.com. 8 rooms, some family-sized, in
modern house run by Rajesh, the son of the
owner of **Apani Dhani** (see above), and
his wife Sarla, an excellent cook. Some
nice big rooms, beautiful old furniture made
by Rajesh's grandfather, very welcoming.
Another guesthouse has opened up calling
itself Tourist Pension near Roop Niwas,
make sure you come to this one.
E-F Hotel Aman, near railway station,
Jhunjhunun, T01592-231090. 10 rooms,
4 a/c, reasonable restaurant, 24-hr checkout.
E-F Hotel Shekawati, off Mukandgarh Rd,
Mandawa, T01592-223036. Simple, basic
rooms, only budget place in town, adequate.
E-G Neelam, opposite Khetan Hospital,
Jhunjhunun. 24 rooms, a/c and air-cooled,
economical with shared facilities, restaurant
serving snacks, slightly shabby.
F-G Sangam, near bus stand, Jhunjhunun,
T0159-232544. Clean rooms, better with bath
at rear, vegetarian meals, best budget option.

🍴 Eating

Sikar District *p280*
🍴 **Natraj Restaurant**, Main Rd, Sikar. Good
meals and snacks, clean, reasonable.

Jhunjhunun District *p280*
🍴🍴 **Roop Niwas Kothi**, Nawalgarh. For
heritage experience (and unreliable service).
🍴 **Shekawati Guest House**, Nawalgarh.
For delicious, hygienically prepared fare.

▲ Activities and tours

Shekhawati *p279*
Camel safaris

A typical 5-day safari might include Nawalgarh–
Mukundgarh– Mandawa–Mahansar–Churu
(crossing some of the finest sand dunes in
Shekhawati); 3-day safaris might include
Nawalgarh–Fatehpur. Also 1-week country
safaris to Tal Chappar Wildlife Sanctuary.
The cost depends on the number in the
group and the facilities provided ranging from
Rs 800-1500 per day. 1-day safaris arranged
by the heritage hotels cost about Rs 800 with
packed lunch and mineral water. **Roop Niwas
Palace**, **Apani Dhani** (Nawalgarh), **Dundlod**
and **Mandawa** (see Sleeping) offer trips.

Horse safaris

Dundlod Fort and **Roop Niwas** at Nawalgarh
(see Sleeping) offer 1-week safaris staying
overnight in royal tents (occasionally in
castles or heritage hotels) to cover the
attractions of the region. The most popular
take in the Pushkar or Tilwara fairs. You can
expect folk music concerts, campfires, guest
speakers, masseurs, and sometimes even a
barber, all with jeep support. You ride 3 hrs
in the morning and 2 hrs in the afternoon,
and spend time visiting eco-farms, rural
communities and *havelis* en route.

Trekking

There are some interesting treks in the Aravalli
hills near Nawalgarh starting from Lohargal
(34 km), a temple with sacred pools. Local
people claim that this is the place recorded
in the *Mahabharata* where Bhim's mace is said
to have been crafted. A 4- to 5-day trek
would take in the Bankhandi Peak (1052 m),
Krishna temple in Kirori Valley, Kot Reservoir,
Shakambari mata temple, Nag Kund (a natural
spring) and Raghunathgarh Fort. The cost
depends on the size of the group and the
facilities. **Apani Dhani**, see Sleeping, arranges
highly recommended treks with stays at the
temple guesthouses and villages for US$50
per person per day (minimum 2 people).

⊖ Transport

Shekhawati *p279*
Bicycle

Apani Dhani, Nawalgarh. Arranges cycle
tours in Shekhawati.

Bus

All major towns in the region including
Sikar, Nawalgarh and Jhunjhunun are linked
by bus with **Jaipur** (3-6 hrs) and **Bikaner**,
and some have a daily service to **Delhi**
(7-10 hrs); it's best to book a day ahead
for these as buses fill up.

Jeep

For hire in Nawalgarh, Mandawa and
Dundlod, about Rs 1500 per day.

Taxi

From **Jaipur**, a diesel Ambassador costs
around Rs 3000 for a day tour of parts of
Shekhawati; with detours (eg Samode)
and a/c cars coming in around Rs 5000.
    Local hire is possible in Mandawa,
Mukundgarh and Nawalgarh. Also see
Car hire in Delhi, page 103, as Shekhawati
lies on a sensible if slightly elongated
route between there and Jaipur.

Train

Most trains through Shekhawati are slow
passenger services, which tend to run to their
own schedule. Most begin their journeys at
Rewari (see Bikaner, page 277), and connect
with **Bikaner** and **Jaipur**. Check locally
for current schedules.

⊙ Directory

Jhunjhunun District *p280*
Banks SBBJ and Bank of Baroda, Mandawa.
In Nawalgarh, SBBJ changes currency and
TCs, but poor rate. **Roop Niwas** can help
get better rates. **UCO Bank** changes
currency in Dundlod.

Contents

Footprint features

Background

History

Settlement and early history

Rajasthan was among the first regions of South Asia to be settled. Similarities between hand axes and cleavers discovered in the Chittaurgarh region of southeastern Rajasthan and those found in the Olduvai gorge in Africa have led archaeologists to suggest a slow diffusion from Africa to India, the Indian tools being much more recent. Rajasthan is particularly rich in Middle Palaeolithic artefacts, dating from between 17,000 and 40,000 years before the present, probably during a considerably wetter period than at present. The settlers made use of even apparently inhospitable environments. In the Marwar region of Rajasthan, sand dunes often enclose shallow lakes which were the source of aquatic food for the inhabitants, while the dunes themselves were covered in thick scrub which supported a rich fauna, a source of food for hunters.

The first settlers

By 3500 BC agriculture had spread throughout the Indus Plains and had reached northwestern India. Between 3000 BC and 2500 BC many new settlements sprang up in the heartland of what from 2500 BC became the Harappan or Indus Valley civilization, including cities such as Kalibangan in Rajasthan. Numerous townships of this Harappan period (2500-1500 BC) have been excavated in Rajasthan, most of them along rivers, near the sea coast, or in hills suitable for stone quarrying. In northwestern Rajasthan Kalibangan was a major town and there are many other sites in the now dried-up river beds of the Ghaggar and Sarasvati rivers.

The Indus Valley civilization was entirely home grown. What stimulated its origins, however, remains unclear, but its emergence as a distinct culture seems to have been sudden. Speculation continues to surround the nature of its language, which is still untranslated. It may well have been an early form of the Dravidian languages which today are found largely in South India. However, as even the most basic characteristics such as whether the script should be read from left to right or right to left have not been conclusively demonstrated, the questions far outnumber the reliable answers.

India from 2000 BC to the Mauryas

By 1700 BC the entire Indus Valley civilization had disintegrated. The causes remain uncertain. Sir Mortimer Wheeler's early explanation that the violent arrival of new waves of Aryan immigrants was responsible has now been discarded. Increasing desertification of the already semi-arid landscape, a shift in the course of the Indus as the result of an earthquake such as that which created the so-called 'Allah's Bund' in Kachchh in 1819, and internal political decay have each been suggested as instrumental in its downfall. Whatever the causes in Rajasthan, some features of Indus Valley culture were carried on by succeeding generations.

Possibly a little before 1500 BC northern India entered the Vedic period. Aryan settlers moved southeast towards the Ganga Valley. Classes of rulers *(rajas)* and priests *(brahmins)* began to emerge. Conflict was common. In one battle of this period a confederacy of tribes known as the Bharatas defeated another grouping of 10 tribes. They gave their name to the region to the east of the Indus which is the official name for India today – Bharat.

The centre of population shifted east from the banks of the Indus to the land between the rivers Yamuna and Ganga, the *doab* (pronounced *doe-ahb*, literally 'two waters'). This region became the heart of emerging Aryan culture, which, from 1500 BC onwards, laid the literary and religious foundations of what ultimately became Hinduism. Little is known of developments in Rajasthan at this time, but the centre of gravity of the emerging Hindu culture was clearly to the north and east.

The first fruit of this development was the **Rig Veda**, the first of four Vedas (literally 'knowledge'), composed, collected and passed on orally by Brahmin priests from 1300 BC to about 1000 BC. The later Vedas show that the Indo-Aryans developed a clear sense of the Ganga-Yamuna *doab* as 'their' territory. Later texts extended the core region from the Himalaya to the Vindhyans and to the Bay of Bengal in the east. Beyond lay the land of mixed peoples and then of barbarians, outside the pale of Aryan society.

The Mauryas

Chandragupta Maurya Within a year of the retreat of Alexander the Great from the Indus in 326 BC, Chandragupta Maurya established the first indigenous empire to exercise control over much of the subcontinent. Under his successors that control was extended to all but the extreme south of peninsular India.

Asoka The greatest of the Mauryan emperors, Asoka took power in 272 BC. He inherited a full-blown empire, but extended it from Afghanistan to Assam and from the Himalaya to Mysore.

Asoka (described on the edicts as "the Beloved of the Gods, of Gracious Countenance") left a series of inscriptions on pillars and rocks were written in *Prakrit*, using the *Brahmi* script, although in the northwest they were in Greek using the *Kharoshti* script. They were unintelligible for over 2000 years after the decline of the Mauryan empire until James Prinsep deciphered the Brahmi script in 1837. Although Buddhist influence was never as strong in Rajasthan as in some parts of India, Asoka left an engraved rock at Girnar near Junagadh in modern Gujarat with 14 of his edicts, indicating that Kathiawad was an important Mauryan stronghold on the west coast of the Indian peninsula.

Through the edicts, Asoka urged all people to follow the code of *dhamma* or *dharma* – translated by the Indian historian Romila Thapar as "morality, piety, virtue and social order".

Sakas The Sakas or Scythians, and other Central Asian tribes, entered from the northwest. They set up rule in Rajasthan before the Christian era. Colonel Tod, in his *Annals of Mewar*, suggests that the Kathi royal families of Kathiawadi states like Jasdan, Jetpur, Bhilkha are direct descendants of the Sakas. Rudraman, one of their major rulers, left edicts which can be seen in suburban Junagadh, Gujarat.

Classical Period – the Gupta Empire AD 319-467

Although the political power of Chandra Gupta and his successors never approached that of his unrelated namesake, nearly 650 years before him, the Gupta Empire produced developments in every field of Indian culture. Their influence has been felt profoundly across South Asia to the present. Many Gupta-period terracottas and artefacts have been found in Rajasthan and are displayed in the state's museums.

Geographically the Guptas originated in the same Magadhan region that had given rise to the Mauryan Empire. Extending their power by strategic marriage alliances, Chandra Gupta's empire of Magadh was extended by his son, Samudra Gupta, who took power in AD 335, across North India. He also marched as far south as Kanchipuram in modern Tamil Nadu, but the heartland of the Gupta Empire remained the plains of the Ganga. Chandra

Gupta II reigned for 39 years from AD 376 and was a great patron of the arts. Trade with Southeast Asia, Arabia and China all added to royal wealth.

Throughout the Gupta period, the Brahmins, Hinduism's priestly caste, were in the key position to mediate change. They refocused earlier literature to give shape to the emerging religious philosophy. In their hands the *Mahabharata* and the *Ramayana* were transformed from secular epics to religious stories. The excellence of contemporary sculpture both reflected and contributed to an increase in image worship and the growing role of temples as centres of devotion.

Eventually the Gupta Empire crumbled in the face of repeated attacks from the northwest, this time by the Huns. By the end of the sixth century Punjab and Kashmir had been prised from Gupta control and the last great Hindu empire to embrace the whole of North India and part of the peninsula was at an end.

Regional kingdoms and cultures

The collapse of Gupta power opened the way for successive smaller kingdoms to assert themselves. After the comparatively brief reign of **Harsha** in the mid-seventh century, which recaptured something both of the territory and the glory of the Guptas, the Gangetic plains were constantly fought over by rival groups.

The Rajputs The political instability and rivalry that resulted from the ending of Gupta power opened the way for new waves of immigrants from the northwest and for new groups and clans to seize power. The most significant of these were the Rajputs (sons of kings). Rajput clans trace their origins to one of three mythical sources. The *Suryavanshi* Sisodias (Guhilot) dynasties claim direct descent from the Sun God. They had their capital at Vallabhi in Kathiawad before moving to Nagda and Chittaurgarh in the seventh century, and ultimately to Udaipur after the Mughal conquest of Chittaurgarh. Further north the Kachhawahas, who also claim descent from the sun, took over the Amber region in AD 967. The *Krishnavanshi* Bhatti Rajputs, like the Jadeja Rajputs of Kachchh-Kathiawad, claim descent from the Moon God and Lord Krishna. They migrated to the western desert in the early 11th century and established Jaisalmer in 1156. According to the legend recorded by Chanda Bardai in his epic *Prithviraja Raso*, written for the Rajput King Prithviraj III of Delhi between 1178-1192, a third myth suggests that the four original Rajput warriors were created out of the sacrificial fire-pit – the *agni kula* – of sage Vashista on Mount Abu. The *rishis* – ascetic sages – called them into being to oppose the *rishis'* enemies. By the sixth century the four clans which claim descent from the sacrificial fire, the Paramaras (Pawar), Parihar (Pratihara), Chauhan (Chahamma) and Chalukya (Solanki or Vaghela) clans, came to control large areas of the Deccan and Malwa.

The chief criterion for inclusion in the lists of Rajput clans was the scale of their estates. New colonization in the medieval period turned previously tribal, and 'untamed', territory into the domain of agriculture, trade and the Hindu mainstream. But alongside the colonization process ran an equally important strand of widening social inclusion into the 'Kshatriya' ranks. Chattophadhyaya illustrates the point by reference to the according of Kshatriya status to formerly tribal groups such as the Medas and Hunas.

Each of the major dynasties established control over specific territories. The Chalukyans (Solankis) took Anhilwara (present day Patan) in 961 AD and became sovereign in the Gujarat region stretching from Mount Abu to Malwa. This period saw the rise of western India's finest Hindu and Jain temples, including those of Modhera, Dilwara, Girnar, Taranga, Kumbhariyaji, Somnath, Osian, Menal, Jhalawar and Bardoli. The Solankis introduced important water harvesting systems while the Chauhans built impressive defence structures such as the hill forts at Ranthambhore and Nagaur in Rajasthan. There were two Chauhan lines, the Sambhar dynasty from Ajmer, which became a national power under Raja Prithviraj, and the Kheechi line which ultimately set up a kingdom at Pawagadh.

Rajput chivalry Through their myths of an essential Rajput identity, the Rajputs fostered a reputation for chivalry, valour and honour in battle and their attitude to women. In the commonly presented idealized view of Rajputs they strove against all odds to preserve the civilization of their ancestors, although they were successively forced to accept the suzerainty of first the Mughals and then the British. Death was preferable to dishonour and, before their greatest battles, when certain defeat was anticipated, their queens and princesses committed mass suicide (*jauhar*) to save themselves from being touched by enemy hands, the men then marching naked to the battlefield. See page 228.

The spread of Islamic power

The Delhi Sultanate From about AD 1000 the external attacks which inflicted most damage on Rajput wealth and power came increasingly from the Arabs and Turks. Mahmud of Ghazni raided the Punjab, Rajasthan and ultimately Gujarat virtually every year between 1000 and 1026, attracted both by the agricultural surpluses and the wealth of India's temples. By launching annual raids during the harvest season, Mahmud financed his struggles in Central Asia and his attacks on the profitable trade conducted along the Silk Road between China and the Mediterranean. The enormous wealth in cash, golden images and jewellery of North India's temples drew him back every year and his hunger for gold, used to re-monetize the economy of the remarkable Ghaznavid Sultanate of Afghanistan, was insatiable. He sacked many wealthy centres in the northwest until his death in 1030.

Muslim political power was heralded by the raids of Mu'izzu'd Din and his defeat of massive Rajput forces at the Second Battle of Tarain in 1192. He made further successful raids inflicting crushing defeats on Hindu opponents from Gwalior to Varanasi. The foundations were then laid for the first extended period of Muslim power, which came under the Delhi sultans.

Qutb u'd Din Aibak took Lahore in 1206, although it was his lieutenant **Iltutmish** who really established control from Delhi in 1211. Qutb ud din Aibak converted the old Hindu stronghold of Qila Rai Pithora in Delhi into his capital and began several magnificent building projects, including the Quwwat-ul-Islam mosque and the Qutb Minar, a victory tower. Iltutmish was a Turkish slave – a *Mamluk* – and the Sultanate continued to look west for its leadership and inspiration. However, the possibility of continuing control from outside India was destroyed by the crushing raids of **Genghis Khan** through Central Asia and from 1222 Iltutmish ruled from Delhi completely independently of outside authority.

In 1290 the first dynasty was succeeded by the Khaljis, which in turn gave way to the Tughluqs in 1320. Despite its periodic brutality, this era marked a turning point in Muslim government in India, as Turkish Mamluks gave way to government by Indian Muslims and their Hindu allies. The Delhi sultans were open to local influences and employed Hindus in their administration. In the mid-14th century their capital, Delhi, was one of the leading cities of the contemporary world but in 1398 their control came to an abrupt end with the arrival of the Mongol Timur.

Timur's limp caused him to be called Timur-i-leng (Timur the Lame, known to the west as Tamburlaine). This self-styled 'Scourge of God' was illiterate, a devout Muslim, an outstanding chess player and a patron of the arts. He cut a bloody swathe through to Delhi and is believed to have been responsible for five million deaths. Famine followed the destruction caused by his troops and plague resulted from the corpses left behind. It was a carnage which, however, offered temporary political opportunity to opponents of Sultanate rule to the south. In 1398 the Tomar Rajput Bir Singh Deo recaptured Gwalior from the Muslims and became Raja of Gwalior, establishing a dynasty which was to leave a profound impression on the development of Rajput architecture.

The period of Empire

The Mughal Empire
The descendants of conquerors, with the blood of Timur (Tamburlaine) and Genghis Khan in their veins, the Mughals came to dominate Indian politics from Babur's victory near Delhi in 1526 to Aurangzeb's death in 1707. Their legacy was not only some of the most magnificent architecture in the world, but a profound impact on the culture, society and future politics of South Asia.

Babur (the tiger) Founder of the Mughal Dynasty, Babur was born in Russian Turkestan on 15 February 1483, the fifth direct descendant on the male side of Timur and 13th on the female side from Genghis Khan. He established the Mughal Empire by leading his cavalry and artillery forces to a stupendous victory over the combined armies of Ibrahim Lodi, last ruler of the Delhi Sultanate and the Rajput Raja of Gwalior, at **Panipat**, 80 km north of Delhi, in 1526. When he died four years later, the Empire was still far from secured, but not only had he laid the foundations of political and military power but he'd also begun to establish courtly traditions of poetry, literature and art which became the hallmark of subsequent Mughal rulers. Babur was charismatic. He ruled by keeping the loyalty of his military chiefs, giving them control of large areas of territory.

Humayun The strength of Babur's military commanders proved a mixed blessing for Humayun, his successor. Almost immediately after Babur's death Humayun was forced to retreat from Delhi by two of his brothers and one of his father's lieutenants, the Afghan **Sher Shah Suri**. Humayun's son Akbar, who was to become the greatest of the Mughal emperors, was born at Umarkot in Sindh, modern Pakistan, during this period of exile, on 23 November 1542.

Humayun found the artistic skills of the Iranian court stunningly beautiful and he surrounded himself with his own group of Iranian artists and scholars. Planning his move back into India proper, Humayun urged his group of artists to join him and between 1548 and his return to power in Delhi in 1555, he was accompanied by this influential entourage.

Akbar One year after his final return to Delhi, Humayun died from the effects of a fall on the stairs of his library in the Purana Qila in Delhi. Akbar 'the Builder of Empire' was therefore only 13 when he took the throne in 1556. The next 44 years were one of the most remarkable periods of South Asian history, paralleled by the Elizabethan period in England, where Queen Elizabeth I ruled from 1558 to 1603. Although Akbar inherited the throne, it was he who really created the empire. At the age of 15 he had conquered Ajmer and large areas of Central India. Chittaurgarh and Ranthambhore fell to him in 1567-1568, bringing most of what is now Rajasthan under his control.

Through his marriage to a Hindu princess he ensured that Hindus were given honoured positions in government, as well as respect for their religious beliefs and practices. He sustained a passionate interest in art and literature, matched by a determination to create monuments to his empire's political power and he laid the foundations for an artistic and architectural tradition which developed a totally distinctive Indian style. This emerged from the separate elements of Iranian and Indian traditions by a constant process of blending and originality of which he was the chief patron.

Akbar deliberately widened his power base by incorporating Rajput princes into the administrative structure and giving them extensive rights in the revenue from land. He abolished the hated tax on non-Muslims (*jizya*) – ultimately reinstated by his strictly orthodox great grandson Aurangzeb – ceased levying taxes on Hindus who went on pilgrimage and ended the practice of forcible conversion to Islam.

Artistic treasures abound from Akbar's court – paintings, jewellery, weapons – often bringing together material and skills from across the known world. Emeralds were particularly popular, with the religious significance which attaches to the colour green in mystic Islam adding to their attraction. Some came from as far afield as Colombia. Akbar's intellectual interests were extraordinarily catholic. He met the Portuguese Jesuits in 1572 and welcomed them to his court in Fatehpur Sikri, along with Buddhists, Hindus and Zoroastrians, every year between 1575 and 1582.

Akbar's eclecticism had a political purpose, for he was trying to build a focus of loyalty beyond that of caste, social group, region or religion. Like Roman emperors before him, he deliberately cultivated a new religion in which the emperor himself attained divinity, hoping thereby to give the empire a legitimacy which would last. While his religion disappeared with his death, the legitimacy of the Mughals survived another 200 years, long after their real power had almost disappeared.

Jahangir Akbar died of a stomach illness in 1605. He was succeeded by his son, Prince Salim, who inherited the throne as Emperor Jahangir (World Seizer). He commissioned works of art and literature, many of which directly recorded life in the Mughal court. Hunting scenes were not just romanticized accounts of rural life, but conveyed the real dangers of hunting lions or tigers; implements, furniture, tools and weapons were made with lavish care and often exquisite design.

Nur Jahan Jahangir's favourite wife, Nur Jahan, brought her own artistic gifts. Born the daughter of an Iranian nobleman, she had been brought to the Mughal court along with her family as a child and moved to Bengal as the wife of Sher Afghan. She made rapid progress after her first husband's accidental death in 1607, which caused her to move from Bengal to be a lady-in-waiting for one of Akbar's widows.

At the Mughal court in 1611 she met Jahangir. Mutually enraptured, they were married in May. Jahangir gave her the title Nur Mahal (Light of the Palace), soon increased to Nur Jahan (Light of the World).

By 1622 Nur Jahan effectively controlled the empire. She commissioned and supervized the building in Agra of one of the Mughal world's most beautiful buildings, the **I'timad ud-Daula** (Pillar of Government), as a tomb for her father and mother. Her father, **Ghiyas Beg**, had risen to become one of Jahangir's most trusted advisers and Nur Jahan was determined to ensure that their memory was adequately honoured. She was less successful in her wish to deny the succession after Jahangir's death at the age of 58 to Prince Khurram. Acceding to the throne in 1628, he took the title of Shah Jahan (Ruler of the World) and in the following 30 years his reign represented the height of Mughal power.

Shah Jahan The Mughal Empire was under attack in the Deccan and the northwest when Shah Jahan became Emperor. He tried to re-establish and extend Mughal authority in both regions by a combination of military campaigns and skilled diplomacy and most of the Deccan was brought firmly under Mughal control.

He also commissioned art, literature and, above all, architectural monuments, on an unparalleled scale. The Taj Mahal may be the most famous of these, but a succession of brilliant achievements can be attributed to his reign. From miniature paintings and manuscripts, which had been central features of Mughal artistic development from Babur onwards, to massive fortifications such as the Red Fort in Delhi, Shah Jahan added to the already great body of outstanding Mughal art.

Throughout this period Rajput rulers adjusted in varying degrees to the dominance of the Mughal emperors. Seeking to maximize their own remaining authority without risking punitive raids which would have destroyed what control they had, many of the clan leaders made direct arrangements with successive emperors which gave them continued effective control over their own territories. Sometimes clan leaders took sides in the internal feuding within the Mughal court. Udai Singh of Udaipur for example gave the young Prince Khurram, the future Emperor Shah Jahan, shelter in his Jag Mandir palace in Lake Pichola when he was fleeing his father Jahangir's wrath, and it is striking that both Jahangir and Shah Jahan had Rajput mothers.

Aurangzeb All this changed with the ascension of Aurangzeb (The Jewel in the Throne) to the throne. He needed all his political and military skills to hold on to an unwieldy empire that was in permanent danger of collapse from its own size.

Aurangzeb realized that the resources of the territory he inherited from Shah Jahan were not enough to sustain the empire's power. One response was to push south, while maintaining his hold on the east and north. Initially he maintained his alliances with the Rajputs in the west, which had been a crucial element in Mughal strategy. However, in 1678 he claimed absolute rights over Jodhpur and went to war with the Rajput clans, at the same time embarking on a policy of outright Islamization. For the remaining 29 years of his reign he was forced to struggle continuously to sustain his power.

The Maratha challenge

A great threat to Mughal and Rajput control of Rajasthan through the 18th century was that of the **Maratha confederacy**. The Marathas were unique in India in uniting different castes and classes in a nationalist fervour for the region of Maharashtra. When the Mughals ceded the central district of Malwa, the Marathas were able to pour through the gap created between the Nizam of Hyderabad's territories in the south and the area remaining under Mughal control in the north.

By 1750 they had reached the gates of Delhi. When Delhi collapsed to Afghan invaders in 1756-1757 the Mughal minister called on the Marathas for help. Yet again Panipat proved to be a decisive battlefield, the Marathas being heavily defeated by the Afghan forces of Ahmad Shah on 13 January 1761. However Ahmad Shah was forced to retreat to Afghanistan by his own rebellious troops demanding two years arrears of pay, leaving a power vacuum. The Maratha confederacy dissolved into five independent powers, with whom the incoming British were able to deal separately. For them, the door to the north was open.

The decline of Muslim power

Aurangzeb never fully came to terms with the rising power of the Marathas, though he did end their ambitions to form an empire of their own. Nor was Aurangzeb able to create any wide sense of identity with the Mughals as a legitimate popular power. Instead, under the influence of Sunni Muslim theologians, he retreated into insistence on Islamic purity. He imposed Islamic law, the *Sharia*, promoted only Muslims to positions of power and authority, tried to replace Hindu administrators and revenue collectors with Muslims and reimposed the *jizya* tax on all non-Muslims. By the time of his death in 1707 the empire no longer had either the broadness of spirit or the physical means to survive.

East India Company and the rise of British power

The British were unique among the foreign rulers of India in coming by sea rather than through the northwest and in coming first for trade rather than for military conquest. The ports that they established – Madras (Chennai), Bombay (Mumbai) and Calcutta (Kolkata) – became completely new centres of political, economic and social activity. Before them Indian empires had controlled their territories from the land. The British dictated the emerging shape of the economy by controlling sea-borne trade.

In its first 90 years of contact with South Asia after the Company set up its first trading post at Masulipatnam, on the east coast of India, it had depended almost entirely on trade for its profits. In 1608 it established its warehouse on the west coast at Surat, already an important port, and it remained the headquarters until it moved to Bombay in 1674. The Company was accepted and sometimes welcomed, partly because it offered to bolster the inadequate revenues of the Mughals by exchanging silver bullion for the cloth it bought.

Alliances In the century and a half that followed the death of Aurangzeb, the British East India Company extended its economic and political influence into the heart of India. As the Mughal Empire lost its power India fell into many smaller states. The Company undertook to protect the rulers of several of these states from external attack by stationing British troops in their territory. In exchange for this service the rulers paid subsidies to the Company. As the British historian Christopher Bayly has pointed out, the cure was usually worse than the disease and the cost of the payments to the Company crippled the local ruler. The British extended their territory through the 18th century as successive regional powers were annexed and brought under direct Company rule.

Progress to direct British control was uneven and often opposed. The Sikhs in Punjab, the Marathas in the west and the Mysore sultans in the south, fiercely contested British advances. The Marathas were not defeated until the war of 1816-1818, a defeat which had to wait until Napoleon was defeated in Europe and the British could turn their wholehearted attention once again to the Indian scene. Even then the defeat owed as much to internal faction fighting as to the power of the British-led army.

In 1818 India's economy was in ruins and its political structures destroyed. Irrigation works and road systems had fallen into decay and gangs terrorized the countryside. Thugs and dacoits controlled much of the open countryside in Central India and often robbed and murdered even on the outskirts of towns. The peace and stability of the Mughal period had long since passed. Between 1818 and 1857 there was a succession of local and uncoordinated revolts in different parts of India. Some were bought off, some put down by military force.

A period of reforms

While existing political systems were collapsing, the first half of the 19th century was also a period of radical social change in the territories governed by the East India Company. **Lord William Bentinck** became Governor-General at a time when England itself was entering a period of major reform. In 1828 he banned the burning of widows on the funeral pyres of their husbands (*sati*) and then moved to suppress the ritual murder and robbery carried out in the name of the goddess Kali (*thuggee*). But his most far-reaching change was to introduce education in English.

From the late 1830s massive new engineering projects began to be taken up; first canals, then railways. However, it was in eastern India that British control was most directly imposed and the consequent changes were most sharply felt. Although much of modern Gujarat was also brought under direct British control, under the governance of Bombay, most Rajput areas remained under their subordinate authority as Rajputana.

British-led innovations stimulated change and change contributed to the growing unease with the British presence, particularly under the Governor-Generalship of the Marquess of Dalhousie (1848-1856). The development of the telegraph, railways and new roads, three universities and the extension of massive new canal irrigation projects in North India seemed to threaten traditional society, a risk increased by the annexation of Indian states to bring them under direct British rule. The most important of these was Oudh.

The Rebellion

Out of the growing discontent and widespread economic difficulties came the Rebellion or 'Mutiny' of 1857 (now widely known as the First War of Independence). Although it had little support among the Rajput rulers and Rajputana remained seemingly uninvolved, no part of India was unaffected. The 1857 rebellion marked the end not only of the Mughal Empire but also of the East India Company, for the British Government in London took overall control in 1858. After the establishment of the British Indian Empire, the Rajput Princely States gained in the appearance and show of power just as they lost its reality.

Pomp and circumstance The British awarded gun salutes on the basis of importance. Rajasthan had 19 'gun salute' states, 17 of them ruled by various Rajput clans, Bharatpur by a Jat dynasty and Tonk by a Muslim Nawab, with countless non-salute chieftains. The princes maintained huge fleets of European and American cars, stables of elephants and horses, chariots and horse-drawn carriages, and travelled in their own royal rail saloon carriages which could be attached to regular trains for their journeys across the subcontinent. Some even had private aircraft. This was a period of grand darbars, parties, banquets, weddings, processions, polo and cricket matches and royal hunting camps. A strict order of precedence was maintained according to gun salutes awarded to each state. The Maharaja of Baroda was entitled to 21-gun salutes, the Maharana of Udaipur to 19-gun salutes, the Maharajas of Jaipur, Jodhpur, Bundi, Bikaner, Kachchh, Kota, Karauli and Bharatpur to 17-gun salutes and so on.

While the show of power was far from reality, for these maharajas came under the British Raj, the princes were given considerable freedom of rule and many of them proved to be capable rulers. Ganga Singh of Bikaner was one of a few rulers who introduced wide-ranging reforms that are landmarks in administration in India. British political agents, collectors and other residents were appointed to look into affairs of state, and when a crown prince inherited the throne as a minor a British representative was selected to handle the state on his behalf. Ajmer was a seat of British administrators, and during the summer months Mount Abu was a popular retreat for British and royal residents of Rajasthan who wanted to escape the heat of the plains.

Yet within 30 years a movement for self-government had begun and there were the first signs of a demand that political rights be awarded to match the sense of Indian national identity. This took varied forms. In Udaipur the Maharishi Dayanand wrote the *Satyarath Prakash* which was a call to restore Hinduism to its 'pure' form, and the founding in 1875 of the Arya Samaj on the basis of these principles placed the emphasis on a return to Vedic Hinduism at the core of its view of Indian national identity, a view which is still a powerful influence through the recently deposed BJP party.

Indian National Congress The movement for independence went through a series of steps. The creation of the Indian National Congress in 1885 was the first all-India political institution and was to become the key vehicle of demands for independence. However, the educated Muslim elite of what is now Uttar Pradesh saw a threat to Muslim rights, power and identity in the emergence of democratic institutions which gave Hindus, with

Mahatma Gandhi

A westernized, English-educated lawyer, Mohandas Karamchand Gandhi, had lived outside India from his youth to middle age. He preached the general acceptance of some of the doctrines he had grown to respect in his childhood, which stemmed from deep Indian traditions – notably *ahimsa*, or non-violence. On his return the Bengali Nobel Laureate poet, Rabindranath Tagore, had dubbed him *Mahatma* (Great Soul). From 1921 he gave up his Western style of dress and adopted the hand spun *dhoti* worn by poor Indian villagers. Yet, he was also fiercely critical of many aspects of traditional Hindu society. He preached against the discrimination of the caste system which still dominated life for the overwhelming majority of Hindus. Often despised by the British in India, his death at the hands of an extreme Hindu chauvinist in January 1948 was a final testimony to the ambiguity of his achievements: successful in contributing so much to India's Independence, yet failing to resolve some of the bitter communal legacies which he gave his life to overcome.

their built-in natural majority, significant advantages. Sir Sayyid Ahmad Khan, who had founded a Muslim University at Aligarh in 1877, advised Muslims against joining the Congress, seeing it as a vehicle for Hindu and especially Bengali, nationalism.

Muslim League The educated Muslim community of North India remained deeply suspicious of the Congress, making up less than 8% of those attending its conferences between 1900-1920. Muslims from Uttar Pradesh created the All-India Muslim League in 1906. However, the demands of the Muslim League were not always opposed to those of the Congress. In 1916 it concluded the Lucknow Pact with the Congress, in which the Congress won Muslim support for self-government, in exchange for the recognition that there would be separate constituencies for Muslims. The nature of the future Independent India was still far from clear, however. The British conceded the principle of self-government in 1918, but however radical the reforms would have seemed five years earlier they already fell far short of heightened Indian expectations.

Mahatma Gandhi Into a tense atmosphere Gandhi returned to India in 1915 after 20 years practising as a lawyer in South Africa. He arrived as the government of India was being given new powers by the British parliament to try political cases without a jury and to give provincial governments the right to imprison politicians without trial. In opposition to this legislation Gandhi proposed to call a *hartal*, when all activity would cease for a day, a form of protest still in widespread use. Such protests took place across India, often accompanied by riots.

The thrust for Independence Through the 1920s Gandhi developed concepts and political programmes that were to become the hallmark of India's Independence struggle. Rejecting the 1919 reforms Gandhi preached the doctrine of *swaraj*, or self rule, developing an idea he first published in a leaflet in 1909. He saw *swaraj* not just as political independence from a foreign ruler but, in Judith Brown's words, as made up of three elements: "It was a state of being that had to be created from the roots upwards, by the regeneration of individuals and their realization of their true spiritual being ... unity among all religions; the eradication of Untouchability; and the practice of *swadeshi*." Swadeshi was not simply dependence on Indian products rather than foreign imports, but a deliberate move to a simple lifestyle, hence his emphasis on hand spinning as a daily routine.

Ultimately political Independence was to be achieved not by violent rebellion but by *satyagraha* – a 'truth force' which implied a willingness to suffer through non-violent resistance to injustice. This gave birth to Gandhi's advocacy of 'non-cooperation' as a key political weapon and brought together Gandhi's commitment to matching political goals and moral means. Although the political achievements of Gandhi's programme continue to be strongly debated the struggles of the 1920s established his position as a key figure in the Independence movement.

By the end of the Second World War the positions of the Muslim League, now under the leadership of **Mohammad Ali Jinnah** and the Congress led by Jawaharlal Nehru, were irreconcilable. While major questions of the definition of separate territories for a Muslim and non-Muslim state remained to be answered, it was clear to General Wavell, the British Viceroy through the last years of the War, that there was no alternative but to accept that independence would have to be given on the basis of separate states.

The transition to Independence and Partition

On 20 February 1947, the British Labour Government announced its decision to replace Lord Wavell as Viceroy with Lord Mountbatten, who was to oversee the transfer of power to new independent governments. It set a deadline of June 1948 for British withdrawal. The announcement of a firm date made the Indian politicians even less willing to compromise and the resulting division satisfied no one.

When Independence arrived – on 15 August for India and the 14 August for Pakistan because Indian astrologers deemed the 15th to be the most auspicious moment – many questions remained unanswered. Several key Princely States had still not decided firmly to which country they would accede. The Muslim Nawab of Junagadh exercized his right to accede to Pakistan, but the Indian Government, arguing that Junagadh had a predominantly Hindu population and lay surrounded by Hindus, insisted on organizing a plebiscite under Indian government supervision, and the Nawab was forced to flee into exile. Equally the future accession of Kashmir remained unclear with results that have lasted to the present day.

The end of the Princely States At Independence the 216 smallest states were abolished and merged into neighbouring provinces. Some 275 Princely States across India, including Rajasthan, had either acceded to the Indian union or signed standstill agreements with the new government while permanent arrangements were agreed. They were integrated initially into five new unions, each with its provincial governor or *Rajpramukh*. A further 61 states were brought under direct central government control. These arrangements, intended as temporary, were short-lived. The first stage of transition was completed in 1950 when they all became part of the Indian Union under an agreement in which the princes retained their titles and government subsidies, known as their privy purses. The region's 18 Princely States were ultimately absorbed into the new state of Rajasthan on 1 November 1956. In 1971 Mrs Gandhi abolished the remaining rights of the maharajas and took away their privy purses.

The successors of royal families have lost power but still retain wide respect and considerable political influence. The palaces, many of them converted to hotels with varying degrees of success, maintain the memory of princely India.

Modern India

India, with an estimated 1.17 billion people in 2009, is the second most populated country in the world after China. That population size reflects the long history of human occupation and the fact that an astonishingly high proportion of India's land is relatively fertile. About 60% of India's surface area is cultivated today, compared with 10% in China and 20% in the United States.

Although the birth rate has fallen steadily over the last 40 years, initially death rates fell faster and the rate of population increase has continued to be nearly 2% – or 18 million – a year. Today over 320 million people live in towns and cities.

Politics and institutions

When India became independent on 15 August 1947 it faced three immediate crises. Partition left it with a bitter struggle between Muslims on one side and Hindus and Sikhs on the other which threatened to tear the new country into pieces at birth. An estimated 13 million people migrated between the two new countries of India and Pakistan.

In the years since Independence, striking political achievements have been made. With the two year exception of 1975-1977, when Mrs Gandhi imposed a state of emergency in which all political activity was banned, India has sustained a democratic system in the face of tremendous pressures. The general elections of May 2004 saw the Congress Party return as the largest single party, with 220 of the 540 Lok Sabha seats. They managed to forge alliances with some of the smaller parties and thus formed the new United Progressive Alliance government under the prime ministership not of the Congress Party's leader, Sonia Gandhi, but of ex-finance minister, Manmohan Singh.

The constitution

Establishing itself as a sovereign democratic republic, the Indian parliament accepted Nehru's advocacy of a secular constitution. The president is formally vested with all executive powers exercised under the authority of the prime minister.

Parliament has a lower house (the *Lok Sabha* – House of the people) and an upper house (the *Rajya Sabha* – Council of States). The former is made up of directly elected representatives from the 543 parliamentary constituencies (plus two nominated members from the Anglo-Indian community), the latter of a mixture of members elected by an electoral college and of nominated members.

India's federal constitution devolves certain powers to elected state assemblies. Each state has a governor who acts as its official head. Many states also have two chambers, the upper generally called the Rajya Sabha and the lower (often called the Vidhan Sabha) being of directly elected representatives. In practice many of the state assemblies have had a totally different political complexion from that of the Lok Sabha. Regional parties have played a far more prominent role, though in many states central government has effectively dictated both the leadership and policy of state assemblies.

States and Union Territories Union territories are administered by the president "acting to such an extent as he thinks fit". In practice Union territories have varying forms of self-government. Pondicherry has a legislative Assembly and Council of Ministers. The 69th Amendment to the Constitution in 1991 provided for a legislative assembly and council of ministers for Delhi, elections for which were held in December 1993. The Assemblies of Union

Territories have more restricted powers of legislation than full states. Some Union Territories – Dadra and Nagar Haveli, Daman and Diu, all of which separated from Goa in 1987 when Goa achieved full statehood – Andaman and Nicobar Islands and Lakshadweep, have elected bodies known as Pradesh Councils.

Secularism One of the key features of India's constitution is its secular principle. Some see the commitment to a secular constitution as having been under increasing challenge from the Hindu nationalism of the Bharatiya Janata Party, the BJP.

The judiciary India's Supreme Court has similar but somewhat weaker powers to those of the United States. The judiciary has remained effectively independent of the government except under the Emergency between 1975-1977.

The civil service India continued to use the small but highly professional administrative service inherited from the British period. Renamed the Indian Administrative Service (IAS), it continues to exercise remarkable influence across the country. The administration of many aspects of central and regional government is in the hands of this elite body, who act largely by the constitutional rules which bind them as servants of the state. Many Indians accept the continuing efficiency and high calibre of the top ranking officers in the administration while believing that the bureaucratic system as a whole has been overtaken by widespread corruption.

The police India's police service is divided into a series of groups, numbering nearly one million. While the top ranks of the Indian Police Service are comparable to the IAS, lower levels are extremely poorly trained and very low paid. In addition to the domestic police force there are special groups: the Border Security Force, Central Reserve Police and others. They may be armed with modern weapons and are called in for special duties.

The armed forces Unlike its immediate neighbours Pakistan and Bangladesh, India has never had military rule. It has around one million men in the army, one of the largest armed forces in the world. Although they have remained out of politics the army has been used increasingly frequently to put down civil unrest especially in Kashmir.

The Congress Party The Congress won overall majorities in seven of the 10 general elections held before the 1996 election, although in no election did the Congress obtain more than 50% of the popular vote. In 1998 its popular support completely disappeared in some regions and fell below 30% nationally and in the elections of September-October 1999 Sonia Gandhi, Rajiv Gandhi's Italian-born widow, failed to achieve the much vaunted revival in the Party's fortunes. Through 2001 into 2002 a change began with the BJP losing power in state assemblies in the north and becoming increasingly unpopular nationally, and the Congress picking up a wide measure of support, culminating in their victory in the May 2004 general election, when Sonia Gandhi nominated Manmohan Singh as prime minister.

Non-Congress parties Political activity outside the Congress can seem bewilderingly complex. There are no genuinely national parties. The only alternative governments to the Congress have been formed by coalitions of regional and ideologically based parties. Parties of the left – Communist and Socialist – have never broken out of their narrow regional bases. The Communist Party of India split into two factions in 1964, with the Communist Party of India Marxist (CPM) ultimately taking power in West Bengal and Kerala. In the 1960s the Swatantra Party (a liberal party) made some ground nationally, opposing the economic centralization and state control supported by the Congress.

At the right of the political spectrum, the Jan Sangh was seen as a party of right wing Hindu nationalism with a concentrated but significant base in parts of the north, especially among higher castes and merchant communities. The most organized political force outside the Congress, the Jan Sangh merged with the Janata Party for the elections of 1977. After the collapse of that government it re-formed itself as the **Bharatiya Janata Party (BJP)**. In 1990-1991 it developed a powerful campaign focusing on reviving Hindu identity against the minorities. The elections of 1991 showed it to be the most powerful single challenger to the Congress in North India. In the decade that followed it became the most powerful single party across northern India and established a series of footholds and alliances in the South. Elsewhere a succession of regional parties dominated politics in several key states, including Tamil Nadu and Andhra Pradesh in the south and West Bengal and Bihar in the east.

Recent developments

By mid-2001 the gloss had worn off the popularity of the BJP and it had suffered a series of scandals, but the prime minister had kept the core of the government together. In July 2001 Pakistan's military ruler General Pervez Musharraf visited New Delhi and Agra for talks at the Indian Government's invitation, but they ended in a shambles.

The attacks on New York and Washington on 11 September and the US-led 'War on Terror' has had major repercussions in India and Pakistan. While the Taliban's rapid defeat brought a new government to power in Afghanistan, strongly supported by India, the Kashmir dispute between India and Pakistan deepened. Both India and Pakistan sought political advantage from the war on terror, and when a terrorist attack was launched on the Indian parliament on 13 December 2001 the Indian government pushed massive reinforcements to the Pakistan border from Gujarat and Rajasthan to Kashmir. India demanded that President Musharraf close down all camps and organizations which India claimed were the source of the attacks in Delhi and Kashmir. Although President Musharraf closed down *Lashkar e Taiba* and *Jaish e Mohammad*, two of the most feared groups operating openly in Pakistan, cross-border firing intensified along the Line of Control in Kashmir and attacks in Kashmir continued. On 16 May 2002 terrorists launched a devastating attack on an army camp in Jammu, killing at least 20 people, and Sonia Gandhi demanded that the Government translate rhetoric into action. Since the change of government in May 2004, however, things have improved dramatically, with the new Indian prime minister seeming to enjoy a genuinely warm rapport with Pakistan's Pervez Musharraf. Progress over the following three years has been slow and is complicated by the continuing unrest in Pakistan itself and the challenge of apparently renewed support for the Taliban in some of its border regions. Work continues, however, on resolving the Kashmir problem.

The 2009 elections saw the **United Progressive Alliance** (UPA) led by the Indian National Congress form the new government. This meant Manmohan Singh became the first prime minister since Nehru to be re-elected after completing a full five-year term. In West Bengal, which had been led by a democratically elected Communist government for over 30 years, the tide turned to the UPA. The Left Front won just 15 of the 42 Lok Sabha seats. Assam and Arunachal also carried a UPA majority, while Sikkim saw a win by the Sikkim Democratic Front.

Culture

Language

Rajasthan has its own distinct language, Rajasthani, one of the Indo-Aryan languages (the easternmost group of the Indo-European family).

Sanskrit As the pastoralists from Central Asia moved into South Asia from 2000 BC onwards, the Indo-Aryan languages they spoke were gradually modified. Sanskrit developed from this process, emerging as the dominant classical language of India by the sixth century BC, when it was classified in the grammar of **Panini**. Sir William Jones, the great 19th-century scholar, discovered the close links between Sanskrit (the basis of nearly all North Indian languages) German and Greek. He showed that they all must have originated in the common heartland of Central Asia, being carried west, south and east by the nomadic tribes who shaped so much of the subsequent history of both Europe and Asia. Sanskrit remained the language of the educated until about AD 1000.

Hindi and Urdu The Muslims brought Persian into South Asia as the language of the rulers. The most striking example of Muslim influence on the earlier Indo-European languages is that of the two most important languages of India and Pakistan, Hindi and Urdu respectively. Most of the modern North Indian languages were not written until the 16th century or after. Hindi developed into the language of the heartland of Hindu culture, stretching from Punjab to Bihar and from the foothills of the Himalaya to the marchlands of Central India, while Urdu became as the language of urban Muslims.

Rajasthani In Rajasthan, the principal language is Rajasthani, while the four most important dialects are *Marwari* in the west, *Jaipuri* in the east, *Malwi* in the southeast and *Mewati* in the northeast. Hindi is rapidly replacing Rajasthani as the lingua franca.

Scripts The earliest ancestor of scripts used in India today was **Brahmi**, in which Asoka's famous inscriptions were written in the third century BC. Written from left to right, a separate symbol represented each different sound. For about 1000 years the major script of northern India has been the Nagari or Devanagari, which means literally the script of the 'city of the gods', though Gujarati has its own running script which developed as part of Gujarat's mercantile tradition.

Numerals Many of the Indian alphabets have their own notation for numerals. This is not without irony, for what in the Western world are called 'Arabic' numerals are in fact of Indian origin. Local numerical symbols are still in use, but by and large you will find that the Arabic number symbols familiar in Europe and the West are common.

The role of English English now plays an important role across India. It is widely spoken in towns and cities and even in quite remote villages it is not usually difficult to find someone who speaks at least a little English. Other European languages are almost completely unknown. The accent in which English is spoken is often affected strongly by the mother tongue of the speaker and there have been changes in common grammar which sometimes make it sound unusual. Many of these changes have become standard Indian English usage, as valid as any other varieties of English used around the world.

Literature

Rajasthan has a long tradition of vernacular poetry in local dialects, but its literature has been profoundly influenced by the wider traditions of literature in India. Sanskrit was the first all-India language. Its early literature was memorized and recited. The hymns of the *Rig Veda* probably did not reach their final form until about the sixth century BC, but the earliest may go back as far as 1300 BC.

The Vedas The *Rig Veda* is a collection of 1028 hymns, not all directly religious. Its main function was to provide orders of worship for priests responsible for the sacrifices that were central to the religion of the Indo-Aryans. Two later texts, the *Yajurveda* and the *Samaveda*, served the same purpose. A fourth, the *Atharvaveda*, is largely a collection of magic spells.

At some time after 1000 BC a second category of Vedic literature, the **Brahmanas**, began to take shape. Story telling developed as a means to interpret the significance of sacrifice. The most famous and the most important of these were the *Upanishads*, probably written at some time between the seventh and fifth centuries BC. The Brahmanas gave their name to the religion emerging between the eighth and sixth centuries BC, Brahmanism, the ancestor of Hinduism. Two of its texts remain the best known and most widely revered epic compositions in South Asia, the *Mahabharata* and the *Ramayana*.

The details of the great battle recounted in the *Mahabharata* are unclear. Tradition puts its date at precisely 3102 BC, the start of the present era and names the author of the poem as a sage, Vyasa. Evidence suggests however that the battle was fought around 800 BC at **Kurukshetra**. It was another 400 years before priests began to write the stories down, a process which was not complete until AD 400. The original version was about 3000 stanzas long, but it now contains over 100,000 – eight times as long as Homer's Iliad and the Odyssey put together. The battle was seen as a war of the forces of good and evil, the **Pandavas** being interpreted as gods and the **Kauravas** as devils. The arguments were elaborated and expanded until about the fourth century AD. A comparatively late addition to the *Mahabharata*, the *Bhagavad-Gita* is the most widely read and revered text among Hindus in South Asia today.

Valmiki is thought of in India as the author of the second great Indian epic, the **Ramayana**, though no more is known of his identity than is known of Homer's. Like the *Mahabharata*, it underwent several stages of development before it reached its final version of 48,000 lines.

Sanskrit literature Sanskrit was always the language of the court and the elite. Other languages replaced it in common speech by the third century BC, but it remained in restricted use for over 1000 years after that period. The remarkable Sanskrit grammar of Panini helped to establish grammar as one of the six disciplines essential to understanding the Vedas properly and to conducting Vedic rituals. The other five were phonetics, etymology, meter, ritual practice and astronomy. Sanskrit literature continued to be written in the courts until the Muslims replaced it with Persian, long after it had ceased to be a language of spoken communication. One of India's greatest poets, **Kalidasa**, contributed to the development of Sanskrit as the language of learning and the arts.

Literally 'stories of ancient times', the *Puranas* are about Brahma, Vishnu and Siva. Although some of the stories may relate to real events that occurred as early as 1500 BC, they were not compiled until the fifth century AD. Margaret and James Stutley record the belief that "during the destruction of the world at the end of the age, Hayagriva is said to have saved the *Puranas*. A summary of the original work is now preserved in Heaven!".

The stories are often the only source of information about the period immediately following the early Vedas. Each *Purana* was intended to deal with five themes: "the creation of the world (*sarga*); its destruction and recreation (*pratisarga*); the genealogy of gods and patriarchs (*vamsa*); the reigns and periods of the Manus (*manvantaras*); and the history of the solar and lunar dynasties".

Muslim influence For considerable periods between the 13th and 18th century, **Persian** became the language of the courts. Classical Persian was the dominant influence, with Iran as its country of origin and Shiraz its main cultural centre, but India developed its own Persian-based style. Two poets stood out at the end of the 13th century AD, when Muslim rulers had established a sultanate in Delhi, Amir Khusrau, who lived from 1253 to 1325 and the mystic Amir Hasan, who died about AD 1328.

The Mughal emperor Babur left one of the most remarkable political autobiographies of any generation, the *Babur-nama* (History of Babur), written in **Turki** and translated into Persian. His grandson Akbar commissioned a biography, the *Akbar-nama*, which reflected his interest in all the world's religions. His son Jahangir left his memoirs, the *Tuzuk-i Jahangiri*, in Persian. They have been described as intimate and spontaneous and showing an insatiable interest in things, events and people.

Colonial period The use of Persian was already in decline during the reign of the last great Muslim Emperor, **Aurangzeb** and as the British extended their political power so the role of English grew. There is now a wide range of Indian literature accessible in English, which has become the latest of the languages to be used across the whole of South Asia.

In the 19th century English became a vehicle for developing nationalist ideals. However, notably in the work of **Rabindranath Tagore**, it became a medium for religious and philosophical prose and for a developing poetry. Tagore himself won the Nobel Prize for Literature in 1913 for his translation into English of his own work, *Gitanjali*.

Science

Calendar By about 500 BC Indian texts illustrated the calculation of the calendar, although the system itself almost certainly goes back to the eighth or ninth century BC. The year was divided into 27 *nakshatras*, or fortnights, years being calculated on a mixture of lunar and solar counting. See page 323.

Views of the universe Early Indian views of the universe were based on the square and the cube. The earth was seen as a square, one corner pointing south, rising like a pyramid in a series of square terraces with its peak, the mythical Mount Meru. The sun moved round the top of Mount Meru in a square orbit and the square orbits of the planets were at successive planes above the orbit of the sun. These were seen therefore as forming a second pyramid of planetary movement. Mount Meru was central to all early Indian schools of thought, Hindu, Buddhist and Jain.

However, about 200 BC the Jains transformed the view of the universe based on squares by replacing the idea of square orbits with that of the circle. The earth was shown as a circular disc, with Mount Meru rising from its centre and the Pole Star directly above it. These views have not completely lost their currency among some Jains today.

Mathematics Conceptions of the universe and the mathematical and geometrical ideas that accompanied them were comparatively advanced in South Asia by the time of the Mauryan Empire and were put to use in the rules developed for building temple altars. Indians were using the concept of zero and decimal points in the Gupta period. Furthermore in AD 499, just after the demise of the Gupta Empire, the astronomer Aryabhatta calculated Pi as 3.1416 and the length of the solar year as 365.358 days. He also postulated that the earth was a sphere rotating on its own axis and revolving around the sun and that the shadow of the earth falling on the moon caused lunar eclipses.

Art and architecture

Both have developed with a remarkable continuity through successive regional and religious influences and styles. Rajasthan has its own distinctive regional styles of both religious and secular building which have continued to evolve right up to the present day.

The Buddhist stylistic influence on early Hindu architecture was profound. The first Hindu religious buildings to have survived into the modern period were constructed in south and east India from the sixth century AD. The early Muslims destroyed much that was in their path. Yet the Islamic architecture which followed was not simply a transplant from another country or region, but grew out of India's own traditions. That continuity reflected many forces, not least the use made by the great Mughal emperors of local skilled craftsmen and builders. The first Emperor, Babur, expressed his admiration for the magnificence of the Rajput palace at Gwalior, and successive emperors tried to emulate and exceed the sumptuousness of Rajput forts and palaces while incorporating key elements from Muslim traditions.

Painting, sculpture, inlay work, all blended skills from a variety of sources and craftsmen – even occasionally from Europe. What emerged was another stepping stone in a tradition of Indian architecture, which wove the threads of Hindu tradition into new forms. The Taj Mahal was the ultimate product of this extraordinary process. Yet regional styles developed their own special feature and the main thrust of Hindu and Muslim religious buildings remains fundamentally different.

Architecture
Hindu temple buildings The principles of religious building were laid down by priests in the *sastras*. Every aspect of Hindu, Jain and Buddhist religious building is identified with conceptions of the structure of the universe. This applies as much to the process of building – the timing of which must be undertaken at astrologically propitious times – as to the formal layout of the buildings. The cardinal directions of north, south, east and west are the basic fix on which buildings are planned. In addition to the cardinal directions, number is also critical to the design, the ultimate scale of the building is being derived from the measurements of the sanctuary at its heart.

Indian temples were nearly always built to a design based on philosophical understandings of the universe. This cosmology of an infinite number of universes, isolated from each other in space, proceeds by imagining various possibilities as to its nature. Its centre is seen as dominated by **Mount Meru** which keeps earth and heaven apart. The concept of separation is crucial to Hindu thought and social practice. Continents, rivers and oceans occupy concentric rings around the mountain, while the stars encircle the mountain in another plane. Humans live on the continent of **Jambudvipa** characterized by the rose apple tree (*jambu*).

The *sastras* show plans of this continent, organized in concentric rings and entered at the cardinal points. This type of diagram was known as a **mandala**. The centre of the *mandala* would be the seat of the major god. *Mandalas* provided the ground rules for the building of stupas and temples across India and gave the key to the symbolic meaning attached to every aspect of religious buildings.

The focal point of the temple, its sanctuary, was the home of the presiding deity, the 'womb-chamber' (*garbhagriha*). A series of doorways, in large temples leading through a succession of buildings, allowed the worshipper to move towards the final encounter with the deity to obtain *darshan* – a sight of the god. Both Buddhist and Hindu worship encourage the worshipper to walk clockwise around the shrine, performing *pradakshina*.

The elevations are symbolic representations of the home of the gods. Mountain peaks such as Kailasa are common names for the most prominent of the towers. In North and East Indian temples the tallest of these towers rises above the *garbagriha* itself, symbolizing the meeting of earth and heaven in the person of the enshrined deity. The basic structure is usually richly embellished with sculpture. When first built this would usually have been plastered and painted and often covered in gems. In contrast to the extraordinary profusion of colour and life on the outside, the interior is dark and cramped but here it is believed, lies the true centre of divine power.

Rajput architecture The Rajputs expressed their power in a variety of architectural forms. Although they were great patrons of Hindu religious art and worship, their most significant architectural legacy has been secular, paying particular attention to the construction of massive forts and lavish palaces. Merchants under Rajput protection also developed superb domestic architecture in their *havelis*. The main period of Rajput building dates from the mid-15th to the mid-18th centuries. It is no accident that this coincides with the period of Mughal dominance in North India, for it was a period during which the Rajputs had a relatively secure hold on power within their own territories, guaranteed in many cases by the superior force of the Mughals with whom for long periods they had close, protected relationships. The Rajput city capitals became the sites of the most extravagant palace building extravaganza in India.

In his book *The Rajput Palaces* Tillotson observed that "A Rajput palace was a symbol of dynasty, and each *raja* sought to outdo his neighbours and his predecessors in the splendour of his building projects". Palaces were sometimes doubled up as fortresses, others were designed and occupied for periods of peace. The standard features included a division into men's and women's quarters (*mardana* and *zenana*), the creation of large open courtyards as public space and much more confined rooms for private residence. The function of the palace was to demonstrate power, wealth and status, and thus the halls of public audience (*diwan-i-am*) played a prominent role and were often richly decorated. The hall of private audience (*diwan-i-khas*) was contained within the private quarters and was on a much smaller scale. Many Rajput palaces include a picture gallery – the *chitra shali* – and a bedroom with inlay mirror work, the *sheesh mahal,* while there would also be armouries and treasuries. The *zenana*, always less prolifically decorated, nonetheless would often have wonderfully constructed *jali* screens of pierced or latticed stone work, through which the women could watch proceedings outside without being seen.

The similarity of some of these features to those of Islamic building in India tempted early scholars to infer that Rajput architecture was simply derivative of Islamic, and in particular Mughal, traditions. Tillotson has argued that this view is mistaken, and points to the clear existence of a distinct Rajput palace complex style in the earliest remaining Rajput capital site of Chittaurgarh which existed well before the Mughals became supreme. A wealth of detail from later palaces, Tillotson argues, can be attributed to earlier Hindu temple models: the use of "square based columns, the *jarokha*, or cradle balcony; the *chajja* or deep eave; the *jali* or pieced stone screen; coloured tile decoration; the lotus rosette, and the first tentative use of the cusped arch."

It is clear that Rajput secular architecture borrowed from the tradition of religious architecture, a tradition of great antiquity. The Solanki, Parmara, Chauhan, Jetwa and Parihar rulers of eighth-13th century AD followed an architectural lay-out which is better known as the Chalukyan style. The Hindu and Jain temples of this period had a multi-columned portico entered through *torana* archways, an assembly hall called a *Sabha mandapam* and a shrine room. The outer walls and inside pillars were decorated with exquisite panels of sculpture depicting gods, goddesses, human and animal figures. Some of them portrayed voluptuous women and erotic friezes. The interior domes were corbelled and carved in detail, some of them had panels of carvings in concentric circles leading to the apex of the dome, superimposed by carved brackets. The interiors of the sanctum were usually plain and rarely had any carvings, certainly no erotica. Some temples like the Sun temple at Modhera had a *kund* where devotees could have a bath before entering the portico of the temple for their worship. Temples such as those at Dilwara and Osian follow this layout and made extensive use of marble and other stones.

This period also saw the building of one of the region's most distinctive features, the highly decorated step well (*baoli* or *vav*). The early works were simple but later in Gujarat more elaborate structures came into existence like the seven storeyed Rani-ki-Vav stepwell of Patan believed to date from AD 1052, the Vikia Vav at Ghumli near Porbandar probably dating to the 12th century and the five storeyed *vav* at Adalaj near Gandhinagar dating from the late 15th century. These step wells had landings between flights of steps, exquisite carvings along the walls and pavilions/ galleries/chambers cooled by air wafting off the water surface. It is believed these galleries may have doubled as caravanserais or as royal chambers for the ruling family to retreat from the heat of the summer sun.

Haveli architecture Rajasthan has a style of domestic residential architecture which reflected the needs and aspirations of the rich and powerful merchant class, the *haveli*, built around a courtyard and ornately decorated. In Rajasthan these *havelis* were built from local stone. The sandstone *havelis* of Jaisalmer, Bikaner, Jodhpur here are masterpieces of stone carving. The Shekhawati mansions had their courtyards decorated with wall paintings, and have been referred to as open-air art galleries. See also page 281.

Minor architectural features Rajput princes also characteristically built commemorative pavilions (*chattris* or *devals*), to mark royal cremation sites. The style of such *chattris* is often replicated in external features on both Rajput and Mughal buildings, including on the Taj Mahal.

Muslim religious architecture Although the Muslims adapted many Hindu features, they also brought totally new forms. Dominating the architecture of many North Indian cities are the mosques and tomb complexes (*dargah*). The use of brickwork was widespread and they brought with them from Persia the principle of constructing the true arch and succeeded in producing a variety of domed structures, often incorporating distinctively Hindu features such as the surmounting finial. By the end of the great period of Muslim building in 1707, the Muslims had added magnificent forts and palaces to their religious structures, a statement of power as well as of aesthetic taste.

European buildings Nearly two centuries of architectural stagnation and decline followed the demise of Mughal power. The Portuguese built a series of remarkable churches in their territories that owed nothing to local traditions and everything to Baroque developments in Europe. Not until the end of the Victorian period, when British imperial ambitions were at their height, did the British colonial impact on public rather than domestic architecture begin to be felt. Fierce arguments divided British architects as to the merits of indigenous design. The ultimate plan for New Delhi was carried out by men who had little time for Hindu architecture and believed themselves to be on a civilizing mission. Others at the end of the 19th century wanted to recapture and enhance a tradition for which they had great respect. They have left a series of buildings, both in formerly British ruled territory and in the Princely States, notably in Rajasthan, which illustrate this concern through the development of what became known as the Indo-Saracenic style. The princes themselves often demonstrated highly eclectic tastes, importing such contrasting styles as

Venetian-Gothic, Greek Doric and other Europeans styles for their new palaces and mansions. British architects like Sir Samuel Swinton Jacob, William Emerson and Charles Mant, as well as local state architects and Parsi architects/builders blended European and Indian features. Victorian, art deco and other European furnishings appointed the palaces, besides traditional arts, crafts, furniture and utensils of the region.

Art

Painting Rajasthan is well known for its wall paintings. Murals were painted on forts, temples, palaces and other historic buildings for centuries, but the fresco technique of Italy (painting on wet plaster) arrived with the Muslims to India. Mudwall painting is popular in Rajasthan, most of these paintings being done on hut walls by women during festivals and family celebrations. High-quality *pichhwais* (temple paintings) are produced in Nathdwara, Udaipur and Bhilwara.

Miniature paintings The early miniature paintings in Western India are believed to originate from the classical murals of the Buddhist caves and ancient Jain art. In the 11th century, paintings adorned palm leaf and cloth-bound manuscripts, principally those of the Jains of Rajasthan and Gujarat. In the 16th century, the Mughals in India introduced Persian and West Asian techniques that strongly influenced the Rajasthani schools.

The Rajasthan Princely States were important patrons of medieval miniature painting and various schools developed in different areas, drawing from local traditions and combining them with Mughal art. While Indian paintings had specialized in full frontal and three-quarter portraits, the Islamic painters introduced profiles. The Rajasthani painters depicted nature with bold colours and emphasized human forms while the Mughals introduced royal, courtly painting. Soon, flamboyant Rajput court culture began to appear as a popular theme but this was tempered by Hindu and Jain elements, local traditions and folklore. Popular tales portrayed by the miniaturists were those from epics like the *Ramayana* and *Mahabharata*, Sanskrit writings like the Puranas and Shringara, iconography of the seasons (*Barah masa* or 12 months), and music (the *Ragamala*). Rajasthani ballads (love stories of Dhola-Maru – Sohni-Mahival, Nala-Damyanti, etc), festivals, historical events, battles and hunts, sports like polo and pig sticking, all found a place, while the painters looked at dunes, hills, forests, orchards and historic buildings for their backdrops.

Miniature paintings were usually done on paper, sheets being bound together to make a firm surface. Mineral and organic colours were applied using squirrel hair and featherquill brushes and adhesives like gum arabic were used for fixing. Terracotta was sometimes brushed over the subject to give the raised effect, enhanced by gold leaf or powder work. Rare and expensive ivory lent itself as a suitable base for prized miniaturist art which were done with transparent colours so that the base of ivory was visible. This was favoured by affluent Jains and royalty who commissioned paintings of religious subjects, portraits and courtly scenes.

Weaving Kota in eastern Rajasthan is known for its Doria saris with hundreds of weavers in the village of Khaitoon working to produce fine silk and cotton textiles with embroidered zari borders. Often the warp and weft threads are dyed in different colours to create a shot effect in Kota. Weavers of Jaisalmer, Jodhpur and other districts work on pit-looms to produce *durrie* rugs, carpets, woollen cloth and other fabrics. Weaving of traditional woollen *durries* also became associated with Bikaner, Jaipur (and Ahmadabad) jails but today attractive *durries* in pastel colours cater to the modern taste. Floor coverings called *jajams* are produced in Chittaurgarh. Handloom weaving on cradle looms is practised throughout Rajasthan.

Printing Hand-held wood blocks are carefully cut to enable patterns in different colours to be printed; up to five blocks may be used for an elaborate design. Children apprenticed to block makers and printers, master the craft by the age of 14 or 15. Traditionally colours were based on vegetable pigments though now many use chemical dyes. Printing is done in a long shed and after the block printing is complete, the fabric is boiled to make the dye fast. Good examples can be seen in the City Museum in Jaipur. Sanganer, just south of the city, is still well known for block-printing.

Tie-and-dye *Bandhani* tie-dye is another intricate process and ancient technique common throughout Rajasthan. The fabric is pinched together in selected places, tied round with twine or thread and then dyed. Afterwards, the threads are removed to reveal a pattern in the original or preceding colour. The process is often repeated, the dyeing sequence going from light to dark colours. Jaipur, Jodhpur and Udaipur districts are well known for their *bandhani*. Another form of dyeing is the *lehariya* of eastern Rajasthan which leaves long lines or bands running diagonally on the fabric surface.

Jewellery Uncut gemstones are strung or set in typical Rajasthani jewellery, Jaipur being particularly famous for its gems and jewellery. Typical items are nose rings, ear ornaments, bangles and necklaces. *Kundan* work specializes in setting stones in gold; sometimes *meenakari* (enamelling) complements the setting on the reverse side of the jewellery.

Pottery The best-known pottery in Rajasthan is the 'Jaipur Blue'. This uses a coarse grey clay that is quite brittle even when fired. It is then decorated with floral and geometric patterns along Persian lines utilizing rich ultramarines, turquoise and lapis colours on a plain off-white/grey background. In the villages, the common pot is made from a combination of earth, water and dung. The coarse pots are thrown on a simple stone wheel, partially dried, then finished with a hammer before being simply decorated, glazed and fired.

Terracotta is one of the world's oldest media of artistic expression. Tribes still pray at shrines of terracotta horses and other animistic figures, made in villages like Bhenswara in the Jalor Bhil belt and Chotta Udepur in eastern Rajasthan, among others. Pottery for water storage, ornamental plants and other utilities are made by Kumhars in most cities, towns and villages. Clay plaques for wall decor are available at Molela near Nathdwara. Pokharan produces attractive red pottery, while Merta near Ajmer is known for its delicate Kagazi pottery.

Embroidery Barmer, Jaisalmer and other districts of the western desert in Rajasthan are well known for their embroidered fabrics set with mirrors and other ornamentation. Leather embroidery is a well known craft in the Jalor, Barmer and Jodhpur districts. The most popular article of production is footwear called *mojdi*, with bold embroidery patterns; Bhinmal in Jalor district is specially well known for its embroidered shoes. Camel leather work is done by the Ustas of Bikaner though this tends to be expensive and is losing popularity.

Wood carving Barmer is known for its woodwork – surprising given the town's location in the desert – perhaps because of its tradition of wood block printing and the camel saddle market. Fancy wood crafts and furnishings are produced for domestic and export markets, sometimes with brass and other metal inlaid patterns. Udaipur is well known for its wooden toys and lacquered wood, Bassi near Chittaurgarh for wooden figures, Jaipur in recent times for wooden furniture. Jodhpur and Sawai Madhopur districts are also well known for their attractive furniture.

Metalware Jaipur city and various districts of Rajasthan are famous for their silver ornaments, utensils and artefacts. Jaipur is particularly well known for its engraved brassware with floral motifs or lacquered effect patterns. Zinc water bags/bottles are made in the desert cities and towns of Rajasthan. Gaduliya Lohars are nomadic smiths in Rajasthan. The swordsmiths of Sirohi, Udaipur and Alwar specialize in metal inlays.

Stone carving The Silavats and other artisans of Rajasthan excel in carving marble, sandstone and other material into beautiful *jali*-work (lattice) utensils and ornamental pieces. Outdoor furniture made from carved marble and other stones are crafted in Sirohi, Kishangarh and other districts of Rajasthan.

Other crafts Other crafts practised in Rajasthan include *khari* (embossed printing using gold and silver), engraving and lacquering brassware and embroidering camel skin. Papermaking is important in the Jaipur-Bagru-Sanganer triangle, zari embroidery at Surat, Jamnagar and Jaipur, and the making of marble bangles or grass tribal jewellery.

Music and dance

Music

Indian music can trace its origins to the metrical hymns and chants of the Vedas, in which the production of sound according to strict rules was understood to be vital to the continuing order of the Universe. Through more than 3000 years of development and a range of regional schools, India's musical tradition has been handed on almost entirely by ear. The chants of the **Rig Veda** developed into songs in the **Sama Veda** and music found expression in every sphere of life, reflecting the cycle of seasons and the rhythm of work.

Over the centuries the original three notes, which were sung strictly in descending order, were extended to five and then seven and developed to allow freedom to move up and down the scale. The scale increased to 12 with the addition of flats and sharps and finally to 22 with the further subdivision of semitones. Books of musical rules go back at least as far as the third century AD. Classical music was totally intertwined with dance and drama, an interweaving reflected in the term *sangita*.

At some point after the Muslim influence made itself felt in the north, northern and southern Indian styles diverged, to become Carnatic (Karnatak) music in the south and Hindustani music in the north. However, they still share important common features: *svara* (pitch), *raga* (the melodic structure) and *tala* (rhythm).

Hindustani music probably originated in the Delhi Sultanate during the 13th century, when the most widely known of North Indian musical instruments, the *sitar*, was believed to have been invented. **Amir Khusrau** is also believed to have invented the small drums, the *tabla*. Hindustani music is held to have reached its peak under *Tansen*, a court musician of Akbar. The other important northern instruments are the stringed *sarod*, the reed instrument *shahnai* and the wooden flute. Most Hindustani compositions have devotional texts, though they encompass a great emotional and thematic range. A common classical form of vocal performance is the *dhrupad*, a four-part composition.

The essential structure of a melody is known as a *raga* which usually has five to seven notes and can have as many as nine (or even 12 in mixed *ragas*). The music is improvised by the performer within certain governing rules and, although theoretically thousands of *ragas* are possible, only around 100 are commonly performed. *Ragas* have become associated with particular moods and specific times of the day. Music festivals often include all night sessions to allow performers a wider choice of repertoire.

Dance

The rules for classical dance were laid down in the Natya shastra in the second century BC, which is still one of the bases for modern dance forms. The most common sources for Indian dance are the epics, but there are three essential aspects of the dance itself, *Nritta* (pure dance), *Nrittya* (emotional expression) and *Natya* (drama). The religious influence in dance was exemplified by the tradition of temple dancers, *devadasis*, girls and women who were dedicated to the deity in major temples. India is also rich in folk dance traditions which are widely performed during festivals.

Folk dance Typical community folk dances of the Rajasthan region are based on the *Rasa* tradition of dancing in circles, clapping hands or striking sticks in unison to set the rhythm. The *Ghoomer* of Rajasthan is generally for women, who clap their hands or strike small sticks to the simple rhythm. The *Ger* of Rajasthan is a dance for men using larger sticks. Combination dances, for both men and women, are also performed. The best period to witness these dances Holi, Gangaur, Navratri and other festivals of Rajasthan.

Kachchhi Ghodi is a dance performed by men riding hobby-horses and sporting swords. The dances are accompanied by songs that recite tales of the Bavaria outlaws of Shekhawati, the Robin Hoods of Rajasthan.

Sidh Naths of Bikaner are deservedly famous for their fire dances. The performers dance on the fire as if it did not exist, and even put burning coals in their mouths, to the beat and rhythm of pipes and drums. The Dholis of Jalore district are known for their drum dance which is a sword, stick and scarf dance performed to powerful beats of five or more drums, as well as cymbals and other percussion instruments.

One of the most colourful dancing communities is the Kalbelia (generally snake charmers and nomadic workers by profession). The women wear embroidered veils called *odhnis*, skirts called *gaghras*, blouses called *cholis* and artistic jewellery, while men wear red turbans. A vigorous dance is the *Terah Tal* of Ramdeora near Pokaran, which has now become a popular dance throughout Rajasthan.

Bhavai is a dance drama, the folk theatre of Gujarat. In Rajasthan tribal dancers recite the tale of the mystic Pabhuji, unravelling a long narrative painting of the hero's life. Langas and Manganiars of western Rajasthan are professional singers whose haunting melodies recall the feel of the desert. Mirasis are professional musicians, usually employed for weddings and celebrations, sometimes accompanied by dancers, while the Naths of Rajasthan are acrobats who perform spell-binding acts to the tune of singing and music.

The pastoral communities of Rajasthan have dances based on the Dandia, Garba, Ger and Ghoomer formations. During Holi in Rajasthan, Bhils perform the Ger-Ghoomar which begins with men in an outer circle and women in the inner circle, but as the dance progresses both sexes get together.

The people

The population of Rajasthan is almost wholly of Indo-Aryan stock. However, they have a much higher percentage of scheduled tribes than the national average.

Tribal peoples

The tribal population of Rajasthan constitutes about 12% of the state's population, nearly double the national average. The Bhils and Minas are the largest groups, but the less well known Sahariyas, Damariyas, Garasias and Gaduliya Lohars are all important. The tribes share many common traits but differences in their costumes and jewellery, their gods, fairs and festivals also set them apart from one another.

Bhils The Bhils comprise nearly 40% of Rajasthan's tribal population with their stronghold in Baneshwar. *Bil* (bow) describes their original talent and strength. Today, the accepted head of all the Rajput clans of Rajasthan – the Maharana of Udaipur – is crowned by anointing his forehead with blood drawn from the palm of a Bhil chieftain, affirming the alliance and the loyalty of his tribe. Rajput rulers came to value the guerrilla tactics of the Bhils, and Muslim and Maratha attacks could not have been repelled without their active support. Furthermore, they always remained a minority and offered no real threat to the city-dwelling princes and their armies. Physically, the Bhils are short, stocky and dark with broad noses and thick lips. They once lived off roots, leaves and fruits of the forest and the increasingly scarce game. Most now farm land and keep cattle, goats and sheep, while those who live near towns often work on daily wages. Thousands congregate near the confluence of the Mahi and Som rivers in Dungarpur district for the Baneshwar fair in January and February.

Minas The Minas are Rajasthan's most widely spread tribal group. They may have been the original inhabitants of the Indus Valley civilization, mentioned in the *Vedas* and the *Mahabharata*, who were finally dispersed into the Aravallis by the Kachhawaha Rajputs. The Minas are tall, with an athletic build, light brown complexion and sharp features. The men wear a loincloth round the waist, a waistcoat and a brightly coloured turban while the women wear a long gathered skirt (*ghaghra*), a small blouse (*kurti-kanchali*) and a large scarf. Most Minas are cultivators who measure their wealth in cattle and other livestock. They worship Siva in temples decorated with stone carvings, and also Sheeta Mata (Shitala), the goddess of smallpox. Like other tribal groups they have a tradition of giving grain, clothes, animals and jewellery to the needy. The forest dwellings, *Mewas*, comprise a cluster of huts or *pals*. Though their marriage ceremony, performed round a fire, is similar to a Hindu one, divorce is not uncommon or particularly difficult. A man wanting a divorce tears a piece of his clothes and gives this to his wife, who then leaves the home carrying two pitchers of water. Whoever helps her unload the pitchers becomes her new husband! Of the tribes of Rajasthan the Minas have progressed the most and only in a few pockets do they follow traditional practices.

Gaduliya Lohars The Gaduliya Lohars, named after their beautiful bullock carts (*gadis*), are nomadic blacksmiths, said to have wandered from their homeland of Mewar because of their promise to their 'lord' Maharana Pratap who was ousted from Chittaurgarh by Akbar. This clan of warring Rajputs vowed to re-enter the city only with a victorious Maharana Pratap. Unfortunately the Maharana was killed on the battlefield, so even today many of them prefer a nomadic life.

Sahariyas The Sahariyas are jungle dwellers, their name possibly deriving from the Persian *sehr* (jungle). They are regarded as the most backward tribe in Rajasthan and eke out a living as shifting cultivators and by hunting and fishing. More recently they have also undertaken menial and manual work on daily wages. In most respects their rituals are those of Hindus. One difference is that polygamy and widow marriage (*nata*) are permitted, though only to a widower or divorcee.

Bishnois With the growing recent interest in environmental conservation the Bishnois of Rajasthan's desert districts have come into prominence. For centuries, they have protected wildlife and vegetation with a religious passion inspired by their medieval leader Jamboji. Jalore, Barmer, Nagaur, Jodhpur and Bikaner district have large groups of Bishnois. Their hamlets, called *dhannis*, comprise picturesque huts with thatch roofing and mud walls. Each *dhanni* is surrounded by vegetation. Antelope and gazelle feel safe in Bishnoi areas and are less shy than anywhere else.

Garasias One of the most colourful tribal communities is the Garasia adivasi, inhabitants of the Aravalli foothills of Sabarkanta and Banaskanta districts in north Gujarat, and Udaipur, Sirohi and Pali districts of Rajasthan. Garasia adivasis claim descent from Rajput men who married Bhil women (*Garasia* = landowner, *adivasi* = original inhabitant) and consider themselves superior to other tribes of the Aravalli foothills. They still own cultivable land and work on fields, the reason for the importance of the spring harvest in the life of this tribal community. Garasia homes are typically made from mud and bamboo decorated during festivals with line art and wall paintings. The women dress in colourful clothes, sport facial tattoos and wear artistic silver and grass jewellery. The men wear turbans of different colours, *kurtas* and ear ornaments, and pride themselves on being skilful archers. Potters make terracotta horses and other figurines for the animistic worship. The community can be seen at their colourful best during tribal fairs in March and April like the Gaur fair near Mount Abu and Chitra Vichitra fair near Poshina. These fairs feature ancestor mourning, music, dancing, revelry and match-making (elopement is not uncommon!).

Rathwas Like the Garasia Adivasis of northern Gujarat, the Rathwa of eastern Gujarat love music, dancing, colourful clothes and attractive ornaments, and are skilled archers. The Rathwas usually live in picturesque village houses, made of mud and roofed with intricately thatched straw, leaves, timber or locally made clay tiles. The interiors of these houses are embellished with a profusion of faunal figures called *pithoras*. The tribes worship at shrines comprising terracotta horses and other animistic clay figures and are strong believers in ghosts, spirits, ancestor worship and the Hindu pantheon. The *pithora* paintings are believed to be magical and ward away evil spirits.

The beautiful villages are often surrounded by agricultural fields, and may be set next to palm groves that the tribes tap for toddy, or in the heart of wooded hill country. Today, many of these tribal people have taken employment as mine workers, farm labourers and watchmen, but traditional handicrafts like wood carving, basket weaving and arrow crafting continue in this tribal belt, and the men still carry bows, arrows and guns when they travel. Ephemeral village markets (*haats*) are a daily event in the Rathwa tribal belt, with one of the largest being the Saturday bazar at Chotta Udepur. The area comes alive with music, dancing, acrobatics and a showcase of colourful tribal dress during the fairs of Dasara and Holi. The Kawant fair offers an interesting insight into the tribes of this region, their clothing, ornaments, music and dancing.

Rabaris The Rabari (also called **Raika** in Rajasthan), the best known of the semi-nomadic herders, are widespread with many distinct subgroups. They have attractive houses in their villages, but travel with camels and cattle in search of pasture seasonally.

Siddis The Siddis live either side of the Rajasthan-Gujarat border, and are believed to have originally come from Africa in the 13th century. Employed by the Gujarat sultanate as mercenary warriors or slaves, some rose to become generals, working to protect important ports like Daman and Diu from Portuguese naval invasions. The Siddis of Gir live in hamlets that would not be out of place in the African bush, and retain many of their traditions and beliefs handed down through generations. Among their many Africans inheritances is the natural sense of rhythm reflected in their drumming and dance performances. They also retain some elements of African dress and custom such as breaking coconuts with their heads and fire-walking.

Jats and Ahirs The Jats inhabit Kachchh and the northwestern arid zone from Gujarat and Rajasthan to the North Western Frontier Province of Pakistan. Their turbans and dress are reminiscent of the days when camel caravans plied from the Near East to the Far East across the desert areas of western India. The Ahirs are an agricultural community of Kachchh. Their women are known for their colourful embroidery.

Religion

It is impossible to write briefly about religion in India without greatly oversimplifying. Over 80% of Indians are Hindu, but there are significant minorities. Muslims number about 120 million and there are over 20 million Christians, 18 million Sikhs, six million Buddhists, two million Jains and a number of other religious groups. Although nearly all these groups are represented in Rajasthan, the balance varies. Buddhism is barely represented, and there are only small communities of Sikhs and Christians. While Hinduism is dominant, there is a significant Muslim minority, and the greatest concentration of Jains in India.

One of the most persistent features of Indian religious and social life is the caste system. This has undergone substantial changes since Independence, especially in towns and cities, but most people in India are still clearly identified as a member of a particular caste group. The government has introduced measures to help the 'backward' or 'scheduled' castes – the *dalits*, meaning 'oppressed' – though in recent years this has produced a major political backlash.

Hinduism

It has always been easier to define Hinduism by what it is not than by what it is. Indeed, the name 'Hindu' was given by foreigners to the peoples of the subcontinent who did not profess the other major faiths, such as Muslims or Christians. The beliefs and practices of modern Hinduism began to take shape in the centuries on either side of the birth of Christ. But while some aspects of modern Hinduism can be traced back more than 2000 years before that, other features are recent.

Key ideas

Some Hindu scholars and philosophers talk of Hinduism as one religious and cultural tradition. Yet there is no Hindu organization, like a church, with the authority to define belief or establish official practice. There are spiritual leaders who are widely revered and there is an enormous range of literature that is treated as sacred. In view of these characteristics, many authorities argue that it is misleading to think of Hinduism as a religion at all. Be that as it may, the evidence of the living importance of Hinduism is visible across India. Hindu philosophy and practice has also touched many of those who belong to other religious traditions, particularly in terms of social institutions such as caste.

Darshan One of Hinduism's recurring themes is 'vision', 'sight' or 'view' – *darshan*. Applied to the different philosophical systems themselves, such as *yoga* or *vedanta*, *darshan* is also used to describe the sight of the deity that worshippers hope to gain when they visit a temple or shrine hoping for the sight of a *guru* (teacher). Equally it may apply to the religious insight gained through meditation or prayer.

The four human goals Many Hindus also accept that there are four major human goals; material prosperity (*artha*), the satisfaction of desires (*kama*) and performing the duties laid down according to your position in life (*dharma*). Beyond those is the goal of achieving liberation from the endless cycle of rebirths into which everyone is locked (*moksha*). It is to the search for liberation that the major schools of Indian philosophy have devoted most attention. Together with *dharma*, it is basic to Hindu thought.

The *Mahabharata* lists 10 embodiments of *dharma*: good name, truth, self-control, cleanness of mind and body, simplicity, endurance, resoluteness of character, giving and

Karma – an eye to the future

According to the doctrine of karma, every person, animal or god has a being or 'self' which has existed without beginning. Every action, except those that are done without any consideration of the results, leaves an indelible mark on that Self, carried forward into the next life.

The overall character of the imprint on each person's Self determines three features of the next life: the nature of his next birth (animal, human or god), the kind of family he will be born into if human and the length of the next life. Finally, it controls the good or bad experiences that the self will experience. However, it does not imply a fatalistic belief that the nature of action in this life is unimportant. Rather, it suggests that the path followed by the individual in the present life is vital to the nature of its next life and ultimately to the chance of gaining release from this world.

sharing, austerities and continence. In *dharmic* thinking these are inseparable from five patterns of behaviour: non-violence, an attitude of equality, peace and tranquillity, lack of aggression and cruelty and absence of envy. Dharma, an essentially secular concept, represents the order inherent in human life.

Karma The idea of *karma*, 'the effect of former actions', is central to achieving liberation. As C Rajagopalachari put it: "Every act has its appointed effect, whether the act be thought, word or deed. The cause holds the effect, so to say, in its womb. If we reflect deeply and objectively, the entire world will be found to obey unalterable laws. That is the doctrine of karma".

Rebirth The belief in the transmigration of souls (*samsara*) in a never-ending cycle of rebirth has been Hinduism's most distinctive and important contribution to Indian culture. The earliest reference to the belief is found in one of the Upanishads, around the seventh century BC, at about the same time as the doctrine of karma made its first appearance. By the late Upanishads it was universally accepted and in Buddhism and Jainism it is never questioned.

Ahimsa AL Basham pointed out that belief in transmigration must have encouraged a further distinctive doctrine, that of non-violence or non-injury – *ahimsa*. The belief in rebirth meant that all living things and creatures of the spirit – people, devils, gods, animals, even worms – possessed the same essential soul. It was an idea that became particularly important for the Jains.

Schools of philosophy

It is common now to talk of six major schools of Hindu philosophy. *Nyaya*, *Vaisheshika*, *Sankhya*, *Yoga*, *Purvamimansa* and *Vedanta*.

Yoga Yoga, can be traced back to at least the third century AD. It seeks a synthesis of the spirit, the soul and the flesh and is concerned with systems of meditation and self denial that lead to the realization of the Divine within oneself and can ultimately release one from the cycle of rebirth.

Vedanta These are literally the final parts of the Vedic literature, the *Upanishads*. The basic texts also include the *Brahmasutra of Badrayana*, written about the first century AD and the most important of all, the *Bhagavad-Gita*, which is a part of the epic the *Mahabharata*. There are many interpretations of these basic texts.

Worship

Puja For most Hindus today worship (performing *puja*) is an integral part of their faith. Acts of devotion are often aimed at the granting of favours and the meeting of urgent needs for this life – good health, finding a suitable wife or husband, the birth of a son, prosperity and good fortune. Puja involves making an offering to God and *darshan* (having a view of the deity). Hindu worship is generally, though not always, an act performed by individuals. Thus Hindu temples may be little more than a shrine in the middle of the street, tended by a priest and visited at special times when a *darshan* of the resident God can be obtained. When it has been consecrated, the image, if exactly made, becomes the channel for the godhead to work.

Rituals and festivals The temple rituals often follow through the cycle of day and night, as well as yearly life cycles. The priests may wake the deity from sleep, bathe, clothe and feed it. Worshippers will be invited to share in this process by bringing offerings of clothes and food. Gifts of money will usually be made and in some temples there is a charge levied for taking up positions in front of the deity in order to obtain a *darshan* at the appropriate times.

Hindu deities

Today three Gods are widely seen as all-powerful: Brahma, Vishnu and Siva. While Brahma is regarded as the ultimate source of creation, Siva also has a creative role alongside his function as destroyer. Vishnu in contrast is seen as the preserver or protector of the universe. Vishnu and Siva are widely represented in sculpture and art (where Brahma is not) and have come to be seen as the most powerful and important. Their followers are referred to as Vaishnavites and Shaivites respectively and numerically they form the two largest sects in India.

Brahma In the literal sense the name Brahma is the masculine and personalized form of the neuter word Brahman. Popularly Brahma is recognized as the Creator. In the early Vedic writing, Brahman represented the universal and impersonal principle which governed the Universe. Gradually, as Vedic philosophy moved towards a monotheistic interpretation of the universe and its origins, this impersonal power was increasingly personalized. In the Upanishads, Brahman was seen as a universal and elemental creative spirit.

By the fourth and fifth centuries AD, the height of the classical period of Hinduism, Brahma was seen as one of the trinity of Gods – *Trimurti* – in which Vishnu, Siva and Brahma represented three forms of the unmanifested supreme being. It is from Brahma that Hindu cosmology takes its structure. The basic cycle through which the whole cosmos passes is described as one day in the life of Brahma – the *kalpa*. It equals 4320 million years, with an equally long night. One year of Brahma's life – a cosmic year – lasts 360 days and nights. The universe is expected to last for 100 years of Brahma's life, who is currently believed to be 51 years old.

By the sixth century AD Brahma worship had effectively ceased (before the great period of temple building), which accounts for the fact that there are remarkably few temples dedicated to Brahma. Nonetheless images of Brahma are found in most temples. Characteristically he is shown with four faces, a fifth having been destroyed by the fire from Siva's third eye. In his four arms he usually holds a copy of the Vedas, a sceptre and a water jug or a bow. He is accompanied by the goose, symbolizing knowledge.

Sarasvati Seen by some Hindus as the 'active power' of Brahma, popularly thought of as his consort, Sarasvati, the goddess of education and learning, is worshipped in schools

Auspicious signs

Some of Hinduism's sacred symbols are thought to have originated in the Aryan religion of the Vedic period.

Om The Primordial sound of the universe, 'Om' (or more correctly the three-in-one 'Aum') is the Supreme syllable. It is the opening and sometimes closing, chant for Hindu prayers. Some attribute the three constituents to the Hindu triad of Brahma, Vishnu and Siva. It is believed to be the cosmic sound of Creation which encompasses all states from wakefulness to deep sleep and though it is the essence of all sound, it is outside our hearing.

Svastika Representing the Sun and it's energy, the svastika usually appears on doors or walls of temples, in red, the colour associated with good fortune and luck. The term, derived from the Sanskrit 'svasti', is repeated in Hindu chants. The arms of the symbol point in the cardinal directions which may reflect the ancient practice of lighting fire sticks in the four directions. When the svastika appears to rotate clockwise it symbolizes the positive creative energy of the sun; the anti-clockwise svastika, symbolizing the autumn/winter sun, is considered to be unlucky.

Six-pointed star The intersecting triangles in the 'Star of David' symbol represents Spirit and Matter held in balance. A central dot signifies a particle of Divinity. The star is incorporated as a decorative element in some Muslim buildings such as Humayun's Tomb in Delhi.

Lotus The 'padma' or 'kamal' flower with it's many petals appears not only in art and architecture but also in association with gods and godesses. Some deities are seen holding one, others are portrayed seated or standing on the flower, or as with Padmanabha it appears from Vishnu's navel. The lotus represents purity, peace and beauty, a symbol also shared by Buddhists and Jains and as in nature stands away and above the impure, murky water from which it emerges. In architecture, the lotus motif occurs frequently.

Om

Svastika

Six-pointed star

Lotus

and colleges with gifts of fruit, flowers and incense. The development of her identity represented the rebirth of the concept of a mother goddess, which had been strong in the Indus Valley civilization over 1000 years before and which may have been continued in popular ideas through the worship of female spirits.

In addition to her role as Brahma's wife, Sarasvati is also variously seen as the wife of Vishnu and Manu or as Daksha's daughter, among other interpretations. Normally white coloured, riding on a swan and carrying a book, she is often shown playing a *vina*. She may have many arms and heads, representing her role as patron of all the sciences and arts.

Vishnu Vishnu is seen as the God with the human face. From the second century a new and passionate devotional worship of Vishnu's incarnation as Krishna developed in the South. By 1000 AD Vaishnavism had spread across South India and it became closely associated with the devotional form of Hinduism preached by **Ramanuja**, whose followers spread the worship of Vishnu and his 10 successive incarnations in animal and

Hindu deities

Deity	Association	Relationship
Brahma	Creator	One of Trinity
Sarasvati	Education and culture, "the word"	Wife of Brahma
Siva	Creator/destroyer	One of Trinity
Bhairava	Fierce aspect of Siva	
Parvati (Uma)	Benevolent aspect of female divine power	Consort of Siva, mother of Ganesh
Kali	The energy that destroys evil	Consort of Siva
Durga	In fighting attitude	Consort of Siva
Ganesh/ Ganapati	God of good beginnings, clearer of obstacles	Son of Siva
Skanda	God of War/bringer of disease (Karttikkeya, Murugan, Subrahmanya)	Son of Siva and Ganga
Vishnu	Preserver	One of Trinity
Prithvi/ Bhudevi	Goddess of Earth	Wife of Vishnu
Lakshmi	Goddess of Wealth	Wife of Vishnu
Agni	God of Fire	
Indra	Rain, lightning and thunder	
Ravana	King of the demons	

human form. For Vaishnavites, God took these different forms in order to save the world from impending disaster.

Rama and Krishna By far the most influential incarnations of Vishnu are those in which he was believed to take recognizable human form, especially as Rama (twice) and Krishna. As the Prince of Ayodhya, history and myth blend, for Rama was probably a chief who lived in the eighth or seventh century BC.

Although Rama (or Ram – pronounced to rhyme with *calm*) is now seen as an earlier incarnation of Vishnu than Krishna, he came to be regarded as divine very late, probably after the Muslim invasions of the 12th century AD. The story has become part of the cultures of Southeast Asia.

Krishna is worshipped extremely widely as perhaps the most human of the gods. Often shown in pictures as blue in colour and playing the flute, he is the playful child stealing butter or the amorous young man teasing the young women looking after the cattle. His advice on the battlefield of the *Mahabharata* is one of the major sources of guidance for the rules of daily living for many Hindus today.

Lakshmi Commonly represented as Vishnu's wife, Lakshmi is widely worshipped as the goddess of wealth. Earlier representations of Vishnu's consorts portrayed her as Sridevi, often shown in statues on Vishnu's right, while Bhudevi, also known as Prithvi, who

Attributes	Vehicle
4 heads, 4 arms, upper left holds water pot and rosary or sacrificial spoon, sacred thread across left shoulder	Hamsa (goose/swan)
Two or more arms, vina, lotus, plam leaves, rosary	Hamsa
Linga; Rudra, matted hair, 3 eyes, drum, fire, deer, trident; Nataraja, Lord of the Dance	Bull – Nandi
Trident, sword, noose, naked, snakes, garland of skulls, dishevelled hair, carrying destructive weapons	Dog
2 arms when shown with Siva, 4 when on her own, blue lily in right hand, left hand hangs down	Lion
Trident, noose, human skulls, sword, shield, black colour	Lion
4 arms, conch, disc, bow, arrow, bell, sword, shield	Lion or tiger
Goad, noose, broken tusk, fruits	Rat/mouse/shrew
6 heads, 12 arms, spear, arrow, sword, discus, noose cock, bow, shield, conch and plough	Peacock
4 arms, high crown, discus and conch in upper arms, club and sword (or lotus) in lower	Garuda – mythical eagle
Right hand in abhaya gesture, left holds pomegranate, left leg on treasure pot	
Seated/standing on red lotus, 4 hands, lotuses, vessel, fruit	Lotus
Sacred thread, axe, wood, bellows, torch, sacrificial spoon	2-headed ram
Bow, thunderbolt, lances	
10 heads, 20 arms, bow and arrow	

represented the earth, was on his left. Lakshmi is popularly shown in her own right as standing on a lotus flower, although eight forms of Lakshmi are recognized.

Hanuman The Ramayana tells how Hanuman, Rama's faithful monkey servant, went across India and finally into the demon Ravana's forest home of Lanka at the head of his monkey army in search of the abducted Sita. He used his powers to jump the sea channel separating India from Sri Lanka and managed after a series of heroic and magical feats to find and rescue his master's wife. Whatever form he is shown in, he remains almost instantly recognizable.

Siva Siva is interpreted as both creator and destroyer, the power through whom the universe evolves. He lives on Mount Kailasa with his wife **Parvati** (also known as **Uma**, **Sati**, **Kali** and **Durga**) and two sons, the elephant-headed Ganesh and the six-headed Karttikeya. To many contemporary Hindus they form a model of sorts for family life. In sculptural representations Siva is normally accompanied by his 'vehicle', the bull (*nandi* or *nandin*).

Siva is also represented in Shaivite temples throughout India by the linga, literally meaning 'sign' or 'mark', but referring in this context to the sign of gender or phallus and *yoni*. On the one hand a symbol of energy, fertility and potency, as Siva's symbol it also represents the yogic power of sexual abstinence and penance. The linga has become the most important symbol of the cult of Siva.

A wide variety of myths appeared to explain the origin of linga worship. The myths surrounding the 12 *jyotirlinga* (linga of light) found at centres like Somnath in Gujarat go back to the second century BC and were developed in order to explain and justify linga worship.

Although Siva is not seen as having a series of rebirths, like Vishnu, he nonetheless appears in very many forms representing different aspects of his varied powers. Some of the more common are: **Chandrasekhara** – the moon (*chandra*) symbolizes the powers of creation and destruction. **Mahadeva**–the representation of Siva as the god of supreme power, which came relatively late into Hindu thought, shown as the linga in combination with the *yoni*, or female genitalia. **Nataraja** – the Lord of the Cosmic Dance. The story is based on a legend in which Siva and Vishnu went to the forest to overcome 10,000 heretics. In their anger the heretics attacked Siva first by sending a tiger, then a snake and thirdly a fierce black dwarf with a club. Siva killed the tiger, tamed the snake and wore it like a garland and then put his foot on the dwarf and performed a dance of such power that the dwarf and the heretics acknowledged Siva as the Lord. **Rudra** – Siva's early prototype, who may date back to the Indus Valley civilization. Virabhadra – Siva created Virabhadra to avenge himself on his wife Sati's father, Daksha, who had insulted Siva by not inviting him to a special sacrifice. Sati attended the ceremony against Siva's wishes and when she heard her father grossly abusing Siva she committed suicide by jumping into the sacrificial fire. This act gave rise to the term *sati* (*suttee*, a word which simply means a good or virtuous woman). Recorded in the *Vedas*, the self immolation of a woman on her husband's funeral pyre probably did not become accepted practice until the early centuries BC. Even then it was mainly restricted to those of the Kshatriya caste. **Nandi** – Siva's vehicle, the bull, one of the most widespread of sacred symbols of the ancient world, may represent a link with Rudra who was sometimes represented as a bull in pre-Hindu India. Strength and virility are key attributes and pilgrims to Siva temples will often touch the Nandi's testicles on their way into the shrine.

Ganesh One of Hinduism's most popular gods, Ganesh is seen as the great clearer of obstacles. Shown at gateways and on door lintels with his elephant head and pot belly, his image is revered across India. Meetings, functions and special family gatherings will often start with prayers to Ganesh and any new venture, from the opening of a building to inaugurating a company, will not be deemed complete without a Ganesh puja.

Shakti, The Mother Goddess **Shakti** is a female divinity often worshipped in the form of Siva's wife Durga or Kali. As Durga she agreed to do battle with Mahish, an *asura* (demon) who threatened to dethrone the gods. Many sculptures and paintings illustrate the story in which, during the terrifying struggle which ensued, the demon changed into a buffalo, an elephant and a giant with 1000 arms. Durga, clutching weapons in each of her 10 hands, eventually emerges victorious. As Kali (black) the mother goddess takes on her most fearsome form and character. Fighting with the chief of the demons, she was forced to use every weapon in her armoury, but every drop of blood that she drew became 1000 new giants just as strong as him. The only way she could win was by drinking the blood of all her enemies. Having succeeded she was so elated that her dance of triumph threatened the earth. Ignoring the pleas of the gods to stop, she even threw her husband Siva to the ground and trampled over him, until she realized to her shame what she had done. She is always shown with a sword in one hand, the severed head of the giant in another, two corpses for earrings and a necklace of human skulls. She is often shown standing with one foot on the body and the other on the leg of Siva.

Gods of the warrior caste Modern Hinduism has brought into its pantheon over many generations gods who were worshipped by the earlier pre-Hindu Aryan civilizations.

The most important is **Indra**, often shown as the god of rain, thunder and lightning. To the early Aryans, Indra destroyed demons in battle, the most important being his victory over Vritra, 'the Obstructor'. By this victory Indra released waters from the clouds, allowing the earth to become fertile. To the early Vedic writers the clouds of the southwest monsoon were seen as hostile, determined to keep their precious treasure of water to themselves and only releasing it when forced to by a greater power. Indra, carrying a bow in one hand, a thunderbolt in another and lances in the others and riding on his vehicle Airavata, the elephant, is thus the Lord of Heaven.

Mitra and **Varuna** have the power both of gods and demons. Their role is to sustain order, Mitra taking responsibility for friendship and Varuna for oaths and as they have to keep watch for 24 hours a day Mitra has become the god of the day or the sun, Varuna the god of the moon.

Soma The juice of the soma plant, the nectar of the gods guaranteeing eternal life, Soma is also a deity taking many forms. Born from the churning of the ocean of milk in later stories Soma was identified with the moon. The golden-haired and golden-skinned god **Savitri** is an intermediary with the great power to forgive sin and as king of heaven he gives the gods their immortality. **Surya**, the god of the sun, fittingly of overpowering splendour, is often described as being dark red, sitting on a red lotus or riding a chariot pulled by the seven horses of the dawn (representing the days of the week). **Usha**, sometimes referred to as Surya's wife, is the goddess of the dawn, daughter of Heaven and sister of the night. She rides in a chariot drawn by cows or horses.

Devas and Asuras In Hindu popular mythology the world is also populated by innumerable gods and demons, with a somewhat uncertain dividing line between them. Both have great power and moral character and there are frequent conflicts and battles between them.

The Nagas and Naginis The multiple-hooded cobra head often seen in sculptures represents the fabulous snake gods the Nagas, though they may often be shown in other forms, even human. Worshipped throughout India, in Rajasthan the *naga* – or *sesa* – is widely revered. The thousand-headed cosmic serpent is seen as the God Vishnu in the form of the snake. **Sesa** has the power to destroy the world at the end of every age by his fiery breath.

Hindu society

Dharma is seen as the most important of the objectives of individual and social life. Hindu law givers laid down rules of family conduct and social obligations related to the institutions of caste and *jati* which were beginning to take shape at the same time.

Caste Although the word caste was given by the Portuguese in the 15th century AD, the main feature of the system emerged at the end of the Vedic period. Two terms – *varna* and *jati* – are used in India itself and have come to be used interchangeably and confusingly with the word caste.

Varna This literally means colour, had a fourfold division. By 600 BC this had become a standard means of classifying the population. The fair-skinned Aryans distinguished themselves from the darker skinned earlier inhabitants. The priestly *varna*, the Brahmins, were seen as coming from the mouth of Brahma; the Kshatriyas (or Rajputs as they are commonly called in Northwest India) were warriors, coming from Brahma's arms; the Vaishyas, a trading community, came from Brahma's thighs and the Sudras, classified as agriculturalists, from his feet. Relegated beyond the pale of civilized Hindu society were the untouchables or outcastes, who were left with the jobs which were regarded as impure.

Jati Many Brahmins and Rajputs are conscious of their *varna* status, but the great majority of Indians do not put themselves into one of the four *varna* categories, but into a *jati* group. There are thousands of different *jatis* across the country. While individuals found it impossible to change caste or to move up the social scale, groups would sometimes try to gain recognition as higher caste by adopting practices of the Brahmins such as becoming vegetarians. Many used to be identified with particular activities and occupations used to be hereditary. Caste membership is decided simply by birth. Although you can be evicted from your caste by your fellow members you cannot join another caste and technically you become an outcaste. Right up until Independence in 1947 such punishment was a drastic penalty for disobeying one's dharmic duty. In many areas all avenues into normal life could be blocked, families would disregard outcaste members and it could even be impossible for the outcaste to continue to work within the locality.

The Dalits Gandhi spearheaded his campaign for independence from British colonial rule with a powerful campaign to abolish the disabilities imposed by the caste system. Coining the term *harijan* (person of God) Gandhi demanded that discrimination be outlawed. Lists – or 'schedules' – of 'backward' castes were drawn up during the early part of this century in order to provide positive help to such groups. The term *harijan* has been rejected by many former outcastes as paternalistic and as implying an adherence to Hindu beliefs which some explicitly reject. Many argue passionately for the use of the secular term *dalits* – the 'oppressed'.

Affirmative action Since 1947 the Indian government has extended its positive discrimination (a form of affirmative action) to scheduled castes and scheduled tribes, particularly through reserving up to 50% of jobs in government-run institutions and in further education, leading to professional qualifications for these groups. Members of the scheduled castes are now found in important positions throughout the economy. Most of the obvious forms of social discrimination have disappeared. Yet caste remains an explosive political issue. Attempts to improve the social and economic position of dalits and what are termed 'other backward castes' (OBCs) continues to cause sometimes violent conflict.

Marriage Even in cities, where traditional means of arranging marriages have often broken down and where many people resort to advertising for marriage partners in the columns of the Sunday newspapers, caste is frequently stated as a requirement. Marriage is generally seen as an alliance between two families. Great efforts are made to match caste, social status and economic position, although the rules which govern eligibility vary from region to region. In some groups marriage between even first cousins is common, while among others marriage between any branch of the same clan is strictly prohibited.

Hindu reform movements

Hinduism today is a more self-conscious religious and political force than it was even at Independence in 1947. Reform movements of modern Hinduism can be traced back at least to the early years of the 19th century. These movements were unique in Hinduism's history in putting the importance of political ideas on the same level as strictly religious thinking and in interrelating them.

The **Arya Samaj**, founded in 1875 at Ajmer by Dayanand Sarasvati, was established to restore India to its Vedic Aryan religious roots. Particularly strong in Rajasthan and northwestern India, the Arya Samaj held that the Vedas contain all knowledge and truth. In its extreme form this has led to claims that references to everything ever invented can be found in the Vedas, including space travel and nuclear weapons, but the Arya Samaj also had a significant social reforming dimension.

The Hindu calendar While for its secular life India follows the Gregorian calendar, for Hindus, much of religious and personal life follows the Hindu calendar. This is based on the lunar cycle of 29½ days, but the clever bit comes in the way it is synchronized with the 365-day Gregorian solar calendar of the west by the addition of an 'extra month' (*adhik maas*), every 2½ to three years.

Hindus follow two distinct eras. The *Vikrama Samvat* which began in 57 BC and the *Salivahan Saka* which dates from 78 AD and has been the official Indian calendar since 1957. The *Saka* new year starts on 22 March and has the same length as the Gregorian calendar. In North India the New Year is celebrated in the second month of *Vaisakh*.

The year itself is divided into two, the first six solar months being when the sun 'moves' north, known as the *Makar Sankranti* (which is marked by special festivals), and the second half when it moves south, the *Karka Sankranti*. The first begins in January and the second in June. The 29½-day lunar month with its 'dark' (*Krishna*) and 'bright' (*Shukla*) halves based on the new (*Amavasya*) and full moons (*Purnima*), are named after the 12 constellations, and total a 354-day year. The day itself is divided into eight *praharas* of three hours each and the year into six seasons: *Vasant* (spring), *Grishha* (summer), *Varsha* (rains), *Sharat* (early autumn), *Hemanta* (late autumn), *Shishir* (winter).

Hindu, and corresponding Gregorian, calendar months:

Chaitra	March-April	Ashwin	September-October
Vaishakh	April-May	Kartik	October-November
Jyeshtha	May-June	Margashirsha	November-December
Aashadh	June-July	Poush	December-January
Shravan	July -August	Magh	January-February
Bhadra	August-September	Phalgun	February-March

Islam

Islam is a highly visible presence in India today. Even after partition in 1947 over 40 million Muslims remained in India and today there are just over 120 million. It is the most recent of imported religions. From the creation of the Delhi Sultanate in 1206, by Turkish rather than Arab power, Islam became a permanent living religion in India.

The victory of the Turkish ruler of Ghazni over the Rajputs in AD 1192 established a 500-year period of Muslim power in India. The contact between the courts of the new rulers and the indigenous Hindu populations produced innovative developments in art and architecture, language and literature. Hindus and Hindu culture were profoundly affected by the spread and exercise of Muslim political power, but Islam too underwent major modifications in response to the new social and religious context in which the Muslim rulers found themselves.

From the middle of the 13th century, when the Mongols crushed the Arab caliphate, the Delhi sultans were left on their own to exercise Islamic authority in India. From then onwards the main external influences were from Persia. Small numbers of migrants, mainly the skilled and the educated, continued to flow into the Indian courts.

Muslim populations Muslims only became a majority of the South Asian population in the plains of the Indus and west Punjab and in parts of Bengal. Elsewhere they formed important minorities, notably in the towns of the central heartland such as Lucknow. In the central plains there was already a densely populated, Hindu region, where little attempt was made to achieve converts.

The **Mughals** wanted to expand their territory and their economic base. To pursue this they made enormous grants of land to those who had served the empire, and new land was brought into cultivation. At the same time, shrines were established to Sufi saints who attracted peasant farmers. By the 18th century many Muslims had joined the **Sunni** sect of Islam.

In some areas Muslim society shared many of the characteristic features of the Hindu society from which the majority of them came. Many of the Muslim migrants from Iran or Turkey, the elite **Ashraf** communities, continued to identify with the Islamic elites from which they traced their descent. They held high military and civil posts in imperial service. In sharp contrast, many of the non-Ashraf Muslim communities in the towns and cities were organized in social groups very much like the *jatis* of their neighbouring Hindu communities. While the elites followed Islamic practices close to those based on the Qur'an as interpreted by scholars, the poorer, less literate communities followed devotional and pietistic forms of Islam. The distinction is still very clear today and the importance of veneration of the saints can be seen at tombs and shrines in Rajasthan.

Muslim beliefs The beliefs of Islam (which means 'submission to God') could apparently scarcely be more different from those of Hinduism. Islam, often described as having 'five pillars' of faith has a fundamental creed; 'There is no God but God; and Mohammad is the Prophet of God' (*La Illaha illa 'llah Mohammad Rasulu 'llah*). One book, the Qur'an, is the supreme authority on Islamic teaching and faith. Islam preaches the belief in bodily resurrection after death and in the reality of heaven and hell.

The idea of heaven as paradise is pre-Islamic. Alexander the Great is believed to have brought the word into Greek from Persia, where he used it to describe the walled Persian gardens that were found even three centuries before the birth of Christ. For Muslims, Paradise is believed to be filled with sensuous delights and pleasures, while hell is a place of eternal terror and torture, which is the certain fate of all who deny the unity of God.

Islam has no priesthood. The authority of Imams derives from social custom and from their authority to interpret the scriptures, rather than from a defined status within the Islamic community. Islam also prohibits any distinction on the basis of race or colour and most Muslims believe it is wrong to represent the human figure. It is often thought, inaccurately, that this ban stems from the Qur'an itself. In fact it probably has its origins in the belief of Mohammad that images were likely to be turned into idols.

Muslim sects During the first century after Mohammad's death Islam split in to two sects which were divided on political and religious grounds, the Shi'is and Sunnis.

The **Sunnis** – always the majority in South Asia – believe that Mohammad did not appoint a successor and that Abu Bak'r, Omar and Othman were the first three caliphs (or vice-regents) after Mohammad's death. Ali, whom the Sunnis count as the fourth caliph, is regarded as the first legitimate caliph by the Shi'is, who consider Abu Bak'r and Omar to be usurpers. While the Sunnis believe in the principle of election of caliphs, Shi'is believe that although Mohammad is the last prophet there is a continuing need for intermediaries between God and man. Such intermediaries are termed *Imams* and they base both their law and religious practice on the teaching of the *Imams*.

The Islamic Calendar The calendar begins on 16 July 622 AD, the date of the Prophet's migration from Mecca to Medina, the Hijra, hence AH (Anno Hejirae). The Muslim year is divided into 12 lunar months, totalling 354 or 355 days, hence Islamic festivals usually move 11 days earlier each year according to the solar (Gregorian) calendar. The first month of the year is *Moharram*, followed by *Safar, Rabi-ul-Awwal, Rabi-ul-Sani, Jumada-ul-Awwal, Jumada-ul-Sani, Rajab, Shaban, Ramadan, Shawwal, Ziquad* and *Zilhaj*.

Jainism

Like Buddhism, Jainism started as a reform movement of the Brahmanic religious beliefs of the sixth century BC. Its founder was a widely revered saint and ascetic, Vardhamma, who became known as **Mahavir** (great hero). Mahavir was born in the same border region of India and Nepal as the Buddha, just 50 km north of modern Patna, probably in 599 BC. Thus he was about 35 years older than the Buddha. His family, also royal, were followers of an ascetic saint, Parsvanatha, who according to Jain tradition had lived 200 years previously.

Mahavir's life story is embellished with legends, but there is no doubt that he left his royal home for a life of the strict ascetic. He is believed to have received enlightenment after 12 years of rigorous hardship, penance and meditation. Afterwards he travelled and preached for 30 years, stopping only in the rainy season. He died aged 72 in 527 BC. His death was commemorated by a special lamp festival in the region of Bihar, which Jains claim is the basis of the now-common Hindu festival of lights, Diwali.

Some Jain ideas, such as vegetarianism and reverence for all life, are widely recognized by Hindus as highly commendable, even by those who do not share other Jain beliefs. The value Jains place on non-violence has contributed to their importance in business and commerce, as they regard nearly all occupations except banking and commerce as violent.

Jain beliefs Jains (from the word *Jina*, literally meaning 'descendants of conquerors') believe that there are two fundamental principles, the living (*jiva*) and the non-living (*ajiva*). The essence of Jain belief is that all life is sacred and that every living entity, even the smallest insect, has within it an indestructible and immortal soul. Jains developed the view of *ahimsa* – often translated as 'non-violence', but better perhaps as 'non-harming'. *Ahimsa* was the basis for the entire scheme of Jain values and ethics and alternative codes of practice were defined for householders and for ascetics.

The five vows may be taken both by monks and by lay people. A Jain must not kill any living being for food, sport or pleasure but the use of force is permissible in defending one's country, society, family or property. Jains practise strict vegetarianism – and even some vegetables, such as potatoes and onions, are believed to have microscopic souls. Where injury to life is unavoidable, a Jain is required to reduce this to a minimum by taking all precautions. The other vows require a Jain to speak the truth, not to steal (or cheat or use dishonest means in acquiring material wealth), to abstain from sexual relations (except with one's spouse for the lay people) and to set a limit on acquiring possessions and to use any surplus for the common good. The essence of all the rules is to avoid intentional injury, which is the worst of all sins.

Like Hindus, the Jains believe in *karma*, by which the evil effects of earlier deeds leave an indelible impurity on the soul. This impurity will remain through endless rebirths unless burned off by extreme penances.

Jains also regard the manner of dying as extremely important. Although suicide is deeply opposed, vows of fasting to death voluntarily may be regarded as earning merit in the proper context. Mahavir himself is believed to have died of self-starvation, near Rajgir in modern Bihar.

Jain sects Jains have two main sects, whose origins can be traced back to the fourth century BC. The more numerous **Svetambaras** – the 'white clad' – concentrated in eastern and western India, wear only two or three unsewn white garments. The **Digambaras** – or 'sky-clad' – among whom the male monks go naked.

Unlike Buddhists, Jains accept the idea of God, but not as a creator of the universe. They see him in the lives of the 24 **Tirthankaras** (prophets, or literally 'makers of fords' – a reference to their role in building crossing points for the spiritual journey over the river of life), the 24 leaders of Jainism, whose lives are recounted in the Kalpsutra – the third century BC book of ritual for the Svetambaras. **Vardhamana Mahavir** (599-527 BC) who followed **Parsvanatha** (877-777 BC), is regarded as the last of these great spiritual leaders. The first and most revered of the Tirthankaras, **Adinatha Rishabdeva**, who lived in pre-historic times, is widely represented in Jain temples.

Jains devote great attention to the care of sick animals and birds and run a number of special animal hospitals. Note the '*parabdis*', special feeding places for birds, in the town.

Buddhism

India was the home of Buddhism, which had its roots in the early Hinduism, or Brahmanism, of its time. Siddharta Gautama, who came to be given the title of the Buddha – or *enlightened one* – was born a prince into the kshatriya caste about 563 BC. By the time he died the Buddha had established a small band of monks and nuns known as the *sangha*, and had followers across northern India. During the early centuries BC and AD Buddhist caves mushroomed across Saurashtra. Buddhist relics can be seen at Talaja near Bhavnagar, Junagadh and surrounds, and at Khambilida near Gondal. Today however Buddhism is practised only on the margins of the subcontinent, from Ladakh, Nepal and Bhutan in the north to Sri Lanka in the south, where it is the religion of the majority Sinhalese community. Most are very recent converts, the last adherents of the early schools of Buddhism having been killed or converted by the Muslim invaders of the 13th century.

Sikhism

Guru Nanak, the founder of the religion, was born just west of Lahore and grew up in what is now the Pakistani town of Sultanpur. His followers, the Sikhs (derived from the Sanskrit word for 'disciples'), form perhaps one of India's most recognizable groups. Beards and turbans give them a very distinctive presence and although they represent less than 2% of the total population of India – and a far smaller proportion in Rajasthan – they are both politically and economically significant.

Sikh beliefs The first Guru, accepted the ideas of *samsara* – the cycle of rebirths – and *karma* (see page 315) from Hinduism. However, Sikhism is unequivocal in its belief in the oneness of God, rejecting idolatry and any worship of objects or images. Guru Nanak believed that God is One, formless, eternal and beyond description.

Guru Nanak also fiercely opposed discrimination on the grounds of caste. He saw God as present everywhere, visible to anyone who cared to look and as essentially full of grace and compassion. One of the many stories about his travels tells of how he was rebuked on his visit to Mecca for sleeping with his feet pointing towards the Qa'aba, an act Muslims would consider sacrilegious. Apologizing profusely, he had replied "If you can show me in which direction I may lie so that my feet do not point towards God, I will do so". His contact with Muslim families when still young prompted him to organize community hymn singing when both Hindus and Muslims were welcomed. Along with a Muslim servant, he also organized a common kitchen where Hindus of all castes and Muslims could eat together, thereby deliberately breaking one of the strictest of caste rules.

Guru Nanak preached that salvation depended on accepting the nature of God. If man recognized the true harmony of the divine order (*hookam*) and brought himself into line with that harmony he would be saved. Rejecting the prevailing Hindu belief that such harmony could be achieved by ascetic practices, he emphasized three actions; meditating on and repeating God's name (*naam*), 'giving', or charity (*daan*) and bathing (*isnaan*).

Many of the features now associated with Sikhism can be attributed to **Guru Gobind Singh**, who on 15 April 1699, started the new brotherhood called the *Khalsa* (meaning 'the pure', from the Persian word *khales*), an inner core of the faithful, accepted by baptism (*amrit*). The 'five ks' date from this period: *kesh* (uncut hair), the most important, followed by *kangha* (comb, usually of wood), *kirpan* (dagger or short sword), *kara* (steel bangle) and *kachh* (similar to 'boxer' shorts). The dagger and the shorts reflect military influence.

In addition to the compulsory 'five ks', the new code prohibited smoking, eating *halal* meat and sexual intercourse with Muslim women. These date from the 18th century, when the Sikhs were often in conflict with the Muslims. Other strict prohibitions include: idolatry, caste discrimination, hypocrisy and pilgrimage to Hindu sacred places. The *Khalsa* also explicitly forbade the seclusion of women, one of the common practices of Islam. It was only under the warrior king Ranjit Singh (1799-1838) that the idea of the Guru's presence in meetings of the Sikh community (the *Panth*) gave way to the now universally held belief in the total authority of the **Guru Granth**, the recorded words of the Guru in the scripture.

Christianity

There are about 23 million Christians in India. Christianity ranks third in terms of religious affiliation after Hinduism and Islam and there are Christian congregations in all the major towns of India.

The great majority of the Protestant Christians in India are now members of the Church of South India, formed from the major Protestant denominations in 1947, or the Church of North India, which followed suit in 1970. Together they account for approximately half the total number of Christians. Roman Catholics make up the majority of the rest. Many of the church congregations, both in towns and villages, are active centres of Christian worship. Origins Some of the churches owe their origin either to the modern missionary movement of the late 18th century onwards, or to the colonial presence of the European powers. However, Christians probably arrived in India during the first century AD. There is evidence that one of Christ's Apostles, **Thomas**, reached India in 52 AD, only 20 years after Christ was crucified. He settled in Malabar and then expanded his missionary work to China. It is widely believed that he was martyred in Tamil Nadu on his return to India in 72 AD and is buried in Mylapore, in the suburbs of modern Chennai. St Thomas' Mount, a small rocky hill just north of Madras airport, takes its name from him. Today there is still a church of Thomas Christians in Kerala. In north India the influence of Christian missions in education and medical work was greater than as a proselytizing force. Education in Christian schools stimulated reform movements in Hinduism itself and mission hospitals supplemented government-run hospitals, particularly in remote rural areas.

Land and environment

Geography

Rajasthan lies on the northwestern edge of the Indian Peninsula, the southernmost of India's three major geological regions. To its north are the alluvial plains of the Ganges and Indus rivers, and to their north again the great mountain chain of the Himalaya.

The origins of India's landscapes Only 100 million years ago the Indian Peninsula was still attached to the great land mass of what geologists call 'Pangaea' alongside South Africa, Australia and Antarctica. Then as the great plates on which the earth's southern continents stood broke up, the Indian Plate started its dramatic shift northwards. About 55 million years ago the northernmost tip of the peninsula collided with the Asian plate, in the next 20 million years bringing the first Himalayan uplift in what are now the western Himalaya. From 36 to five million years ago the peninsula continued its northward movement under the Asian plate but also rotated in an anticlockwise direction, pushing up a succession of parallel mountain ranges from Himachal Pradesh eastwards through Nepal to the eastern Himalaya. The Indian Plate is still moving north under the Tibetan Plateau at a rate of up to 2.5 cm a year. This movement continues to have major effects on the landscapes of the entire region. The Himalaya are still rising, in places by several millimetres a year, and along the faulted junctions of the Indian and the Asian plates are some of the world's most active earthquake zones. The western borders of Rajasthan are particularly affected by this seismic activity.

The ancient rocks of the peninsula have also been disturbed by its continuing thrust under the Asian plate, the ancient sandstones of the Vindhyan ranges in southeastern Rajasthan and the Aravallis showing evidence of the buckling power of the impact.

The crystalline rocks of the peninsula are some of the oldest in the world, some being over 3100 million years old. Over 60 million years ago a mass of volcanic lava welled up through cracks in the earth's surface and covered some 500,000 sq km of southern Gujarat, Rajasthan and Madhya Pradesh, while stretching south to Maharashtra and northern Karnataka.

Rajasthani landscape Running like a spine through Rajasthan the **Aravalli hills** are one of the oldest mountain systems in the world. They form a series of jagged, heavily folded ranges, stretching from **Mount Abu** in the southwest (1720 m) to Kota and Bundi in the east. Mount Abu is granite but the range has a mixture of ancient sedimentary and metamorphic rocks, and Rajasthan is the source of the glittering white **Makrana marble** used in the Taj Mahal. The ancient sandstones of the Vindhyan mountain system of Madhya Pradesh extend northwards into southeastern Rajasthan, eroded in places to form great cliff-topped scarps overlooking the often fertile alluvial plains below, as at Ranthambhore and Bundi.

The watershed between the eastward draining Chambal river system, which ultimately flows into the Bay of Bengal, and the Luni which flows into the Arabian Sea, runs along the crest line of the Aravallis from Udaipur in the southeast to Jaipur in the northwest.

To the west of this line is the arid and forbidding **Thar Desert**, with its shifting sand dunes and crushingly high summer temperatures. Carol Henderson has written that James Tod, the first British emissary to the region, was constantly reminded that the names for the region – *Marwar, Maroosthali*, or *Maru-desh*, mean 'the land of death'. Before Partition from Pakistan Jaisalmer and Bikaner dominated the overland routes to the west. However, the Great Indian desert is not completely barren but covered with shrubs and trees, interspersed with farmland, and fed by rivers like the Luni. Sand dunes rise over 70 m in Jaisalmer, Jodhpur, Bikaner and Barmer districts. The Indira Canal and other projects have greened vast stretches of the desert, making them suitable for cultivation and plantation, though they have not entirely achieved what was envisaged. Salt lakes like Sambhar and Tal Chapper, and dry beds of rivers like the Luni, are frequently seen in the desert and arid stretches of the Aravallis.

Jodhpur lies on the edge of this arid tract, the link between the true desert and the semi-arid but cultivable regions to the east. To the southeast of the Aravalli divide are the wetter and more fertile river basins of the Chambal and its tributaries, though even here there are some outstandingly barren rocky hills and plateaus.

Around Jaipur and Bharatpur, cultivated land is interspersed with rocky outcrops such as those at Amber. In the south the average elevation is higher (330-1150 m). Around Bharatpur the landscape forms part of the nearly flat Yamuna drainage basin. Mewar, the southeast region of modern Rajasthan, with Udaipur and Chittaurgarh as two of the region's former capitals, is hilly, and drains northeastwards into the only perennial river of southern Rajasthan, the Chambal. The surface geology of the southeast has been modified greatly by the great volcanic lava flows which have weathered to give rich black soils, especially fertile when irrigated and well drained.

Climate

The Tropic of Cancer runs through the southernmost tip of Rajasthan, and the climate of the region reflects this tropical position at the northwestern corner of the Indian subcontinent.
The monsoon In common with the rest of India, the climate of Rajasthan is dominated by the monsoon. What makes the Indian monsoon quite exceptional is not its regularity but the depth of moist air which passes over the subcontinent. Over India, for example, the highly unstable moist airflow is over 6000 m thick compared with only 2000 m over Japan, giving rise to the bursts of torrential rain which mark out the wet season. However, most of Rajasthan is to the north of the main rain-bearing southwesterlies, and rainfall decreases sharply from the southeast to the northwest, which is true desert. Rajasthan's location on the margins of pure desert has made much of it particularly susceptible to climatic change throughout settlement history, and fossil sand dunes found as far east as Delhi testify to the advance and retreat of the desert over the last 5000 years.
The wet season The monsoon season in Rajasthan lasts approximately three months. It brings an enveloping dampness which makes it very difficult to keep things dry. However, nowhere receives more than 1000 mm a year, and the rain comes mainly in the form of heavy isolated showers. Rainfall generally decreases towards the northwest, Rajasthan merging imperceptibly into genuine desert.
Winter In winter high pressure builds up over Central Asia. Most of India is protected from the cold northeast monsoon winds that result by the massive bulk of the Himalaya and daytime temperatures rise sharply in the sun. In winter the daily maximum in most low-lying areas is 22-28°C and the minimum 8-14°C, but the air is often almost bitingly dry. The sharp drop in temperature on winter nights makes warm clothing essential between late November and mid-February. To the south the winter temperatures increase having minima of around 20°C. Despite the night-time cold, Rajasthan often has beautiful weather from November through to March.
Summer From April onwards northwestern India becomes almost unbearably hot. Except in the hills the summer maxima exceed 46°C and the average from May to August

is 38°C. In winter the daily maximum in most low-lying areas is 22-28°C and the minimum is 8-14°C. The Aravallis, notably Mount Abu, offer welcome relief in the hot season and are noticeably colder in winter.

At the end of May the upper air westerly jet stream, which controls the atmospheric system over the Indo-Gangetic plains through the winter, suddenly breaks down. It re-forms to the north of Tibet, thus allowing very moist southwesterlies to sweep across South India and the Bay of Bengal. They then double back northwestwards, bringing rain across the Indo-Gangetic Plains to northwest India.

Vegetation

The dry tropical monsoon climate gives Rajasthan a quite distinctive natural vegetation. Dry deciduous woodland is the most common cover in the wetter areas, shading to desert vegetation in the arid west. Today forest cover has been greatly reduced as elsewhere in India, mainly as a result of the need for agricultural land.

Deciduous forest Neither of the two types of deciduous tree dominant elsewhere in India, sal (*Shorea robusta*) and teak (*Tectona grandis*), are common in Rajasthan, teak only being found in the Aravallis and sal absent altogether.

Western Rajasthan has distinct desert vegetation like the **sewan grasslands** near Jaisalmer, Phog which grows on sand dunes, **capparis**, a cactus-like euphorbia, **aak** or **calotropis**, all three of which are fairly succulent and sustain life in the desert. **Kharjal** (*Salvadora persica*) and the thorny **khejra** (*Prosopis cineraria*) are trees of the desert. The second is often used for a dish called *ker-sangri* that is part of the Marwar diet, while rohira, a truly desert tree, is used by wood carvers of Barmer and other desert towns.

Flowering trees Many Indian trees are planted along roadsides to provide shade and they often also produce beautiful flowers. The **silk cotton tree** (*Bombax ceiba*), up to 25 m in height, is one of the most dramatic. The pale greyish bark of this buttressed tree usually bears conical spines. It has wide spreading branches and keeps its leaves for most of the year. The flowers, which appear when the tree is leafless, are cup-shaped, with curling, rather fleshy red petals up to 12 cm long while the fruit produce the fine, silky cotton which gives it its name.

Other common trees with red or orange flowers include the dhak, the gulmohur and the Indian coral tree. The smallish (6 m) deciduous **dhak** (*Butea monosperma*) has light grey bark and a gnarled, twisted trunk and thick, leathery leaves. The large, bright orange and sweet pea-shaped flowers appear on leafless branches from late March to May. The 8- to 9-m-high umbrella-shaped **gulmohur** (*Delonix regia*), a native of Madagascar, is grown as a shade tree in towns. The fiery coloured flowers make a magnificent display after the tree has shed its feathery leaves. The scarlet flowers of the **Indian coral tree** (*Erythrina indica*) also appear when its branches with thorny bark are leafless.

Often seen along roadsides the **jacaranda** (*Jacaranda mimosaefolia*) has attractive feathery foliage and purple-blue thimble-shaped flowers up to 40 mm long. When not in flower it resembles a gulmohur, but differs in its general shape. The valuable **tamarind** (*Tamarindus indica*) has a short straight trunk and a spreading crown. An evergreen with feathery leaves, it bears small clusters of yellow and red flowers. The noticeable fruit pods are long, curved and swollen at intervals. In parts of India, the rights to the fruit are auctioned off annually for up to Rs 4000 (US$100) per tree.

Fruit trees The large, spreading **mango** (*Mangifera indica*) bears the delicious, distinctively shaped fruit that comes in hundreds of varieties. The **banana plant** (*Musa*), actually a gigantic herb (up to 5 m high) arising from an underground stem has very large leaves which grow directly off the trunk. Each large purplish flower produces bunches of up to 100 bananas. The **papaya** (*Carica papaya*) grows to about 4 m with the large hand-shaped leaves clustered near the top. Only the female tree bears the fruit, which hang down close to the trunk just below the leaves.

Of all Indian trees the **banyan** (*Ficus benghalensis*) is probably the best known. It is planted by temples, in villages and along roads. The seeds often germinate in the cracks of old walls, the growing roots splitting the wall apart. If it grows in the bark of another tree, it sends down roots towards the ground. As it grows, more roots appear from the branches, until the original host tree is surrounded by a 'cage' which eventually strangles it.

Related to the banyan, the **pipal** or **peepul** (*Ficus religiosa*), also cracks open walls and strangles other trees with its roots. With a smooth grey bark, it too is commonly found near temples and shrines. You can distinguish it from the banyan by the absence of aerial roots and its large, heart-shaped leaf with a point tapering into a pronounced 'tail'. It bears abundant 'figs' of a purplish tinge which are about 1 cm across.

Acacia trees with their feathery leaves are fairly common in the drier parts of India. The best known is the **babul** (*Acacia arabica*) with a rough, dark bark. The leaves have long silvery white thorns at the base and consist of many leaflets while the flowers grow in golden balls about 1 cm across.

The **eucalyptus** or **gum tree** (*Eucalyptus grandis*), introduced from Australia in the 19th century, is now widespread and is planted near villages to provide both shade and firewood. There are various forms but all may be readily recognized by their height, their characteristic long, thin leaves which have a pleasant fresh smell and the colourful peeling bark.

The wispy **casuarina** (*Casuarina*) grows in poor sandy soil, especially on the coast and on village waste land. It has the typical leaves of a pine tree and the cones are small and prickly to walk on. It is said to attract lightning during a thunder storm.

Bamboo (*Bambusa*) strictly speaking is a grass which can vary in size from small ornamental clumps to the enormous wild plant whose stems are so strong and thick that they are used for construction and for scaffolding and as pipes in rural irrigation schemes.

Flowering plants Many other flowering plants are cultivated in parks, gardens and roadside verges. The attractive **frangipani** (*Plumeria acutifolia*) has a rather crooked trunk and stubby branches, which if broken give out a white milky juice which can be irritating to the skin. The big, leathery leaves taper to a point at each end and have noticeable parallel veins. The sweetly scented waxy flowers are white, pale yellow or pink. The **bougainvillea** grows as a dense bush or climber with small oval leaves and rather long thorns. The brightly coloured part which appears like a flower, is formed by large papery bracts, not by the petals, which are quite magnificent.

The **hibiscus** has an unusual trumpet-shaped flower as much as 7 or 8 cm across. A very long 'tongue' grows out from the centre and varies in colour from scarlet to yellow or white. The leaves are somewhat oval or heart-shaped with jagged edges.

On many ponds and tanks the floating plants of the **lotus** (*Nelumbo nucifera*) and the **water hyacinth** (*Eichornia crassipes*) are seen. Lotus flowers which rise on stalks above the water can be white, pink or a deep red and up to 25 cm across. The very large leaves either float on the surface or rise above the water. The rather fleshy leaves and lilac flowers of the water hyacinth float to form a dense carpet, often clogging the waterways.

Crops Rajasthan may have been the original home of millet cultivation in South Asia. The semi-arid climate means that millet, wheat and barley remain the staple cereal crops, though rice is grown on some irrigated land. There are many different sorts of **millet**, but the ones most often seen are finger millet, pearl millet (*bajra*) and sorghum (*jowar*). **Sugar cane** (*Saccharum*) is another commercially important crop. This looks like a large grass which stands up to 3 m tall. The crude brown sugar is sold as jaggery and has a flavour of molasses. **Cotton** (*Gossypium*) is also grown. The cotton bush is a small knee-high bush and the cotton boll appears after the flower has withered. This splits when ripe to show the white cotton lint inside. The Malwa region of southeastern Rajasthan and the neighbouring districts of Madhya Pradesh have been centres of cultivation of the **opium poppy** (*Papaver somniferum*) for at least 500 years. It is grown on tiny plots under strict government supervision, but provides a highly distinctive white patchwork character to the landscape. See page 230.

Wildlife

Conservation

Alarmed by diminishing numbers of wild animals and the rapid loss of wildlife habitat the Indian Government established the first conservation measures in 1972, followed by the setting up of national parks and reserves. Some 25,000 sq km were set aside in 1973 for Project Tiger. Tigers have been reported to be increasing steadily in several of the game reserves, but threats to their survival continue, notably through poaching. The same is true of other, less well known species. Their natural habitat has been destroyed both by people and by domesticated animals (there are some 250 million cattle and 50 million sheep and goats). Rajasthan has some of India's best known parks, including Ranthambhore and Bharatpur. The Indian Government has defined national parks as areas in which no human activity is allowed, whereas in wildlife parks some grazing and minor forest produce collection can be permitted. The entry fee for foreigners and vehicle charges at some parks have been raised dramatically in recent years.

The cat family

The **tiger** (*Panthera tigris*), which prefers to live in fairly dense cover, is most likely to be glimpsed as it lies in long grass or in dappled shadow. Unlike the lion, it leads a quite solitary life. It is more nocturnal and depends on cover for hunting, the reason it is more difficult to spot. Rajasthan has two tiger reserves. Ranthambhore offers better chances of spotting a tiger over a two- or three-day visit than Sariska, the other tiger reserve. The tiger is a magnificent animal, richly coloured with bold stripes, up to 10 ft long and weighing about 200 kg. Females are smaller and weigh 20% less than the males. You will often hear of tiger sightings in the hills of Rajasthan but you are unlikely to see one outside the two tiger reserves.

The **leopard** or **panther** (*Panthera pardus*), as it is often called in India, is far more numerous and widespread than the tiger, but is even more elusive. The hills of Rajasthan have a sizeable panther population but they are not often seen, being nocturnal and shy. Male panthers average 7 ft in length, females being shorter. The typical colour is dull yellow with black rosette markings that become solid black spots on the head, neck, limbs and belly, and a whitish underside. Panther sightings are not uncommon in the Kachida Valley of Ranthambhore National Park and they are also seen in the arid hills of Pali and Jalore district as the cats here have turned on livestock following the decimation of their natural prey like the gazelle. They often visit villages and waterholes. The panthers in these arid areas, close to the desert, are paler in colour than those of the hilly forest tracts, and sometimes also smaller.

The colour and markings of the **leopard cat** make it look like a miniature panther. They are seen in forest areas. The jungle cat is more common, having adapted to a variety of habitats from grasslands, thorn scrub, forests, agricultural areas, surrounds of wetlands and even proximity to towns and villages. Its longer legs and shorter tail distinguish the jungle cat from the domestic and other lesser wild cats. The jungle cat varies in colour from sandy grey in the arid areas to a brighter yellowish grey in greener areas. The **fishing cat** hunts at the marshes of the Keoladeo Ghana Sanctuary of Bharatpur, Rajasthan. Besides being adept at fishing with its paw and feeding on molluscs, it also hunts mammals and birds. Fishing cats do not enter the water but grab fish or mollusc from rocks and other vantage points on the shores of the marshlands.

The desert zone is home to the **desert cat**, which has greyish yellow fur marked with black spots, striped cheek and a black ring on its tail.

The **caracal** is an agile, medium-sized cat with pointed, tufted ears, and a short tail. They are rarely seen though present in many scrub jungles of the Gujarat-Rajasthan belt.

The dog family

The **Indian wolf** has become an endangered species, not least because it tends to turn on livestock, making it a target for pastoral communities. The scrublands of Kumbhalgarh Sanctuary have shown a proliferating population of wolves. Wolves have different methods of hunting depending on the habitat. In the desert the wolf hunts by chasing its prey at a steady pace waiting for its quarry to get tired, while in areas that are more vegetated the strategy is to hunt by surprise. Wolves grow to about 75 cm at shoulder and 95 cm in length. Holes in rocks and ground are their favoured homes in drylands. In the desert they may dig burrows on the dunes, while in the forests they will find shelter in bushes.

The **jackal** (*Canis aureus*), a lone scavenger in towns and villages, looks like a cross between a dog and a fox and varies in colour from shades of brown through to black. It feeds on carcasses and the prey of larger carnivores but will hunt smaller game and when in large packs can even bring down deer, antelope and gazelle. The bushy tail has a dark tip. It is a common sight while driving through Rajasthan after dark. Their howling is often heard at dawn, dusk and sometimes at night.

There are two kinds of fox found in this region. The **Indian fox** is common in the plains and is grey in colour. The **white-footed desert fox** is distinguished from the Indian fox by its white-tipped tail as opposed to the black-tipped tail of the latter and black markings on its ears. The habitats of the desert and Indian fox overlap in the western Rajasthani desert.

The dreaded **wild dog** or **dhole** has been sighted at Sariska and Ranthambhore national parks as recently as January 2001, though they had previously been thought to have become extinct in Rajasthan.

Other carnivores

The **sloth bear** (*Melursus ursinus*), about 75 cm at the shoulder, lives in broken forest, but may be seen on a lead accompanying a street entertainer who makes it 'dance' to music as a part of an act. They have a long snout, a pendulous lower lip and a shaggy black coat with a yellowish V-shaped mark on the chest. The sloth bear is present in many wildlife parks of the Aravallis including Ranthambhore and Kumbhalgarh in Rajasthan, but are not easily seen as they are active after dusk and shy of human presence. Being short-sighted they are known to be nervous and attack human visitors to their habitat. Bears are omnivores. They will hunt other animals, feed on termites and other invertebrate and climb trees for fruits, berries and flowers.

The **common mongoose** (*Herpestes edwardsi*) lives in scrub and open jungle. It kills snakes, but will also take rats, mice and chicken. Tawny coloured with a grey grizzled tinge, it is about 90 cm in length, of which half is pale-tipped tail. The **ratel or honey badger** is seen at Sariska.

Deer, antelope, oxen and their relatives

Once widespread, these animals are now largely confined to the reserves. The deer, unlike the antelopes that inhabit the grass and scrub, are animals of the forests and are rarely seen outside the wildlife sanctuaries.

The largest **deer** and one of the most widespread, is the magnificent **sambhar** (*Cervus unicolor*) which can be up to 150 cm at the shoulder. It has a noticeably shaggy coat, which varies in colour from brown with a yellowish or grey tinge through to dark, almost black, in the older stags. The sambhar is often found on wooded hillsides and lives in groups of up to 10 or so, though solitary individuals are also seen. The sambhar is common in Ranthambhore, Sariska, and Bharatpur national parks. The small **chital** or **spotted deer** (*Axis axis*), only about 90 cm tall, are seen in herds of 20 or so, in grassy areas. The bright rufous coat spotted with white is unmistakable; the stags carry antlers with three tines. It is seen in good numbers at Ranthambhore, Sariska and Bharatpur.

Antelopes live in open grasslands, never too far from water. The beautiful **blackbuck** or **Indian antelope** (*Antilope cervicapra*), up to 80 cm at the shoulder, occurs in large herds. The distinctive colouring and the long spiralling horns make the stag easy to identify. The larger and heavier nilgai or blue bull (*Boselaphus tragocamelus*), like the blackbuck and chowsingha, is one of a kind in its genus. The largest antelope in India, the Nilgai has a very small cone shaped horn in ratio to its height of 130 cm. The mature bull is iron grey in colour, the juveniles are tawny. The females are tawny and hornless. They are often seen in sparsely wooded hills and fields in batches of four to ten. The very graceful **chinkara** or **Indian gazelle** (*Gazella gazella*) is only 65 cm at the shoulder. The light russet colour of the body has a distinct line along the side where the paler underparts start. Both sexes carry slightly S-shaped horns. Chinkara live in the desert and can thrive on minimal vegetation and obtain water from succulent leaves. Fleet-footed and graceful, the chinkaras can be seen widely and in good numbers in the Desert National Park of Jaisalmer district and in the surrounds of Bishnoi villages of Jodhpur, Nagaur, Jalore, Barmer and Bikaner districts. The **chowsingha** or **four-horned antelope** is the only animal in the world with two pairs of horns. Unlike the blackbuck they prefer forests to grasslands. Being diminutive in size and favouring the woodlands they are difficult to spot though they are present in good numbers at Sariska and Ranthambhore national parks, and sanctuaries like Kumbhalgarh and Sitamata.

The commonest member of the **oxen** group is the **Asiatic wild buffalo** or **water buffalo** (*Bubalus bubalis*). About 170 cm at the shoulder, the wild buffalo, which can be aggressive, occurs in herds on grassy plains and swamps near rivers and lakes. The black coat and wide-spreading curved horns, carried by both sexes, are distinctive. The **Indian bison** or **gaur** (*Bos gaurus*) can be up to 200 cm at the shoulder with a heavy muscular ridge across it. Both sexes carry curved horns. The young gaur is a light sandy colour, which darkens with age, the old bulls being nearly black with pale sandy coloured 'socks' and a pale forehead.

The **wild boar** (*Sus scrofa*) has mainly black body and a pig-like head, the hairs thicken down the spine to form a sort of mane. A mature male stands 90 cm at the shoulder and, unlike the female, bears tusks. The young are striped. Quite widespread, they often cause great destruction among crops.

One of the most important scavengers of the open countryside, the **striped hyena** (*Hyena hyena*) usually comes out at night. It is about 90 cm at the shoulder with a large head with a noticeable crest of hairs along its sloping back.

Monkeys

The **common langur** (*Presbytis entellus*), 75 cm, is a long-tailed monkey with a distinctive black face, hands and feet. It is the main primate of the Rajasthan region and is common at Sariska National Park, Sitamata sanctuary and other wildlife reserves. They are adaptable and are frequently seen in gardens of large cities and around Hanuman temples where they are fed. The **rhesus macaque** (*Macaca mulatta*), 60 cm, is more solid looking with shorter limbs and a shorter tail. It can be distinguished by the orange-red fur on its rump and flanks.

Squirrels

Palm squirrels are very common. The **five-striped palm squirrel** (*Funambulus pennanti*) and the **three-striped palm squirrel** (*Funambulus palmarum*) are 30 cm long (about half of which is tail). The five-striped is usually seen in towns. **Flying squirrel** is reported from Sitamata sanctuary but are rarely seen. The **common giant flying squirrel** (*Petaurista petaurista*) are common in the larger forests of India. The body can be 45 cm long and the tail another 50 cm. They glide from tree to tree using a membrane stretching from front leg to back leg which acts like a parachute.

Bats

The two bats most commonly seen in towns differ enormously in size. The larger so-called **flying fox** (*Pteropus giganteus*) has a wing span of 120 cm. These fruit-eating bats roost in large noisy colonies where they look like folded umbrellas hanging from the trees. In the evening they can be seen leaving the roost with slow measured wing beats. The much smaller **Indian pipistrelle** (*Pipistrellus coromandra*), with a wing span of about 15 cm, is an insect eater. It comes into the house at dusk to roost under eaves and has a fast, erratic flight.

Other mammals

Two subspecies of **Indian hare** are present – the *black-naped* is usually seen in the more wooded area, and the desert in western Rajasthan and other arid areas. The **pale hedgehog** is common, the long-eared species being seen in the desert, while **gerbils** are typical rodents of the desert, their bounding movement reminiscent of a miniature kangaroo. The **Indian elephant** (*Elephas maximus*) has been domesticated for centuries and today it is still used as a beast of burden. There are no wild elephants in Rajasthan.

Birds

Rajasthan is one of the most prolific birding areas in India. During the winter birds gather in large assemblages at lakes and parks, including those in towns, cities and villages and while travelling between destinations a birder will find a fabulous variety of birds.

Dry land and desert birds   The endangered **great Indian bustard** is often sighted in the Desert National Park of Jaisalmer district and in the scrub and grass of Bikaner, and has spectacular breeding displays. The **houbara bustard** is a winter visitor to western Rajasthan.

The **black-bellied** or **imperial sandgrouse** is another winter visitor, flocking in large numbers at Gajner lake and waterholes in the Thar Desert National Park for their daily drink. **Spotted sandgrouse** is frequently seen during the winter months in the drylands. The **common Indian sandgrouse** breeds in the arid belt of western Rajasthan. **Painted sandgrouse** frequent the wooded areas and taller grasses.

The **grey francolin** or partridge is a common sight in the countryside of Rajasthan, and its challenging cries can be heard almost everywhere. The painted francolin frequents forested areas like Kumbalgarh and Ranthambhore.

Water and waterside birds The *jheels* (marshes or swamps) of Rajasthan form one of the richest bird habitats in India. The magnificent **sarus crane** (*Grus antigone*, 150 cm) is one of India's tallest birds. The bare red head and long red legs and grey plumage make it easy to identify. **Demoiselle cranes** are seen in good numbers near Jodhpur, specially at Khichan where they are fed by the villagers. **Siberian cranes** visit Bharatpur but are becoming very rare as they are often lured to traps on their way south each winter. There are also large stork heronries at Bharatpur.

The **openbill stork** (*Anastomus oscitans*, 80 cm) and the **painted stork** (*Ibis leucocephalus*, 100 cm) are common too and are spotted breeding in large colonies. The former is white with black wing feathers and a curiously shaped bill. The latter mainly white, has a pinkish tinge on the back and dark marks on the wings and a broken black band on the lower chest. The bare yellow face and yellow down-curved bill are conspicuous.

Rosy, spotbilled and other **pelicans** are frequent visitors to many lakes including Sardar Sammand and Keoladeo Ghana National Park. White, black and glossy **ibises**, **spoonbill** and various **herons** including the little and cattle egrets and grey heron are frequently seen in Rajasthan's wetlands. Greater and lesser **flamingos** are occasionally seen in Rajasthan. These long-necked rosy white birds, with heavy bills, are graceful and attractive. When seen in flight, lesser flamingos can be distinguished by their shorter trailing legs. Alaniya dam near Kota, and the River Luni in western Rajasthan attract flamingos in good numbers.

By almost every swamp, ditch or rice paddy up to about 1200 m you will see the **paddy bird** (*Ardeola grayii*, 45 cm). An inconspicuous, buff-coloured bird, it is easily overlooked as it stands hunched up by the waterside.

The commonest and most widespread of the Indian kingfishers is the jewel-like **common kingfisher** (*Alcedo atthis*, 18 cm). With its brilliant blue upper parts and orange breast it is usually seen perched on a twig or a reed beside the water.

Birds of open grassland, light woodland and cultivated land The **cattle egret** (*Bubulcus ibis*, 50 cm), a small white heron, is usually seen near herds of cattle, frequently perched on the backs of the animals.

The **rose-ringed parakeet** (*Psittacula krameri*, 40 cm) is found throughout India up to about 1500 m while the **pied myna** (*Sturnus contra*, 23 cm) is restricted to northern and central India. The rose-ringed parakeet often forms huge flocks, an impressive sight coming in to roost. They can be very destructive to crops, but are attractive birds and are frequently kept as pets. The pied myna, with its smart black and white plumage is conspicuous, usually in small flocks in grazing land or cultivation. The all-black **drongo** (*Dicrurus adsimilis*, 30 cm) is almost invariably seen perched on telegraph wires or bare branches. Its distinctively forked tail makes it easy to identify.

Weaver birds are a family of mainly yellow birds, all remarkable for the intricate nests they build. The most widespread is the **baya weaver** (*Ploceus philippinus*, 15 cm) which nest in large colonies, often near villages. The male in the breeding season combines a black face and throat with a contrasting yellow top of the head and the yellow breast band. In the non-breeding season both sexes are brownish sparrow-like birds.

India's national bird, the magnificent **peafowl** (*Pavo cristatus*, male 210 cm, female 100 cm), is more commonly known as the peacock. Semi-domesticated birds are commonly seen around towns and villages. In the wild it favours hilly jungles and dense scrub.

Reptiles and amphibians

Snakes India is famous for its reptiles, especially its snakes which feature in many stories and legends. In reality, snakes keep out of the way of people. Four main species of venomous snakes are seen in Rajasthan, the Indian **cobra** is the best known. The **common krait** has the most toxic venom but is less aggressive than the cobra and also more nocturnal and shy. **Saw-scaled viper** is common in the plains, rocks and desert areas of Rajasthan. The saw-scaled viper uses a locomotion called side winding to negotiate the hot sands of the desert dunes. **Russel's viper**, with its chain-like markings, inhabits forests like Ranthambhore.

A large snake favoured by street entertainers is the cobras. The various species all have a hood which is spread when the snake draws itself up to strike. They are all highly venomous and the snake charmers prudently de-fang them to render them harmless. The best known is probably the **spectacled cobra** (*Naja naja*), which has a mark like a pair of spectacles on the back of its hood. The largest venomous snake in the world is the **king cobra** (*Ophiophagus hannah*) which is 5 m in length. It is usually brown, but can vary from cream to black and lacks the spectacle marks of the other. In their natural state cobras are generally inhabitants of forest regions.

Equally venomous, but much smaller, the **common krait** (*Bungarus caeruleus*) is just over 1 m in length. The slender, shiny, blue-black snake has thin white bands which can sometimes be almost indiscernible.

The **Indian rock python** (*Python molurus*), about 4 m in length, is a 'constrictor' which kills it's prey by suffocation. The python point at Bharatpur is a good place to see them.

Lizards In houses everywhere you cannot fail to see the **gecko** (*Hemidactylus*). This small harmless, primitive lizard is active after dark. It lives in houses behind pictures and curtain rails and at night emerges to run across the walls and ceilings to hunt the night flying insects which form its main prey. It is not usually more than about 14 cm long, with a curiously transparent, pale yellowish brown body. At the other end of the scale is the **monitor lizard** (*Varanus*), which can grow to 2 m in length. They can vary from a colourful black and yellow, to plain or speckled brown. They live in different habitats from cultivation and scrub to waterside places and desert.

The desert areas of western Rajasthan are home to **spiny-tailed lizard**, an omnivore that feeds on desert succulent vegetation, as well as termites and other insects, but their numbers are declining as they are sought after by 'medicine men' for their so-called aphrodisiac qualities.

Crocodiles The most widespread crocodile is the freshwater **mugger** or **marsh crocodile** (*Crocodilus palustris*) which grows to a length of 3-4 m. Muggers are often seen at reservoirs like, Sitamata and Kumbalgarh sanctuary lakes, Jaisammand Lake, and Ranthambhore National Park. The only similar fresh water species is the **gharial** (*Gavialis gangeticus*) which lives in large, fast flowing rivers. Up to twice the length of the mugger, it is a fish-eating crocodile with a long thin snout and, in the case of the male, an extraordinary bulbous growth on the end of the snout. They are found along the River Chambal in eastern Rajasthan.

Books

Art and architecture

Burton, TR *Hindu Art*, British Museum P. Well illustrated; broad view of art and religion.
Cooper, I and Dawson, B *Traditional Buildings of India*, Thames & Hudson.
Michell, G *The Hindu Temple*, Univ of Chicago Press, 1988. An authoritative account of Hindu architectural development.
Ramaswami, NS *Temples of South India*, Chennai, Maps and Agencies, 1996, and **KR Srinivasan**'s *Temples of South India*, 3rd ed, New Delhi, National Book Trust, 1985, good background information.
Sterlin, H *Hindu India*. Köln, Taschen, 1998. Traces the development from early rock-cut shrines, detailing famous examples; clearly written, well illustrated.
Tillotson, G *The Rajput Palaces*, Yale, 1987; *Mughal architecture*, London, Viking, 1990; *The tradition of Indian architecture*, Yale 1989. Superbly clear writing on Indian architecture under Rajputs, Mughals and the British.

Rakesh, P and Lewis, K *Shekhawati: Rajasthan's painted houses*. Also well illustrated.

Current affairs and politics

French, P *Liberty or Death,* Harper Collins, 1997. Well researched, serious, but very readable.
Granta 57 *India: the Golden Jubilee*. Superb edition devoted to India's 50th anniversary of Independence, 22 international writers give brilliant snapshot accounts of India today.
Khilnani, S *The idea of India*, Penguin, 1997. Excellent introduction to contemporary India.
Silver, RB and Epstein, B *India: a mosaic*. New York, NYRB, 2000. Distinguished essays on history, politics and literature. Amartya Sen on Tagore, Pankaj Mishra on nuclear India.
Tharur, S *India: from midnight to the millennium*. Viking, 1997.
Tully, M *No full stops in India*, Viking, 1991. An often superbly observed but controversially interpreted view of contemporary India.

Cities, sites and places

Delhi
Barton, G, and Malone, L *Old Delhi: 10 easy walks*. Delhi, Rupa, 1988. Interesting companion for exploring the old city, helpful maps.
Kaul, H, Ed *Historic Delhi: an anthology*. Delhi, OUP, 1985.
Miller, S *Delhi Adventures in a Megacity*. Penguin 2008. A non-fiction bestseller.
Sainty, S *Lost monuments of Delhi*. Delhi, Harper Collins, 1997. A booklet covering Islamic architecture in brief.
Sengupta, R *Delhi Metropolitan*. Penguin 2008.
Sharma, YD *Delhi and its neighbourhood*. Delhi, ASI, 1972. History, architecture and site details.

Shekhawati
Cooper, I *The painted towns of Shekhawati*, Mapin, Allahabad, 1994. Photos and maps.

History: medieval and modern

Beames, J *Memoirs of a Bengal Civilian*. A readable insight into the British Raj in the post-Mutiny period, London, Eland, 1991.
Edwardes, M *The Myth of the Mahatma*. Presents Gandhi in a whole new light.
Gandhi, R *The Good Boatman* Viking/Penguin 1995. An excellent biography by one of Gandhi's noted grandson's.
Gascoigne, B *The Great Moghuls*, London, Cape, 1987.
Keay, J *India: a History*, Harper Collins, 2000. A major new popular history of the subcontinent.
Nehru, J *The discovery of India*, New Delhi, ICCR, 1976.
Robinson, F (ed) *Cambridge Encyclopaedia of India*, Cambridge, 1989. An introduction to many aspects of South Asian society.

Spear, P and Thapar, R *A history of India*, 2 vols, Penguin, 1978.
Wolpert, S *A new history of India*, OUP 1990.

History: pre- and early history

Allchin, B and R *Origins of a civilisation*, Viking, Penguin Books, 1997. The most authoritative up-to-date survey of the origins of Indian civilizations.
Basham, AL *The Wonder that was India*, London, Sidgwick & Jackson, 1985. One of the most comprehensive and readable accounts of the development of India's culture.

Language

Snell, R and Weightman, S *Teach Yourself Hindi*. An excellent, accessible teaching guides with cassette tapes.
Yule, H and Burnell, AC (eds) *Hobson-Jobson*, 1886. New paperback edition, 1986. A delightful insight into Anglo-Indian words and phrases.

Literature

Chatterjee, U *English August*. London, Faber, 1988. A wry modern account of an Indian civil servant's year in a rural posting.
Chaudhuri, N Vivid, witty and often sharply critical accounts of India across the 20th century. *The autobiography of an unknown Indian*, Macmillan, London; *Thy Hand, Great Anarch!*, London, Chatto & Windus, 1987.
Kanga, F *Trying to grow*, Bloomsbury, 1989. Mumbai life seen through the experiences of a Parsi family.
Mistry, R *A fine balance*. Faber, 1995. A tale of the struggle to survive in the modern Indian city.
Naipaul, VS *A million mutinies now*, Penguin, 1992. 'Revisionist' account of India turns away from the despondency of his earlier books (*An Area of darkness* and *India: a wounded civilisation*).

Narayan, RK Gentle and humorous novels and stories of South India: *The Man-eater of Malgudi* and *Under the Banyan tree and other stories, Grandmother's stories*, London, Penguin, 1985.
Ramanuja, AK: *The collected essays*. Ed by V Dhawadker. New Delhi, OUP, 1999. Brilliant essays on Indian culture and literature.
Roy, A *The God of Small Things*. Indian Ink/Harper Collins, 1997. Excellent first novel about family turmoil in a Syrian Christian household in Kerala.
Rushdie, S *Midnight's children*, London, Picador, 1981. India since Independence, with funny and sharp critiques of South Asian life in the 1980s. *The Moor's Last Sigh*, Viking, 1996, is of particular interest to those travelling to Kochi and Mumbai.
Scott, P *The Raj Quartet*, London, Panther, 1973; *Staying on*, Longmans, 1985. Outstandingly perceptive novels of the end of the Raj.
Seth, V *A Suitable Boy*, Phoenix House London, 1993. Prize-winning novel of modern Indian life.
Weightman, S (ed) *Travellers Literary Companion: the Indian Sub-continent*. Invaluable introduction to the diversity of Indian writing.

Music and cinema

Menon, RR *Penguin Dictionary of Indian Classical Music*, Penguin New Delhi 1995.
Mohan, L *Bollywood, Popular Indian Cinema*, Joshi (Dakini).

People

Bumiller, E *May you be the mother of one hundred sons*, Penguin, 1991. An American woman journalists' account of coming to understand the issues that face India's women.
Holmstrom, L *The Inner Courtyard*. A series of short stories by Indian women, translated into English, Rupa, 1992.

Lewis, N *A goddess in the stones*. An insight into tribal life in Orissa and Bihar.
Varma, PK *Being Indian*. Penguin 2004.
Bijapurkar, R *We are like that only*, Penguin 2007. To understand consumer India.
Lloyd, S *An Indian Attachment*, London, Eland, 1992. A very personal and engaging account of time spent in an Indian village.

Religion

Doniger O'Flaherty, W *Hindu Myths*, London, Penguin, 1974. A sourcebook translated from the Sanskrit.
Jain, JP *Religion and Culture of the Jains* , 3rd ed. New Delhi, Bharatiya Jnanapith, 1981.
Qureshi, IH *The Muslim Community of the Indo-Pakistan Sub-Continent 610-1947*, OUP, Karachi, 1977.
Rahula, W *What the Buddha Taught*.
Singh, H *The heritage of the Sikhs*, 2nd ed, New Delhi, 1983.
Waterstone, R *India, the cultural companion*, Duncan Baird, Winchester, 2002. India's spiritual traditions brought up to date, well illustrated.
Zaehner, RC *Hinduism*, OUP.

Travel

Dalrymple, W *City of Djinns*, Indus/Harper Collins, 1993, paperback. Superb account of Delhi, based on a year living in the city. *The Age of Kali*, published in edited form in India as *In the court of the fish-eyed Goddess*, is his second anecdotal but insightful account.

Fishlock, T *Cobra Road*, London, John Murray, 1991. Impressions of a news journalist.
Frater, A *Chasing the monsoon*, London, Viking, 1990. Prize-winning account of the human impact of the monsoon's sweep across India.
Hatt, J *The tropical traveller: the essential guide to travel in hot countries*, Penguin, 3rd ed, 1992. Wide ranging and clearly written, based on extensive experience and research.
Keay, J *Into India*, London, John Murray, 1999. Seasoned traveller's introduction to understanding and enjoying India.

Wildlife and vegetation

Ali, S *Indian hill birds*, OUP.
Ali, Sand Dillon Ripley, S *Handbook of the birds of India & Pakistan* (compact ed).
Cowen, DV *Flowering Trees and Shrubs in India*.
Ewans, M *Bharatpur: Bird Paradise*, Lustre Press, Delhi.
Grimmet, R, and Inskipp, C and T *Pocket guide to Birds of the Indian Sub-Continent*. 1999.
Ives, R *Of tigers and men*, Doubleday, 1995.
Kazmierczak, K and Singh, R *A birdwatcher's guide to India*. Prion, 1998, Sandy, Beds, UK. Well researched and carrying lots of practical information for all birders.
Nair, SM *Endangered animals of India*, New Delhi, NBT, 1992.
Polunin, O and Stainton, A *Flowers of the Himalaya*, OUP, 1984.
Prater, SH *The Book of Indian Animals*.
Sippy, S and Kapoor, S *The Ultimate Ranthambhore Guide*, 2001. Informative, practical guide stressing conservation.
Thapar and Rathore *Wild tigers of Ranthambhore* OUP, 2000.

Contents

Footnotes

Language

Hindi words and phrases

Pronunciation
a as in *ah*   i as in *bee*
nasalized vowels are shown
as an *un*
o as in *oh*   u as in *oo* in book

Basics
Hello, good morning,
  goodbye *namaste*
Thank you/no thank
  you *dhanyavad* or
  shukriya/nahin shukriya
Excuse me, sorry *maf kijiye*
Yes/no *ji han/ji nahin*
Never mind/that's all right
  koi bat nahin

Questions
What is your name? *apka nam
  kya hai?*
My name is ... *mera nam... Hai*
Pardon? *phir bataiye?*
How are you? *kya hal hai?*
I am well, thanks, and
  you? *main thik hun, aur ap?*
Not very well *main thik nahin
  hun*
Where is the...? *kahan hai...?*
Who is? *kaun hai?*
What is this? *yeh kya hai?*

Shopping
How much? *Kitna?*
That makes (20) rupees *(bis)
  rupaye*
That is very expensive! *bahut
  mahanga hai!*
Make it a bit cheaper! *thora
  kam kijiye!*

The hotel
What is the room
  charge? *kiraya kitna hai?*
Please show the room *kamra
  dikhaiye*
Is there an air-conditioned
  room? *kya a/c kamra hai?*

Is there hot water? *garam pani
  hai?*
... a bathroom/fan/ mosquito
  net *... bathroom/pankha/
  machhar dani*
Is there a large room? *bara
  kamra hai?*
Please clean it *saf karwa dijiye*
Are there clean sheets/
  blanket? *saf chadaren/
  kambal hain?*
Bill please *bill dijiye*

Travel
Where's the railway
  station? *railway station
  kahan hai?*
How much is the ticket to
  Agra? *Agra ka ticket kitne
  ka hai?*
When does the Agra bus
  leave? *Agra bus kab jaegi?*
How much? *Kitna?*
Left/right *baien/dahina*
Go straight on *sidha chaliye*
Nearby *nazdik*
Please wait here *yahan
  thahariye*
Please come at 8 *ath bajai ana*
Quickly *jaldi*
Stop *rukiye*

Restaurants
Please show the menu *menu
  dikhaiye*
No chillies please *mirch nahin
  dalna*
...sugar/milk/ice ...*chini/
  doodh/baraf*
A bottle of water please *ek
  botal pani dijiye*
Sweet/savoury *mitha/ namkin*
Spoon, fork, knife *chamach,
  kanta, chhuri*

Time and days
right now *abhi*
month *mahina*

morning *suba*
year *sal*
afternoon *dopahar*
evening *sham*
night *rat*
today *aj*
tomorrow/yesterday
  kal/kal
day *din*
week *hafta*
Sunday *ravivar*
Monday *somvar*
Tuesday *mangalvar*
Wednesday *budhvar*
Thursday *virvar*
Friday *shukravar*
Saturday *shanivar*

Numbers
1	*ek*	2	*do*
3	*tin*	4	*char*
5	*panch*	6	*chhai*
7	*sat*	8	*ath*
9	*nau*	10	*das*
11	*gyara*	12	*barah*
13	*terah*	14	*chaudah*
15	*pandrah*	16	*solah*
17	*satrah*	18	*atharah*
19	*unnis*	20	*bis*
100/200		*sau/do sau*	
1000/2000		*hazar/*	
		do hazar	
100,000		*lakh*	

Basic vocabulary
Words such as airport,
bank, bathroom, bus, doctor,
embassy, ferry, hotel, hospital,
juice, police, restaurant, station,
stamp, taxi, ticket, train are
used locally though often
pronounced differently
eg *daktar, haspatal.*
and *aur*
big *bara*
café/food stall *dhaba/hotel*
chemist *dawai ki dukan*
clean *saf*

closed *band*	newspaper *akhbar*	this *yeh*
cold *thanda*	of course, sure *zaroor*	town *shahar*
day *din*	open *khula*	water *pani*
dirty *ganda*	police station *thana*	what *kya*
English *angrezi*	road *rasta*	when *kab*
excellent *bahut achha*	room *kamra*	where *kahan/kidhar*
food/ to eat *khana*	shop *dukan*	which/who *kaun*
hot (spicy) *jhal, masaledar*	sick (ill) *bimar*	why *kiun*
hot (temp) *garam*	silk *reshmi/silk*	with *ke sathh*
luggage *saman*	small *chhota*	
medicine *dawai*	that *who*	

Food and drink

Eating out is normally cheap and safe but menus can often be dauntingly long and full of unfamiliar names. Here are some Hindi words to help you.

Meat and fish
chicken *murgh*
fish *macchli*
meat *gosht, mas*
prawns *jhinga*

Vegetables (sabzi)
aubergine *baingan*
cabbage *band gobi*
carrots *gajar*
cauliflower *phool gobi*
mushroom *khumbhi*

onion *piaz*
okra, ladies' fingers *bhindi*
peas *matar*
potato *aloo*
spinach *sag*

Styles of cooking
Many items on restaurant menus are named according to methods of preparation, roughly equivalent to terms such as 'Provençal' or 'sauté'.

bhoona in a thick, fairly spicy sauce

chops minced meat, fish or vegetables, covered with mashed potato, crumbed and fried

cutlet minced meat, fish, vegetables formed into flat rounds or ovals, crumbed and fried (eg prawn cutlet, flattened king prawn)

do piaza with onions (added twice during cooking)

dum pukht steam baked

jhal frazi spicy, hot sauce with tomatoes and chillies

jhol thin gravy (Bengali)

Kashmiri cooked with mild spices, ground almonds and yoghurt, often with fruit

kebab skewered (or minced and shaped) meat or fish; a dry spicy dish cooked on a fire

kima minced meat (usually 'mutton')

kofta minced meat or vegetable balls

korma in fairly mild rich sauce using cream/yoghurt

masala marinated in spices (fairly hot)

Madras hot

makhani in butter rich sauce

moli South Indian dishes cooked in coconut milk and green chilli sauce

Mughlai rich North Indian style

Nargisi dish using boiled eggs

navratan curry ('9 jewels') colourful mixed vegetables and fruit in mild sauce

Peshwari rich with dried fruit and nuts (northwest Indian)

tandoori baked in a tandoor (special clay oven) or one imitating it

tikka marinated meat pieces, baked quite dry

vindaloo hot and sour Goan meat dish using vinegar

Typical dishes
aloo gosht potato and mutton stew

aloo gobi dry potato and cauliflower with cumin

aloo, matar, kumbhi potato, peas, mushrooms in a dryish mildly spicy sauce

bhindi bhaji okra fried with onions and mild spices

boti kebab marinated pieces of meat, skewered and cooked over a fire

dhal makhani lentils cooked with butter

dum aloo potato curry with a spicy yoghurt, tomato and onion sauce

matar panir curd cheese cubes with peas and spices (and often tomatoes)

murgh massallam chicken in creamy marinade of yoghurt, spices and herbs with nuts

nargisi kofta boiled eggs covered in minced lamb, cooked in a thick sauce

rogan josh rich, mutton/beef pieces in creamy, red sauce

sag panir drained curd (panir) sautéd with chopped spinach in mild spices

sarson-ke-sag and **makkai-ki-roti** mustard leaf cooked dry with spices served with maize four roti from Punjab

shabdeg a special Mughlai mutton dish with vegetables

yakhni lamb stew

Rice

bhat/sada chawal plain boiled rice

biriyani partially cooked rice layered over meat and baked with saffron

khichari rice and lentils cooked with turmeric and other spices

pulao/pilau fried rice cooked with spices (cloves, cardamom, cinnamon) with dried fruit, nuts or vegetables. Sometimes cooked with meat, like a biriyani

Roti – breads

chapati (roti) thin, plain, wholemeal unleavened bread cooked on a tawa (griddle), usually made from ata (wheat flour). Makkaikiroti is with maize flour.

nan oven baked (traditionally in a tandoor) white flour leavened bread often large and triangular; sometimes stuffed with almonds and dried fruit

paratha fried bread layered with ghi (sometimes cooked with egg or with potatoes)

poori thin deep-fried, puffed rounds of flour

Sweets

These are often made with reduced/thickened milk, drained curd cheese or powdered lentils and nuts. They are sometimes covered with a flimsy sheet of decorative, edible silver leaf.

barfi fudgelike rectangles/diamonds

gulab jamun dark fried spongy balls, soaked in syrup

halwa rich sweet made from cereal, fruit, vegetable, nuts and sugar

khir, payasam, paesh thickened milk rice/vermicelli pudding

kulfi cone-shaped Indian ice cream with pistachios/ almonds, uneven in texture

jalebi spirals of fried batter soaked in syrup

laddoo lentil based batter 'grains' shaped into rounds

rasgulla (roshgulla) balls of curd in clear syrup

sandesh dry sweet made of curd cheese

Snacks

bhaji, pakora vegetable fritters (onions, potatoes, cauliflower, etc) deep-fried in batter

chat sweet and sour fruit and vegetables flavoured with tama rind paste and chillies

chana choor, chioora ('Bombay mix') lentil and flattened rice snacks mixed with nuts and dried fruit

dosai South Indian pancake made with rice and lentil flour; served with a mild potato and onion filling (masala dosai) or without (ravai or plain dosai)

iddli steamed South Indian rice cakes, a bland breakfast given flavour by spiced accompaniments

kachori fried pastry rounds stuffed with spiced lentil/ peas/potato filling

samosa cooked vegetable or meat wrapped in pastry triangles and deep fried

utthappam thick South Indian rice and lentil flour pancake cooked with spices/onions/ tomatoes

vadai deep fried, small savoury lentil 'doughnut' rings. Dahi vada are similar rounds in yoghurt

Glossary

Words in italics are common elements of words, often making up part of a place name

A

aarti (arati) Hindu worship with lamps

abacus square or rectangular table resting on top of a pillar

abad peopled

acanthus thick-leaved plant, common decoration on pillars, esp Greek

achalam hill (Tamil)

acharya religious teacher

Adi Granth Guru Granth Sahib, holy book of the Sikhs

Adinatha first of the 24 Tirthankaras, distinguished by his bull mount

agarbathi incense

Agastya legendary sage who brought the Vedas to South India

Agni Vedic fire divinity, intermediary between gods and men; guardian of the Southeast

ahimsa non-harming, non-violence

akhand path unbroken reading of the Guru Granth Sahib

alinda veranda

ambulatory processional path

amla/amalaka circular ribbed pattern (based on a gourd) at the top of a temple tower

amrita ambrosia; drink of immortality

ananda joy

Ananda the Buddha's chief disciple

Ananta a huge snake on whose coils Vishnu rests

anda literally 'egg', spherical part of the stupa

Andhaka demon killed by Siva

anicut irrigation channel (Tamil)

anna (ana) one sixteenth of a rupee (still occasionally referred to)

Annapurna Goddess of abundance; one aspect of Devi

antarala vestibule, chamber in front of shrine or cella

antechamber chamber in front of the sanctuary

apsara celestial nymph

apse semi-circular plan

arabesque ornamental decoration with intertwining lines

aram pleasure garden

architrave horizontal beam across posts or gateways

ardha mandapam chamber in front of main hall of temple

Ardhanarisvara Siva represented as half-male and half-female

Arjuna hero of the Mahabharata, to whom Krishna delivered the Bhagavad Gita

arrack alcoholic spirit fermented from potatoes or grain

aru river (Tamil)

Aruna charioteer of Surya, Sun God; Red

Aryans literally 'noble' (Sanskrit); prehistoric peoples who settled in Persia and North India

asana a seat or throne (Buddha's) pose

ashram hermitage or retreat

Ashta Matrikas The eight mother goddesses who attended on Siva or Skanda

astanah threshold

atman philosophical concept of universal soul or spirit

atrium court open to the sky in the centre In modern architecture, enclosed in glass

aus summer rice crop (Apr-Aug) Bengal

Avalokiteshwara Lord who looks down; Bodhisattva, the Compassionate

avatara 'descent'; incarnation of a divinity

ayacut irrigation command area (Tamil)

ayah nursemaid, especially for children

B

babu clerk

bada cubical portion of a temple up to the roof or spire

badgir rooftop structure to channel cool breeze into the house (mainly North and West India)

badlands eroded landscape

bagh garden

bahadur title, meaning 'the brave'

baksheesh tip 'bribe'

Balabhadra Balarama, elder brother of Krishna

baluster (balustrade) a small column supporting a handrail

bandh a strike

bandhani tie dyeing (West India)

Bangla (Bangaldar) curved roof, based on thatched roofs in Bengal

bania merchant caste

banian vest

baoli or vav rectangular well surrounded by steps

baradari literally 'twelve pillared', a pavilion with columns

barrel-vault semi-cylindrical shaped roof or ceiling

bas-relief carving of low projection

basement lower part of walls, usually with decorated mouldings

basti Jain temple

batter slope of a wall, especially in a fort

bazar market

bedi (vedi) altar/platform for reading holy texts

begum Muslim princess/woman's courtesy title

beki circular stone below the amla in the finial of a roof

belvedere summer house; small room on a house roof

bhabar coarse alluvium at foot of Himalayas

bhadra flat face of the sikhara (tower)

Bhadrakali Tantric goddess and consort of Bhairav

Bhagavad-Gita Song of the Lord; section of the Mahabharata

Bhagiratha the king who prayed to Ganga to descend to earth

bhai brother

Bhairava Siva, the Fearful

bhakti adoration of a deity

bhang Indian hemp

bharal Himalayan blue sheep

Bharata half-brother of Rama

bhavan building or house

bhikku Buddhist monk

Bhima Pandava hero of the Mahabharata, famous for his strength

Bhimsen Deity worshipped for his strength and courage

bhisti a water-carrier

bhogamandapa the refectory hall of a temple

bhumi literally earth; a horizontal moulding of a sikhara

bidi (beedi) Indian cigarette, tobacco wrapped in tendu leaves

bigha measure of land – normally about one-third of an acre

bo-tree (or Bodhi) *Ficus religiosa*, pipal tree associated with the Buddha

Bodhisattva Enlightened One, destined to become Buddha

bodi tuft of hair on back of the shaven head (also *tikki*)

Brahma Universal self-existing power; Creator in the Hindu Triad.

Brahmachari religious student, accepting rigorous discipline (eg chastity)

Brahman (Brahmin) highest Hindu (and Jain) caste of priests

Brahmanism ancient Indian religion, precursor of modern Hinduism

Buddha The Enlightened One; founder of Buddhism

bund an embankment

bundh (literally closed) a strike

burj tower or bastion

burqa (burkha) over-dress worn by Muslim women observing purdah

bustee slum

C

cantonment planned military or civil area in town

capital upper part of a column

caryatid sculptured human female figure used as a support for columns

catamaran log raft, logs (*maram*) tied (*kattu*) together (Tamil)

cave temple rock-cut shrine or monastery

cella small chamber, compartment for the image of a deity

cenotaph commemorative monument, usually an open domed pavilion

chaam Himalayan Buddhist masked dance

chadar sheet worn as clothing

chai tea

chaitya large arched opening in the façade of a hall or Buddhist temple

chajja overhanging cornice or eaves

chakra sacred Buddhist wheel of the law; also Vishnu's discus

chala Bengali curved roof

Chamunda terrifying form of the goddess Durga

Chandra Moon; a planetary deity

chankramana place of the promenade of the Buddha at Bodh Gaya

chapati unleavened Indian bread cooked on a griddle

chaprassi messenger or orderly usually wearing a badge

char sand-bank or island in a river

char bagh formal Mughal garden, divided into quarters

char bangla (char-chala) 'four temples' in Bengal, built like huts

charan footprint

charka spinning wheel

charpai 'four legs' – wooden frame string bed

chatt(r)a ceremonial umbrella on stupa (Buddhist)

chauki recessed space between pillars: entrance

chaukidar (chowkidar) night-watchman; guard

chaultri (choultry) travellers' rest house (Telugu)

chaumukha Jain sanctuary with a quadruple image, approached through four doorways

chauri fly-whisk, symbol for royalty

chauth 25% tax raised for revenue by Marathas

cheri outcaste settlement; slum (Tamil Nadu)

chhang strong mountain beer of fermented barley maize rye or millet or rice

chhatri umbrella shaped dome or pavilion

chhetri (kshatriya) Hindu warrior caste

chikan shadow embroidery on fine cotton (especially in Lucknow)

chikki nut crunch, a speciality of Lonavla

chit sabha hall of wisdom (Tamil)

chitrakar picture maker

chlorite soft greenish stone that hardens on exposure

chogyal heavenly king (Sikkim)

choli blouse

chorten Himalayan Buddhist relic shrine or a memorial stupa

chowk (chauk) a block; open place in a city where the market is held

chunam lime plaster or stucco made from burnt seashells

circumambulation clockwise movement around a shrine

clerestory upper section of the walls of a building which allows light in

cloister passage usually around an open square

coir fibre from coconut husk

corbel horizontal block supporting a vertical structure or covering an opening

cornice horizontal band at the top of a wall

crenellated having battlements

crewel work chain stitching

crore 10 million

cupola small dome

curvilinear gently curving shape, generally of a tower

cusp, cusped projecting point between small sections of an arch

D

dacoit bandit

dada (dadu) grandfather; elder brother

dado part of a pedestal between its base and cornice

dahi yoghurt

dais raised platform

dak bungalow rest house for officials

dak post

dakini sorceress

Dakshineshvara Lord of the South; name of Siva

dan gift

dandi wooden 'seat' carried by bearers

darbar (durbar) a royal gathering

dargah a Muslim tomb complex

darshan (darshana) viewing of a deity or spiritual leader

darwaza gateway, door

Dasara (dassara/dussehra/dasse hra) 10-day festival (Sep-Oct)

Dasaratha King of Ayodhya and father of Rama

Dattatraya syncretistic deity; an incarnation of Vishnu, a teacher of Siva, or a cousin of the Buddha

daulat khana treasury

dentil small block used as part of a cornice

deodar Himalayan cedar; from deva-daru, the 'wood of the gods'

dervish member of Muslim brotherhood, committed to poverty

deul in Bengal and Orissa, generic name for temple; the sanctuary

deval memorial pavilion built to mark royal funeral pyre

devala temple or shrine (Buddhist or Hindu)

devasthanam temple trust

Devi Goddess; later, the Supreme Goddess

dhaba roadside restaurant (mainly North India) truck drivers' stop

dhal lentils, pulses

dhansak Parsi dish made with lentils

dharamshala (dharamsala) pilgrims' rest house

dharma moral and religious duty

dharmachakra wheel of 'moral' law (Buddhist)

dhobi washerman

dhol drums

dhooli (dhooli) swinging chair on a pole, carried by bearers

dhoti loose loincloth worn by Indian men

dhyana meditation

digambara literally 'sky-clad' Jain sect in which the monks go naked

dighi village pond (Bengal)

dikka raised platform around ablution tank

dikpala guardian of one of the cardinal directions mostly appearing in a group of eight

dikshitar person who makes oblations or offerings

dipdan lamp pillar

distributary river that flows away from main channel

divan (diwan) smoking-room; also a chief minister

Diwali festival of lights (Oct-Nov)

diwan chief financial minister

diwan-i-am hall of public audience

diwan-i-khas hall of private audience

do-chala rectangular Bengali style roof

doab interfluve, land between two rivers

dokra tribal name for lost wax metal casting (cire perdu)

dosai (dosa) thin pancake

double dome composed of an inner and outer shell of masonry

Draupadi wife-in-common of the five Pandava brothers in the Mahabharata

drug (durg) fort (Tamil, Telugu)

dry masonry stones laid without mortar

duar (dwar) door, gateway

dun valley

dupatta long scarf worn by Punjabi women

Durga principal goddess of the Shakti cult

durrie (dhurrie) thick handloom rug

durwan watchman

dvarpala doorkeeper

dvipa lamp-column, generally of stone or brass-covered wood

E

eave overhang that shelters a porch or veranda

ek the number 1, a symbol of unity

ekka one horse carriage

epigraph carved inscription

eri tank (Tamil)

F

faience coloured tilework, earthenware or porcelain

fakir Muslim religious mendicant

fan-light fan-shaped window over door

fenestration with windows or openings

filigree ornamental work or delicate tracery

finial emblem at the summit of a stupa, tower, dome, or at the end of a parapet

firman edict or grant issued by a sovereign

foliation ornamental design derived from foliage

frieze horizontal band of figures or decorative designs

G

gable end of an angled roof

gadba woollen blanket (Kashmir)

gaddi throne

gadi/gari car, cart, train

gali (galli) lane; an alley

gana child figures in art

Gandharva semi-divine flying figure; celestial musician

Ganesh (Ganapati) elephant-headed son of Siva and Parvati

Ganga goddess personifying the Ganges

ganj market

ganja Indian hemp

gaon village

garbhagriha literally 'womb-chamber'; a temple sanctuary

garh fort

Garuda Mythical eagle, half-human Vishnu's vehicle

Gauri 'Fair One'; Parvati

Gaurishankara Siva with Parvati

ghagra (ghongra) long flared skirt

ghanta bell

ghat hill range, hill road; landing place; steps on the river bank

ghazal Urdu lyric poetry/love songs, often erotic

ghee clarified butter for cooking

gherao industrial action, surrounding home or office of politician or industrial manager

giri hill

Gita Govinda Jayadeva's poem of the Krishnalila

godown warehouse

gola conical-shaped storehouse

gompa Tibetan Buddhist monastery

goncha loose woollen robe, tied at waist with wide coloured band (Ladakh)

Gopala (Govinda) cowherd; a name of Krishna

Gopis cowherd girls; milk maids who played with Krishna

gopuram towered gateway in South Indian temples

Gorakhnath historically, an 11th-century yogi who founded a Saivite cult; an incarnation of Siva

gosain monk or devotee (Hindi)

gram chick pea, pulse

gram village; gramadan, gift of village

gudi temple (Karnataka)

gumbaz (gumbad) dome

gumpha monastery, cave temple

gur gur salted butter tea (Ladakh)

gur palm sugar

guru teacher; spiritual leader, Sikh religious leader

gurudwara (literally 'entrance to the house of God'); Sikh religious complex

H

Haj (Hajj) annual Muslim pilgrimage to Mecca

hakim judge; a physician (usually Muslim)

halwa a special sweetmeat

hammam Turkish bath

handi Punjabi dish cooked in a pot

Hanuman Monkey devotee of Rama; bringer of success to armies

Hara (Hara Siddhi) Siva

harem women's quarters (Muslim), from 'haram', Arabic for 'forbidden by law'

Hari Vishnu Harihara, Vishnu-Siva as a single divinity

Hariti goddess of prosperity and patroness of children, consort of Kubera

harmika the finial of a stupa in the form of a pedestal where the shaft of the honorific umbrella was set

hartal general strike

Hasan the murdered eldest son of Ali, commemorated at Muharram

hat (haat) market

hathi (hati) elephant

hathi pol elephant gate

hauz tank or reservoir

haveli a merchant's house usually in Rajasthan

havildar army sergeant

hawa mahal palace of the winds

Hidimba Devi Durga worshipped at Manali

hindola swing

hippogryph fabulous griffin-like creature with body of a horse

Hiranyakashipu Demon king killed by Narasimha

hiti a water channel; a bath or tank with water spouts

Holi spring festival (Feb-Mar)

hookah 'hubble bubble' or smoking vase

howdah seat on elephant's back, sometimes canopied

hundi temple offering

Hussain the second murdered son of Ali, commemorated at Muharram

huzra a Muslim tomb chamber

hypostyle hall with pillars

I

lat pillar, column

icon statue or image of worship

Id principal Muslim festivals

iddli steamed rice cake (Tamil)

Idgah open space for the Id prayers

ikat 'resist-dyed' woven fabric

imam Muslim religious leader

imambara tomb of a Shiite Muslim holy man; focus of Muharram procession

Indra King of the gods; God of rain; guardian of the East

Ishana Guardian of the Northeast

Ishvara Lord; Siva

iwan main arch in mosque

J

jadu magic

jaga mohan audience hall or ante-chamber of an Orissan temple

Jagadambi literally Mother of the World; Parvati

Jagannath literally Lord of the World; particularly, Krishna worshipped at Puri

jagati railed parapet

jaggery brown sugar, made from palm sap

jahaz ship: building in form of ship

jali literally 'net'; any lattice or perforated pattern

jamb vertical side slab of doorway

Jambudvipa Continent of the Rose-Apple Tree; the earth

Jami masjid (Jama, Jumma) Friday mosque, for congregational worship

Jamuna Hindu goddess who rides a tortoise; river

Janaka Father of Sita

jangha broad band of sculpture on the outside of the temple wall

jarokha balcony

jataka stories accounts of the previous lives of the Buddha

jatra Bengali folk theatre

jauhar (jauhar) mass suicide by fire of women, particularly in Rajasthan, to avoid capture

jawab literally 'answer,' a building which duplicates another to provide symmetry

jawan army recruit, soldier

jaya stambha victory tower

jheel (jhil) lake; a marsh; a swamp

jhilmil projecting canopy over a window or door opening

-ji (jee) honorific suffix added to names out of reverence and/or politeness; also abbreviated 'yes' (Hindi/Urdu)

jihad striving in the way of god; holy war by Muslims against non-believers

Jina literally 'victor'; spiritual conqueror or Tirthankara, after whom Jainism is named

Jogini mystical goddess

jorbangla double hut-like temple in Bengal

Jyotirlinga luminous energy of Siva manifested at 12 holy places, miraculously formed lingams

K

kabalai (kavalai) well irrigation using bullock power (Tamil Nadu)

kabigan folk debate in verse

kachcha man's 'under-shorts' (one of five Sikh symbols)

kacheri (kutchery) a court; an office for public business

kadal wooden bridge (Kashmir)

kadhi savoury yoghurt curry (Gujarat/North India)

kadu forest (Tamil)

Kailasa mountain home of Siva

kalamkari special painted cotton hanging from Andhra

kalasha pot-like finial of a tower

Kali literally 'black'; terrifying form of the goddess Durga, wearing a necklace of skulls/heads

Kalki future incarnation of Vishnu on horseback

kalyanamandapa marriage hall

kameez women's shirt

kanga comb (one of five Sikh symbols)

kankar limestone pieces, used for road making

kantha Bengali quilting

kapok the silk cotton tree

kara steel bracelet (one of five Sikh symbols)

karma impurity resulting from past misdeeds

Kartikkeya (Kartik) Son of Siva, God of war

kashi-work special kind of glazed tiling, probably derived from Kashan in Persia

kati-roll Muslim snack of meat rolled in a 'paratha' bread

kattakat mixed brain, liver and kidney (Gujarat)

keep tower of a fort, stronghold

kere tank (Kanarese)

keystone central wedge-shaped block in a masonry arch

khadi woven cotton cloth made from home-spun cotton (or silk) yarn

khal creek; a canal

khana suffix for room/office/place; also food or meal

khanqah Muslim (Sufi) hospice

kharif monsoon season crop

khave khana tea shop

kheda enclosure in which wild elephants are caught; elephant depot

khet field

khola river or stream in Nepal

khondalite crudely grained basalt

khukri traditional curved Gurkha weapon

kirpan sabre, dagger (one of five Sikh symbols)

kirti-stambha 'pillar of fame,' free standing pillar in front of temple

kohl antimony, used as eye shadow

konda hill (Telugu)

kos minars Mughal 'mile' stones

kot (kota/kottai/kotte) fort

kothi house

kotla citadel

kovil (koil) temple (Tamil)

Krishna Eighth incarnation of Vishnu

kritis South Indian devotional music

Kubera Chief yaksha; keeper of the treasures of the earth, Guardian of the North

kulam tank or pond (Tamil)

kumar a young man

Kumari Virgin; Durga

kumbha a vase-like motif, pot

Kumbhayog auspicious time for bathing to wash away sins

kumhar (kumar) potter

kund lake, well or pool

kundan jewellery setting of uncut gems (Rajasthan)

kuppam hamlet (Tamil)

kurta Punjabi shirt

kurti-kanchali small blouse

kutcha (cutcha/kacha) raw; crude; unpaved; built with sun-dried bricks

kwabgah bedroom; literally 'palace of dreams'

L

la Himalayan mountain pass

lakh 100,000

Lakshmana younger brother of Rama

Lakshmi Goddess of wealth and good fortune, consort of Vishnu

Lakulisha founder of the Pashupata sect, believed to be an incarnation of Siva

lama Buddhist priest in Tibet

lassi iced yoghurt drink

lath monolithic pillar

lathi bamboo stick with metal bindings, used by police

lena cave, usually a rock-cut sanctuary

lingam (linga) Siva as the phallic emblem

Lingaraja Siva worshipped at Bhubaneswar

lintel horizontal beam over doorway

liwan cloisters of a mosque

Lokeshwar 'Lord of the World', Avalokiteshwara to Buddhists and form of Siva to Hindus

lunette semi-circular window opening

lungi wrapped-around loin cloth, normally checked

M

madrassa Islamic theological school or college

maha great

Mahabharata Sanskrit epic about the battle between the Pandavas and Kauravas

Mahabodhi Great Enlightenment of Buddha

Mahadeva literally 'Great Lord'; Siva

mahal palace, grand building

mahalla (mohulla) division of a town; a quarter; a ward

mahamandapam large enclosed hall in front of main shrine

mahant head of a monastery

maharaja great king

maharana Rajput clan head

maharani great queen

maharishi (Maharshi) literally 'great teacher'

Mahavira literally 'Great Hero'; last of the 24 Tirthankaras, founder of Jainism

Mahayana The Greater Vehicle; form of Buddhism practised in East Asia, Tibet and Nepal

Mahesha (Maheshvara) Great Lord; Siva

Mahisha Buffalo demon killed by Durga

mahout elephant driver/keeper

mahseer large freshwater fish found especially in Himalayan rivers

maidan large open grassy area in a town

Maitreya the future Buddha

makara crocodile-shaped mythical creature symbolizing the river Ganga

makhan butter

malai hill (Tamil)

mali gardener

Manasa Snake goddess; Sakti

manastambha free-standing pillar in front of temple

mandala geometric diagram symbolizing the structure of the Universe

mandalam region, tract of country (Tamil)

mandapa columned hall preceding the temple sanctuary

mandi market

mandir temple

mani (mani wall) stones with sacred inscriptions at Buddhist sites

mantra chant for meditation by Hindus and Buddhists

maqbara chamber of a Muslim tomb

Mara Tempter, who sent his daughters (and soldiers) to disturb the Buddha's meditation

marg wide roadway

masjid literally 'place of prostration'; mosque

mata mother

math Hindu or Jain monastery

maulana scholar (Muslim)

maulvi religious teacher (Muslim)

maund measure of weight about 20 kg

mausoleum large tomb building

maya illusion

medallion circle or part-circle framing a figure or decorative motif

meena enamel work

mela festival or fair, usually Hindu

memsahib married European woman, term used mainly before Independence

Meru mountain supporting the heavens

mihrab niche in the western wall of a mosque

mimbar pulpit in mosque

Minakshi literally 'fish-eyed'; Parvati

minar (minaret) slender tower of a mosque

mitthai Indian sweets

mithuna couple in sexual embrace

mofussil the country as distinct from the town

Mohammad 'the praised'; The Prophet; founder of Islam

moksha salvation, enlightenment; literally 'release'

momos Tibetan stuffed pastas

monolith single block of stone shaped into a pillar

moonstone the semi-circular stone step before a shrine (also chandrasila)

mouza (mowza) village; a parcel of land having a separate name in the revenue records

mridangam barrel-shaped drum (musical)

muballigh second prayer leader

mudra symbolic hand gesture

muezzin mosque official who calls the faithful to prayer

Muharram period of mourning in remembrance of Hasan and Hussain, two murdered sons of Ali

mukha mandapa, hall for shrine

mullah religious teacher (Muslim)

mund Toda village

muqarna Muslim stalactite design

mural wall decoration

musalla prayer mat

muta limited duration marriage (Leh)

muthi measure equal to 'a handful'

N

nadi river

nadu region, country (Tamil)

Naga (nagi/nagini) Snake deity; associated with fertility and protection

nagara city, sometimes capital

nakkar khana (naggar or naubat khana) drum house; arched structure or gateway for musicians

nal mandapa porch over a staircase

nallah (nullah) ditch, channel

namaaz Muslim prayers, worship

namaste common Hindu greeting (with joined palms) translated as: 'I salute all divine qualities in you'

namda rug

Nandi a bull, Siva's vehicle and a symbol of fertility

nara durg large fort built on a flat plain

Narayana Vishnu as the creator of life

nata mandapa (nat-mandir; nritya sala) dancing hall in a temple

Nataraja Siva, Lord of the cosmic dance

nath literally 'place' eg Amarnath

natya the art of dance

nautch display by dancing girls

navagraha nine planets, represented usually on the lintel or architrave of the front door of a temple

navaranga central hall of temple

navaratri literally '9 nights'; name of the Dasara festival

nawab prince, wealthy Muslim, sometimes used as a title

niche wall recess containing a sculpted image or emblem, mostly framed by a pair of pilasters

Nihang literally 'crocodile': followers of Guru Gobind Singh (Sikh)

nirvana enlightenment; literally 'extinguished'

niwas small palace

nritya pure dance

O

obelisk tapering and usually monolithic stone shaft

oriel projecting window

P

pada foot or base

padam dance which tells a story

padma lotus flower, Padmasana, lotus seat; posture of meditating figures

paga projecting pilaster-like surface of an Orissan temple

pagoda tall structure in several stories

pahar hill

paisa (poisa) one hundredth of a rupee

palanquin covered litter for one, carried on poles

palayam minor kingdom (Tamil)

pali language of Buddhist scriptures

palli village

pan leaf of the betel vine; sliced areca nut, lime and other ingredients wrapped in leaf for chewing

panchayat a 'council of five'; a government system of elected councils

pandal marquee made of bamboo and cloth

pandas temple priests

pandit teacher or wise man; a Sanskrit scholar

pankah (punkha) fan, formerly pulled by a cord

parabdis special feeding place for birds

parapet wall extending above the roof

pargana subdivision of a district usually comprising many villages; a fiscal unit

Parinirvana the Buddha's state prior to nirvana, shown usually as a reclining figure

parishads political division of group of villages

Parsi (Parsee) Zoroastrians who fled from Iran to West India in the 8th century to avoid persecution

parterre level space in a garden occupied by flowerbeds

Parvati daughter of the Mountain; Siva's consort

pashmina fine wool from a mountain goat

Pashupati literally Lord of the Beasts; Siva

pata painted hanging scroll

patan town or city (Sanskrit)

patel village headman

patina green film that covers materials exposed to the air

pattachitra specially painted cloth (especially Orissan)

pau measure for vegetables and fruit equal to 250 g

paya soup

pediment mouldings, often in a triangular formation above an opening or niche

pendant hanging, a motif depicted upside down

peon servant, messenger (from Portuguese *peao*)

perak black hat, studded with turquoise and lapis lazuli (Ladakh)

peristyle range of columns surrounding a court or temple

Persian wheel well irrigation system using a bucket lift

pettah suburbs, outskirts of town (Tamil: *pettai*)

pice (old form) 1/100th of a rupee

picottah water lift using horizontal pole pivoted on vertical pole (Tamil Nadu)

pida (pitha) basement

pida deul hall with a pyramidal roof in an Orissan temple

pietra dura inlaid mosaic of hard, semi-precious stones

pilaster ornamental small column, with capital and bracket

pinjra lattice work

pinjrapol animal hospital (Jain)

pipal Ficus religiosa, the Bodhi tree

pir Muslim holy man

pitha base, pedestal

pithasthana place of pilgrimage

podium stone bench; low pedestal wall

pokana bathing tank (Sri Lanka)

pol fortified gateway

porch covered entrance to a shrine or hall, generally open and with columns

portico space enclosed between columns

pradakshina patha processional passage

prakaram open courtyard

pralaya the end of the world

prasadam consecrated temple food

prayag confluence considered sacred by Hindus

puja ritual offerings to the gods; worship (Hindu)

pujari worshipper; one who performs puja (Hindu)

pukka literally 'ripe' or 'finished'; reliable; solidly built

punya merit earned through actions and religious devotion (Buddhist)

Puranas literally 'the old' Sanskrit sacred poems

purdah seclusion of Muslim women from public view (literally curtains)

pushkarani sacred pool or tank

Q

qabr Muslim grave

qibla direction for Muslim prayer

qila fort

Quran holy Muslim scriptures

qutb axis or pivot

R

rabi winter/spring season crop

Radha Krishna's favourite consort

raj rule or government

raja king, ruler (variations include rao, rawal)

rajbari palaces of a small kingdom

Rajput dynasties of western and central India

Rakshakas Earth spirits

Rama Seventh incarnation of Vishnu

Ramayana Sanskrit epic – the story of Rama

Ramazan (Ramadan) Muslim month of fasting

rana warrior (Nepal)

rangamandapa painted hall or theatre

rani queen

rath chariot or temple car

Ravana Demon king of Lanka; kidnapper of Sita

rawal head priest

rekha curvilinear portion of a spire or sikhara (rekha deul,

sanctuary, curved tower of an Orissan temple)

reredos screen behind an altar

rickshaw three-wheeled bicycle-powered (or two-wheeled hand-powered) vehicle

Rig (Rg) Veda oldest and most sacred of the Vedas

Rimpoche blessed incarnation; abbot of a Tibetan Buddhist monastery (gompa)

rishi 'seer'; inspired poet, philosopher

rumal handkerchief, specially painted in Chamba (Himachal Pradesh)

rupee unit of currency in India

ryot (rayat/raiyat) a subject; a cultivator; a farmer

S

sabha columned hall (sabha mandapa, assembly hall)

sabzi vegetables, vegetable curry

sadar (sadr/saddar) chief, main especially Sikh

sadhu ascetic; religious mendicant, holy man

safa turban (Rajasthan)

sagar lake; reservoir

sahib title of address, like 'sir'

sahn open courtyard of a mosque

Saiva (Shaiva) the cult of Siva

sal a hall

sal hardwood tree of the lower slopes of the Himalayan foothills

salaam literally 'peace'; greeting (Muslim)

salwar (shalwar) loose trousers (Punjab)

samadh(i) literally concentrated thought, meditation; a funerary memorial

sambar lentil and vegetable soup dish, accompanying main meal (Tamil)

samsara transmigration of the soul

samudra large tank or inland sea

sangam junction of rivers

sangarama monastery

sangha ascetic order founded by Buddha

sangrahalaya rest house for Jain pilgrims

sankha (shankha) the conch shell (symbolically held by Vishnu); the shell bangle worn by Bengali women

sanyasi wandering ascetic; final stage in the ideal life of a man

sarai caravansarai, halting place

saranghi small four-stringed viola shaped from a single piece of wood

Saraswati wife of Brahma and goddess of knowledge

sarkar the government; the state; a writer; an accountant

sarod Indian stringed musical instrument

sarvodaya uplift, improvement of all

sati (suttee) a virtuous woman; act of self-immolation on a husband's funeral pyre

Sati wife of Siva who destroyed herself by fire

satyagraha 'truth force'; passive resistance

sayid title (Muslim)

schist grey or green finely grained stone

seer (ser) weight (about 1 kg)

sepoy (sepai) Indian soldier, private

serow a wild Himalayan antelope

seth merchant, businessman

seva voluntary service

shahtush very fine wool from the Tibetan antelope

Shakti Energy; female divinity often associated with Siva

shala barrel-vaulted roof

shalagrama stone containing fossils worshipped as a form of Vishnu

shaman doctor/priest, using magic, exorcist

shamiana cloth canopy

Shankara Siva

sharia corpus of Muslim theological law

shastras ancient texts defining temple architecture

shastri religious title (Hindu)

sheesh mahal palace apartment with mirror work

shehnai (shahnai) Indian wind instrument like an oboe

sherwani knee-length coat for men

Shesha (Sesha) serpent who supports Vishnu

shikar hunting

shikara boat (Kashmir)

shisham a valuable building timber

sikhara curved temple tower or spire

shloka (sloka) Sanskrit sacred verse

shola patch of forest or wood (Tamil)

sileh khana armoury

sindur vermilion powder used in temple ritual; married women mark their hair parting with it (East India)

singh (sinha) lion; Rajput caste name adopted by Sikhs

sinha stambha lion pillar

sirdar a guide who leads trekking groups

Sita Rama's wife, heroine of the Ramayana epic

sitar classical stringed musical instrument with a gourd for soundbox

Siva (Shiva) The Destroyer in the Hindu triad of Gods

Sivaratri literally 'Siva's night'; a festival (Feb-Mar)

Skanda the Hindu god of war; Kartikkeya

soma sacred drink mentioned in the Vedas

spandrel triangular space between the curve of an arch and the square enclosing it

squinch arch across an interior angle

sri (shri) honorific title, often used for 'Mr'; repeated as sign of great respect

sridhara pillar with octagonal shaft and square base

stalactite system of vaulting, remotely resembling stalactite formations in a cave

stambha free-standing column or pillar, often for a lamp or figure

steatite finely grained grey mineral

stele upright, inscribed slab used as a gravestone

step well (vav) vertical shaft leading down to a well, with elaborately carved walls

sthan place (suffix)

stucco plasterwork

stupa hemispheric Buddhist funerary mound

stylobate base on which a colonnade is placed

subahdar (subedar) the governor of a province; viceroy under the Mughals

Subrahmanya Skanda, one of Siva's sons; Kartikkeya in South India

sudra lowest of the Hindu castes

sufi Muslim mystic; sufism, Muslim mystic worship

sultan Muslim prince (sultana, wife of sultan)

Surya Sun; Sun God

svami (swami) holy man; a suffix for temple deities

svastika (swastika) auspicious Hindu/ Buddhist cross-like sign

swadeshi home-made goods

swaraj home rule

swatantra freedom

T

tabla a pair of drums

tahr wild goat

tahsildar revenue collector

taikhana underground apartments

takht throne

talao (tal, talar) water tank

taluk administrative subdivision of a district

tamasha spectacle; festive celebration

tandava (dance) of Siva

tank lake dug for irrigation; a masonry-lined temple pool with stepped sides

tapas (tapasya) ascetic meditative self-denial

Tara literally 'star'; a goddess

tarkashi Orissan silver filigree

tatties cane or grass screens used for shade

Teej Hindu festival

tehsil subdivision of a district (North India)

tempera distemper; method of mural painting by means of a 'body', such as white pigment

tempo three-wheeler vehicle

terai narrow strip of land along Himalayan foothills

teri soil formed from wind blown sand (Tamil Nadu)

terracotta burnt clay used as building material

thakur high Hindu caste; deity (Bengal)

thakur bari temple sanctuary (Bengal)

thali South and West Indian vegetarian meal

thana a police jurisdiction; police station

thangka (thankha) cloth (often silk) painted with a Tibetan Mahayana deity

thug professional robber/murderer (Central India)

tiffin snack, light meal

tika (tilak) vermilion powder, auspicious mark on the forehead; often decorative

tikka tender pieces of meat that have been marinated and barbecued

tillana abstract dance

tirtha ford, bathing place, holy spot (Sanskrit)

Tirthankara literally 'ford-maker'; title given to 24 religious 'teachers', worshipped by Jains

tonga two-wheeled horse carriage

topi (topee) pith helmet

torana gateway; two posts with an architrave

tottam garden (Tamil)

tribhanga triple-bended pose for standing figures

Trimurti the Hindu Triad, Brahma, Vishnu and Siva

tripolia triple gateway

trisul the trident chief symbol of the god Siva

triveni triple-braided

tsampa ground, roasted barley, eaten dry or mixed with milk, tea or water (Himalayan)

tso lake (Ladakh)

tuk fortified enclosure containing Jain shrines

tulsi sacred basil plant

tykhana underground room for use in hot weather (North India)

tympanum triangular space within cornices

U

Uma Siva's consort in one of her many forms

untouchable 'outcastes', with whom contact of any kind was believed by high caste Hindus to be defiling

Upanishads ancient Sanskrit philosophical texts, part of the Vedas

ur village (Tamil)

usta painted camel leather goods

ustad master

uttarayana northwards

V

vahana 'vehicle' of the deity

vaisya the 'middle-class' caste of merchants and farmers

Valmiki sage, author of the Ramayana epic

Vamana dwarf incarnation of Vishnu

vana grove, forest

Varaha boar incarnation of Vishnu

varam village (Tamil)

varna 'colour'; social division of Hindus into Brahmin, Kshatriya, Vaishya and Sudra

Varuna Guardian of the West, accompanied by Makara (see above)

Vayu Wind god; Guardian of the Northwest

Veda (Vedic) oldest known Hindu religious texts

vedi (bedi) altar, also a wall or screen

veranda enlarged porch in front of a hall

vihara Buddhist or Jain monastery with cells around a courtyard

vilas house or pleasure palace

vimana towered sanctuary containing the cell in which the deity is enshrined

vina plucked stringed instrument, relative of sitar

Vishnu a principal Hindu deity; the Preserver (and Creator)

vyala (yali) leogryph, mythical lion-like sculpture

W

-wallah suffix often used with a occupational name, eg rickshaw-wallah

wav (vav) step well, particularly in Gujarat and western India (baoli)

wazir chief minister of a raja (from Turkish 'vizier')

wazwan ceremonial meal (Kashmir)

Y

yagya (yajna) major ceremonial sacrifice

Yaksha (Yakshi) a demi-god, associated with nature

yali see vyala

Yama God of death, judge of the living

yantra magical diagram used in meditation; instrument

yatra pilgrimage

Yellow Hat Gelugpa Sect of Tibetan Buddhism – monks wear yellow headdress

yeti mythical Himalayan animal often referred to as 'the abominable snowman'

yoga school of philosophy stressing mental and physical disciplines; yogi

yoni a hole symbolising female sexuality; vagina

yura water channel (Ladakh)

Z

zamindar a landlord granted income under the Mughals

zari silver and gold thread used in weaving or embroidery

zarih cenotaph in a Muslim tomb

zenana segregated women's apartments

ziarat holy Muslim tomb

zilla (zillah) district

Advertisers' index

Acknowledgements

A guidebook is nothing if not a work of collaboration, and this book doubly so, having been handed down by several generations of previous authors. As such, the authors are indebted to Robert and Roma Bradnock for their founding work in creating the first edition of *Footprint Rajasthan*, and to Matt Barrett and David Stott for their work on the second and third editions.

Credits

Footprint credits

Project editor: Jen Haddington
Layout and production: Emma Bryers
Maps: Kevin Feeney
Colour section: Rob Lunn
Series design: Mytton Williams
Cover design: Robert Lunn

Managing Director: Andy Riddle
Commercial Director: Patrick Dawson
Publisher: Alan Murphy
Publishing Managers: Felicity Laughton,
Nicola Gibbs, Jo Williams, Jen Haddington
Marketing and PR: Liz Harper
Sales: Diane McEntee
Advertising: Renu Sibal
Finance and administration:
Elizabeth Taylor

Photography credits

Front cover: Alamy/Robert Harding
(Hawa Mahal, Jaipur).
Back cover: Imagestate Media Partners Ltd -
Impact Photos/Alamy (Cloth merchant, Jodhpur).
Page 1: Jeremy Richards/Shutterstock.
Pages 2-3: thefinalmiracle/Shutterstock.
Page 6: Blaine Harrington III/Alamy; Jeremy Richards/
Shutterstock; Regien Paassen/Shutterstock; Robert
Harding PL Ltd/Alamy; Michele Burgess/Alamy.
Page 7: Lonely Planet Images/Alamy; brianindia/
Alamy; Indian Gypsy/Alamy; Cardaf/Shutterstock.
Page 8: Lebedinski Vladislav/Shutterstock.

Manufactured in India by Nutech
Pulp from sustainable forests

Footprint feedback

We try as hard as we can to make each
Footprint guide as up to date as possible
but, of course, things always change. If you
want to let us know about your experiences –
good, bad or ugly – then don't delay, go to
footprinttravelguides.com and send in
your comments.

Publishing information

Footprint Rajasthan
4th edition
© Footprint Handbooks Ltd
January 2011

ISBN: 9781907263156
CIP DATA: A catalogue record for this book
is available from the British Library

® Footprint Handbooks and the Footprint
mark are a registered trademark of Footprint
Handbooks Ltd

Published by Footprint
6 Riverside Court
Lower Bristol Road
Bath BA2 3DZ, UK
T +44 (0)1225 469141
F +44 (0)1225 469461
footprinttravelguides.com

Distributed in the USA by Globe Pequot Press,
Guilford, Connecticut

Every effort has been made to ensure that
the facts in this guidebook are accurate.
However, travellers should still obtain
advice from consulates, airlines, etc about
travel and visa requirements before travelling.
The authors and publishers cannot accept
responsibility for any loss, injury or
inconvenience however caused.